CANADA'S
ALL-TIME #1 BESTSELLER
ABOUT THE 1000 MEN WHO RUN CANADA

This superseller is about money and power—who has it, how they got it, how they keep it, how they use it, how they abuse it.

You'll meet the men of fabulous wealth—the superrich who run Canada—1000 men who form an "invisible government." Inbred, secretive, puritanical, tough-minded, iron-willed, they are dedicated to preserving the status quo—*their* status quo.

Peter C. Newman names names, the men and institutions where real authority resides. He traces the elaborate personal networks that connect the power elite. He shows how authority moves and how power is jealously guarded to ensure it remains with the super elect. Trenchant, exciting, frightening, this is one of the most explosive and important books of the decade.

THE CANADIAN ESTABLISHMENT

"It's my firm testimony, as an expatriate, that this is the best guide anyone will ever encounter to Canada and the Canadians."
—John Kenneth Galbraith

The Canadian Establishment

Peter C. Newman

Volume One

Seal Books
are published by
McClelland and Stewart-Bantam Limited
Toronto

THE CANADIAN ESTABLISHMENT
*A Seal Book / published by arrangement with
McClelland and Stewart Limited*

PRINTING HISTORY
McClelland and Stewart edition published November 1975
2nd printing .... December 1975
3rd printing .... November 1976
Seal edition / April 1977

Cover photograph courtesy of Bob Young

ISBN 0-7704-1500-8

PRINTED IN CANADA

For my daughter, *Ashley*,
who knows why

I thought that my invincible power
would hold the world captive,
leaving me in a freedom undisturbed.
Thus night and day I worked at the chain
with huge fires and cruel hard strokes.
When at last
the work was done,
I found that it held me in its grip.

—Rabindranath Tagore

Contents

Acknowledgments   xiii
Author's Note   xv
Foreword   xvii

I. Personal Power

1. The World of Bud McDougald   3
2. The Flash of Paul Desmarais   43

II. Veto Power

3. The Bankers: Guardians of the Temple   91
4. The Withering Pride of Neil McKinnon   135

III. Corporate Power

5. The Theology of Free Enterprise   153
6. The Frightened Men in the Corner Offices   175
7. Working the System   191

IV. Money Power

8. The El Dorado Crowd   285
9. The Immaculate Passions of Nelson Morgan Davis   343

V. Network Power

10. Present at the Creation: CD's Boys   357
11. The Ties That Bind   397
12. Clubland on the Rocks   417
13. The Canadian Establishment: A Tentative Sounding   443

Appendices

The Sturgeon Lake Pack   453
The Jet Set   455
The Top One Hundred Club   457
The Canadian Business Establishment   466
The Munitions and Supply Gang   476
The Exchange Control Board Alumni   488
The Wartime Prices and Trade Grads   490
The Five Lakes Fishing Club Crowd   496
The Ottawa Mandarins   500
C.D. Howe's Secret Insiders   503
The Private School Fraternity   504
The Harvard Business School Club   509

Index   525

Acknowledgements

Anonymity is all too often the price of candour, and since some of my research involved off-the-record discussions, acknowledgements by name of all my sources is not possible. Where no printed origin is indicated in the text, quotations are from my on-the-record interviews.

This book bears the imprint, as does everything I have written or ever will write, of the long happy apprenticeship I served under the late Ralph Allen, my mentor and friend. I am most grateful to Lloyd Hodgkinson, the publisher of *Maclean's*, for allowing me the freedom and opportunity to write this book, although neither its tone nor its contents bears the sanction of Maclean-Hunter Limited.

Martin Lynch, the immensely knowledgeable assistant news editor of the Toronto *Globe and Mail*, and Janet Craig, McClelland and Stewart's editor, have been invaluable companions during the long and sometimes painful creation of this book. Their wise counsel and inspiration, their dedication to detail, accuracy, and, I am sure, exasperating attempts to correct my use of an adopted language, have left me with a greater debt than I can describe or repay. Christina Newman's talents illuminated parts of this book as they have all of my previous works. I wish to thank Arlene Arnason, my assistant, for her warm-hearted and unflagging help in every phase of the manuscript's preparation.

The appreciation in which I hold Jack McClelland is very much more than the lively sense of obligation a writer feels for his publisher. His imaginative support kept this project alive through the many difficulties that continually threatened its survival. My gratitude must also encompass Stan Kenton and his music for providing some badly needed exhilaration and cadence during the pre-dawn hours when I did my writing.

This book owes its existence to many others not mentioned here; only the responsibility for its imperfections is fully my own.

April 1, 1969–August 31, 1975   P.C.N.

Author's Note

The books that will eventually make up this series of probes into the Canadian Establishment should be read as parts of one integrated work. The first volume deals mostly with Canada's business Establishment, this country's dominant and dominating elite. The overwhelming influence of U.S. investment and American culture on Canada; the workings of government and its interface with the private sector; the rise of the Jewish Establishment; a delineation of the legal profession's growing clout; the curious role of the press lords—these and many other essential themes will be explored in subsequent volumes.

Foreword

This first volume in a journalist's attempt to analyse the workings of the Canadian Establishment grew out of some six hundred interviews and half a dozen years of research and observation.

Before this project began, I spent more than a decade on various writing assignments in Ottawa and saw that slumbering town transformed. National politics, which had been the great national yawn during the King-St. Laurent era, became the country's leading spectator sport. At the time, along with every other power-conscious inhabitant of the capital, I was quite certain the universe, at least the part of it unfolding over that thirteenth of the earth's surface which is Canada, was centred on Parliament Hill and that nothing very significant or interesting ever happened in the hinterland.

Visiting business executives—men familiar with the smell of cigars, who sat around the Rideau Club managing somehow to look a trifle bewildered and pompously ingratiating at the same time—seemed in their appearance and message to be the emissaries of some alien mercantile order. The senior power, I was sure, would always reside in politics, not business, conferred by revocable mandate rather than entrenched position.

More or less by coincidence, I moved to Toronto just as the conflict between the private and public sectors began to manifest itself more openly, with the men who occupy the corporate board rooms challenging political power and finding themselves challenged in return. I started to move around in the republic of business, a stranger in a strange land, meeting the men who work in large corner offices at the top of large corner buildings where the furniture is antique and so are the secretaries, as befits the breeding and importance of the occupants, even when they turn out to be hard-edged American multinational buccaneers who have nothing to do with being quietly classy and everything to do with the ethics of Genghis Khan.

I began to meet the heads of large corporations and even larger banks, men who were secretive, strong-

minded, short-haired, puritanical, uptight, and yet somehow good-natured in their arrogance and often
compellingly interesting. I found that most of them inhabited not merely a different climate from ordinary men
but almost a different meteorology.

My fascination grew as I learned to discern the subtle
differences between wealth and power, between influence
and control. A few of the individuals I met were friendly,
most of them engrossing, all of them cagey. Having previously confined their limited dealings with journalists to
public relations departments, they regarded me with a
mixture of the traditional British attitude toward the press
("blackguards with their eyes to the keyhole") and the
much freer American approach ("buddies at the bar
where the whisky of the powerful flows"). Since I
seemed to fit into neither category, I was treated warily
but not excluded entirely from their confidence. Many
of the men I saw had never granted an open session to a
journalist before.

By choice and by necessity, I laboured on the other
side of the barricades from my subjects. I am grateful for
their indulgence, but I do not expect they will endorse my
findings.

In researching and organizing this book, I have not
tried to fit the Canadian Establishment into any quantita-
tive sociological categories. Recognizing the validity of
the concept that power resides in various elites, I have
concentrated instead on trying to define and detail their
qualitative workings, origins, interconnections, rivalries,
styles of operation. No bloodless audit of the Establishment's common strains, this is a journalist's tentative
exploration of its members' essences, flaws, values,
strengths, and motives—who they are, what they do, and
how they get away with it.

I

Personal Power

CHAPTER ONE

The World of Bud McDougald

He may well be the least known
and most admired member of the
business Establishment. Without
question, he is the most powerful.

If the Canadian business Establishment has a grand master, that all-powerful figure has to be a nearly invisible Toronto capitalist named John Angus "Bud" McDougald. He is the archetype of the tycoons the radicals love to fanaticize about. His life style, his sense of personal imperative, his manners, his use of metaphor, his looks, his view of public power and private prerogative—everything about him is perfect. He is obsessively secretive, tough, chivalrous, ultra-rightwing in his outlook, and self-confident to a degree that goes beyond mere pride and becomes something very much simpler, like self-absorption. Because he has never lost at anything he's tried, winning has become the only tolerable condition of life for him. During the half century he has spent building up his corporate holdings and personal fortune, McDougald's claim to uncommon privilege has been nurtured by the obsequiousness of the many lesser men who have found comfort in deferring to his certitudes.

The very rich are different from the merely rich. Those insolent, side-burned financial gunslingers who talk fast and deal hard, who know all the right buzzwords and think they're somebodies (in their striped shirts, flowing ties, and vented double-breasteds) because they've put a few million-dollar deals together—they don't even know Bud McDougald exists. But should one of them nibble at any of his enterprises, a hint in the right banker's ear can cut the intruder down to size and leave him thrashing about with the empty energy of a master of ceremonies on an afternoon television quiz show.

McDougald shuns public notice. Unlike E.P. Taylor,

whose enlarged mantle he now carries, McDougald deliberately cultivates the absence of a visible personality. Few Canadians are aware of his existence, and even those Establishment insiders who operate away from his immediate orbit know him less by sight than by reputation. McDougald is really not very much interested in what people think of him. He understands power very well, where it resides and how to exercise it. Discretion is best, anonymity even better. He senses that those of his would-be peers who appear on radio and television, in magazines and newspapers, do so because they are still in the process of testing the stretch of their authority. Bud McDougald knows precisely where he fits. At the very top.

He may well be the least known and most admired member of the business Establishment. Without question, he is the most powerful.

His critics tend to dismiss McDougald as a nineteenth-century buccaneer, tragically out of touch with current political and economic realities. But if McDougald fits any century—and this is a dubious proposition, since his kind of entrepreneur belongs to a system rather than an age—he might well claim sanctuary in the seventeenth-century England of Thomas Hobbes, who saw life as "a perpetuall and restless desire of power after power that ceaseth onley in Death." One of the few McDougald contemporaries who appreciated the spirit that has propelled them both was Lord Beaverbrook. "A man must feel those early deals right down to the pit of his stomach if he is going to be a great man of business," Beaverbrook wrote in his autobiographical *Men and Power*. "They must shake the very fibre of his being as the conception of a great painting shakes the artist. The money brain is, in the modern world, the supreme brain. Why? Because that which the greatest number of men will strive for will produce the fiercest competition of intellect."

This is the ethos McDougald lives by, but he expresses it in a less grandiose, more interesting way. Viewed from his specialized sensibility, a rough airplane trip across the Atlantic (with a fellow Catholic who happens to be a bishop) can trigger thoughts about power and the limitless boundaries of its exercise. "One day," he recalls, "I was coming back from London on a Pan

American plane—my wife and I were on it—when Bishop Sheen got on and sat near us. It was an old Stratocruiser, and we started out for New York. We were out about an hour and we were supposed to go to Shannon first, when the pilot said we were going to have to change our course. We were going to Reykjavik, Iceland. He said we were going to run into some pretty rough weather, and we'd better tighten our seat belts. It was the worst trip I was ever on in an airplane. You could see the old wings just flapping. My wife said to me, 'Give me fifty dollars, quickly.'

"I said, 'What do you want fifty dollars for? Here I am all strapped in.'

" 'Well, give me a hundred dollars, then.'

"I said, 'What do you want a hundred dollars for?'

" 'Well,' she said, 'there's Bishop Sheen. I want to give it to him so he'll pray for us.'

"I said, 'Don't worry about him, he's full out now. What's good for the bishop will be all right for us . . . .'

"We landed in Iceland, about midnight. It was broad daylight. It was an American base [Keflavik] and all those GIs had come down to the plane to see Sheen, and they greeted him and so on, and I just thought, now there's a fellow, if he wanted to twist that power, what damage he could do. But he didn't do it. A few weeks later, funnily enough, I was having lunch with Cardinal Spellman in New York. He used to call me every once in a while just to compare notes. He was quite a fellow. He called me this day, and he said, 'Bud, is there any chance you'll be in New York soon?'

"And I said, 'Well, it just happens I am going to be there, why?'

"He said, 'Well, Louis B. Mayer who's one of my friends is getting old and his health isn't very good, and he's gotten in with what I think are bad people who are trying to get control of Metro-Goldwyn-Mayer. You probably know something about them; come and have lunch.'

"I said, 'I'll join you at the Palace on Madison Avenue,' which I did.

"Sheen happened to be there for lunch on that particular day, and when I was introduced to him he said, 'Oh, you're the fellow who wouldn't let your wife give me that hundred dollars. I'm mentioning it on my program tonight,' and he did. But what I was thinking of was the power that man had at that time; it was fantastic."

WELL INTO HIS SIXTIES, MCDOUGALD HAS A PHYSICAL APPEARANCE THAT IS ENGAGING and, at a distance, surprisingly youthful. The cheek lines that run from his nose to the corners of his mouth form a precise isosceles triangle. The blue-grey eyes are always watchful, alert to every move, each nuance, any signal that might betray a visitor's true motive. His grooming is beyond the impeccable: the three-piece suits are fashioned, at £271 each, by the firm of Huntsman's, one of Savile Row's most exclusive tailors; the English bench-made shoes are carved from the skins of young alligators.

His manner of speaking is somehow lulling, without highs or lows—the last visit to his Toronto house by Prince Philip; the rose-cultivating skills of his head gardener; the socialist tendencies of Pierre Elliott Trudeau; his triumphs at the British racetracks; the new Massey-Ferguson plant being built in Poland; the real reason the Packard Motor Car Company went out of business; the advice he gave President Eisenhower about dealing with the Russians; the broken valve on the propane tank that heats his swimming pool—everything is discussed in the same tone. There is little sense of irony in his makeup. Bud McDougald has never taken a drink. He doesn't smoke or eat sweets; he hasn't had a cavity for thirty years.*

---

*McDougald has strong feelings against liquor, though he serves all the best brands. When pressed, he explains how he became an abstainer: "My father's home was run like a gentleman's house. He didn't drink, but he served everything. If you wanted a whisky and soda you got it, if you wanted a glass of milk you got it, if you wanted a tomato juice you got it; it didn't matter what you wanted. And there was no emphasis put on it. At that time, the Ontario Temperance Act was in force and the smart thing for the young fellows to do was to go to the bootleggers. Well, all I had to do is to go to my father's house and get them anything they wanted. There was no difference at all between a whisky and soda and a glass of milk. And as a result, I rebelled against alcohol because I thought these fellows were just a bunch of hicks, running down to a joint on Chestnut Street to buy some rotgut when all I had to do was ask my friends to my father's house and give them a drink in a civilized way. And then when the crash came in '29 there were so many young fellows I knew who had been very successful in the boom days who had been hitting it up pretty hard, and they weren't able to take it, so they went to the bottle to prop them up. Many never recovered."

The harsher side of McDougald's nature is tempered by a kind of Henry James charm—a sense of the urbane, a faith in manners, the restriction of passion, deep respect for privacy and the proper order of things. It is this facet of his character that allows the outsider to sense that even in the face of all his power there exists a cast of sadness in Bud McDougald's world. Although he has set himself up above the wearing constraints of ordinary lives, happiness has not visibly followed. He seems dimly aware of some loss to which he cannot put a name. Somehow the anticipated satisfactions keep eluding him; more success doesn't bring anything he couldn't have had before. Except perhaps the absence of fear. "I admire guts more than anything else in other people," he says. "There are so many people you can trip up because you can outsmart them. Not because you're smart, but because they're afraid. They think you've got something up your sleeve that isn't there."

The extent of McDougald's fortune is difficult to estimate. The combination of his personal stock holdings and his position as chairman and president of Argus Corporation gives him direct control over industrial and commercial assets worth $2 billion, including Dominion Stores, Massey-Ferguson, Hollinger Mines, Domtar, and Standard Broadcasting.* "We're proprietors," he says of the Argus setup, "and that's where you get the reputation for being tough. Because you can say what you mean and not be afraid of losing your job." McDougald also exercises voting control over Crown Trust (with $811 million in its custody); is a dominant force and member of the executive committee of the Canadian Imperial Bank of Commerce (assets $20.2 billion); is a member of the advisory board of the First National Bank in Palm

---

*With sales in 1974 of $1.3 billion, Dominion Stores is the largest food retailer in Canada and its annual volume is growing 10 per cent faster than the industry average. Massey-Ferguson is the world's second-largest manufacturer of agricultural implements, with annual sales of $2 billion from thirty-nine plants located in a dozen countries. Domtar's sales are approaching $910 million, with huge paper, chemical, and packaging operations. Hollinger's main assets are a 60 per cent interest in Labrador Mining and a 15 per cent investment in Iron Ore Company of Canada, as well as an 11 per cent stake in Noranda Mines. Standard Broadcasting owns Canada's two largest radio stations (CFRB in Toronto and CJAD in Montreal) and in 1975 was successful in its bid for Bushnell Communications, which owns TV stations in Ottawa, Cornwall, and Deseronto, Ontario.

Beach, Florida; and is a director of several major international corporations including the $1.5 billion Avco conglomerate.

He is reputed to keep about $10 million in cash and gold at the main Toronto branch of the Commerce. One estimate with which he doesn't quarrel places his personal wealth in excess of $250 million. An indication of his income comes from his tax bill. A few years ago, Percy Finlay, a corporation lawyer and Hollinger director, weary of McDougald's endless lamentations about the iniquities of the federal government, asked him: "Bud, why do you think you have the right to complain so much about this country?" They were in the Toronto Club at the time, surrounded by the local big money men sipping their pre-luncheon Scotch and sodas.

McDougald didn't even glance around before he gave his answer. "Because," he said, "I'm the only man in this room who's paid personal income tax of more than a million dollars every year for the past sixteen years."

THE DIMENSIONS OF BUD MCDOUGALD'S COMMERCIAL HEGEMONY are hard to overestimate. More than any other Canadian businessman, he has used his indigenous power base to build up remarkable circles of influence both in Europe and in the United States. Even if few Canadians can pretend to be his intimates, in London, Geneva, New York, and Palm Beach he is no recluse.

In such settings, McDougald is transmuted into a citizen of the world. "What I claim," he says, "is that if you're in an international type of operation as we are, and you really want to get through to the local community, you've got to be one of them. I find I can get business done an awful lot easier that way." He has little trouble masquerading as a Canadian, an Englishman, and an American all at the same time. Once he was having tea with his friend Sir Harmar Nicholls, a British M.P., on the terrace of Westminster, when two Labour members came by, took one look at McDougald in his morning coat, and, assuming he was a new Tory backbencher, tried to enlist him in a scheme to tear down St. Paul's Cathedral for a housing project. McDougald became so vehement in defence of the British traditions represented by St. Paul's that the Labourites abandoned the idea on the spot.

When he's in London, McDougald stays in a special suite at Claridge's Hotel with bay windows angled to allow him an unobstructed view of his Phantom VI Rolls-Royce parked on the street below, so that he can signal the chauffeur when he's on his way down. The oversized limousine is decorated in royal colours and lent to the Queen for ceremonial occasions. "I've been at Claridge's for twenty-five years and it's like a clearing-house for the world," he says. "It's amazing; you stick around there for a week and you can see your connections from all over the globe."

McDougald likes London on weekends when it is silent and free of people. His man knows the roads well and drives him down to the country houses for Saturday and Sunday luncheons. Among his closest acquaintances are the Marquess of Abergavenny, chairman of Ascot,* and Lord Crathorne, a former British minister of agriculture. McDougald stables most of his hackney horses in England, is a member of both Epsom and Ascot, and knows the royal family well enough that on his 1967 visit to Toronto Prince Philip chose to stay with him, as did Princess Anne and her husband, Captain Mark Phillips, when they came to open the 1974 Royal Agricultural Winter Fair in Toronto.†

McDougald's stature in London can be measured by his membership in three of England's most exclusive clubs:

White's, which dates from 1693, was rated by Anthony Sampson in his *Anatomy of Britain* as "the most arrogant of them all," and has a twenty-year waiting list;

Buck's, which has had on its roster Lord Mountbatten, Lord Tweedsmuir, the Prince of Wales, and the Duke of Gloucester;

The Turf, whose membership includes sixteen dukes, though the late Aga Khan and a former Duke of Atholl

---

*The most illustrious ancestor of Lord Abergavenny was Warwick the Kingmaker, who toppled two Plantagenet kings before he was killed in battle in 1471.

†That particular royal occasion turned out to be something of an Argus affair. Besides staying at the McDougalds', the royal pair was entertained at a special reception given by E.P. Taylor at his farm near Oshawa, and later the same day they dined with Mrs. Eric Phillips, McDougald's sister-in-law and widow of a former Argus partner.

are said to have been blackballed. The lavatory of the Turf still has four chamber pots which, before the days of proper plumbing, were proffered by footmen to members with weak bladders—even if one resident lord much preferred to use the fireplace. (Maurice Baring, the novelist and son of Lord Revelstoke, the banker, tells a story about being entertained at the Turf by the Earl of Westmorland. When, at the end of the meal—*vol-au-vent* and *crêpes suzette*—he praised both the food and the service, the waiter broke down in tears and said: "I have been employed here man and boy for forty years, sir, and that's the first kindly word I've ever had.")

McDougald's penchant for the British way of life caused an embarrassing moment for Vacy Ash, the former head of Shell Canada and a long-time McDougald associate. Ash once called McDougald at his winter home in Palm Beach, and the phone was answered by a stranger with a heavy English accent. "Wellington *heah*," he announced. Ash thought he was speaking with the latest in McDougald's long line of British butlers, hesitated, and came within a hair's breadth of making a terrible *faux pas*.

It was, of course, the Duke of Wellington, direct descendant of Napoleon's conqueror, now on the board of Massey-Ferguson and a good buddy of Bud's.

THE AMERICAN HEADQUARTERS OF THE MCDOUGALD EMPIRE is a large Mediterranean-style villa on Palm Beach's Ocean Boulevard, next to the former mansion of the much-married Marjorie Merriweather Post Close Hutton Davies May.*

McDougald bought the house from one of the du Pont heirs in 1960, when the mansion he had been leasing for many years from Rick Bay was turned into the southern White House for President John F. Kennedy.† The present

---

*Until she died in 1973, Mrs. Post was the high priestess of Palm Beach society along wth Mrs. Stephen "Laddie" Sanford, who once told a friend: "I have been blessed with one of the most beautiful homes in the world. I look out through the window on the ocean—and I can't help feeling it's mine."

†While he was occupying Rick Bay's home, he met both King Ibn Saud, then ruler of Saudi Arabia, and his son, Crown Prince Faisal, who were renting the house across the road. The Arabs used to slaughter four lambs at a time on the living-room carpet and roast them in the fireplace.

villa, which has eighteen bathrooms and attempts a Basque
effect with tile roof and sloping eaves, looks so unusual
that a local postcard company once issued its likeness to
illustrate Palm Beach's unique architecture. McDougald
promptly ensured his privacy by buying all the available
copies and having the plates destroyed.*

The Palm Beach that Bud McDougald inhabits is very
different from the Florida glimpsed by Canadian tourists.
One of the last and most garish resorts of the American
upper classes, it has more Caddies, Connies, and Rollses
than any other place its size. The luxury shops along
Worth Avenue sell precious dachshunds cast in bronze,
Royal Doulton porcelain flying horses, and lovebirds
hand-blown of Bohemian crystal. (One boutique called
Au Bon Goût charges a fifty-dollar membership just to
shop, a ploy that keeps the tourists from interfering with
the big spenders.) There's four o'clock tea at the Breakers Hotel, but life centres on the Everglades and the Bath
and Tennis clubs. Probably the only swimming club in
the world that still has a by-law against the display of
bellybuttons, the Bath and Tennis is a great Moorish castle
built in 1926. It charged a charter membership of
$10,000, but $250,000 had to be returned because the
quota was so quickly filled. McDougald is a vice-president of the Bath and Tennis, a governor of both clubs,
and a director of the Everglades Protective Syndicate.†
He's also a governor of the Good Samaritan Hospital and
since 1962 has been a shareholding member of the advisory board of what may well be the most unusual bank

*The house is a rare example of the bizarre creativity of Addison Miz-
ner, an artist, prizefighter, and self-taught architect whose trademark was
his forgetfulness. Mizner built one house (for the Rasmussen family)
without a staircase and left the kitchen out of another. When Harry K.
Thaw, the confessed slayer of Stanford White, saw one of Mizner's more
outlandish creations, he is supposed to have whispered: "My God, I shot
the wrong architect."

†In 1950, a local real estate firm attempted to buy some Everglades
property for a housing project. The developer thought he would catch the
members off guard by making his move in the summer, when most of
them were away from Palm Beach. But they flew in, a hundred strong, to
meet at New York's Metropolitan Club and defeated the proposal. Mc-
Dougald is, of course, a member in his own right of the Metropolitan,
which was founded by J.P. Morgan around 1900 because he was angry at
not being able to get a friend into the then more prestige-laden Union
Club. Another McDougald habitat is the New York Yacht Club, which
is actually a land-locked mansion on West 44th Street in the heart of
Manhattan. In 1974 McDougald was part of the New York Yacht Club
syndicate that sponsored Intrepid in the America's Cup race.

in the United States. Although few outsiders are aware of it, the First National Bank in Palm Beach is a transplanted miniature Switzerland. The modest-looking institution has just two branches (one of them at a shopping mall) and a net annual income (for 1974) of only $2.9 million. But its total deposits run close to $750 million.* The bank's secret is that it pays no interest on deposits. This simple device means that the U.S. tax authorities don't have to be notified about individuals' holdings—where they came from or how they got there. Washington, in turn, has no reason to report on the depositors to the countries, including Canada, with which it has reciprocal taxing arrangements. The bank's customer list reads like a blue book of the world. The only public clue to the bank's true significance is the stature of its directors and advisory board members.†

McDougald spends most winters in Palm Beach, scheduling the annual meetings of the Argus companies close together in the spring so that he has to make only a few quick journeys north. When he commutes it's in a jet owned by Sugra Limited.‡

"People think I go to my winter house in Palm Beach just to lie in the sun," he says. "But I don't ever get time. I operate the same as I do in Toronto. Palm Beach is quite a clearing house. It's easier for me to be in Palm Beach in the winter with the various interests that we have than it is to be in Canada. That particular stratum of people we deal with are coming and going, people are moving all the time. You can fly from Paris or London to Miami, then straight out to the West Coast if you want to, out to Los Angeles or San Diego. So I see all kinds of

---

*The bank also operates vaults with 43,000 square feet of storage capacity and more than five thousand oversized safety deposit boxes for furs, silver collections, paintings, and other personal effects of the very rich.

†As well as Bud McDougald, they include Charles White, former chairman of the board, Republic Steel Corporation; Harold Sweatt, former chairman of the board, Honeywell Inc.; Frank Prior, former chairman of the board, Standard Oil of Indiana; Clifford Hood, former president, U.S. Steel Corporation; Stanton Griffis, former investment banker and U.S. ambassador to Poland, Egypt, Argentina, and Spain; Ed Warren, former president, Cities Service Corporation; Semon E. "Bunkie" Knudsen, chairman and president, White Motor Corporation; Mead Johnson, former president, Mead Johnson & Co.; Marion Epley, former chairman of the board, Texaco Inc.; and Benjamin Oehlert, Jr., former ambassador and senior vice-president, Coca-Cola Company.

‡That's Argus spelled backwards.

our people in Palm Beach all winter long. Then, with our various other things, such as iron ore, which we're heavily interested in, that's a Cleveland operation. Their executives are up and down all the time; they have ranches, for instance, in lower Georgia where they shoot quail and that sort of thing, so I hold a lot of meetings in Palm Beach that normally you'd have either in Cleveland or Canada."

YOU DRIVE PAST THE INCONGRUOUSLY COUNTRIFIED MAIL BOX with the Green Meadows sign on it, through the colonial-style picket fence, up the manicured driveway lined with weeping willows, catch sight of the McDougalds' magnificent Toronto residence, and it's *Tara*, by God. Formerly stretching over three hundred acres, it's in inner suburbia now, reduced to a mere nineteen acres in a 1969 deal with the North York Council that permitted McDougald to keep a barn within city limits in return for disposing of his extra land for badly needed housing construction. McDougald has been offered $2 million for the balance of the property, but he won't sell. The McDougald estate, its lawns treated to give them the quality of the bluegrass horse country of Kentucky, consists of a large Georgian stable with indoor training ring for the eight resident thoroughbreds, separate cottages for the chauffeur and gardener, several outbuildings, a large swimming pool, and a *thirty*-car garage. But it is the gleaming mansion, with its white pillars and handcrafted shutters—large enough to require a permanent staff of six servants—all there within sight of the city's apartment towers, stabbing aimlessly at the sky, that makes the visitor blink in disbelief.

The front hall has a fireplace, blue-and-white wallpaper, a huge bowl of seasonal flowers on an Adam table, and a grandfather clock made by Robert Macadam of Dumfries. The sunroom is done up in white wicker with pink chintz. The pale green and gold decor of the drawing room provides an elegant setting for the richness of the Queen Anne furniture; the dining room has the inevitable Sheraton table with ecru lace mats. The walls are crammed with paintings of horses by the world's best-known equestrian artists: George Stubbs, Sir Alfred Munnings, Ben Marshall, John Fernelly, J.F. Herring, Raoul Millais. There's a majestic canvas of Bud McDougald in the dining room by Sir James Gunn, who painted the state portrait of the Queen in 1954, and a striking painting in the sitting room of Mrs. McDougald by Pietro Annigoni.* The pantry has special cabinets for seven sets of exquisite china, including a complete Lowestoft service. The dessert silver is made of gold.

The McDougalds have no children. The upstairs quarters of Mrs. McDougald (whose real name is Maude but everyone calls Jim) are dominated by pink. Her bedroom is pink, her study is pink, and there's even a pink dog's dish in her pink bathroom. An intelligent and attractive presence, Mrs. McDougald was once an Olympic figure skater, a golfing champion, and rode a motorcycle for the Red Cross during World War II. She has trouble with her poodles. Their sire, called Pete the Poodle, was purchased in England and when he was one year old, she went overseas to recruit a proper mate for him. But Pete couldn't wait, and while she was gone he got mixed up with a Welsh terrier. The puppies with their crossed bloodlines were quietly put out for adoption ("Cutest things you ever saw, but you couldn't have them about the place").

A large part of the McDougalds' lives is taken up with horses. But they don't pursue their hobby with the ferocity of E.P. Taylor, who once told them they were bad for the horse business because they become too fond of their animals. They won't sell horses that can't win races any longer and once bought a nursemaid pony for a colt whose mother "went bonkers," according to Jim. Their racing colours (French grey and cerise) are not extensively recognized, though one of McDougald's entries called Idiot's Delight won his first race at Ascot, and Mrs. McDougald's Musketeer Miss has done well on Canadian tracks. McDougald is much prouder of his champion hackneys, which have been judged tops in the international horse world. He helped revive fox hunting in

---

*Not to be outdone, Mrs. Eric Phillips, Mrs. McDougald's sister, had her portrait painted by Salvador Dali *and* by Pietro Annigoni.

Toronto after World War II and once had three hundred guests to a pre-hunt breakfast of Melton Mowbray pork pie.

One of McDougald's more relaxing hobbies is showing visitors his collection of classic automobiles. The temperature-controlled garages of Green Meadows house thirty cars. There are five Rolls-Royces, including a 1913 Silver Ghost that is the most valuable Rolls in captivity; a 1928 model 38-250-SS supercharged Mercedes-Benz with a custom handmade body; the 1924 Isotta Fraschini Type B originally built (out of tulip wood) for Alfonso XIII, King of Spain; a 1909 Hupmobile; a 1920 Kissel Gold Bug; and various Bentleys, Packards, Bugattis, and Alfa Romeos and four custom-built Cadillacs, one of which McDougald uses for his drives to the Argus Corporation head office in downtown Toronto.

THE DAILY CIRCUIT IN ONE OF HIS MANY LIMOUSINES is not really greatly different from Bud McDougald's initial trek to the Toronto financial district in late 1926. His father, who ran a successful investment house called D.J. McDougald and Company, had given him a grey 1924 model 30/98 Vauxhall Velox. Easily capable of travelling more than a mile a minute, the hand-built masterpiece of machinery was the top sports car of its day. Bud was eighteen at the time. The elder McDougald had arranged for him to get a clerk's job at Dominion Securities Corporation, but there was a condition attached to the gift of the car. "I either had to take the streetcar down to the office or the family chauffeur would drive me down, with his Prussian uniform, leggings, and so on," McDougald remembers. "So the day I reported for work as an office boy I arrived in the $9,000 Vauxhall with the chauffeur in his Prussian uniform and went in and sat down at a little desk with an ENQUIRY sign on top of it and an enunciator to answer buzzers. They all thought, 'This is a great office boy—we'll fix him.' I got quite a lot of criticism but I still did it, because I liked it better than coming by streetcar. I was old enough to drive myself, but the basis that I was brought up with was that if you're not prepared to defend yourself, then you'd better not do it. I was allowed to take the family chauffeur every morning, providing I got off at the front door of the office. If I ever got out at the corner and walked along to avoid the teasing, I'd have got a whaling —or my father would never have allowed me to use the chauffeur again. But as long as I was prepared to stand up and take the criticism, then I could have him."

The senior McDougald's insistence that his son be allowed to do just about anything provided that he was prepared to defend his actions produced an unorthodox upbringing. McDougald's ancestors on both sides had been Scottish crofters in the 1770s. A great-grandfather on his mother's side, W.A. Murray, had emigrated to Canada and eventually became Timothy Eaton's predecessor as "the merchant prince of Toronto." McDougald's grandfather was chairman of the Eastern and Western Land Corporation, a large real estate trust set up to capitalize on the migration of settlers into western Canada in the decade before World War I. An uncle, Senator Wilfrid Laurier McDougald, was one of the chief figures in the Beauharnois scandal that shook Mackenzie King's Liberals in the early thirties. As a youthful guest at the senator's Montreal estate, Bud remembers being impressed with the horses that pulled a large lawn-cutting device. They all wore rubber shoes.

Bud McDougald himself grew up in his father's Rosedale mansion and sporadically attended two of Toronto's best private schools. He was enrolled at Upper Canada College for several years but is remembered there mainly for tying the rear axle of Principal William Lawson "Choppy" Grant's Model T to a tree branch so that when the unmechanically minded school head got into his car and gunned the motor, the wheels just spun in the air until Bud cut him down. Poor old Choppy never did catch on. The experience left McDougald permanently scornful of the teaching profession.* Whenever he takes

---

*While he was attending UCC's prep school, McDougald insisted on driving a Briggs and Stratton Buckboard, so that he wouldn't have to go by streetcar. Since he was only twelve at the time, this was against city and school regulations, and the prep school headmaster, J.L. "the Duke" Somerville, would cane him every time he was caught. After one round of four successive and increasingly painful beatings, Somerville asked how long McDougald intended to keep using his car, since he knew he would be beaten every time he did. "If that's the price I have to pay,

time to muse about his education, he will confess with mock sadness: "Left school at fourteen and I've regretted it all my life." Then, as the listener lowers his eyes in courteous acknowledgement of all those missed years of wisdom, Bud McDougald delivers the punch line: "Biggest mistake I ever made. *Should have left when I was twelve!"*

During a brief stint at St. Andrew's College following his polite dismissal from Upper Canada, young Bud came into his own at last. He went into business for himself. He started a small mouthwash company in Galt, Ontario (later sold at a large profit); he launched a partnership with Sam Kalles, a Toronto tailor who eventually built up a chain of clothing stores; and he became a bookie. The CPR then had a track running through both the northern end of the St. Andrew's property and the western tip of the Thorncliffe racetrack park. Bud would jump out classroom windows between periods, hop a freight, and bet his chums' pocket money on the races. He eventually acquired five horses of his own. Because he was underage, all these transactions had to be carried out in the name of Fred English, a local riding instructor. McDougald soon discovered that he could predict race results more accurately than his classmates, who had access only to the racing forms. He never failed to pay off at the published odds, but he didn't always bet as instructed—so he often ended up with extra cash.

Since he showed no signs of trying to pass any exams ("I just couldn't waste the time; I had too many things going"), his father sent him off to tour Europe with a private tutor. Early in 1926 he abruptly decided to enrol in Cambridge University ("You could get into Sidney Sussex College quite easily if you knew your way around"). He took lodgings in the Carlton Hotel in London, but the general strike intervened, and McDougald found himself

---

then I am quite prepared to pay it," young Bud declared. The Duke gave him one more beating, then told him he had earned the right to drive to school. This is probably the lesson McDougald remembers best from his whole formal education. On a more practical level, he used to help out at a soda fountain in Sutton, Ontario, during the summer holidays, and he recalls that milk shakes were ten cents each or fifteen cents with an egg in them. The owner, who was making a considerable markup on the eggs, told him that instead of asking if customers wanted an egg at all, he should simply demand whether they wanted one egg or two. "I've used that philosophy on a lot of occasions since," McDougald admits.

pulling a milk cart through the St. John's Wood area of northwest London. It was while making these rounds that he decided England was washed up and he would return to Canada and the job his father had obtained for him at Dominion Securities.

"Dominion Securities was a great education," he recalls. "If I was going to do it over, I'd do exactly what I did again. But you can't do it now, because they don't have office boys. New people are all overschooled now. They come in as statisticians, BAS or Masters of Business Administration, and they have no practical knowledge. I learned the hard way. Within a week every partner knew who I was because I answered their buzzers. Some of them thought I was fairly bright, and they'd give me jobs to do. In those days all the partners of the Dominion Securities were top-notch financiers. E.R. Wood, who was president, and Arthur White, who succeeded him—those were the type of people who taught me. Not some professor who couldn't earn a living in the outside world." Harry Bawden, then a partner at Dominion Securities, recalled afterwards that by the time McDougald was seventeen, he "knew more about finance than most men ever know. It was a kind of intuitive thing with him. He had a feel for finance like Mozart had for music."

He cleaned inkwells, clipped the *Wall Street Journal* and the *Financial Post,* drank mid-morning coffee with the other messengers (to find out what was happening "below stairs"), ran out for ham sandwiches, and often stayed until midnight. "One of my jobs at night was to go around to all the partners' filing drawers, pick up their correspondence, and take it up to the filing department. I'd stay up there late, reading all their letters, and I knew more about some of the deals they were working on than all the partners put together." Within two years, McDougald had been appointed the firm's syndicate manager and had signed a cheque to the CNR on a $70-million bond issue before he was twenty.

The 1929 crash wiped out his father's firm as well as cutting the value of McDougald's own private portfolio. Instead of reducing his increasingly expensive life style, McDougald chose to push himself even harder. In 1934, just ten days before his marriage to Maude Eustace Smith,

he invested $10,000 cash in a short-lived partnership with
a group of American promoters. The deal happened to
fall through on his wedding day. The ceremony had been
planned for three o'clock in the afternoon, but at 2.15
p.m. McDougald was still at his office with Pete Campbell,
his best friend and legal adviser, trying to find some
way out of the mess. After hurrying home to change into
his striped trousers, he asked Campbell to invite his erstwhile partners to the wedding reception. It was there, in
a series of tense whispered asides between the champagne
toasts proposed by family and friends, that a settlement
was finally negotiated.

During the next decade, while he was still with Dominion Securities, McDougald became interested in a series
of outside ventures that enhanced both his reputation and
his bank account. He built a large tanker using the then
unique financing technique of showing the British shipyard a long-term charter contract with Shell Oil instead
of making a down payment. He sold and bought companies, merged their assets, split their stocks, and became recognized as one of Bay Street's shrewdest
promoters. His credit rating and his connections were so
good that at one point he was able to obtain Bank of
Commerce financing for a venture that involved cash
loans greater than the bank's combined capital and reserves. ("I never had any trouble getting money. My
problem has always been getting something that was
worth putting money into.")

His dealings were temporarily halted by a serious heart
attack in 1938. But he recovered and spent most of
World War II as head of Haldenby and White, Dominion
Securities' stock-trading operation, which allowed him
even deeper penetration of the Street's inner circles of
influence. McDougald became known as the toughest
member of the Canadian financial community. ("I don't
fool around," he says. "I mean, I call a spade a spade
and if something's wrong, I take a tough position on it.
I don't fold. But I wouldn't say that was being tough.")

Harry Bawden recalls meeting Ted Gooderham at
about this time, when the scion of the Ontario liquor fortune had just been to see McDougald. "I told him," reported Gooderham, " 'Bud, I can remember when you

were a boy. You used to say you'd make a million dollars. Well, you little bugger, you've done it!' And you know what Bud replied? 'Well, don't forget this, Ted. It took me seventeen years to learn how and five years to do it.'"

THE ASCENT OF BUD MCDOUGALD INTO THAT STRATO-SPHERE of the Canadian Establishment that divides the adjudicators of power from those who merely belong goes back to his partnership with E.P. Taylor. Though they were not each other's after-hours favourites, the two men understood and complemented each other in the development of Argus into one of Canada's dominant corporate entities.

In the thirties, Edward Plunket "Eddie" Taylor had used his grandfather's Brading Breweries in Ottawa as a starting base to merge, buy up, and pressure in various ways some thirty beer-making concerns into his huge Canadian Breweries, which eventually became the world's largest brewing organization.*

In 1945, along with several dollar-a-year men he met while serving in wartime Ottawa, Taylor formed a closed-end investment fund called Argus Corporation, modelled after Floyd Odlum's Atlas Corporation of New York. Taylor retained his initial controlling interest by folding in his Breweries stock in return for a majority control of Argus. He described the Argus approach as searching for companies "that will grow not only with the country, but faster than the country; companies where no very large shareholder exists, so that we can acquire enough stock to give us an important voice in policy decisions." What Taylor really wanted was to acquire management control of profitable large companies without tying up the excessive amounts of capital required to buy up a majority of shares. Argus was launched with equity capital of only $8.5 million ($6 million of it taken up by the

*For example, when the directors of Canada Bud Breweries, which operated two small Toronto plants, turned down a Taylor offer for an exchange of shares with his Brewing Corporation of Canada, Taylor instructed London and Toronto brokers to "put a substantial volume of orders into the market between June 11 and June 14 [1934] as this is a critical period and the market quotation on our shares is of paramount importance to the success of our deal." They did as requested, the stock quotations went up, the shareholders of Bud traded in their stocks, and the Canada Bud directors capitulated.

original group of directors) and preferred stock worth $4 million. During the next decade, Argus experimented with many holdings, including a brief period of trying to run Peruvian International Airways, but the Argus portfolio eventually settled into the comfortable—and profitable—groove of controlling six of the largest Canadian operations in their fields.

Until he withdrew to manage his investments in Nassau and elsewhere in the world, it was Taylor who gave Argus its public face.* He was condemned by Socialists as "the crushing Croesus of big business" and by Canadian Communists as "E(xcess) P(rofits) Taylor—the mad miser of millions." His photograph in the sports pages of the nation's newspapers, accepting his latest racing award, binoculars perched on portly stomach, became the symbol of Canadian capitalism run rampant.†

---

*For a detailed description of E.P. Taylor's more recent activities, see Chapter 8.

†Although Taylor provided most of the innovative push, it was other partners who actually ran the Argus companies. M.W. "Wally" McCutcheon was the Argus "axe-man," pruning the executive suites of acquired companies. When Argus got control of Dominion Tar and Chemical (Domtar) in 1951, McCutcheon failed to fire only one of the senior executives, because he was on holidays and couldn't be reached. But during the next ten years he also built up the company from a medium-sized business selling $25 million of house-building products to a major industrial enterprise with sales of $325 million. McCutcheon left Argus in 1962 for a brief fling at Canadian politics, including a short and bizarre term as John Diefenbaker's minister of Trade and Commerce. He died in 1969. His Argus holdings, reputedly worth $25 million, were held by Gormley Investments Ltd., which sold a block of the common stock in 1975 to the McDougald group.

Lt.-Col. Eric Phillips, who distinguished himself with the British Army in World War I (winning both the D.S.O. and the M.C.) was probably the toughest-minded member of the Argus group. A senior Toronto lawyer once observed that "if you cut Eric up into little pieces, you'd have a thousand razor blades." Originally married to a daughter of Sam McLaughlin, he ran a large Oshawa glass factory and headed an important Crown corporation during World War II. Phillips loved motorboats, and when he couldn't get the Grew company to fix his own on schedule, he bought the firm instead. He died in 1964. Grew remains his estate's chief holding company, with Bud McDougald voting his widow's Argus interests.

George Montegu Black, whose father owned Western Breweries in Winnipeg, was running another Crown corporation (Canadian Propellers) during the war when he met Taylor. It was Black who really turned Canadian Breweries into a profitable operation, partly by his ruthless decentralization of its operations. He resigned abruptly in 1958 when Taylor wanted to reverse this process, even though he was offered a five-year contract at double his salary of $75,000 a year to stay. Black remains on the boards of Argus, Dominion Stores, and Standard Broadcasting but seldom ventures out of his Bayview mansion north of Toronto. Since 1958 he has spent most nights reading the works of Toynbee and books on Napoleon. He sometimes refights the Battle of Waterloo with his own sets of toy soldiers. He seldom goes to sleep until 4 a.m. The business Establishment has written Black off as a recluse, yet in his lonely way he has become its most literary member.

For the first ten years of Argus's existence, Bud McDougald remained in the shadows as a partner of Taylor, McDougald Limited, a promotional entity used to acquire possible takeover prospects for the parent company. In 1946, for example, Purity Flour Mills was persuaded to sell off its five profitable bakeries to Taylor, McDougald—a decision possibly facilitated by the fact that McDougald was on the Purity board. The bakeries were in turn sold to Dominion Stores, where they became General Bakeries Limited, which eventually grew into Canada's second-largest baking company. Taylor, McDougald realized a tidy profit on the deal. Such transactions became a highly profitable pattern for realized capital gains. It was also McDougald who brought Dominion Stores within the Argus orbit. But his most profitable—and controversial—acquisition was St. Lawrence Corporation, a holding company that controlled several large Quebec paper-making companies. The Argus subsidiary involved was Arbor Corporation, set up in 1950 according to the Taylor, McDougald formula. Arbor bought 200,000 shares of St. Lawrence over the next five years at prices that were never disclosed. (During that interval, St. Lawrence shares had sold for as low as $28.50, and even in 1954 they could be bought for $37.50.) In 1955 Argus paid Arbor $15 million for the St. Lawrence stock, or $75 a share. This gave the Arbor shareholders a capital gain of anywhere up to $9 million. At the 1955 annual meeting that ratified this transaction, the Argus board of directors was increased from sixteen to seventeen and Bud McDougald was "elected" to fill the "vacancy."

Still another Argus paper tiger called Taymac Investments was used to sell Argus the 250,000 Hollinger shares it had acquired for $7,125,000—or $28.50 a share. The original Taymac purchase price was kept secret, but Hollinger stock was selling for as low as $19 at the end of 1960. The Argus purchase was raised through a bank loan which in turn was repaid from the proceeds of a $10-million issue of Argus redeemable preferred shares. The *Financial Post* estimated that the Taymac directors (McDougald, Taylor, Phillips, and McCutcheon) netted a capital gain of at least $1,250,000.

The Massey-Harris and Ferguson acquisitions were the most dramatic of all. During his first year in wartime Ottawa, Taylor had made friends with James Duncan, the Massey president then serving as deputy minister for air in the Department of National Defence. They both lived in the Chateau Laurier Hotel and often dined together, with Duncan forecasting the great plans he had for the postwar expansion of the agricultural implement firm he'd joined in 1911 and risen to head. Taylor began quietly to buy into Massey-Harris and by the winter of 1945 had acquired 55,000 of the company's preferred shares, transferring them into common stock one minute before the deadline specified by a little-noticed company by-law—a move that wrenched control away from a syndicate headed by Toronto financier J.H. Gundy. With 8 per cent of the equity stock, Taylor became the largest single shareholder in Massey-Harris and managed to displace nine of the sixteen directors and replace them with his own nominees.

Under Duncan's presidency, Massey-Harris sales increased fivefold between 1941 and 1955, but Taylor felt there had been too much emphasis on overseas operations and that Duncan acted more like an ambassador than a salesman. Despite record sales of $412 million in 1957, the year showed an over-all loss of $4.7 million. After a final disagreement over dividend policies, Taylor abruptly fired Duncan and when he was accused of being ruthless blandly retorted: "Me ruthless? Certainly not. But when I'm right and management's consistently wrong, of course I get rid of management." Eric Phillips moved into the Massey chairmanship, cut executive salaries by half, sent an eight-girl chorus line on a 10,000-mile safari to enliven the company's sales meetings, and within twelve months turned the previous year's loss into a $13-million profit. By the end of 1974, the company was selling agricultural implements, diesel engines, and construction machinery worth more than $1.7 billion on five continents. A major impetus in its growth had been the acquisition, in 1953, of the industrial empire run by the eccentric Irish inventor, Harry Ferguson. Although Duncan was still president of Massey at the time, it was McDougald's cunning that facilitated the takeover and later forced Ferguson out of the Massey chairmanship.

Harry Ferguson was a madcap genius, so absurdly punctilious that he insisted his shoelaces be put in with exactly equal lengths of end remaining; his sheets had to have precisely the same overhang on both sides of the bed; and supper had always to be served precisely at seven. In 1948, when his research group produced a new tractor he decided to introduce it in the ballroom of Claridge's Hotel before a white-tie audience. Angered by a Russian reporter's scepticism over the machine's manoeuvrability, Ferguson jumped into the driver's seat, started it up, and after executing a minuet amid the scurrying socialites, drove the belching machine through Claridge's carpeted lobby and down the hotel steps into the street.

Ferguson's designs led the agricultural implement world, but the firm was haphazardly managed and in 1953 Ferguson decided to sell his controlling interest to the Massey group. He agreed to become titular chairman of the newly formed Massey-Harris-Ferguson Limited, but the negotiations bogged down at the cash value of the Massey-Harris stock he would receive for his British company: Ferguson wanted $17 million; the Argus directors offered $16 million. McDougald finally flew to England, determined to negotiate a settlement.

As they were driving in McDougald's Rolls through the Cotswold village of Broadway, Ferguson asked him to stop. "In Ireland we have a way of settling such matters," he said. "Let's toss for it." They did. Ferguson lost. McDougald promptly had the coin mounted on a silver cigar box with the engraved inscription:

TO OUR FRIEND AND PARTNER HARRY FERGUSON
A GALLANT SPORTSMAN
TAILS HE CALLED, BUT HEADS IT WAS
THE $1,000,000 COIN

The deal made Ferguson the new industrial combine's chairman and largest shareholder. But within a year McDougald was back in England on a very different mission: to rid the Massey-Harris-Ferguson board room of the "gallant sportsman," who turned out to be not quite enough of a silent partner to suit the Argus management.

At the end of six stormy weeks, Ferguson still wouldn't resign, insisting that he didn't need the cash from his enforced sale of Massey stock. But McDougald knew the old man was secretly busy exploring an Italian engineering venture for which he required new capital.

Killing time in London, McDougald one day dropped in on Oscar Johnson, his favourite art dealer, to have him arrange a meeting the following Thursday with Sir Alfred Munnings to commission yet another horse portrait. Johnson explained that he couldn't meet McDougald on the appointed day because he was negotiating the purchase of a Constable from Lord Glenconner for Harry Ferguson. McDougald decided to test Ferguson's intentions. He insisted on an appointment with Ferguson for the same Thursday and said that if they couldn't reach an agreement that day he'd fly back to Canada the following morning. On the preceding Wednesday, McDougald asked his wife to call casually at the Johnson gallery. She was told by the excited art dealer that her husband could now see Munnings on Thursday after all, because Ferguson had cancelled his appointment to view the Constable. When Mrs. McDougald reported the conversation to her husband back at Claridge's, he knew that the six weeks of delays had been just a bargaining position. He drew up a final offer and Ferguson capitulated the next day.

THE ARGUS CORPORATION MULTIPLIED ITS INFLUENCE through the fifties and sixties. A random sampling of the Toronto Stock Exchange on June, 5, 1964, for example, shows that fully 10 per cent of all the shares traded that day had been in Argus-owned enterprises. The Taylor stocks were consistent market leaders, and Bud McDougald was in the thick of every acquisition. "What allows me to see when a deal is really good?" he observed. "Well, you've got to be around to begin with. It's unlikely that you'll ever run into a good proposition if you're just on the golf course and not moving around. One thing leads to another. I never had a written agreement in my life with anybody on a deal, never. Eddie Taylor and I never had an agreement and we never had a dispute over money. We had plenty of arguments over policy, but never have I been cheated in my life by anybody. Maybe it's because I was always able to know who I was dealing with. I always went on the principle if a written agreement was necessary it wasn't worth bothering with."

In 1958, the Argus operation moved into its present quarters at 10 Toronto Street, north of the King Edward Hotel. Erected in 1853, the building was originally Canada's most elegant post office and later housed several federal departments until it was taken over by the Bank of Canada in 1935 as its Toronto branch. Taylor had the structure completely renovated to resemble one of the original British merchant banks—all done up in the Adam style with silk wall-coverings, Georgian mouldings, crystal chandeliers, and a staircase with velvet swags for handrails. There's an elevator that runs up only one floor.

When he reached sixty-eight in 1969, Taylor resigned from the Argus presidency and Bruce Matthews became the holding company's executive vice-president. Except for a few secretaries, one accountant, and an economist, McDougald and Matthews are now the building's only occupants, and Argus itself has moved into a relatively sedate if still highly influential period of consolidation.

The only recent major shifts in the Argus portfolio were surrender of the controlling interest in Canadian Breweries to Rothmans of Pall Mall Canada in 1968 (for a profit of $17.7 million) and the 1973 retreat from trying to gain control of B.C. Forest Products with the sale of 500,000 shares to Noranda. By the end of 1974, Argus was still the dominant shareholder in five large Canadian corporations with the following portfolio:

Company	Number of common shares	Percentage of outstanding shares	Indicated market value
B.C. Forest Products Ltd.	500,000	6.6%	$ 6,000,000
Dominion Stores Ltd.	2,000,000	23.6%	29,500,000
Domtar Ltd.	2,500,000	16.9%	55,000,000
Hollinger Mines Ltd.	1,042,000	21.2%	23,445,000
Massey-Ferguson Ltd.	2,850,000	15.6%	37,762,500
Standard Broadcasting Corp.	2,687,475	47.7%	20,491,997
			$172,199,497

The holding company's board comprised the heads of each controlled corporation plus the professional Argus directors themselves who, among them, occupied twenty-six chairs in the various captive board rooms. As the accompanying chart indicates, the Argus universe is really operated by three men: Bud McDougald, who is either chairman of the board or chairman of the executive committee of all the Argus companies except Domtar (where he is only a director and member of the executive committee); Max Meighen, who is a member of all the executive committees (as well as being chairman of the Argus executive committee) and chairman of the Domtar board; and Bruce Matthews, who sits on all the boards and acts as Argus's chief operating officer.*

By holding the largest single block of stock, controlling each company's executive committee, and having the various corporate presidents sit on the Argus board, McDougald can run this impressive empire as if each part of it were in fact a wholly-owned subsidiary. ("I don't get into the nitty-gritty of any business; I only get into the policy end of things.")

Bruce Matthews describes the Argus control as an informal consultative process. "We have a little session after most board meetings and go over what was said and what sort of decisions were taken (if any), what atmosphere was created at the time," he says. "We've adopted the view that Argus is part of a transitional stage in Canadian business. As shareholder control by individuals or families disappears and it is no longer possible to be a direct proprietor, there is a place for our kind of semi-proprietary operation through syndicate ownership. Only this way, if something catastrophic happens to group management or there is a failure of some other sort, can a major shareholder exert his influence in the best interests of the company."

Matthews, whose father had been a lieutenant-governor of Ontario, is probably the most civilized man ever

---

*Two companies float within the Argus orbit without being part of it. They are Crown Trust, which along with the dominant McDougald interest includes two other Argus directors (Thomas McCormack and Allen McMartin), and Canadian General Investments, controlled by Max Meighen, which includes two Argus directors (Bruce Matthews and Alex Barron).

DOMINION STORES LTD.
*JOHN A. McDOUGALD
*Chairman of the Board
Chairman of the
Executive Committee*
*Thomas G. McCormack
Chief Executive Officer
*Thomas G. Bolton
President
L. H. M. Ayre
*Alex Barron
*Stewart G. Bennett
*George Black, Jr.
Pierre Daigle
*Bruce Matthews
*Max Meighen
André Monast
Mitchell L. Wasik

HOLLINGER MINES LTD.
*JOHN A. McDOUGALD
*Chairman of the
Executive Committee*
*Allen A. McMartin
Chairman of the Board
*Albert L. Fairley, Jr.
President
Hon. Edouard Asselin
L. H. M. Ayre
David M. Dunlap
*Percy Finlay
Duncan McMartin
Bruce Matthews
*Max Meighen

MASSEY-FERGUSON LTD.
*JOHN A. McDOUGALD
*Chairman of the
Executive Committee*
*A. A. Thornbrough
*President and Chief
Executive Officer*
The Marquess of Abergavenny
Alex Barron
Henry Borden
Lord Crathorne
Charles L. Gundy
Gilbert Humphrey
J. D. Leitch
*Bruce Matthews
*Max Meighen
J. E. Mitchell
A. M. Runciman
J. G. Staiger
*E. P. Taylor
Trumbull Warren
*Colin W. Webster
The Duke of Wellington

The Argus Corporation

ARGUS
CORPORATION LTD.

*JOHN A. McDOUGALD
*Chairman of the Board
President*
*Bruce Matthews
Executive Vice-President
*Max Meighen
*Chairman of the
Executive Committee*
David G. Baird
*Alex Barron
*George Black, Jr.
H. J. Carmichael
*Dixon S. Chant
W. C. Thornton Cran†
*Albert L. Fairley, Jr.
Thomas G. McCormack
D. A. McIntosh
Allen A. McMartin
James N. Swinden
*E. P. Taylor
A. A. Thornbrough

*Members of the Executive Committee
†Died, June 1975.

28

to occupy an Argus executive office. He first met McDougald when they were at Upper Canada College together. After commanding the Second Canadian Division as a much-decorated major-general during World War II, he entered his family's investment company, which included in its portfolio control of the Excelsior Life Insurance Company. He was Lester Pearson's first choice for governor general (after George Vanier died), but the appointment was not made because Matthews's previous post as president of the National Liberal Federation would have made it politically suspect. Matthews is in his mid-sixties; his shoes have a military shine, his bald head is elegant, and he is consciously but easily the very model of the gentleman of old English-Canadian stock. His room, as he calls his office, has silver cigarette boxes, silver ashtrays, silk lampshades, and on a side table there are photographs of King George VI and his queen in silver frames. Whenever tea or coffee is brought in, it arrives on a silver tray with china that has a Romanesque band of navy and gold.

Down the hall, Bud McDougald uncharacteristically sips Richmello instant coffee out of plain china cups and munches on standard Dominion Store cookies. But this is the office where the real power resides. And its repository is not in the easily traceable ownership of Argus shares. McDougald owns outright only 275 shares of Argus. But at the same time, he is president and controlling shareholder of Ravelston Corporation, the holding company of a holding company which owns more than a million shares (about 61 per cent) of the Argus common stock. Max Meighen, Bruce Matthews, the Phillips estate, and George Black are the other Ravelston partners.* "Nobody can buy into Argus unless we want to sell it to him," McDougald has always insisted.

---

*E.P. Taylor owns 10.34 per cent of Argus common stock through Windfields Farm Ltd. and a family holding company called Cay West S.A. His holdings are part of the Ravelston arrangement until June of 1976. The Ravelston partners have first call on each other's stock so that no outsider can get in. The no-raiding provision extends even beyond the grave. When another generation of owners comes along, should any combination of partners want to sell their Ravelston shares at a premium (because the prize at stake would be control of Argus), the other partners are guaranteed an equally high price for their holdings. (Ravelston is the name of a place in Scotland where McDougald's great-grandfather, William Allan Murray, was born in 1814. It is now a district of Edin-

The last man to try it was Paul Desmarais of Power Corporation. He had originally accumulated 10.37 per cent of Argus common stock on the open market through one of his subsidiaries (Shawinigan Industries) from 1965 to 1969; then he waited to be invited on the board. Nothing happened. In the winter of 1972, while he was in Palm Beach looking for a site for his new villa, Desmarais asked McDougald about the possibility of acquiring a controlling interest in Argus. "You'll just have to wait your turn, Paul," was the reply, and as soon as the Power Corporation chairman was out the door, McDougald turned to a friend and added: "But it's *not* coming."

ON SUNDAY, MARCH 23, 1975, BUD MCDOUGALD WAS RELAXING AT HIS PALM BEACH PALACE when he received an urgent request from Paul Desmarais for a meeting. Looking determined and unusually nervous, the Power Corporation chairman arrived a few moments later, sat down in one of McDougald's five living rooms, and came to the point: he was about to launch a $150-million bid for control of Argus; his host should lead the Toronto holding company's shareholders in accepting his offer of $22 for each common share (then trading at $15.25 to $16.50) and $17 for each Class C preferred share (then worth $12.75). McDougald was flabbergasted. "I said, 'Paul, for God's sake, don't bother arguing with me, Argus just isn't for sale. I'm going to croak someday and your turn may come—if, as, and when that happens. I've got no interest in your deal, so just forget it.' Desmarais seemed to accept that and I took him to the Everglades Club. We had lunch in a friendly way and afterwards I dropped him on Worth Avenue where he wanted to do some shopping. And that was the end of that."

Late that evening, W.G. "Bill" Cluett (of Cluett, Peabody, the Arrow Shirt people), the Everglades Club president, suddenly died, and McDougald, who is not

burgh and the Ravelston mansion house, owned for a time by a branch of the Murray family, is now the Mary Erskine School for Girls; the formal gardens, which provided some of the features of Tully-Veolan in Walter Scott's novel *Waverley*, are now the school's playing fields.)

only a governor of the club but also a director of the syndicate that controls it, became preoccupied with choosing a successor. Picking a new head of the Everglades is a process only slightly less formal than deciding the papal continuity in Rome. Club governors meet in solemn conclave on the first juridical day after the incumbent's passing and no one is allowed to disturb them. Desmarais telephoned the club on Monday morning to inform McDougald that he was proceeding with his bid despite the Argus chairman's warning. But the Everglades steward refused to put him through. He left a number, and when McDougald finally called back, it turned out to be a pay phone at the Palm Beach airport. Desmarais spent the rest of the day flying across the continent aboard his private JetStar.* He landed at the Palm Springs airport in California and was immediately driven to the El Dorado Golf Club at Palm Desert. He remained there for most of the next month, living in a villa lent to him by Fred Mannix, the Calgary industrialist. His only house guest was Senator Louis Gélinas; his most important new acquaintance was Gerald Ford, who came to play golf at the El Dorado Club on March 22. Desmarais did phone through to McDougald once more, on the evening of March 24, to advise the Argus chairman that his lawyers had told him to report their negotiations to the SEC. McDougald, angry now, replied that as far as he was concerned no negotiations had taken place, and hung up.

At 11.12 a.m. the following day, with no advance notice, Power launched its bid for Argus. By the time the stock exchanges ordered a halt to trading in Argus shares three minutes later, the common stock had jumped a dollar and the Class C shares were up $2.38. Significantly, Power common finished the day up only 38 cents. It was as though the financial Establishment had, in those crucial 180 seconds, already decided who would be the eventual winner in this contest of Goliaths. In Ottawa, the Power offer blew up into a major political issue and Pierre Trudeau established a royal commis-

---

*The $3-million plane was purchased by Desmarais from Henry Ford II. Its gold-coloured interior has five seats, a sofa, a bar, a kitchen, and a stereo system.

sion to examine "the economic and social implications for
the public interest of major concentrations of corporate
power in Canada."

Then began a strange interlude in McDougald's career.
The mysterious tycoon who never talked to reporters became, at least for the month that followed, the most accessible of men, personally answering the telephone to
anyone who called. Because his Palm Beach residence
has no office, McDougald converted Felix du Pont's
former private shower, a ten-foot-square cubicle with
windows overlooking the Atlantic, into his command post,
equipping it with a desk, a wastebasket, a pencil sharpen-
er, and two telephones. On the Wednesday morning following the Power bid between 9.30 and 12.30, Mrs.
McDougald logged thirty-two calls.

"I kept asking people," McDougald remembers, "what
are you talking about? Fight Power Corporation? There's
no fight. The war's over. There *isn't* any war. And
Desmarais? I don't know how anybody could live till he
was forty-nine and be so naïve and green in that deal.
The board room of Power must be just like Alice in
Wonderland. It's just fantastic. Take a fellow like Earle
McLaughlin [chairman of the Royal Bank]. He knew
the facts. The Royal was our main banker, right from the
day Argus started. He's a director of Power. I assume
he approved this deal. He loaned them the money."

What only McDougald's intimates realized at the time
was that even under the pressure of the Desmarais bid
McDougald had desperately wanted to retain the public
silence he had never broken. The real reason he began
to speak out was that the Power offer came at a particularly awkward moment for Argus, just as four major
deals were moving into their crucial stages of negotia-
tion. Standard Broadcasting, controlled by Argus, was in
the process of purchasing Capital Radio, a large British
private broadcaster aimed at the London market. The
British principals, as well as members of the Independent
Broadcasting Authority, threatened to break off the talks
should the ownership of Argus change hands. At the same
time, in Canada, Standard had made a $10-million bid
for Bushnell Communications in Ottawa, subject to approval by the CRTC. Pierre Juneau, the commission's chair-

man, requested that Argus publicly declare its intentions. And so, in his sixty-eighth year, Bud McDougald for the first time in his life went on radio and in a two-minute broadcast over CFRB Toronto (which Standard owns) denounced the interlopers who had dared challenge his power.

At the same time, in his capacity as chairman of Massey-Ferguson, McDougald was negotiating with S.E. "Bunkie" Knudsen, head of the White Motor Corporation, for a huge diesel plant at Canton, Ohio, which he wanted as an alternative source of engines to Massey's strife-torn branch at Peterborough, in the English Midlands. McDougald had persuaded the White Motors chairman to sign over the factory merely in return for Massey's taking over the $40 million in outstanding municipal debentures that had been used for the factory's original financing. Now Knudsen wanted out of the deal if Desmarais was going to be involved. McDougald managed to calm him down.

The most delicate bargaining of all concerned the 1.6 million Massey-Ferguson cumulative redeemable preferred shares then due to be issued. Wood Gundy, lead firm in the thirty-member underwriting syndicate, had sent John Abell, one of its vice-presidents, to Palm Beach, where several of Massey's directors were spending the winter, to tidy up the details. "There was a whole army of people in my house," McDougald recalls. "Because the takeover bid was overhanging the market, dealers were beginning to get worried about taking commitments on these shares. The way Massey had been run under the Argus umbrella, they felt that was one thing, but under this other group, it might be something else. . . . Well, there I was, sitting in Palm Beach with some of the Massey directors, still negotiating on the amount and the price. And as we talked, the thing was sinking further, till finally the syndicate people claimed the best they could sell was $20 millions. 'Well,' I said, 'that's just an insult to Massey. But let's get the thing cleaned up. If you're willing to take on another $5 million, we'll settle for that.' Abell called Toronto and came back to tell me there was a new quirk in the deal. Greenshields and

Nesbitt, Thomson, members of the Massey syndicate, were actively soliciting Argus shares on Power's behalf.

"I was so mad, I said to Abell, 'I don't like ungrateful people—this was only two weeks after we had given Nesbitt a $30-million bond issue in Dominion Stores—I don't like disloyal people, and I don't like people sabotaging their client's account. There's only one thing to do: kick them out of this Massey financing altogether. Just kick them out. Don't let them withdraw, because that'll give the impression maybe they thought the issue wasn't good.' Poor Abell figured this was pretty rough stuff and pointed out that he'd got all this banking group already signed up and both Greenshields and Nesbitt were in it.

" 'Well,' I told him, 'there's only one chink in your so-called armour, and that's me. In the dining room there are all those papers sitting out there, waiting for me to sign up. There's going to be no deal at all unless you go to the telephone right now and tell both those people that they're being kicked out for disloyalty and sabotage. And when you've finished, you call the other members of the banking group and explain the reason they were kicked out—not let out, but *kicked out.*'

"I stood there while Abell did it. This was something new in Canadian finance. At one point he asked me who was going to take up their shares, and I said: 'Don't worry about that. I'll take them up personally if I have to, so get on with it.'

"'I'll give Abell full credit. He did it. He kicked them out. It was quite a shock to them. As I say, it wasn't allowed to get around that they simply weren't part of the deal; they were kicked out. The very minute the other dealers heard that Greenshields and Nesbitt had been kicked out, they knew we meant business. That was the turning point. Before the day was over, we had the $40 million for Massey and the issue was oversubscribed the following morning."*

---

*Deane Nesbitt's version of this transaction is that "Mr. McDougald was misinformed on the subject of our soliciting shares of Argus on behalf of Power Corporation, prior to being removed from the Massey banking group. Mr. McDougald had Nesbitt, Thomson and Greenshields removed on April 1. The Power Corporation offer was not mailed until

The Royal Bank, which had granted Desmarais the $150-million credit for his bid, now began to get nervous and started sending out feelers, trying to lay off at least $50 million on another bank. McDougald somehow got wind of the attempt, and when the chairman of the Commerce (where he is a senior director) phoned to get his assessment, he enthusiastically supported the loan. To McDougald it was the best banking deal he'd ever seen, because he knew the Commerce would simply get its stand-by fee on the $50 million, without ever actually having to advance the money.

AT THIS POINT, E.P. TAYLOR, WHO HAD NOT BEEN ACTIVE IN ARGUS MANAGEMENT SINCE 1971 but in the public mind continued to personify Canadian business power and prestige, openly joined the fray. Actually, Taylor had been in on the deal from the beginning, when he entertained Desmarais and Lord Hardinge at his Nassau estate early in March. Caryl Nicholas Charles Hardinge (whose title dates from 1846, when Field Marshal Sir Henry Hardinge was named governor-general of India) had spent much of his working life as a partner with the London stockbrokers Kitcat and Aitken. He had first met Taylor when he came to Ottawa in 1926 as a young aide-de-camp to the Earl of Willingdon, then governor general, and emigrated to Montreal in 1952. He shared with Taylor an interest in racehorses and as chairman of Greenshields had been chief underwriter for the New Providence Development Company in the Bahamas. Desmarais's connection with Taylor was more recent. Taylor's daughter had decorated his Montreal house and

---

April 3, and there certainly was no solicitation prior to April 4. Even after being advised that we had been 'kicked out' of the banking group, we made a policy decision to support the Massey-Ferguson financing, and so advised Wood Gundy. We applied in the selling group for 60,000 shares, which was the net amount of what our banking group position would have been. Initially, we were allotted 50,000 shares, but on reapplication we were allotted an additional 15,000 shares. In this way we remained associated with the offering of Massey-Ferguson preferred shares; we gave very important support to the financing and certainly contributed to the successful placing of the issue. A test of the market had been made at 9¾ per cent, and the real turning point in obtaining the $40 million came when Wood Gundy, manager of the syndicate offering the shares, announced the increase in the dividend rate from 9¾ per cent to 10 per cent."

the two men had established a friendship based on mutual respect and personal compatibility.

At 1.30 p.m. on April 17, a week before the Power offer for the Argus shares was due to expire, Taylor, who was about to board his private Hawker Siddeley jet at Toronto airport, made a statement to the *Globe and Mail* that he was tendering his 1,250,000 Class C Argus shares (worth $21.25 million) to Power Corporation, but stipulated that the announcement should be held until after the close of that day's stock market. The story appeared in the *Globe*'s bulldog edition, which reaches the street in the evening, well after the markets across Canada have closed. When it broke, McDougald had only one comment: "Mr. Taylor is perfectly free to do what he wishes. He's over twenty-one."

The Taylor manoeuvre didn't cause the expected stir. When the Power offer closed, holders of only 3 per cent of the common shares had accepted its terms, though 3,987,812 Class C shares were turned in, giving Desmarais 50.8 per cent of the total issued participating equity stock in Argus, but not control, since the Class C shares carry no vote.* The unsuccessful offer had cost Power about $70 million. Perhaps before he undertook his foray, Paul Desmarais ought to have examined closely one of Bud McDougald's thirty automobiles. On the side of each vehicle, so small it's hardly visible, is part of the McDougald coat of arms and the McDougald motto: VINCERE VEL MORI (Conquer or Die).

MCDOUGALD STILL EXPENDS MOST OF HIS TIME ON ARGUS AFFAIRS, though he also runs Crown Trust,† is a director

---

*In late May of 1975, McDougald increased his hold by buying (through Ravelston) a further 10 per cent of Argus common shares (at $30 each) from the Wallace McCutcheon estate and made arrangements for another 8 per cent with the Jackman interests. H.N.R. Jackman, chairman of Empire Life, became an Argus director on June 26, 1975. Throughout the McDougald-Desmarais confrontation, Hollinger, controlled by Argus, was standing by with $50 million cash for any contingency.

†Now listed as chief of the company's advisory board, McDougald has been a director of Crown Trust since 1941. His uncle, John McMartin, who was one of the original backers of the Hollinger mine in Timmins, left an estate so large that a trust company (then called Trusts and Guarantee) was established to handle its administration. Bud McDougald's father was John McMartin's chief executor. McMartin's son Jack and

of both Sangamo Company Limited (the world's largest manufacturer of electric meters) and Avco Corporation, a huge U.S. conglomerate whose subsidiaries include large defence plants, motion picture production houses (*A Touch of Class* and *The Day of the Dolphin* were among the recent releases), radio and TV stations, a credit-card system (Carte Blanche), as well as land development projects, consumer finance, and insurance operations.

As he grows older, McDougald has retreated into a philosophy of life that attributes everything imperfect to the collective impulses of the liberal society in which he lives. "Our trouble today," he complains, "is the courts, the parole boards, the universities and the churches." He is an avowed anti-nationalist (he has no patience, he says, with the Walter Gordons, as though there were more than one) and believes that governments should "stay out of business and especially stay out of harassing business, which is what they're doing." He admits he has never felt the inclination to run for public office to put his beliefs into practice because of "the sort of people you have to meet—all that terrible going to strawberry festivals and the like."

"C.D. Howe," he says, "was the last man to bring business and government together. You could deal with CD. If there was some problem where the government was involved, you could talk to him. He didn't have to yank in a half a dozen deputies to advise him. He knew what you were talking about. And he'd make a decision just like that. It wouldn't necessarily always be in your favour but he knew what it was all about and he could decide so that you could get on with it. I don't know a cabinet minister now who would dare give you a decision on anything without bringing in all his deputies. They're

his nephews Allen and Duncan showed little interest in business, and the younger McDougald gradually took over the firm, amalgamating it with Crown Trust, a medium-sized Montreal operation, in 1946. In addition to his own considerable holdings, McDougald votes the 26 per cent still held by the McMartins, who now live in Bermuda. John McMartin's niece, Melba, once bought a sixty-four-carat diamond the size of a man's thumb joint, but only wore its paste imitation. Her cousin Jack used to march into Montreal bars and with his walking stick smash every bottle behind the counter. Weary bartenders let him enjoy himself, because they knew they could charge him a flat $1,000 fee per performance. When Melba's brother Duncan was an RCAF instructor near Calgary during World War II, one Friday the pay failed to arrive and he wrote a cheque to cover the station's payroll.

only front men for their departments. They're nothing. Louis St. Laurent was right at the top of the heap before he went into the government. He did it as a patriotic move, that's the only reason. And gave up a lot to do it. But other than St. Laurent I don't know anybody in government who hasn't bettered his position."

A friend once attempted to have McDougald name one, any *one*, politician, living or dead, who might have possessed redeeming qualities. After rejecting half a hundred names, McDougald softened a little at the mention of Abraham Lincoln, reluctantly conceding that perhaps he wasn't all that bad. Then he added: "But, he wasn't as good as John Wilkes Booth."

McDougald's political creed, though that may be too grand a category for it, is a simplistic loathing of state intervention in any form. "There's no percentage in being socialistic," he preaches. "I mean, some of the most successful fellows I know started with nothing and have done pretty well, and they're not socialists. A lot of the people that inherited large sums of money are very sympathetic, but they never give anything away. I've found that out. I've watched them pretty carefully. Members of the second generation have a complex; they're ashamed of something. They're sometimes socialist, because they couldn't do it on their own, so they're trying to justify it. But they never give any of their own money away."*

Because he made most of his own fortune himself, McDougald regards the sons of the rich as dilettantes. He was once having dinner with Bobby Kennedy in the Everglades Club in Florida, a Disney World sort of place with a sliding roof that opens up over the dance floor on clear starry nights. When the young senator tried to score a few dints in his political intransigence, McDougald pretended to go along with the lecture. In mock earnestness he confessed that he'd finally seen the light. Why didn't they both do something about all the social needs the young Kennedy had been listing? "I put Bobby on the

---

*Despite his opposition to socialism, McDougald was one of the largest contributors to the 1972 campaign of John Harney, the NDPcr from Scarborough West Riding—mainly so that he could beat the incumbent Liberal. McDougald was also a substantial contributor to the McGovern candidacy of 1972.

spot that night," he remembers with some relish. "I said, 'You just turn over everything Joe set up for you, and I'll match it. We'll give it all to a charity of your choice and that will set a good example for some others.' But Bobby wasn't very much in favour of that. It really shut him up."*

THE LION IN WINTER. THE VIALS OF WRATH HAVE BEEN RETREATING WITHIN BUD MCDOUGALD ever since his second major heart attack in 1966, when he spent most of nine weeks unconscious inside an oxygen tent in an intensive-care unit. He is seldom abusive now, dimly aware that absolute power no longer holds men or causes. His pursuit of money has become more of a diversion than food for his soul.†

Relaxing with a friend, he will tell the story of a childhood encounter that probably affected him—and his approach to life—more deeply than any other single experience. "Years ago I was on my way to Mexico with my father. We went from Chicago to St. Louis, Missouri, on a special train called the Banner Blue, and when we came into the railroad station in St. Louis, the trains used to come alongside each other, and right beside my father's railroad car I looked across on the next track, and here was a fellow in another private car with a grand

---

*McDougald's own charitable activities were highlighted by his successful $5-million campagn for St. Michael's Hospital in Toronto. When it was over, he sent out letters to each of the 17,000 subscribers, explaining what had been accomplished with their money. St. Michael's still hangs a portrait of him, painted by Sir James Gunn, in the place of honour in its board room. He also donated $200,000 to the Royal Agricultural Winter Fair in Toronto for construction of a private elevator and refurbishing of the chairman's quarters. He quietly contributes generous amounts to several Catholic institutions particularly in Western Canada.

†This doesn't mean that he will pass up opportunities to expand his wealth. In 1968, the Lycoming division of Avco, of which he is a director, was beaten in its bid for a large order of jet engines for the Lockheed L-1011 TriStar by Rolls-Royce, which guaranteed a fixed price instead of insisting on the escalator clauses more usual in development contracts. McDougald figured that no company should be that confident of its product and immediately began to sell Rolls stock short. He believes he was the only investor to make a fortune out of the British firm's bankruptcy in February, 1971. He used a similar tactic in 1950, when a letter he wrote to the president of Packard to get an instruction booklet for a 1918 touring car he had purchased brought a reply that "Packard is a progressive company: we are not interested in the past, only the future." To McDougald this indicated bad management. He sold Packard stock short and made a killing when the company ran into financial difficulties two years later.

piano in it. This was at seven o'clock in the morning, and I was having breakfast and the fellow in the other car was going up and down doing his scales, just going like that until he nearly drove me crazy. That night we went to dinner at somebody's house and then to a concert by Paderewski. He was a great pianist and premier of Poland at the same time. Because I was young, the hostess took me under her wing and I sat next to her while we heard this great concert. She turned to me and said, 'You know, Bud, isn't it wonderful to be so lucky to have that talent, to be able to play so easily?'

" 'Well,' I said, 'I've got a little special news on that one. I saw that bird this morning at seven o'clock, and if you think he just got it by having talent, you're all wrong. He has the talent but he works hard. I saw him doing his scales at seven o'clock this morning.'

" 'And that's why he's drawing ten dollars a ticket.' "

CHAPTER TWO

The Flash of Paul Desmarais

He has turned himself into a fully
emancipated entrepreneur, perhaps
the only one in the country, a man
who can attempt any corporate foray
he wants, can do it because he has
the money, the energy, the imagination,
and no apparent guilt.

So still was the forest that Paul Desmarais could hear the
beat of the pheasant's wings a hundred yards across the
clearing. From where he was standing, on the tip of Ile
aux Ruaux, Desmarais could look up the rushing St.
Lawrence River, past Ile d'Orléans to the distant copper
rooftops of Quebec City, glimmering green in the late afternoon sun. Red maples dotted the far shore like flecks
of blood. A stiff east wind beat the hunters' walkways
into brown cement.

On his way back to the old farmhouse where dinner
was being cooked, Desmarais hugged himself, as though
he could feel in his bones the chill of the Canadian mood
during that historic Thanksgiving weekend of 1970. Five
days earlier James Cross, the British trade commissioner
in Montreal, had been kidnapped by the Front de Liberation du Québec, setting off the October Crisis. As the
head of Power Corporation, the largest agglomeration of
economic power in the hands of a French Canadian,
Desmarais had been warned by the Montreal chief of
police to keep out of sight, and so with his best friend,
Pierre Genest, he had decided to seek the seclusion of
Ruaux.*

---

*The island had been purchased in 1960 by Bill O'Brien, a Montreal
investment executive, and turned into a private shooting preserve called
Club aux Brigands. It soon became the most exclusive hunting club in
Canada, with membership limited to seven (the others: Edgar Bronfman,
the New York distiller; Fred Mannix, the Calgary construction executive;
Frank McMahon, the Palm Beach oil tycoon; Frank Augsbury, of Og-
densburg, N.Y., the head of Hall Corporation Shipping Ltd. of Montreal;
and the late Art Mayne, executive vice president of the Royal Bank).
Only one member can use the island at a time. Few guests are wel-

43

As Paul Desmarais approached the island's ancient farm building, he could see Pierre Genest—a heavy, cheerfully brilliant Toronto lawyer with one of those vivid faces that has the blood close to the skin—motioning him inside. Marc Lalonde, then principal secretary and chief adviser to the Prime Minister of Canada, was calling on the island's radio-telephone hookup.*

Trudeau and Desmarais were close but fairly recent allies. It had been in the offices of Power Corporation at regular Friday night meetings early in 1968 that the plans for Trudeau's leadership candidacy had first been hatched. In August of 1968, two months after Trudeau had swept the country, the new prime minister had flown to visit Desmarais at Murray Bay, where he has a summer home. When Desmarais had picked the P.M. up at the local airport in one of the two Rolls-Royces he keeps there, Trudeau casually inquired what it was like to drive a Rolls. Desmarais stopped the car, got in the back seat, and, as Trudeau took the wheel, exclaimed: "This is the first time I've ever been driven by a prime minister!"

The mood was very different now. In Ottawa, Trudeau had just been informed that Pierre Laporte had been kidnapped; a secret revolutionary manifesto named the Power Corporation chairman as the FLQ's next priority target; a platoon of plainclothesmen had already been posted to Desmarais's Montreal house. Desmarais was being warned to get himself off Ruaux; the federal authority could no longer guarantee his safety.

When you're running a $7-billion operation, there is always a way of getting yourself off an island. Within minutes, Desmarais had contacted the yards of Davie Shipbuilding (one of his companies' subsidiaries) at Lauzon,

---

comed, Prince Philip being an exception. O'Brien has stocked Ruaux with pheasant, put down a grass airstrip, and restored the primitive farmhouse originally used by doctors who operated a nearby quarantine station during the great cholera epidemics of the Irish migrations in the 1840s. Local lore has it that one of the medical residents had been extracting the dying immigrants' gold teeth in lieu of payment, and when remorse finally overtook him, he lay down on a cot and cut his throat. Because untreated wood preserves bloodstains for a very long time, they are still on the farmhouse floor. The winter silence of Ruaux is broken by the occasional brave fox from the mainland that catches the pheasants' scent, hops a floe, and gorges on the captive birds, only to be hunted down himself at spring breakup.

*Other callers that day included Maurice St. Pierre, chief of the Quebec Provincial Police, and Desmarais's brother Louis.

just a few miles upstream, and ordered a tug to pick him
up on Monday. The tugboat captain called back to report
that Ruaux's tidal flats would not allow him to land.

By coincidence, the Royal 22nd Regiment kept a land-
ing craft of World War II vintage near Quebec City.
With its shallow draught, the barge could transfer the
hunters from Ruaux to the Davie tug.

A PURPLE STREAK LYING OVER CAP TOURMENTE WAS
ALL THAT REMAINED of that strange Saturday as Desmarais
paced around the farmhouse. His good friend Genest was
beside him, hunched over the foundations of his strong
legs, looking as solid and faithful as an old Byzantine
church. Like a man going outdoors after a heavy rain
and seeing the world with a kind of heightened sensitiv-
ity, Desmarais had reason to reflect on the past week's
turbulent events. Only three years before he had gone to
Hawaii at another crucial moment in Quebec history. A
semi-official Union Nationale document had come to light
outlining the provincial government's confidential five-year
plan for Quebec independence. After refusing to disown
the scheme, Premier Daniel Johnson had flown to Hawaii
for a rest. Without anyone's knowledge or permission,
Desmarais promptly joined him there, taking along a *La
Presse* reporter and Marcel Faribault, the Montreal constitutional expert. The three men walked along the beach
and debated the issue; then Johnson told the journalist
from *La Presse* (which Desmarais owns) that he would
support a federalist constitution and that his administration had been given "no mandate to build a Great Wall
of China around Quebec."

That was a sweet time for Paul Desmarais. That was
the way he liked to deal himself in on history. It seemed
to those who knew him best that Desmarais sometimes
treated politicians with the deference due sleepwalkers:
men who must be led, but ever so gently, lest they should
ever wake up to the fact. As he climbed in the orbits of
influence, Desmarais seemed to gain the sense that somehow his personal destiny was merged with that of his
province and of his country.

PAUL GUY DESMARAIS HAS MOVED UP IN CANADA'S POSTWAR BUSINESS HIERARCHY so quickly and so quietly that only a few top insiders know him well or have even heard his footsteps. A corporate gambler on a grand scale who has mastered the free enterprise system to reap its boldest dividends, he is the business Establishment's most intriguing figure. Within French Canada, he is considered something of an outsider—a man who was born and raised in Ontario, who established and enlarged his impressive credit sources entirely through sympathetic support from the large Wasp financial institutions. At the same time, members of English Canada's Establishment regard him as their chief ambassador from contemporary Quebec—endowing him with almost occult powers as they try to understand a part of the country and a state of mind that they view with only slightly less comprehension than the rumblings of some distant, mythical Transylvania.

Paul Desmarais is the most vital money man we have and the most essentially Canadian. He has no equivalents in either French or English Canada, yet he couldn't exist anywhere else. He is unique—and uniquely Canadian —because he didn't look to New York or London to find out how to be; he knew from his native wits how to play on Canada's two cultures while getting the best out of both. Above all, he has turned himself into a fully emancipated entrepreneur, perhaps the only one in the country, a man who can attempt any corporate foray he wants, can do it because he has the money, the energy, the imagination, and no apparent guilt.

Desmarais fits no stereotypes. He is like some rare breed of cat, prowling the corporate jungles, free of the hidebound timidity that holds back would-be challengers. Ever since he moved into contention as an important entrepreneur during the mid-sixties, there has been a discernible pattern in the nature of his postures and presences that gives his career the cumulative cadence of a great stage performance. He has fashioned his role from moment to moment, from one corporate *coup* to the next, taking on psychic weight as his empire has expanded, guarding his self-imposed public silence, preserving the air of the mysterious intruder a-hum with improbable energies.

He is fearless, and this may be his secret—more than intellect or even moxie. He isn't afraid. He knows he can outwit or outcharm (and if necessary outbully) anybody he needs to deal with. He is shrewd, a man who has drawn his most useful experience from the streets, from hanging around the garages, community rinks, drug stores, and pool halls in Sudbury, where he grew up. The English have never possessed any mystery for him. "I just never had any fear of the English and their institutions, like the banks, for example," he says. "They don't do business on an English or French basis but on a business basis. I had to fight to speak French where I came from, but I was always talking to English Canadians, playing hockey with them, going to school with them, and everything else. I knew that the ball game was there and that I was allowed to play."

The fact that Paul Desmarais is a French Canadian is responsible in no small measure for his success. The men who control the large private capital pools with which he deals—the Royal Bank, the CPR, the Canadian Imperial Bank of Commerce, Cemp Investments (Bronfman money), and Genstar Limited (the Canadian investment front for La Société Générale de Belgique)—have a vested financial interest in holding Canada together. More by osmosis than by intent, Desmarais has somehow caused them to believe that if *he* should fail, the cause of Quebec in Canada would be lost and Quebec might separate. "I feel," he admits, "that as a Quebecker involved in the national economy, I have an added responsibility to succeed. A successful French Canadian destroys the separatists' argument that success is impossible within Canada. So they attack him and try to knock him down to justify their position and discourage others from trying."

To those French Canadians who believe in both federalism and capitalism, Desmarais provides a useful symbol of what can be achieved within the system. But to the radical nationalists he has come to personify the enemy. At one point during the long and violent strike and lockout at *La Presse* in October of 1971, fifteen thousand demonstrators marched on the building, many carrying placards that read *"DESMARAIS AU POTEAU"* ("Desmarais to the gallows"), and burned him in effigy.

Desmarais sees himself as the forerunner of Quebec's hoped-for graduation into the big business ethic. "Quebec is a closed-in society financially," he says. "You don't see many French Canadians who are presidents of any of our national business institutions—you know, banks, insurance companies, trust companies, oil companies, mines, steel companies, transport or pipeline or anything—you name it. What I want them to do is get out there and participate and feel part of it. Once they understand what the game's all about, well, they'll say there's nothing to this and they'll feel at home. It'll be great."

PAUL DESMARAIS'S APPEARANCE IS NOT SIMPLE TO CAPTURE. He seems to invent himself for each occasion, changing his demeanour, his very essence, according to the impression he wants to leave. There is the temptation to throw off a one-dimensional portrait of him as resembling a bit player in a French film about Gallic high jinks in a Mont Blanc ski resort. But he is very much more than that. Whatever role he happens to be playing, the stern centre of the man remains inviolate: his natural physical elegance; the six-foot two-inch frame, bent like a parenthesis, moving with a deliberately slowed stride; the brown eyes disengaged from whatever may be occupying his mind; the shrug, so elusive that it could be carefree or serious, confirming a joke or a promise; the tube of his long, vented, three-piece dark blue suits; his greying cowlick of hair; his almost successfully disguised stutter; the thumbs that curve outward, signalling a hot temper.

Anyone meeting Desmarais for the first time finds himself overwhelmed by the man's vivacity, his special quality of being alive to any possibility that might exist. Desmarais possesses all of the natural French-Canadian charm, but somehow he is not cowed, not burdened by the hierarchical society of Quebec with its dark resentments of the English. He shares the fun and closeness he enjoys within his own family and is most himself when he's telling stories about his father, Aunt Blanche's funeral, or the time his Uncle Clovis sold the Polish government some gold-plated lead bars.

As he mimics his middle-class relatives, it's evident that no man could be easier with his background: "My father's got enough pep to kill us all. He's seventy-four. Every October he gets a new Buick, drives around Sudbury for a month, then he and my mother drive all the way to Florida. I told him a few years ago, 'Listen, Dad, you're going to kill yourself.' I was very mad. 'This doesn't make any sense at all. What you've got to do is take your car and put it in your garage and I'm going to buy you a ticket and you're going to take the plane to Florida instead of driving. I'll provide you with an identical car on your arrival.' I had an interest in Avis Rent-a-Car at the time so I asked them to give him an identical car, a blue Buick with the same radio, same buttons, same everything, except for the licence plate. So my mother persuaded my father to avoid the big drive and accept my offer. So, by geez, they did it.

"When I called to ask how he was doing, he said, 'Oh, fine.' I asked him how he liked his Avis car. 'Oh, fine.' I wanted to know when he was coming back. He said, 'Well, your mother and I have decided that we're going to travel from Florida to California; then we're going up to Vancouver and we're coming back on the Trans-Canada.'

"I said, 'With an Avis car?'

"He replied, 'Oh no, I have my own car.'

" 'How did you do that?' I asked him.

" 'Well, you know, I offered the return portion of my ticket to Pierre [Paul's brother, then in Sudbury] and his wife. I wanted him to have a little holiday. So he drove my car down and took your plane ticket to return.'

"I said, 'God bless you, Pop. Take your car and drive it all the way to Moscow.' "

SUCH STORIES AND THE GUSTO WITH WHICH HE TELLS THEM MAKE IT EASY to lose sight of the imposing economic influence Paul Desmarais has accumulated within Power Corporation of Canada, the $7-billion corporate commonwealth he controls through Gelco and Nordex, his private holding companies.

A complex maze of interlocking shareholdings and

directorships places Desmarais at the top of an amazing pyramid that includes Canada's largest mutual fund (Investors Group); an important trust company (Montreal Trust); third-largest life insurer (Great-West Life and Imperial Life combined); third-largest finance company (Laurentide); largest ship operator on the Great Lakes (Canada Steamship Lines); largest shipyard (Davie Shipbuilding); third-largest trucking company (Kingsway Transports); fourth-biggest newsprint maker (Consolidated-Bathurst); largest domestically owned bus line (Provincial-Voyageur); and dozens of other enterprises, including a large ranch in Australia. It is difficult for the ordinary Canadian to exist a week without enriching Paul Desmarais, however indirectly. In 1974, Power's combined revenues totalled nearly $1 million per working day.

Unlike most of his rivals, by holding 51 per cent or more of Power Corporation, Desmarais actually *owns* all but one of the seventy companies that make up the huge conglomerate.* His enemies insist that no one should be so powerful, that if money makes men ugly, new money makes them uglier still, because they haven't learned to disguise their avarice behind masks of pretension.

It is impossible to trace how this unique empire was put together without first taking full account of Desmarais's personality. A long time ago, he learned an important secret: the Canadian Establishment is starved for irreverence. Some of its notable members who have been bested by Desmarais in his various dealings (and the list is long) behave like the mythical character whose head has been cut off in a duel and he doesn't realize it until he tries to sneeze. Desmarais pokes fun at their stuffy, sedate airs, addresses them with profanities more usually heard at waterfront bars, and they lap it up. Perhaps it's because they recognize in Desmarais's high candour a way they will never be: an individual with a superbly developed sense of the absurd operating in a world filled

---

*These companies are owned in the sense that Desmarais has voting control of Power Corp. which in turn is their majority shareholder. The exception is Consolidated-Bathurst, where he has the largest single block (37 per cent) of stock and controls all of the seats on the board of directors.

with men who feel comfortable with themselves only if they set their countenances in the stern look of a suspended storm.

Still, the Establishment is by no means unanimous in accepting Desmarais. Its members can't ignore his presence or the daring of his intuitive leaps, but they occasionally treat him as though they were fraternity brothers dealing with an affable graduate student who holds two part-time jobs and gets the best marks. They seem always to be circling around him, trying to learn his tricks, testing him with those intimidating pauses they muster up so well. They still occasionally try to make him feel like a novice praying in the chill at the rear of the Establishment abbey—though none would deny that he is safely within the fold for all that.* Their most effective weapon is to discount—just a little—the market worth of Power's shares. The daily swing in the company's price-earnings ratio is a mirror reflecting the business Establishment's verdict of Desmarais's worth.

DESMARAIS TREATS EACH NEW BUSINESS DEAL LIKE A POLITICAL CONQUEST. As negotiations progress toward their climax, he takes on the urgent persuasiveness of a politician coming up to polling day in a closely fought campaign. He has the knack of making people believe in him. "Paul is probably the only businessman in Canada who can make a pitch to a board of directors for the takeover of their own company and leave them in heat," says one observer of the process. His style of corporate politics invites involvement, generating energy in others convertible to his use.

Desmarais understands very well that a politician needs no deep sense of motivation for his attempts to keep continually enlarging his power base. His life depends on it. He knows how to calculate his real options, how much of what is desirable can be attained, which

---

*In addition to being a director of the various Power subsidiaries, Desmarais is on the boards of Brascan, Brinco, Hilton of Canada, Siemens Canada, Kaiser Resources, and Standard Brands. He is not able to join a bank board because he controls Montreal Trust, and the 1967 revision of the Bank Act prevented the interlocking of trust company and bank boards.

tensions can be withstood, all the subtle ways in which commitments can be matched with available power. The trick is never to stop expanding your constituency, because there's no other way to keep your mandate alive. "You're never too big," Desmarais says of Power Corporation. "If you get big like ITT, you're criticized for being too big—being multinational, pulling the strings here and there, trying to run the world. But if you put a limit on your growth, then you're dead the minute you reach it."

Because he practises their beguiling arts to such advantage, Desmarais feels compatible with politicians, likes to spend time in their company, and sees little wrong with trying to influence their decisions: "There isn't enough flexibility and communication between businessmen and politicians, not enough willingness for each to understand the legitimate needs of the other."

Desmarais's best friend in politics was Daniel Johnson, but he has known intimately all the Quebec premiers of his time.* Robert Bourassa is on the phone to him at least twice a week. "The Premier," reports a friend who knows them both well, "leans heavily on Desmarais for advice in all sorts of areas, tells Paul the government's troubles, treats him like a father confessor." Relations between the two men cooled considerably when Bourassa halted Desmarais's bid for the Quebec City daily *Le Soleil* in 1973.

The channels of influence that link Power Corporation and the federal Liberal party carry considerable two-way traffic. For Paul Desmarais, the ultimate expression of power is to *feel* history as it is being made. It's when he is being consulted by the prime minister and premiers on options before they become policies that he really begins to fulfil every great entrepreneur's dream: that his stewardship will be judged by criteria beyond those found at the bottom line of his balance sheets. Desmarais genuinely believes that it is his mission to act as a broker between government and business on behalf of Confederation. Should shipbuilding contracts and other forms of

---

*One of Daniel Johnson's sons became secretary of Power Corporation in 1973. A lawyer, he had a Ph.D. from the University of London and is a graduate of the Harvard Business School.

patronage flow out of his dealings with Ottawa and Quebec City, well, those are just the fringe benefits. He always wants to be in the *know*. Government announcements seldom catch him by surprise.

That process requires the establishment of communication links near the summit of Ottawa's decision-making pyramids. The easiest way to achieve such synergy is to hire away some of the capital's more effective young shakers who want to move on, are capable of operating in the business environment, and still retain their Ottawa contacts. Desmarais's chief aide is John Rae, who was executive assistant to Jean Chrétien in Indian Affairs. The bright and affable older son of Saul Rae, Canada's ambassador to the United Nations, Rae was preceded by Claude Frenette, who ran Maurice Sauvé's office when he was Minister of Forestry in the Pearson cabinet.* Sauvé himself later became vice-president, administration, of Consolidated-Bathurst, a Power subsidiary. Bryce Mackasey spent his two years' banishment from the Trudeau cabinet as a consultant to Canada Steamship Lines, another Power Corporation subsidiary. Paul Martin, Jr., who organized his father's 1968 leadership campaign, now operates CSL for Power. Bill Teron, president of Central Mortgage and Housing Corporation, Tony Hampson, president of the Canada Development Corporation, Maurice Strong, Undersecretary-General of the United Nations, Louis Desmarais, who is vice-chairman of the Canada Development Corporation, and several others have all worked for Power Corporation in senior capacities. Power's board includes not only Jean-Luc Pepin, an ex-minister of Trade, Commerce and Industry in the Trudeau government, and Jean-Paul Gignac, president of Sidbec, the steel company owned by the Quebec government, but also John Robarts, the former premier of Ontario, and Alfredo Campo, chairman of Petrofina Canada (Petrofina's president is Pierre Nadeau, a member of the three-man Royal Commission on Corporate Concentration, set up in 1975). Desmarais's connections with the federal

---

*When Frenette, then a vice-president of Power, won the presidency of the Quebec Liberal Federation by beating out an anti-reform candidate, Pierre Trudeau burst into his hotel room, hugged him, and said: "We beat the bastards; now we can get something done."

Conservatives aren't as direct, but Robert Stanfield has visited his Montreal house, and the Tories did get sizable campaign contributions from him in 1972 and 1974.

When Warnock Hersey International had closer ties with Power Corporation, it owned a luxurious beach villa in Jamaica. In the early sixties, several Liberal cabinet ministers used to pass the key quietly around among themselves and spend free time there. Montreal Trust, another Power operation, acts as the main depository for financing Quebec's federal and provincial Liberal parties.

Desmarais makes little attempt to justify his predilection for surrounding himself with ex-politicians: "Not to hire a guy because he has been a politician is stupid. We want good people in Ottawa and Quebec City. If we can use their talent after they've retired or have been defeated, I would be the first one to hire them or offer them a seat on our boards. To hell with the people who say that we do it for political favours. Why should former politicians who have served the country well be discarded if they can still render good service in the private sector or anywhere else?"

Desmarais is also one of the few members of the business Establishment who unabashedly support Pierre Trudeau, and he lunches with the P.M. privately at least twice a year. "Some people tell me that the present government is overly socialistic. I disagree," he says. "The Trudeau government is right for this critical period in our history. Trudeau is not a socialist. We all want the maximum freedom possible to accomplish our different ambitions. In today's Canadian context, and in the world's complex economic and political climate, I trust Trudeau to take decisions protecting the liberty of the individual commensurate with the survival and well-being of our society."

Apart from that mild heresy, his free enterprise philosophy could have been copied from a chamber of commerce pamphlet: "We are reaching the crossroads where I suppose governments will have to decide whether or not there is any role left for private enterprise in our society or whether government, through Crown corporations, regulatory agencies, excessive taxation, or outright takeovers, will control everything. The net result of all this, of course, is that individual initiative is stifled by red tape created by super-Big-Brother government acting, supposedly, in the best interests of the community. I believe in a vigorous private sector because if companies do not perform, they are out of business. They must perform or die. That does not apply to governments, and if governments fail, the collectivity never really knows how much it has lost."

Besides Trudeau himself, Desmarais's best cabinet friends are Jean Chrétien and Marc Lalonde. During the summer doldrums following the 1974 election campaign, Desmarais's guests on fishing trips to Anticosti Island included Simon Reisman, then deputy minister of finance, as well as Trudeau and his son Justin. There is a photograph now permanently ensconced in Desmarais's office of the Prime Minister fishing on Anticosti's Jupiter River.

The Jupiter is reputed to be the best salmon stream in North America and for six years one of Desmarais's companies owned all of Anticosti, the largest piece of freehold property on earth. The 135-mile-long island, whose western tip lies about four hundred miles northeast of Quebec City, guards the frothing mouth of the St. Lawrence River. Discovered by Jacques Cartier in 1535, Anticosti has been privately held since the reign of Louis XIV. Its most unusual landlord was Henri Menier, the chocolate manufacturer from France who acquired the property in 1895 and turned it into a sylvan fiefdom. He built himself a thirty-room *château* and an eighteen-mile railway, stocked his retreat with salmon, beaver, deer, caribou, and moose. He loved to spend his mornings astride a gold throne from which he would issue instructions to his employees and settle disputes among the island's eight hundred permanent residents.

In 1926, Anticosti was sold for $6.5 million to a group of Canadian paper companies headed by Sir Herbert Holt, who sent in three thousand lumberjacks and built five ships to bring the wood to his mills. Because of the high initial investment, Anticosti timber cost ten dollars more per cord than other Quebec pulpwood and by 1934, shareholders in the Holt venture were referring to their investment as the "Ain't-It-Costly" Corporation. Eventually, the island became part of the Consolidated-

Bathurst merger that Power put together in 1966. Desmarais often went to the island for weekends of fishing and poker with a floating group of young high-rollers, including John Rae and Paul Martin, Jr., from his own company, Pierre Genest, and James Coutts, the Toronto management consultant who emerged during the 1974 election campaign as the *éminence grise* to Pierre Trudeau.*

After three years of bargaining, Anticosti was expropriated in 1975 by the Quebec government for a provincial park at a price of $23.8 million, although it was carried on Consolidated-Bathurst's books at $4.9 million. Desmarais's request to maintain his fishing rights on the Jupiter was denied.

STILL, THE JUPITER IS NOT THE ONLY PLACE WHERE PAUL DESMARAIS CAN ENTERTAIN HIS FRIENDS. For winter weekends there's the lodge at Ste Adèle, right up on Mont Gabriel, that he gave his wife, Jackie, one year for Christmas. Originally owned by the O'Connell family, it commands the magnificent panorama of the Laurentians; it has an indoor swimming pool, season-round servants, and a special Japanese bath house. In the winter of 1975, Desmarais built himself a $180,000 winter villa at Delray Beach in Florida.† Power has a private Jet-Star to make his commuting easier.

His main residence, on Ramezay Road in Westmount, was decorated by Lou Edwards, E.P. Taylor's daughter. The large living room, done in lemon and pale aqua, has a stunning Diego Rivera canvas as its central focus. He keeps three cars in Montreal, including a Mercedes-Benz 600, equipped with mobile telephones. Although he be-

---

*Desmarais's favourite games are poker and cribbage. Pierre Genest, who went to university with him, recalls that they played cribbage for twenty-five cents a game, and at the end of one year's residence he owed Desmarais $1,100. John Robarts tells a story about one trip to Texas by private jet when no one had brought any cards and Desmarais insisted they make bets on the serial numbers of the folding money in their wallets.

†He's a member there of the St. Andrews Club, which also includes Charlie Burns, the head of Burns Bros. and Denton; Donald G. "Bud" Willmot, chairman of Molson Companies; George Mara, chairman of the Olympic Trust; Karl Scott, the former head of Ford of Canada; Richard Corbet, the Toronto mining man and director of Canada Permanent Trust; and Leonard Lumbers, chairman of Noranda Manufacturing.

longs to three of Montreal's important clubs—the Mount Royal, the St. James's, and the St. Denis—Desmarais prefers to lunch at the Queen Elizabeth Hotel's Beaver Club restaurant. He has a regular waiter and his own corner table reserved there every day, unless his secretary phones to cancel by noon.

Desmarais's favourite *pied-à-terre* is La Malbaie (Murray Bay), near the mouth of the Saguenay River. In its unobtrusive way, Murray Bay remains the most prestigious international resort in Canada. The Cabots of Boston still go there, as do the Tafts of Ohio and the Hamilton Fishes of New York.* Desmarais owns the property that, formerly belonged to Leo Timmins, of Hollinger Mines fame, on the Boulevard des Falaises, to which he has added a swimming pool, sauna, and tennis court. He keeps a 1906 Cadillac on the property as well as his own motorcycle and the two Rolls-Royces, one of which is fitted with a horn that sounds like a steam locomotive. His neighbours at Murray Bay include Power director Wilbrod Bherer (chairman of Canadian Vickers) and Jack Porteous, his chief legal adviser.

It was through a summer meeting at Murray Bay with Dick Berlin, a former president of the Hearst Corporation, that Desmarais first gained entrée into international finance. His contacts include Vittorio Vaccari, the Italian tycoon, Jean-Jacques Servan-Schreiber, Senator George Smathers, who was a close friend of John F. Kennedy's, John Connally, and Roy Thomson. "When I saw Lord Thomson in London last Thursday," Desmarais reported after one overseas trip, "he told me he was eighty-one and a half. I said, 'For God's sake, what are you doing with the half?' So he says, 'At my age, every half year counts.' He said that he was doing a lot of deals, but that these were very tough times. In order to cut costs he charges fifty pence for his own lunch in his private dining room. He said by imposing restrictions on himself these

---

*Sir Frederick Williams-Taylor, a former general manager of the Bank of Montreal, spent the summers of his retirement at Murray Bay, eating every evening with his wife in the Manoir Richelieu's main dining room. He would invariably make a grand entrance, allowing his evening cape to slide from his shoulders to the floor, and in a penetrating voice ask the maître d': "Anyone notable or distinguished here tonight, Chris?" And Chris would always reply: "Well, *you* are here, Sir Frederick."

economies flow through all the way down the line. He has a remarkable memory. He talked about his interests in Thailand; told me he has two hotels on the beach at such and such a place, a newspaper there, and another outfit somewhere else. I don't know how he keeps track of it all. He encouraged me to invest in Asia where there is no Canadian presence, although there are terrific opportunities. He gave me about five deals we should be making in that area."

Desmarais's most important U.S. connection is Alden Winship "Tom" Clausen, president and chief executive officer of the San Francisco-based Bank of America. With assets of $58 billion, it is the world's largest bank. Clausen has already acquired a 5 per cent interest (342,105 common treasury shares) in the Desmarais-controlled Investors Group of Winnipeg and a 20 per cent share in Montreal Trust. The relationship is bound to expand. "I got to know Tom Clausen before he became the bank's president," says Desmarais. "They weren't very active in Canada, so I told them they should be and that we'd be delighted to have some kind of relationship with them, but if we did, we'd have to control the Canadian company. They could take 49 per cent, but we would have to control it. So, since then, we have developed many associations. They are very helpful to us on a technical basis, and more importantly, if we decide to do some investments outside of Canada, being the biggest bank in the world, they can be tremendous allies."

THIS EMPHASIS ON "ALLIES" IS VERY MUCH IN THE DESMARAIS TRADITION of behaving like the compleat corporate politician. He makes few enemies who might be willing to combine against him. Cash settlements to displace executives of the companies he takes over are generous. David Kilgour, the president of Great-West Life Assurance Company in Winnipeg, fought a tough rearguard action in 1969 to prevent Desmarais's takeover, but he was rewarded with a severance settlement (negotiated through Fraser Elliott, the Montreal lawyer, by John Turner, Kilgour's son-in-law) amounting to $500,000 on top of his pension.

Paul Desmarais knows how to coddle the powerful. When John Aird, the Toronto lawyer who has become an important access to Establishment power, caught a bad cold in Montreal during the winter of 1974, Desmarais kept sending fresh handkerchiefs to his hotel room by Cadillac and telephoning to make sure he was comfortable. "Paul," says Aird, "has flair. He creates an atmosphere of electricity around him. He doesn't clutter up his mind with details. He is very direct. Having decided he wants to do something, he has the guts to take a tremendous plunge and counts on his native shrewdness to overcome what he knows are going to be the problems."

It is also part of Desmarais's political nature that he prefers to deal with people face to face. He writes no more than a dozen personal letters a year. "I'd rather see somebody than talk to him on the telephone or write a letter," he says. "If I want to see a banker or one of our own people, I'd much rather get out of my office and go and see him. Then they know what I've said and they understand what I mean."

Desmarais's own office functions as Power Corporation's control centre, but only those who know where to look can find it. The foyer of the Canada Steamship Lines headquarters at 759 Victoria Square in Montreal is like a museum, with old-fashioned glass cases exhibiting elaborate models of the company's historic passenger liners —the *Tadoussac*, the *Montreal*, the *Saguenay*—dugout canoes and huge beavers carved out of balsam. The building's list of tenants makes no mention of Power Corporation, but the visitor who ascends to the seventh floor finds himself facing a set of electronically locked plate glass doors which swing open readily enough provided that he is recognized by the receptionist.

Power Corporation is run from half a dozen rooms here. Telephones seldom ring; nothing very important seems to be going on. The decor combines the gaudy look of an expensive courtesan's drawing room done up in *chinoiserie nouvelle* with the stately imprint of the National Gallery of Canada laid incongruously on top. The wallpaper has thick red stalks of bamboo crisscrossing a brown tiger pattern—except in the board room, which seems to be papered with distorting mirrors, though it's actually a high-quality aluminum foil. There are marble chairs, Oriental cabinets, bamboo sofas, and large bronze castings scattered about. What's really bizarre is that the walls are crowded with one of the most valuable corporate collections of Canadian art in the country. Dozens of canvases by A.Y. Jackson, Clarence Gagnon, Maurice Cullen, Goodridge Roberts, Frederick Varley, James Wilson Morrice, David Milne, Tom Thomson, Homer Watson, Jean-Paul Lemieux, and Franz Johnston valiantly hang on their bamboo-and-tiger backdrops, looking as comfortable as nuns in a discotheque. Desmarais's own office has three Krieghoffs, a Gagnon, a Cullen, and a large canvas by Samuel Scott of London Bridge in 1772.

He spends most of his time attending board meetings of his own companies, soothing his various constituencies, moving in when problems or conflicts come up, practising what the Harvard Business School has dubbed "the crisis management technique." The textbooks claim it's a method for "helping senior executives make up their own minds"; a more precise description might be that whenever there's a crunch or corporate disagreement of any kind, Desmarais moves in to impose his will. "We give management a lot of freedom," he says, "but we move in during times of crisis, or if they ask for help. I think it's important that the guys run their own show; they establish their five-year plans and we study and approve them and then they go out and run their own companies. If they don't run into any trouble, they don't get any trouble from us. If they run into trouble, they often come to us for help. Also, they come to us for advice if they want to do something important materially affecting the approved five-year plan. We have damn good discussions and it just adds another safety valve to the decision process."

Every company has its own directors, but the same small cadre of Power Corporation nominees dominates each board. Many of the operations are run by former Power executives. Paul Paine, who heads Montreal Trust, was executive vice-president of the parent company; Bill Turner, of Consolidated-Bathurst, was a president of Power; the chairman of Canada Steamship Lines is Louis, Paul Desmarais's brother. The most important head office incumbents are Peter Curry, who in 1973 became Power's president; Jean Parisien, a bookish Montreal chartered accountant who has been with Desmarais from the beginning; Frank Knowles, a wise and amiable accounting genius who knows where all of Power Corporation's secrets are buried; and John Rae, the lean and swift young Desmarais assistant. Curry, a former chairman of Great-West Life and an ex-Winnipeg Blue Bomber, has an imposing bearing, a quick mind, and the rare ability to deduce trends from apparently disconnected events.

But Paul Desmarais is the undisputed boss. *Le patron.* The operating officers of Power subsidiaries possess limited authority. Paul Martin, Jr., the president of Canada Steamship Lines, for example, has a capital spending limit of $250,000. Higher amounts must be approved by his board. But it's a Catch-22 situation, because the majority of CSL directors are also on the board of Power. Despite the existence of eight separate boards, Desmarais and his deputies can make all the important decisions, although they deliberately decentralize their authority and allow the CEO's of the various companies a lot of leeway.

"When Paul walks into a board room, he likes to know he has 51 per cent of the votes in his pocket," says a Power executive. "It's a security thing. He doesn't want to have to depend on others or admit the possibility of somebody trying to creep in and take anything away from him." Voting control also allows Desmarais to consolidate subsidiary earnings under Power's corporate umbrella, making it a more attractive stock-market buy than if it were merely a portfolio holding.

ACQUISITION IS PAUL DESMARAIS'S ART FORM. He places strategy over process, corporate takeovers ahead of spawning new enterprises. His skill is a capacity to recognize patterns where none previously existed, to pull together vague ideas and remote possibilities into tactics for growth by corporate conquest. Like a precocious child, he can visualize the final structure by looking at a pile of building blocks. With his seventy companies and nearly $7 billion in assets, he has yet to establish a single new enterprise. "I can't think of anything I started from scratch," he admits. "We've taken a lot of things that were very disorganized and in real trouble and brought them back. It's not my temperament to start something from scratch; I'd rather take something that is there and build it up. I'm in a hurry. Starting something from scratch is too slow a process."

Most of Power's growth has come as a result of Desmarais's reverse takeover method. It is a case of the minnow swallowing the whale—with the whale's knowledge and consent. The target company, in effect, pays for its own demise. "What you do," Desmarais explains, "is sell your assets to a company and with the proceeds buy the shares of the company that just acquired you. But what you have to have is something of substance first to sell. You can borrow from the bank and from other people. Like Québec Autobus; I eventually sold it to Provincial, and that was a way to get some money out of Provincial back into our own hands. We owned 100 per cent of Provincial Transport. As our position improved over the years and we made more money, we could borrow more because we could support higher debt to do other things, which is what we did."

This is a bit like playing both sides of a chessboard but it works, and it's legal. Except for his very early investments, nearly all of Desmarais's acquisitions have been achieved through reverse takeovers. His main problem in staging these bids is to avoid wasting time with people who haven't the power to make the deals he's after. Dozens of takeover proposals arrive at Desmarais's office every month, though few get past his efficient winnowing system. Still, the dilemma persists: how to find the man who holds the *real* power in any situation. "If he has the power of *decision,* that's what counts," says Desmarais. "If you can carry the deal through, and if you have a problem and explain it, and he says it can be resolved this way, or it can't be resolved and that's it—then you know you've dealt with the guy who has power."

THIS RESTLESS SEARCH FOR THE SOURCES OF MORE POWER is rooted so deep inside Paul Desmarais that he must have been born with it. Sudbury, the land he comes from, is harsh and unyielding, teaching its own lessons. His father, Jean Noel Desmarais, left Northern Ontario only long enough to attend the University of Ottawa, and his son followed him there in 1946. Pierre Genest, who roomed with Desmarais, claims he has changed very little: "Paul was very much like he is today. He loved to get into things, to run things, to influence people. He was treasurer of the student federation, but he remained the man behind the scenes. Candidates who ran for office sort of had to get his blessing, or they wouldn't get in."

More remarkable is the fact that during his second year of university he worked out a complicated but feasible scheme by which an outsider might be able to capture stock control of the CPR. After graduating from the University of Ottawa with a Bachelor of Commerce degree, he went to Osgoode Hall to become a lawyer. Young Desmarais tried the course three times but could never pass the exams in Legal History, one of the easier subjects. The law couldn't hold his interest; he was too anxious to get out in the business world. His opportunity materialized in the form of a small family-owned transportation company which, in 1951, had sixteen old buses, debts of $384,000, and the franchise to run from Sudbury to the International Nickel Company operations at nearby Copper Cliff. It was his rescue of this failing enterprise that set the pattern of his career. He seldom talks about those beginnings now. But every once in a while, when the company is good and all the poker chips have been cashed in, he'll reminisce. And when he does, nobody can tell the story the way Desmarais does:

"It was my grandfather who started, in 1916, a railway between Sudbury and Copper Cliff; it was called the Sudbury–Copper Cliff Suburban Electric Railway Company. It never really made any money. When my grandfather died, he left one quarter of the business to my mother, one quarter to my uncle, and he had a partner who owned 50 per cent. My uncle died and my mother bought his interest, so then she had 50 per cent. She operated the business and made some money during the war, but, of course, then there were no cars or gas. Excess taxes took all the profits off the top, but after the war the family was under the impression that this was a very good business and they should just convert the streetcars to buses, and they bought out the other 50 percent from my grandfather's original partner's estate. Well, of course, as the people in the town of Sudbury made high salaries, they all bought cars as soon as they could, and the proportion of bus travellers went down. By 1950, the company was in real trouble. My father, who had a successful law practice, decided that we should sell the company for what we could get.

"I had built up my dream that I would some day become a lawyer; I'd be in Sudbury and I'd become president of that little company and expand it into something else in the area, maybe have bus lines going to North Bay and the Sault and that sort of thing. So I told him, 'Listen, if you're going to sell it, why don't you let me buy it?'"

"In fact, he gave it to me. He was disappointed, because he was like most French-speaking Canadians; he thought I should continue my studies and get my profession first: 'Once you are a lawyer, then if something goes wrong, you can always go back to your practice.'

"But I said, 'Let me try it for the summer and I promise I'll go back to Osgoode in the fall.' Well, of course, I got so damned involved in the company that I asked him if it would be possible to just stay for another year. Every week I'd have to get three thousand dollars for the payroll, and when you haven't got the money, three thousand dollars, I want to tell you, is a hell of a lot of dough. So I'd borrow three thousand from Monseigneur Coallier one week; another week I borrowed from my sister's father-in-law, who was an undertaker. For two weeks I paid my bus drivers with tickets, until some wives came in to tell me they couldn't buy any groceries with my bus tickets.

"Another time I went to see one of my good friends; his name was Léo Portelance. He used to have a lumber operation. Now, this would always happen Friday nights, and the drivers, the union, would say, 'If we're not paid, Monday morning you're going to have a strike and that'll be the end of it.'

"So, I went to see Portelance at his cottage on Sunday

afternoon and I said, 'Listen, Léo, you've got to lend me three thousand dollars or I'm out of business.'

"He said, 'Listen, you've been going on for months now borrowing three thousand dollars all over the place, and people are just kidding you; they know damn well you'll never be able to make it.' He'd had quite a few drinks and he used to carry a lot of money. So he took a wad of hundred-dollar bills out of his pocket. He had a fire going in his fireplace, and he said, 'I'll show you what I mean.' He takes a hundred-dollar bill and throws it in the fireplace.

"I said, 'What the hell are you doing?'

"He answered, 'I'd rather throw the damn money in the fireplace than lend it to you. For Christ's sake, when will you wake up? Why don't you just fold this thing up?'

"The Royal was my banker at the time. When I got into trouble, I went in to cash some payroll cheques. The manager who ran the Sudbury branch at the time used to take a drink, and he was usually under the influence by ten o'clock in the morning when I came to talk to him —he retired a year after that—and geez, I walked in and he was way at the back of the bank, and he says, 'Desmarais, we don't want any of your business in this bank.'

"And I said, 'What do you mean?'

" 'We've got enough of your cheques flying all over the place; we're not going to cash any more of your cheques, do you understand?' And loud, loud, loud—everybody in the bank heard this.

"I didn't have any choice, so I said, 'Well, to hell with you,' and I walked out. So I said to myself: 'Hell, I can't keep doing this. But as long as I keep the buses going, I have a chance to find a permanent solution with Inco and I'm sure they're going to do something.'

"I went back home and about eleven o'clock called Les Beattie, who was then vice-president of Inco. He had a summer camp on Ramsey Lake, and I took a chance and, geez, I was afraid to ask him for money, but he was my last hope. Mrs. Beattie answered the phone and said, 'Mr. Beattie is just getting into his car. He's going to take the train to Toronto.'

" 'Oh, would you please stop him and get him back into the house?'

"He came back and I was lucky to get him. I said, 'Mr. Beattie, there won't be any bus service tomorrow to Copper Cliff. I need three thousand dollars to pay some wages, otherwise I'm dead.'

"He said, 'What's the meaning of calling me at this time? I can't be giving you three thousand dollars. You have to find a permanent solution to these problems. We can't carry on like this . . . .'

"I said, 'I'm sorry, but you're my last hope. I haven't got any chance unless you're willing to give it to me and then we'll try to work something out.'

"He said, 'You've got to work something out with the creditors and once you do that, once you have a formula, come and see me and we'll see what we can do about it. But, meanwhile, I'll give you the three thousand dollars.'

"So that's the morning I went to the Royal Bank with Beattie's promise for three thousand dollars. I walked in, and before I could explain what I wanted, the manager told me, 'No more business for you, kid.'

"I went to the Banque Canadienne Nationale. I walked into the bank and told the manager, Joe Langelier, 'You're going to cash my cheque for three thousand dollars.'

"The fellow says to me, 'No, I'm not going to cash any of your cheques for three thousand dollars.'

"I said, 'I've got credit.'

"And he said, 'What do you mean?'

"I said, 'International Nickel! They're going to give me credit for three thousand dollars. All you have to do is call Mr. Beattie in Toronto.'

"He said, 'I'm not calling Mr. Beattie in Toronto and that's that.'

"I grabbed the phone and called Mr. Beattie. I said, 'I'm with the Banque Canadienne Nationale.'

"And he said, 'I thought you were at the Royal.'

"I said, 'I've been thrown out at the Royal. I want you to tell this guy I've got credit for three thousand dollars.'

"So the banker says, 'Is that Mr. Beattie himself?'

"I said, 'Yes.'

"So, the bank manager grabbed the phone and said,

'Mr. Beattie, we're a French-Canadian bank and we don't do any business with International Nickel. We think you should have a deposit here.'

" 'God,' I said, 'you're wasting my time—if you want a deposit from Inco, do it on your own time.' In fact, they gave the Banque Canadienne Nationale a deposit and gave me the three thousand dollars, and I kept going for another week.

"In the meantime, I worked out a five-year plan. I remember I worked it out on a roll of wallpaper because I could project all the years on one piece of paper; and I went to see Beattie with my piece of rolled-up wallpaper under my arm, and as I walked in he said, 'What is it this time?'

"I said, 'I think I've got the solution.' So, I handed him my plan and he unrolled it and anchored it at both ends with a couple of ashtrays. The crux was that I needed $138,000 to start the plan, which would allow me to pay arrears in employer's income tax, all secured creditors and everybody else to whom we owed money. The unsecured creditors were taking 10 per cent in cash and the balance in 4 per cent preferred stock. Industrial Acceptance Corporation was going to be paid over a period of time.

"So he said, 'Well, you know, we're not going to give you $138,000 . . . .' I still remember him grabbing the two ashtrays and the wallpaper rolling up again.

"When I got out of there, I had a meeting with my creditors and they bought the plan. After many meetings back and forth, Inco came through. My brother Louis and Jean Parisien were a great help then. We got the company going. I had very loyal workers—a head mechanic by the name of Dixon, a dispatcher by the name of Chassé, and guys like that who really worked like hell, and we pulled it off. The upshot of it was that I convinced Inco to buy the run from Sudbury to Copper Cliff. With the proceeds we paid off part of our debts and were left with the city bus operation.

"Inco had the mine in Copper Cliff and we were carrying their workers—not very many; about ten buses a day were involved. Inco wanted to have a good bus service. Beattie said, 'Listen, we have to resolve this problem because we need the service. We can't have a bankrupt company telling us tomorrow morning there will be no service. Let's resolve this damn thing.' So they effectively gave me $138,000 for the run and we owed about $380,000. So, I made an arrangement with the creditors, paid off the bank and some of the secured debts.

"I was in the bus company for about five years, went back to law school in my second year, and then heard from Pierre Genest that Gatineau Bus in Ottawa-Hull was for sale. By this time I had about $100,000 in cash that I had made in Sudbury, and during the 1955 Easter holidays I went out to see the chief financial officer of Gatineau Power, Code Brittain, a real gentleman. I walked into his office and said, 'I want to buy your bus line.'

"He said, 'That's fine, everybody knows it's for sale. How much do you want to pay for it?'

" 'Well,' I said, 'I've seen the books and would pay $275,000.'

"He said, 'I think that's probably acceptable. How are you going to pay us?'

"I said, 'I'm going to pay you in cash.'

" 'Well,' he said, 'that's just fine. When do you want to do it?'

" 'Well,' I said, 'I have to go to the head office of the Banque Canadienne Nationale in Montreal and I'll borrow the money there. I already have it cleared with the local office at Sudbury and I have $100,000 in cash.'

"He asked me if I wanted an option. 'Well,' I said, 'it takes me only about a day to go to the bank's head office in Montreal and come back—I'll need a three-day option.'

"And he said, 'How much do you want to pay for it?'

" 'Oh,' I replied, 'fifty thousand dollars.'

"Brittain looked surprised. 'Fifty thousand for a three-day option! Are you sure?'

"With a flourish I took out my cheque book and wrote this big cheque for fifty thousand dollars and, boy, was I a big shot, and I threw it on his desk. He gave me a letter and said, 'You'd better be here by Friday or you'll lose your fifty thousand dollars.'

"Well, I went to the bank, and Louis Hébert was then

the manager of that area. He's now chairman of the bank. Louis was sitting behind his desk in a little office about the size of my bathroom. So, I came in and he looked at me with surprise and said, 'Monsieur Desmarais, we haven't made a commitment to lend you $175,000. I met your father some years ago in Sudbury and I was under the impression we were making a loan to him.'

" 'Well,' I said, 'I'm the owner of the bus lines and I'm the guy who is buying Gatineau Bus.'

" 'Oh, no, this just isn't possible,' he said. 'You've got $100,000 and I suppose your business might be worth a couple of hundred thousand dollars. Why do you want to overextend yourself and buy something you don't know much about in the province of Quebec? You can't do that. You will lose all your money! Why would Gatineau sell if it is a good business?'

"The upshot of it was that, by geez, he wouldn't give me the money. So I took the train back to Ottawa. I was thinking about my fifty thousand dollars. I was cut down to size. So, I walked into Brittain's office and he just sat back, looked at me, and said, 'Well, have you got your money? Tomorrow's Friday, and without the money you lose the fifty thousand dollars.'

"By that time I was practically in tears, and I said, 'Well, do you think I could get my fifty thousand dollars back? Here is a letter from the Sudbury branch of my bank telling me they recommended the loan. I thought everything was all right.'

" 'Well,' he said, 'we'll give you back your fifty thousand dollars. Don't worry. But don't do that again. I would have given you an option for nothing. Here's what we'll do. We want to sell and there aren't that many buyers. You need a bank loan; why don't you come and see our bankers, the Bank of Montreal?'

"And I said to him, 'Listen, I have an old connection with the Royal Bank. I'll go and see them, if you'll call them and explain what I am up to.' I had become pretty friendly with Lorry Martin, the Royal Bank manager in Sudbury. Jack Bankes was in Ottawa then, and in about half an hour, hell, he lent me the money. I've been with the Royal Bank ever since.

"I was with Gatineau for four years. We made some

money and then I decided to sell the business because I figured my whole interest was worth about a million dollars. Then I was going to go back to law school, go back to Sudbury and be a guy, you know, who has a bit of money, a good practice with my father and my brother, and the little bus business, which would have been terrific. So I arranged to sell Gatineau for $300,000 to the Bisson brothers in Hull. (Jack Porteous was my lawyer in that transaction and still is in all important things I do.) I went to the bank to deposit their postdated cheques with Jack Bankes, and I said, 'I'm a rich man! I'm all set!'

"But as I came out of the bank, by chance I met Jim Walker, who was a bus salesman for General Motors. It was a hot, hot day. I had built a pool behind my house in Rockcliffe, and I said to Jim, 'Why don't you come and have a swim with me?'

"When he came home after five o'clock, I told him of my plan to retire. He said, 'You're stupid! You know there's every opportunity for you in the province of Quebec. You might be able to buy Québec Autobus. Shawinigan Water and Power are worried about the government expropriation and a local bus service is not a popular thing at any time, regardless of who owns it, and they would love to sell it.' I called Jack Porteous, who knew Jack Fuller, chairman of Shawinigan, and he confirmed that Québec Autobus was for sale.

"This was in 1959, and the negotiations took a full year. When the closing came, I could muster about half a million dollars in cash. But I had to pay $2 million for it. With the help of Jack Fuller, who was also a director of B.A. Oil, I borrowed $800,000 from B.A. Oil on the condition that I took my gas from them, and I borrowed $700,000 from Industrial Acceptance Corporation on their buses. The reason IAC lent me the money was because in Sudbury, when I got started, I owed them $60,000 and they were secured creditors. The main unsecured creditors wanted to pass them off as unsecured creditors because the IAC security was worthless old broken-down buses. They weren't worth a damn and by giving IAC preferred stock instead of cash, the unsecured creditors would have a higher percentage of cash to take home. So, I said, 'No, we have an obligation to IAC and we're going to carry it out exactly as we're supposed to.'

"By geez, I met the fellow who had been manager of IAC then—a guy by the name of Bauslaugh, who, by then, had been promoted to the head office in Montreal. Just by pure chance he was in Sudbury, making a tour of his branches, when I was looking for that $700,000 to finance the purchase of Québec Autobus. I came face to face with him, and I said, 'Geez, you're the man I want. You're going to lend me some money.'

"He said, 'Sure. You come on over to head office and if you can convince us the credit's good, we'll lend you the money.' So IAC lent me $700,000, B.A. $800,000 and the Royal (secured by Bisson cheques and other security) put in my money—$500,000. So I bought Québec Autobus. A year after, I met Bud Drury, who was a member of the Association of Bus Owners for the Province of Quebec, and at their annual meeting asked him, 'Do you want to sell Provincial Transport?' "

THE NEGOTIATIONS TO ACQUIRE PROVINCIAL TRANSPORT COMPANY lasted more than a year. Desmarais had turned the Québec Autobus operation around from a loss of $60,000 for the year before he bought it to a profit of $350,000 during his first twelve months of operation. But he was a newcomer to the financial world, and when he approached Greenshields Incorporated to help him finance the deal, they turned him down. J. Louis Lévesque, the French-Canadian financier from New Brunswick, made possible the sale of the bonds which allowed him to buy up 50.8 per cent of Provincial's shares.

The purchase changed his life, not so much because it brought Desmarais to the top of a large enterprise for the first time, but because it brought him to Montreal. "I wasn't exposed to many opportunities in Sudbury," he says. "But when I got out, spent some time in Toronto, and later bought the bus line in Ottawa and went to live there, it opened things up for me. I met different people and we talked about different things. When I came to

Montreal in 1960, I was in seventh heaven—so many things to do, so many deals to make, so much fun to be had."

Provincial became, for a time, the centre of Desmarais's life. "If there had been no Greyhound in the U.S.," he says, "I am sure I would have created it and it would have been an easy process of just continuing to acquire bus lines as I did in Ontario and Quebec. When I tried to move into the States, I was blocked off by Greyhound, and when I tried to move out West, Greyhound was there also. So that from the point of view of growing, the business could only expand at its normal pace and no longer through acquisition. Therefore, if I wanted to continue growth, I had to diversify. The base for diversification was the bus line. It's like building Standard Oil—they started buying one oil company and then bought them all; or building a railroad—you just keep on laying track. In my case, it has been a repetition of the reverse takeover process."

The technique of reverse takeover was especially relevant to Provincial Transport. Over the next decade, in the process of raising the funds to expand his holdings, Desmarais managed to sell the company to himself four times, folding it into various new entities, always at higher assessed values. When a strike of bus drivers occurred in 1962, Desmarais realized that if he were going to keep moving up, he must both diversify his holdings and find some easily accessible cash.

THE INSTRUMENT THAT PROVIDED BOTH THESE REQUIREMENTS was a subsidiary of the Gatineau Power Company called Gelco Enterprises Limited. Gatineau had received $12.5 million when New Brunswick nationalized its hydro properties and lent $7,450,000 of it to Gelco for a thirty-year period at an interest rate of only 4 per cent. In 1961, by making an offer through Triarch Corporation (which managed Gelco's investments) for an initial 450,000 shares at a dollar each, Desmarais was able to obtain effective control of the Gelco treasury with approximately 20 per cent of the Gelco shares. Provincial Transport was sold at book value to Gelco for

6,531,776 common shares of Gelco valued at $1.20 per share, bringing Desmarais's holding of Gelco to about 80 per cent of its common shares. A total of $2.7 million was spent to obtain complete ownership of Gelco. In 1964, Desmarais liquidated some of the Gelco portfolio to buy a controlling interest (51.2 per cent) in Imperial Life, a middle-sized Toronto insurance company founded in 1896, which then had assets of $332 million. Part of this money was raised by selling Provincial Transport to Gelco—in return for more Gelco shares.*

Now the reverse takeover minuet really got going. In 1965, Desmarais folded Imperial Life and Provincial Transport into Trans-Canada Corporation Fund, a conglomerate of fifteen medium-sized Quebec operations put together by J. Louis Lévesque. The transaction was worth $32 million ($14 million of it for the bus company), and Desmarais emerged with 56 per cent of the Trans-Canada stock, giving him control over assets worth $60 million including both Imperial and Provincial, which came back to him as the new proprietor (he had achieved effective control by this time) of Trans-Canada.

It was at this point that Desmarais began his detour from straight commercial expansion into the controversial area of communications. In 1967, he formed (with Jacques Francoeur) Les Journaux Trans-Canada, which bought eight Quebec newspapers: *La Tribune, La Voix de l'Est, Le Nouvelliste, Dimanche-Matin, Le Petit Journal, Photo Journal, Dernière Heure,* and *Hebdos Métropolitains.* In a separate, much more significant transaction, he also acquired *La Presse,* Quebec's largest daily, which carried with it CKAC, Canada's largest French-language radio station, and the weekly *La Patrie.* This deal, which was financed by the Royal Bank, became a main source of earnings for Trans-Canada. The following year he formed a subsidiary of Gelco called Gesca Ltée to hold these assets. This transfer was financed by a $19.7-million income debenture from Gesca in favour of Trans-Canada, which in effect provided that all earnings and any realized changes in the in-

---

*Gelco remains the main Power Corporation holding company, with Desmarais owning 75 per cent of the shares and Jean Parisien the balance.

cremental value in the equity of Gesca would accrue to the shareholders of the Trans-Canada Corporation Fund. In August of 1973, Gesca acquired the former Union Nationale organ *Montréal-Matin** and sold off some of the smaller publications to Jacques Francoeur. Along with some other television stations acquired along the way, CKAC was also spun off, so that Gesca's final holdings became five Quebec dailies with a combined circulation of more than 400,000: *Montréal-Matin* and *La Presse* (Montreal), *La Tribune* (Sherbrooke), *Le Nouvelliste* (Trois-Rivières), and *La Voix de l'Est* (Granby). "What I was trying to do in buying up the papers," says Desmarais, "was to give Quebec that same sort of clout from the point of view of chains of newspapers that Southam, Thomson, and FP have. Because there is no way that a newspaper today, an independent owner of a newspaper, can stand a strike or bad times or generate the cash needed to take advantage of new technology."

WITHIN SEVEN YEARS OF ARRIVING IN MONTREAL, PAUL DESMARAIS HAD AUTHENTICATED his talent for the intricacies of high finance. But he remained a local phenomenon, a man on the margin of really significant money. As he searched for some path into the business world's upper reaches, his attention was drawn by Claude Frenette to the potentials of Power Corporation of Canada. The company had been formed in 1925 by Nesbitt, Thomson and Company, the Montreal investment house, to bring together its holdings (then worth $6 million) of seven private hydro development stocks and an eventual 25 per cent controlling interest in Canadian Oil Companies. Nothing much happened to Power for the next thirty-five years except that its portfolio grew to a value of $52 million. Then the government of British Columbia nationalized B.C. Electric Company and later bought Power's interest in East Kootenay Power; Quebec took over the Shawinigan Water and Power and Northern

---

*Gabriel Loubier, leader of the Union Nationale (temporarily called Unité Québec), said at the time that he wouldn't dare offer his paper to Power Corporation "because if I did, I'd have to go around in a tank with armed guards." Then he promptly sold it to Paul Desmarais.

Quebec Power Company shares; and Shell bought its Canadian Oil Companies (White Rose) interest. In the space of a few years Power found itself with about $100 million in cash and not quite sure what to do with it.

Peter Thomson, who represented the Nesbitt, Thomson interests and was then running the company, brought in Maurice Strong as executive vice-president in 1962 to handle the re-investment and diversification drive. Strong had put in time as an apprentice fur trader for the Hudson's Bay Company at Chesterfield Inlet, received his early financial training at James Richardson and Sons in Winnipeg, and by the age of twenty-two was financial adviser to the large Dome Exploration operation in Calgary. His own management company quickly built Ajax Petroleums into Canadian Industrial Gas and Oil, one of the largest Canadian independents.

When he joined Power, Strong made some major moves into Bathurst Paper and Consolidated Paper as well as Canada Steamship Lines, Laurentide Financial Corporation, and Dominion Glass—all of which would turn out to be valuable long-term holdings. Under his direction a profitable ($10 million) but unsuccessful bid was launched for McIntyre Porcupine Mines. Strong left the company in 1966 (after running Power's assets up to $214 million) to head Canada's foreign aid program. He was succeeded by Bill Turner, a Harvard MBA who had previously sold Jeeps around the world for Willys-Overland Export Corporation of Toledo, Ohio. Turner acquired control of Laurentide Finance and Dominion Glass and merged the Consolidated and Bathurst paper operations. The Strong-Turner combo had transformed Power Corporation from an inactive, closed-end trust into an expanding conglomerate.

Desmarais moved in on Power during the spring of 1968 with yet another complicated reverse takeover bid. It called for Power to exchange the stock of his Trans-Canada Corporation on a share-for-share basis for a new issue of 5 per cent cumulative redeemable convertible Power preferreds with a par value of twelve dollars.*

---

*The transaction provided an important clue to the sources of Desmarais's financing. Some 2.2 of the 3.5 million Trans-Canada shares deposited were held by Roythree, a nominee name for the Royal Bank of Canada. Presumably the stock had been pledged as security for a previous Desmarais loan.

Gelco, Desmarais's private holding company, then made an offer for 250,000 of the 6 per cent participating preferred Power shares that carried ten votes each to give Desmarais about 31.4 per cent of the voting stock. By May 1968, Desmarais was running the company and Peter Thomson had moved into the background as deputy chairman. Thomson held his 30 per cent of Power's voting shares through Warnock Hersey International, an eclectic conglomerate that owned hotels, plastic billboard companies, and chemical-testing laboratories, as well as steel and furniture plants. Thomson was not very interested in business and spent much of his time cruising out of the Coral Harbour Yacht Club in the Bahamas aboard the *Moby Dick II*, a converted 82-foot cruiser, formerly a U.S. Navy PT boat.* Both Power and Warnock Hersey were cash hungry, and to cure this condition Desmarais sold 1.6 million shares of Northern and Central Gas Corporation, which had been part of the Power portfolio, for $21 million. He then created a $19-million income debenture, maturing in the year 2020, of Gesca Ltée, the Gelco subsidiary that owns *La Presse*. Gelco used part of this revenue to buy, for $7.2 million, 600,000 of the 6 per cent participating preferreds in Power held by Warnock Hersey. It was through this complex interchange that Desmarais raised his holdings of Power Corporation over the magic 50 per cent mark, leaving him in full control.

None of these manoeuvres helped solve Power's basic problems. Laurentide Finance, a Vancouver subsidiary, needed a $9-million injection after being caught in the undertow of the Atlantic Acceptance scandal. Robert Campeau, the Ottawa builder, moved his real estate and construction complex first into and then out of Power, taking a $13.5 million loss in the process. By the end of 1970, Desmarais announced the omission of fourth-quarter dividends. The stock slipped from a 1970 high of $12 to $4.60. "We got into a lot of difficulty around 1970," he recalls. "Right after we took Power over everything just fell apart. We were much too diversified. We had con-

---

*The *Moby Dick IV* has since been replaced by the *Non Oblitus*, a luxurious 95-foot, $500,000 cruiser.

struction companies, insurance companies, furniture factories, newspapers, racetracks, property companies, bus companies, travel agencies, resorts, steel tank companies, radio and television stations, major interests in shipping, pipelines, pulp and paper, glass, trucking, etc. We were dealing with a huge number of people who were dealing in different endeavours, all going different directions at the same time with no control. We got rid of a lot of incompatible interests that were too small or didn't fit in."

At about this time, Power needed more cash to finance Desmarais's efforts to raise his 16 per cent holdings in Consolidated-Bathurst through a share exchange offering. The paper company was in trouble, and as the largest but not majority shareholder, he didn't see much point in trying to rescue it unless he could gain the resultant financial benefits. Montreal's financial community (particularly W.A. Arbuckle, one of its respected elder statesmen) rebuffed Desmarais's share exchange offer for the outstanding Consolidated-Bathurst stock. Richard Lafferty, a Montreal investment counsellor, commented at the time that this was a case of "a financial group trying to get the earnings of its own holding company higher by taking over from the public shareholder an operating company where there are sufficient potential earnings to offset the dilution involved. It is essentially a financial manipulation to compensate for their own inability to develop earnings through any creative endeavour."

Desmarais remained stuck with a minority holding but all of the responsibility for resurrecting a sick enterprise. "When things went well, before Connie got into trouble, Power Corporation was just a shareholder," he recalls. "When things went wrong, then Power Corporation got the blame as the *major* shareholder and, in fact, we were stuck with the reputation of having bungled it. However, we did something about it. But then we decided that we weren't going to get into this kind of a mess again and not be able to control it because of our minority interest position. If you're going to correct a bad situation and spend a lot of time doing it, you should benefit by it, which means you need more of the equity. Why, hell, if you buy 10 per cent of something and work like hell to rebuild it, what's the percentage?" Even though Power managed to gain only an extra 20 per cent of the Consolidated-Bathurst stock through its exchange offer, Bill Turner was transferred from Power to the paper company's presidency. Within two years he had turned it around, and in 1973 Dominion Glass was also placed under his management.

Not the least of Power Corporation's problems in 1970 was that, despite the tremendous pressure his company was under, Desmarais never once broke the stride of his rush for expansion. Five years before, he had acquired (through Imperial Life) 900,000 shares of Investors Group from the Canadian Imperial Bank of Commerce. Set up in 1940 as a subsidiary of Investors Diversified Services Incorporated of Minneapolis, the company had passed into Canadian control in 1957, when Webb and Knapp (Canada), Dominion Securities Corporation, the Royal Bank, and the Commerce all took up large blocks. With assets of about $3 billion, Investors had built up an impressive collection of subsidiaries selling mutual funds, investment certificates, and pension plans. In early 1970, Desmarais acquired most of the remaining Investors shares held by the two banks through an issue of a million treasury shares from Power. But he was still short of a majority. It was Buck Crump, then chairman of the CPR and a close friend of Desmarais's, who made it possible for Desmarais to gain control. Through its affiliate, Canadian Pacific Investments, CPR had picked up a block of Investors stock. Crump phoned Ian Sinclair (then president of the railway) from Winnipeg at nine o'clock one morning in February of 1970 and asked him to make the $12.8-million deal that transferred a million shares of CPI's holdings of Investors to Power in return for some of its stock in Consolidated-Bathurst and Northern and Central Gas. Along with the transfer of the highly profitable Investors Group to Power's earnings came a 24 per cent interest in Montreal Trust and eventual control of the Great-West Life Assurance Company. The minority holding in the trust company was eventually boosted to 51 per cent by Investors Group's purchase of its stock on the open market.

The original Great-West acquisition had been a much more complicated affair. Desmarais was having dinner one winter evening in 1969 with Neil McKinnon, then chairman of the Canadian Imperial Bank of Commerce, at Winston's in Toronto, when the banker casually inquired whether he realized that control of Great West was "on the street" and that a branch of the Bronfman family was after it.

Great-West was an ultra-conservative operation (with business in force of more than $8 billion) which had grown by absorbing five other companies.* Late in 1968, Edper Investments, a trust set up for Edward and Peter, the sons of Allan Bronfman, a vice-president of Distillers Corporation-Seagrams, had bought control of the Great West Saddlery Company, a former leather operation (it had supplied the first saddles issued to the North West Mounted Police) that had been turned into a small conglomerate. Although its stock had ranged in value from 46 cents to $24.00 during 1969, Saddlery proceeded to offer $76 million for Great-West Life in the form of an exchange consisting of six of its treasury shares plus $30. David Kilgour, the president of Great-West Life, who had led the insurance industry's bitter struggle against the Pearson government's pension plan, was determined to keep his company from being sold out from under him. He managed to persuade Henry Langford, chairman of the Ontario Securities Commission, to suspend trading in it for five days. (The only public explanation for the suspension offered by Langford was that "the company had asked for it.")

Desmarais flew to Winnipeg the morning after his dinner with McKinnon for lunch with Dick Malone, publisher of the Winnipeg *Free Press*, and a briefing on the local situation. It turned out that the Saddlery management had set up a bucket shop with five telephones in the Fort Garry Hotel, trying to sign up Great-West shareholders all over the country.† The Bronfman group already held 194,000 of the insurance company's shares.

---

*In 1894, Great West acquired the Dominion Safety Fund Association; in 1932, the Columbia Life Assurance Company of Vancouver; in 1940, the Western Empire Life Assurance Company; in 1943, the Universal Life Assurance and Annuity Company; and in 1944, the Mutual Home Security Association.

†Chief organizer of the Great West Saddlery takeover bid was a Vancouver insurance salesman called Gordon Minchin, a former heavyweight boxing champion of the RAF.

Desmarais realized that he would have to raise the necessary $76 million fast, while the stock exchange prohibition was still in force. Malone put him in touch with Max Bell, chairman of the FP newspaper group, who was then vacationing at Palm Beach. Desmarais contacted his financing group (the Royal Bank, Canadian Pacific Investments, and the Commerce) and then flew to Florida for a session with Bell. The Calgary financier agreed to underwrite part of the cost, but in the meantime, Desmarais's other partners had come through, joined by the Bank of America. The $76 million was finally raised through the issuing by Investors Group (in which Desmarais then had a 30 per cent interest) of $40 millions' worth of convertible preferred shares plus three million common shares at twelve dollars each. By the end of April, 1969, Investors had obtained 51 per cent of Great-West, including the 194,000 shares that had been turned in on the Saddlery offer.*

BY THE SUMMER OF 1972, JUST WHEN CANADA'S FINANCIAL COMMUNITY thought that Desmarais might take a brief respite in his rampaging expansion, he staged the ultimate reverse takeover: Power Corporation swallowed itself. The genesis of this formidably complicated transaction was his growing control over Canada Steamship Lines. Power had purchased 300,000 shares of CSL in May of 1963 from Algoma Steel. Another big block was bought from the McConnell-owned Commercial Trust, and by July, 1968, Power controlled 30 per cent of the transportation company. Then in March, 1969, that good old horse Provincial Transport was sold to CSL for $17 million as part of an internal reverse takeover that brought Power's holdings in CSL to 50.5 per cent. In November of 1971 Desmarais made an open offer for CSL shares at $40—$10 above their quoted market value. The offering cost Power $60 million, but it moved Desmarais's ownership ratio to 99.5 per cent, giving him total

*Max Bell's participation turned out to be unnecessary, but Desmarais offered it to him anyway, as a point of honour. Bell declined, but Malone extracted a pledge from Desmarais that he would never move Great-West's head office from Winnipeg.

control of a conservatively managed company that had no debt, a cash flow of $20 million a year, and untapped borrowing capacity.

At the same time, the Trudeau government had included a little-noticed provision in its 1972 budget permitting deduction of interest expense on funds borrowed for the purpose of acquiring other companies. This wrinkle prompted Desmarais to sell part of Power's assets to CSL for $145 million, of which $70 million was in cash. That repaid the Royal Bank for the $60 million (lent at 1 per cent over prime) that was used to pay off the CSL shareholders, leaving $10 million in Power's treasury. Power had thus been transformed from a conglomerate into a diversified operating company. In one stroke, Power's term-debt and working capital deficit had been liquidated. At the same time, the heavy interest charges assumed by CSL (about $7 million a year, which was the interest on Power's $75-million note to CSL) could be used by CSL to minimize the taxes paid on its profitable subsidiaries—those subsidiaries now constituting all of Power's companies except the Gesca newspaper empire.*

---

*One anomaly in this comfortable arrangement is a 14 per cent holding in the common (voting) shares of Argus Corporation. Power Corporation's original 10.4 per cent of the common shares was bought by Gelco Enterprises in 1967 and transferred to Shawinigan Industries in 1969. The balance accrued to Power in the spring of 1975 through an offer of $17 for the Class C preferred shares and $22 for the common. Under this offer Power acquired 3,987,812 Class C and 58,696 common shares in April. Power continued buying Argus stock in May, picking up 57,458 Class C and 7,906 of the common. This amounted to about 60 per cent of the Class C. The cost to Power was more than $70 million. Desmarais told shareholders at the annual meeting on April 30, 1975, that Power at the end of his 21-day offer held 50.8 per cent of the total issued participating equity shares of Argus. Of this bid, Desmarais says: "During the winter of 1975, Bud and I met frequently in Palm Beach. I made a number of informal proposals and Bud told me that he had received many other offers. I told him, however, that all of these had been informal and that I would bring him a formal proposal approved by my board. Some time in March, I gave him our formal offer, which he undertook to present to his board. He did, however, point out to me that if the offer became public in the interim, he would deny it. I explained that the Power offer was approved by my board, financed by the banks, and the OSC disclosure rules had to be met. For example, we had to advise the chairman of the OSC that we were talking. I expressed the hope that he would phone his directors in Jamaica, Barbados, and the Bahamas as soon as possible and give me a reply so as to avoid the possibility of a leak. Bud said it would take some time to reach the directors, so that we would have to take the risk of leaks. We know the results. Power now owns over 50 per cent of the equity in Argus, without voting control. I am confident, however, that the board of directors of Argus will always act in the best interests of all its shareholders."

The ownership links that exist between the various Power companies are surprising. Liverpool Plains Pastoral Company Proprietary Limited, for example, is a $1-million sheep ranch in New South Wales north of Sydney. Ocean Lines Limited is a Bermuda-based shipping operation. John N. Brocklesby Transport operates most of the heavy cranes in Montreal harbour. Canaus Investments Incorporated is a Panamanian corporation used as a blind trust for offshore purchases.

POWER CORPORATION'S MASSIVE RESTRUCTURING KEPT DESMARAIS OCCUPIED through most of 1972 and 1973. Then came the stock market collapse of 1974, which seemed to leave even a man of his nerve very little space to manoeuvre. It was a mark of his audacity that he became one of the very few Canadian businessmen to turn the depressed share prices to his own advantage. A reconstruction of how Desmarais was able, in less than three days of hectic activity, to emerge with a $15-million paper profit demonstrates in sharp relief all the elements that have become his corporate style: the flexibility to alter strategies in mid-deal; his insistence on secrecy and thorough planning; his telephone access to virtually unlimited credit; and above all, his ability to deal so fast that what's actually taking place becomes clear to others only in retrospect. What follows is a chronology of the week that began on Thursday, November 14, 1974:

Tom Bell, the chairman and chief executive officer of the Abitibi Paper Company, announces an offer at $18 for 49 per cent (or 4.8 million shares) of the Price Company, one of Canada's five largest newsprint producers. (With paper mills in Quebec, Newfoundland, and Louisiana, Price had annual sales of $230 million. It had a strong balance sheet with a good cash position. The company's 1974 earnings were expected to be about $3 a share and, with a market price of only $12, Price was selling at the unusually low multiple of four times earnings.)

The senior executives of Price are enjoying a sales conference at La Sapinière, the famous Laurentian hotel, when news of the takeover bid is telephoned to C.R. Tittemore, the company's chief executive officer, who immediately rushes back to his head office in Quebec City. The Abitibi offer for the Price stock takes advantage of an obscure paragraph in the Ontario Securities Act to circumvent the usual twenty-one-day waiting period. By making the bid through the Montreal and Toronto exchanges (with shareholders having to turn in their stock to Wood Gundy representatives by 9.45 a.m. on November 19) instead of the usual mailing to shareholders, Bell has cut the time margin to only three working days.

At 9.30 a.m. on Friday, November 15, Arthur Pattillo, chairman of the Ontario Securities Commission, telephones John A. Tory, an Abitibi director and the company's chief legal adviser, and asks that he and J.R. Kimber, president of the Toronto Stock Exchange, come to the OSC offices after lunch. (At 2.15 p.m. Monday a letter is hand-delivered to Pattillo from the Canada Permanent Trust Company officially protesting against the short duration of the trade-in period.) Pattillo warns Tory and Kimber that he could suspend trading in the Price stock and requests a forty-eight-hour extension of the offer, but he later accepts the compromise of one extra day. At about the same time in Quebec City, Tittemore issues a statement advising Price shareholders to hold out for an alternative bid, because the Abitibi offer doesn't reflect the true value of his company.

What he has in mind is the possibility of inspiring an offer from Domtar, the newsprint arm of Argus Corporation. Domtar holds 7 per cent of Price shares. All day Friday, Argus tries to line up institutional support for a share-exchange-plus-cash offer, but there isn't enough time, and on Saturday morning Bud McDougald, the Argus chairman, orders the bid abandoned. Tittemore immediately retracts his advice to Price shareholders.

Then, over the weekend, a new group enters the

picture. From London arrive three men representing Associated Newspapers Group, the holding company of Viscount Rothermere. They are Vere Harmsworth, the company's chairman and chief executive officer, Michael Shields, its managing director, and Peter Saunders, the company secretary. Although Associated Newspapers' most visible business is publishing the *Daily Mail* and the *Evening News,* its assets also include a major oil find in the North Sea and an 18.9 per cent interest in Price. The three men, all Price directors, reject the Abitibi bid and together with Tittemore and Bob Morrow (the vice-chairman of Price and a partner in the Montreal law firm of Ogilvy, Cope, Porteous, et al.) set out to find an alternative bidder.

Paul Desmarais has spent the previous week in Paris. He arrives home Friday at midnight, and the next morning John Rae briefs him on the Abitibi situation. Nothing much happens because on Sunday evening Desmarais flies to Winnipeg for an Investors Group directors' meeting. He has an early session Tuesday morning with Bill Turner, president of Consolidated-Bathurst, the newsprint complex controlled by Power Corporation. The two set up a task force* to discuss whether they should make an offer for the Price stock and how it should be financed.

At noon, Desmarais telephones Bob Morrow, the Rothermere lawyer, to invite Associated Newspapers into an alternative bid. This is hardly a new thought for Morrow, who seems to have been waiting for the call. He arrives with Tittemore, and the three British negotiators join them at six o'clock. During the next two hours, they agree to proceed with the offer. Desmarais and Bill Turner spend less than twenty minutes on the telephone lining up the $80 million in credit from the Royal Bank and the Bank of

---

*Besides Desmarais and John Rae, present for Power Corporation are Peter Curry, Jean Parisien, and Frank Knowles, while Consolidated-Bathurst is represented by Bill Turner, Spike Irwin, Oscar Stangeland, Des Campbell, Tim Wagg, and Norm Grundy. Also in attendance is the paper company's main legal adviser, Ken Howard, a senior partner in Ogilvy, Cope, Porteous.

Montreal needed to float the deal. It then takes several hours for the two lawyers—Morrow and Howard—to translate Desmarais's characteristically complicated scheme into a three-page legal document that both parties sign. The arrangement calls for Associated to exchange its shares in Price on a two-for-one basis for Consolidated-Bathurst treasury stock. By the end of that long evening, 930,385 Consolidated-Bathurst shares have been traded for 1,860,770 shares of Price. This gives Associated a minority position (13 per cent) in Consolidated-Bathurst (in which Desmarais still maintains a solid 38 per cent), but it makes Consolidated-Bathurst the largest shareholder in Price. "Until the next annual meeting, we are in *de facto* control of the Price Company," Bill Turner declares. "We think we know where at least 50 per cent of the shares are."

Under existing securities legislation, a company can attempt a private offering to no more than eight shareholders. Desmarais and Turner poll the largest institutional shareholders in Price—Domtar, the Canadian Pacific Pension Fund, Cemp Investments, Standard Life, the Royal Bank, the Bank of Montreal, Royal Trust, and the Caisse de Dépôt—but the total is less than 50 per cent, and they decide to make a public *pro rata* offer to all stockholders for four million shares at $20—two dollars more than was bid by Abitibi. The negotiations finally wind up at 3 a.m. Three tired Englishmen, Tittemore, and Rae straggle into Ben's all-night delicatessen and eat some smoked-meat sandwiches; then the Power Corporation host discovers he doesn't have enough cash to pay the bill. Tittemore, who has just lost control of his company, chips in.

Six hours later, just 45 minutes before the Abitibi offer is due to expire, Consolidated-Bathurst announces its counter offer and the stock exchanges suspend trading in Price shares, giving Abitibi until 2 p.m. the following day to come up with another bid. Rare excitement sweeps through the offices of the security analysts in Toronto and Montreal. The new company formed by the merger of Consolidated-Bathurst and Price would be the world's largest newsprint producer, with annual sales of $1 billion.*

Next day, a heavy snowstorm hits Montreal and Bob Morrow, the Rothermere negotiator, is stuck for five hours on the Champlain Bridge. But he is not required. At 1.45 p.m., just fifteen minutes before the expiry of the Power Corporation deadline, Abitibi raises its bid to $25. The exchanges give Desmarais until 4 p.m. to respond, but instead he calmly tenders his 1.8 million Price shares. This gives him a gain of $25 million in cash plus the 900,000 remaining Price shares, then having a market value of $22.5 million.†

HAVING TURNED A PAPER PROFIT OF NEARLY $15 MILLION IN THIRTY-FOUR HOURS, with no investment involved, Desmarais might have been thought to be at least temporarily content with his achievements. Yet he remains as restless as ever. Introspection is not one of his favourite habits, but occasionally the bewilderment of someone not quite at home with himself bubbles up to reveal a glimpse of the real man within: "If you think too much about the kind of man you are, you can get very confused . . . . I sometimes get in a depressed condition when I ask myself: why don't you stop, for with everything you have there is a corresponding responsibility—and after a while it becomes a heavy burden. But the fascination to go on to greater heights grows also. You have to strike a reasonable position between risk and conservatism, between growth and consolidation."

---

*The eventual Abitibi-Price combination resulted in an even larger producer of newsprint.

†In March, 1975, Domtar announced that it had tendered its holding of 684,525 shares of Price common under the Abitibi offer; 361,258 shares (53.77 per cent) were accepted, resulting in an after-tax realization of $8.6 million and leaving a holding of 323,267 Price shares. On April 1, Domtar sold this as a block to Abitibi for $4.6 million at $14.12 a share; Abitibi thus raised its holding in Price to 54 per cent from 50.7 per cent, and Domtar eliminated a holding it picked up in 1961 by gaining control of St. Lawrence Corporation, which had acquired the shares in 1956, mainly from the estate of I.W. Killam.

There is a large zone of unrest inside Paul Desmarais. It is the deep existential dread of there ever being a vacuum in his affairs, and he will take any risk to fill it. This may well be the ultimate source of his success. He will never be satisfied. You can imagine him wondering if there isn't something else. *I've made all this money,* he seems to be thinking, *but what else can I do? I'm not yet fifty. I'm the richest French Canadian there ever was. I have an office full of Krieghoffs and Chippendale chairs, an ambassador's son as my assistant. Cabinet ministers come and play poker with me. I own the O'Connells' place in the Laurentians and the old Timmins mansion at Murray Bay. E.P. Taylor's daughter did my Montreal house, The Governor General throws special receptions for me. My wife is beautiful and I can entertain eighty relatives at a time. I don't have to bow to anybody. Here I am, done up in my gorgeous three-piece dark blue cashmere suit with a Patek Philippe gold watch and custom-made, valet-shined shoes. What else can I do? There must be something I can turn my wits to . . .*

II

Veto Power

CHAPTER THREE

The Bankers:
Guardians of the Temple

Administering more than $100 billion
in assets, the men who run Canada's
banks rule the nation's economy.
They decide who will succeed and
who will fail, acting as arbiters of the
system—the fiscal father
confessors of us all.

There are some streets where, when you walk down them, what you think about is Money. Only that. One, of course, is Wall Street in New York, and another is Threadneedle Street in the centre of the City in London. Yet the kind of money you think about is very different on each of those streets. On Wall, you think of Fast Money— big figures being hustled in aggressive voices by men (with well-barbered necks) drinking bonded Bourbon or Scotch straight up in Oscar's, around the corner from Lehman's bank. On Threadneedle, what you can still observe is Discreet Money being courted behind the daffodils in the window boxes and whispered about in biscuit-coloured Bentleys driven up from Kent and Surrey.

On four grey blocks in downtown Toronto, which run along King Street west from Yonge to York and down Bay to Front, you can conjure up yet another kind of financial image: Careful Money. Money saved up by high school principals, widows with rockers on their verandahs, retired railway engineers. Money guarded by canny men with tellers' eyes: Canada's bankers—those extraordinarily ordinary individuals who operate the safest and one of the most profitable banking systems on earth. They exercise a great deal more financial authority than any other group in the country. Administering more than $100 billion in assets, the men who run Canada's banks rule the nation's economy. They decide who will succeed and who will fail, acting as arbiters of the system—the fiscal father confessors of us all.

The $650 millions' worth of bank buildings lining that corridor of power on Toronto's King Street include the head offices of the Canadian Imperial Bank of Commerce, the Toronto-Dominion Bank, and the Bank of Nova Scotia. Here also are the chief regional offices for the Bank of Montreal and the Royal Bank, whose headquarters remain in Montreal, although more and more of their vital decisions are being made in Toronto.* The wind blows down that stretch of King as though through a tunnel, and just after high noon every weekday, as the typists swirl by in platform shoes and eye paint, black limousines with tinted windows nose into it, chauffeur-driven, miraculously immune to parking tickets. Out of these cars step the corporate men on their way to wring some of that Careful Money from the bankers over lunches held in private dining rooms that resound with phrases like "extending our lines of credit" and "watching our debt-equity ratio." What the corporate men acknowledge by coming to these blocks (and blocks not unlike them in Vancouver, Calgary, Winnipeg, Montreal, Saint John, Halifax, and St. John's) is the predominant influence of Canada's bankers.

It is the banks that run the private intelligence network that allows the men at the command posts of Canadian business to keep in touch. The executive board meetings of the five largest banks represent the greatest source of non-governmental power in the country. During these deliberations are formed, strengthened, and multiplied the kinships through which the Canadian Establishment protects its existence and swells its authority. The corporations represented on each bank's board of directors trace the bloodlines of big business power in Canada. The clusters formed by this interlacing of friendships, shared concerns, open doors, and common policies decide who gets what portion of the $40 billion in loans that the banks have outstanding at any one time (see ac-

---

*The mammoth new structures the two banks will be occupying by 1976 are testimonials to this shift. The Montreal's $200-million, 72-storey skyscraper will be the largest bank building anywhere, housing fifty thousand office workers and visitors per day, its glass-and-marble face automatically washed every sixty hours. The Royal's two triangular towers, clad in bronze reflecting glass, will cost at least $100 million.

The Big Five Canadian Banks and Their Corporate Clients*

Royal Bank of Canada

Abitibi Paper Co. Ltd., Toronto
Algoma Steel Corporation Ltd., Sault Ste Marie
Asbestos Corporation Ltd., Montreal
Blakeny Concrete Products Ltd., Moncton
British Columbia Forest Products Ltd., Vancouver
Canadian Fuel Marketers Ltd., Montreal
Canadian Liquid Air Ltd., Montreal
Canadian Pacific Ltd., Montreal
Christopher Enterprises Ltd., Vancouver
Comstock International Ltd., Toronto
Eastern Air Lines Inc., New York
Imasco Ltd., Montreal
Imperial Oil Ltd., Toronto
International Paper Co., New York
Mannix Co. Ltd., Calgary
Maritime Steel & Foundries Ltd., New Glasgow
Melchers Distilleries Ltd., Montreal
Metro Centre Developments Ltd.
New Providence Development Co. Ltd., Nassau
Noranda Mines Ltd., Toronto
Otis Elevator Co. Ltd., Hamilton
Pacific Petroleums Ltd., Calgary
Petrofina Canada Ltd., Montreal
Power Corporation of Canada Ltd., Montreal
Sandwell and Co. Ltd., Vancouver
Saskatoon Trading Co. Ltd., Saskatoon
Simpsons Ltd., Toronto
Thomson Newspapers Ltd., Toronto
Westcoast Transmission Co. Ltd., Vancouver
Woodward Stores Ltd., Vancouver

Canadian Imperial Bank of Commerce

Argo Construction Ltd., Montreal
Argus Corporation Ltd., Toronto
Bell Canada, Montreal
Bowes Co. Ltd., Toronto

---

*This list of companies represented on the boards of the Big Five Canadian banks in the spring of 1975 does not include some interests represented by lawyer-directors.

Brascan Ltd., Toronto
British Columbia Telephone Co., Vancouver
Budd Automotive Co. of Canada Ltd., Kitchener
Canada Cement Lafarge Ltd., Montreal
Canada Life Assurance Co., Toronto
Canada Packers Ltd., Toronto
Canron Ltd., Montreal
Cooper Construction Co. Ltd., Hamilton
Crang & Ostiguy Inc., Montreal
Crown Zellerbach Canada Ltd., Vancouver
N. M. Davis Corporation Ltd., Toronto
Dominion Tanners Ltd., Winnipeg
Domtar Ltd., Montreal
Drayton Group of Investment Trusts, London
Falconbridge Nickel Mines Ltd., Toronto
Ford Motor Co. of Canada Ltd., Oakville
A. E. Hickman Co. Ltd., St. John's
Hollinger Mines Ltd., Toronto
Imperial Optical Co. Ltd., Toronto
International Multifoods Corp., Minneapolis
M&M Systems Research Ltd., Edmonton
MacMillan Bloedel Ltd., Vancouver
Massey-Ferguson Ltd., Toronto
McLarens Foods Ltd., Toronto
Moosehead Breweries Ltd., Saint John
National Life Assurance Co. of Canada, Toronto
Noranda Mines Ltd., Toronto
Northern and Central Gas Corporation Ltd., Toronto
Placer Development Ltd., Vancouver
James Richardson & Sons Ltd., Winnipeg
Shell Transport and Trading Co. Ltd., London
Simpsons-Sears Ltd., Toronto
TransCanada PipeLines Ltd., Toronto
Upper Lakes Shipping Ltd., Toronto
Weyburn Livestock Exchange Ltd., Weyburn

Bank of Montreal

Alberta Gas Trunk Line Co. Ltd., Calgary
Alcan Aluminium Ltd., Montreal
B.C. Sugar Refinery Ltd., Vancouver
Bell Canada, Montreal
Brinco Ltd., Montreal
Buckwold's Ltd., Saskatoon
Canada Cement Lafarge Ltd., Montreal

Canadian Corporate Management Co. Ltd., Toronto
Canadian Forest Products Ltd., Vancouver
Canadian Industries Ltd., Montreal
Canadian Pacific Ltd., Montreal
Century Sales & Service Ltd., Edmonton
Crosbie Services Ltd., St. John's
Dawson Construction Ltd., Vancouver
T. Eaton Co. Ltd., Toronto
Federal Industries Ltd., Winnipeg
Hambro Canada Ltd., Toronto
House of Seagram Ltd., Montreal
International Nickel Co. of Canada Ltd., Toronto
Laiterie Laval Ltée, Montreal
Jos. A. Likely Ltd., Saint John
McGavin ToastMaster Ltd., Vancouver
Molson Companies Ltd., Toronto
Morgan Trust Co., Montreal
Petrofina Canada Ltd., Montreal
Prenor Group Ltd., Montreal
Richardson Securities of Canada, Winnipeg
Rolland Paper Co. Ltd., Montreal
Rothmans of Pall Mall Canada Ltd., Toronto
Sobeys Stores Ltd., Stellarton, N.S.
Standard Life Assurance Co., Montreal
Steel Co. of Canada Ltd., Toronto
Sun Life Assurance Co. of Canada, Montreal
Wabasso Ltd., Montreal
Western Tractor Ltd., Regina

Bank of Nova Scotia

Alberta Energy Co. Ltd., Edmonton
Alberta Gas Trunk Line Co. Ltd., Calgary
Algoma Central Railway, Sault Ste Marie
Ayre & Sons Ltd., St. John's
Canada Life Assurance Co., Toronto
Cominco Ltd., Vancouver
Dominion Foundries and Steel Ltd., Hamilton
Great Canadian Oil Sands Ltd., Toronto
Gulf Oil Canada Ltd., Toronto
Inter-Ocean Grain Co. Ltd., Winnipeg
MacCulloch & Co. Ltd., Halifax
Maclaren Power & Paper Co., Buckingham, Que.
Robert McAlpine Ltd., Toronto
McCain Foods Ltd., Florenceville, N.B.

Minas Basin Pulp and Power Co. Ltd., Hantsport, N.S.
Molson Companies Ltd., Toronto
Moore Corporation Ltd., Toronto
New Brunswick Telephone Co. Ltd., Saint John
Noranda Mines Ltd., Toronto
Numac Oil & Gas Ltd., Edmonton
Oshawa Group Ltd., Toronto
Weyerhaeuser Canada Ltd., Vancouver

Toronto-Dominion Bank

Bell Canada, Montreal
British Steel Corporation (Canada) Ltd., Hamilton
Cemp Investments Ltd., Montreal
Cominco Ltd., Vancouver
Consumers' Gas Co., Toronto
Continental Can International Corp., New York
Dominion Construction Co. Ltd., Vancouver
Du Pont of Canada Ltd., Montreal
T. Eaton Co. Ltd., Toronto
Excelsior Life Insurance Co., Toronto
Finning Tractor & Equipment Co. Ltd., Vancouver
Goodyear Canada Inc., Toronto
Gulf Oil Canada Ltd., Toronto
Harding Carpets Ltd., Toronto
Hiram Walker-Gooderham & Worts Ltd., Windsor
IBM Canada Ltd., Toronto
International Nickel Co. of Canada Ltd., Toronto
London Life Insurance Co., London, Ont.
Maclean-Hunter Ltd., Toronto
Maritime Telegraph & Telephone Co. Ltd., Halifax
Miron Company Ltd., Montreal
Mobil Oil Canada Ltd., Calgary
N.M. Paterson & Sons Ltd., Thunder Bay
Poole Construction Ltd., Edmonton
Procter & Gamble Co. of Canada Ltd., Toronto
Rio Tinto-Zinc Corporation Ltd., London
Thomson Newspapers Ltd., Toronto
UAP Inc., Montreal
Union Carbide Canada Ltd., Toronto
Westinghouse Canada Ltd., Hamilton

companying cluster representations).* The bankers' om-
nipotence is exercised through their ability to withhold
favours, to keep the interlopers they consider unsuitable
from joining not only their own clusters of influence but
any other clusters as well. This veto-power constitutes the
chief element of the bankers' might.

The banks encounter little opposition to either their
hegemony or their methods. Canadians believe in banking.
They write four million cheques, money orders, and drafts
on their twenty-six million accounts every working day,
making them the largest per capita users of bank services in the world. There are more bank branches (6,878
at latest count) than taverns in the country. (Julien
Côté, director-general of Canada's Olympic Lottery,
found a solution to the problem of slow initial ticket
sales outside Quebec by marketing through the banks.
"In English Canada people really trust the banks," he said,
"and that was how we solved our credibility troubles. Sales
in Ontario tripled for the second draw just because people
heard the banks had started to make the tickets available.")

Canada's chartered banks are huge bureaucracies that
make up one of the most concentrated banking systems
anywhere.† Professor Daniel Baum of Osgoode Hall Law
School has written: "Governmental efforts in the field of
banking have been directed toward the creation of an
economically powerful system capable of maintaining a
strong competitive position vis-à-vis other financial institutions. The relationship between the bank and the
customer has been of only incidental concern. The government has benefited from this result by achieving more
effective control over national monetary policy."‡

By mid-1975, only five of the ten Canadian banks had
assets large enough to place them in contention as national institutions exercising significant economic clout.

---

*The surest way to establish the banking connection of any company
not represented on bank boards is to look up the identity of the street-
level branch bank in its head-office building.
†Thirty-three Canadian banks were open for business at the time of
Confederation and a total of 157 bank charters were granted between
1820 and 1970, though sixty-two of them were never taken up. Some
forty-five banks failed (with losses of about $15 million) and forty-one
other banks were absorbed through mergers. If Canada had as many
banks proportionately as the U.S., there would be approximately fourteen hundred independent banks in this country, instead of ten.
‡In the *Georgetown Law Journal 59* (May 1971): 1127.

The chart below shows these five and their smaller contemporaries with their assets in the spring of 1975.

The industry's Big Five account for 91 per cent of all banking assets; the Royal alone controls nearly a quarter of the system's wealth.* In a 1967 brief to the Commons Committee on Finance, Trade and Economic Affairs, R.G.D. Lafferty, the Montreal investment dealer, characterized Canadian banking as "a nationwide, monolithic structure with participants being governed by manuals and regulations designed to mold the system into a cohesive form that responds to a narrow management structure surrounded by interlocking directorates . . . a banking machine which responds to the policies of the hierarchy and not to the desires of the consumer."†

	(Assets in millions of dollars)
Royal Bank	$ 23,700.8
Commerce	$ 20,743.3
Montreal	$ 18,490.8
Nova Scotia	$ 15,293.2
Toronto-Dominion	$ 13,274.8

The five smaller banks were:

Banque Canadienne Nationale*	$ 4,592.7
Banque Provinciale du Canada*	$ 2,825.9
Mercantile Bank of Canada	$ 905.3
Bank of British Columbia	$ 535.7
Unity Bank of Canada	$ 152.8
TOTAL ASSETS	$100,515.3†

*Both the BCN and BPC would, in the context of any other system, be considered major banks. Under the dynamic presidency of Germain Perreault, the BCN plans to be operating fifty branches outside Quebec by 1980.
†Bank assets have doubled since 1971, following a record 180 per cent increase during the sixties. At the end of 1960, they totalled only $16.9 billion. By 1970, banks held 35 per cent of the total assets of all Canadian financial institutions, including insurance companies, trusteed pension plans, mortgage and loan companies, finance companies, credit unions, and mutual funds.

Acting as middlemen between savers and spenders, banks make their profit out of the difference between what they pay for money (mostly the interest they grant

*Only three banks in North America, the Bank of America, the First National City and the Chase Manhattan, are larger than the Royal, which employs a staff of thirty thousand in fifteen hundred branches.
†Shortly after his testimony, the Royal withdrew from handling Lafferty's private and business bank accounts.

depositors) and what they get for money (mostly the interest they collect on loans). Published net profit figures are not very meaningful because they can so easily be distorted by pushing extra earnings into any number of contingency reserves.* Bankers measure real profits by their "balance-of-revenue" accounts—the difference between earnings generated and expenses paid. Except for the Bank of Montreal, the Big Five showed large balance-of-revenue gains for 1974, compared to the previous twelve months:

	(Gains in millions of dollars)	*(Gain or loss relative to 1973)*
Royal Bank	$211	+ 9.8%
Commerce	$206	+13.6%
Montreal	$109	—17.2%*
Nova Scotia	$138	+27.6%
Toronto-Dominion	$139	+35.1%

*This sharp drop in profit prompted some serious doubts in the investment community about the Bank of Montreal's management capabilities. The bank's performance has been declining ever since 1935, when it ceased to act as the federal government's chief fiscal agent. It had previously been the most illustrious financial institution in Canada. Sir Lomer Gouin, who was premier of Quebec for fifteen years, once declared that he would rather have been president of the Bank of Montreal. Part of the problem has been the Montreal's uninspired hiring practices, while the Royal Bank, under James Muir and Earle McLaughlin, has been recruiting the fastest guns in the industry. They include Jock Finlayson, its deputy chairman at head office, Rowlie Frazee, its executive vice-president and chief general manager, and Doug Gardiner, its deputy chairman in Toronto, who (along with Ced Ritchie, chairman of the Nova Scotia, and Dick Thomson of the Toronto-Dominion) are the ablest bankers in the country. Another reason for the disparity in earnings is that the Royal has accommodated much more rapidly to shifting its centre of gravity from Montreal to Toronto. Until recently, the Montreal tended to regard Toronto (as one of its competitors puts it) as "a distant outpost with a sizable beaver catch." (The Montreal didn't hold a national directors' meeting in Toronto until 1960.) At the same time, the Bank of Montreal has made little effort to integrate itself into the new Quebec. Only one of its senior head office executives (M.A. Massé) is a French-speaking Canadian. Addressing a dinner marking the bank's 150th anniversary in 1967, Arnold Hart, the Bank of Montreal's chairman, said not a single word in French. Jean Drapeau pointedly told the audience: "I am so happy to be mayor of a city with the same name as your bank." But his sarcasm was wasted; the Bank of Montreal men merely looked at each other in smug agreement.

---

*The fastest-growing sector of Canadian banking is its foreign business, with 280 full-scale branches and 4,500 agencies operated abroad, holding $26 billion in foreign currency assets. The Royal is part of the Orion banking group, in which it joined with the Chase Manhattan (the third-largest U.S. bank), the National Westminster (the second-largest British bank), and the Westdeutsche Landesbank (Germany's largest) in one of the most powerful alliances of banking interests ever forged. The Montreal is one of four equal partners in an Australian merchant bank (the Australian International Finance Corp.). The Toronto-Dominion is heavily committed in Asia and is part of the huge London-based Midland and International Banks Ltd. With six other banks, the Nova Scotia owns the United International Bank Ltd., which makes no loans of less than a million dollars.

MONEY IS NO JOKE IN THIS COUNTRY, AND BANKING IS VERY MUCH MORE THAN JUST A BUSINESS. It is a calling. Senior bankers, especially the chairmen of the Big Five —the men who set the tone and the policies for the whole system—regard themselves as chief custodians of the free enterprise ethic. They take inordinate pride in operating the levers of the machinery that keeps business expanding, consumers spending, and the economy functioning.* The bankers discharge their powers with the self-conscious virtue of representative elders at a Presbyterian synod meeting: never pushy, seldom impatient, always careful, gracious, proper, and, above all, serene in the security of their faith. They view banking as a beneficial discipline, foreordained to reward the worthy and the able.

The men who head each of the five most powerful financial institutions are very distinct individuals, but they have one trait in common with all other first-rate bankers: the inclination to identify themselves so totally with their work that they have come to regard banking decisions as genuine extensions of their personal feelings. This produces in most bankers an approach to their profession that gives it a strange resemblance to the priestly calling. They seem to regard the handling of money not so much as a means of gaining power or prestige for themselves as an end in itself. Currencies must be tended like delicate flowers by God's own anointed gardeners—themselves.

The banks deliberately instill in their employees the same feeling that exists inside the hierarchies of the church or the foreign service, that to reach the top you must start at the bottom and mutely accept the many disciplines along the way. "You just have to live, eat, and breathe banking if you're going to be any good at it,"

---

*Their self-imposed role as guardians of the free enterprise system sometimes leads the bank chairmen to the conclusion that everyone enjoying the benefits of Canadian society should have a similar outlook, regardless of his economic status. William Nicks, late chairman of the Nova Scotia, advanced the theory to his bank's annual meeting in 1970 that paying income tax was good for the poor. "The objective of removing large numbers of people from the tax roll is contrary to the long-run interest of a participatory society," he said. "No matter how small, the act of filing a tax return and paying a levy helps to bring home the fact that nothing is free and that new services mean new taxes."

says Dick Thomson,* who became president of the Toronto-Dominion when he was only thirty-nine. Bankers tend to talk about being "in the service," as if banking were an activity somehow set apart from the strivings of ordinary mortals. At the Royal, all managers have to sign a witnessed oath of secrecy every twelve months, pledging not to disclose the bank's or the customers' financial dealings. According to John Coleman, a former deputy chairman at the Royal, "We're like priests in a confessional and have to keep everything we hear in confidence, even when we're in on both sides of a deal." This combination of zeal and secrecy makes senior bankers intensely private individuals. Except for compulsory attendance at annual meetings of shareholders, the occasional appearance before parliamentary committees, and rare luncheon-club speaking engagements, they prefer to remain in the shadows—men marked by twin passions: the first for credit risks that will not default, the second for anonymity.

The bankers move softly, "talking things over," foreclosing on loans only as a last resort. Circumspection is everything: it is the inflection in a banker's voice that counts.† Earle McLaughlin (who as chairman of the Royal could easily have broken Paul Desmarais's march to power in 1970, when Power Corporation got into difficulties with Consolidated-Bathurst, or have done con-

---

*Thomson personifies the new breed of Canadian bankers. Unlike most of his predecessors, he came from a highly placed banking family (his father was vice-chairman of the Commerce); he studied engineering at the University of Toronto and in 1957 received a Master of Business Administration degree from Harvard. He joined the TD immediately after graduation and only eight years later was named assistant general manager. He became president of the bank in 1972.

†All that circumspection has produced a relatively safe system. There were no bank failures during the Great Depression of the thirties, although operations were severely curtailed, with outstanding loans reduced by $655 million between 1929 and 1933. One bank in difficulty was the Weyburn Security Bank, all of whose thirty branches were in southern Saskatchewan. The Imperial Bank absorbed it in January, 1931, eliminating the only chartered bank of the time whose head office was in Western Canada. The last major failure was that of the Home Bank in 1923. Too many bad loans had been made (some to directors) and the record books were juggled to conceal losses. A vice-president of the Home and five directors were charged with fraud, but their convictions were quashed on appeal. A royal commission reported that several Ontario cabinet ministers had withdrawn their money from the failing bank two days before its doors closed. The inquiry also revealed that Col. James Cooper Mason, the general manager, had placed the funds he borrowed from the Home in other banks for safekeeping.

siderable damage to the Webster fortune when the family was in trouble with its Quebecair deal) is the prime example of a bank chairman who eschews the very idea that he possesses power of any kind. "Power is something political," he says. "What we have is *responsibility*."*

Responsibility is a concept that bankers understand. It is the supreme middle-class virtue. Despite their exalted place in the country's fiscal firmament, they are middle-class men and mighty proud of it. Fitted more by temperament than by birth for their high station, they are the primitives of Canadian business. They cannot be fitted into any forest of Canadian family trees. With a few (though increasing) exceptions, they grew up in small towns where the banks provided the only passport to the outside world for bright boys whose parents couldn't afford to send them to university. "The old story in New Brunswick," McLaughlin recalls, "was that a young man could either cut wood, grow potatoes, or join the Royal."

There is little nepotism in the banks. Unlike the investment-dealer community, which perpetuates the influence of established wealth and the right private schools, the bankers function as an elite without elitist credentials. No matter how high they rise, most bankers retain a kind of green-eyeshade, good-boy-who-got-terrific-marks aspect about them. They are dutiful soldiers, dutiful sons, dutiful husbands—steadfast ecclesiasts in a heretical world. Their relationship to businessmen is somehow reminiscent of that between public servants and politicians —two very different species, operating in a symbiotic partnership.

Unlike the brasher corporate men, who relish the knowledge that anywhere they go people will move for them, give way, run errands, *jump*, bankers lead muted lives. (Graham Towers, when he was governor of the Bank of Canada, once found himself at a hotel in the Maritimes without enough cash to pay his bill. When a suspicious cashier demanded identification before he would honour his cheque, Towers tried with considerable

---

*Apart from McLaughlin's position as chairman and dominant personality at the Royal, he is also a director of Power Corporation, Genstar Ltd., Metropolitan Life, Algoma Steel, Canadian Pacific, and General Motors Corp. (Detroit), a position he took over from Col. Sam McLaughlin, his first cousin once removed.

embarrassment to avoid revealing who he was but finally pulled out a dollar bill and reluctantly showed the startled cashier his signature, then decorating all of Canada's paper currency.) Although chairmen of the Big Five receive salaries in the $200,000-a-year range, they seldom indulge themselves in visible luxuries and feel (or pretend) pious amusement at such ostentations as fat yachts, thin mistresses, thoroughbred horses, and dollar cigars. They tend to find their diversions on golf courses and at summer cottages, very much as they would if they were still branch managers.

They operate from offices furnished like *Forsyte Saga* drawing rooms, meant to convey the impression that instead of being men of power they are merely the guardians at the gates. They seldom step outside their head offices, even for lunch, preferring to entertain clients in the banks' own executive dining rooms, which serve discreet cocktails followed by meticulously prepared meals.* It is here, away from the noise and confusion of everyday commerce, over silver platters and escutcheoned china, that the chairmen solidify the contacts that lead to the big-dollar deals.

IN ALMOST EVERYTHING THEY DO, THE SENIOR BANKERS RELY ON TRADITION AND PRECEDENT. Canada's early bankers were a stuffy lot, acting as if they were doing depositors a favour by accepting their money. Banks issued their own currencies (until 1935) and their operating heads were generally knighted by British monarchs.

When Floyd Chalmers, later president of Maclean-Hunter and chancellor of York University, was a young *Financial Post* editor in Montreal during the early twenties, he was granted an interview by Sir Frederick Williams-Taylor, general manager of the Bank of Montreal. "My appointment was for around twelve o'clock," Chalmers recalls. "I had about half an hour with him and then, at half-past twelve, he stood up—he looked im-

---

*Quiche Lorraine is the specialty at Commerce headquarters in Toronto, which also features a special drink made of apple juice and ginger ale with a touch of Angostura bitters; the Royal's chef roasts the best salted almonds in the country.

maculate to me—and went behind a screen. He said: 'Keep on talking.' And he changed his striped trousers to another set of striped trousers. He came out and put on his grey gloves. He thanked me for coming in, pressed a button, and an attendant in a froglike uniform opened the door of his office. Williams-Taylor walked as far as the inner door of the bank leading to the street. Two attendants there opened the double doors; another attendant opened the door outside. Still another one, with a broom (because this was in early winter), swept the steps to his car, where a uniformed chauffeur was waiting to take him to the Mount Royal Club for lunch. This kind of protocol reflected the character of the banks which, at that time, didn't have much interest in the public or small businessmen—except to try to impress them."*

One of the most influential bank directors at that time was Albert Brown, a director of the Royal between 1912 and 1938. He was so parsimonious that when he was courting his wife, who lived in Quebec City, he wrote her a letter daily but mailed them only once a week to save on postage. He insisted that each of his three male assistants constantly carry a notebook. If Brown caught one unprepared, he would immediately begin to dictate a letter which the unfortunate assistant would have to take down on the starched cuff of his shirt. Brown once caned a young CNR messenger because the boy had the nerve to whistle while riding in the same elevator with him.

The banks were so rigid in their ways that when one young clerk had the temerity to write a letter to his head office on a typewriter, it brought a reply to the effect that

---

*Writing in *Maclean's*, Sir Frederick spelled out the seven commandments that in his view led to the ideal life:

"First—INTEMPERANCE is the greatest handicap with which a young man can burden himself. If you touch stimulants before you are twenty-five years of age you are a fool.

"Second—CONCENTRATION is invaluable in any career. If you want easy proof of its value try it in a game of tennis or golf, or any game, but above all in the game of life.

"Third—OCCASIONAL INTROSPECTION is highly advantageous.

"Fourth—THE CARE OF THE BODY automatically improves the mind. In playing games one gets mental relaxation—physical rejuvenation.

"Fifth—MONEY MAKING is a natural tendency in these days, but never forget that the men who make the acquisition of riches their sole object in life are poor creatures at best.

"Sixth—PUNCTUALITY is the easiest and rarest of virtues.

"Seventh—WORK is the open sesame to every portal."

"if you cannot pen a legible hand, you had best resign." Robert Service, the Yukon poet, on the other hand, was turned down for a messenger's job by the Bank of British North America at Dawson in 1898 on the grounds that "there must be something wrong with a man who would be eager to get so menial a position when he can sign his name in such a beautiful hand." Service was finally accepted by the Bank of Commerce and served as a clerk in Dawson while writing his *Songs of a Sourdough*.

THE KIND OF MAN WHO HAS TRADITIONALLY RISEN TO THE TOP IN THE CANADIAN BANKING SYSTEM has held very definite, if resolutely non-eccentric, views. James Muir, late chairman of the Royal, was probably the prototype of the breed. William Zeckendorf, the New York real estate developer, once commented: "Jim kept things simple: if you were his friend, you could do no wrong; if you were his enemy, you could do no right. And if you were worth considering at all, you were in one category or the other." Muir's personality and that of most other senior bankers is a reflection of their passion for certainty. They feel compelled to control the environment in which they are operating. Their world is one in which everyone, especially subordinates, plays out his assigned role, where words carry the same message to all concerned and risks exist only as accidents.

In an era when institutional power structures are being fragmented, the banks stand apart. They are enormous sharply vertical pyramids with authority flowing to the places and projects where it is required, subject always to the final authority of the man at the top. He rules on the basis of a self-defined mandate that rests not on any constitution or formal set of instructions but rather on the enormous moral suasion he imposes through the weight of his office. Climbers at various levels of the pyramid seem to know instinctively what the chief executive officer wants done. The chairmen safeguard their positions by naming outside directors (their own appointees) to nonoperating vice-presidencies.* These nominees preside

---

*These vice-presidents are usually paid $10,000 a year on top of directors' fees.

over board meetings during the absence of the chairmen and act as a kind of palace guard to protect them against overly impatient successors. Bank chairmen enjoy remarkably lengthy tenures, usually either dying in office or reaching such a state of advanced irrelevance that their replacement becomes a necessary salvage operation.* Except for the Bank of Montreal, which has been recruiting, with increasing panic, a succession of outsiders, the new chairmen usually emerge from the third echelon of a bank's executive structure, because incumbents tend to select those closest to them as much for their loyalty as for their abilities.

Conditions for juniors have improved considerably over the situation before World War II, when bank employees could not marry without the manager's permission and only after their salaries had risen to a princely $1,500 a year, or at least $1,200, with the balance guaranteed by the parents of either. The perfect banker is categorized as "a good evaluator of people and risks," with recruiters constantly on the lookout for those elusive "clean-cut" young men who once populated Canadian high schools.† University graduates are rapidly being moved into staff functions, but there remains a residue of resentment against them as potential troublemakers who ask a lot of questions and tend to be dissatisfied with routine assignments.‡ "The banks," says Gordon Sharwood, a for-

---

*A dramatic exception to the customarily smooth transition among bank chairmen was the ouster in 1973 of Neil McKinnon as chief of the Commerce. This incident is described in the chapter that follows.

†The banks still try to control what employees wear. A Commerce handbook for women tellers states: "Clothing should be simple in style, properly fitted and coordinated in colors; dresses that are too tight or too short are not suitable, nor are bulky sweaters or faddish stockings. Basic jewelry is acceptable, but items that are extreme in style, or designed for evening wear (such as bangles, oversized earrings and most sparkling jewelry), should be avoided. Plain basic pumps and flat shoes are preferred, and they always should be in good condition; casual or extreme styles, including moccasins, boots and sneakers, are undesirable."

‡Turning ordinary mortals into bankers is a tough and touchy assignment. With a total payroll of 115,000 and an annual turnover of 35 per cent for women and 14 per cent for men, the banks are constantly recruiting, training, and educating. About nine thousand middle-rank bank employees take courses from the Institute of Canadian Bankers; a few especially promising candidates are awarded university scholarships; and everyone learns on the job. All the banks sponsor a variety of problem-solving seminars and group-dynamics cash-ins, but there is one learning institution that possesses an ambience all its own. Deep in that part of wealthy Toronto where the mansions begin to have curved driveways guarded by urn-topped gateposts stands a neo-Georgian pile called Burnside, once the home of Josephine Burnside, elder daughter of Timothy

mer chief general manager of the Commerce, "look for people who get high marks and have some aptitude with figures. But they don't go after the aggressive sales-oriented guys who knock on the doors of IBM or Procter and Gamble. They usually end up with the solid, solemn, good citizen types, and if they get the other kind they don't generally keep them very long."

Branch managers due for promotion are invited to their bank's annual meeting, where head office executives can look over their wives to see if they could back up their husbands in more senior postings. Two reports are filed annually on most employees, one by the supervisor and one by a bank inspector, categorizing the subject's performance according to a rigid grading system. Hardly anybody is fired except for embezzlement, heavy drinking on the job, or trying to organize a tellers' union.*

A BANK EMPLOYEE'S STATUS HAS LITTLE TO DO WITH HIS TITLE OR SENIORITY: the important factor is his "discretionary limit"—the amount of money he can lend on the basis of his own signature.† In medium-sized branches

---

Eaton. The two-acre estate, acquired by the Commerce in 1963, has a gazebo and a fountain in the garden, a *porte-cochère* at the main entrance, and a system of twenty-four bells for maids in the kitchen. This is the Canadian Imperial Bank of Commerce Staff College. It accommodates thirty executives for two or three weeks at a time. In the large formal garden, among some forty varieties of carefully planted trees and shrubs, is the original bird fountain, bearing the inscription: WHEN THE BIRDS ARE HERE, ARE THE ANGELS?

*Loans that go sour (referred to as "impaired") can get the man who made them into trouble; he is not asked to make good the damage, but he has "blotted his copybook," and if he doesn't improve he isn't promoted. The highest tribute a bank can pay to an up-and-coming credit man is to appoint him to a branch that operates in the needle-trades areas of Winnipeg, Toronto, or Montreal, where small businesses often go bankrupt. Survival there means certain promotion.

†Salaries are tied in directly with the credit size of a branch; thus managers of shopping-centre banks, where there are heavy deposits but not much big lending, are paid less than those of downtown operations that handle business borrowings. Branch managers' salaries range between $12,000 and $35,000 a year, not including fringe benefits, which can be considerable. For example, when E.A. Royce, who spent forty-four years with the Bank of Montreal before being appointed chairman of the Ontario Securities Commission, was manager of the bank's main branch in Ottawa in the early 1950s, his salary was $9,000, but he also had free membership in the Rideau Club, the use of a chauffeured limousine, a $3,000 expense allowance, and a Rockcliffe house for which he was charged a rent of only $150 a month. In his final year at the Montreal (1969), as one of its regional general managers Royce was getting $40,000 in salary, $13,000 in bonuses, and $18,000 in expense accounts, plus the subsidized use of a bank-owned house. This was a fairly typical arrangement. Contributory pension benefits are generous, amounting to 70 per cent of salaries.

the manager might follow what is known as the five-and-ten limit (this means he can lend up to $5,000 on his own signature without collateral and a further $10,000 on the basis of negotiable collateral). At the main big-city branches, managers may exercise discretionary lending powers of up to $250,000, and regional vice-presidents can go as high as a million. Anything larger goes through to head office.*

The major loan decisions, the discretion that counts— this is the mandate of the approximately three hundred directors who occupy the bank board rooms. They constitute the most important economic elite in the country, placing the indelible mark of their personal interests, corporate loyalties, and philosophical predilections not only on bank policies but also on nearly every significant economic decision taken by the private sector. The bank boards distill business power. Among them, the three hundred directors hold more than three thousand directorships of corporations with assets totalling $700 billion.

The bank directors are drawn from the corporate clusters interconnected with each of the banks. All but four of the top one hundred Canadian bank directors (ranked on the accompanying table according to the amount of the corporate assets with which they are involved) sit on the boards of the three largest banks. Each bank maintains special relationships with these client-directors and also with selected underwriters, law firms, auditing houses, trust and insurance companies. Some sixty-three bank directors sit on the boards of Canada's sixteen largest insurance firms, which control 83 per cent of their industry. Here is a tabulation of the extent of interlocking between banking and insurance board rooms:

---

*Limits differ between banks. The discretionary lending powers of management at the Commerce were recently raised from $2 million to $5 million. Page Wadsworth has decentralized the bank's operations by appointing five senior vice-presidents and raising regional loan limits to $1 million. The Nova Scotia keeps regional lending limits down to $250,000; the Toronto-Dominion sends any loan over $1 million to its board for approval.

Insurance Company	Directors also on board of:				
	B of M	CIBC	RBC	B of NS	TDB
Sun Life	8	2	3		1
Manufacturers Life		2			2
Prudential Life			1		
London Life					1
Great-West Life	1		1		
Canada Life	1	2		2	1
Mutual Life		1	1	2	
Metropolitan Life			1		
Confederation Life	2	2			1
Standard Life	4		1		
Crown Life	2	1		3	
North American Life		1	2		1
Imperial Life	2	1		1	
Dominion Life			1		
National Life		1	1	1	1
Monarch Life		1			
	20	14	12	9	8

Each of the large banks has a special relationship with a trust company (the Royal with Montreal Trust, the Montreal with Royal Trust, the Commerce with National Trust, and the Nova Scotia and Toronto-Dominion with Canada Permanent; the Nova Scotia's link had been with Eastern and Chartered Trust until that company and Canada Permanent merged in 1967).* Canada's thirty-five major trust companies administer $40 billion in estates in addition to other accounts. Among them they have in their orbit of influence something like half of the market value of all the Canadian-owned industrial stocks on the Montreal and Toronto stock exchanges. They also provide other bridges to the banks. Major-General A.L. Penhale, for example, was chairman of the Sherbrooke advisory committee of Royal Trust while he was also a director of the Royal Bank, which is closely connected to Montreal Trust, the Royal Trust's main competitor. This kind of daisy chain can be endless. At one time, the chairman of Mutual Life Assurance, who was also a Royal Bank director, had sitting on his board the chair-

---

*While Canadian banks are not permitted to own more than 10 per cent of any trust company's shares, the Bank of America holds 20 per cent of Montreal Trust, a subsidiary of Paul Desmarais's Power Corp.

Canada's Top One Hundred Bank Directors and Their Corporate Connections

Name	Bank Connection	Number of Director-ships	Assets of Companies Involved (in Millions of Dollars)	Main Corporate Interest
McLaughlin, W.E.	Royal Bank	23	31,389	Royal Bank
Coleman, J.H.	Royal Bank	20	20,435	Royal Bank
Wingate, H.S.	Montreal	15	20,378	International Nickel Co.
Sinclair, I.D.	Royal Bank	20	20,185	Canadian Pacific
Hart, G.A.	Montreal	12	18,777	Bank of Montreal
Matthews, Beverley	Toronto-Dominion	14	18,415	McCarthy & McCarthy
Rolland, L.G.	Montreal	18	18,209	Rolland Paper Co.
Webster, C.W.	Royal Bank	27	17,754	Canadian Import Ltd.
Moore, J.H.	Commerce	8	17,315	Brascan Ltd.
Kerr, J.W.	Commerce	9	17,098	TransCanada PipeLines
Covert, F.M.	Royal Bank	29	17,016	Stewart, MacKeen & Covert
Mayne, A.F.*	Royal Bank	29	16,918	A.F. Mayne & Associates
Vincent, Marcel	Montreal	5	16,820	Bell Canada
Lank, H.H.	Toronto-Dominion	15	16,771	Du Pont of Canada
Monast, André	Commerce	15	16,327	St. Laurent, Monast & Waters
Sinclair, James	Montreal	8	15,571	Canada Cement Lafarge
Crump, N.R.	Montreal	20	15,504	Canadian Pacific
Fairley, A.L.	Commerce	9	15,466	Hollinger Mines

*Died September 1972.

110

Leitch, J.D.	Commerce	10	15,369	Upper Lakes Shipping
Crabtree, H.R.	Montreal	16	15,208	Wabasso Ltd.
Smith, J.H.	Commerce	5	15,185	Canadian General Electric
Scrivener, R.C.	Commerce	7	15,137	Bell Canada
Richardson, G.T.	Commerce	24	15,084	James Richardson & Sons
Mackenzie, M.W.	Commerce	7	14,763	Retired (Chemcell Ltd.)
McDougald, J.A.	Commerce	30	14,602	Argus Corp.
Scully, V.W.T.	Montreal	5	14,600	Steel Co. of Canada
Manning, E.C.	Commerce	11	14,522	M & M Systems Research
Lang, H.J.	Commerce	7	14,389	Canron Ltd.
Arbuckle, W.A.	Montreal	25	14,278	Arbuckle Govett & Co.
Ostiguy, J.P.W.	Commerce	15	14,179	Morgan, Ostiguy & Hudon
Clyne, J.V.	Commerce	5	14,155	MacMillan Bloedel Ltd.
Cooper, R.W.	Commerce	10	14,123	Cooper Construction Co.
Duquet, J.E.L.	Royal Bank	17	14,117	Duquet, MacKay & Wellon
Lambert, A.T.	Toronto-Dominion	21	13,984	Toronto-Dominion Bank
Pratte, Claude	Royal Bank	16	13,960	Létourneau, Stein, Marseille
Thomson, P.N.	Royal Bank	43	13,655	Power Corp.
Powis, Alfred	Commerce	25	13,615	Noranda Mines
Rogers, R.G.	Commerce	8	13,594	Crown Zellerbach Canada
Davis, N.V.	Montreal	4	13,548	Alcan Aluminium Ltd.
Blumenauer, G.H.	Royal Bank	7	13,374	Otis Elevator Co.
McKinnon, Neil*	Commerce	10	13,200	CIBC
Mayberry, T.M.	Commerce	3	13,148	Retired (Firestone Tire)
Leach, A.S.	Montreal	12	13,101	Federal Grain Ltd.

*Died August 1975,

111

Name	Bank Connection	Number of Directorships	Assets of Companies Involved (in Millions of Dollars)	Main Corporate Interest
Rathgeb, C.I.	Royal Bank	9	12,962	Comstock International Ltd.
Twaits, W.O.	Royal Bank	3	12,930	Imperial Oil
Beaupré, T.N.*	Royal Bank	9	12,892	Domtar
Notman, J.G.*	Commerce	17	12,889	Westmount Life
Deutsch, J.J.	Commerce	2	12,878	Queen's University
Richardson, J.E.	Commerce	8	12,798	B.C. Telephone
Molson, H. de M.	Montreal	6	12,741	Molson Companies Ltd.
MacIntosh, A.J.	Commerce	12	12,707	Blake, Cassels & Graydon
Lumbers, L.G.	Royal Bank	18	12,689	Noranda Mines
Wood, E.C.	Royal Bank	10	12,635	Genstar Ltd.
Ash, W.M.V.	Montreal	6	12,618	General Bakeries Ltd.
Cooper, M.A.	Commerce	22	12,578	Falconbridge Nickel Mines Ltd.
Taylor, E.P.	Royal Bank	13	12,560	New Providence Development Co.
Nielsen, A.R.	Toronto-Dominion	6	12,531	Mobil Oil Canada Ltd.
Desruisseaux, Paul	Royal Bank	21	12,467	Melchers Distilleries Ltd.
Tory, J.A.	Royal Bank	17	12,438	Tory, Tory, DesLauriers
Woodward, C.N.W.	Royal Bank	6	12,395	Woodward Stores
Penhale, A.L.	Royal Bank	10	12,362	Asbestos Corp. Ltd.
Bell, T.J.	Royal Bank	8	12,331	Abitibi Paper
Holbrook, D.S.	Royal Bank	6	12,297	Algoma Steel Corp.

*Died March 1974.

112

Mannix, F.C.	Royal Bank	4	12,290	Bowfort Services Ltd.
Hicks, A.R.	Montreal	4	12,288	Sun Life Assurance
Gill, E.C.	Commerce	2	12,282	Canada Life Assurance
Christopher, A.B.	Royal Bank	13	12,277	Nelsons Laundries Ltd.
Riley, C.S.	Commerce	7	12,202	Dominion Tanners Ltd.
Barrow, J.C.	Commerce	7	12,192	Simpsons-Sears Ltd.
Thornbrough, A.A.	Commerce	3	12,178	Massey-Ferguson Ltd.
Simpson, J.D.	Commerce	5	12,159	Placer Development
Burton, G.A.	Royal Bank	7	12,148	Simpsons Ltd.
Macdonnell, P.L.P.	Royal Bank	12	12,139	Milner & Steer
Davidson, I.D.	Commerce	9	12,102	Retired (Canadian Shell)
Scott, Karl E.	Commerce	5	11,944	Ford of Canada
Létourneau, Roger	Montreal	12	11,870	Létourneau, Stein, Marseille
Paré, Paul	Royal Bank	4	11,855	Imasco Ltd.
Mockridge, H.C.F.	Montreal	10	11,842	Osler, Hoskin & Harcourt
Ogilvy, I.A.	Royal Bank	8	11,837	Ogilvy, Cope, Porteous
Pollock, C.A.	Royal Bank	7	11,822	Electrohome Ltd.
McMahon, F.M.	Royal Bank	3	11,8-9	Retired (Westcoast Transmission Co.)
Wadsworth, J.P.R.	Commerce	4	11,798	CIBC
Hermant, S.M.	Commerce	4	11,733	Imperial Optical Co.
Anderson, D.S.	Royal Bank	4	11,670	Metro Centre Developments
McLagan, T.R.	Royal Bank	12	11,663	Canada Steamship Lines
McLean, W.F.	Commerce	4	11,636	Canada Packers
MacKeen, J.C.*	Royal Bank	21	11,550	Nova Scotia Light & Power
Bleckwell, E.H.	Royal Bank	3	11,577	Du Pont of Canada

*Died October 1972.

Name	Bank Connection	Number of Director-ships	Assets of Companies Involved (in Millions of Dollars)	Main Corporate Interest
Greenwood, L.G.	Commerce	2	11,529	CIBC
Hunter, G.R.	Commerce	8	11,499	Pitblado & Co.
Gibbings, C.W.	Royal Bank	6	11,369	Commissioner, Canadian Wheat Board
Hickman, E.L.	Commerce	18	11,338	A.E. Hickman Co.
Black, G.M., Jr.	Commerce	8	11,305	Argus Corp.
Thomson, H.W.	Commerce	6	11,295	CIBC
Elliott, R.F.	Commerce	21	11,274	Stikeman, Elliott, Tamaki
Pinder, H.C.	Royal Bank	8	11,273	Saskatoon Drug & Stationery Co.
Rattenbury, Nelson*	Commerce	8	11,140	Northern Industries Ltd.
Baillie, A.W.	Commerce	8	11,119	Bowes Co. Ltd.
Moore, T.F.	Commerce	3	11,112	Retired (Imperial Oil)
East, M.A.	Commerce	4	11,097	Retired (John East Iron Works)

NOTE: This list was taken from the bank directors' lists as of March, 1972. Some highly influential businessmen were not included because their major interests are in private corporations, which do not make public their asset positions. That is why David Kinnear, then chairman of the T. Eaton Company and a Bank of Montreal director and a Toronto-Dominion director, and a Bank of Montreal director, Leo Kolber, head of the Bronfman-owned Cemp Investments Ltd. and a Toronto-Dominion director, and Nelson Davis, head of N.M. Davis Corp. and a Commerce director, among others, are not listed.

*Died May 1973.

114

men of two other banks and a director of a third. At the same time, Mutual held a 20 per cent interest in a large trust company allied to yet another of the competing Big Five banks.*

CANADIAN BUSINESSMEN ASPIRE TO BANK BOARDS THE WAY POLITICIANS SIGH FOR THE SENATE, and once appointed seldom surrender the honour until the mandatory retirement age of seventy-five. (The late Colonel R.S. McLaughlin, for instance, was a director of the Dominion Bank and its successor, the Toronto-Dominion, from 1917 to 1959.) "For a Canadian, becoming a bank director," says Charles Rathgeb, the head of Comstock International Limited, who is on the Royal board, "is the summit of one's business career. The banks are very powerful in the sense that no individual in Canada, to my mind, can do much without the support of the chartered banks. I hope there'll always be room in this country for the banks to support the individual entrepreneur."

The affection pulls both ways. "Our directors are of considerable help to management," says John Coleman, formerly of the Royal. "The product of banking is the same, so it's the personal contact that counts. If we hear of corporate business coming up, we'll look at the names of the company's directors and try to get at them through our own board and *their* connections. If we heard a big deal was coming up in the West, we wouldn't hesitate a minute to call up one of our Prairie directors to see if he could get us some of the action."

Whether the banks make greater use of their directors or the directors make more use of the banks is a moot point. The ground rules are well understood by everyone involved: a bank gets any given piece of business because it knows the potential borrower—one of the "right" people—a little better than its rivals. The men who supply these contacts (the agents of the networks that keep each of the banks expanding) are the board members who

---

*Each of the banks has a link with one of the large investment dealers. A.E. Ames and Co. does most of the floor trading for the Bank of Montreal; Dominion Securities has a link with the Commerce; and the Royal Bank is close to Wood Gundy.

know exactly what's happening within their own industries, which firms are poor risks, what the prospects are for new ventures. In return, the directors gain a great deal of business intelligence themselves—from their fellow directors, from briefings by bank economists, and from the chairmen, who report on the innermost concerns of the Bank of Canada governor himself. "When I went on the board of the Commerce," says Con Riley, president of Dominion Tanners in Winnipeg, "it was to replace Peter Curry. And if you live in the West, in what I call the short grass country, it's pretty handy to be connected with a large Eastern board. You get a kind of feel for what's going on in the financial heartland, which is basically in Toronto. I don't know whether I do the bank any good, but I think they do me some good."

"I've brought a lot of business to the Royal," says Frank Covert, the Halifax lawyer who has been on the bank's board since 1956. "I engineered several purchases and takeovers for Roy Jodrey, and even though he was on the board of the Nova Scotia, he always let me take my clients to the Royal —when we bought Moirs Chocolates and Ben's Bakery, for example, which used to be Commerce accounts."

The Big Five extend their regional influence by recruiting every important bank account they can. In Vancouver, for example, the twenty directors who serve on their boards* represent such a concentration of wealth and influence that there aren't enough important names left to decorate the Bank of British Columbia's own board,† and, what is more significant, there aren't enough major corporate accounts outstanding to allow the regional bank much growth potential.

---

*Big Five directors in B.C. (with the name of their main company followed by that of the bank) include Ian Barclay (B.C. Forest Products, Royal), H. Clark Bentall (Dominion Construction, Toronto-Dominion), F.E. Burnet (Cominco, Toronto-Dominion), A.B. Christopher (Christopher Enterprises, Royal), Graham Dawson (Dawson Construction, Montreal), A. John Ellis (chairman, Canada Development Corporation, Montreal), Gerald Hobbs (Cominco, Nova Scotia), T.H. McClelland (Placer Development, Commerce), Allan McGavin (McGavin Toast-Master, Nova Scotia), John Prentice (Canadian Forest Products, Montreal), J. Ernest Richardson (B.C. Telephone, Commerce), Forrest Rogers (B.C. Sugar, Montreal), Robert Rogers (Crown Zellerbach, Commerce), Thomas Rust (Weyerhaeuser, Nova Scotia), P.R. Sandwell (Sandwell and Co., Royal), James Sinclair (Canada Cement Lafarge, Montreal), Denis Timmis (MacMillan Bloedel, Commerce), H. Richard Whittall (Richardson Securities, Montreal), C.N.W. Woodward (Woodward Stores, Royal), W. Maurice Young (Finning Tractor, Toronto-Dominion).

†A 9.92 per cent holding in the Bank of British Columbia was acquired in the spring of 1975 by the Metropolitan Trust Co., making the Toronto-based company the bank's largest single shareholder.

Bank directors are entitled, among their other privileges, to use of the bank's private aircraft (the Royal, the Montreal, and the Toronto-Dominion operate their own jets). "If you're travelling in England, Europe, the United States or in the Caribbean, it's very handy to be able to drop into the local bank and say: 'I'm a director of the Bank of Nova Scotia and need some accommodation,'" says John Aird, the Toronto lawyer. "And it really works beyond the ramifications of being a director of one bank. For instance, if you're in a town where there's a Royal Bank and you go and tell the manager you are a director of the Bank of Nova Scotia, you're going to be looked after."

Exactly how much the directors have to do with actually running the banks is less clear. "There are a lot of policy things you consult your board on," says Earle McLaughlin, "but the day-to-day running of the bank is in the hands of the professionals, same as any company." Allen Lambert, chairman of the Toronto-Dominion, sees the main functions of his board as "assessment of management and replacement of it when needed, so that management can't just get into place and stay there regardless of how it performs, plus examination of all major loans."

Stephen Jarislowsky, a leading Montreal investment counsellor, is more cynical. "The average bank director," he maintains, "isn't there for anything except window-dressing, and in order to keep his company within the confines of the bank's group."

No one, in or out of the banking system, recalls a board ever actually having reversed any important bank policy. "I haven't heard, even by the grapevine, of any director who made things difficult for management," says E.P. Neufeld, the former University of Toronto professor of economics who is the best-known authority on Canadian banking. Some directors occasionally complain that they are asked merely to rubber-stamp management's decisions. But few bank shareholders seem worried that they are not adequately represented by the directors they elect.*

"Almost the sole purpose of appointing directors to

*At the 1970 annual meeting of the Banque Canadienne Nationale, a resolution was passed by shareholders congratulating "each and every one of the bank's directors for the excellent results achieved during the past financial year."

banks is that they bring and retain business," says Tony Griffin, chairman of Home Oil and several other large companies. "The thing that really bothers me is that the banking system, through constant consolidation, has become a pretty monolithic structure, and this is bound to have an effect in institutionalizing attitudes, making the banks much less flexible. So far, the banking system has served Canada not too badly, but I'm wondering, looking down the line a little, whether this monolithic structure is going to serve as well in the future."

Procedures differ, but most board meetings are followed by lunch in the bank's dining chamber—and it is during the informal chatter before and after the actual meetings that the gossip is exchanged, intelligence is traded, and a new consensus is formed. The Bank of Nova Scotia has the most formal board procedure: every director is allotted a large agenda book, especially prepared for the meeting, and his own blue-satin-lined, name-plated birchwood chair, which he gets to keep when he leaves the board.

According to the Bank Act, directors must own at least 2,500 shares in a bank before they can be named to its board. At today's market prices, this can mean an investment of at least $40,000. Bankers like to point out that it is this requirement that prevents the boards from reflecting the real character of the communities in which they operate. But the banks don't really want their boards to include anyone but representatives of big business. A confidential survey commissioned by the Commerce in 1972 showed this breakdown of the principal occupations of the 221 men and one woman* who sat around the board room tables of the Big Five:

Occupational Range of Directors

Industry or Field	CIBC	B of M	ROYAL	T-D	B of NS
Banking	7	6	6	4	4
Manufacturing and Construction	6	7	6	6	1
Law	5	7	7	5	5
Shipping and Trading	3	3	6	1	2

*By mid-1975 there were two women on the CIBC board, Dr. F. Marguerite Hill, physician-in-chief of the Women's College Hospital in Toronto, and Sister Catherine Wallace of Fredericton, N.B.

Radio and Communications	2	1		2	1
Food and Retail	4	9	5	5	4
Investment Holding Companies	4	2	2	4	
Automobile Industry	4	1		1	
Mining	3	3	2	1	2
Forest Products	3	2	4	2	4
Oil and Chemicals		4	1	4	3
Investment Community	2				2
Pipelines and Power	1	2	2	1	
Public Figures and Politicians	4	2			
Steel and Engineering	2	1	1	1	2
Insurance	3	2		1	3
Academic and Other	2		1		1
TOTAL	55	52	43	38	34

The same study tabulated the following geographical distribution for the Big Five boards:

Geographic Spread of Directors*

Location	CIBC Directors	CIBC Branches	B of M Directors	B of M Branches	ROYAL Directors	ROYAL Branches	T-D Directors	T-D Branches	B of NS Directors	B of NS Branches
Ontario	27	677	10	379	11	461	19	452	17	344
Quebec	8	184	20	204	16	189	8	81	1	74
British Columbia	4	216	6	138	3	160	2	89	2	91
Alberta	2	156	3	104	2	113	3	74	2	80
Manitoba	3	75	3	68	2	88	1	46	1	29
Saskatchewan	1	106	2	64	1	102	1	42	1	39
Nova Scotia	1	29	2	30	2	82	1	4	4	60
New Brunswick	1	21	1	24		27		6	1	41
Newfoundland	1	15	2	31		20		1	1	49
Yukon/NWT/PEI		25		7		9		3		12
U.S.A.	2	21	1	6	1	1	2	6	1	4
U.K.	2	2	2	2	2	2	1	2	3	7
Caribbean		47			3	102				92
Europe and other	3			5		2				7

*This total does not differentiate between directors of Canadian companies and the twenty-two domestic directors representing Canadian subsidiaries of foreign corporations.

The bank boards convene according to different schedules. The Royal and the Nova Scotia meet once a week, the Toronto-Dominion every second Thursday, the Commerce the first Thursday of the month, the Montreal on alternate Tuesdays. Probably the most spectacular board room is that of the Royal, on the forty-first floor of Place Ville Marie. Its table, fashioned of Brazilian teak, is forty-eight feet long and eleven feet wide. When it was being installed, bank officials wanted to add microphones, because they felt the directors at its far end would not be able to hear the chairman. McLaughlin killed the idea when he was told a good sound system would cost $40,000. "That could mean an eventual $80,000, and that's too much," he said. "I'll shout!"

According to the Bank Act, whenever loans to any director's companies are being discussed, he must leave the room or risk a $5,000 fine. It's a great theory and directors *do* walk out to a chorus of chuckles and self-disparaging remarks. But these loans are seldom turned down.* In the autumn of 1974, for example, Laura Secord Candy Shops, a subsidiary of John Labatt Limited (represented on the Commerce board mainly by Jake Moore, president of Brascan, which controls Labatt's), was granted $24 million in assistance, even though the company was insolvent at the time, having suffered an operating loss of $5.3 million during the previous twelve months. Although Laura Secord's own parent company had refused to guarantee its credit, board minutes show only that Sydney Hermant, reported to be the largest shareholder of the bank, asked for a more precise definition of the difference between an outright loan and a "letter of comfort," while Neil McKinnon, the former chairman, wondered about the propriety of the proposed transaction. No one else raised any questions, and the assistance was routinely approved.†

---

*The banks will not disclose any figures on how high a proportion of their credit is extended to their own directors. The only estimate ever published was in the report of the Royal Commission on Banking and Finance, which appeared in 1962. It stated that about 30 per cent of all authorized credit lines of $100,000 or more were "to directors, their firms or corporations of which they were officers or directors."

†Laura Secord was ultimately rescued by being merged with the profitable Catelli pasta operation in Montreal, a subsidiary of Ogilvie Flour Mills Co. Ltd., which, in turn, is 99.7 per cent owned by Labatt's.

IN BANKING, CONTACTS ARE EVERYTHING. When William Zeckendorf was making his move into Canada during the mid-fifties, he was given an introduction by John J. McCloy, then chairman of the Chase Manhattan Bank, to James Muir, then chairman of the Royal. "In Canada," Zeckendorf noted at the time, "unlike the United States, banking is a membership business. Once you're affiliated with one particular bank, that bank expects you to be loyal to it and to bank exclusively with it. In exchange, it gives loyalty to you and will support your efforts."

When Zeckendorf started to line up financing for Montreal's huge Place Ville Marie development, he couldn't get enough tenants. Suspecting the trouble arose from prejudice against himself (both as an American interloper and as a Jew) and resentment of the Chinese architect Ieoh Ming Pei, Zeckendorf telephoned Muir. "Jim," he said, "you know we're not getting anywhere with this damn renting."

"Why the hell should you get anywhere? That goddamn Chinaman is stopping you."

"No, you're stopping us."

"I'm stopping you?"

"Jim, your enemies, the ones who hate you, won't take space here. The ones who love you don't believe in us. There's a gang-up on the part of the other banks—the Bank of Montreal, the Imperial, the Commerce, the Nova Scotia, the Toronto-Dominion."

"You're crazy."

"I'm not crazy."

"Well, what do you want me to do about it?"

"Move."

"I should move? Move? You're mad."

"Move, Jim. We'll call the new tower the Royal Bank of Canada Building in Place Ville Marie. You'll be king of the hill, towering over the whole of Montreal. The business will come to you."

"You're out of your mind. We have the biggest bank in Canada in the biggest bank building in Canada."

"I'll buy it from you."

"You've got no money to buy it."

"Now, think it over. I'm coming up tomorrow morning to a directors' meeting."

"Och, I'm going to England. I don't get back for two weeks. Forget it."

Three weeks later Zeckendorf had persuaded Muir to move his head office into Place Ville Marie and to sign a lease for an annual rental of $2.6 million.

As soon as Neil McKinnon, then head of the Commerce, learned of the Royal's plans, he acquired a property across Dominion Square and began to put up an even higher skyscraper. Muir made no visible response, but at the last minute he had Zeckendorf add three extra floors to make Place Ville Marie the tallest building in the Commonwealth at the time. McKinnon eventually retaliated by putting a TV antenna on top of *his* building, so that it stuck up a few feet higher than the Royal's banking palace.

Besides generating new business from tenants, bank buildings tend to give the bankers themselves a psychological boost. Allen Lambert, who piloted through the construction of the $160-million Toronto-Dominion Centre in downtown Toronto (which succeeded Place Ville Marie as the tallest building in the Commonwealth until Neil McKinnon's new fifty-seven-storey Commerce Court next door was topped off in 1971, and which in turn was supplanted as tallest by the Bank of Montreal's new Toronto headquarters), is convinced that the new headquarters have altered the image of his bank. "Of the Big Five," he says, "we were the smallest bank. Certainly large enough to do anything we wanted, but what was important is that we *appeared* to be the smallest. Since the building opened, it's given our people a tremendous lift, an opportunity to attract the brightest young recruits, and to establish relationships with many major new accounts."*

Another banker whose building provides him with a psychological lift is Earle McLaughlin of the Royal. He

---

*This approach is a decided departure from the days when genteel gloom was the deliberately fostered atmosphere of Canadian banking. Banks equated fiscal stability with an appearance of fortresses on the outside and Dickensian counting houses on the inside. The accent was on dark wood panelling, yards of frosted glass, protective grilles, and scratchy pens on chains. During the visit of King George VI and Queen Elizabeth in 1939, when Vancouver buildings along the royal route were to be given an exterior cleaning, the banks objected on the grounds that their coating of grime gave them an appearance of dependability.

proudly points out to his board-room visitors (peering down from the top of Place Ville Marie at the Bank of Montreal's headquarters on Place d'Armes) that on a clear day "all I have to do is get out my binoculars to tell who Arnold Hart is having lunch with."

Since most wooing of new accounts takes place during the elegant lunches bankers hold for prospective clients, guest lists are discreetly guarded. Though the bankers agree with each other on every principle in their system of values, competition for large corporate accounts can be fierce.

When the late James Muir heard that the Murchison group of American pipeline financiers was coming up to Montreal with considerable investment capital and no established banking connections, he decided to meet their private car on the overnight train from Chicago at the Windsor Station. But as he was pacing the platform he spotted a Bank of Montreal Cadillac pulling up. According to the ARRIVALS board, the train was twenty minutes late. Muir leapt into his own limousine and drove to Montreal West, the second-to-last stop for the train before it reached Windsor Station. He jumped on the private car just as it was pulling out and persuaded the U.S. investors to get off at Westmount, the next stop, rather than face fighting the traffic of midtown Montreal. He signed them up, while back at Windsor Station the man from the Montreal was still puzzling over his visitors' mysterious disappearance.

"There is no business in this country any more competitive than banking," says Donald Anderson, a former executive vice-president of the Royal. "To get new accounts, you offer your personality and demonstrate your familiarity with the client's business." When Anderson was manager of the Calgary branch, he and an associate, Jack Bankes, later the Royal's vice-president in Toronto, decided to donate a trophy for the proposed Oilman's Golf Tournament, being sponsored by a group within the Petroleum Club. Because there was an agreement among banks at that time that no bank-sponsored trophy could be worth more than twenty-five dollars, Anderson and Bankes decided to pay for the cup out of their own pockets. When Muir heard about this proposal, he immediately arranged for the purchase of a hallmarked silver rose bowl for $1,800. It became the Royal Bank Trophy, which is still awarded every year at the Oilman's Golf Tournament, though how the Royal circumvented the twenty-five-dollar limit has never been made clear.

BECAUSE THEY ARE SO BIG, POWERFUL, AND OMNIPRESENT, THE BANKS ARE ULTRASENSITIVE to any whisper of collusion. Bank chairmen act as if they didn't know each other's first names ("Earle *who* . . . ?" they ask, with wintry humour). There is no private hideaway where they meet, though during the fifties when Gordon Ball was chairman of the Montreal and James Muir chairman of the Royal, they used to get together away from prying eyes at the Longchamps racetrack, near Paris. Yet they belong to the same clubs, move in similar circles, and know each other's habits so intimately that when Arnold Hart's private chauffeur suddenly died on September 16, 1971, Earle McLaughlin sent over a personal note of sympathy. The Big Five will not hire staff away from each other; if one bank turns down a loan, the odds are high that no other bank will touch it.*

The banking industry's official co-ordinating organization is the Canadian Bankers' Association, with headquarters in the Toronto-Dominion Centre. The CBA also lobbies the federal government on behalf of the banks and is considerably aided in these activities by having as its executive director J. Harvey Perry, who was a senior official in the finance department between 1936 and 1952 (along with Mitchell Sharp, Louis Rasminsky, and Bob Bryce) and knows his way around Ottawa very well.†

Whenever a bank captures a major account from a

---

*One joint enterprise the banks openly discuss is their policy on their charitable donations by advising one another what fund requests they'll honour. The Royal, Montreal, and Commerce each usually contribute 1 per cent of the target figure to national campaigns such as those of hospitals and universities, with the Nova Scotia and the Toronto-Dominion giving approximately 0.6 per cent and the smaller banks a *pro rata* amount. Because most other businessmen want to know how much the banks are giving before committing themselves, capital campaigns can succeed or fail according to the bankers' initial reactions.

†He retired as executive director of the CBA in mid-1975 but continues as a full-time consultant until the decennial revision of the Bank Act in 1977.

competitor (the Labatt switch from the Nova Scotia to the Commerce in 1967, for example) it's an event that shakes the business world. The transition is usually a gradual process. "The business community is pretty small, and nobody smacks anybody in the eye deliberately," says one former bank executive. "What usually happens is that the president of a company may be a member of the same club or have a summer cottage near an executive or a director of the bank that's trying to get his business. Discreetly it's suggested to him that he start a small account with the new bank—'just to get the feel of it.' He's flattered by all the attention being paid to him, and more and more credit lines are switched to his new banking connection. The process is so gradual that his existing banker doesn't realize he has lost the account until it's too late."

Corporations sometimes play banks off against each other to get the best deal possible, and some of the more aggressive corporate giants have representatives on more than a single bank board. At one point during the mid-sixties, the chairman of Inco was on the board of the Montreal, the company's executive vice-president was on the Nova Scotia, and its president was on the Toronto-Dominion. Eight of the directors on the board of Argus Corporation sit on a total of five bank boards. Gulf Oil splits its business between the Toronto-Dominion and the Nova Scotia; E.P. Taylor maintains all of his corporate business with the Royal, but when he became the guiding force of the Ontario Jockey Club he allowed it to keep its accounts at the Commerce. Eaton's divides up its banking between the Toronto-Dominion and the Montreal.*

Because banks offer the same product and very nearly the same quality of service, competition takes the subtle form of personal relationships. "Public criticism of the banks usually focuses on the lending side of our operations, accusing us of all having the same rates, but I don't see how you can have a different rate for any given credit line," says Bob MacIntosh, executive vice-president of the

---

*Until the early thirties, Eaton's was a Royal account. Through a clerical error, the company allowed one of its accounts to run up a million-dollar overdraft. When a bank accountant telephoned Eaton's and asked them to cover it, the department store sent over a million in cash and at the same time switched its banking connection.

Nova Scotia. "Let's say that Bell Canada was getting its money for 9 per cent from the Bank of Montreal and we were to come along and offer 8 per cent. First of all, the Montreal would match it, because they wouldn't want to lose the account, and then they might try to retaliate by undercutting us with somebody else. The same kind of thing happens in the consumer field. If one bank raises its rate on deposits or lowers its interest on loans and you don't, you start to get calls from branches all over the country, saying: 'You jokers, what are you up to down there? We're going to lose seven depositors across the street this afternoon.' So you quickly come into line. There can really be only one price for money; it's an undifferentiated product."

An example of how the competition among banks works was provided in 1970 by the abrupt decision of Leonard Walker, then president of the Bank of Montreal, to cut the prime interest rate from 8½ per cent to 8 per cent, effective June 15. Nothing happened for a week. Walker began to get nervous and placed full-page ads in dailies across the country, appealing to the public to support his decision with new deposits. That broke the resistance. By noon of the day the ads appeared, the Royal and then the Toronto-Dominion tumbled into line and were followed by all the others by the end of the day.

Occasionally, the bank chairmen deliberately conspire to set identical policies. In the summer of 1959, when the chartered banks were carrying on their feud with Bank of Canada governor Jim Coyne, James Muir telephoned Neil McKinnon and asked him to convene in his office all of the Toronto bank presidents. He himself would bring the Montreal presidents down with him for a meeting, so that they could decide on a monetary policy different from that being advocated by the central bank. McKinnon, who had spent the previous Sunday at his cottage in Muskoka drafting a circular for distribution to all Commerce branches that set out a new policy on loan limits, chaired the secret conclave. At the end of the meeting, Muir asked McKinnon if he could have a copy of the circular for his own bank. "You'd better rephrase it," McKinnon warned him.

On June 12, 1972, at a meeting in Winnipeg between

Louis Rasminsky, then governor of the Bank of Canada, and the chief general managers of the Big Five, an informal agreement was negotiated setting interest-rate ceilings on bank deposits of $100,000 or more. This confidential pact, which became known among bankers as the Winnipeg Agreement, in effect removed interest rates as a competitive element, because up to then the banks had all been bidding against each other for large fixed-term deposits. The Winnipeg Agreement, which had the sanction of the Minister of Finance, was terminated on January 16, 1975, because the short-term rates for money had fallen well below the set ceilings.

ANY BANKING SYSTEM HAS FOUR MAIN FUNCTIONS: keeping safe the funds entrusted to it, facilitating commerce by making loans available at the appropriate moment through lines of credit, transmitting the central bank's credit influence, and using its prestige and financial resources in a creative way to serve the national interest. It is in this fourth role that the Canadian banking system is least effective.

The banks like to think of themselves as passive instruments, neutral intermediaries between lenders and borrowers who cannot afford the luxury of tempering their decisions with any hint of social conscience. They can muster little concern if a loan is used to build a plant that will pollute a river system. "It is not the responsibility of the banks to sit in judgement on such matters," Arnold Hart of the Montreal once remarked. "Now, if the government said we shouldn't lend to a certain industry because they're going to pollute the atmosphere, we might disagree thoroughly, but we would have to abide by their edict." The bankers take a similar approach to the issue of foreign domination of the Canadian economy, preferring low-risk loans to the Canadian subsidiaries of U.S. corporations to backing Canadian entrepreneurs. Each bank maintains a list of Canadian businesses for sale to foreign contacts.

"We have an efficient banking system in this country," Claude Ryan, the respected editor of Montreal's *Le Devoir*, told a convention of the Institute of Canadian Bankers in 1973, "and I do not know many citizens who would seriously dream of substituting for this system a monopolistic state-operated regime. It is clear, on the other hand, that in their present organization the banks are working hand in hand with the financial, commercial, and industrial elites of the country and have, in consequence, become far too much removed from the working classes. It is also clear that they can easily arrive amongst themselves at tacit agreements which are tantamount to decisions of an oligopolistic nature." Some of the younger bankers—notably Bob MacIntosh of the Nova Scotia, Dick Thomson of the Toronto-Dominion, André Bisson, who heads the Nova Scotia's Quebec operations, and Rowlie Frazee of the Royal—have been advocating a slightly more enlightened approach. "Just as it is unacceptable for the politician to consider that his sole objective should be to get reelected, so it is unacceptable for the businessman to consider that his sole objective is to make a profit," Frazee proclaims. "For both politician and businessman, the only acceptable basic purpose is to meet the needs of society. Both government and business are institutions set up and maintained by society to fill its needs, and if a society's institutions don't seem to be doing this, then sooner or later society will change them."

Not enough, perhaps, to make a saint jump up and down, but a start.

THE RESTRAINTS THAT EXIST ARE APPLIED ON THE BANKS THROUGH THE BANK OF CANADA. Its governor exercises what the private bankers privately describe as "immoral suasion," gently but persuasively issuing the edicts that implement the country's monetary policies. Fred McNeil, deputy chairman of the Montreal, describes the process this way: "Over teacups he almost makes his suggestions, and we sometimes almost dispute them, but when the Governor says, 'Gentlemen, I think we ought to do it this way'—we do it."*

---

*A soft approach doesn't always work with Canadian subsidiaries of U.S. corporations. The American-controlled Mercantile Bank will not subscribe to Bank of Canada directives because Washington's anti-trust laws will not allow U.S.-controlled companies to enter into any agreements

The Bank of Canada was set up to offset the near-collapse of confidence in the Canadian financial system brought about by the depression of the thirties. It was charged with regulating "credit and currency in the best interest of the economic life of the nation" and generally promoting "the economic and financial welfare of the Dominion." It is not a bank in the sense that it accepts deposits from individuals or makes loans to companies, its primary duty being to see that there is the right amount of money in existence at any given moment in the development of the country's economy—seldom a simple assignment.*

The governor's authority is supreme. He has the power to overrule even his own board of directors, a body of twelve businessmen who meet seven times a year, though such a veto has to be referred to Cabinet for confirmation. The relationship between the Bank of Canada and the federal government has always been touchy, probably because any institution that has the power to create money is naturally subject to political pressures. In general, when Bank of Canada decisions have been popular, govern-

---

that make them act as part of a group. The First National City Bank of New York retains 24 per cent of the Mercantile's ownership and effectively controls its operations, which include eleven branches; 89 per cent of its loans are in the $1-million-plus category. In 1959, when the Bank of Canada suggested that finance companies should keep their loans below a set total, General Motors Acceptance Corp. would not agree to the limit.

*The Bank of Canada achieves changes in the money supply by increasing or lowering the funds that the Canadian banking system as a whole is able to lend and invest. It can do this because under the Bank Act each chartered bank is required to maintain cash reserves with the central bank equal to at least 4 per cent of its notice deposits and 12 per cent of its demand deposits (in force until the 1977 revision of the Bank Act). If the Bank of Canada wants to increase the funds of the banking system it buys government securities in the open market, and pays for them with cheques drawn on itself. These cheques are eventually deposited by the individuals who sold the government bonds at their own chartered banks. These banks, in turn, return the cheques to the Bank of Canada. The cheques are then credited to their accounts at the central bank—thereby increasing the cash reserves they have on deposit. Because this raises their reserves to more than the minimum requirement, they can then increase their loan and investment operations. If, on the other hand, the Bank of Canada wants to reduce the money supply, the whole procedure is simply reversed. The central bank sells government bonds from its portfolio in the open market and accepts in payment cheques drawn on the accounts the buyers maintain with the chartered banks. The Bank of Canada charges these cheques against the cash reserves of the chartered banks on deposit with it—reducing their totals below the required levels. To bring up their reserve ratio, the chartered banks have to increase their cash deposits with the central bank, thus slowing down the rate at which they can lend money to their customers.

ments have gladly accepted the responsibility for helping to formulate them; when they have caused controversy, the politicians have sternly pointed to the bank's antiseptic independence.

"The smugness of the banks," says Max Saltsman, the NDP's financial critic, "derives from the fact that they are virtually an instrument of government policy; as long as they follow it, they can't fail. They are almost inseparable from government activity, not only in terms of carrying out monetary directives but because so many of their deposit-creating powers are at the discretion of Ottawa. At the same time, the *private* banks are completely and absolutely dependent on the goodwill of governments, because their power rests on the renewable charters they are granted, charters that are the equivalent ·of a licence to print money."

Nationalizing the banks was for years a priority item in the CCF-NDP platforms, and whenever the bankers come up before a parliamentary committee they expect the subject to be raised. "One time," Saltsman recalls, "I decided to have some fun. I knew they were waiting for me, as the NDP's spokesman on banking, to come out for nationalization, and you could tell by the rustle of papers when I got up to speak that they were ready. So I told them I wouldn't disappoint them by not asking a question along those lines, and there was some polite laughter. But then I said: 'Rather than my making a statement that you might think outrageous, let's be reasonable today; you tell me why banks *shouldn't* be nationalized.' Well, that seemed to throw them right off because their answers weren't oriented that way, so they started saying things like, 'You're asking us to say, "Stop beating your wife," ' and stuff like that, but they never answered my question."

Except for the occasional aberration, such as the independent-minded stewardship of James Coyne, relations between the chartered banks, the Bank of Canada, the Department of Finance, and the Cabinet are so cosy that outsiders try hard to become part of it. "We are not, as a trust company, required to subject our activities to control by the Bank of Canada," Ken White, president of Royal Trust, told *Executive* magazine in September,

1974. "Voluntarily, however, we have established a close liaison with the Bank of Canada people. We're in daily touch with them. They know us well; they understand what we're doing; and if we meet a sticky question we talk to them. For example, a few years ago we had a chance to take a big deposit in foreign currency. I said to myself: 'I think the Bank of Canada would be interested. I'll ask them what they think we ought to do with it.' As it turned out, it was going to embarrass them quite a bit. They said: 'Gee, we wish you wouldn't do it. Could you direct that deposit to the banking system?' We said we would.'"

The chief lobbying objective of the bankers in Ottawa is the decennial review of the Bank Act, and seldom did they gain more than during the 1967 revision. It allowed them into the conventional mortgage field for the first time, reduced their required cash ratio, and removed interest-rate ceilings—a combination of factors that has allowed them to double their rate of asset expansion since the new act was passed. By the mid-seventies, with another revision in the works, the bankers are busy gathering support for a new set of demands.*

The chairmen meet regularly with the governor at least three times a year (in Ottawa, Montreal, and Toronto), with the minister of finance dropping in for lunch during the Ottawa sessions, usually held in June. There are separate regular briefings with the general managers and bank economists, but probably the most important annual occasion is the Canadian Bankers' Association dinner, which alternates between Toronto's York Club and the Seigniory Club, at Montebello, Quebec. It was during one of those assemblies in the early sixties, chaired by Louis Rasminsky and Walter Gordon, then minister of finance, that the real nature of the relationship between the central bank and

---

*The bankers' requests will include changes in the Bank Act which would permit their entry into factoring (the buying and managing of money owed to others) and leasing operations, which now account for an annual turnover of close to $6 billion, most of it handled by Canadian subsidiaries of international financial houses. Approximately 250 foreign banks now operate in Canada, escaping the limits imposed by federal legislation by the simple expedient of not calling themselves banks. Another 150 "suitcase" bankers regularly visit Toronto, Montreal, and Vancouver to transact their business out of hotel rooms. They are also gaining an increasing share of the short-term money market by issuing paper backed by their parent institutions.

the federal government was subtly defined. The two men had been having a dispute over the course of the country's monetary policies of which the private bankers had heard rumblings, and this seemed to be the right occasion to get their differences into the open.

It was the usual mellifluous affair, a fine roast beef dinner in the Fountain Room of the Seigniory Club. Gordon spoke first, wittily and forcefully, ending his talk with the outspoken thought that, well, we'll listen to you, Louis, but I'm so plainly right that it's only a courtesy, after all. Rasminsky then stood up, elegant as always, waited for the room to become completely quiet, and said that he would tell a story which he felt was all he need say in reply to the honourable minister. He had just returned from Europe, as they all knew, since earlier in the day he'd done a *tour d'horizon* of what he had learned there. But he hadn't told them that one of the highlights of his visit had been a dinner with the governor of the Bank of France. They had been discussing relationships with governments, more particularly cabinets, and at one point the Frenchman had leaned over to Rasminsky and said to him: "Louis, we practise a fine profession. In assessing its merits it might bear remembering that in the years I've been governor, I've seen twenty-two ministers of finance come and go."

With that, Louis Rasminsky bowed to Walter Gordon and sat down.

Whether or not the governor's performance was justified in the face of the fiscal and monetary policies in dispute at the moment, certainly his manner of assurance and superiority personified perfectly the prevailing attitude of Canadian bankers. Their allegiance to the *status quo* has changed remarkably little during a century and a half of immensely profitable operation.

There is a story, apocryphal perhaps, about a middle-rung manager in one of the Big Five being toasted at his retirement dinner, after fifty years of faithful service. The bank chairman wound up his tribute with a flourish. "Now, won't you think back in your career," he said. "Won't you think about everything that happened and tell us what has been the most important *change* you've seen during your long and rewarding stewardship?"

The departing banker paused to ponder the import of the question for some moments, blinked, and then blurted out: "Air conditioning!"

CHAPTER FOUR

The Withering Pride
of Neil McKinnon

At some point after he'd been forced
to leave the Commerce, he must have
travelled to the darkest places inside
himself, and come back numbed.

The massive oak door to the elegant apartment tower near Upper Canada College is guarded by two rumpled, unjacketed doormen, looking out of place and very Canadian there among the Jacobean chairs, Oriental rugs, and dark tiled floors, scattering cigarette ashes over all that chaste splendour, getting ready to pull out their portable radio for the game between the Philadelphia Flyers and Toronto Maple Leafs.

Neil McKinnon resides one floor below the penthouse. Only Mrs. George Drew has a better view across the city which from that height seems eternally enchanting, no matter what the hour or the season. He is a small man, tanned, with freckles on his forehead, who tends to wear grey, summer-weight suits, slightly too large for him in the shoulders, with ties—black and grey prints—too narrow for the fashion. He looks very expensive but neutral, somehow, like a Swiss ambassador to the Court of St. James's. The apartment is large and comfortable, filled with the right paintings, floating pink silks, *matelassé* grey sofas, and the de rigueur Sheraton dining table (*have the Canadian rich completely cleaned England out of Sheraton tables and sideboards?*) set with hand-embroidered place mats, crystal, and some kind of silver ding-dong in the middle.

Neil McKinnon moves among his comforts like a very powerful man with all the accoutrements of big money but none of the ease. Even though he operated in circles of influence that no Canadian banker has attained since the days of Sir Herbert Holt, he has never quite shaken

135

off the air of a chartered accountant in pursuit of the Holy Grail.

Born in the Northern Ontario mining town of Cobalt, where he went to work for the Bank of Commerce when he was only fourteen, McKinnon rose to become for seventeen years Canada's top banker, only to be relieved of his power by a directors' *coup d'état* late in 1973. Now in his mid-sixties, he is a little bewildered and more than a little hurt, but somewhere deep inside him that yearning kid from Cobalt is still there and you can visualize him as a young man in bow tie and heavy knit sweater, walking out on a Sunday afternoon, holding the hand of a girl with bright blue eyes and rosy complexion: a knitting-book portrait, slightly larger than scale.

The pain that he occasionally betrays by a word, a glance, or a gesture dates from his dethronement as chairman of the Canadian Imperial Bank of Commerce. He refuses to discuss the details, but it must have scared the hell out of him, made him feel vulnerable when he thought he never would be vulnerable again. After all, when you grew up in Cobalt, where, as he says, "if you didn't work, you didn't eat—it was as simple as that"; and when you've achieved everything he'd achieved, with chauffeured limousines at his call and private aircraft flying him to board meetings in Philadelphia, Buenos Aires, Hong Kong; and above all, when you've exercised that headiest of banking powers, the supreme right to veto or approve loans for fifteen or fifty million dollars—when you've done all that and done it exquisitely well for most of twenty years, you think you've armoured yourself against anything life can throw at you. But it turns out that you're not armoured against hurt, and this explains the look of perplexity in Neil McKinnon's eyes. At some point after he'd been forced to leave the Commerce, he must have travelled to the darkest places inside himself, and come back numbed. *How could this happen to me? I always got to work on time, slaved my ass off, moved the bank's assets from two to seventeen billions, my liquidity ratios were never out of line. It damn well isn't fair.*

A deposed strong man, he is vastly influential still, his fiscal wisdom sought by central bankers, board chairmen, chief executive officers, and investors on three continents.

But it is only when he talks about past business triumphs that the hurt look disappears. This is how it was. This is what the boy who was the Cobalt teller had the talent for —being hard-nosed, parsing those balance sheets, smelling the risks, calculating the multipliers, writing in the escape clauses, reactivating old contacts. He'd run the bank and ruled his world on this kind of shrewdness and it had all worked for him until he tested his pride and principles against the consensus of the system, and it broke him.

THERE WILL NEVER BE ANOTHER BANKER quite like Neil John McKinnon. The trait that most clearly isolated him from his colleagues and competitors was the way he used his position as Chief Executive Overlord of the Commerce between 1956 and 1973. The influence that Canadian bank chairmen wield is very real, but it is usually a delegated form of authority, in the sense that it flows from the job rather than from the man. McKinnon ignored such subtleties. Unlike his fellow bankers, who preferred to exercise their leverage as an expression of their institutions' collective wills, McKinnon had the personal power and he used it.

It was this vaulting self-confidence that made Neil McKinnon both the best banker of his generation and the only chairman of a major Canadian bank ever to be removed by his own board of directors.

McKinnon's self-confidence was due in large measure to his airy dismissal of what has been the surest strength of most Canadian bankers: success by inadvertence. Sustained by nothing more than an instinctive response to the call of nearly three decades of continuous economic growth, their loan decisions stood more than a reasonable chance of being vindicated. Until the early seventies, this tended to become such an automatic process that few bank chairmen bothered either to examine their own mandates or to study very deeply the world environment in which they did business and made their profits.

McKinnon was different. He had a kind of sixth sense about banking. He could size up credit risks in a few minutes' scrutiny—his eyes, ice-grey marbles in aspic—of a prospect's balance sheet. He knew how to inject a multiplier into his deals so that the return on large loans wouldn't be limited to the basic principal and interest; how to trade off his clients' strengths against their weaknesses; just how far to float a new venture and when to sever its credit lifeline. He acted as if he had done everything before so that he knew exactly what to expect. "What a man has learned over the years," he once said, "gets under his skin. It enters into the marrow of him and becomes part of his personality so he knows instinctively how to act and what to decide in any set of familiar circumstances."

McKinnon was decisive and he was tough. When he was assembling land for the $100-million Commerce Court development in downtown Toronto, he discovered that one of the few substantial pieces of real estate outstanding was John Bassett's *Telegram* property on Melinda Street. The bank's lawyers had been hesitating about how to approach Bassett for months when McKinnon picked up the telephone and asked if he intended to sell.

"Sure," Bassett replied with equal dash, and named his price: $3,200,000.

"Well, my price is $2,800,000," said McKinnon.

"You want to split the difference?"

"Okay."

The whole deal took sixty seconds.

More important than any of this, McKinnon had a clear understanding of the banker's function. He rejected the romance-of-the-counting-house approach, preferring to view himself in the double role of a guardian of the funds entrusted to his care and a creative risk taker in their disbursement. The game was always to minimize the downside risk. Because uncertainty is more hazardous than predictable disaster, the next best thing to controlling the economic environment is *knowing* what's most likely to happen.

To keep himself ahead of events, McKinnon travelled continually, touching the many discreet bases of his private intelligence network. It included ministers of finance, central bank directors, and merchant bankers who talked freely to him because he brought them at least as much knowledge as he took away. The world he moved in consisted of those semi-visible, autonomous men who created the Western world's credit before the Arabs assumed that prerogative. They spoke to each other in a code that made words mean the same thing, no matter what language they were actually using. In London, he would call on Sir David Barran, chairman of Shell, Lord McFadzean, deputy chairman of the Midland Bank, and Harry Oppenheimer of the South African diamond trust. Then he would hop over to the continent for meetings with Baron Hubert Ansiaux, governor of the Banque Nationale de Belgique, and the Swiss money men in Geneva.* McKinnon's most interesting contact was André Meyer, head of the house of Lazard Frères in New York. Meyer lives in an apartment that he has turned into an art gallery at the Carlyle Hotel and works out of a small office at the top of Rockefeller Plaza. He negotiates multibillion-dollar mergers, acts as a clearing house for international monetary gossip, and manages the private investment portfolios of Jacqueline Onassis, Gianni Agnelli, the Rockefeller brothers, the Boel family of Belgium, and the Cowdrays of Britain. Probably the most influential private banker in the U.S., Meyer once referred to McKinnon as the shrewdest man he knew.

NEIL MCKINNON'S PROBLEM WAS THAT HE UNDERSTOOD POWER better than he understood talent. When it came to dealing with the men who worked for him, he used his intelligence as a rapier instead of a security blanket in which they might share his confidences. Impatient with subordinates who wanted reasons and assurances, he made most of the big decisions himself. "Neil ran the Commerce as if he were a giant amaranthine plant, a kind of flower which allows no vegetation to flourish in its vicinity," remarked one of Toronto's more literary financiers. "He couldn't tolerate crown princes. He would bring good people forward, then cut them down."

Because the Establishment in Canada has bestowed on the banks a faintly clerical character, the appointment of

---

*During the mid-sixties, McKinnon became the only Canadian banker granted an interview by Alexei Kosygin. When he arrived at the Kremlin, he was surprised to see the Russian dictator leafing through the Commerce's latest annual report. After a while, Kosygin mused: "I would like to own half of a bank like this myself."

new presidents is made to appear as smooth and untroubled as a papal selection, without the telltale white plume. McKinnon turned his own succession into a game of musical chairs. In 1963, he abruptly appointed Page Wadsworth, an old friend (each had been best man at the other's wedding), president of the Commerce. A year later Wadsworth found himself deputy chairman in charge of the Quebec district, with W.M. Currie, the bank's chief general manager, moved into the presidency. Currie's term lasted less than four years, when he was suddenly demoted to deputy chairman in charge of British Columbia; L.G. Greenwood, who had succeeded Currie as chief general manager, was named president. Three years later, Greenwood in turn found himself presiding over the Quebec region and Wadsworth arrived back in Toronto—the only man to make president *twice*. None of this made much difference because McKinnon ran the bank, anyway. His shadow dominated every decision. "We hardly dared go to the bathroom without Neil's permission," one of his subordinates confessed at the time. McKinnon grew so secretive about his—and the bank's—intentions that at the 1965 annual meeting Hugh Bruce, a Toronto lawyer speaking for a group of unhappy shareholders, complained that "there is far less information in the Commerce's annual statement than in that of the Moscow Narodny Bank of London, which is wholly owned by what most people consider to be the world's worst dictatorship." When he went on overseas visits, McKinnon would often lock his office door, leaving no one with ready access to important bank documents.

The financial community didn't find McKinnon's games particularly upsetting because the Commerce was doing well and the switches involved internal officials they hardly knew. What really shook their confidence in McKinnon's judgement was his treatment of Gordon Sharwood and Robert Winters. Unlike most bankers, when Sharwood joined the Commerce in 1956 he was already a certified member of the Canadian Establishment. His father had been vice-president, treasurer, and a director of CIL; he had been educated in comfortable circumstances at Selwyn House School, Bishop's College School, McGill, Oxford, and Harvard. In 1968, after a series of lightning promotions, Sharwood was named, at only thirty-seven, the bank's $90,000-a-year chief general manager. An open, gregarious individual with a sparkling intelligence, he began transforming the Commerce image. The word was out that McKinnon had found his eventual heir at last. But a tension developed between the two men, partly because of Sharwood's open approach to banking and at least a little because, even if they moved in the same social circles, it was for very different reasons: McKinnon because of his rank, Sharwood because of his upbringing. On the morning of August 26, 1969, as he sat at breakfast leafing through the *Globe and Mail*, Sharwood spotted a two-paragraph news story announcing the promotion of a colleague, Russell Harrison, then regional general manager for Quebec. It informed the astonished Sharwood that Harrison had just been appointed to his job.*

Robert Winters, a former minister in the St. Laurent cabinet and principal contender with Pierre Elliott Trudeau for the prime ministership of Canada, was another, less obvious McKinnon victim. Winters's ability, both in politics and in business, had been a matter of considerable debate. At the Toronto Club he was sometimes referred to as "an Eisenhower with brains," though many considered the qualifier undeserved. Full of good-natured arrogance, he loved big offices and jiggled a set of keys in his pocket or ran the bows of his spectacles over his shiny, perfect teeth as he talked. When he left the chairmanship of Rio Algom to re-enter politics in 1965, he was given a tax-free pension settlement of $499,000, and to the insiders it seemed a bargain. A rude partisan, he once told the Alberta Liberal Association that "at heart 75 per cent of the people of Canada are Liberals. They're ours for the asking." But he'd been a protégé of C.D. Howe, a fellow MIT graduate (the touches of Back Bay Boston still in his voice), and *looked* as if he knew exactly what he was doing—with that disarming smile, the perpetual tan, and the jiggling keys. In the spring of 1968, after Winters

---

*Sharwood later became the moving spirit of a large and imaginative financial conglomerate that included Guaranty Trust, Acres Limited, Traders Group, Canadian General Securities, Canadian Insurance Shares, and Aetna Factors Corporation.

had lost out to Trudeau for the Liberal leadership (by only 249 votes on the fourth ballot), he was approached by McKinnon to take over the presidency of Brazilian Light and Power,* one of the country's largest multinationals and an important Commerce account. Within sixteen months, McKinnon felt that Winters had not fought hard enough against a bid for control by International Utilities Corporation of Philadelphia and lined up the necessary majority of Brascan directors to depose Winters from the presidency to the chairmanship.†

What came into play now was an Establishment consensus, never really expressed but forming just the same, that Neil McKinnon had somehow misjudged the mechanics of power. Bob Winters and Gordon Sharwood (not to mention the ragtag of Commerce presidents) had been McKinnon's instruments and he had cut them down. This went against an important Establishment tenet: once you're part of a system of authority, you must look after your own, because if you don't the whole chain of influence that safeguards your own position disintegrates. The men you must depend on to protect your back begin to ask themselves: "Maybe I'm next?"

Although McKinnon was not yet aware of it, by the spring of 1971 his iron hold was being questioned among the only group that possessed the countervailing force to bring him down—the Canadian Imperial Bank of Commerce's own board of directors.

PLOTS TO DETHRONE A MAN OF POWER are never simple to disentangle; long after McKinnon had left the Commerce chairmanship, the Canadian financial community still wondered how it had all happened. At the time, the Commerce board had fifty-seven directors, but only the dozen main participants were directly involved.

One of the board's early agitators against McKinnon was Herb Smith, a former president of Canadian General Electric and a director of de Havilland Aircraft and Sun

---

*The name of Brazilian Light and Power was changed to Brascan in June, 1969.

†Winters died a month later while playing a set of doubles at the Carmel Valley Tennis Club in California.

Life of Canada. Smith found an appreciative audience in Jake Moore, the former Clarkson, Gordon accountant who had become president of Labatt's and then, under McKinnon's sponsorship, had succeeded Winters in the Brascan presidency. McKinnon had also placed Moore on the boards of the Commerce and CPR, but the two men had become estranged over a hushed-up episode involving the possible takeover by Simpsons of the Hudson's Bay Company department store operations.

Negotiations between the two retailing giants had been so delicate that at first they couldn't even agree on a meeting place. Allan Burton, the head of Simpsons (who divided his corporate banking between the Commerce and the Royal), had refused an invitation to London and the British executives of the Bay wouldn't come to Toronto. They countered with Bermuda. New York was finally picked as a suitable middle ground, but after a week of offers and counter-offers no agreement could be reached. It was during these negotiations that Burton discovered Jake Moore (then a director of Simpsons) had bought about 6.6 per cent of the Bay's stock through a Brascan holding company. This could have been either in anticipation of a takeover bid or as a long-term hold. Burton and McKinnon adhered to the former view. The situation resolved itself when Moore quietly left the Simpsons board, but his relations with McKinnon cooled considerably.

During the early autumn of 1971, whispers reached McKinnon that Moore, Smith, and a few other directors had been interrogating Commerce executives about his dominant brand of leadership, expressing particular dissatisfaction with the bank's lagging assets-to-loans ratio. It was McKinnon's insistence on maintaining the Commerce in a state of high liquidity—cash on hand—that had depressed the bank's earnings below their potential. McKinnon felt no reason to have himself investigated, but he saw little harm in trying to defuse the situation by appointing a committee of directors to delineate the powers of bank executives. He felt its report would be simple enough to shelve and forget. To his mild surprise, five of the most important Commerce directors promptly volunteered to join Moore and Smith in the assignment. They were:

1. Bob Scrivener, chairman and chief executive of Bell Canada and a director of Power Corporation;

2. Bill McLean, president (and largest shareholder) of Canada Packers as well as a director of Canadian General Electric;

3. Jack Leitch, president of Upper Lakes Shipping and a director of Massey-Ferguson, Canada Life, Dominion Foundries and Steel (Dofasco), and American Airlines;

4. Howard Lang, chairman and president of Canron Limited in Montreal and a director of Sun Life, CPR, Dofasco, and Texaco Canada; and

5. André Monast, a partner in Louis St. Laurent's former Quebec City law firm and a director of Noranda Mines, Confederation Life, Canada Cement Lafarge, and Dominion Stores.

The seven-man committee met eleven times during the first five months of 1972, with one evening spent listening to McKinnon's version of how the bank should be run. Jack Leitch had been the original chairman but it was Bill McLean who presented the final report. The document began with a warning: "The committee is concerned about the primary responsibility of the board of the Bank to ensure that a program exists to provide for an orderly succession for top-management positions with a minimum loss of momentum and with a minimum risk in the appointment of . . . the next chairman and the next president."

Then the dissenting directors took aim at their real target, Neil McKinnon: "The committee recognizes the outstanding role the Chairman has played in bringing the Bank to its present state of development. It became increasingly apparent during the course of our studies, however, that the business of the Bank is rapidly changing and that the pressure on Bank executives has grown tremendously. The large number of changes in senior executive officers in recent years not only invites a potential loss of public confidence but has adversely affected morale within the Bank." The committee recommended unanimously that the Chairman (they never referred to McKinnon by name) henceforth limit himself to conducting board meetings and acting as a consultant to Page Wadsworth, then the Commerce's president and chief executive officer.

McKinnon treated the report with bemused indifference. He wrote a short letter to the dissenting directors on May 25, 1972, dismissing their findings as "superficial, contradictory, incomplete and containing demonstrable misstatements of fact."

At the full directors' meeting that August, the board meekly endorsed the committee's report with little debate. At that point, neither McKinnon nor the directors seemed to be aware of the magnitude of what had happened. The endorsed document clearly deprived the chairman of all his executive functions, including the vital authority of appointment. The great man's powers seemed to have vanished in a season.

But nobody had dared spell this out to Neil McKinnon. For most of the next four months he ran the Commerce as before. Then, on December 8, when McKinnon sent a memo to Russell Harrison, asking him to provide the board with some data about outstanding loans, he got back instead a curt note from Page Wadsworth: "Last Friday afternoon, you sent a memorandum to the executive vice-president and chief general manager requesting certain information be presented to the board meeting this coming Thursday. The new by-laws of the bank provide that the chairman of the executive committee may require the president to present such data only if he is advised. Your action was initiated without his being advised. I must therefore ask that any further requests be sent directly to the president." In its roundabout, hesitant, and anonymous fashion, this directive cut McKinnon off from even *discussing* policy with bank officials.

At last it dawned on the furious chairman that something serious was in train here. He chose to fight back, not by attempting to reclaim the bank's executive powers, but on an issue of monetary principle. On July 6, 1972, a month before the directors voted to reduce his authority, McKinnon had taken up most of the directors' meeting with warnings that the Commerce's liquidity ratio was too low in relation to loans outstanding. Even the dry prose of the board's minutes couldn't entirely disguise the emotional tone of McKinnon's plea: he had spent most of the depression of the thirties in the bank's credit department, and the last time there had been similarly excessive loan ratios was in 1929; during every period of tight money since, the Commerce had maintained more liquidity than any other Canadian bank, enabling it to serve regular customers; this was not the time to abandon the sound practices of the past.

Then, on a Sunday night in March of 1973, for the first time in its history, the Commerce "went to the window." This is an ultra-secret bail-out that grants Canadian chartered banks short-term Bank of Canada funds whenever their loans temporarily overtake their assets. The Commerce was forced to draw down $50 million (though a further $86 million in U.S. deposits had to be quickly converted into Canadian funds) to meet its Monday morning obligations. The bank's solvency was never in question. But its request was considered serious enough to prompt a letter from the Bank of Canada, requesting an accounting of the Commerce's liquidity prospects. To Neil McKinnon this was the ultimate affront, the vindication of his concerns. A few days later, when he asked Russell Harrison whether the bank would now at last curtail its new loans acquisitions, he was told that, on the contrary, the Commerce was out signing up more low-risk, high-profit prospects.

McKinnon left for a long European journey to do some uncharacteristic brooding. "Our world is coming to an end," an old Dutch financier told him. "Nobody resigns any more. We've moved from an age of principle to an age of expediency." On May 10, aboard a friendly banker's yacht in the Mediterranean, McKinnon composed an explosive counterattack. He pointed out that the bank's authorized lines of credit amounted to more than $6.1 billion, raising its loans ratio to 79 per cent, which, added to the 14 per cent in compulsory primary and secondary reserves the chartered banks must hold, meant that 93 per cent of the Commerce's assets were committed, leaving a paltry 7 per cent for day-to-day clearings. "The principle adhered to for many years by the Chairman of operating a sound bank always in a position to meet its commitments," he noted, "has given way to an objective of maximizing near-term profits." The document ended with a Churchillian declaration—McKinnon would not preside over the dissolution of his empire. "The Chairman is seriously concerned about the financial condition of the Bank," he wrote. "He finds himself in the untenable position of carrying responsibility in the eyes of many directors, shareholders, customers and the public at large, without influence over the course of the Bank's affairs. After nearly 48 years' service with this institution of which more than 25 years have been spent in positions of most serious responsibility during which the Bank has shown the greatest growth in its history, I do not propose to sit here and watch the financial position of the Bank deteriorate into a totally unmanageable situation."

THE FINAL CONFRONTATION TOOK PLACE at the bank's board meeting on June 7. It started at 10 a.m., but instead of the customary leisurely luncheon break, the directors didn't disperse until 5.20 in the afternoon. The dispute centred on the interpretation of McKinnon's long letter. His opponents, led by the dissenting group of seven that had drafted the original report downgrading his powers, claimed that McKinnon wanted the board to vote non-confidence in management and that a choice had to be made between disowning management or firing the chairman. His defenders barely managed to prevent a move to ask for McKinnon's resignation on the spot.

The bank's executive committee agreed to study the McKinnon document. At the same time, the Commerce management was given an overwhelming vote of confidence. In the final vote of the afternoon, Nelson Davis, chairman of the N.M. Davis Corporation, and Bud McDougald, chairman and president of Argus, were nominated to negotiate with McKinnon.

Next morning, McDougald and Davis received hand-delivered letters from Bill McLean, urgently stating his demand that they force the chairman's resignation by the weekend. The two men were meanwhile attempting to salvage a compromise that might have allowed McKinnon to stay on for another year as chairman of the executive committee—more a protocol than a policy-setting function. What really terrified the Commerce hierarchy was that news of the squabble might leak out, damaging the bank's credibility.

The coolest man around was Neil McKinnon himself. While his friends were trying to sustain the remnants of his vanishing authority and his enemies were determined to humble him, he continued to view the struggle as a question of principle. He had placed an ultimatum before the board on the liquidity issue and was awaiting its verdict.

When the board met on October 4, McKinnon sat gazing around the huge board-room table, watching his squabbling fellow directors (most of them his own appointees), and saw only one way out. The dissidents had won few permanent converts; most board members felt so uncomfortable with the very idea of arguing inside a bank board room that a show of strength by McKinnon's allies would probably have carried the day. But McKinnon's love (no other word will do) for the Commerce overcame his fighting spirit. To crush the revolt would hurt his bank. So he quietly announced that he would not stand for re-election at the annual meeting on December 11, 1973, and walked out.

The One Hundred and Seventh Annual General Meeting of Shareholders, the Canadian Imperial Bank of Commerce, went precisely according to schedule. There was not a hint of unpleasantness. No one asked why the Chairman was retiring two years early. Nobody seemed to be aware—then or later—that anything out of the ordinary was taking place. The Establishment had closed in on itself. The departing chairman made an innocuous farewell speech. A properly rehearsed shareholder seconded it. The meeting clapped him on his way.

And Neil McKinnon stood there, smiling, trying hard not to intrude too much into his own privacy. He had, after all, said good-bye his own way a few minutes before the meeting started. Walking by one of the bank's executive offices, he had noticed the dissenting directors, along with some of the bank's executives, gathering to toast their victory. They were noisy and happy, behaving in the high good spirits of the lifting of a siege.

Neil McKinnon, still King of the Commerce, walked in and stood there, dead still at the doorway, and stared at them for a long moment. Then the about-to-be-de-

posed Chairman turned to leave and shot back over his
shoulder a farewell that silenced the revellers: "I just
wanted to see what a room full of sons of bitches looks
like."

POSTSCRIPT

On the sun-shrill afternoon of August 4, 1975, as he was
snorkling in ten feet of water off his private island in
Lake Rosseau in Muskoka, Neil McKinnon suffered a heart
attack and drowned. John Aird, whose place is on an
adjoining island, tried to rescue him, but it was too late.
Two days later, when the stock markets re-opened after
the long weekend, the Canadian Establishment paid its
final tribute to the McKinnon influence. Commerce shares
dropped a full point.

III

Corporate Power

CHAPTER FIVE

The Theology of
Free Enterprise

Adherents of the creed genuinely believe
that virtue can be certified by worldly
accomplishment, that success is tangible
evidence of holy favour. They have limited
tolerance for the meaning of heaven or hell, recognize
little logic in pain or compassion. The real
enemies are chaos and Big Government.

Whenever Canada is examined as a society it is almost
always considered in terms of its identity crisis, bicultural
problems, or agonies as a pygmy nation in thrall to one or
another overdeveloped empire. The country is rarely
viewed through the prism of its status as one of the
world's most successful capitalist states. Yet, that's what
we are—a capitalist society run by clusters of interlocking
elites.

The men who operate this system are much more interested in exercising power than in any process of self-
analysis. Attempts at introspection throw most of them
into inarticulate confusion. But whenever they hear the
catch phrase "free enterprise," something inside them
clicks to attention. The real buzzword, of course, is "business," which is said reverentially, as in "Well, that's business . . ." or "But it's *good* for business . . ."—statements
that leave ignored the most flamboyant distortions of how
any egalitarian society should operate.

The businessmen's faith is more a collection of attitudes
than any carefully conceived theology. But it does follow a
catechism of sorts. All men and the actions of all men, the
orthodox believe, are essentially a product of the marketplace; everyone therefore and everything has its price.*

---

*At the same time, they reject both the cold-blooded approach of old-
line capitalists such as Sir James Dunn, who was reported to have been
ecstatic when fire destroyed the CSL vessel *Noronic* in Toronto harbour
on September 17, 1949, because he was in the process of accumulating
the company's stock and the catastrophe drove down its price, and the

Pure free-enterprisers hold that man can be motivated to help society only by helping himself; they regard any form of incentive not based on the profit motive as hopelessly romantic. Adherents of the creed genuinely believe that virtue can be certified by worldly accomplishment, that success is tangible evidence of holy favour. They have limited tolerance for the meaning of heaven or hell, recognize little logic in pain or compassion. The real enemies are chaos and Big Government.

Power is no judge of values, but it acts instinctively to create order because no order can exist without power and no power exists without order. That's why businessmen place so much emphasis on institutions and hierarchies in which people know and keep their place. It is this deeply felt faith in institutions that is at the heart of the capitalist ethic.

According to this creed, freedom has about it an indivisible quality. Since economic freedom and political freedom are inseparable, it follows that democracy and capitalism necessarily reinforce each other. Private property thus becomes not only the basis for the free enterprise system but also the source of individual freedom. (The link here seems to be that if the individual has private property, it is more difficult for the state to deprive him of liberty.) This doctrine holds that dynamic capitalism has the best chance of producing the higher living standards in which democracy can flourish; that the free enterprise system must always triumph because it builds on individual and collective self-interest.

Out of such dogma emerges the businessman's stoutest conviction: that every piece of social legislation proposed by any government constitutes a potential affront to future liberties and must be opposed by all available means. To most members of the Canadian Establishment, the idea of a tolerable social reformer stops well short of Pope John XXIII.

The shout that David Kilgour, president of Great-West Life, directed in 1963 at Ottawa's pension plan ("Let's

---

antics of New Rich buccaneers like Harold Ballard, president of Maple Leaf Gardens, who was charged with forty-seven counts of theft and fraud and was convicted in 1972 of defrauding his company of $82,000 and taking part in the theft of another $123,000.

raise a storm! Let's make it a good one! The strongest, most lightning-packed, angry wind that has blown around Parliament Hill for a long time!") finds strong echoes among Canadian business leaders:

Ian Sinclair, chairman, Canadian Pacific Limited: "We need to counter the raucous clamour that the private sector is not performing, that it is 'ripping off' exorbitant profits, that it is a relic of the past. A weak and indecisive government is not prepared to stand up and be counted and present the true facts. . . . Every dollar removed from the capital market, because it has been taken by taxation from the pocket of the would-be investor, is a dollar denied to Canadian business. It is the volume of expenditure of governments which limits the range of private business activity."

Bill McLean, president, Canada Packers: "Being a businessman has a negative influence when dealing with government. Business has become impotent. In a sense there's been a revolt against all established institutions—they've gone out of style. My views are coloured by my background and upbringing but I think we are moving left too fast. I'm especially concerned by the barrage of rules and regulations. If business doesn't prosper, governments will not have the taxes to provide the economic base for transfer payments."

Bud Willmot, chairman, Molson Companies: "As government legislation and regulations encroach on the economic system, affecting such prerogatives as financial resource allocation, investment in underdeveloped areas, executive compensation, and the quality-of-life restrictions, we will see a gradual narrowing of the decision-making parameters for corporate executives. It would appear that if, and I say *if*, the death of corporate enterprise occurs, it will not be as a great cataclysmic event such as a revolution or the election of an avowed socialist government but simply through the interplay of trends which are already at work. Indeed, there are those who would argue that 'free enterprise' as it is called has already expired in a historical sense and that it will simply become a label associated with the industrial era through which we have already passed."

Bud McDougald, chairman, Argus Corporation: "Governments should just run the affairs of the country. They shouldn't be buying their seats back in the Commons by spending taxpayers' money just to get themselves elected and they shouldn't be trying to kill off the people who are creating the nation's wealth."

Leo Kolber, president, Cemp Investments: "Our political leaders seem to go out of their way to discourage the formation of pools of capital. In every which-way: first of all, the Foreign Investment Review Act won't let foreign capital in. Then, our laws militate against accumulating capital yourself. It's virtually impossible to get a top executive motivated to the point where he accumulates capital. It's nice that our government is on a great big giveaway program, and it's very difficult for a guy in my position to say that people shouldn't have benefits. It doesn't come out sounding properly, I understand that. But I also understand that the government doesn't seem to know where the hell the money's going to come from. It's nice that they're going to have a guaranteed wage and free medicine, free this and free that, and at the same time discourage pools of capital. Where does it come from? It's a difficult subject to discuss because, God knows, I have benefited greatly from the free-enterprise system. I started off with two cents in my pocket, but everything I've earned I've earned on my own. And I've contributed—in my opinion anyhow—a hell of a lot. I've helped make the wheels go round. You need literally hundreds of guys like myself, who are willing to work long hours and weekends and nights and holidays and push, because we just happen to have the drive and ambition. Whether it's ego or sickness or neurosis, it doesn't matter. But you've got to make the achievers of this world live in an ambience that allows them to fulfil their particular pretension. And in doing that, they benefit the country greatly. Look, we have a bloody welfare system here where in many, many instances people at the low end of the scale are well advised to stay home and do nothing. That's not good for mental health. I'm not trying to become a great psychiatrist here, but it's not good, and it's also terrible for business."

Stephen Jarislowsky, Montreal investment counsellor: "We're going through a change in class structure. The meek are not just inheriting the earth, they are grabbing it. While our capitalist system, to work properly, doesn't permit this, the politicians must inevitably look at the vote. About 90 per cent of Canadian households earn under $14,000, so the vote of the rest doesn't count. Socialism is happening, whether we agree with it or not, and it's probably irreversible. The 10 per cent of the people with funds to invest are locked out of the democratic process."

Alf Powis, president, Noranda Mines: "Ideally the government should set the rules under which business operates in a reasonably stable way, rules that aren't subject to violent, year-to-year change. What business complains about are very rapid shifts in what the rules are, and shifts for reasons that we don't consider very good ones. Politicians have to be political. But they also have a responsibility to give leadership. The terrible problem we've got in Canada is that everybody is preoccupied with the distribution of wealth and nobody is paying enough attention to the fact that you first have to create the wealth you're trying to distribute. . . . The average businessman is a rotten politician. Even C.D. Howe, in the end, was a rotten politician and brought a government down. If you're in business, you're used to getting on with things, doing things, and to hell with compromise, you go straight down the road. Politicians have to be a lot more flexible."

David Collier, president, General Motors of Canada: "What the people of North America need to realize is that with the loss of a free-choice, competitive market, it is only a step away from the loss of a free-political-choice society. Government today often tells business not only what it must not do, but what it must do, and—more than that—how to run business. Corporate responsibility becomes meaningless in that atmosphere."

Roy Thomson, press lord: "The welfare state robs people of incentive. If, in my early days, there had been family allowances and old age pensions and all the rest of it, I wouldn't have done what I did. They say business is the law of the jungle. I think it's the law of life. If you want to live and you want to prosper, you've got to be ambitious. You've got to be ready to sacrifice leisure and pleasure, and you've got to plan ahead. I was forty years old before I had any money at all. But these things don't happen overnight. Now, how many people are there who will wait that long to be successful, and work all the time? Not very many. Maybe they're right. Maybe I'm a bloody fool. But I don't think I am."

Lord Thomson's oath of allegiance to the Protestant ethic is deep within the Canadian business tradition. It is a view of life that stresses the more sombre virtues, the quiet good feeling of a hard day's work well done, the idea that the good man always more than earns his pay, a kind of fierce pragmatism in which the hard-and-fast, here-and-now aspects of life alone deserve reality.

The idea of the Protestant ethic as state religion appeals to most businessmen. They have little trouble stretching their creed toward heaven. It is a view of life reflected in the prayers repeated at Junior Chamber of Commerce meetings ("We believe that faith in God gives purpose and meaning to human life; that economic justice can best be won by free men through free enterprise . . .") and the invocation at monthly gatherings of one of the organizations of geological scientists in Calgary ("O Lord, who put the treasures beneath the earth, help us, Thy servants, to find them . . .").*

---

*Some American entrepreneurs tailor their appeals to more individual requirements. In 1948, when Wallace Johnson, who was to become a founding figure in Holiday Inns, was fighting a rezoning battle with the municipality of Memphis, he used the following text for his daily prayers: "O Lord, make us one of the greatest leaders of the nation in the building of men and homes, and help the city officials of Memphis to understand that this is our goal, so they will help us instead of hinder us. O Lord, help me to be one of the biggest businessmen in the country, and if it be Thy will, let me be a vice-president of the National Home Builders' Association. Amen."

IT IS ONE OF THE DEEP PARADOXES OF CANADA'S ECONOMIC
HISTORY that more often than not government provided
the fiscal answer to some of the most rugged free enter-
prisers' prayers. Our businessmen have loudly touted the
capitalist ethic without really believing it. A true capitalist
tradition requires faith in free enterprise unhindered by
any sense of sin, something like the way Eskimos must
have felt about sex before the missionaries came. But the
founding economic class in Canada, as R.T. Naylor has
pointed out,* had *mercantile* roots, accumulating its wealth
through circulation rather than production. This has led
not to independent capitalist development, but to the per-
petuation of a colonial mentality and risk-free *under*-
development. The men who have prevailed in the running
of the country's private sector since Confederation have
persisted for their own purposes (mostly the desire to
attract foreign capital on which to get rich) in seeing
economic development as desperately risky, feeling always
the need of a protector in the form of either outside
investment or government aid.

"At a time when American conservative intellectuals
were freeing the individual for the progressive Darwinian
struggle, Canadian thinkers, owing more to Burke than to
Darwin, insisted that the state should provide some
measure of moral direction for the society," wrote Viv
Nelles in a recent analysis of Ontario's mixed economy.†
"For them, loyalty to the British crown signified more than
just a choice of a particular set of representative institutions; it implied as well an organic view of society
within which the crown and the institutions of government
moulded the character of the individual, measured wealth
against commonwealth, and presided over just and orderly social change." Crown ownership of natural resources was a joint heritage from French seigneurial and
British freehold systems.

The idea of developing a joint economy with public
money backing private enterprise was initially forced on
Canada by the threat of American dominance. "The pub-

---

*R.T. Naylor, "The Rise and Fall of the Third Commercial Empire of
the St. Lawrence," in *Capitalism and the National Question in Canada*,
edited by Gary Teeple (Toronto: University of Toronto Press, 1972).
†H V. Nelles, *The Politics of Development: Forests, Mines and Hydro-
Electric Power in Ontario, 1849–1941* (Toronto: Macmillan, 1974).

lic involvement in canals and railroads took place step by step to protect the Canadian political economy (indeed Confederation itself) against American expansionism," according to Herschel Hardin, a British Columbia playwright who has probably come the closest to defining the Canadian identity.* "Only by publicly organized investment could a country like Canada, with its small domestic market and lesser population, keep within hailing distance of the great U.S. spectacle and defend itself. . . . The public enterprise tradition in Canada has sustained the culture of private enterprise. When we undertook the Pacific railroad, and during the Second World War when public enterprise flourished, we felt we had come into our own, which indeed we had. By contrast, in the one period when creating new Crown enterprises was largely neglected —the post-war years—Canadians' entrepreneurial will disintegrated. It was a period not simply of sell-out, of abject lack of confidence, and of blind giving of concessions to others in the desperate hope they would provide us with industry and jobs. It was also a period when, despite the impact on the national psyche of the Second World War, Canadians began to talk morosely and endlessly about an identity crisis. Public enterprise and financing are at the core of what Canada is all about, economically speaking."

This two-way partnership between business and government has resulted in some strange alliances. Probably the most ostentatious admission of a businessman's political dealings came out in the last will of Lord Strathcona, the former Hudson's Bay factor who wound up heading both his old company and the Bank of Montreal, as well as being one of the chief financiers (and beneficiaries) of the building of the CPR. His will, distributing an estate of $17 million (an amount that didn't truly reflect his wealth because most of his money had already been given away to his heirs), included provisions for cancelling the debts owed to him by Sir Richard Cartwright and Sir George Foster, formerly the ministers of finance in Liberal and Conservative governments.

The trouble some of the less ethical enterpreneurs have in dealing with governments is that politicians tend not to

---

*Herschel Hardin, *A Nation Unaware* (J.J. Douglas, Vancouver, 1974).

stay bought; they can at best be rented. Politicians generally find that the best way to solicit funds from businessmen is to anchor their campaigns to specific causes. When Ross Thatcher became Saskatchewan's Liberal leader in 1959, for example, he had no war chest and asked his friend Mel Jack, the supreme backroom-stager of the Conservative party, for help. (When Thatcher had been with the CCF in the federal House, he, Jack, and Jimmy Sinclair of the Liberals ran a floating bar in each other's homes during the early fifties.) Jack set out to organize two dinners, one at the National Club in Toronto, with Bob Winters as host, and the other at the Mount Royal Club in Montreal, put on by Bill Bennett, the former assistant to C.D. Howe. Thatcher made a simple pitch: if they gave him enough money, he would go out and fight socialism. From the ninety men at the two meals, he raised $189,000 in cash.*

THE LINES BETWEEN BUSINESS AND GOVERNMENT BECAME BLURRED during World War II, when dollar-a-year men swarmed into Ottawa and set out (along with C.D. Howe) to run the economy. The business creed became, for a while at least, the official standard for defining the national interest. For the next decade, the same men drifted between Cabinet and business board rooms. When Louis St. Laurent entered the government, for instance, he resigned as a director of Metropolitan Life Insurance; when Brooke Claxton left the Liberal cabinet, it was to take over as president of the same company. Governments saw themselves as creators of a climate in which free enterprise could prosper. "I think all of us recognize," St. Laurent told the Commons on May 14, 1953, "that there are some things which it is more appropriate to have done by public authorities than by free enterprise. But I think

*Such appeals don't always work. When Senator Grattan O'Leary was collecting funds for the Tory leadership campaign of Robert Stanfield as a way of saving the two-party system, he went to see Neil McKinnon at the Commerce and was given $5,000. J. Grant Glassco, then head of Brazilian Light and Power, also donated $5,000 but reminded O'Leary that in the same building there was a man (Henry Borden, nephew of Sir Robert Borden, the former prime minister and a fellow Nova Scotian) who was much richer than either he or McKinnon. O'Leary went to see him and a week later he received Borden's cheque. It was for $100.

we are all most happy when free enterprise does what is required to be done and public authorities do not have to intervene."

But starting with the fiery Prairie populism of John George Diefenbaker, economics became, quite simply, a branch of politics. The nation's legislators, sensing that business was losing public support, decided that the acquisitive impulse was not necessarily man's noblest instinct, that businessmen weren't the best brains or the most enjoyable company, that they constituted a faction to be propitiated, not a force to be followed. Then, during the mid-seventies, business itself seemed confused, losing its access to capital, misjudging its markets, battered by a recession it did not foresee and could not handle.

Too many businessmen had distorted their own system of values by subscribing to the notion that they could be ethical without being moral, that the main operative restraint was to show maximum profits without going to jail. The environmental devastation of the Sudbury basin by Inco and Falconbridge, for example, had become so complete that U.S. astronauts used the area to practise moonwalking before the Apollo flights.

The $135-million Atlantic Acceptance scandal tainted 286 corporations, shaking the whole North American capital market. (Although it wasn't known at the time, Atlantic's collapse came so close to causing a credit panic that in the first two months of the company's default, the Bank of Canada had to increase the money supply by $1 billion.) The "Harbourgate" affair that came to light in the spring of 1975, in which charges of conspiracy to defraud the public of $4 million were laid against fourteen chief executives of dredging companies, including some pillars of the Establishment, further eroded public faith in Canadian capitalism.*

"The only alternative to the further expansion of government to fill the vacuum of economic leader-

---

*Among the accused were Hugh Martin, chairman of Marwell Dredging and Canadian Dredge & Dock Co., a high-ranking Liberal stalwart and director of the Canada Development Corp.; Harold McNamara, chairman of Bovis Corp. and McNamara Corp.; Gérard Filion, former president of Marine Industries Ltd. and former head of the Canadian Manufacturers' Association; and Jean Simard, a part-owner of Marine Industries and director of twenty other companies.

ship," wrote Professor Abe Rotstein, an associate professor in the Department of Political Economy at the University of Toronto, "is a renaissance of Canadian business, willing and able to step into the breach and reassert control as proximate representatives of the Canadian interest. Canadian business should understand that it is its own failure to fill the power vacuum which is at the heart of the emergence of the new government corporations and initiatives with which it feels itself suddenly surrounded."

PART OF THE TROUBLE BUSINESSMEN HAVE IN DEALING WITH OTTAWA IS THE CHARACTER OF THE CITY ITSELF. It is a place of corridors, with everyone constantly on the point of arrival or departure. Bureaucrats rich in caution, clever, industrious, curiously cool, their desks neat, their clothes inconspicuous, their haircuts inoffensive, pass their days poring over fat dossiers. Their decisions have a provisional air, like commutation orders that the intended victim is never quite certain will really be signed. It all seems like a huge paper factory with a negative purpose, where the right things are usually done for the wrong reason, an environment unequipped for an overdose of anything natural. The total effect is that of an upside-down insane asylum, with most of what is publicly presented adding up to fantasy and much of what is privately transacted being real.

The businessmen and the bureaucrat-politicians view each other across a chasm of misunderstanding. They are not only different men, they are different *kinds* of men. The denizens of Ottawa see corporate executives essentially as marauders, selfish plutocrats who wear cutaways and have dollar signs for watch fobs, Neanderthal creatures who walk around with raw knuckles, because they keep scraping the ground.* The executives who fly into the capital on uncomfortable forays regard the govern-

---

*Lord Keynes caught this mood in 1938 when he wrote in a private letter to Franklin Delano Roosevelt: "You could do anything you liked with businessmen if you could treat them (even the big ones) just as wolves and tigers, but as domestic animals by nature, even though they have been badly brought up and not trained as you would wish."

ment men as misguided quasi-radicals who could never meet a payroll, don't understand very much about anything, and never seem to realize that their only purpose in life should be to provide custodial care for those whom the private sector rejects.

They complain that more and more money is being spent by the federal government, but what really concerns them is the shift of more and more *power* from private to public hands. They resent the myriad regulations,* the length of time it takes for regulatory agencies to hand down rulings, and the fact that their decisions can't be appealed.† "Anything where the government has got you by the balls, I think your chance of getting rich out of it is very bad," Lord Thomson complains. "As soon as you start to make more money than they think is good for you, they'll put in more restrictions."

The government-business feud broke into the open with the debate in 1970 on Ben Benson's White Paper on Tax Reform, which coincided with Ron Basford's new competition bill and Bryce Mackasey's revised labour code. Even though Pierre Trudeau is the first Canadian prime minister to come out of an affluent urban background,‡ he has become the chief target of every businessman's anger. Since he is also being attacked by most of the country's social reformers, it may be that he has been more successful than any of his predecessors since Mackenzie King in attaining the ideal state of Canadian political grace: he is occupying the political centre while moving simultaneously both to the left and to the right.||

Trudeau has acquired few genuine friends inside the

---

*There is rumoured to be one civil service regulation that states: "If you are absent from work owing to illness or injury on the date on which you joined the Pension Plan (or, if this is a non-working day, then the next preceding working day), you will not be entitled to death benefits until you return to work."

†For example, TransCanada PipeLines requested a 4½ per cent rate increase, in August of 1969. It took the National Energy Board forty-five months to put it through, involving 156 days of hearings that took 15,000 pages to transcribe.

‡Only two prime ministers are usually thought of as having favoured big business. But one of them, Arthur Meighen, came from a Western Ontario hamlet (Anderson, near St. Marys) and an Ulster Presbyterian background, sustaining himself by a belief in hard work and plain living; the other, R. B. Bennett, didn't become rich until he was an adult.

||To tag Trudeau with any recognizable ideology, it is probably necessary to move into the existentialism of the French philosopher Jean-Paul Sartre, who claims that each individual is what he makes of himself— that "man invents himself through exercising his freedom of choices."

Canadian financial community.* Only three important members of the business Establishment feel particularly close to him: John Aird and John Godfrey, the Toronto lawyers who are his former and present chief fund-raisers, and Paul Desmarais, the Power Corporation chief. But there are other businessmen with whom Trudeau has friendly relations. They include Allen Lambert, chairman of the Toronto-Dominion Bank, Bill Wilder, chairman of Canadian Arctic Gas Pipeline, Harrison McCain of New Brunswick, and Stu Keate, publisher of the *Vancouver Sun*. Urged on by Senator Keith Davey and James Coutts, the P.M. has repeatedly tried to establish closer rapport by meeting businessmen in small groups, but somehow the chemistry isn't there.†

In mid-December of 1974, when the economy had turned sour, a two-hour lunch at 24 Sussex Drive was organized at the business community's request, with James Coutts acting as the middleman. Only five senior business ambassadors were invited: Bill Wilder of Canadian Arctic Gas, Jake Moore of Brascan, Peter Gordon of Stelco, Paul Desmarais of Power, and Doug Gibson, the Toronto corporate consultant.‡

---

*Lester Pearson's network was a bit wider, including Jack Clyne and John Nichol in Vancouver, Philip Chester and Brig. Richard Malone in Winnipeg, Bill Harris, John Aird, and Tony Griffin in Toronto, and Charles Bronfman and Hartland Molson in Montreal.

†At a private meeting on April 18, 1972, Trudeau's guests were Roy Bennett of Ford Canada, W.J. Cheesman of Westinghouse Canada, R.J. Richardson of Du Pont Canada, W.O. Twaits of Imperial Oil, Robert Bonner of MacMillan Bloedel, Paul Leman of Alcan, W.F. McLean of Canada Packers, Alfred Powis of Noranda Mines, A.A. Thornbrough of Massey-Ferguson, Marcel Vincent of Bell Canada, and D.G. Willmot of Molson Industries.

‡On May 15, 1975, a much larger group met Trudeau and finance minister John Turner: J.C. Barrow of Simpsons-Sears, T.J. Bell of Abitibi Paper, Thomas G. Bolton of Dominion Stores, John F. Bulloch of the Canadian Federation of Independent Business, Fred Burnet of Cominco, J.W. Burns of Great-West Life, R.J. Butler of Eaton's, J.W. Cameron of Alcan, Alistair Campbell of Sun Life, Arthur Child of Burns Foods, William Clerihue of Celanese Canada, David C. Collier of General Motors of Canada, George Crompton of the Retail Merchants' Association, George Currie of MacMillan Bloedel, Peter Gordon of Stelco, L. Edward Grubb of Inco, Alex D. Hamilton of Domtar, Eric Hamilton of CIL, William Hamilton of the Employers' Council of British Columbia, Jean-Claude Hébert of Bombardier, Samuel Hughes of the Canadian Chamber of Commerce, J. Taylor Kennedy of Canada Cement Lafarge, Harrison McCain of McCain Foods, W. Earle McLaughlin of the Royal Bank, Fred McNeil of the Bank of Montreal, W.K. Mounfield of Massey-Ferguson, David Nichol of Weston's, Charles Perrault of the Conseil du Patronat du Québec, Alfred Powis of Noranda, Henry de Puyjalon of the Canadian Construction Association, Charles Rathgeb of Comstock International, R.G. Reid of Imperial Oil, Michael Schurman of Schurman Construction, F.H. Sherman of Dofasco, E.K. Turner of the Saskatchewan Wheat Pool, and Walter G. Ward of Canadian General Electric.

To document their conviction that Trudeau is really a socialist in pragmatist's clothing, his critics quote from an article he wrote in *Vrai* during the late fifties, attacking the role of the church in Quebec's economic development: "They told us that the Popes were against state ownership, with the result that Ontario Hydro got fifty years' head start over Quebec."

Under Trudeau, Ottawa's interventionist grip on the economy has been tightening.* The retroactive legislation preventing the sale of Denison Mines to a Canadian subsidiary of the U.S.-owned Continental Oil Company, the institution of export taxes on petroleum products, the monitoring of food and steel prices, the tax increases on mining profits, the financing of Panarctic Oils Limited as a joint public-private venture, and, particularly, the growing vigilance of the Department of Consumer and Corporate Affairs in attacking the monopolistic practices of large Canadian corporations—these are some of the specific targets for the complaints levelled at Trudeau from inside corporate board rooms.

They find his anti-monopoly drive especially galling. Despite their unqualified allegiance to free enterprise, most Canadian businessmen don't, in fact, like to compete. When they extol the virtues of capitalism, they are really describing an oligarchic economy with little scope or need for competition.†

---

*The federal initiatives have been accompanied by more direct nationalization measures sponsored by various provincial governments. This has included not only the NDP administrations of British Columbia, Saskatchewan, and Manitoba but also the Conservative regimes of Alberta (which took over Pacific Western Airlines) and Newfoundland (which nationalized the power assets of Brinco). Dealing with provincial governments, even those headed by unabashed free-enterprisers, is difficult for businessmen who have a different interpretation of what political mandates mean and require. "People seemed to have trouble seeing W.A.C. Bennett when he was premier of B.C., though I never did," recalls Jack Clyne, the former chairman of MacMillan Bloedel. "But I never saw him for very long. If I stayed more than half an hour, either he'd get mad or I'd get mad, so we always used to limit our conversations to about twenty minutes."

†The difference between a monopoly and an oligopoly is that several large firms instead of one company control the price system of a service or commodity. History's most savage monopoly was probably the quinine cartel. Before the invention of synthetic substitutes during World War II, the world's 500 million malaria sufferers depended on quinine made from the bark of Javanese cinchona trees. To maintain its high price, the quinine cartel's hired arsonists regularly burned half the harvest of the life-giving substance.

EVER SINCE 1888, WHEN A GROUP OF TORONTO UNDER-TAKERS was discovered to be keeping coffin prices artificially high, Canada's anti-combines investigators have provided some spectacular illustrations of firms that overcharge consumers if they can escape into the economic no-man's land where prices are set by clandestine intercompany dealings. Ottawa's justice department agents have uncovered price-fixing agreements among the manufacturers and distributors of such commodities as oatmeal, fruits and vegetables, car accessories, matches, sugar, wire fencing, galoshes, quilted goods, eyeglasses, tires, flour, gasoline, bread, coal, cigarettes, toilet paper, false teeth, and cement.

Canada became the first nation to legislate against the modern type of industrial combine by adding a section to the Criminal Code directed at flourishing monopolies in oatmeal, stoves, barbed wire, coal, and coffins. The Combines Investigation Act was written and guided through Parliament in 1910 by Mackenzie King, then minister of labour. A further revision of the act in 1923 set up a permanent investigating organization, headed by King's private secretary, Fred McGregor. One of the most rigid combines was in the rubber industry. The manufacturers of rubber footwear, for example, not only agreed to observe identical prices but also set up elaborate sales-quota arrangements. Companies exceeding their allotments paid their surplus profits to firms that failed to meet sales quotas. Every manufacturer had to make a substantial deposit at a central office as proof of his allegiance. During the rubber companies' trial, the Toronto fire department complained that it had just received four identical tenders for rubber hose.

The case that focused the most national attention on the work of the Combines Investigation Branch was the report charging a price conspiracy among Canadian flour millers. When Ottawa took the wartime controls off flour on September 15, 1947, the millers immediately raised prices by identical amounts. McGregor impounded their files and found undeniable evidence of price-setting.*

*One of the more bizarre practices was documented in a file seized from the Quaker Oats Company of Canada. It contained a description of the tendering procedure for a U.S. Army contract during the building

The law at that time required anti-monopoly reports to be made public within fifteen days of their printing. The yellow-covered 121-page copies of the findings (charging that eleven milling companies, controlling 70 per cent of the market, were operating an illegal combine) landed on the desk of justice minister Stuart Garson on April 22, 1949. Parliament had prorogued on April 20 for a general election without action on the report. Cabinet had split on the issue, with C.D. Howe insisting that the millers' decision was in keeping with the orders of the Wartime Prices and Trade Board. When the government refused to release the investigation's findings even after the election, McGregor resigned in protest, on October 29, 1949. The report was finally tabled in the House of Commons nine days later. The Opposition benches exploded. George Drew demanded that the Liberals dissolve Parliament because of the delay. "In 1649," proclaimed M.J. Coldwell, the leader of the CCF, "an English king was beheaded for doing exactly what the government has done." The flour millers were never prosecuted.

An even more rigid cartel was the wooden-match monopoly, formed by companies associated with Ivar Kreuger, the Swedish millionaire who at one time owned a hundred and fifty factories in twenty-eight countries producing 65 per cent of the world's matches. In 1923 Kreuger bought a match plant at Berthierville, Quebec, from the Rockefeller family and five years later merged it with the match business of the E.B. Eddy Company at Hull, then controlled by R.B. Bennett. This made the Swedish financier's newly formed Eddy Match Company Canada's only producer of wooden matches. As competing plants were established, Eddy flooded their sales areas with underpriced brands. Columbia Match Company, which set up a large factory at St. Johns, Quebec, in 1929, for a while was the most successful competitor. "No doubt you will watch their efforts and see that they are care-

---

of the Alaska Highway. The American colonel in charge of purchasing found that six Canadian flour mills had submitted identical bids. Using a deck of cards, he eliminated four of the six millers in a series of high-low cuts. Then he and a lieutenant cut the deck again: the king of diamonds won the round for Quaker Oats by beating out the ten of spades, which had turned up representing Lake of the Woods Milling Co. Ltd.

fully attended to if they attempt to take any of our business," G.W. Paton, the president of Eddy, instructed A.G. Woodruff, one of his vice-presidents, in a confidential interoffice memo soon after Columbia's incorporation. After three years of battling Eddy's low-priced "fighting brands," Columbia was forced into bankruptcy. Eddy executives secretly purchased the plant and operated it as the Commonwealth Match Company.

Eddy was tried and convicted as a monopoly in 1951. Because the company had maintained the firms it absorbed as separate corporations—to give the appearance of competition within the industry—the fine totalled $85,000 instead of a meaningful amount. Eddy's grasp on the Canadian market was hardly splintered, because a section of the law providing for the break-up of monopolies was not yet in force.

One problem with combines cases is that prosecution of charges takes so long. In the fall of 1948, for instance, the combines investigators noted that the prices of Canadian writing, blotting, and book papers were remarkably similar and that since 1935 only three new companies had joined the fine-paper industry. A full-scale inquiry was launched. Three years of searching through the files of forty-five paper mills were followed by two years of private hearings to gather oral evidence and allow the firms to state their defence. The transcript of these sessions amounted to a million words. The report, charging Canada's fine-paper industry with having maintained a competition-restraining combine over the past seventeen years, was issued in 1952. The trial of the companies in the Supreme Court of Ontario began on January 11, 1954. It lasted seventy-one days; more than twenty million words of evidence were taken. The judge took five hours to read his ruling, which found most of the companies guilty. After a hearing before the Ontario Court of Appeal, the case reached the Supreme Court of Canada in the fall of 1956. This court delivered its judgement on May 13, 1957, confirming the decision in a twenty-four-page single-spaced document. Twenty-seven of the fine-paper companies were fined a total of $242,000 in November, 1957—almost a decade from the beginning of the investigation.

The effectiveness of past combines prosecutions has been fatally weakened by the insignificance of fines imposed. In January, 1958, for instance, eleven shingle manufacturers paid the courts the maximum fine of $10,000 each for having operated a combine in the $30-million-a-year asphalt-roofing industry since 1932.

Until recently, the pace of anti-monopoly prosecutions has been hesitant, almost lackadaisical. The conviction of the Electric Reduction Company of Canada by the Supreme Court of Canada in 1970 for its 1959 merger with Dominion Fertilizers was the combines branch's first monopoly conviction in seventeen years. The fine of $150,-000 imposed in 1974 on the Irving newspaper interests in New Brunswick was for the first conviction under the section of the law that prohibits mergers from harming the public since the Eddy Match case.* But the Trudeau government has raised the fines,† and under proposed new legislation, guilty executives would not only have to pay personal penalties of up to a million dollars but could also go to jail for five years.

FACED WITH THESE AND OTHER ONSLAUGHTS ON THEIR PROFITS, a few business leaders have been making tentative efforts to don a mantle of corporate responsibility. Even though the *status quo* is quaking beneath their feet, only a tiny enclave within the Canadian Establishment is yet aware of the need for a fresh response. This enlightened minority recognizes the approaching disappearance of *laissez-faire* capitalism and with its passing the need to reach an appropriate accommodation with the new forces that are grabbing a larger share of society's powers, particularly the various levels of government administration. "Business now clearly must hitch its wagon to the rising star of social capitalism in this country," wrote Don Carlson, the publisher of the *Financial Times of Canada,* who first tried to define the new ideology. "This

---

*The Irving conviction was reversed on appeal in 1975.
†In the spring of 1974, seven cement companies, including Canada Cement Lafarge Ltd., whose B.C. operations were headed by Jimmy Sinclair, Pierre Trudeau's father-in-law, were fined $432,000 for conspiring to fix base mill cement prices.

would be a more constructive response, more contemporary than entrenchment against the unfolding political and economic system, alien though this system is to the past experience of business. . . . Social capitalism as charted by our public leaders is increasingly blessed by public mandate. The only sensible reaction by the private sector is to use its considerable expertise to help build self-restraint into the Canadian Grand Plan. Elected and bureaucratic planners need to be inspired—or embarrassed—into providing this missing component in their avant-garde programming. . . . But business can accomplish more—in the public interest and in its own self-interest—by going beyond mere submissive adaptation to the new roles being planned for it. Some perceptive Canadians believe that new kinds of business initiatives can contribute to practical economic policy within the broader context of Canada's unfolding social capitalism."

Whether they realize it or not, even some diehard adherents of free enterprise are becoming converts to the philosophy of John Maynard Keynes (a concept nearly forty years old), accepting the function of government as the chief energizer and stabilizer of the economy. "It is in the national interest for government and business to get closer together to solve the problems at hand," Peter Gordon, the president of the Steel Company of Canada, told the Hamilton chapter of the Financial Executives' Institute in the spring of 1975. "I'm not suggesting that the public and private sectors can be completely compatible. But there are obvious areas for mutual co-operation and joint enterprise, which combine the ability of industry to get things done in the most efficient way with the responsibility of the government to uphold the legitimate public interest."*

No one has tried harder to reconcile the two factions than Bob Wisener, a graduate of the Royal Canadian Naval College and a former governor of the Toronto Stock Exchange. For two weekends every autumn since the mid-fifties, Wisener has thrown open Rosehill, his sum-

---

*An independent government investigation of Stelco's operations found the company not guilty of having unduly increased its profit margin during recent price increases.

mer compound on Sturgeon Lake (near Bobcaygeon, Ontario), to groups of business executives and top-level bureaucrats, three dozen at a time, for off-the-record, free-for-all confrontations.

These unstructured occasions allow the ambassadors of both sides to exchange intuitions, deceptions, and obsessions while lounging around Wisener's Italian gardens, golf course, and private beach. The 1973 gathering, just after Ottawa had implemented its capital gains tax measures, was highlighted by a noisy argument between Alf Powis, the Noranda president, and Simon Reisman, then the finance deputy, who ended the exchange by shouting, "You fat cats will just have to pay more taxes!" and diving into Sturgeon Lake.* "There have been some moments that have been sort of fun," says Wisener, a large man with a sardonic sense of humour. "But it isn't what's discussed during the weekends that creates something. It's the phone calls that go on for the next year between the people who meet there. They see that the other fellow doesn't have horns. The businessmen realize that the Ottawa guys have real problems. They've just got to do things that are politically acceptable, because if they don't, they aren't going to be there any more."

The concept that most clearly separates the two groups, no matter how friendly their plenipotentiaries may become, is the idea of profit as the ultimate measure of individual achievement and happiness. "Capitalism revolves around profit," says Jack Clyne, the former Mac-Millan Bloedel chairman. "If you do away with the profit motive you are acting in a manner totally contrary to the human instinct. Money in itself doesn't bring happiness. But often the *pursuit* of money does." According to this bottom-line philosophy, there can never be too much profit,† and pursuit of profit excuses almost everything, even idealism (Canadian industrial profits run to about $10 billion a year). Walter Gordon, whose nationalistic measures made him the devil incarnate along Toronto's Bay

---

*For a complete list of the executives and bureaucrats who attended this Sturgeon Lake conference, see Appendix A.

†"If I had unlimited wealth and the CRTC would let me have all the electronic media I wanted," John Bassett, president of Baton Broadcasting Inc., told the *Windsor Star*, "I'd be a real pig. I like it. And if you're in business, you want more, you want to be a real pig."

Street during the sixties, found that by the early seventies businessmen who had studiously avoided him for years were suddenly crossing the street to greet him. "At first," he says, "I thought they might be changing their minds on the foreign ownership issue. But then I quickly discovered that it was because my company, Canadian Corporate Management, was making a good profit, and they must have figured that anyone who can make money can't be all bad."

The shift in position of a few businessmen does not amount to a reformation. The typical Establishmentarian's search for understanding begins not in wonder but in the reduction of an increasingly confusing world to safe old values. Outlining what he considered to be the typical career pattern for ambitious young Canadians, Harry Jackman, the head of Dominion and Anglo Investment, told a parliamentary committee hearing on the Benson White Paper in 1970: "He begins by learning his trade; he saves his small stake, borrows from the bank, starts a business and, if successful, creates employment and provides goods and services for the people. In his forties he may start making some money. In his fifties his standard of living is pretty well established. Because of the general affluence, domestic servants are almost impossible to get. Probably corporatewise or personally he becomes an automatic saver or provider of capital. . . ."

It's been a while since the average Canadian youngster saw his future in quite this Horatio Alger spirit. But Jackman and most other members of the business Establishment continue clinging to the notion that somehow, at some dim time in the not too distant future, society will return to what they like to think of as normal. However unlikely this is to happen, their faith that it is still possible feeds their souls and keeps them from the wind.

CHAPTER SIX

The Frightened Men
in the Corner Offices

The Chief Executive Officers of many large
corporations are men in flight, harried
individuals driven by the necessity of coming
down to their bottom lines with ever better
results. Life becomes an endless
sequence of moving sales and profit targets.

To most people a generation ago, and to some people
still, the stereotype of the really big businessman is the
flinty-eyed tycoon, the dollar-cigar empire builder who
practises a Darwinian ethic that allows only the fittest to
survive. Yet this kind of domineering old titan, who was
epitomized by Sir Herbert Holt and Sir James Dunn, has
long since been replaced by smooth managerial types who
feed the furnaces of their ambitions by meshing group
effort instead of pioneering new dimensions of economic
exploitation.

Unlike its predecessors, this new breed of corporate cat
seldom emerges into public light. The Chief Executive
Officers appear scowling from the financial pages of the
daily newspapers only once a year, entering or leaving
their stockholders' meetings—men with ice picks in their
eyes, swimming across the rented hotel ballrooms in
broad, hand-shaking strokes, generally followed by lawyers and PR men in split-T formation.

Whenever they speak, it is with the unmistakable accent of power, proudly proclaiming how humble they feel
about operating the levers of the economic machinery
that keeps the nation functioning. These corporate chief-
tains tend to be obsequious to their equals and tough on
those who work for them. As long as they are manoeuvring blocks of money or trying to shift power—as long as
they are holding the floor—they are dynamic and alive to
shifting possibilities. But when they pause to express their
innermost thoughts and feelings, their certitudes usually

fade into evasion and doubt. Even during their brief moment of glory they seem unable or unwilling to measure their self-esteem against original dreams, as if they comprehended only vaguely the time and place of their own incarnation.

The Chief Executive Officers of many large corporations are men in flight, harried individuals driven by the necessity of coming down to their bottom lines with ever better results. Life becomes an endless sequence of moving sales and profit targets.

"This is a commercial company, and our epitaph is written in dollars per share returned to stockholders," Harold Geneen, the head of ITT, once told a meeting of his executives, defining the corporate philosophy. The essence of this approach is that life can be lived according to calculable rules, that results are more important than process, that what really matters most is a kind of implacable momentum toward a common goal. This creed makes its practitioners immune from devoting much commitment to the larger economic and social issues. Career tends to replace conscience. Corporate men eventually become what they appear to be. By granting them indulgences, by endowing their endeavours with meaning, by rationalizing their every uncertainty, their corporate affiliations take on a divine quality. The cardinal sin is to possess a sense of the absurd, not to be a true believer.

Loyalty is the supreme virtue. Clinging to existence means clinging to office. Virtually no personal sacrifice is too great if it helps fulfil corporate objectives. During the 1975 Hamilton Harbour trial, when asked why he had destroyed documents connected with the case after the RCMP visited his office, Horace Rindress, a former president of J.P. Porter Company, a Montreal dredging company, replied: "For twenty-two years I put that company ahead of myself. I came second."

THE MOST PRESSING PROBLEM AMONG CHIEF EXECUTIVE OFFICERS IS HOW TO MANAGE THEIR TIME MORE EFFECTIVELY. "The worst thing about running a big business is that there are so many people you have to see," E.P. Taylor complained when he was still operating as a corporate president. "Most of them are well meaning, well intentioned, but some of them may be crazy, have crazy ideas. They may be inventors. They may want a loan. But out of politeness, because you're selling a certain product, you have to see them. Sometimes friends call up and they're really just passing this person on to you. That takes up an awful lot of time. They always want to see the top guy. You can't shove them off as easily as you'd like to."

George Black, who was Taylor's choice to run Canadian Breweries, was one of the most successful organizers of his personal timetable. "The perfect executive is the man who has nothing to do," he contends. "That's not quite possible, of course, but I came pretty close when I was president of Canadian Breweries. All I did was to have a chat once a month with my key vice-presidents and remain accessible to them." Every CEO tries hard to cut down the number of executives reporting to him, so that he can devote his energies to policy rather than operating matters. Ian Sinclair, for example, CEO of the huge Canadian Pacific complex, sees only six divisional heads on a regular basis. "One of the problems," he says, "is maintaining a balance between these people, because everyone thinks his area is Number One. You *want* them to think that. They always imagine that somebody else is getting more of your time, more of your forward thrust, more of the allocation of the scarcest of all resources, money, and you have to keep threading it, and the way you thread it best is by getting on the ground with them. That's why I make a point of talking airlines in Vancouver, talking oil in Calgary, talking real estate in Toronto, and shipping in London or Bermuda."

The Sinclair approach is followed by the CEOs of most companies. Bill McLean, the easy-going president of Canada Packers, has the heads of the company's four operating divisions plus George Dickson, his executive vice-president, reporting to him; Charles Bronfman has regular contact with only three of his senior executives;* Bud Willmot, while he was CEO of Molson Industries, ex-

---

*They are Mel Griffin, executive vice-president and chief operating officer, House of Seagram Ltd., David Roche, executive vice-president, marketing, and Len Babich, senior vice-president, finance.

ercised "a span of control over six senior group vice-presidents." At the Royal Bank, a recent structural re-organization has placed most of the operating power in the hands of Rowlie Frazee, the executive vice-president and chief general manager, with Earle McLaughlin almost exclusively concerned with long-term prospects and overseas opportunities.

One of the minor ways executives save time is to use a form of linguistic shorthand with each other. In part, this is a kind of "witch doctor" syndrome—words and phrases that are used because they *sound* impressive.

One U.S. management consultant made up the following table, which allows executives in any situation to come up quickly with what appear to be thoughtful, contemporary-sounding comments:

Column 1	Column 2	Column 3
0. integrated	0. management	0. options
1. total	1. organizational	1. flexibility
2. systematized	2. monitored	2. capability
3. parallel	3. reciprocal	3. mobility
4. functional	4. digital	4. programming
5. responsive	5. logistical	5. concept
6. optional	6. transitional	6. time-phase
7. synchronized	7. incremental	7. projection
8. compatible	8. third-generation	8. hardware
9. balanced	9. policy	9. contingency

The busy executive merely thinks up any three-digit number and then selects the corresponding buzzword from each column. For instance, 980 comes out as "balanced third-generation options," a suitably meaningless phrase that can be dropped into almost every conversation on any subject. "No one will have the remotest idea what you're talking about," Philip Broughton, the table's author, points out. "But the important thing is that they're not about to admit it."

The executive preoccupation with time, its uses and abuses, sometimes even extends to periods away from the office. The CEOs complain about "useless" leisure and prefer spending winter holidays in the South with enough

work or customers along to make the journey "worthwhile." Corporate man is so enthralled by the electric
stream of problems and events that engulf him daily that
to be disconnected from the current for more than a
week can cause a minor identity crisis. "The worst days
to me are holidays, Saturdays, and Sundays, because I'm
the only one who wants to work," F. P. Taylor said on his
seventy-fourth birthday. "Every day is the same to me.
I travel a lot in my jet. It goes 530 miles an hour."*
The more valuable such men feel, the more expensive
their time becomes, so that eventually they literally cannot afford to have much "free" time. Arthur Child, for
example, CEO of Burns Foods Limited in Calgary, works
ten hours a day, seven days most weeks, and hasn't taken
an extended holiday since 1966. His company's official
biography states: "Arthur Child has no social or sports
interests whatsoever. For the most part his time is spent
at his office, his home, or travelling on business."

To compensate for their dedication, the CEOs receive
every consideration money can buy. A 1974 survey by
Heidrick and Struggles Incorporated, a firm of international management consultants, showed that 73 per
cent of Canadian presidents in companies with sales of
more than $100 million were getting salaries of at least
$100,000. (At the same time, the Canadian operating
heads of U.S. subsidiaries with similar dollar volumes were
averaging $195,000.) The three highest-paying jobs in
the country ($250,000 a year plus side benefits) are the
chairmanships of Imperial Oil, Inco, and the Bank of
Montreal. But salaries are a decreasingly important proportion of executive earnings. A study by H.V. Chapman
and Associates has documented that 28 per cent of the income of CEOs is derived from various bonus arrangements. More than half of all company presidents enjoy
company-owned or leased cars. Their take-home pay is
boosted through a variety of schemes, including interest-
free loans, deferred-pay contracts (arranging for annual
retainers *after* retirement, when tax levels are lower),

---

*The Hawker Siddeley jet is painted in Taylor's racing colours: tur-
quoise and gold.

deferred profit-sharing schemes, stock options,* and phantom dividend plans.† Retirement provisions are generous,‡ particularly if a president is dismissed or pushed aside by a merger. In 1968, when Charles Specht was forced out of the MacMillan Bloedel presidency, he was given four months' full pay (at $120,000 a year) plus a $200,000 bonus. J. Howard Hawke, the vice-chairman of Jannock Corporation, a Toronto holding company, got $187,500 spread out over forty-eight instalments when Bud Willmot and a group of his associates took over the company in the spring of 1975. W.J.R. Paton, the Jannock chairman, was granted $60,000 a year for life. Hawke then became president and CEO of Bache and Company Canada.

Another way of rewarding the CEOs is to provide them with the appropriate turf for their decision making. In the corner offices‖ from which they operate, carpets (Persian, not broadloom) are thick,§ ceilings sound-proofed, telephone bells dulled. Swivel chairs bend, tilt, and respond, like good horses, to the slightest impulse of their riders. Lights are controlled by rheostats which can create a gentle glow for introspection or a full blaze for action. Desks, once wooden fortresses bristling with penholders and knick-knacks, now have pristine surfaces and no drawers. Bars and refrigerators are almost standard equipment, though most CEOs maintain such facilities in

---

*Probably the most generous Canadian stock-option arrangement was set up by Frank McMahon, president of Westcoast Transmission, in 1956. He allocated 154,687 shares to himself at 5 cents each and another 200,000 shares at $5.97. Two years later he had realized a profit of $6.4 million. (During the 1960 election campaign in British Columbia, McMahon threatened to cancel $450 millions' worth of construction projects if the voters didn't re-elect a strong Social Credit government.)

†Participants are credited with a certain number of corporate units, each of which is equivalent to a share of company stock (even when there is none issued) but costs the participant nothing. The bonuses that are paid out are equal to the actual dividends that would have been payable on the equivalent number of actual shares. These are, in effect, performance shares, and the executive's compensation will depend on how much he has been able to drive up the worth of his company's stock.

‡They can go on for a long time. Sir George Bury, for instance, who retired as a CPR vice-president in 1918, lived to 92 and collected well over half a million dollars in pension cheques.

‖It's doubtful if there is a single chief executive officer of any Canadian corporation who is *not* in a corner office. The Reichmanns, a family of developers, capitalized on this in 1972 by completing a building with ten irregular sides at King Street and University Avenue in Toronto. Each floor has eight corner offices.

§The ultimate status symbol is to have an oriental rug on top of broadloom.

separate suites that serve as private dining rooms.* Monogrammed silver and crested china help create the Georgian atmosphere that the majority of top executives seem to prefer. The look they strive for evokes the safe, nineteeth-century glories of unbridled capitalism—a combination of panelled walls, Adam fireplaces, Sheraton tables, breakfront libraries, writing commodes, Regency wine coolers, and paintings of bloody British hunting scenes. There is a subtle attempt to impress on the visitor the notion that the occupant's power is not corporate but personal.

This mood is not always easy to capture, especially inside the austere glass skyscrapers from which most of the important companies now operate. But you can do it if you try. Charles Gundy, chairman of Wood Gundy, has converted his suite in Toronto's TD Centre into a Georgian drawing room, complete with white panelling, inlaid wood floors, cornices at the top of the walls, and windows walled in halfway up and converted into small-paned Georgian bays.

The CEO's home expresses his wife's personality; his office tends to reflect the man himself. Frequently these working chambers are sadly impersonal, revealing little about their occupants' joys or sorrows, nothing of their dead and living dreams, no hint of why they had been (or conceived themselves to have been) put on the face of the earth. There are exceptions. Charles Bronfman kept a large plastic noughts-and-crosses coffee table near his desk, but got rid of it when he underwent a change of outlook following his purchase of the Montreal Expos. "I was very uptight in those early days," he says, "and I guess many of the people I dealt with were also uptight. I put in the noughts-and-crosses set because I wanted to create an atmosphere which, in effect, told my visitors this is only a game. . . . Now that I *know* business is only a game I don't need the noughts-and-crosses any longer to remind me."

Earle McLaughlin, the Royal Bank chairman, has added

*Not only invitations to the executive dining room but the *times* for which they are tendered can be important. Until recently, there were two sittings at the Metropolitan Life head offices' private eating chambers in Ottawa: at 11.45 a.m. and at 1 p.m. Executives knew that when they made the latter sitting, they really had arrived.

an antique touch to his suite in Place Ville Marie by installing a large Royal Navy sea chest and an ancient Chinese abacus.* E.P. Taylor has hunting scenes with titles like "The Death of the Bear" and "The Hog at Bay" decorating his anterooms. Ian Sinclair of Canadian Pacific expresses his faith in the work ethic by keeping a photograph of two giant Clydesdales straining in their harnesses above his desk. Steve Roman, chairman of Denison Mines, has a giant painting in his office of a bear killing a reindeer, with some wolves in the background waiting to take possession of the dying prey.

Probably the most valuable office art collection is owned by Aikins, MacAulay and Thorvaldson, the Winnipeg law firm. John MacAulay, the senior partner, has distributed some of his private treasures, including seventeen A.Y. Jacksons, among the offices. Northern and Central Gas Corporation has integrated eighty-five paintings into the design of its Toronto head office.

The most lavish office in Canada belongs to Ken Thomson, heir to the publishing empire. At the top of the Thomson Building, across Queen Street from Toronto's new city hall, it occupies almost an entire floor and is reached by private elevator. Somehow the layout manages to remain vaguely utilitarian, even though it seems much more suitable to an art gallery. The office houses *eighty-three* Krieghoffs as well as numerous Cullens, Gagnons, and Emily Carrs and half a dozen showcases containing exquisite miniatures fashioned from ivory, boxwood, and Renaissance jewels. "I like beautiful, delicate things that you can hold in your hand," he says.

More mundane executive-suite furnishings have deep totemic significance. A mahogany desk outranks walnut, but walnut outranks oak, and cherry outranks everything else. The number of windows in any businessman's office provides an important clue to his status.† The strangest office arrangement of all time may have been the red beacon that John Bradfield maintained outside his presidential

---

*It is glued in position at $10,196,159,299, the amount of the bank's assets at its hundredth anniversary in 1969.

†Allen Lambert, chairman of the Toronto-Dominion Bank, wins this contest hands down. His large modern chamber on the eleventh floor of the TD Centre has fourteen windows.

suite at Noranda between 1956 and 1962. J.Y. Murdoch, the temperamental lawyer and mining pioneer who had incorporated Noranda in 1923 and held on to its presidency for the next thirty-three years, decided in 1956 to appoint himself chairman. He ran the company, until he died in 1962, out of the living room of his Rosedale mansion, even though most of his time seemed to be spent drinking. So that his staff wouldn't learn how he was receiving his marching orders, Bradfield had the red light installed, turned it on whenever Murdoch called with instructions or advice, and absolutely forbade anyone to enter his office while it was flashing.

What has really come to symbolize prestige among members of Canada's business Establishment in the mid-1970s is the private jet. These aircraft—their cabins furnished with leather-upholstered sofas, Gucci lap robes, backgammon sets from Hermes of Paris, and colour-co-ordinated bars—perform the same status functions once rendered by private railway cars and yachts.*

The ultimately sumptuous plane belonged to Sam Hashman, the Calgary builder, who converted a seventy-nine-passenger BAC One-Eleven airliner into a twenty-one-seat flying bungalow complete with dishwasher. Probably the most important aircraft in the country is the Gulfstream II bought in 1974 by Inco for its chairman, Edward Grubb. The $5-million plane, one of six owned in Canada, is the most expensive of the business jets.† Because Grubb already had a $1-million Westwind, he hesitated to order the new plane until he had prepared elaborate studies on the additional productivity the Gulfstream would add to his working day. Inco's board of directors didn't take his charts very seriously but surprised Grubb at the end of a long board meeting by officially presenting him with a $5-million gift certificate so that he could get his plane. What makes the aircraft significant is that it has, in effect, become Inco's head office. Caught between reluctant recognition of the fact that most of its

---

*For a complete list of Canada's business jets, including a description and the cost of each type of aircraft, see Appendix B.
†The others are used by Marsh Cooper, president of Falconbridge; Jack Armstrong, chairman of Imperial Oil; Alf Powis, president of Noranda; Steve Roman, chairman of Denison Mines; and John Lobb, chairman of Northern Electric.

profits originate in Canada and a desire to keep running the company from New York, Inco has split its management into financial and marketing departments (still run out of New York) and the operating division, now run from Toronto. There is so much commuting by senior executives from both ends that most of their decisions seem to be reached in the air, somewhere over Poughkeepsie, N.Y.

UNLIKE THE WEALTHY, CHIEF EXECUTIVE OFFICERS HAVE LITTLE AMBIVALENCE IN THEIR FEELINGS ABOUT THE EXERCISE OF POWER. They like it. Yet their authority, like that of bankers, is delegated, remaining an inherent function of the job rather than the individual. This authority of incumbency perishes when the holder is removed from his particular desk. The alert CEO realizes that he is easily replaceable, that there is no substitute for ownership, that the only real security lies in establishing a strong equity position in the corporation that employs him. "The hired top corporation man," wrote Ferdinand Lundberg, "is much like the cormorant, or fishing bird, still used in China. A strap is fastened around the animal's neck, permitting him to breathe but not allowing him to gulp his catch. He dutifully brings the fish back to the boat. Now and again (paydays) the strap is loosened and he is allowed to swallow a fish. The bird is a percentage participant in the process, which was established by and for others."*

Some CEOs have been buying up shares in their operations for their own accounts, partly as a kind of self-induced incentive to be more profit-minded, but mostly because becoming part-owners aggrandizes their authority. Arthur Child of Burns Foods, for example, now owns more than 4 per cent of his company, making him second only to Howard Webster as an individual shareholder.

Child is a prototype of the successful Canadian CEO. Educated at four universities, including the Harvard Busi-

---

*F. Lundberg, *The Rich and the Super-Rich* (New York: Lyle Stuart, 1968).

ness School, he became chief auditor of Canada Packers
at twenty-eight and assumed the Burns presidency in 1966,
when Howard Webster was trying to rescue the Calgary
firm from bankruptcy. Child turned it around, more than
tripling sales and turning a profit of $4,571,000 in 1974.
"To do the things I've done in this company," he says,
"takes a tremendous strength of will. When you make
decisions involving people, there's always a balance between what's good for the individual and what's good
for all the employees. What's good for the employees always has to prevail as far as I'm concerned, and that's
not just being profit-minded. That's protecting the other
six thousand jobs we have here, because if all my decisions were based only on what was good for the individual I'd be running the company down and be
jeopardizing the future of the company. In this process,
I'm just as tough on myself as I am on the others. Very
few people really know how tough you have to be."

One man who has managed the difficult jump from being a CEO to becoming a *de facto* owner is John "Jake"
Henderson Moore. Exercising both executive power and
effective control over the huge (assets, $2 billion)
Brascan empire, his grasp also extends to voting rights
over the largest single block of stock in the Hudson's
Bay Company (sales, $1 billion). A graduate of Ridley
and the Royal Military College at Kingston, he became a
partner in the London, Ontario, office of Clarkson, Gordon and Company and in 1953 moved over to one of his
accounts, John Labatt Limited, as treasurer. Named president five years later, he pumped the company's sales up
from third to first place in the Canadian beer market. In
1964, members of the Labatt family decided to sell their
controlling interest to Jos. Schlitz of Milwaukee. But the
anti-trust division of the U.S. justice department got a
court ruling that ordered Schlitz to sell its holding. Moore
and other Labatt officers and friends, after lining up
help through Triarch Corporation, a Toronto financial
house, eventually set up Jonlab Investments and, with
Brazilian Light and Power (later Brascan) and Investors
Group of Winnipeg, bought the Schlitz-owned shares in
1967, heavily geared up by a loan from the Commerce.

About two years after swinging the repatriation of the Labatt's stock, Moore replaced Bob Winters as CEO at Brascan—a manoeuvre achieved through the influence of Neil McKinnon of the Commerce, who was opposed to Winters's lack of opposition to the proposed purchase of the Canadian company by International Utilities Corporation of Philadelphia.* A few months later, in February, 1970, the two million shares of Brascan (an 8 per cent interest) that IU had accumulated by then were purchased by Moore and placed in Jonlab, with the cash ($23.4 million) being raised by Jonlab's sale of its Labatt's stock to Brascan. Moore could sponsor this manoeuvre because he simultaneously controlled Jonlab and was the CEO of Brascan, which held a controlling interest in Labatt's. (In 1970 he went out on the open market and purchased, on Brascan's account, a 6.6 per cent share—also the largest single block—of stock in the Hudson's Bay Company.)† Moore's personal stake in Jonlab's shares (13 per cent) netted him at least $5 million in profits on these deals.‡

THE RESULTS OF SUCCESSFUL MANAGEMENT ARE OBVIOUS, ITS MEANS MYSTERIOUS. Most Canadian corporations are run by Chief Executive Officers on a "management by exception" basis—their support staff make all day-to-day operational decisions except those broad policy matters and high-expenditure items that remain their personal prerogatives. They hop from crisis to crisis, spending most of their time at meetings with the vice-presidents who report to them, reading reports, affirming or modifying proposals that bubble up from below. As heads of large corporations, they are, in effect, the

---

*International Utilities Corp. changed its name in 1973 to IU International Corp.
†For the details of this deal, see Chapter 4.
‡Jonlab went on to acquire Triarch Corp. and repatriate it—51 per cent control of Triarch having been acquired by U.S. interests soon after the Schlitz deal. Jonlab also picked up Elliott & Page, the investment counsellors, and First Toronto Corp., as well as the largest interest in Canadian Cablesystems Ltd. and Commerce Capital Corp. Ltd. In September, 1975, Brascan—which held 41 per cent of Jonlab's non-voting stock—offered $13.48 million for all the remaining issued shares of Jonlab, which held 8 per cent of Brascan's stock.

presidents of small republics, and part of their success depends on how well they can spot and groom successors.

The process of natural selection through which new CEOs emerge is based on a combination of factors. They must want the top job with a passion. "It's just a case of endocrine glands, that's all," James Muir, a former chairman of the Royal Bank, used to claim.* "If you're born with endocrine glands of a certain nature, there's nothing you can do to satisfy yourself until you get to the top." To achieve ultimate power, the climbers (moving up the corporate ladders on little cat feet) must prove themselves acceptable to the men who already hold it. There are certain things they have to do, certain attitudes they have to share, certain tests they have to pass, and then it's theirs. To possess the talent, to reek of good intentions and probity is not enough. In manners, political beliefs, life styles, even choice of wives, the potential successors must fit in with the incumbent's own prides and prejudices. To grab the brass ring, the candidate must submerge his own feelings, reflecting instead his superior's every mood, gesture, frown, or opinion. Potential non-believers, doubters, scoffers, the "oddballs with negative attitudes," are not considered "tough" or "realistic" enough to make it all the way. The long, compromising climb upward can create some strange alliances. But in the corporate game the distance between affection and opportunity is short. There is nothing wrong with having idealistic thoughts and dreams, just so long as they're never mentioned.

Few corporations leave succession at the top to chance. Some CEOs keep PYM (Promising Young Men) lists in their desk drawers; others prefer to revitalize their firms by bringing in outsiders. Bell Canada's Management and Resource Committee (a subcommittee set up by the directors) plots the company's presidency ten years ahead, with deliberate alternation between French-speaking and English-speaking appointees. The Royal Bank has a sys-

---

*Muir himself was so anxious to start his own banking career that he skipped lunch and joined the Peebles branch of the Commercial Bank of Scotland as a clerk within an hour of graduating from secondary school on July 17, 1907.

tem of understudies for executives so that at least three men are ready to move into every senior slot. ("If I wasn't a director and vice-president of the Royal, I'd be raiding them," says Ian Sinclair, the Canadian Pacific chairman. "They're so loaded with talent, it just makes you drool.")

But major appointments occasionally do happen by chance. James Kerr, the CEO of TransCanada PipeLines, was a vice-president of Canadian Westinghouse in 1958 when he traded his Army-Navy football tickets to watch the World Series with Dr. Richard Hearn, the retired chairman of Ontario Hydro. Hearn had been scouting around for a qualified engineer to head the then controversial pipeline company, and Kerr was offered the job as he watched the New York Yankees clobber the Milwaukee Braves.

The most expensive recruitment in Canadian corporate history was the wooing of D.G. "Bud" Willmot from the presidency of Anthes Imperial (originally a St. Catharines plumbing and heating supply operation) to become CEO of Molson Industries Limited (the Toronto-based conglomerate that grew out of the Montreal brewery). Between 1949 and 1967, Willmot had turned the modest Anthes operation into a consistent moneymaker, and when Molson's began to diversify, its directors paid $74 million to buy out Anthes so they could get him as part of the deal. (In addition to a hefty salary boost, Willmot received some $10 millions' worth of Molson stock yielding $350,000 in annual dividends.)

Life at the top is financially rewarding, spiritually draining, physically exhausting, and short. Few CEOs stay in office more than a decade, although the term of their influence is usually stretched when they switch from being president to the much less onerous responsibilities involved in becoming chairman of the board. But eventually they too pass into the shadows, tasting something of the disappointment experienced by the many ambitious climbers who, stuck at some midway point on the corporate ladder, never make it at all.

Failure inside the business environment is subtle and intensively subjective. Pay continues; subordinates still obey orders; colleagues are affable. Yet there rises up, overnight it seems, a palpable consensus that the man is done. There is no appeal. The mushroom treatment begins.*

This up-or-out ethic forces some executives to live constantly with the fear of failure, wondering when and how it will come to them. It's a process that toughens the nerve ends. Too often the years of self-repression in the cause of corporate advancement sap humanity's juices in a man. When the bottle is uncorked, its content has evaporated. There is no one left inside.

---

* "You're fed lots of fertilizer, kept in the dark for six months, and then canned," according to one of its victims.

CHAPTER SEVEN

Working the System

*It sometimes seems as if members of
Canada's Establishment spend
most of their waking hours on one
mammoth conference call. Few business
secrets or rumours last more than a
day as the private possession of any
group. For those addicted to the
personal exercise of power, corporate
machinations can provide a giddy,
almost sexual sensation.*

The business Establishment's true adherents —men with hairy forearms, resonant voices, and eyes of surpassing indifference—live out their careers in a kind of perpetual Indian summer. Little seems to disturb their easy confidence, born of peering over extended nostrils at less exalted mortals and judging themselves superior.

They know how to work the system.

At the stratospheric financial altitudes in which they operate, what matters is not what they do but whom they *know*, what entrees they can provide. The idea is always to be extending your reach, consolidating your contacts, knowing something that somebody else doesn't know. At this level, it is knowledge, not money, that creates power. The network of private schools, clubs, weddings, funerals, receptions, board meetings, country weekends, and other rounds of encounters provides an effective bush-telegraph for the barter system according to which the Establishment game is played. Deals are made, information is traded, tips are exchanged, recommendations quickly granted or withheld.* Each time, personal debits and credits are carefully noted.

---

*In these higher circles, information has achieved the status of currency. A man's dossier of contacts is very much more important than the functional details of the deals he is engaged in. As well as the informal channels of communication, important exchanges of intelligence go on at the regular meetings of the Conference Board's Canadian Council (whose directors include Roy Bennett of Ford, Ed Grubb of Inco, Alf Powis of

All of this manoeuvring and scheming goes on within the Establishment's carefully prescribed confines, even if business deals occasionally turn into feuds. After the struggle between Power and Argus in the spring of 1975, John A. McDougald, the central pillar of Canada's business Establishment, complained with some justification: "I really don't know what the Establishment is. Here's the Royal Bank, who've been the prime bankers of Argus since the day we started; here's Greenshields, that Argus have been very friendly with and good to for twenty years; here's Nesbitt, Thomson, the same thing—and in spite of all this, they turned against us as soon as the Power Corporation bid came up. . . . People talk about corporate power. There is no such thing. It's personal power that counts. You'll never change that. Whose hands it's in— that's what it all boils down to."

Even when its cohesion is severely strained, the Establishment's habits of trust usually triumph over any tendencies toward suspicion. The process of elite accommodation can be very strong. Like every other elite, the business Establishment operates by exclusion; those who belong behave toward one another very differently from the way they treat everyone else. ("The world of the economic elite," John Porter noted, "appears as a complex network of small groupings interlocked by a high degree of cross membership. Throughout this network runs a thin, but nonetheless perceptible, thread of kinship.")

That an Establishment exists is beyond dispute. How it is perceived depends on the observer. This is the way some of its charter members define their club:

Ian Sinclair, chairman, Canadian Pacific: "You can't operate on a large scale without being associated with the people who run the country's financial institutions. And

---

Noranda, Bob Scrivener of Bell Canada, and Earle McLaughlin of the Royal Bank) and the Canadian Economic Policy Committee of the C.D. Howe Research Institute (whose members include Roy Bennett, Ed Grubb, Alf Powis, Bob Scrivener, and Earle McLaughlin). Another regular international meeting ground is provided by the closed conferences of the Bilderberg Group, which takes its name from a hotel in Holland and is sponsored by Prince Bernhard of the Netherlands. Colin Brown, the insurance super-salesman (he averages two or three million dollars in sales a year) from London, Ontario, regularly charters two DC-8s to fly groups of Canadian executives to the Masters Golf Tournament in Augusta, Georgia.

the people who run the financial institutions have to get input by being on boards of industrial or service companies. And so there is this interplay. In that sense there is an Establishment.

"But people get the idea that in every company there's just one man with power. He's the visible fellow. What you do is build management teams. But one man's got to make the final decision. You listen to things and then you say, 'Goddammit, this is what we're going to do,' and everybody supports you or gets off the team. That's just the way it has to be. But basically, even if you're the visible part, you're still a team operator. A company like Canadian Pacific: no one can run it. It's impossible, and with the theory of management that we're working on, with the profit centre concept, that breaks it down even more."

Leo Kolber, president, Cemp Investments: "There is a Canadian Establishment of sorts, but it's regionalized; some of it is cross-country. Canada would be much poorer if there weren't that Establishment, because the wheels of commerce would go around much, much more slowly. It creates common interests, ways of being helpful to one another, great sources of information. The speed of communication becomes easier when you know one another. . . . The public has this horrendous idea of so-called bigness. In fact, Canada doesn't have bigness; that's one of our great economic weaknesses. The government now has a royal commission to investigate bigness. I do hope they do their job properly. I think they'll find that there is no bigness. Just try to name a dozen pools of private capital in this country."

Richard M. "Dick" Thomson, president, Toronto-Dominion Bank: "Canada is a relatively small country and certainly the business community at the senior level becomes that much smaller. It's centred basically in Toronto and Montreal, though there are certain smaller groupings in perhaps another five cities. It's very easy in Canada for the senior businessmen to know each other. The people who come and go are the presidents of some of the foreign-controlled corporations. So, because of its smallness and the knowledge everybody has of everyone else, it makes for an easy kind of community to keep track of. To get into the Establishment is a matter of proving yourself over a period of time. To be kept out of it, you would have to do something very brash, do something illegal, have a very wild private life. I can think of more ways to describe how you would not be a part of it than I can think of things to say about getting into it. Obviously, there's no charter, no drawn-up regulations."

Donald G. "Bud" Willmot, chairman, Molson Companies: "I don't like the term 'Establishment.' It has connotations of power and large sectors of society have hopes and anticipations that naturally lead them to be critical of any so-called Establishment. It does exist, however, but it's made up of responsible people who do great things for Canada. One of the good things is that communications, for example, between government and the private sector can be so much more effectively handled because of the small size of the country. I've had the pleasure of being in certain small-group situations where the pulse of the economy, the thoughts of the private sector, the concerns of the elected representatives, and so on, were brought together very effectively, which would be difficult to do in other countries with a social structure similar to ours."

Richard Rohmer, Toronto lawyer-novelist-air force general: "Members of any Establishment all know each other and have some degree of business and social connection. That certainly exists in Canada, but it's readily accessible to those who can get in by dint of their performance. Being accepted by the Establishment gives you, more than anything else, a right of access to any of its other members. You can open any door in the country. You find out whether or not you're part of it, when you try to open those doors."

Stephen Jarislowsky, Montreal investment counsellor: "The power structure in Canada is based on cities, based on banks, based on regions. It's all a very cosy arrangement. Businessmen are probably one of the only groups who really know the country from coast to coast because they travel in the West, in the Maritimes, in Montreal and Toronto. . . . The boys in the leading companies all know each other. The fellows in all the financial operations at least have a pretty good understanding of each other. There's competition beyond that, and I think a lot of people in Ottawa underestimate the competition that does take place."

John Craig Eaton, chairman, Eaton's of Canada: "I guess you could say we represent the Canadian Establishment, but it's a funny word. I imagine it means the *status quo*—who's in power, as opposed to the now more violent fringes of society."

George Black, corporate director and former president, Canadian Breweries: "Oh, sure, there's an Establishment in Canada. It consists of about a thousand wealthy families. It works by exclusion, but once in a while a new name pops up, like Paul Desmarais, and then he has to be included in. What it consists of is a sharing of attitudes, even if the people involved don't have the same politics. Nobody tries to exercise very much power or to show off his money because we tend to be a nation of brooders. But even if they don't exercise it or abuse it, money is power."

W.F. "Bill" McLean, president, Canada Packers: "There is a certain kinship among us. I feel that if I get out of my depths in something, I can go to one of these guys I know and ask him. We consult a lot. Though I honestly don't think an Establishment exists, if some fellow had a plan for a new bank and someone we knew trusted him, well, that wouldn't do him any harm."

Robert A. Wisener, Toronto investment dealer: "We live in one of the few dynamic business communities still small enough that you can know it from coast to coast. It would take me all of five minutes to get a rundown on anybody in the Canadian business world. This is quite a remarkable thing. You can't do it in the United States because it's too big. You can't do it in England because you just don't have access to all those people. And here it's not just from Toronto. You can do it just as well from the West Coast or Winnipeg. Winnipeg's tuned right in to the whole thing. There may be a small difference between the French business community and the English one, but there are an awful lot of bridges being built."

Douglas Fullerton, former chairman, National Capital Commission, corporate director, and pivotal business-government co-ordinator: "Power is building your network. Those who have a good network are constantly expanding their power; those who haven't don't—no matter how much wealth they may have. You build your network through personal charm, exchanging favours, and money, but most of all by having information to exchange. One test is if you can always get through on the telephone—if the people who count, whether you've met them or not, know your name. The network operates through a combination of friendship, respect, fear, and hope ('this is a guy who may be able to help me sometime') or just pure charm. It's not family or money that counts, but performance. The process favours the guy who has scored a few goals."

Donald C. "Ben" Webster, president, Helix Investments Limited: "It takes about twenty or thirty years to become part of the real Establishment. The reason it takes so long is that money isn't the only thing that counts. It matters whether you've been honest or you haven't been caught being dishonest. You've got to be a performer, and you can't be in a business that seems to hurt the public, or hurt other people. The business Establishment is a very loose confederation of interests. You operate by knowing people, meeting them in various ways, in common sorts of things. You must also be talking the same language, just like doctors, who can understand each other quickly. It's led by brokers, merchant bankers, people like that, who are not wealthy themselves. The large money is made in industry, or in real estate and shipping. The financial people are usually very intelligent and well dressed and really work hard for a living, working every day, while the man in industry, once he gets things going, can relax a bit, as a rule."

Charles R. Bronfman, president, House of Seagram, Montreal: "There's an Establishment in every part of Canadian society. In the Jewish community, for example, there's an Establishment in that, and most people know damn well when they're in or out of it. In Canadian business there's been an Establishment for a long time. I've been happy to see it changing, because it was such a tight-knit group at one time, with interlocking boards and so on and so forth, that it seemed as if a dozen people basically ran the business end of the country. But now you see a guy like Paul Desmarais all of a sudden come along and uproot a lot of things, and you see some of the young French-Canadian businessmen starting to come alive. . . . It's pathetic, when you think of it, that my father was the first Jewish director of the Bank of Montreal. I mean, that's almost incredible. And then you had all those token French-Canadian directors. This is all definitely changing, and changing for the good."

John C. Parkin, Establishment architect: "The most interesting phenomenon of the Canadian Establishment is that it constantly out-breeds, which is its particular strength. There really isn't a hell of a lot of intermarriage. There are new people all the time. So our Establishment tends not to be self-perpetuating in that sense, except in Newfoundland and possibly in London, Ontario."

Charles I. "Chuck" Rathgeb, chairman, Comstock International Limited: "The Canadian business scene kind of reminds me of the way it used to be in the Canadian Navy right at the beginning of the war in that everybody knew everybody else. The Establishment is mostly based on business friendships, some on personal friendships, obviously, but it's good for the country as long as there's no exclusivity. I don't think it is a club, it's too big for that. There's no group of people sitting around and saying this is what Canada is going to do or anything of that nature;

it's a very loosely formed model. There is room for the newcomer to join in, as new industries and new activities start up. How does a newcomer prove himself, at what point is he admitted? It's simply a matter of accomplishment, of what he's doing in his business. It's performance, not family, that counts." ──

Alf Powis, president, Noranda Mines Limited: "Obviously, there is a group of people in Canada who are running corporations and they tend to know each other. Once you get into a certain position, you've got shared problems with people who are in similar positions. Automatically, I'm going to share certain attitudes, a lot of attitudes, with Peter Gordon at Stelco, for example, just because we're all up against the same sort of thing. Okay, if that then constitutes an Establishment, it certainly exists. . . . But we're different in some ways from the group which preceded us. We've been trained differently, to start with. We've perhaps grown up differently. I was barely alive during the depression. An awful lot of the older people had to live through it. (Maybe we're going to live through it again, and I'll get that experience sooner than I want.) Another difference is that fundamentally I'm a hired gun, while people like Bud McDougald and Nelson Davis are looking after their own money. I don't have any money to speak of; I'm a manager. But we share the same attitude toward profit. One of the things that bothers hell out of me is all the crap thrown out about profits. I would certainly like to think that I'm as heavily oriented toward profit as Bud McDougald."

Gordon Sharwood, chief executive officer, Guaranty Trust Company: "Being part of the Establishment is essentially sharing the trust and knowledge you have with others. You see somebody in the washroom of the Toronto Club and you say, 'Did you hear that so-and-so is doing this-and-that?' and you become a part of this sort of informal network of intelligence that gets put together through snatches of conversation all over the place from all sorts of people. If you go to the perpetual receptions that are always going on, you exchange little bits of gossip. Information gets exchanged to those who are part of the

Establishment, and not quite so easily to those who are not."

John Robarts, *corporate director, former premier of Ontario*: "I'm not sedate enough to be a real Establishment member. They all wear those menopausal suits, and I find myself secretly laughing at them and wanting to ask: 'When did you last get roaring drunk at Winston's during noon hour?' "

CONTRAILS OF THE ESTABLISHMENT'S PATHS KEEP CROSS-
ING THROUGH LONG LIFETIMES IN UNLIKELY PLACES.
When Ian Sinclair was a young undergraduate at Wesley College, in Winnipeg, his history teacher was Jack Pickersgill, then just back from Oxford and not yet into politics. Three decades later, Sinclair, now chairman of the CPR, found himself dealing with his former professor, first as minister of transport in the Pearson government and later as president of the Canadian Transport Commission. Recently, Sinclair's CPR helped finance Pickersgill's memoir of the St. Laurent years through a grant to Carleton University. In 1923, when Jack Clyne was studying law at the University of British Columbia, he was nominated for a Rhodes Scholarship. The field had been narrowed down to himself and one other candidate whose chances were poor because he played no sports. Clyne organized an interclass rugby competition and encouraged his rival to play. Ten minutes into the game, the neophyte broke his arm, which was enough to impress the Rhodes judges with his sportsmanship. And that was how Norman Robertson, who later became Canada's top diplomat, got to Oxford.*

---

*Sports has long been an important catalyst for business Establishment contacts. If there is such a thing as a sports Establishment it should include the Bronfmans (Expos for the Cemp group and Canadiens for the Edper group), the Molsons of Montreal; two Websters in Montreal, R. Howard, trying for a big-league baseball franchise in Toronto, and his nephew Lorne; and John Bassett and two Bassett sons in Toronto, along with three young Eatons and two sailing Gooderhams, Bill and George, and a Gooderham cousin, Peter Maclachlan. Also under sail: the Olands of Halifax; Loi Killam and George O'Brien in Vancouver; and in Toronto, Gerhard Moog, Robert Grant, W Bernard Herman, Jim Crang, Paul Phelan, Burke Seitz, Gordon Fisher, Douglas Hatch, Walter Zwig, and Bruce Sully (who drives over from Goderich). At the track: E.P. Taylor and his son, Charles, Charlie Burns, George Hendrie, Jack

A unique institution that has bound five generations of Canada's business Establishmentarians together is Clarkson, Gordon and Company, the Toronto accountancy house. With branches in eighteen cities, 176 partners, and a total payroll exceeding two thousand, it is the oldest and most illustrious auditing firm in Canada. Its imprimatur on a balance sheet is tantamount to a royal seal of approval. "But," Barbara Moon pointed out in a profile of the company,* "to the connoisseurs of the Canadian Establishment, Clarkson, Gordon is something more interesting; it is the unofficial but effective finishing school —the only one in Canada aside from certain fashionable Toronto and Montreal law firms and investment houses —for young men of the Upper Class."

For reasons not entirely documented, the secret badge of the true Clarkson, Gordon man has become the garters most of them use to hold up their executive-length socks. A.J. "Pete" Little, a Clarkson, Gordon alumnus, now a director of Brascan, was startled at one annual meeting to hear his old firm's audit attacked by several shareholders. The discussion ended when Eric Warren, a prominent stockholder and Gutta Percha heir, stood up and declared: "I trust the Clarkson, Gordon audit because Pete Little has his garters on." Founded in 1864 by Thomas Clarkson, a British emigrant (who married three times and had sixteen children), the firm became two partnerships in 1913, when Colonel H.D.L. Gordon (Upper Canada College, Royal Military College) lent his name and prestige to the accounting practice and four of the Clarksons ran the trustee and bankruptcy partnership. Gordon's sons Walter and Duncan have since been partners in the busi-

---

Stafford, Conn Smythe, John Mooney, J.E. Frowde Seagram, George Gardiner, Jack Diamond, and J. Louis Lévesque. (The strong Alberta entry has been broken up by the deaths of Max Bell and Wilder Ripley, and their erstwhile partner Frank McMahon now races out of California.) The football moneybackers: David Loeb (Ottawa Rough Riders); Sam Berger (Montreal Alouettes); Bill Hodgson and Sam Belzberg (Toronto Argonauts); and Bob Kramer of Regina (godfather to the Saskatchewan Roughriders). Men-about-sports: the Hatches, the McNamaras, Chuck Rathgeb, George Mara, Harold Ballard, and Sydney Cooper in Toronto; Colin Brown of London, Ontario; Clayton Delbridge, Jim Pattison, Poldi and Peter Bentley, Herb Capozzi, and Coley Hall in Vancouver (and Peter Graham, operating in San Diego); Dr. Charles Allard and Zane Feldman in Edmonton; Ben Hatskin in Winnipeg; and the Piggott family in Saskatoon.

*In the *Globe Magazine*, May 1, 1965.

ness, which has rapidly expanded into management consulting.*

To have arrived in the Establishment, you feel that you know its fellow members, even though you've never met. "It's a small business community and there are very definite loops of knowledge," says Gordon Sharwood of Guaranty Trust. "The other night, for example, I met Harrison McCain from New Brunswick for the first time. 'I know all about you, Sharwood,' he told me, and of course I knew all about him."

To the dispassionate observer, it sometimes seems as if members of Canada's Establishment spend most of their waking hours on one mammoth conference call. Few business secrets or rumours last more than a day as the private possession of any group. For those addicted to the personal exercise of power, corporate machinations can provide a giddy, almost sexual sensation.

What makes it practical for the business Establishment to act and feel so unanimously on most issues is the tight concentration of corporate power. A relief map of Canadian companies would not show a plateau with the occasional bulge, but region after region of high mountain ranges, with the top hundred peaks giving the whole economy its essential contours. Of Canada's 170,000 active corporations, the hundred largest control more than half the country's $300 billion in corporate assets.† As Appendix C illustrates, nearly two-thirds of these corporations are U.S. or foreign owned.‡ Their presidents, chairmen, and directors act merely as surrogates, colonial administrators responsible to invisible men in a foreign land,

---

*Clarkson, Gordon's ex-partners have included V.W.T. Scully, chairman of the board, Steel Company of Canada; W.L. Gordon, Minister of Finance; J.G. Glassco, president, Brascan; J.H. Moore, president, Brascan; E.C. Freeman-Attwood, executive vice-president, Brascan; E.H. Orser, president, T. Eaton Company.

†Since 1900, nearly five thousand large Canadian companies have disappeared through mergers and takeovers. Some of the more striking offspring of corporate marriages are Acklands, Canada Cement Lafarge, Carling O'Keefe, Dominion Textile, Jannock, Domtar, Molson Companies, Neonex, Noranda, Stelco, and Standard Brands. Aside from the chartered banks and the CDC, only five major investment pools now exist: Argus Corp., Power Corp., Cemp Investments, Brascan, and Canadian Pacific Investments.

‡The Americans have no trouble identifying shifts in Canadian corporate power. The position of serving on the advisory committee of the Chase Manhattan Bank has moved from Bob Winters of Brascan, to Maj.-Gen. Bruce Matthews of Argus, to Ian Sinclair of the CPR.

transitory creations of offshore head offices who exercise little real clout and despite their very considerable collective authority figure only marginally in any audit of personal business power on the Canadian scene.* Most, though not all, U.S. companies treat Canada as a slightly backward extension of their northern sales territories, reflecting the advice of Jacques Maisonrouge, head of the IBM World Trade Corporation, who has noted that "for business purposes, the boundaries that separate one nation from another are no more real than the equator."

The Americanization of Canadian business will be a topic covered in a later volume, but few members of Canada's Establishment have resisted the trend, making them members of the only elite in world history that has cheerfully participated in its own demise. E.P. Taylor's attitude is typical: "If it weren't for the racial issue in the U.S. and the political problems they have, I would think that the two countries could come together. . . . I'm against this trend of trying to reduce American ownership in Canadian companies. I think nature has to take its course."

This let's-surrender-with-profit syndrome has prevented Canada's capitalist class from ever attaining any strong consciousness of itself. "As a nation, we seem to have lacked some vital fibre of the spirit in the challenging days after World War II," wrote W.A. Wilson. "Constantly told by our government and our business leaders that it was inevitable, we largely turned over to the Americans the development of this country during a period of exceptional opportunity. Led by government and business, Canada became the only advanced country which actively sought economic colonization by the United States."†

A good case can perhaps be made for the proposition that the institutions housing the greatest influence in the

---

*There are exceptions. Roy Bennett, who heads Ford of Canada, which is Canada's largest corporation (because Ford-U.S. channels most of its foreign sales through its Canadian subsidiary), has become a real presence in this country. (In 1974, his operations showed a 19.8 per cent return on equity—three times better than the results of his parent corporation.) Bill Twaits, who served as president or chairman of Imperial Oil for fourteen years, turned himself into one of the Canadian business community's most respected spokesmen. When he retired in 1974, he was offered some forty directorships, but Imperial still asked him to give up Box 39-B, which he had proudly held at the Royal Agricultural Winter Fair since 1960.

†*Montreal Star*, February 16, 1974.

country are the hotels that ring most Canadian airports. The smug and savvy men who are the foreign owners of the lion's share of this country's industrial and natural resource wealth daily land their private jets in Montreal, Toronto, Calgary, and Vancouver. In Toronto, dozens of limousines are booked in advance for the five-minute transfer to the local Hilton, Howard Johnson's, Cara Inn, or Constellation Hotel.* Canadian operations managers (flanked by nervous accountants) arrive to give their reports in private suites that combine office and sleeping facilities. Orders are issued. The following morning (or the same day, if there is one more territory to straighten out), the parent-company executive is ferried back to his waiting jet. He departs as quietly as he came.

THE AUTHORITY OF THE MEN WHO RUN THE MAJOR CORPORATIONS can be understood only in the context of the institutions they operate. The corporate order is a system of private governments lacking the restraints of public accountability. The large companies not only dominate their own industries but become centres of power around which are clustered satellite enterprises (and men) whose fates are determined by their actions. The big corporations comprise organized markets, and the men who rise to dominate them hold sway over empires that extend far beyond their official titles.

In their classic study of this phenomenon, Adolf Berle and Gardiner Means documented that ownership of modern U.S. corporations has become so diffused that most of them no longer are instruments of private property.†

---

*In Toronto alone, there are now ten large hotels adjoining the International Airport at Malton. Their average occupancy rate in 1974 was 91.7 per cent. They have golf courses, gymnasiums, and some of the fanciest dining rooms in the city. The shower in the Presidential Suite at the Constellation has an optional nozzle mounted under the standard fixture for executives who wish to freshen up without getting their hair wet. The toilet has a wall telephone.

†A.A. Berle, Jr., and Gardiner C. Means, *The Modern Corporation and Private Property* (New York: Commerce Clearing House, 1932). John Kenneth Galbraith took this theory one step further by claiming, in his *The New Industrial State* (Boston: Houghton Mifflin, 1967), that the real power has been passing from up-front executives to corporate bureaucracies whose authority flows out of their technical knowledge. This "technostructure" is much more interested in growth than in profits, since the prestige and salaries of its members depend more on long-term expansion than on short-run returns.

With the growing separation between control and owner-ship, American corporations have become dominated by their managements. This is much less true in Canada, where power has tended to flow instead to corporate di-rectors. "The board is the formalized means of establishing power relations," says Wallace Clement in *The Canadian Corporate Elite*. "As stock ownership became widely dis-persed, major owners were forced to formalize their con-trol through this body." As arbiters between owners and managers, the directors perform a crucial function. Few limits exist on the exercise of their authority.* They can move factories without moving their employees, fire presi-dents, ignore shareholders, hatch new company towns or, as one British Columbia court case confirmed, sell a company's entire assets.

The *Financial Post's Directory of Directors* lists four-teen thousand names, but fewer than a thousand of the named individuals possess any significant clout. Qualifica-tions for becoming a director differ, though one absolute essential is the ability (unless you happen to be a majority stockholder) to stay awake during board meetings. Anoth-er supremely important virtue seems to be the knack of being able to conduct yourself through a meeting with social grace, breaking tensions with engaging small talk and charming little asides. The suitable director must, above all, have a cast of mind not dissimilar from that of his colleagues. "It's like a club," says John A. McDougald, the Argus chairman. "You tend to invite on your board directors you get on with."

As the success of corporations grows increasingly de-pendent on the ability to minimize tax burdens and deal with government regulatory agencies, more and more places around board-room tables are being filled from the large law firms. "In many countries, a directorship is offered as a plum to a deserving someone whom the company can do something for," noted the late Russell

---

*Ownership and control are so separate that most directors have to own only a relatively small qualifying holding in the companies they oversee. In the CPR, for example, directors must hold a minimum of two thousand shares. The entire board, comprising twenty-four of the most influential businessmen in the country, owns a combined total of only 0.17 per cent of the outstanding CPR stock, yet sets the company's policies.

Bell, a former head of Greenshields and Company. "But in Canada, a director is usually chosen for what he can contribute to the company." Besides exercising policy control, directors impose their power on management through their boards' audit and executive compensation committees.

Exceptions to all this are the boards that still include one or more members who hold a majority of their company's stock.* For example, the board of Canada Packers, which is controlled by Bill McLean through his family's foundation, is made up mainly of inside managers, even though with annual sales of more than $1.5 billion it is Canada's tenth largest corporation.

A recent survey by the Conference Board showed that only 20 per cent of directors are inside managers, that the average age of all Canadian directors is fifty-eight and that each one receives up to $10,800 in annual retainers and per-meeting fees. Two classes of directors may be unique to Canada. There is an expanding roster of Establishment names willing to lend their prestige as a token presence on American boards—men like Marcel Bélanger of Quebec City, John Nichol of Vancouver, Dr. Murray Ross of Toronto, Davidson Dunton of Ottawa, and John O'Brien of Montreal. A more interesting group are the professional directors, still few in number, who have no permanent corporate links but float between large corporations offering their considerable expertise to boards that invite their participation. They include Tony Griffin, now a director of fifteen corporations; A.J. Little (four); J. Douglas Gibson (thirteen); Floyd Chalmers (fourteen); William Arbuckle (twenty-one); John Robarts (ten); Don Anderson (fourteen); George Mara (nine); D.A. McIntosh (seventeen); Louis Rasminsky (seven); and Francis Winspear (six).

"Business policy must start somewhere," says Winspear, an Edmonton industrialist (Winham Investments) and re-

---

*When Arthur Vining Davis, who owned the controlling block of stock in the Aluminum Company of America and resigned as chairman at ninety "because of the pressure of other business," was confronted by an obdurate group of directors who voted against one of his pet propositions, he settled the argument by telling them: "Some days we count the votes around this table and other days we weigh them. Today we'll weigh them."

tired accountant, "and it should best start with men who have experience, imagination, and vitality. This, of necessity, must represent a small group in any business community." The group is made even smaller by the fact that through mazes of interlocking directorships, one man can exert many times the equivalent of his private influence. The intelligence (information, not necessarily grey matter) that goes into business decisions is derived largely from the informal chatter that goes on before board meetings and the luncheons that follow. Shared directorates provide a unique and important means of intercorporate communication. Horizontal interlocks include directors who serve on boards of competing companies (until recently, for example, Oscar Lundell, a Vancouver lawyer, was a director of both Crown Zellerbach and B.C. Forest Products); vertical interlocks unite a company with one of its main suppliers (J. Norman Hyland, for instance, is a director of both MacMillan Bloedel and Pacific Press —the West Coast's largest producer and largest purchaser of newsprint). About a quarter of Canadian corporate directors have significant interlocking connections.* "Conflicts of interest are rampant in the system," says Douglas Fullerton, formerly of the National Capital Commission, who has wide contacts inside the business community. "The almost incestuous nature of the interlocking directorate structure inhibits competition and change, hindering acceptance of new ideas."†

One of the few moves Ottawa has taken against this practice was to prohibit bank directors from sitting on the boards of trust companies as well. The measure draws a characteristically caustic comment from Bud McDougald. "This theory on interconnecting directorates is all bunk," he says. "I was a director of Crown Trust for at least twenty-five years. I was a director of the Bank of Com-

---

*The boards of the chartered banks provide the most important concentrating influences (for details, see the table on pages 110–114). Other boards that perform this function include TransCanada PipeLines, CPR, Bell Canada, MacMillan Bloedel, Inco, Steel Company of Canada, Power Corp., Argus Corp., Brascan, Simpsons, Sun Life, and Royal Trust.

†Legal in Canada, interlocking directorates are prohibited in the U.S. In 1971 Ron Basford, then minister of consumer and corporate affairs, introduced legislation to set up a "competitive practices tribunal, with powers to prohibit interlocks that have the effect of significantly lessening competition." It disappeared from the Commons Order Paper and has not been revived.

merce for the same length of time. On the board of the
trust company we had seventeen directors of various banks
—the Commerce, the Montreal, the Royal, and the
Toronto-Dominion. For instance, Eric Phillips was on the
Crown Trust board; he was also a director of the Royal.
Vacy Ash was president of Shell Oil and a director of the
Bank of Montreal, and so on. Never in my entire career
did I ever see anything that would smack of a conflict of
interest. Because that class of fellow doesn't have a conflict of interest. If he did, he wouldn't be on that board, as
far as I'm concerned. The people who make all these
charges are the kind of people that, if they were in these
positions, *would* have conflicts of interest. They plugged all
the holes so the net result of the 1967 Bank Act revision
was that we had to retire seventeen directors off the board
of the Crown Trust. It didn't do the banks or the trust
company any good. It didn't do anybody any good. If I
had ever seen where anybody had taken advantage of
something they had learned at the trust company or at the
bank, because I was quite close to both at the time, I
would have fired them like that, but there never was. Still,
the people that write these acts, this is the way their minds
work. They think: 'If I were in that position I'd do such
and such, so we'd better plug that hole.' "

THE GROUP THAT PROVIDES DIRECTORS WITH THEIR MAN-
DATES—and should be the most vitally concerned with
their performance and their ethics—is blissfully ignored
by everyone concerned. Shareholders in Canadian companies have been disfranchised by both their own timidity
and most directors' arrogance in dealing with them. "The
annual shareholders' meeting of most corporations has
turned into a ritualistic farce in which the main objective of executives seems to be to meet their legal
requirements with the least possible fuss and embarrassment," Ronald Anderson, the *Globe and Mail*'s financial
columnist, has noted. "The annual meeting is carefully
structured and conditioned in a way that keeps the initiative firmly in the hands of management. Ordinary shareholders, even those who are long term investors in a
company's shares and who are genuinely interested in the

corporation's welfare, can expect an abrupt and uninformative response to any questions they may raise."*

The definitive statement on management-shareholder relations may have been made by a director and general manager of Cassiar Asbestos Corporation, who looked out at the glum faces staring back at him during one of the company's annual meetings and broke the deep silence with this comment: "If you're as confused about the asbestos business as we are, I don't blame you for not asking questions." In 1965, at the first confrontation between shareholders and directors of Windfall Oils and Mines, after a stormy royal commission inquiry into the directors' questionable ethics (which boosted the price of the shares from 57 cents to $5.60 and back down again), not a single shareholder asked a question. The entire annual meeting lasted exactly twelve minutes.† At the 1974 Bank of Montreal annual meeting (which followed its disastrous decline in profits), no shareholder volunteered any comments (as opposed to the 1973 meeting, when one shareholder rose and asked Arnold Hart, the chairman: "Why don't you have a reception with a few drinks the way they do after Seagram's annual meeting, or at that other bank?").

One of the few organized shareholder uprisings took place in 1954, when directors of Coleman Collieries, which operates coal mines in the Crowsnest Pass region, of Alberta, mailed bondholders a request that they exchange their 5 per cent first-mortgage certificates (which included a provision for sharing in any petroleum discoveries on company land) for a new issue at a lower over-all interest rate and with no oil rights. Notice of the December 29 annual meeting to discuss the switch didn't reach most shareholders until December 20. Meanwhile a rumour had leaked out that the company had made a deal with a U.S. petroleum firm to explore some land on which it had drilling rights.

---

*Globe and Mail, October 4, 1974.

†A dramatic exception to this silent treatment was the frequent performance of the late W.R. "One-Share" Sweeny, a former New Jersey cab driver, who bought small shareholdings so that he could badger directors for better results and more information. He wasn't above making deals with company presidents *not* to ask questions for an appropriate consideration and eventually acquired a black Rolls-Royce and the Concourse Building in downtown Toronto on the proceeds.

Only six irritated bondholders, who battled stormy weather for the 165-mile drive from Calgary in a taxi, reached the town of Coleman in time. But at the meeting it turned out that F.J. Harquail, then managing director of Coleman Collieries, had voting control of Hillcrest Collieries, which held 92 per cent of a subsidiary named Hillcrest Mohawk Collieries. Hillcrest Mohawk's main asset was $3.5 millions' worth of Coleman bonds— enough to outvote the dejected, travel-weary bondholders.

The company that stages the strangest annual meetings is Premier Trust of Toronto. Its general manager since 1934 has been a crusty lawyer named Thomas B. Holmes, who held the presidency from 1940 till 1974, when he stepped down for his son, Thomas H., a doctor. The elder Holmes, who remains general manager, operates on the simple assumption that shareholders are entitled only to the information they may be able to drag out of him; if they get too obstreperous, he merely overrules their requests. At Premier's 1951 annual meeting, as shareholders began yelling for a more adequate disclosure of the company's true profit position, Holmes shouted back: "You're out of order! You're all out of order!" A farmer-shareholder from St. Catharines stood up and made an impassioned plea. "This meeting," he said, "reminds me of my old hen on the farm. She is slopping around and all of a sudden she senses danger. She sounds the alarm and all the hens flop underneath the trees. *That's what's going on here!*" Moved by his oratory, fellow shareholders took up the chant and started dancing around Holmes, yelling: "*He thinks we're all chickens— we're just plucked fowl!*" The meeting lasted eight hours, but Holmes never once relented, even after one of his appointees was referred to as "a skunk."

CANADA'S BUSINESS ESTABLISHMENT OPERATES LIKE SOME MINIATURE SOLAR SYSTEM, with orbits of influence grouped around the particularly powerful stars in its firmament. It consists of sets of overlapping orbits without a common centre. Power is what counts, and power means the ability to get your own way, to shape events, to make things happen or stop them from taking place.

The list of the 175 most influential Canadian businessmen in Appendix D is based partly on the author's observations but more significantly on a kind of floating consensus among the Establishment itself about who counts and who doesn't. These are the pivotal people, the power brokers who carry the proxies for the great law firms and financial institutions, the congenial operators of the system.

Some have hacked their way onto this list, assembling power by conquest, like some latter-day Machiavelli freed from geographical restraints. Others have appeared quietly, almost anonymously. For example, George Hitchman, Ted McDowell, C.M. Laidley, and H.E. Wyatt are included only because they happen to be the officers of four of the large banks who approve major corporate loans. The next group in this category would probably be the invisible men who manage the country's large private pension plans, which now have assets of about $36 billion, increasing at an annual rate of $2 billion. Always, the list is changing.

POWER IS APPLIED THROUGH ONE OF FIVE MAJOR AND THREE MINOR GEOGRAPHICAL CLUSTERS ACROSS THE COUNTRY. This is how they work:

Montreal

MONTREAL REMAINS THE COUNTRY'S MOST CHARMING METROPOLIS, the only large town, other than Quebec City, where the visitor can become aware of a strong sense of history and a feeling of continuity along with it. This tingle of past glories comes from the Mountain, the St. Lawrence River, the archbishop's palace, the restored buildings around Bonsecours Market, restaurants like Chez La Mère Michelle and Ste Amable, and, of course, the overwhelming French presence. There are still men here whose great-grandfathers auctioned the beaver pelts, ran the sawmills, built the railways, dredged the rivers, founded the elites that first exploited the Canadian hinterland.

Yet there prevails among the English a sombre mood

of acquiescence after the fear that built up during the sixties and reached its crescendo in the dark days of October, 1970. Montreal has the air of a place that's lost something. And what Montrealers have lost (at least what the English-Canadian Establishment has lost) is the feeling that they live in the centre of the action—the chic, vital, terrific, necessary place to be if you're a Canadian entrepreneur.

English-speaking businessmen have become a careful lot. Because they are the people who have traditionally run the city's—and the province's—economic life, taken the risks, provided the leadership and the jobs, little very new or exciting is happening. Montreal is no longer the centre of banking, finance, or manufacturing. The decline of the Bank of Montreal, the token presence of the Royal Bank and the CPR, both of which do much of their important wheeling and dealing elsewhere, the quiet shifts of key head-office personnel by the Molson family, Texaco Canada, IAC, and Royal Trust, among others, are all symptoms of the decline. Even Paul Desmarais, Montreal's one great vital business force of the seventies, now spends most of his time and energy away from the city, trying to break into Toronto. English-speaking Montrealers who aren't "old family" are moving away, while outsiders (Ian Sinclair at Canadian Pacific, Peter Curry at Power Corporation, William Mulholland at the Bank of Montreal) are being brought in to head the big firms.

Montreal has become like Boston or Philadelphia in the eighties and nineties, as New York outstripped them by grabbing the business power that counted. Toronto may be crass, brash, may not have the super-elegant women or the super-*raffinée* cooking in the restaurants, but it is intensely alive. To the dispassionate Torontonian, English Montreal's upper-class women, with their untouchable coiffures and matched-to-their-costumes purses of leather from Hermes of Paris, seem a little old-style, hidebound, out of it, as they drink and dine and dance at the Ritz, and so do the earnest men in the three-piece dark suits who are with them.

Even the old families have been reduced to making limp gestures against the onrushing realities of the twentieth century. The descendants of Sir Hugh Allan were so in-

furiated by Pierre Berton's treatment of the shipowner's
dealings with the Pacific railway that they telephoned all
their friends to boycott his books.* One of the Allan great-
granddaughters couldn't resist the temptation and was
spotted sneaking into Morgan's to read snatches of the
first volume behind the clerks' backs, memorizing all the
illicit details.

Many old-family English Montrealers project two somewhat contrary reactions to the sad state in which they
find themselves: slight surprise and a kind of relief. They
always thought the rest of Canada was a bore. It's relaxing,
now, to sink back into the elegance of times past and go
right on believing that Toronto is a place where only
vulgar money-managers want to live, and that what lies
west of Toronto is something no civilized person con-
siders.

Montreal looks inward, faces east—across the Atlantic
—to England and France, and dreams of the past; Toronto looks outward, faces south to the United States, and
dreams of the future.

This absence of vitality in Montreal's English community is traceable to many factors. The Square Mile
(where the wealthy old families lived before and after
the turn of the century) was decimated by World War I.
The CPR fortunes moved into third-generation hands and
ceased taking investment initiatives. Business first began
its exodus when Sir Henry Thornton formed the CNR in
1922 out of the bankrupt shells of the Canadian Northern, the Grand Trunk, and the Grand Trunk Pacific, allowing the Bank of Commerce in Toronto to become a
major force in national railways. Meanwhile the Ontario
government had been financing railway construction into
its own northland as early as 1902, which triggered the
Cobalt, Porcupine, and Kirkland Lake mining booms. The
riches of the Canadian Shield thus came under Toronto's
dominance. While Montrealers continued to regard the
mining market as "a bit undignified," speculative wealth
poured into Toronto. Amalgamation of the Toronto

---

*Because the Royal Trust Company sponsored the television adapta-
tion of Berton's *The National Dream*, the Allan descendants reportedly
withdrew their still substantial fortune from the firm's care.

Stock Exchange and the Standard Stock and Mining Exchange in 1934 contrasted with the Montreal Stock Exchange's insistence on relegating mining stocks to trading on the floor of the lesser Montreal Curb Market.*

None of this had much visible effect on the English Montrealers of the thirties, forties, or fifties, who lived out their lives with an imperviousness that Dickens would have found entirely contemporary. JAMM† still ruled the roost.

St. James Street, once the chief metaphor for Canadian capitalism, has suffered the most ignominious decline. The floor of the old Montreal Stock Exchange has been turned into a theatre, and there are empty buildings sporting hopeful FOR RENT signs, second-rate shops, and greasy restaurants. Business has moved up the hill to cluster around Place Ville Marie. The main Wasp holdouts left on St. James are the Bank of Montreal and Nesbitt, Thomson, which is housed in the former head office of the Merchants' Bank, the old Allan bank, which was absorbed by the Montreal in 1921. "There has certainly been a move away from Montreal," admits Paul Desmarais, the Power Corporation chairman. "Toronto is now the power centre. It has the advantage also of being the provincial capital and is without a doubt the country's financial centre. In Montreal, you still have two of the big banks headquartered here, but their presence in Toronto is very real, especially with those two new huge buildings. All the financing in the mining industry has been done traditionally in Toronto. It's become the decision centre. Money and people go where the action is."

One problem that has continually plagued English Montrealers is that their numbers are too small to afford them much of a provincial or federal power base. Financial power eventually moves—for its own protection—to where there is also political power, and that may be the ultimate reason why the core of Canada's business

---

*The Montreal Curb Market became the Canadian Stock Exchange in 1953; in January, 1974, the Montreal Stock Exchange absorbed the CSE listings.

†That's the Junior Associates of the Montreal Museum of Fine Arts, to which all the young bluebloods belonged.

Establishment has permanently altered its address from Montreal to Toronto.

AT THE MOMENT, WASPS STILL DOMINATE THE ECONOMY OF QUEBEC, BUT THE PROVINCE'S SURVIVING BUSINESS ESTABLISHMENT is gradually being taken over by French-speaking Canadians who live either in Montreal or in Quebec City. French Canada's own most dynamic business presence (though he comes from Sudbury) is Paul Desmarais.

Probably only about a dozen French Canadians qualify in the context of the national business Establishment: André Charron (president of Lévesque, Beaubien), Jacques Courtois (the lawyer, bank vice-president, and Tory fund-raiser), Jean de Granpré (president of Bell Canada), Claude Hébert (war hero, independently wealthy corporate executive), Pierre Nadeau (CEO of Petrofina and Royal Commissioner), Jean Ostiguy (head of his own investment house), Paul Paré (CEO of Imasco and a major influence in both the French and the English communities), Yves Pratte (chairman of Air Canada), and Lucien Rolland (the paper company president and corporate director).

Among others with more of a province-wide influence are René Amyot (Quebec City lawyer and corporate director), Pierre Arbour (Caisse de Dépôt), Louis Beaubien (the senator and Tory fund-raiser), Philippe de Gaspé Beaubien (head of Télémedia), Laurent Beaudoin (president of Bombardier), Roger Beaulieu (lawyer and corporate director), Michel Bélanger (Montreal Stock Exchange president), André Bisson (Quebec chief of the Bank of Nova Scotia), Robert Boyd (president of the James Bay Energy Corporation), Marcel Caron (the senior Montreal partner of Clarkson, Gordon), Marcel Cazavan (chairman of Caisse de Dépôt), Guy Charbonneau (insurance agency executive and chief Tory fund-raiser), Etienne Crevier (insurance executive), Charles Demers (corporate director), Robert Demers (lawyer, ex-treasurer of the Quebec Liberal party, and chief government negotiator during the FLQ crisis of 1970; now head of the Quebec Securities Commission), Louis

Desmarais (CEO of Canada Steamship Lines), Marc
Dhavernas (financier and corporate director), Jacques
Francoeur (newspaper publisher), Claude Frenette (the
province's most idealistic entrepreneur), Louis P. Gélinas
(Liberal senator and corporate director), Jean-Paul
Gignac (CEO of Sidbec-Dosco), Roland Giroux (president
of Hydro-Québec and chief financial adviser to Premier
Bourassa), Louis Hébert and Germain Perreault (Banque
Canadienne Nationale), Bernard Lamarre (consulting
engineer), Léo Lavoie (of the Banque Provinciale),
Raymond Lavoie (CEO of Crédit Foncier Franco-Canadien
and corporate director), Jean Lesage (the former premier), Roger Létourneau (Quebec City lawyer and cor-
porate director), J. Louis Lévesque (a capitalist in the
E.P. Taylor tradition), André Monast (Quebec City lawyer and corporate director), Jean-Michel Paris (Caisse
de Dépôt), Jean Parisien (deputy chairman of Power
Corporation), Gérard Parizeau (the insurance man),
Pierre Peladeau (newspaper publisher), Laurent Picard
(the former CBC president, now in charge of Marine
Industries), Marcel Piché (lawyer and corporate director), Gérard Plourde (CEO of UAP Inc.), Jean-Marie
Poitras (CEO of Laurentian Mutual Assurance, Quebec
City), Claude Pratte (the Quebec City lawyer and corporate director), Maurice Riel (lawyer and chief Liberal
fund-raiser), Alfred Rouleau of Lévis (who heads the
Caisses Populaires), and Antoine Turmel (of Provigo).

This roster's most significant omission is that it lists no
Simards, until recently the wealthiest and most powerful clan in Quebec. Buffeted by scandal, internal rivalries,
and weak management, the heirs to the Simard fortune
no longer exercise an influential presence in the province,
though they maintain their political clout through Robert
Bourassa, a Simard son-in-law.

Joseph Simard's private duchy at Sorel encompassed a
forest of industrial installations worth a billion dollars,
strewn around the junction of the Richelieu and St.
Lawrence rivers. His place at the top of Liberal patronage
lists had allowed him to buy, in 1937, the federal government's shipyards at Sorel and a large dredging fleet for
only a million dollars. Wartime federal contracts followed
that eventually placed one of North America's largest and

most profitable naval armament works under Simard's control. He and his brothers built thirty Liberty ships, dozens of minesweepers and corvettes; their private tanker and dredging fleets ranged the world. Among them, the Simards were directors of forty-six companies building everything from garbage trucks to the RCN's flagship icebreaker, *Labrador*. Every venture they touched seemed to turn a profit. In 1953, Joe Simard sent to Seattle for the seven-hundred-ton schooner *Fantome*, which he acquired by paying her overdue docking charges. The *Fantome* had been abandoned in Seattle by A.E. Guinness, the Anglo-Irish brewing millionaire, at the outbreak of World War II. One of the most luxurious vessels ever built, requiring a crew of forty, she had only eight passenger cabins and a built-in fresh-milk dispenser—a deck locker to accommodate a sea-going cow. Simard bought the yacht because he wanted to put her two auxiliary engines into one of his tugboats. But a personal inspection persuaded him to wait for a customer. When Aristotle Socrates Onassis, the Greek shipowner, saw the *Fantome*, he immediately bought her for many times Simard's investment, as a wedding present for Prince Rainier and Grace Kelly.

Whenever the Simard shipyard ran out of work, Joseph or Edouard or Ludger would simply pay Ottawa a visit, and orders would magically follow. The family also stage-managed the provincial Liberals. Georges-Emile Lapalme, who led the party before Jean Lesage, recalled how, in 1950, he was, in effect, handed the job, when he was a Member of Parliament. He was called to Sorel by Edouard Simard and told: "The prophet Elie* and myself wish to remind you that a job is open in Quebec. Mr. Godbout has resigned as leader of the Liberal party. There will be a convention in the spring. The prophet Elie wishes you to know that we are thinking of you and that you would certainly be chosen if you were a candidate. That is also my opinion."

In 1958, Joseph Simard's niece Andrée married Robert

---

*His way of referring to Senator Elie Beauregard, who was then Speaker of the Senate and Louis St. Laurent's chief organizer in Quebec.

Bourassa, a young Montreal lawyer who had studied at Oxford and Harvard, been secretary of a royal commission, and who in 1970 became Quebec's twenty-second premier. Marine Industries, the Simard holding instrument, eventually came under control of the Quebec government through the province's General Investment Corporation, and in mid-1975, the company was negotiating a merger with Bombardier. The six Simard nieces and nephews had previously continued to hold 21.2 per cent of Marine through a family trust called La Compagnie de Charlevoix. Mme Bourassa, her brother Claude (a minister in the Bourassa government), and another brother (René) and sister (Michelle) each also owned 23.7 per cent of Clauremiand Limited, another family holding apparatus, which in turn controlled 73 per cent of Paragon Business Forms, which became an important supplier of office equipment to the Quebec government. This was the conflict of interest, first revealed in *La Presse*, that triggered the decline in the Premier's popularity. At about the same time, a crown prosecutor in the Hamilton Harbour dredging scandal claimed that a consortium of three companies, Marine Industries, J.P. Porter, and McNamara, had agreed to pay a competitor $400,000 for submitting an artificially high bid in 1971 to deepen the St. Lawrence channel off Ile d'Orléans—the largest single dredging project ever undertaken in Canada. J.P. Porter is controlled by the Simard interests, and Jean Simard was charged in regard to the alleged contract rigging. Long before any of these scandals surfaced, the bulk of the Simard fortune had been quietly channelled out of Canada (through yet another holding company, called Simcor) into Bahamas tax havens for investment in Texas oil and other offshore ventures.

THE JEWISH SECTOR OF THE BUSINESS ESTABLISHMENT IN QUEBEC is also in the process of changing its leadership. Dominated for most of three decades by Samuel Bronfman (who died in 1971), its unofficial interim chief spokesman is Lazarus Phillips, a founding partner of the Phillips and Vineberg law firm, former vice-president of the Royal Bank, director of seven large corporations, ex-senator, Talmudic scholar, confidant of the rich, art collector, philosopher, gentleman. Born in 1895, when it was not easy being Jewish in Canada, Phillips grew up painfully conscious of the example Montreal Jews had to provide for their cousins in other parts of Canada. At the turn of the century, a maternal uncle, Lazarus Cohen, was the second-richest Jew in Canada, having made a fortune dredging the St. Lawrence for the Laurier government. His other uncle, Hersh Cohen, was chairman of the Montreal Council of Orthodox Rabbis. Phillips has inherited both these mantles and wears them with pride. His most important connection was with Samuel Bronfman, whose go-between he was for nearly fifty years. An important Liberal power broker (who arranged, among other things, for Pierre Trudeau to get the Mount Royal nomination in 1965, when not a single French-speaking riding in the province would take him), Phillips was named to the Senate in 1968, the moment Bronfman was safely past the age limit of seventy-five. Because of the compulsory retirement rule, his own term lasted only twenty-four months. When he left, on the eve of Yom Kippur in 1970, Grattan O'Leary called him the greatest senator in the history of Canada, and his colleagues responded with a standing ovation.

Phillips's courtly manners, his infinite tolerance, and his life style represent the zenith of Jewish acceptability. His Tudor stone house in the upper reaches of Westmount is a monument to personal tastes and values. The eighteenth-century living room is full of French impressionists; a Chippendale dining room is decorated with bits of chinoiserie; there is a Napoleonic Empire room upstairs—everything put together with great regard for its authenticity. He loves *faience,* the glazed earthenware from Italy, and is particularly proud of his matched pair of crystal chandeliers that once belonged to the Duke of Newcastle, Secretary for War at the time of the Crimean altercations. The total effect is dazzling, yet slightly out of its place and time; the only Canadian object in sight is the original version of the tri-colour, three-maple-leaf Canadian flag that Lester Pearson sent him in 1965.

THE THIRD AND STILL MOST IMPORTANT STRAIN IN QUE-
BEC's business Establishment is subdivided into clusters
around the great corporations whose head offices domi-
nate Montreal's skyline: Sun Life (Alistair Campbell and
Thomas Galt); the Royal Bank (Earle McLaughlin, Jock
Finlayson, and Rowlie Frazee); the Bank of Montreal
(Arnold Hart, Fred McNeil, and William Mulholland);
Alcan (Nathanael Davis, Paul Leman, and David Cul-
ver); the McConnell interests (Derek Price, Peter Laing,
and Peter McEntyre); Consolidated-Bathurst (Bill Tur-
ner); Iron Ore Company (Bill Bennett); Royal Trust (Con
Harrington and Ken White); Canron (Howard Lang and
Cliff Malone); Genstar (August Franck); Bell Canada
(Robert Scrivener); Canadian National (Robert Bandeen);
Seagram (Charles Bronfman); Cemp Investments (Leo
Kolber); Trizec (James Soden); and Steinberg's (Sam
Steinberg). These clusters, in turn, are linked through in-
vestment men (Deane Nesbitt, David Torrey, Neil Ivory,
Michael Scott, Dominik Dlouhy, Peter Kilburn, James
Pitblado, Alex Tomlinson, Stephen Jarislowsky,* John
Scholes) and lawyers (J. Angus Ogilvy, Brock Clarke,
Fraser Elliott,† Jean Martineau, Philip Vineberg, Fran-
çois Mercier, and Jack Porteous). Declining in influence
is an old guard composed of Herb Lank, Lord Hardinge,
William Arbuckle, Robert Fowler, and Hartland Molson,
though in Establishment argot it is said about them that
"when the chips are down they still cut the mustard."

Apart from Desmarais and the bankers, the most powerful businessman in Montreal is Ian Sinclair, chairman and
chief executive officer of Canadian Pacific and director
of twenty-three other firms. An intense, commanding full-
back of a man with unblinking eyes that have the opaque
quality of peeled grapes, Sinclair is one of the few non-

---

*Born in Berlin and fluent in six languages, Jarislowsky is a graduate
of Cornell, the University of Chicago, and Harvard. He is retained as
an investment counsel by ten large Canadian corporations and holds
some of the most stimulating and unorthodox opinions within the Canadian business community. A slight man with a mild accent, he works in
a penthouse off Sherbrooke Street surrounded by a jungle of plants and
ancient Costa Rican archaeological stones.
†Chief English fund-raiser for the Liberal party in Quebec, Elliott
spent both the 1972 and 1974 election nights at Trudeau's elbow. A
knowledgeable art collector, he made most of his fortune by getting into
Canadian Aviation Electronics at its start.

operating-railwaymen ever to head the company. For most of its colourful history, the CPR's presidents travelled around the system in their private railways cars with the pomp and fanfare of royal processions. N.R. "Buck" Crump, Sinclair's predecessor, had *Laurentian,* his private car, fitted with lights, so that he could inspect the condition of the tracks he was passing over long into the night. The car also had a panel of instruments that allowed him to read out the locomotive's performance. Sinclair has no railway car and if he did, he wouldn't have time to use it. A lawyer who joined CP's legal department in 1942, he has totally transformed a hidebound transportation company into a huge, free-swinging, multinational conglomerate that within the next five years will become one of the free world's major concentrations of economic power. The CP group of companies already has assets of about $4.5 billion, but during 1975 and 1976, capital expenditures of nearly $2 billion are being budgeted, and long-term projections call for even faster growth.

The CP holdings have become so enormous that they generate a cash flow that allows the company to act as its own banker. Besides having a stockpile reserve of $80 million, it keeps more than $200 million continually circulating in the short-term money market. Through Canadian Pacific Investments, CP controls Algoma Steel in Sault Ste Marie, which operates Canada's third-largest steel mill; Great Lakes Paper Company in Thunder Bay; Pan-Canadian Petroleum in Calgary, the largest independent Canadian-owned producer and seeker of oil, actively exploring potential strikes from the Mackenzie Delta down through Montana and Colorado into offshore Texas; CP Air, one of the world's great (and best) airlines; Cominco, which owns the large Trail smelter in B.C. and controls Pine Point Mines in the Northwest Territories, the Black Angel Mine in Greenland, the Aberfoyle group of mines in Australia, and the Rubiales zinc-lead mine in northern Spain; Fording Coal in the Elk Valley of southeastern B.C.; Pacific Logging on Vancouver Island; Marathon Realty, which has large holdings in most Canadian city cores; and one of the world's largest hotel operations, which includes plans for the development or management of eight hotels in Mexico, two hotels in Germany, and two in Israel. CPI also holds more than 12 per cent (the largest single block, worth about $83 million) of the voting stock in MacMillan Bloedel, as well as growing proportions of ownership in Husky Oil, Northern and Central Gas Corporation, Rio Algom, TransCanada Pipe-Lines, and Union Carbide Canada.

Sinclair runs this empire with unbridled enthusiasm and a much greater regard for his own bottom line than for any of Canada's national policy goals. He builds his container ships in Japan and operates them through a Bermuda subsidiary because that's the most profitable formula. Despite CPR's history of government grants (adding up to an original $106 million and 44 million acres of land), Sinclair despises the idea of subsidies. "You're ultimately judged by your bottom line," he says, "and I'm happy to have that discipline. It's the only true discipline. One of the things about subsidies I find very, very bad is that they tend to get people not to think seriously enough about what should be changed or done away with, because they say it doesn't really cost us money. Now, that's a very vicious thing, but I've seen it creeping in. You run an extra car on a train. Maybe you really don't need it, but you get a little bit of flak the odd time if you take it off, so you get rid of the flak by running the extra car with the understanding that really most of it is paid by the government, anyhow. That's a dangerous thing. Once it starts, you lose the discipline of the bottom line."

Sinclair's authority is based on personal toughness and unsurpassed negotiating skill. "I know you can't kiss all the girls. You've got to lose sometimes," he says. "When you're negotiating, you start from the premise that you don't just do things to be popular, that you can't be liked by everybody, that the best you can hope for is to be respected. I have the advantage of having been a barrister, and I only remember the cases I lost and the lessons they taught me. I like to strike a deal that gives the other guy a chance to back down gracefully and that's fair to both sides. But I like to get just a smidgen more than the balance. I enjoy trying to get that."

His most spectacular success was the way he obtained the 25 per cent of Algoma Steel shares held by Mannesmann AG in 1973. The deal was brought to Sinclair by Charlie Burns, the Toronto investment dealer, who settled all details except the conditions of payment. Both sides remained far apart on the terms by which the $60 million would change hands, and finally Sinclair flew to Düsseldorf for a showdown. Egon Overbeck, the German negotiator, had been a member of the German General Staff during the Nazi blitzkriegs of World War II, had been wounded seven times, and was considered to be the toughest industrialist in Western Germany. He sat down in an office across from Sinclair and emerged four hours later, shaking his head. "The reason I'm not smiling," he said, "is that I'm not the least bit happy with the transaction we've just completed." Sinclair's conditions had carried the day.

About the only people who really baffle Sinclair are politicians. Being tough hasn't done him much good around Ottawa. "One of the most amazing times I had was with Mike Pearson," he recalls. "I went to Ottawa with the then head of the Canadian National, Norman MacMillan. We were in a very, very touchy labour situation, and Mr. Pearson asked if he could have a chat with us off the record. He didn't agree with what I was saying, so I was prepared for his comeback. After we'd had dinner, he said: 'Now, that's very interesting, Sinclair, that's very interesting, but the Toronto Maple Leafs are playing and we're going to watch that, and then we'll have a chat afterwards.' I thought to myself, 'Boy, by the time I get through that bloody game, I won't remember how I've put some of this bloody stuff, and he'll be able to say, "Now you said this," and I won't want to argue with him if it's fairly close.' So anyway, we watched the game, and in his quiet way he worked away at me. Finally, I phoned Buck Crump in Montreal. He asked me: 'What did you decide?' And I said, 'I'll be goddamned if I know. I know who won the hockey game and I know I'm going back tomorrow, but I'm buggered if I know what I decided. Except I know Pearson doesn't agree with me. That I know.'"

Halifax

EVER SINCE THEY JOINED TOGETHER IN UNEASY ALLI-
ANCE TO FORM THIS COUNTRY, Canada's provinces have
been vying with each other—like spoiled children arguing
over who ate the largest slice of a birthday cake—about
which of them really got the worst deal in Confederation.
This dubious honour almost certainly belongs to New
Brunswick and Nova Scotia.

Their entry coincided with the end of the brief, bright
age of sail that saw the Maritimes lead the sparsely populated Dominion into becoming the fourth-greatest ship-
owning and shipbuilding nation in the world. The windships
placed Nova Scotia and New Brunswick businessmen at
the economic forefront of the times, prompting them to
start banks, insurance companies, and world-wide cargo
brokerage operations.

The demand for ever more tonnage was accelerated by
the California gold rush (1849), the Australian gold rush
(1851), the Crimean War (1854), and the Indian Mu-
tiny (1857). By 1853, Atlantic shipyards were sending
nearly five hundred large ships a year down their slipways.
Canada's Bluenose fleet swept the oceans, while the yards
continued to refine their techniques, producing magnificent
windjammers capable of loading 3,600 tons deadweight,
which regularly earned the highest classification from
Lloyd's Register—14A1.

But by the 1880s, steel-hulled steamships had taken
over the bulk of ocean traffic, and the Maritimers lacked
the capital and technology to make the switch.* Meanwhile, Canada's trade patterns were switching from north
and south to the longer, tariff-shielded east-west channels
enshrined in Sir John A. Macdonald's National Policy.

---

*An exception was Samuel Cunard (1787–1865), who was agent in
Halifax for the East India Company and operated sailing ships running
to New England, Newfoundland, and Bermuda. He was a shareholder in
the company that in 1831, in Quebec, launched an early steamship, the
wooden paddle-wheeler Royal William, and in 1840 founded one of the
world's great steamship lines, using ships built on the Clyde. Under competition from the U.S.-owned Collins Line, Cunard started cutting back
Halifax calls on his Liverpool-Boston run in the early 1850s, and in the
late 1860s dropped Halifax and concentrated on New York. Cunard
didn't restore regular service to Canada until 1911—and that was to
Montreal.

It has taken the Maritimes Establishment most of a century to recover from this blow, which gradually became based less in economics than in a kind of self-induced Rip Van Winkle lethargy. Otherwise realistic men spent their lives sighing for the days when the tidal terminal of every creek and river was marked by the tall angular silhouettes of the great sailing ships. "We refused to believe that steel would ever replace wooden ships and the world passed us by," says Harold Connolly, a former Nova Scotia premier, now in the Senate. "We sold our lumber at the cheapest prices in the world because we wouldn't grade it. We threw our apples into barrels, unloaded them at Liverpool, and took whatever they would bring. Whenever we managed to build up a thriving business like a trust company, we quickly sold it to a central Canadian competitor, invested the proceeds in 'sure-fire' securities, and lived off the interest. We became the world's champion sitters. The older among us smoked our pipes, sat upon the front stoops, and said to one another, 'What a great people we are! Isn't Canada a fortunate country to have Nova Scotia from which to draw its grey matter?'"

It was this psychic defeatism that turned Maritimes businessmen toward their governments to form temporary coalitions with the only force they considered powerful enough to bargain effectively with the central economic and political authorities. The lines between public and private enterprise grew increasingly blurred, prompting K.C. Irving's classic comment: "I don't think politics and business mix. New Brunswick is too small for politics."

But in the mid-1970s this attitude began to change. "The old men still sit on their stoops and make themselves feel good with talk of past glories," Senator Connolly says. "But a small core of younger men have finally realized that unless we do things for ourselves, the chances of someone else doing them is remote. So, for the first time in my more than seventy years here, there is real growth. This is especially true of the Halifax-Dartmouth and Canso areas."

No matter where they originate or where they eventually end up, the lines of established business power in Nova Scotia lead to Frank Manning Covert, the nephew of a lawyer and former lieutenant-governor who was president of Eastern Canada Savings and Loan Company. Son of a doctor who died when Frank was fourteen, he graduated from Dalhousie Law School and articled under the late James McGregor Stewart, Canada's greatest collector of Kipling manuscripts, who became vice-president and director of the Royal Bank and several other large Canadian corporations. Covert spent two war years in Ottawa as a lawyer in Munitions and Supply, then joined the RCAF and won the DFC. "I have no special talents except the ability to work," he says, "but I've come into contact with all of the men in Nova Scotia who have, in my lifetime, done great things in the business and political worlds. I sat at the feet of Angus L. Macdonald, campaigned for James Ilsley, worked for C.D. Howe, and acted as a legal adviser to Roy Jodrey, Fred Manning, George Chase, Ralph Bell, some of the Sobeys, the MacCullochs, and others."

Born at Canning in Kings County and planning to retire to Hunts Point, near Liverpool on the South Shore, within the sound of the heaving Atlantic, Covert is one of the few Maritimers who have been totally accepted by every branch of the Upper Canadian Establishment. He is a non-pukka type with a tiny Vandyke who acts as if he were constantly surprised that anyone should be bothered listening to him, while at the same time tossing out, like some bored lover's gifts, comments around board-room tables that have an uncanny way of turning out to be incisive solutions to issues at hand. Somehow all this happens in a manner that allows the chairman to believe *he* thought up the whole thing, and Covert is always the first to congratulate him. That's a rare art, and it's part of the explanation for the fact that Covert has been invited to accept the directorships he holds.*

The balance of Nova Scotia's Establishment comprises at least a dozen businessmen of national stature:

---

*As well as being senior Maritimes director for the Royal Bank, Covert sits on the boards of Sun Life, IAC Ltd., Trizec Corp., Petrofina Canada, Molson Companies, Standard Brands Ltd., Phoenix Assurance, Maritime Paper Products, Ben's Holdings Ltd., Great Eastern Corp., Maritime Steel & Foundries Ltd., National Sea Products, Minas Basin Pulp & Power, Canadian Keyes Fibre Co., Sydney Engineering & Dry Dock, Home Care Properties, Eastern Telephone & Telegraph, Acadian Lines Ltd., Lindwood Holdings, Maritime Accessories Ltd., Bowaters Mersey Paper, and Canning Investment Corp.

R.B. Cameron, a contractor who was a millionaire by thirty, controls Maritime Steel and Foundries and is becoming active in the development of tidal power. In 1968, Cameron was called in to be chairman and president of Sydney Steel Corporation, the provincial Crown company that took over the money-losing Cape Breton operations of Dominion Steel and Coal Corporation. By January, 1969, he reported a profit of about $2.5 million. He succeeded the late John C. MacKeen on the board of the Royal Bank and is reported to own a hundred thousand shares of Royal stock.

The Connor-Smith-Morrow holdings are concentrated in National Sea Products, the province's largest fishing operation. The Smith family has close to 16 per cent of the company, the Morrow family 10 per cent, and the Connors just over 6 per cent, mostly through holding companies. A 7 per cent block was acquired recently by the Jodrey family through Minas Basin Pulp and Power.

Gordon Hughes lives quietly at Hampshire Court in Windsor, Nova Scotia; he is Gerry Regan's frequent tennis partner and one of the Premier's main fund-raisers. He is the dominant shareholder in Evangeline Savings and Mortgage Company and Scotia Bond Company, a director of John Labatt and the Canada Development Corporation, and for two terms his presence decorated the governing councils of the CRTC.

Charles E. MacCulloch is head of the province's largest lumber and hardware chain, chairman of Industrial Estates, and a leading developer. He started out as a carpenter, became a house builder, and now owns much of the serviced land around Dartmouth. MacCulloch originally got the Scotia Square development off the ground and brought Eaton's and Simpsons together at his Micmac Mall on the other side of the harbour. On the boards of the Bank of Nova Scotia and Maritime Life Assurance, he exercises a growing influence.

Donald McInnes is a Halifax lawyer now on nine national boards including the Bank of Nova Scotia and Bell

Canada; his influence is waning as he approaches retirement.

Ralph Medjuck has become the single most powerful real estate operator in the Maritimes. He is a director of Central and Nova Scotia Trust, and most of his investments are channelled through two firms, Centennial Properties and Commercial Developments (Maritimes).

Victor Oland, a former lieutenant-governor, is a declining influence since his family's brewing business was sold to Labatt's in 1971, but he is still on the boards of the Bank of Montreal and Texaco Canada.

A. Gordon Archibald is chairman and CEO of Maritime Telegraph and Telephone, Canada's third-largest investor-owned phone company, and chairman of Island Telephone, its PEI subsidiary. He's a director of the TD Bank, Stanfield's, and two insurance companies.

William, David, and Donald Sobey of Stellarton, which adjoins New Glasgow and Trenton in Pictou County, are chief inheritors of the impressive business empire put together by Frank Hoyse Sobey. Their father started out as a butcher, eventually building up a chain of movie theatres and supermarkets and ending up with dominant blocks of stock in Dominion Textile, Anthes Imperial, Canadian Salt, and several other large corporations held through Empire Company, the family's investment trust. Among them the Sobey brothers sit on twenty-seven boards.

John Jodrey and David Hennigar are the son and grandson of the late Roy Jodrey, who was one of the most successful investors of his generation. Born to a Gaspereau Valley cabinetmaker, Jodrey left school at thirteen to become an apple-picker. Somehow he got hold of a book about building power dams and threw one up across the Avon River to provide a source of local electricity. When he was bought out for $250,000 by the Nova Scotia Light and Power Company in 1927, he got extra loans from the Bank of Nova Scotia and plunged heavily into stocks.

The 1929 crash all but wiped him out. For a while he owned only one suit and hid in bed while his wife pressed it before he went out. But gradually he was able to build more dams, bought land and stocks, and expanded his Minas Basin Pulp and Power Company.

A blocky, pasty-faced Baptist with a carthorse capacity for hard work, he lived at Hantsport in austere seclusion, spending most nights slouched on his living-room sofa, reading company balance sheets to the accompaniment of a constant replaying of his Stephen Foster record collection. When he went to Toronto, New York, or Montreal, it was usually to buy stocks or attend board meetings. He eventually became director of fifty-six companies with $3.5 billions' worth of assets stretching from Newfoundland to Venezuela. His largest holdings were in the former Dominion Steel and Coal Corporation, Noranda, Fraser Companies, Algoma Central Railway (in which, at one point, he had stock worth $8 million), the Bank of Nova Scotia (he was a director and one of the largest shareholders, with holdings worth an estimated $10 million), and Crown Life. Prompted by his friend Charlie Burns of Toronto, Jodrey acquired the Crown Life stock owned by George McCullagh, publisher of the *Globe and Mail*, and eventually became the company's largest shareholder. (The Jodrey family still holds about 13 per cent of Crown, worth nearly $20 million.)

The real key to Jodrey's success was that he understood and mastered the art of using bank credits. Unlike most investors, who worry how they'll pay off their bank loans, Jodrey would borrow ten to twelve million dollars, mostly from the Bank of Nova Scotia, buy stocks with the proceeds, and watch their value appreciate.

"Roy started buying securities through my office," Burns remembers. "He would never say 'Buy me a hundred or a thousand shares,' but just 'Buy me some Mining Corporation,' and that could mean fifty or twenty thousand shares. I'd never had a client like that before. He would come back to my office, having spent the day on the Street, and he'd sit there and write in his diary for fifteen minutes and not even talk to me.

"I'd say, 'Roy, I think you ought to buy some Hudson's Bay Oil and Gas. This western market is starting to look pretty hot, and my research fellows tell me it's under-priced.' He'd tell me to buy some and write in his note-book: 'Charlie Burns says Hudson's Bay Oil and Gas is a good buy,' almost as if he was putting you right on the spot."

The way Jodrey picked his stocks was to call on a dozen or so of the key trend-setters along Bay Street to ask them what they thought was worth buying. He would record each opinion in his notebook and usually come up with a fairly clear consensus. The real worth of the stock was less important than the fact that Toronto's financial opinion makers *thought* it was moving up. Eventually, word got around to watch what Jodrey was buying, and that in turn drove his stocks even higher.

Winnipeg

THE WEST IS A LAND OF LONG MEMORIES. During the Great Depression of the thirties, Canada's Prairies, and Saskatchewan in particular, suffered the worst drop in material living standards of any area in the civilized world. Most of the money that wasn't lost during that terrible decade stayed frightened for a long time. In Winnipeg, a quarter of the houses were owned by the city for back taxes right up until 1941.

The roots of Prairie discontent stretch back to the turn of the century when the Western territories struck the bargains that brought them into Confederation. The issues then (and now) were tariffs and freight rates, but more significant was the feeling that the industrialized East was using political means to subjugate the West, to turn it into a hinterland exploitable by the railway and manufacturing interests of Montreal and Toronto. This mood was best caught in the apocryphal oath uttered by the mythical farmer who returns home one afternoon to find that a hailstorm has ruined his crops, his house has been struck by lightning, and his wife has run away with the hired man. He inspects the damage, runs out to the highest point of what's left of his farm, shakes his fist at heaven, and shouts: *"Goddamn the CPR!"*

Not so long ago, Western farmers felt themselves at the very forefront of Canadian civilization. They had wrested the country from the wilderness. But now they feel abandoned: their way of life lost, control of their existence given over to the moneyed navel-gazers and midnight philosophers from the big Eastern cities—men who never had to serve harsh apprenticeships, never knew what it was like to work the night harvests with fires that spread from horizon to horizon, as the straw stacks were set alight so that threshing crews could see to toil until midnight when the dew mercifully brought operations to a halt. They mourn the disappearance of honesty, simplicity, fidelity, and all the homely virtues, longing for a time when people did a little business so they could socialize, rather than socialize in order to do business.

Winnipeg has always stood slightly apart from both Prairie discontents and Eastern ambitions, acting more as an emporium where East and West could meet to trade, building up the fortunes of its old families in the process. Not quite East, not quite West, not quite rich, not quite poor, Winnipeg became a midway house in the Canadian mosaic.

This worked fairly well until the Canadian Wheat Board took over from the Winnipeg Grain Exchange in 1935. Of the grain-merchant families—the Richardsons, Smiths, Bawlfs, Meladys, Sellerses, Searles, Leaches, Gooderhams, Hargrafts, Gillespies, Heffelfingers, Patersons, Purveses, McCabes, Parrishes, and Heimbeckers—few remain with operations under the family name, with the notable exceptions of the Richardsons (whose country elevators bear the Pioneer mark), the Patersons, and the Parrishes and Heimbeckers, with their P&H elevators.

In its heyday, when the Prairies' wholesale structure and grain trade made Winnipeg a booming metropolis, it also became a centre of thought, fostered by the great John W. Dafoe of the *Free Press* and his famous Sanhedrin. But many intellectual activists who followed—Jack Pickersgill, James Coyne, Arnold Heeney, Claude Isbister, and Mitchell Sharp—moved to Ottawa, to be tamed inside the federal bureaucracy. A new, more business-oriented elite emerged, consisting of Elmer Woods* (Monarch

---

*Elmer Woods was so implicitly trusted by every branch of the Manitoba Establishment that at one point he became chief bagman for *both* the provincial Liberal and Conservative parties.

Life), Culver Riley (Canadian Indemnity), Ken Powell (K.A. Powell Limited), Clarence Atchison (Investors Syndicate), Brigadier Dick Malone (*Free Press*), Peter Curry (Great-West and Sovereign Life), Dick Murray and Don McGiverin (Hudson's Bay Company), Gordon Osler (Osler, Hammond and Nanton), George Black (Western Breweries), David Kilgour (Great-West Life), John MacAulay (law), Harry Sellers (Federal Grain), Gordon Smith (Reliance Grain), A.E. Tarr (Monarch Life), Joseph Harris (Great-West Life), and the Richardsons.

But by the mid-seventies nearly all of these men had either died, retired, or left Winnipeg. In the late fifties, when Duff Roblin and John Diefenbaker moved into political power, most of the Manitoba Establishment remained bound to the remnants of the Liberal party, a branch of the Manitoba Club, making them viceroys in a conquered province, men out of touch with their own environment, able to seek political expression only through the federal Liberal party, with which they felt deep ideological differences.

Hived out of grain merchandising by government fiat and left without the influence of any other dominant industry, like lumber in B.C., oil in Alberta, or potash in Saskatchewan,* Manitoba's new business Establishment has yet to take definite shape. The Establishment that *does* exist converged for one glittering private occasion in November of 1974, when Sol Kanee (chairman of Soo Line Mills and himself an enlightened pillar of Winnipeg's cultural and economic life) gave a great dinner at the Fort Garry Hotel in honour of the first visit to the city by Gerald Bouey as governor of the Bank of Canada. In addition to the local heads of the Big Five banks, who

*There is a lot of wealth in Saskatchewan, but not very much national economic influence. Among the important businessmen are R.J. Balfour (Conservative M.P. and corporate director); Dr. David Baltzan, head of a family of five doctors (hotels and property); Sid Buckwold (Buckwold's Ltd., wholesalers; senator and bank director); H.A. Crittenden (TV); D.L. Fuller (Producers Pipelines); Donald Kramer (Kramer Tractor); Herb Pinder (pharmacies; corporate director and bank director); E.A. Rawlinson (radio and TV); W. Erle Roger (Weyburn Livestock Exchange; bank director); John B. Sangster (investor); George Solomon (Western Tractor; bank director); Benjamin Torchinsky (Agra Industries); Jack Turvey (Interprovincial Steel & Pipe); David M. Tyerman (lawyer, corporate director, bank director); and Norman Whitmore (corporate directorships including Canadian Pacific and Molson Companies).

are constantly being transferred, the guest list included just about every Establishmentarian in town:*

J.W. Burns
President,
Great-West Life Assurance

Albert D. Cohen†
President,
General Distributors of
    Canada

W.F. Griffiths
Chairman,
Canada Safeway

George Heffelfinger
President,
Highcroft Enterprises

R.H. Jones
President,
Investors Group

Charles Kroft
Chairman,
Tryton Investment

F.A. Lang
President,
Canadian Premier Life
    Insurance

A. Searle Leach
Chairman,
Federal Industries

K.B. MacMillan
President,
Pioneer Grain

Arthur Mauro
President,
Transair

E.R. O'Neill
President,
Westfair Foods

Kenneth A. Powell
President,
Kenwal Enterprises

Gregory Purchase
Vice-President, Western
    Stores,
T. Eaton Co.

R.P. Purves‡
President,
Inter-Ocean Grain

George Richardson
President,
James Richardson & Sons

C.S. Riley
President,
Dominion Tanners

---

*With the possible exceptions of Doug Everett (senator, president of Royal Canadian Securities, and a Liberal bagman), Dick Hunter (lawyer and corporate director), Richard C. Malone (publisher of the *Free Press*), Paul Morton (theatres and television), and Ron Williams (publisher of the *Tribune*).

†Albert Cohen, who now controls Metropolitan Stores, made a fortune by becoming the first North American businessman to believe in Japanese portable radios. He obtained the Canadian agency for Sony in 1955 and built up his General Distributors organization into a major national chain. He may be the only Canadian entrepreneur who was admired for his verve and daring by Ian Fleming, author of the James Bond series.

‡Purves has been an important influence in re-establishing Winnipeg's thriving Commodity Exchange (until 1972 the Grain Exchange), now specializing in gold trades.

Donald S. Rogers
President,
Gambles Canada

H.W. Sutherland
Senior Vice-President,
Hudson's Bay Co.

A.M. Runciman
President,
United Grain Growers

Alan Sweatman
Partner,
Thompson, Dorfman,
Sweatman

Saul Simkin
Chairman,
BACM Industries

Harold Thompson
President,
Monarch Life Assurance

Harold Sneath
President,
Manitoba Pool Elevators

Garson Vogel*
Chief Commissioner,
Canadian Wheat Board

Daniel Sprague
Chairman,
James B. Carter

No matter how many others might have been invited, the name on the list that really counts is that of George Richardson. Just as the $60-million Lombard Place at Portage and Main that they occupy casts its elegant shadow over downtown Winnipeg, the Richardson family dominates the city's—and the province's—power structure.

A combination of Irish curiosity and Loyalist sobriety has marked the passage of four Richardson generations to always greater riches. The first Richardson† made his fortune selling grain to northern New York State during the American Civil War from his wooden storehouses around the Bay of Quinte and along the shore of Lake Ontario. The first Manitoba office was opened in 1880—before the

---

*Vogel, an introspective, duty-laden, 25-year veteran of the public and private Canadian wheat trade, is probably the most powerful man in Western Canada. His decisions in the highly volatile world grain markets can mean differences of millions of dollars to the region's income. His operations are so large that on any given day the wheat board usually has an outstanding balance with the Canadian banks of more than a billion dollars.

†It was under the original Richardson's stewardship that the company acquired its continuing distaste for publicity. In 1857, the year of the founding of the business, Richardson's name seems to have appeared in the newspapers only once, when he was listed as attending a champagne breakfast for John A. Macdonald. All the Richardson advertising and public relations is handled by one employee, Patrick Burrage. For a long time the company's ads usually limited themselves to proclaiming: "ACTIVE IN ALL PHASES OF THE CANADIAN GRAIN TRADE."

railway reached Winnipeg. James was succeeded by his sons George (president from 1892 to 1906) and Senator Henry W. (president, 1906–1918), but the real empire-building took place under George's son James, who became head of the firm on his uncle's death, after serving with the Allied Wheat Commission, and ran it until 1939. He expanded the Pioneer Grain division into world markets, built radio stations, grubstaked prospectors, set up Canada's first large airline, and helped finance Herbert Kalmus's initial experiments with Technicolor movies.*

When James Richardson died, at the outbreak of World War II, his place was taken by his widow, the former Muriel Sprague, who held the presidency until 1966, when their son James (who left in 1968 to join the Trudeau cabinet) became chairman and chief executive officer and their son George became president.† Seventh head of the Richardson family, George Taylor Richardson is a tall, imperial man who exudes a kind of institutional grace. (He is, after all, *the* Richardson.) Proud of his office atop the Lombard Place complex, he loves to show off the gadgets near his desk which allow him to close the drapes across his windows and tune into a closed-circuit TV camera trained on the latest stock market quotations a few floors below. He flies his own helicopter and has a private heliport on the roof next to his office. A fussy, parsimonious man, he loves to make the repairs on his own tractor at Briarmeade Farm where he lives. After the recent opening of a new Richardson branch office in Edmonton, he sneaked back at night and rearranged the paintings hung in the manager's office more to his personal taste.

---

*In their heyday, the Winnipeg grain merchants made huge profits, even though they stoutly maintained that their commissions added only a quarter of a cent to the price of a bushel. When one Saskatchewan farm leader came to town, James Richardson drove him around Wellington Crescent, pointing out the grain dealers' mansions. The puzzled visitor's only recorded comment was: "All this on a quarter of a cent?"

†It was in 1966, too, that the investment-dealing and stock-brokerage arm of the family business changed its name from James Richardson and Sons (a partnership with the same name as the grain company's but without the "Limited") to Richardson Securities of Canada. The senior company, James Richardson and Sons Limited, has only four beneficial shareholders, represented by family trusts. They are James and George Richardson and their sisters Kathleen and Agnes (whose husband is William Benidickson, a Liberal senator). The family companies are Intercolonial Trading Corp. Ltd., Interprovincial Trading Corp. Ltd., Westmead Ltd. (James), Valley Investments Ltd. (George), Kamarin Investments Ltd. (Kathleen), and Senga Ltd. (Agnes backwards).

The true dimensions of the business empire he heads are a rigorously guarded secret, but according to the estimates of colleagues, the Richardsons' personal fortune totals at least $450 millions. This galaxy of privately owned companies has annual sales of well over $100 million, yielding net revenues of more than $4 million. Among its chief assets: Canada's largest (in terms of both value and volume) retail securities operation, with thirty-four offices across the country; 452 orange and yellow Pioneer Grain elevators in addition to the huge terminal elevators at Thunder Bay and Vancouver; Buckerfield's, Topnotch, Green Valley, and Trouw of Canada—major feed and fertilizer factories; three large insurance firms; Marine Pipeline Construction of Canada, which is the country's largest oil and gas pipeline construction company; Systems Equipment, a Winnipeg-based manufacturer of modern accounting systems; Patricia Contractors, a land-clearing and road-building subsidiary; Mohawk Navigation, which owns a fleet of Great Lakes ships; not to mention several firms engaged in distributing fuel in Kingston, breeding Hereford cattle, selling real estate, and exploring for oil. Richardson maintains offices in Chicago, New York, Grand Cayman, London, Geneva, Frankfurt, Hong Kong, and Tokyo. In addition to belonging to all of the standard North American stock and commodity exchanges and the Hong Kong Stock Exchange, the firm is the only Canadian member of London's Cocoa Terminal Market Association and United Terminal Sugar Market Association. All operations are connected by direct high-speed teletype lines.

Richardson spends two or three days a week on out-of-town journeys of inspection. As well as looking after his family's interests, he is a vice-president of the Canadian Imperial Bank of Commerce, on the board of Hudson's Bay Oil and Gas, and a director (and major shareholder) of International Nickel. But his major outside activity is wearing the proud mantle of Governor of the Hudson's Bay Company, the first Canadian to do so, his forerunners having mostly belonged to the nobility of Scotland or England. Under his governorship, the Bay has expanded its full-scale cross-country department store merchandising, its oil exploration (through Siebens Oil and Gas), and its real estate transactions (through Markborough Properties).

Richardson spends at least a day a week on Bay affairs, visits a dozen northern branches every summer, and occasionally likes to do some comparison shopping by personally browsing through Eaton's or Simpsons. Although fewer than two thousand of the Bay's seventeen thousand employees remain in town, he has no intention of moving the company's head office. The relationship of Winnipeg and the Richardsons is far too interdependent for that.

Partly because the rest of the Winnipeg Establishment (with the exception of Albert Cohen, Sol Kanee, Con Riley, and Alan Sweatman) is so comatose, George Richardson probably looms larger than any other single presence in any Canadian urban power structure. But he is a shy man who seldom flexes his power, lives quietly, works up there at the top of the Lombard tower, an angel of silence brooding over the city.

St. John's

OF CANADA'S TWO ISLAND PROVINCES,* NEWFOUNDLAND HAS THE TIGHTER POWER STRUCTURE, dominated by a few families with solid political connections. The traditionally overwhelming influence of the Water Street overlords— the Macphersons, the Winters, the Harveys, the Murrays, the Bowrings, the Perlins, the Ayres, the Crosbies, the Steers, the Pratts, the Outerbridges—endures, even if it is expressed in different forms of business acumen and not all of the families have survived the economic disfranchisement they felt at the time of Confederation in 1949.

---

*Prince Edward Island's economy is too small to have developed much of an Establishment. The wealthiest Islander is Carl Burke, founder of Maritime Central Airways and still a large shareholder in Nordair. He now owns the Charlottetown Hotel and several motels, including some Florida real estate. The Schurmans of Summerside are the most powerful family, operating the Maritimes' largest contracting firm, and are important financial backers of the Liberal party. Other important businessmen include Harry MacLauchlan (motels); H.B. Willis (potatoes); J.A. Simmonds (dairies); W.A. Rix (metal processing and fish plants for export); Walter Pickard (heavy equipment); Austin Scales (fertilizer); C.M. McLean (food processing); David MacKay (potatoes) and Walter Hyndman (insurance). The largest landowner in the province is Howard Webster of Montreal, who runs a 7,000-acre spread near Dundas on the eastern end of the Island, held through Little Pond Ltd. and Dundas Farms Ltd. Webster raises beef cattle and carries on quality breeding operations.

The original St. John's aristocracy were provisioners to the British fleets, the commissioners who grew rich behind Newfoundland's special colonial privileges and tariff barriers, gradually diversifying their holdings into retail outlets, fishing operations, construction, and local politics. They became the island's "black kings," agents with whom the occupying British garrison commanders and governors made their private and profitable arrangements, in return for keeping the native population from becoming more than reasonably restless.

All this changed when Joey Smallwood brought the island into Confederation. With some notable exceptions, the old families lost their drive, retreated into coupon clipping, or left Newfoundland altogether. Stores and wholesale operations moved in from the mainland, displacing the Water Street monopolies. Under the Smallwood stewardship, most of the province's natural resource wealth was given away, leased, or sold with sometimes spectacular, more often disastrous, consequences to outsiders like Alfred Valdmanis, Edmund de Rothschild, John C. Doyle, and John M. Shaheen.

Four families* dominate Newfoundland's Establishment:

The Lundrigans of Corner Brook. William James, the father, and Arthur Raymond, the son, have built up their family firm into one of the Atlantic provinces' largest contracting operations—all with the generous assistance of Liberal administrations in St. John's, which have awarded them contracts of more than $50 million.

The Ayre family of St. John's. Lewis is its most influential member, Fred having moved to Toronto as managing director of the expanding Bowring Brothers chain. But it's Lewis, not Fred, who belongs to the Toronto Club, even though he still does business from an address on Water Street. A director of eight large corporations (including the Bank of Nova Scotia, Dominion Stores, and

*Six other families also count, but on a much smaller scale: the Hickmans (automobiles and insurance); the Outerbridges (coal, shipping, stores); the Bells (wholesaling); the Collingwoods (insurance, furniture); the Monroes (fishing); the Lakes (fish processing). The chief Tory bagman is Dick Greene; the main Liberal fund-raiser is Derek Lewis.

Hollinger Mines), the senior Ayre is also chairman of Newfoundland Telephone, the Ayre's stores, Blue Peter Steamships, and many other island enterprises.

The Pratt brothers of St. John's. Ewart and Calvert run the family merchandising business (Steers Limited), but are also into fishing, insurance, and steamships.

The Crosbies of Newfoundland. It's doubtful if any other business family—in Newfoundland or on the mainland—maintains such a tortuous relationship with incumbent and potentially incumbent politicians. "Crosbies," wrote Harry Bruce, "fight to excel in business, and in Newfoundland, more than anywhere else, dramatic business success depends on government money. Therefore, Crosbies fight, too, on the political fronts of the province. Both secretly and openly. To complete the pattern, they marry into families who have also fought to excel in business or to influence whatever political movements suit their particular ambitions."*

Andrew Crosbie, the family's current godfather, is well aware of his connections. "Government is probably responsible for 75 per cent of construction in Newfoundland," he says. "If you're not popular with government, there have been ways by which maybe you didn't get the business." According to one estimate, the Smallwood government pumped at least $50 million into Crosbie construction companies between 1950 and 1972. Presumably, the balance of the Crosbies' cluster of companies (which have annual sales of $100 million and employ twenty-four hundred) achieved comparable results.

In that cluster the most prominent gem is Eastern Provincial Airways, Canada's fourth-largest airline, but it also includes thirty-six other firms that run merchant ships, hotels, trucking operations, newspapers, insurance agencies, cocktail bars, and factories that make everything from hospital equipment to bulletproof doors. Andrew's national influence is exerted through his seat on the Bank of Montreal board—he succeeded Arthur Lundrigan. Crosbie's brother John, whose latest incarnation is as

Maclean's, June and July, 1975.

minister of fisheries in the Conservative government of Frank Moores, was, for two stormy years in the Smallwood cabinet, alternatively Smallwood's heir presumptive and bitterest foe. He quit the Liberals to join the Tories in 1971.

The dynasty was founded by Sir John Chalker Crosbie, an exuberant freebooter who became finance minister in Newfoundland's colonial administration of the twenties. It was Ches, the eldest of his eleven children, who turned the primitive conglomerate left by Sir John into a modern commercial enterprise.

The Crosbie influence has no equal in Newfoundland. The brothers have even acquired the trappings associated with Old Money: the interior of John's house, unpretentious on the outside, is lavishly furnished with *objets d'art*; Andrew has a convertible Rolls-Royce; his wife, Joan, drives a Mercedes.

Toronto

TORONTO IS THE EMPIRE CITY, the Canadian Technopolis. The 240-square-mile city state spreads its arrogance across the country, dispassionately dispensing money, heroes, culture, alienation, advice, and predestiny. If Montreal is a city of backgrounds and Vancouver a city of style, Toronto is a city of power.

Its two and a quarter million inhabitants—at least those inside the magic circles whose members go about, thumbs hooked in vest pockets, deciding the order of Canada's economic universe—practise the exhilaration syndrome. They expend their days (and some of their nights) in an intense, far from typically Canadian drive to become the guys who count. Having once made it, they want to feel the *thrill* of flexing their clout.

This is very different from political power, which tends to be carefully husbanded, camouflaged by slogans, smiles, and supplications. Unlike the tides of shifting authority inside the political courts of Ottawa, the Toronto power structure works on a simple principle: either you're in or you're out. And if you're in, you're on top, swinging with the high-rollers who know how to certify the elect.

Power in Toronto is constantly on the move, being

snared by some, eluding others. Fashions change. Names disappear from contention. Telephones stop ringing. Hardly anyone has time to notice, for instance, that the FOOFS (Fine Old Ontario Families) aren't in charge any more. There's a restaurant in the Massey house on Jarvis Street, hordes of long-haired students from Etobicoke pound through Falconer Hall, the Gooderham mansion has been turned into a club, a developer lives in Lady Eaton's former house on Old Forest Hill Road, no one cares who belongs to the Rosedale Golf Club any more except its members, and the Cawthras are all but forgotten.

It's the technostructure that counts now—the anonymous-looking lawyers in their anonymous offices behind receptionists' doors decorated with galloping cadences of names stretching toward the ultimate ampersand; the accountants, salesmen, engineers, architects, and financiers. They are men in perpetual motion, more familiar with the flight schedules to Cleveland and the hotels of Buenos Aires than the main streets of Winnipeg or the vistas of Vancouver. They live on top of one another, trading off fragments of their psyches, constantly trying to stretch their authority, knowing they're only as good as their last deal. "We all need to be within a thousand feet of each other. That's how business gets done," says Michael Koerner, an international investor who works out of one of the Toronto-Dominion towers.

For Canadians who don't share the pull of this country's version of the Big Apple, Toronto can be an alienating experience. The manners of its natives have their own gradations, their culture its own blend, their ambition its own imperatives.

Members of the Toronto Establishment are constantly trying to gauge the state of their own influence. The quickest test is to know that, no matter who they may be calling, they can always get through on the telephone. (If you're asked to hold, you're slipping. If you're asked for your number, forget it.) Another indication is the invitations they get to the intimate dinner parties organized at the Toronto Club by Bill Harris, a cheerfully enlightened investment man who brings in top Canadian, American, and British politicians and bureaucrats for confidential briefings on public issues. "I remember that the first discussion we ever had about the Canadian dollar going on a floating exchange rate," says Gordon Sharwood, "was at one of Bill's dinners attended by Wynne Plumptre and Bob Bryce from Ottawa."

Keeping plugged in is the name of the game. "Because we operate on the same network, we can talk to each other in a kind of shorthand," says John Aird, a Toronto lawyer who sits on a dozen important corporate boards. "Your whole life gets to be a series of judgemental decisions you're required to take. For me, they're the cumulative effect of whatever it is that makes John Aird run, what books I've read, the last people I've talked to, what input I've had sitting around board-room tables. I'll be on the telephone and somebody will ask my opinion. Bang. I've got to have done my homework, to have confidence in what I'm going to say. All my cumulative education, cumulative disciplines, are brought into focus at that given moment. And it happens many times every day."

Aird, who keeps a red toy Dr. Strangelove telephone on his desk as a memento of his time on the Permanent Joint Defence Board, resigned from the Senate in 1974 to head the Institute for Research on Public Policy. Formerly chief national fund-raiser for the Liberal party ("I went through six elections and became known as the best collector the *Tories* ever had because all my calls were on the basis of preserving the two-party system"), he is a grandson of Sir John Aird, who headed the Bank of Commerce. Educated at Upper Canada College, where he played football well enough that he was asked to turn out for the Toronto Argonauts, he married a Housser (the original promoters of Tampax) and began his law practice by becoming a prospector. Scratching for gold out of Yellowknife, Hay River, and other mining camps, he gradually built up contacts across the country. "I gained my appreciation of the Canadian North and the western provinces and got to know a lot of people. When some of them came to Toronto, I was the only lawyer they knew." He still travels a hundred thousand miles a year, even though he's now comfortably ensconced on the boards of the Bank of Nova Scotia, the Molson Companies, Consolidated-Bathurst, Famous Players, and Algoma Central (in which he also has the largest stockholding). His major international board is Amax Incorporated, the world's largest molybdenum operation, where he shares the board room with such U.S. luminaries as George Ball, William A. M. Burden, and Arthur Dean.

Aird has become an important figure within the Canadian business Establishment, and his influence is spreading rapidly. A careful, conscientious lawyer with a low-key instinct for power, he is constantly oiling and expanding his personal network: Paul Desmarais, Arnold Hart, Lucien Rolland, Deane Nesbitt in Montreal; George Richardson and Sy Leach in Winnipeg; Bob Pierce and Eddie Galvin in Calgary; Frank Covert in Halifax; John Nichol and Dick Whittall in Vancouver; the late Sir Denys Lowson in London.

The wheels go round, and somehow Toronto always ends up in the middle. Even though Canada is becoming politically more and more decentralized, economically it is being drawn ever more tightly within Toronto's orbit. While Vancouver and Calgary are emerging as important decision-making centres, they can never marshal all the necessary facilities in one place rapidly enough. Whether you're building a shopping centre in Prince George, financing a motel in Brandon, putting up a pulp mill at La Tuque or fashioning yourself a handy offshore tax haven in the Cayman Islands, Toronto is the only place in the country that has the concentration of expertise, enough money, the *alternatives* that can make it all happen. Blake, Cassels and Graydon, one of the town's many legal factories, has seventy partners who among them are capable of handling any proposition put to them.

TORONTO IS THE ONLY CANADIAN CITY WHERE MEMBERS OF THE LOCAL BUSINESS ESTABLISHMENT almost automatically qualify for cross-country status. Nearly three-quarters of the certified members of Canada's national business Establishment live in the Toronto commuter-shed. They can be divided into five main categories:

1. *The Money Men.* Probably a billion dollars in various forms changes hands during the average Toronto working-day. Many men handle the complex details behind these transactions, but fewer than two dozen make the most important decisions about who is going to get how much money and on what terms. The list is headed (as any Canadian list that sets out the priorities of financial realities must be) by the bankers: Allen Lambert, Dick Thomson, and F.G. McDowell at the Toronto-Dominion; Ced Ritchie, George Hitchman, and Bob MacIntosh at the Bank of Nova Scotia; Page Wadsworth, Russ Harrison, and C.M. Laidley at the Commerce; Hartland MacDougall at the Montreal; and Doug Gardiner at the Royal.

The 1974 stock market panic left investment dealers with reduced authority. But they can still make their advice felt, and they do run what remains of the capital market. The most influential among them are Charlie Burns at Burns Brothers and Denton; Charles Gundy and C.E. Medland at Wood Gundy;* Hal Jackman at Empire Life; Ward Pitfield at Pitfield, Mackay, Ross; Stewart Ripley at Metropolitan Trust; Gordon Sharwood and Alan Marchment at the Guaranty Trust group; Douglas Ward at Dominion Securities Harris; David Weldon at Midland Doherty; and J.W. Whittall at Reed Shaw Osler, the insurance brokers.

2. *The Corporate Men.* What differentiates this highly influential platoon of chairmen and presidents from other executives is that through the multitude of seats they hold on other boards, their influence is felt far beyond the confines of their own corporations. Among the most important are J.A. Armstrong (Imperial Oil), Tom Bell

---

*Wood Gundy is Canada's largest and most powerful investment house. Its modern incarnation was fashioned by William Wilder, who was the firm's president from 1967 until 1972, when he left to build the Mackenzie Valley pipeline. During the 1970 market slump he cut a million dollars out of the company's overhead by, among other things, forcing executives to purchase their own flowers for their offices. Besides its huge money market operations, the company maintains some major ownership positions: control of Simpsons Ltd., for example, is divided between the Burton family and large shareholders of Wood Gundy, each group holding 8 per cent. Wood Gundy's 1974 gross revenue was $51 million on assets of $733.2 million.

(Abitibi Paper), Roy Bennett (Ford of Canada), Ed Bovey (Northern and Central Gas), G. Allan Burton (Simpsons), Marsh Cooper (Falconbridge), Nelson Davis (N.M. Davis Corporation), A.E. Diamond (Cadillac Fairview), Peter Gordon (Stelco), Edward Grubb (Inco), James Kerr (TransCanada PipeLines), Jack Leitch (Upper Lakes Shipping), Bruce Matthews (Argus Corporation), Jerry McAfee (Gulf Oil), John A. "Bud" McDougald (Argus Corporation), Bill McLean (Canada Packers), Jake Moore (Brascan Limited), Dean Muncaster (Canadian Tire), Douglas Peacher (Simpsons-Sears), Alf Powis (Noranda), Charles Rathgeb (Comstock International Limited), Galen Weston (Weston's), Bud Willmot (Molson Companies), William Wilder (Canadian Arctic Gas Pipeline), and Ray Wolfe (Oshawa Group).

3. *The Professional Directors*. Rather than being tied to any one large corporation, they float between various board rooms, offering advice and collecting directors' fees. The most influential among them are John Aird, the lawyer; John Coleman, former deputy chairman of the Royal Bank; J. Douglas Gibson, former executive vice-president of the Bank of Nova Scotia; John Godfrey, lawyer and chief national Liberal fund-raiser; A.G.S. Griffin, Triarch Corporation; Alex MacIntosh, lawyer and corporate director; Beverley Matthews, lawyer and corporate director; John Leighton McCarthy, lawyer and corporate director; D.A. McIntosh, lawyer and corporate director; B.H. Rieger, Canadian Corporate Management; John P. Robarts, former Ontario premier, now on ten major boards; William Twaits, former chairman of Imperial Oil; James and John Tory, twin lawyers and corporate directors; Floyd Chalmers, former publisher, now corporate director; A.J. "Pete" Little, former partner in Clarkson, Gordon, now corporate director; George Mara, entrepreneur and corporate director; and Joseph Sedgwick, lawyer and corporate director.

4. *The Media Lords*. Among them, these men control much of what Canadians read and see: John Bassett (Baton Broadcasting); Donald Campbell (Maclean-Hunt-

er); Murray Chercover (CTV); Gordon Fisher (Southam Press); Beland Honderich (Toronto Star, Comac Communications, Harlequin Enterprises); Richard Malone (Globe and Mail; FP Publications); and Ken Thomson (Thomson Newspapers).

5. *The New Boys.* Pushing up fast is a group of men in their thrusting thirties and forties who will eventually inherit the places at the Establishment's banquets. They are more aware than their predecessors of the social environment in which they operate, international in their outlook, relentless in their dealings, unsentimental, and tough. Although the members of this group operate independently, its natural leaders are two of the young Eaton brothers (Fred and John) and two of the Bassett boys (John and Doug). Also important are Ted Rogers (broadcasting), Michael Koerner (international investment), Conrad Black (newspapers), Bob Korthals (banking), Gary Van Nest (investments), John Carmichael (equipment leasing), George Cohon (hamburgers), Don McCarthy (food products), Michael Sifton (publishing),* Julian Porter (lawyer), Michael de Pencier (publisher), Jerri Mandel (mufflers), S. Bruce McLaughlin (construction), Ted Burton (Simpsons), Gordon Bongard (Bongard, Leslie), Latham Burns (Burns Brothers and Denton), Peter Allen (John C.L. Allen Limited), and Jim Coutts (politics).†

---

*A joint master of the Toronto and North York Hunt clubs and a former subaltern, Sifton owns one of Canada's few indoor polo fields.

†Some of these young jocks have formed themselves into the Sahara Desert Canoe Club, a Sunday-morning hockey team, which practises in Maple Leaf Gardens and includes (on an irregular basis) Johnny Bassett, John Craig Eton, Peter Eby (managing director, Burns Brothers and Denton), Ron Barbaro (partner of Win-Bar Insurance Agencies), Rudy Bratty (lawyer, land developer, and part-owner of the Toronto *Sun*), George Cohon (president, McDonald's Restaurants of Canada), Bill Bremner (chairman of Vickers and Benson), Kenneth McGowen (joint founder of Mac's Milk, president of Cloverlawn Investments), Joseph Kane (lawyer, former coach of the Varsity Blues and Toronto Marlboros), George Eaton (vice-president of Eaton's of Canada), Gordon Gray (president, A.E. LePage real estate), Ronald Chisholm (lawyer), Irving Gerstein (president, Peoples Jewellers), Joseph Garwood (controller, Baton Broadcasting), Allan Beattie (lawyer), Jack Stott (president, Bulk-Lift Systems), Allan Flood (secretary-treasurer, Bulk-Lift Systems), John Finlay (lawyer), Hugh McLelland, Joseph Peters (president, Peters Wiles real estate), Steve Stavro (president of Knob Hill Farms grocery stores and a founder of the North American Soccer League), Nick Trbovich (president, Servotronics Inc., Buffalo), Harry Shier (secretary-treasurer, OSF Industries Ltd.), and Ed Winkler (president, Winkler Lighting, and president of Toronto Globals of the Ontario Fastball League).

ABOVE AND BEYOND THESE CIRCLES OF POWER, THERE
CONTINUES TO EXIST Social Toronto, whose goings-on are
meticulously recorded by the *Globe and Mail*'s Zena Cherry
and McKenzie Porter of the *Sun*. It's a British-oriented
leisure class whose adherents seem to spend half their
lives on horseback. This crowd of gentlemen farms in
and around King, twenty miles north of the downtown
area. It includes Major-General Churchill Mann at View
Hulloa Farm; Bud Willmot, owner of Kinghaven Farms;
Charles Burns, squire of Kingfield Farms; and Harold
Crang, who owns the Glenville Farms in Newmarket.
Other Toronto Establishmentarians who move in the horse
latitudes are Charles "Bud" Baker, chairman of the Ontario Jockey Club, of Northcliffe Farms; Conn Smythe,
whose farms in the Caledon Hills conceal gravel pits;
Jack Leitch; and Tom Mulock of Mulock Farms at Newmarket.

Describing a typical event in this set's lives, McKenzie
Porter wrote in 1972: "I was a guest at the Crang farm
when seventy-five muddy men and women came back
from the field and trooped into the beautiful old house,
pink-cheeked and exhilarated, for a hunt breakfast, while
servants outside coaxed steaming horses into vans. In an
ambience of roaring log fires, panelled walls, oil paintings,
crystal, silver, whisky, and roast oxen, the scene suggested
an interior from a collection of eighteenth-century English sporting prints."

The largest racing stable (apart from E.P. Taylor's,
which is now run out of his spread in Maryland) is owned
by George Gardiner, who maintains 140 thoroughbreds
on a farm near Caledon and makes an annual profit of
$500,000 on his racing and breeding activities. Gardiner's
fortune was partly inherited from his father, Percy (who
made it in scrap metal and the stock market), but is also
based on his canny investments in western oil stocks.

Million-dollar houses aren't rare among the Toronto rich.
Fred Billes, a director of Canadian Tire Corporation and
son of one of the brothers who launched the chain, has
hired the Establishment architect John C. Parkin to put up
a $1.5-million mansion off Bayview Avenue. Until recent-
ly, Joseph Berman, executive vice-president of Cadillac
Fairview, lived happily in his $2-million house on High

Point, off the Bridle Path, with its tennis-court-sized living room and three swimming pools. But it wasn't—well, quite right, somehow. So he has now commissioned architect Raymond Moriyama to build him a really big house at King. This one will be worth $3 million, the most expensive Toronto residence since Sir Henry Pellatt, the tycoon of another age, threw up Casa Loma.

Calgary

TALKING TO ALBERTA'S POWER BROKERS—RESOLUTE MEN WITH WEATHERED COUNTENANCES AND PIERCING EYES—you can sense the forty years of snubs, well caught and well remembered, they've been storing up against Toronto businessmen and Ottawa politicians. Now that they have become lords of the technology of the hour (fully 88 per cent of Canada's oil supplies, not counting the tar sands, and 81 per cent of the natural gas lies within Alberta), their mood has changed. Good men with great dreams who have had their nervous systems strained beyond endurance, they are determined to find the appropriate equalizer that will guarantee their rightful stature.

They feel alienated from the national political process, suspicious of the Eastern Establishment, certain that the Toronto and Montreal crowds' proximity, contacts, and affiliations allow them to play a better game of Ottawa poker, to be constantly receiving more favourable consideration. Like the meeting and marrying of many drops of rain sliding along a wire to form a sudden gusher, Alberta's discontents are bursting in unexpected directions.

What is at stake here, among other things, is destruction of a stereotype, the notion, still dear to the hearts of many Eastern Canadians, of Albertans as half-tamed cowboys with Broderick Crawford faces, Texas twangs, and Stetson hats over bad, pomaded haircuts. At another level, it is a revival of the on-again-off-again allure of Prairie separatism, which has always been the Western gut response to Ontario imperialism. This was an essential element in the early ideological thrusts of the United Farmers of Alberta, the Progressives, the federal wings of the CCF and Social Credit.

The impetus behind these political movements flashed onto the national stage for one final moment as part of John Diefenbaker's "One Canada" approach. However untidy and disappointing his efforts turned out to be, they were firmly rooted in the brave notion that regional aspirations could be translated into national policies, that this country was not, after all, merely a series of appendages to the commercial empire of the St. Lawrence. But peering down from their penthouses, the great adjudicators of the Eastern power blocks saw the man from Prince Albert only as some sort of unfathomable electoral accident, a political street-singer who had to be silenced.

It appeared briefly as if the West's estrangement might end with Pierre Trudeau's election to the Liberal leadership, since he seemed to be offering a wide-open style of government. Instead, like most of his predecessors, he became caught up in the concerns of Ontario (where the nation's industrial future was being moulded) and Quebec (where the struggle for national unity was being waged).

With the *political* process momentarily closed to them —even if such confederations of anger as the small separatist groups led by John Rudolph and Milt Harradence find the occasional spotlight—the Albertans who count are reaching out for national *economic* power, trying to bull their way into the Canadian business Establishment.

THE PROCESS IS WELL UNDER WAY. GONE ARE THE DAYS of the monetary pilgrimages to Toronto for financing that could be extracted only under exorbitant, ultra-safe conditions. "Like a massive, crunching continental drift, the balance of Canadian power and growth has begun inching westward," Jack McArthur wrote in the *Toronto Star*. "It's still well within Ontario. But if it continues to move it will crack old social and economic structures and amid much strain and controversy provide the climate for new ones." Calgary already has the third-largest number of corporate head offices (after Toronto and Montreal), the fourth-busiest airport, and the fastest-growing city core in the country. With a gross provincial product approaching $10 billion, Alberta is Canada's third-richest province, and most of its 1.7 million citizens have long since passed from a rural to an urbanized life style.

Because a majority of the province's corporate executives are merely a coterie around the great multinational owners of most of the oil and gas leases, the only group that possesses the clout to stand up to both Ottawa and the Eastern Establishment is the provincial government of Peter Lougheed. A Harvard Business School grad with shower-fresh good looks and deep convictions about his own sanctity, Lougheed is something less than a pure free-enterpriser, at least in the sense that he sees nothing wrong with "centralizing control" in government hands. During the summer of 1974, in one of those sudden flashes that might have pleased an E.P. Taylor or a Paul Desmarais, Lougheed's government suddenly took over Pacific Western, Canada's third-largest airline, for $32 million.*

The half-dozen key Lougheed advisers involved in the final stages of the PWA decision are known as the Patio Group, because they usually meet on the patio of Lougheed's Edmonton house. The innermost of the inside circles, they include Chip Collins, the ex-Mannix executive who is now deputy provincial treasurer; federal and intergovernmental affairs minister Don Getty, an oil millionaire and former Edmonton Eskimo quarterback who has the best brain (and handsomest face) on the Tory front benches; agriculture minister Hugh Horner, of the fabled Horner clan (whose members believe that no true Canadian should be born east of Portage la Prairie); education minister Lou Hyndman, who ably represents the government's social conscience in Cabinet; Merv Leitch, formerly attorney general, now provincial treasurer; and Peter Macdonnell, who is the Premier's most important go-between (mostly by telephone) with the national Establishment. Son of the late J.M. Macdonnell, a former president of National Trust and Conservative cabinet minister, his grandfather was Sir George Parkin, principal of

*Before making the final decision, industry minister Fred Peacock tried to encourage Ron Southern, president of Atco Industries and a PWA shareholder and director, to make the takeover bid but was told interest rates were too high to make it a viable proposition. The government's offer was organized by R.B. Love, a Calgary lawyer, and J.H. McKibben, a vice-president of National Trust.

Upper Canada College from 1895 to 1902 and organizing secretary of the Rhodes Scholarship Trust, and his uncles included Vincent Massey and W.L. "Choppy" Grant, another famous principal of UCC. A senior partner in the Edmonton law firm of Milner and Steer, Macdonnell is Lougheed's chief fund-raiser outside Alberta. His background, his supremely civilized style, and his expanding connections through directorships in the Royal Bank, North American Life Assurance, and Home Oil plug him into the very heart of the Eastern Establishment.

Other important business influences around Lougheed are R.S. Dinkel, a Calgary lawyer who acts as Lougheed's campaign adviser; John Ballem, the novelist-lawyer who is Lougheed's former law partner; Fred Mannix, the pipeline, construction, and coal multimillionaire;* J.R. McCaig, president of Trimac, the bulk-commodity transporters; Ron Southern, the head of Atco Industries (prefab housing); Rod McDaniel, a Calgary oil consultant and chief Tory fund-raiser; Don Lougheed, the Premier's brother, who is a vice-president of Imperial Oil; David Mitchell, the former head of Great Plains Development, who was named by Lougheed to run the Alberta Energy Company; David Wood, an old friend who now works for Western Co-operative Fertilizers and masterminds the Premier's public relations; and Bob Blair, president of Alberta Gas Trunk Line.

Blair, a deceptively unassuming Queen's University chemical engineer who wears cowboy boots and a broom moustache, has suddenly emerged as Alberta's most important businessman. His company, which is the government's policy vehicle in the natural gas industry and handles all its transmission within Alberta's borders, is pushing for an all-Canadian pipeline down from the Beaufort Sea through the Mackenzie Delta into west-central Alberta. A subsidiary called Alberta Gas Ethylene is planning a $250-million chemicals plant at Red Deer. Blair is a

---

*The Mannix group is one of the country's largest construction operations. Subsidiaries of the privately held company (Loram International Ltd.) include Exploram Minerals Ltd., Techman Ltd. (engineering services), Manark Industrial Sales Ltd. (supply company), Empire Development Co. Ltd. (mining exploration), Pembina Pipe Line Ltd. (oil transmission), Loram Construction Inc. (railway rehabilitation), Manalta Holdings Ltd. (land development), and Manalta Coal Ltd. (coal stripping).

member of three important eastern boards, the Bank of Montreal, Canron, and Dofasco, as well as the Economic Council of Canada, and his influence has skyrocketed, though he's made plenty of enemies along the way.

THE ADVENTUROUS HIGH-ROLLERS WHO ONCE GAVE THE ALBERTA BUSINESS COMMUNITY ITS FLAVOUR—Bobby Brown of Home Oil, Frank McMahon of Pacific Petroleums, Neil McQueen of Del Rio and Central Leduc, and Max Bell of Calvan Consolidated—are all gone. Bell, who was by quite a wide margin the most interesting member of this group, made his original oil strike in Turner Valley in 1936. Moving on to the Redwater field in 1948 with F. Ronald Graham and Wilder Ripley, he organized Calvan Consolidated, which he sold out to Petrofina in 1955 for $35 million. He came very close to capturing control of both the Hudson's Bay Company and the CPR, ending up by selling his $6 millions' worth of HBC stock at a large profit and remaining the railway's largest single shareholder, with stock worth a reported $50 million. Bell, who controlled the *Calgary Albertan* and the Victoria dailies, became a major newspaper publisher in 1959 when he and Victor Sifton of the Winnipeg *Free Press* formed FP Publications, which later owned nine papers, including the *Globe and Mail*, the *Vancouver Sun*, the *Ottawa Journal*, and the *Montreal Star*.

Bell was a careless dresser, and the cash cage teller at the *Ottawa Journal* once refused to cash his cheque for fifty dollars until she could check on his credentials. An impatient man, he was visiting Moscow in the spring of 1964 when he found himself caught in the crowds lining the streets to watch the May Day parade. Realizing that he couldn't break through the police lines to get back to his hotel, he took off his jacket, rolled up his sleeves, joined the young Marxists, and marched back to his room.

Alberta Ranches, which Bell owned in partnership with Frank McMahon, Wilder Ripley, and Vance Longden, ran seventy thoroughbreds. He was an intuitive handicapper, and his Meadow Court, which he bought for $9,000 in 1963, won both the Derby at Epsom and the Irish Derby, eventually earning close to $2 million. His greatest ambition was to win the Kentucky Derby. He tried seven times but never succeeded. A staunch Presbyterian, anti-nationalist, and free-enterpriser, he kept in his Calgary office the original anvil that his grandfather, one of Western Canada's first blacksmiths, had used in the 1880s. He owned a palatial home on Twin Islands in British Columbia that had sixteen bedrooms with monogrammed blankets, but he was rarely there and eventually sold it to a German prince. He spent little time aboard his yacht, the 137-foot *Campana*. A non-smoker and non-drinker (his friend Jim Coleman, the sportswriter, once quipped that Bell's idea of debauchery was "to have three flavours of ice cream in the same dish"), he kept himself in top physical shape and conducted some directors' meetings while flexing his muscles with an elastic arm developer. He once startled a group of editors in Victoria by walking across his hotel room on his hands.

TODAY'S ALBERTA ENTREPRENEURS ARE A FAR TAMER BREED. Calgary's power structure remains an anomaly. Nearly all of the largest companies are headed by the Canadian managers of American subsidiaries, most of whom receive their daily marching orders via the computer printouts that arrive from Tulsa, Dallas, Phoenix, or New York.

The business Establishment that does exist (besides some of the Lougheed intimates listed previously) includes Peter Bawden (oil drilling), Robert Campbell (PanCanadian Petroleum), Arthur Child (Burns Foods, and a director of, among other firms, Allendale Mutual in Providence, Rhode Island, which is the largest fire insurance company in the world), Harry Cohen (General Distributors), James Cross (Canada's second-largest rancher), N.R. "Buck" Crump (the former CPR chairman), William Dickie (lawyer and corporate consultant), Ian Doig (Bache and Company Canada), Jack Gallagher (Dome Petroleum), Eddie Galvin (Canadian Industrial Gas and Oil), Kelly Gibson (Pacific Petroleums), Donald Harvie (Petrofina, and one of the heirs to the Eric Harvie fortune), R.F. Jennings (Standard-General Construction), Gerald Knowlton, whose real estate firm specializes in office leasing, Richard Matthews (MacKimmie Matthews; lawyer and corporate director), Carl Nickle (Conventures), Arne Nielsen (Mobil Oil), Ross Phillips (Home Oil), John Poyen (Canadian Petroleum Association), Smiley Raborn (CanDel Oil), Daryl Seaman (Bow Valley Industries), Arthur Smith (power broker), Rodney Touche (investor), and Marsh Williams (Calgary Power).* This contingent is backed by a small group of influential businessmen and corporate directors living in Edmonton: Dr. Charles Allard (Allarco Developments), Louis Desrochers (lawyer, McCuaig Desrochers), E.W. King (Canadian Utilities and Alberta Power), Don Love (Oxford Development Group), D.R.B. McArthur (Inland Cement), William McGregor (Numac Oil and Gas), Stan Milner (Chieftain Development), Hoadley Mitchell (engineer, Mitchell and Associates), H.J. Sanders Pearson (Selkirk Holdings and Century Sales and Service, and former head of the old Taylor, Pearson and Carson automotive wholesale and broadcasting business), G.E. and J.E. Poole (Poole Construction), Frank Spragins (Syncrude), and D.K. Yorath (International Utilities companies).

It's a lively group operating in an incubator atmosphere that guarantees growth and, even more important, financial independence from all those Eastern bastards who have been busily exploiting Alberta since it joined Confederation in 1905. "All that Bay Street stuff is finished," says John Ballem. "What we want from Ontario now is its industries, not its money. There's not that much anger any more. Who could be angry at people who live in Toronto? I feel sorry for them."

Saint John

ALTHOUGH THE POWER STRUCTURE OF NEW BRUNSWICK IS TOTALLY DOMINATED by the feudal impulses of the Irvings

---

*As well as exercising business clout at home, Calgarians have demonstrated a remarkable ability to pursue dollars to the ends of the earth. Canadian-owned petroleum enterprises are heavily international in their orientation, and many local oilmen carry two business cards: one in English and one in Arabic. The main operators outside Canada are Tom Brook, Jack Pierce, Bill Siebens, Peter Bawden, and Home Oil.

and the McCains, the province's economy is developing fast enough to be throwing up a growing number of entrepreneurs.* Some of the most interesting are:

John Burchill of Newcastle runs the family's sawmill interests and sits on the board of New Brunswick Telephone, the Bank of Canada, and the Industrial Development Bank. If anyone can bestride the Miramichi River, the Burchills do.

Chester Campbell, Fredericton's largest tractor and construction equipment dealer, is on the board of N.B. Telephone as well as that of Central and Nova Scotia Trust.

Reuben Cohen, Moncton, has put together a financial mini-empire, encompassing control of Central and Nova Scotia Trust and dominant holdings in Eastern Canada Savings and Loan and the Maritime Life Assurance Company. A lawyer with a large private art collection, he is also becoming important in real estate investments. In mid-1975, in company with Montreal investment man Leonard Ellen, he acquired a 25 per cent interest in Crown Trust.

Kenneth Cox of Saint John is president of N.B. Telephone and has achieved national stature through his directorships in the Bank of Nova Scotia and North American Life Assurance.

Gilbert Finn, St. Anselme, is president of Assomption Mutual Life, chairman of Mother's Own Bakery, and leader of the province's Acadian business community. He is the only director of a chartered bank (Banque Provinciale of Montreal) who also sits on the board of the Bank of Canada.

Whidden Ganong runs the family candy factory at St. Stephen and is a director of N.B. Telephone.

---

*Although it's controlled by Bell Canada, N.B. Telephone concentrates on its board much of the province's business power. Eight names on this list are N.B. Telephone directors.

Horace Hanson, Fredericton, is a lawyer with important financial connections through the Central and Nova Scotia Trust Company.

Mitchell Franklin of Saint John owns and operates (with Halifax partner Peter Herschorn) expanding chains of movie theatres and hotels, including the Lord Nelson in Halifax.

Alfred Landry, Shediac, the senior partner of Moncton's largest law firm, is on the boards of N.B. Tel., Mother's Own Bakery, and Assomption Mutual.

Joseph Likely, Saint John, is big in construction, concrete, and dredging; he's a director of the Bank of Montreal and N.B. Tel.

Leonard Lockhart, Moncton, heads the family-owned building supply firm of Lockharts Limited and is chairman of N.B. Tel.

Hugh Hazen Mackay, Rothesay, is a director of Pitfield, Mackay and the Canada Permanent companies and a Conservative fund-raiser. He's the son of the late Hugh Mackay—lumberman, financier, and former leader of the Conservatives in New Brunswick.

James MacMurray of Saint John is the local partner for Richardson Securities and on the boards of several New Brunswick firms. He also acts as chief bagman for the Tories.

Andrew McCain, Florenceville, is operating head of the McCain potato complex and also on the board of N.B. Tel. He is an important Liberal bagman.

Donald McLean, Black's Harbour, manages Connors Brothers, now a Weston subsidiary, but his family remains influential.

Philip Oland, Saint John, is head of the family-owned Moosehead Breweries, a director of the Commerce. A good committee man, he wants to be lieutenant-governor of the province.

Patrick Rocca, Saint John, runs the Rocca group of construction companies, which have become the province's largest builders of shopping centres and redevelopers of Saint John's downtown core. He enjoys flying to Montreal on weekends to watch the hockey games.

Joseph Streeter, Saint John, an occasional Liberal bagman, now works for Pitfield, Mackay. His family owns Minto Coal Company.

George Urquhart, Moncton, a former Irving manager, heads the Sumner group of companies, hardware wholesalers and building supply dealers. The group was bought in 1972 by Hugh Russel Limited of Toronto.

THE PERSONAL POWERHOUSE ON THE PROVINCE'S BUSINESS SCENE—now that K.C. Irving has fled to the tax haven of Bermuda—is Harrison McCain, the blunt and self-confident head of the multinational $100-million conglomerate based on the humble New Brunswick potato.* "The McCains," wrote Walter Stewart,† "bestride Victoria and Carleton counties, in the heart of New Brunswick's rich potato belt, like a colossus; they own practically everything in sight, and what they don't own they run, and what they can't run, they have under contract, and anything they don't own, run or hold under contract, they watch very warily indeed."

The McCain operating methods are a hybrid combina-

---

*The McCain empire was originally based on McCain Produce Ltd., Canada's largest exporter of seed and table potatoes, which was founded by Andrew McCain, Sr., who left his six children a modest fortune when he died in 1953. Andrew and Robert, the two elder brothers, stayed in growing and selling unprocessed potatoes, but Harrison and Wallace established McCain Foods Ltd. As well as processing 250,000 pounds of potatoes per hour, largely for export, this newer company also owns a large fleet of truck-trailers (through Day & Ross Ltd.); a farm machinery plant (Thomas Equipment); a Holstein breeding operation (MacBan Sales Agency Ltd.); export subsidiaries in Europe, Australia, and the Caribbean; and several fertilizer and cold storage companies. Its manufacturing operations (french fries, pizza, frozen vegetables and desserts) are located at Florenceville and a new plant at Grand Falls, which was built with a $5.5-million grant from the federal government.
†Walter Stewart, *Hard to Swallow* (Toronto: Macmillan, 1974).

tion of the kind of para-military tactics practised on Peruvian cattle ranches and the something less than benign paternalism of the old Southern plantations. (Agricultural technicians keep in touch by walkie-talkie as they inspect the potato fields, while the farmers live an almost indentured existence, to the point of having to make up the difference personally in bad years when deliveries don't match their contracts.)

Most of the McCains reside on River View Drive, overlooking Florenceville. After a recent visit, Harry Bruce wrote in *Maclean's*: "As you move south on River View Drive, the St. John River Valley slides along below your left and eastern elbow; like a huntsman's dream, the voluptuous fields and the wooded hills fade to the sky for miles; and, close at hand, on both sides of your car, there are these houses, modern mansions really, and it's doubtful if any dwellings anywhere in Canada speak so eloquently of New Wealth. One has great white pillars out front, as though its owner had never recovered from a love affair with *Gone with the Wind*. Surely, you think, these houses do not belong here. They must be foreigners. Torontonians maybe. It must have cost a dozen fortunes to pluck them off the tame lawns of Toronto's superaffluent Bayview Village and set them down here so that their Importance can observe the river and, each morning of another profitable day, can greet the sun as it rises over tens of thousands of acres of potato fields. But no appearance could be more deceiving. For no family anywhere could possibly be more *in* place than the McCains are on River View Drive; and their homes, no matter how they might offend some presumptuous stranger's delicate eye for the historical mood of the valley, belong up here as surely as God made big, white spuds."*

The grandeur of the McCains seems out of place only because it's a throwback to another era. The great New Brunswick merchant families—the Millers of Campbellton, the Piries of Grand Falls, the McLeans of Charlotte, the Taits of Shediac, the Kents of Bathurst—treated their districts like fiefs, running the stores, controlling the markets, holding the mortgages, dominating the politics. The Mc-

Maclean's, November, 1973.

Cains and their miniature kingdom at Florenceville perpetuate the tradition of these feudal dynasties, but their only genuine twentieth-century descendant was Kenneth Colin Irving, the last and most splendid of their line.*

"Every New Brunswicker knows—though he may not be aware of knowing it—that K.C. Irving is a lot more than just a man," wrote Russell Hunt and Robert Campbell.† "K.C. Irving is a social phenomenon on the same level of importance as a revolution or a war. And his importance is equally difficult to measure. You can't do it, for instance, by counting up how much his companies own or how much they earn, because the figures simply aren't available. Nor can the Irving power be neatly or easily measured. If there ever was a company town covering 28,000 square miles, with a population of 600,000, New Brunswick is it; and the company is K.C. Irving Ltd.—a company that was begun by Irving and his father in 1926 as a Ford dealership, but which has grown in less than fifty years to be the single most powerful economic force in eastern Canada."

Irving was born in 1899 at Buctouche, an oyster-fishing village on New Brunswick's east coast where his father operated sawmills and a general store. After brief stints at Dalhousie and Acadia universities, young Irving established the local dealership for the Model T and became Imperial Oil's agent for Kent County. By 1924, he was selling so much gas and oil that Imperial suddenly disfranchised him to take over distribution for its own account. An outraged Irving got a bank loan, put in storage tanks, and built his own service stations, painting them red, white, and blue, the same colours as Imperial's, determined to challenge the outsider's supremacy. Within four years, his company was a success and he moved his operations to the five-storey garage in Saint John that remained his headquarters for the next forty-three years. He started a

---

*It's hardly a coincidence that the two most successful McCain brothers —Harrison and Wallace—apprenticed under Irving. By the time he was thirty, Harrison had risen to be Irving Oil's sales manager for New Brunswick; Wallace, at twenty-three, was already manager of the Irving-owned Thorne's Hardware operation. They left in 1957 to start up their own enterprises. Harrison is married to Billie, daughter of former Liberal premier, chief justice, and lieutenant-governor John McNair (who died in 1968). Wallace is married to Margaret Norrie, daughter of Senator Margaret Fawcett Norrie of Truro, N.S. Margaret McCain inherited money from her father, a mining engineer.

†Russell Hunt and Robert Campbell, *K.C. Irving—The Art of the Industrialist* (Toronto: McClelland and Stewart, 1973).

construction company to build his stations, went into shipping, bus lines, and lumber, acquired the Saint John Shipbuilding and Dry Dock Company. One of his most profitable deals was the purchase, in 1945, of the New Brunswick Railway Company, for a reported $1 million. It had no rolling stock to its name but held title to a million acres of choice timber stands. During World War II, Irving operated Canada Veneers, the leading supplier of fuselages for the famous Mosquito fighter-bombers.

His immense energy combined with the country-store clerk's shrewdness that characterized his deals kept the roster of his enterprises lengthening so that eventually Irving controlled a hundred companies employing one in every twelve of the province's workers and owned fully one-tenth of New Brunswick's land area. In partnership with Standard Oil of California, he put up a $50-million refinery near Saint John, and with the heirs of Simon Patino, the Bolivian tin king, financed exploitation of the base-metal deposits near Bathurst, N.B. His gasoline stations grew into a chain of two thousand outlets. He acquired every English-language newspaper and most of the important radio and TV outlets in the province. There was no single public stock offering in any of his enterprises, so that his personal ownership remained undiluted, and their earnings never had to be disclosed. The *New York Times* in 1971 assessed the worth of Irving's empire at $600 million. "K.C. Irving *is* New Brunswick," Brigadier Michael Wardell, publisher of the Irving-owned Fredericton *Daily Gleaner,* boasted with not a little justification.

A tearless Presbyterian who didn't drink, smoke, or swear, Irving was ruthless and unfeeling in pursuing business interests to the point of stopping farmers from trying to appropriate as firewood the odd loose log left at a river's edge after his great spring drives. In the fall of 1973, four young fishermen were fined $700 for daring to dip their lines in Irving's private fishing pond near the salmon-rich Miramichi. "The corporate aspects of K.C. Irving, impressive and mysterious as they are, do not begin to match his personal aspects," reported Ralph Allen after meeting him.* "He is a lean man, very hard and wary. He looks

_____
*In *Maclean's*, April 18, 1964.

like a print of an English bare-knuckles fighter, a James
Figg or a John Broughton or a Cheshire Hero. He is six
feet tall, with wide shoulders and a narrow waist. He is
as bald as an iceberg, his eyes are deep and gray, his jaw
is square and strong and his aquiline nose is a little off-
centre, as if it had been hit by a lucky punch."

He worked a sixteen-hour day, running his empire by
means of a private radio network connected into his office
in Saint John's Golden Ball garage. Constantly in motion,
he was always aboard one of his four airplanes, three
cars, or innumerable ships, inspecting, probing, cutting the
fat, driving up the profits. "His concept of 'pleasure' must
have been exactly the same as his concept of 'work,'"
remarked Ned Belliveau, a public relations adviser, who
grew to know him well. "Irving had a splendid fishing
lodge on the superb Restigouche River, next to the Ristigouche Salmon Club.* But when Irving's guests went
off to fish, KC would stay on the front porch shuffling
papers."

His corporate structure, which no outsider ever managed to disentangle, was so complicated that in the summer
of 1971, when the seamen on one of his tankers, the
Irving Ours Polaire, wanted to get their union certified,
they literally couldn't discover the name of the corporation
that owned the ship.†

His machinations reportedly included a complicated
method of escaping Canadian taxes by funnelling his im-
ports of crude oil from the Persian Gulf or Venezuela
through dummy offshore corporations. This system was
best described by Charles McElman during a speech in the
Canadian Senate on March 10, 1971: "The oil goes
physically to the Saint John refinery. But on paper it goes
to that convenient tax haven, the Bahamas. Two companies become involved. For purposes of discussion we will
call them Eastern Trading and Western Trading. Eastern
is a Bahamian company, which buys crude at the low
source price. Eastern sells the crude to Western, the Canadian company, at a vastly inflated price. The price is so

---

*See Chapter 12 for a description of this club.
†The ship was out on a twenty-year charter to Irving Oil, even though
its actual ownership was unevenly divided among J.D. Irving Ltd., Kent
Line Ltd., Universal Sales Ltd., and Engineering Consultants Ltd., vari-
ously held Irving subsidiaries.

high that the poor refinery operation is in trouble. Some years it cannot even show a profit or pay the national wage rate to its employees. Other years it can squeeze out a small profit and pay a correspondingly small corporate tax to the Federal Government."

His arrangements with the province were also generous. In 1964, the New Brunswick Legislature passed an act on behalf of the Irving-controlled East Coast Smelting and Chemical specifying that "The Company, with the approval of the Lieutenant Governor in Council, may, without the consent of the owner thereof or of any person interested therein, enter upon, take possession of, expropriate and use such lands and privileges, easements, servitudes, rights and interests in such and appertaining to such lands, including riparian rights, but excluding mineral rights, as the Company shall deem necessary or useful."

Irving had little use for politicians who wouldn't perform exactly as he expected. Premier John McNair, the Liberal who governed New Brunswick from 1940 to 1952, for example, was staunchly supported until Irving noticed that a tiny bus service he was operating from St. Anthony in Kent County to Moncton wasn't bringing in enough profit, because some of the people along its route insisted on using car pools. Irving was outraged. He demanded that McNair outlaw car pools. When the Premier diplomatically pointed out that this was hardly a matter within his jurisdiction, Irving lost faith in McNair and backed his Conservative opponent.

But it was the politicians who finally drove Irving out of Canada. Premier Richard Hatfield's new succession duties legislation, which followed changes in the federal budget, was due to go into effect on January 1, 1972, and the federal capital gains tax became effective at the same time. Nine days earlier, K.C. Irving quietly departed for Nassau and later settled into the former Trimingham mansion in Bermuda. His operations were taken over by three sons, Jack (known as Gassy), Jim (Oily), and Arthur (Greasy).

It was left to the Irving-owned Saint John *Telegraph-Journal* to write this epitaph: "Is New Brunswick richer or poorer, not in a financial sense but in every other way, because he has taken his leave? Is New Brunswick richer or poorer? Does the sun shine? Is there water in the ocean?

Is it dark at night? There are some questions which do not need answers. There are some questions for which everyone knows the answer."

Vancouver

CRANES MOVE AWKWARDLY AGAINST THE SKYLINE. The Mies van der Rohe glass-and-steel towers crowd the old gas stations, the three-storey walkups and furriers' stores, as the city rebuilds itself every ninety days, or so it seems.

Vancouver is the Canadian Establishment's frontier. The fiscal gunslingers are more *macho* here than anywhere else; the potential stakes are higher. If you're lucky, you survive; if you're luckier still, you get to stay.

Frontier towns, even those as sophisticated as Vancouver, are places (and states of mind) to escape to— habitats to lose and find yourself in. Living on a frontier implies existing on the edge of undiscovered potential, in yourself as well as your environment. It's this kind of inner excitement that makes Vancouver Canada's most sensuous city.

What Vancouver doesn't have is the kind of integrated self-assurance, that "I-am-important-and-what-could-be-more-fitting" attitude that goes with the Montreal rich and the Toronto powerful. It's not just that those cities are older in terms of having been in existence longer, but that they are more accustomed to wielding power. Corporate authority was flowing out of Toronto when Granville Street was still a trail through the forest and out of Montreal long before that. The very idea of indigenous British Columbia corporate power, in anything but its most primitive forms, is a postwar phenomenon.

There's hardly anybody still important in Vancouver whose own experience, or at least that of his father or grandfather, didn't encompass the actual hard work of his trade. Men who started out in the bush by buying a saw and went on from there. This is very different from the roots that nourish the great power centres of Eastern Canada, where the men who count have usually been removed for three or four generations from the actual labour on which their wealth is based. They have been raised in the private schools and hushed offices, grown up surrounded by antiques, been sent on chaperoned tours, through Europe; they have mommies and daddies who were also raised on these things, and that's why they don't feel so raw, so vulnerable, so eager, or so self-aware.

This contrasting ambience reflects itself in unexpected ways: the thinly disguised anti-Semitism of the Vancouver Club, for example, which comes out of the unease of the powerful here. If you're not sure of your right to be exclusive, you go to any length to protect what exclusivity you have. In Toronto, the clubs can afford to have a couple of assimilated Jews around and it doesn't scare members out of their rights. But in Vancouver, that remains too large a leap. (Some of Vancouver's cultured European Jews sadly turn themselves into Anglicans, and even then it doesn't work.)

This same search for self-assurance also begets the flight into self-gratification that characterizes Vancouver's Establishment. Here is the fittest elite in the country. They're always jogging around Shaughnessy, splashing in their pools, sailing their fifty-footers out of the RVYC, tootling up to their chalets at Whistler, wintering at Palm Desert or on Maui, summering on Savary or Hernando.

United by a common perception about the kind of life they hope to share, cut off by the Rockies and their self-induced astigmatism from considering alternatives, the members of Vancouver's Establishment thrive on an intensification of interconnections—in work, at the clubs, at hockey games, and, one gathers, in bed. Someone always seems to be running off with somebody's wife, marrying somebody's daughter, merging with somebody's widow, forming a family coalition to stop or start something. (Much mention is made of wives. There is a certain respect for the woman born to wealthy parents and a great deal of respect for the man shrewd enough to snag one.)

Everybody talks about the same things. A few years ago it was the miracle of Simon Fraser University. How beautiful it all was, because it had been built by Arthur Erickson, B.C.'s very own architect, forced into unheard-of quick production by B.C.'s own Gordon Shrum (and fashioned out of cement from B.C.'s own cartel). Now everybody talks about Dave Barrett's most recent indiscretion, Arthur Erickson's new government building, John

Turner's next visit, Jack Clyne's latest farewell address, Allan Fotheringham's sources, and Jack Webster's nerve.

What nobody talks about, or wants to hear, is gossip of Ottawa or news from Toronto. B.C. is the only mainland province in Canada that hasn't produced a prime minister or opposition leader in its own right. Who cares? The Toronto men arrive in their pressed suits and white shirts, braving their jet-lag, bursting with all these fantastic insights, and nobody wants to listen. In this way, Vancouver is like the spoiled daughter of a *nouveau riche* millionaire. She wants it all. And the only way she can be sure she has it all is to insist that nobody else have anything. Most loyal Vancouverites try to block Toronto's very existence out of their collective memories, refusing to believe that anything important, interesting, or beautiful can ever happen there.* If it is thought about at all, Toronto is regarded as some distant imperial centre of less consequence economically than Tokyo, culturally than San Francisco, and emotionally than London. At the same time, whenever the B.C. boosters deign to come east, they act like wild-eyed ambassadors from a misty Shangri-la beyond the Rockies, mercilessly raving on about their non-existent winters and postcard scenery, dismissing suggested qualifications as attacks, not just on their taste, but on their honour.

BECAUSE OF BRITISH COLUMBIA'S RELATIVE NEWNESS, fewer power centres are formed around established wealth. Individual clout tends to be transitory, related directly to corporate, municipal, provincial, and philanthropic hierarchies. An Establishment certainly exists. But entry is not very difficult and upward mobility can be rapid. (The quickest way to tell who's really important in Vancouver is to visit his office in one of the new downtown towers. The higher it is, the better, of course, but what

---

*Part of the problem in communication is due simply to the time zone differences. By the time most Vancouverites reach their offices, it's close to the lunch break in Toronto. Much of the day's power adjusting and trading have already been done and most key people are leaving for lunch. By the time they get back, the B.C. man may be out to lunch himself, and when *he* returns, his Toronto contact has probably gone home to beat the traffic on the Don Valley Parkway.

really counts is whether or not it's located in the building's *northwest* corner, with a prime view of the harbour and mountains.)

The B.C. economy is made up of fewer than a hundred major companies, some of them empire-size, which make huge investments and large profits, mainly in mining and logging. The capital required is so immense that much of it has had to be imported, transferring control of something like two-thirds of the province's economy to outsiders.

With so many dominant corporations—B.C. Telephone,* Crown Zellerbach, Placer Development, Lornex Mining, Kaiser Resources, Laurentide Financial Corporation, B.C. Forest Products, Brenda Mines, and Kelly, Douglas among them—owned by non-B.C. residents, the local business Establishment represents only a fraction of disposable power.† The Canadian Pacific enjoys a particularly strong presence. It is the biggest shareholder (12.3 per cent) in the province's largest company (MacMillan Bloedel) and controls (60 per cent) B.C.'s second-largest corporation (Cominco). The railway also has 100 per cent of CP Air (which, if it were a separate operation, would rank as the province's tenth-largest firm); another subsidiary, Marathon Realty, manages some of Vancouver's most valuable real estate holdings; Pacific Logging and Fording Coal are two more growing CP operations. The province's best-known hotel—the Empress in Victoria—is also CP-owned.‡

The fortunes made by the imaginative pioneers who first exploited the province's natural wealth have either been dispersed or become money without much power attached. Harvey Reginald MacMillan, the most impressive member of this group, made his first profit from an ice-cream stand he set up for visiting farmers while he was a

---

*It is controlled by Anglo-Canadian Telephone Company in Montreal, which is 83 per cent owned by General Telephone and Electronics Corp. of New York.

†Howard Urquhart, president and CEO of Rayonier Canada, a subsidiary of ITT, must get approval from the U.S. for any expenditure of more than $25,000.

‡Ian Sinclair is hardly David Barrett's favourite businessman. But the Premier asked him to leave the office only once: when the CP chairman flew in all the way from Montreal to request that cleaning staff at the Empress be exempted from B.C.'s new minimum wage legislation.

student at the Ontario Agricultural College in Guelph. In 1915, he resigned as B.C.'s chief forester and four years later, with one stenographer, started a timber export business. By 1935 he was the world's largest charterer of merchant shipping and making so much money selling other companies' timber that a group of B.C. firms decided to set up an export agency, Seaboard Lumber Sales, and its affiliate, Seaboard Shipping. MacMillan began buying up sawmills and laid the groundwork for the giant MacMillan Bloedel complex. He's lived in retirement since the early 1960s, with most of his estate divided among two daughters (Mrs. Gordon Southam and Mrs. John Lecky) and philanthropic enterprises. W.J. Van Dusen, a long-time MacMillan associate, is now chairman of the Vancouver Foundation.* Frank McMahon, who made his fortune out of Pacific Petroleums and West-coast Transmission, now commutes between the tax haven of the Bahamas and his mansion in Palm Beach. Gordon Farrell, whose family controlled B.C. Telephone and who put together Ocean Cement, now spends most of his time growing orchids. Fred Brown, a real shaker, who held directorships in twelve major corporations, died in 1970.† Charles Bentall, the founder of Dominion Construction, died at ninety-two in 1974. Of the Spencers (who sold their department stores to Eaton's in 1948), perhaps the most interesting survivor is Barbara, a friend of Jack Kennedy's from Harvard days who was one of the two women from Canada he invited to his inauguration in Washington. She used to ranch in the Cariboo and was the first woman director of the Cariboo Cattlemen's Association but gave up the isolated life several years ago and

---

*In 1973, the board of directors of the Vancouver Foundation, which exists "to facilitate the application of private resources to the public good," included Van Dusen as chairman, H.M. Boyce (Gordon Farrell's son-in-law and chairman, Yorkshire Trust Company), Donald M. Clark, Q.C. (son of one of the last two surviving generals from the Canadian Corps of World War I), J. Norman Hyland (a former president of B.C. Packers), J.O. Wilson, former chief justice of the B.C. Supreme Court, J. Lyman Trumbull (long-time businessman and husband of Senator Norman Paterson's sister), and W.T. Brown (president of Odlum Brown & T.B. Read Ltd.).

†His funeral was a gathering of Vancouver's business Establishment. Pallbearers included C.D. Anderson, L.L.G. Bentley, P.C. Birks, H.N. Burgess, H.R. Butler, A.B. Christopher, C.N. Effinger, H.M. Gale, C.C.P. Gray, J.S. Keate, G.C. King, V.F. MacLean, E.C. Mainwaring, Dr. R.F. McKechnie, G.B. McKeen, J.A. McLallen, C.H. McLean, Dr. J.A. McLean, J.A. McMahon, and N.R. Whittall.

now lives in the Okanagan. The Graham interests surface
only occasionally (such as their 25 per cent holding in
Okanagan Helicopters) through a Montreal-based investment company, Graymont. The Wallaces,* Pembertons,
Walkems, Letsons, Tuppers, Hanburys, and Malkins have
virtually disappeared from contention, but various Bell-
Irvings still appear on corporate boards. The Koerner
fortune is now administered from Toronto by Walter's
son Michael.† The Reifels, who made their money in
brewing and distilling and by selling liquor that found its
way down the coast to the U.S. in the late twenties and
early thirties, are now represented mainly by George H.
Reifel (son of George C., whose name is borne by a
waterfowl refuge at the mouth of the Fraser) and Charles
"Chuck" Wills, a cousin who was the youngest officer to
get a command in the Royal Canadian Navy during World
War II and is a member of the Farris law firm and
corporate director. (The liquor trade down the coast was
carried out by a number of companies, among them Consolidated Exporters, which operated such craft as the five-

*Clarence Wallace owned the *Fifer*, one of the largest pleasure boats
to sail out of Vancouver in postwar years; 104 feet long, she was worth
a million dollars. But the great days of yachts in Vancouver were the
years between the wars, and many of the more famous craft put in time
as rumrunners. They included the clipper-bowed *Moonlight Maid* (207
feet, 798 tons), which in the thirties was operated as a yacht by theatre
man Willis P. Dewees after service on Rum Row under the name
Kuyakuzmt, and Eric Hamber's 380-ton *Vencedor*; both had been owned
previously by J.W. Hobbs, who built the Marine Building and was one
of the great Vancouver promoters of the Prohibition era. Joe Hobbs
later started the Great Glen cattle ranch, a Wild West spread in the West
Highlands. It included Inverlochy Castle and became a Scottish showplace. The lovely *Moonlight Maid* was broken up in 1948. Eric Hamber,
one of the province's leading businessmen, outlived the *Vencedor*, which
had started life as the schooner *Exmouth II*. He died in 1960 (the same
year as Victor Spencer, whose yacht was the *Deerleap*), with no direct
heirs; a provincial park in the wilderness of the Rockies bears his name.
Graham Dawson now owns his Vancouver house. Joe Hobbs sold his
Highland ranch in 1961 and retired to his castle. He died in 1963. In
1958 Hamber sold his showplace Minnekhada Stock Farms in Coquitlam
to Clarence Wallace, who sold 1,030 acres of the tract in 1975 to Daon
Development, which was acting as an intermediary for an agency of the
NDP government and turned over the property for $2 million. Wallace kept
seven hundred acres of marsh for wildfowl shooting. His nephew Stuart, a
lawyer, recently became president of Premier Cablevision Ltd., which
operates cable TV systems in Victoria, Vancouver, Coquitlam, Oakville,
Toronto, Ireland, and the United Kingdom.
†Alaska Pine, the Koerner company founded in 1939, acquired the
Killam-owned B.C. Pulp and Paper in 1951 in partnership with Abitibi.
In 1954 Rayonier Inc. bought control of the company, renamed Alaska
Pine & Cellulose Ltd., for $25 million. Walter Koerner remained chairman
of Rayonier Canada Ltd. until 1972, and a nephew, Peter Sloan, is still
a vice-president. Leon Koerner, who died in 1977, spent most of the last
decade of his life as the West Coast's most enlightened philanthropist, a
mandate later perpetuated by his brother.

masted schooner *Malahat* and the three-masted *Coal Harbour*.)

The business Establishment (which comes closer in Vancouver to being the *social* Establishment than it does anywhere else) includes:

Ian Barclay, Ashbury College and Harvard graduate, son of a Montreal judge, is president of B.C. Forest Products (controlled by Noranda and Mead Corporation), a Royal Bank director, and serves on the Economic Council of Canada.

Morris Belkin owns Belkin Packaging in partnership with B.C. Sugar. Not really a member of the Establishment, he's important because he may be the only Vancouver businessman David Barrett takes seriously, because he once worked for him.

Clark Bentall is head of Dominion Construction and its affiliated firms, besides having a seat on the Canada Trust, Toronto-Dominion Bank, Cominco, and Scott Paper boards.

L.L.G. "Poldi" Bentley dominates the Canadian Forest Products-Cornat complex, which is British Columbia's largest privately owned operation. As well as Bentley, it includes his son, Peter, his brother-in-law, John G. Prentice, and Prentice's son-in-law, Ron Longstaffe.*

Douglas McK. Brown, a partner of Russell and DuMoulin, extends his influence eastward through his directorship in Crown Life.

W. Thomas Brown, a highly respected investment dealer (Odlum Brown & T.B. Read), was a member of the Royal Commission on Banking and Finance in the early 1960s.

Arthur Christopher, a school dropout, made his original fortune by putting together a national chain of laundries

---

*For details of this operation, see Chapter 8.

(Nelsons) which was sold to Steiner American Corporation in 1968. He now sits on the boards of MacMillan Bloedel and the Royal Bank. Never quite an insider, he's remembered for the time his 57-foot yacht put into Savary Island flying the Nelsons Laundries flag from her spreaders.

Ronald Cliff is chairman of Inland Natural Gas and on the board of nineteen other companies. An accountant who loves flying, he is active in the Vancouver Symphony Association and Hockey Canada. His wife's father, Fred Brown, was chairman of Pacific Press.

Graham Dawson heads his family construction firm and is a director of Canada Life Assurance, the Bank of Montreal, and Kaiser Resources, in addition to being on the National Trust advisory board. Vancouver's most tight-fisted millionaire, he once complained to a golf partner, after he'd lost the game and discovered he owed 25 cents, that he had provided a round of chocolate bars at the ninth hole and therefore shouldn't have to pay the full amount.

Clayton Boston "Slim" Delbridge, a financier and former publisher of Vancouver's old third daily paper, the *News-Herald,* is chairman and president of Pacific Press but stands in danger of becoming known mainly as Allan Fotheringham's father-in-law. He was president of the B.C. Lions in 1964, the only year they won the Grey Cup.

Jack Diamond, head of the B.C. Jockey Club and chancellor of Simon Fraser University, acts as the leader of Vancouver's Jewish community.

A. John Ellis, B.C. operating head for the Bank of Montreal, is the chairman of the Canada Development Corporation, which maintains its token headquarters in Vancouver but is really run from Toronto by Tony Hampson.

Frank Griffiths is a chartered accountant who has become important in Canadian television. He heads Western

Broadcasting, which controls the Vancouver Canucks. His wife is a Ballard (pet food).

William Hamilton is a deceptively mild-mannered former cabinet minister in the Diefenbaker government who comes as close as any member of the Vancouver business community to earning the accolade of statesman. Now president of the Employers' Council of B.C., he's chairman of Century Insurance and Fidelity Life.

Gerald Hobbs, a highly visible and unabashedly powerful presence, runs the vast and expanding Cominco empire, which now includes mining ventures in Australia, Greenland, and Spain. He's also a director of B.C. Telephone, the Bank of Nova Scotia, MacMillan Bloedel, and Pacific Press.

Stu Keate, of the *Vancouver Sun,* probably influences the local (and national) Establishments more than any other newspaper publisher in the country, acting as an enlightened and enlightening conduit between the makers and consumers of public opinion.

Thomas Ladner is the son of Leon Ladner, who read law with Sir Charles Hibbert Tupper and became one of John Diefenbaker's closest confidants. The younger Ladner now runs one of the fastest-growing law firms in the country. He is a director of seventeen corporations (including Confederation Life and Molson Companies) and through Hastings West Investment helps funnel large doses of Hong Kong money into the country.

Victor MacLean, a grandson of Robert Kelly, one of the founders of Kelly, Douglas, stepped down in 1974 as chairman and president of the wholesale grocery and supermarket operator (which, like another pioneer B.C. food supplier, Malkin's, is owned by Weston's).

Hugh Martin, a former Liberal campaign chairman whose name has come up in federal dredging charges, heads a large construction and hotel operation besides being a director of CP Air and Interprovincial Steel and

Pipe. (He's a former son-in-law of Gordon Farrell; his second wife, Danae, is a Greek whose previous husband, shipowner Panos Gratsos, took off with Iby Koerner's daughter.)

Allan McGavin, born in Scotland, educated at Upper Canada College, the Army and Navy Academy in San Diego, and the Ontario Agricultural College in Guelph, is the head of Vancouver's largest bakery operation and sits on eleven important boards, including the Bank of Nova Scotia, Hudson's Bay Company, and John Labatt.

George McKeen, son of the late Liberal senator Stanley McKeen, inherited a tug and barge fleet and industrial holdings. He merged the family's Straits Towing with the Cosulich family's RivTow Marine. The merged company, RivTow Straits, is now run by the Cosuliches. McKeen is an officer or director of several companies in the Cornat group, acquired recently by Canadian Forest Products, and a director of Dawson Construction and Daon Development. He's on the advisory committee of Crown Trust.

John Nichol—a rich man's son, a lieutenant-governor's grandson, former president of the National Liberal Federation, ex-senator, investor, sometime owner of Hernando Island, whose lots were sold to fifty selected families—is a highly influential power broker. Most of his activities flow through Springfield Investment. He's a director of Crown Zellerbach Canada, Time Canada, Bethlehem Copper, and associated with Western Approaches, which in 1975 was awarded the licence for Vancouver's third English-language television station.

James Pattison is very much outside the Establishment, yet financially significant. Pattison's father worked as a door-to-door piano tuner before acquiring the car dealership that gave a start to young Jimmy's machinations. Until June, 1975, he drove a $30,000 Cadillac.* He plays

---

*The custom automobile had velvet upholstery, colour TV, a refrigerator, a telephone, a robe and pillow, shag rugs made of crushed velvet, and a remote-control starter that allowed Pattison to start the car from his office or bedroom, so that it was either heated or air-conditioned by the time he was ready to step into it.

trumpet at the Glad Tidings Temple on Fraser Street twice every Sunday and when Howard Hughes was staying at the Bayshore, he had his office telescope trained on the American millionaire's hotel window to see if he could pick up any tricks. "Who else but Jimmy Pattison," wrote Allan Fotheringham in *Impetus,* "could walk into the Vancouver Club, that varicose-veined reservoir of tasteful tweed dignity, wearing a white tie with blue polka dots the size of Saskatchewan hailstones, a blue-and-white checked shirt and a suit of black, white and blue stripes. *Wide* stripes. Who else?"

Pattison's main company, Neonex International, became the glamour conglomerate of the late sixties. Starting with his 1968 purchases of Northern Paint Company and Overwaitea, a B.C. chain of grocery stores whose name (over-weight tea) seems to puzzle outsiders, he went on a rampage of monthly acquisitions until his pace was stopped in an unsuccessful attempt to take over Maple Leaf Mills. More cautious now, Pattison has installed a computer to watch his cash flows.

John Pitts, chairman and president of Okanagan Helicopters, a McGill engineering graduate and a Harvard MBA, is a director of a number of companies, including B.C. Sugar, B.C. Tel, and Crows Nest Industries. A partner with him in several companies a few years ago was George O'Brien, also a Harvard MBA, whose main interest in recent years has been ocean racing.

John W. Poole, president of Daon Development, one of Vancouver's fastest-growing developers, came to the Coast from the Prairies and is rapidly moving Daon's operations into Alberta. Daon changed its name from Dawson Developments in 1973; its chairman is still Graham Dawson; 1974 profits were up 86 per cent over 1973's.

J. Ernest Richardson, the beleaguered chairman of B.C. Tel, is a Dalhousie law graduate who moved out to Vancouver from the presidency of Maritime Telegraph and Telephone; he's a director of MacMillan Bloedel and the Canadian Imperial Bank of Commerce.

Forrest Rogers is the fourth son of B.C. Sugar founder B.T. Rogers. His influence is waning, but he does maintain national connections as a Bank of Montreal director. A nephew, Peter Cherniavsky, is president and managing director of B.C. Sugar. (An abrupt, bulldog character, Rogers picked up the phone one morning and was surprised to find himself being asked about rising sugar prices by Pat Burns, one of Vancouver's open-line radio hotshots. "Mr. Rogers, this is Pat Burns, CJOR; you're on the air before forty thousand listeners . . ." Rogers cut in with "The hell I am!" and hung up.)

Robert Rogers, one-time protégé of E.P. Taylor and now chief executive officer of Crown Zellerbach Canada, is a director of seven national corporations, including the Canadian Imperial Bank of Commerce, Genstar, Royal General Insurance, and Hilton Canada. His strong personality helps to expand his considerable influence.

Percy Ritchie Sandwell, chairman of his own international engineering consulting firm, extends his authority through several key directorships, including a seat on the board of the Royal Bank. His Athabasca Columbia Resources is active in real estate and trucking.

Peter Paul Saunders, a Hungarian by birth and by persuasion, has been deeply involved in Vancouver's financial life for twenty-five years, currently as CEO of Cornat Industries, the conglomerate recently purchased by Canadian Forest Products.

James Sinclair, a Rhodes Scholar, was once fisheries minister in the St. Laurent government. He is slowly phasing himself out of his many directorships. A charmer with a lively sense of humour, he is none too comfortable as Pierre Trudeau's father-in-law and worked for John Turner during the Liberal leadership convention.

Austin G.E. Taylor is the son of the Vancouver financier, rancher, and horseman Austin C. Taylor (who made his first million by his early twenties and who lent the federal government an interest-free $2 million during

World War II). Taylor Senior died in 1965. Taylor Junior was known in his youth as Firp (after the Argentine heavyweight boxer Luis Angel Firpo, the Wild Bull of the Pampas). His sister Patricia is Mrs. William Buckley, wife of the *National Review* editor (and sometime New York mayoral candidate), and his stepdaughter Lisa and Chunky Woodward's son John were married in 1974. Taylor Senior's showplace estate on Vancouver's southern slope (built for B.T. Rogers by the late Charles Bentall) has been converted into an Erickson-designed townhouse and apartment development, Shannon Mews.

Denis Timmis is chief executive officer of MacMillan Bloedel, a director of Canadian Pacific, Canadian General Electric, and the Canadian Imperial Bank of Commerce. Formed out of a series of mergers, "MacBlo" is North America's seventh-largest forestry operation and Canada's biggest manufacturer and exporter of forest products. Sales in 1974 exceeded $1.4 billion for a net profit of $72 million; assets are increasing at the rate of a million dollars a week. The entire complex, which consists of about 130 separate companies employing 23,000, is slowly and imperceptibly being moved out of B.C., beyond the reach of its socialist politicians. (Already, more than 35 per cent of MacBlo's earnings are being generated outside its home province.)

Alexander Walton, a former Vancouver manager for the Bank of Montreal and brother of the composer Sir William Walton, is still active in business through Marlfair Holdings. Until recently he spent much of his time collecting funds for the federal Liberals and advising on high-level patronage.*

H. Richard Whittall, a deputy managing partner of Richardson Securities of Canada, has quickly become the most powerful day-to-day influence in the Vancouver busi-

---

*The senior fund-raiser for the Liberals in B.C. is L.C. "Jolly" Jolivet, president of General Bearings Ltd. His opposite number for the Tories is Frank Dorchester, an insurance man; lawyer Gowan Guest also collects for the Tories. The chief fund-raiser for the Socreds (who get the largest donations for provincial campaigns) is investment man Austin Taylor.

ness community. A director of eleven companies (including the Bank of Montreal), he replaced James Sinclair as deputy chairman of Canada Cement Lafarge in 1973. His sister, Diana, was formerly married to the late wartime fighter pilot George "Buzz" Beurling and is the wife of George van Roggen, a lawyer and Liberal senator. Whittall's brother, Judd, is the head of Reed Shaw Osler, a national firm of insurance brokers based in Toronto.

Charles Namby Wynn "Chunky" Woodward, grandson of the department stores' founder, has multiplied the chain's sales (from $96 million to $505 million) since he took over eighteen years ago. A perfectionist,* Woodward could exercise a great deal of influence (he is a Royal Bank director), but prefers instead to spend his spare energies at his Douglas Lake Ranch, a half-million-acre spread that runs up to 14,000 head of cattle and is one of the biggest ranches on the continent.

W. Maurice Young, chairman and CEO of Finning Tractor, is a director of Safeway Stores (the California-based parent of Canada Safeway), the TD bank, and Northern Electric. Boosted by the booming B.C. economy of the 1960s and early seventies, Maury Young helped build the tractor and machinery distributorship of his father-in-law, Earl Finning (a transplanted Californian who died in 1965), into the second-largest Caterpillar agency in the world, with forty-odd service depots throughout B.C. and the Mackenzie Valley and annual earnings of $7.3 million. He is a Master of Science from MIT.

Moving up fast, though they're not yet certified members of the Establishment, are *Robert Wyman,* a youthful UBC Commerce graduate who is reviving Pemberton Securities; *Bob Lee,* real-estate sales chief and a director of Wall and Redekop Corporation, which among other things converted the Austin Taylor estate into townhouses and apartments; he's a conduit for Hong Kong money

---

*In 1964, Woodward rode for Queen Elizabeth and Prince Philip at the Royal Windsor Horse Show. He rode superbly. When he was asked to perform for them again, he refused because he didn't think he could surpass the original performance.

into B.C. real estate; *Jim Rhodes,* B.C. Petroleum Corporation, a B.C. government agency; *Pat Reynolds* of Bethlehem Copper; *Gowan Guest,* the lawyer; *Bruce Howe,* the young group vice-president (pulp and paper) who has shot up through the MacMillan Bloedel hierarchy at record speed; *Larry Killam,* the redeveloper who launched the restoration of Gastown from a waterfront skidroad into an area of restaurants and boutiques; and the three young partners of Brown, Farris and Jefferson Limited, a financial consulting house that is moving into the risk-capital market.*

The only French Canadian who belongs to the Vancouver Establishment is *Jacques Barbeau.* Married to a daughter of Walter Owen, the lieutenant-governor (who himself married the widow of Dal Grauer, the former chairman of B.C. Electric), Barbeau wears three-piece navy-blue suits and aviator glasses, has longish (but not too long) hair, works in his own law office in a building with a spectacular view at a table without drawers instead of a desk, has a clipper ship mounted on the wall and his copy of the *Harvard Law Review* out on a side table. None of this represses his vivacity or wit. "Some people around here keep inspecting me," he says. "Then they come up and sort of whisper: 'You don't *look* French.'"

ONE OF THE FEW TOTEM ESTABLISHMENT FIGURES B.C. HAS PRODUCED IN RECENT TIMES is John Valentine Clyne, a lawyer-industrialist whose power has a charismatic base that has held beyond institutional authority, so that his retirement from the chairmanship of MacMillan Bloedel in 1972 hardly diminished him. "At first glance," Alexander Ross wrote about him,† "Clyne is pure Big Business; the well-cut suit, the paunch, the steely bespectacled gaze. But anyone exposed to his mind for more than twenty minutes revises the first impression. There is a certain gaiety here, a whiff of old Noel Coward drawing-room

---

*They are Michael J. Brown (a 1960 Rhodes Scholar and son of W. Thomas Brown, the investment dealer, who was a 1932 Rhodes Scholar); J. Haig deB. Farris, an economics and law graduate (whose father is Chief Justice of B.C.); and Jack R. Jefferson, economics and law graduate from the University of Winnipeg.
†In *Maclean's,* Aug. 6, 1966.

comedies that you catch in a nicely turned phrase or a theatrical wave of the hand. And then there is this tremendous intellect: he reads until two in the morning nearly every night, and has been known to quote Euripides and McLuhan in the same breath."

What has marked Clyne's passage through the many worlds in which he has excelled is a good-humoured indifference to criticism. He believes that being nice to everybody is socially dishonest, that all decisions carry with them some principle worth defending regardless of the consequences. "Too many people want to be loved," he says. "You must always be choosing between right and wrong. You must always *judge*."

Clyne is a self-made man. His father died when he was two years old, and he spent his teen-age summers as a cowboy in the Cariboo and a placer miner in the Monashee Mountains, earning his university tuition. He studied admiralty law in London and was there during the 1926 general strike:

"The first three days of the strike I joined what they called the 'flying squad' and we went out and would sit around the police station and wait until the riot call came. Then we'd pile into police trucks (these were covered vans and we'd be sitting inside), and when we got to a scene of trouble, you'd hear the shouting outside and there'd be half regular policemen and half specials. The unions had ordered there should be no movement on wheels in London, no vehicle of any kind unless it carried their badge, and so the crowds were upsetting buses and burning them. Our own van would be attacked. We would hear them outside banging, trying to stop it, and as soon as the driver would stop we had to get out quickly. We were instructed to go right straight into the mob with our billies but not under any consideration to hit downwards, not to hit anybody on the head. We cleared up quite a few mobs.

"Then a call went out for mounted police volunteers because half of them were in hospital, they were such obvious targets. People would get upstairs and throw things out windows at them. They had broken arms, bruises, and so I decided to volunteer. In fact, there was quite a bit of competition for that because there were a lot of cavalry officers home on leave. So we had to turn up at Buckingham Palace—that's where they kept the horses. We tried out, and I remember I was very nervous. I'd done a little riding in England because I'd been out with friends who had a country house near Stowe, and I was invited out there to ride to hounds, but I hadn't done that much riding and I remember the first time we were told to mount. There was an old cavalry colonel who was teaching us, and I was used to a Western saddle. I had ridden the English saddle, of course, but by God I remember I was so anxious to be up I just went right over, under the horse's neck or around it. But nobody noticed and I was selected. So I spent the rest of the strike riding around the docks. They issued us a sort of helmet. It wasn't a regular policeman's helmet, it was sort of an army thing, and we had these long sticks. But the horses did most of the work for you. In a crowd, when you were trying to force them to move back, the horse would go right in, turn around, and use his rump. They were marvellously trained animals."

After he returned to Vancouver, Clyne was quickly recognized as an outstanding practitioner of maritime law, and in 1947 when the Canadian Maritime Commission was established, he moved east and became its first chairman.* He so impressed the Ottawa Establishment that by 1950 he was being offered the presidency of the CNR:

"CD wanted me to take it, Louis St. Laurent wanted me to take it, and so did the Simards, but I didn't

---

*While he was in Ottawa, Clyne got a first-hand insight into the power of the civil service. During an Export Trade Policy Subcommittee meeting, attended by three deputy ministers, a decision was made that Clyne knew went directly against the government policy of the day. "I informed the deputies of this fact, and there was dead silence. Then Cliff Clark [Deputy Minister of Finance] leaned over the table and said: 'Jack, you say that this is contrary to government policy?' I said: 'Yes, it is,' and gave him the reason. He just leaned back in his chair with this beatific smile and said: 'Well, if that's the case, we'll just have to change government policy.' "

want to because I wanted to go back out west and practise law. Worst of all, Donald Gordon was a good friend of mine, and he really wanted it. I was having lunch at the Rideau Club one day and Garson, who was then minister of justice, said, 'Jack, you know the lawyers in British Columbia. We've got to appoint a judge out there. Do you have anybody you would recommend?'

"A great light broke over me, and I said, 'Stuart, me!'

"He said, 'Oh hell, you wouldn't take the judgeship.'

"And I said, 'Certainly I would.'

" 'Well,' he said, 'heavens, if you want it, I'm quite sure there wouldn't be any trouble.'

"Garson made the recommendation, and then there was hell to pay. CD phoned me and said, 'For Christ's sake, Jack, what the hell do you think you're doing? This is coming before Cabinet and I'm opposing it. I'll hold it up.'

"I told him: 'CD, I want to go back to British Columbia.'

"And he said, 'Are you crazy? You mustn't do this.'

"Eventually they appointed me, and when I left Ottawa, Howe sent me a letter in which he wrote: 'You walked out of the stream of life which you ought not to have done. I prophesy that you will not be on the Bench more than ten years.' He was right.

"I enjoyed being a judge enormously, but one day in the mid-fifties, H.R. MacMillan came around to see me, told me he had to retire, and started talking about people that would succeed him. Finally he said: 'You know, Jack, I think you ought to take my place.'

"I said, 'Yes, that would be a hell of a good idea' —I assumed he was joking. But he said, 'No, I'm serious.' We talked about it for about six months, and finally I thought, well, here is something that would be exciting, so I did it."

During his sixteen years at "MacBlo," Clyne marched the company's sales to $966 million from $160 million. His biggest coup was the acquisition of Powell River Company, announced in the summer of 1959 and completed on December 31 of that year. Billed as an amalgamation, the corporate marriage was so stormy that within seventeen months a dozen Powell River executives had resigned. This is Clyne's recollection of the final showdown with Harold Foley, Powell River's chairman and vice-chairman of the merged company:

"About a year after the merger, a serious dispute arose between us concerning the ownership of shares in a subsidiary, which I maintained were held in trust for the company and which Foley said were owned beneficially by certain individual shareholders. As a result of this dispute and its implications, I asked Foley for his resignation and he resigned at the following meeting of directors.

"Some time later, Foley approached several of the directors of MacMillan, Bloedel and Powell River with a proposal to sell five million shares of MacMillan, Bloedel and Powell River Limited to St. Regis, an American competitor. The group of the old Powell River directors who were then directors of the merged company indicated to Foley or to the representatives of St. Regis that they were prepared to accept the offer, which would net them about three dollars above the market price. They were not, however, able to raise the full five million shares among themselves but were only able to assemble two and a half million, so they decided to approach H.R. MacMillan and Prentice Bloedel to see if they would join in the deal. At that time the issued shares of the company were twenty million, so a holding of five million would make St. Regis the largest shareholder and would hand over to it the effective control. H.R. MacMillan told the representatives of the Powell River group that the whole matter should be immediately brought to my attention as the chairman of the company, which was done. I told the representative of the Powell River group of directors that the whole deal was en-

tirely improper; the price at which the Powell group
of directors were prepared to sell would give them a
profit of three dollars a share over the market, which
was not available to the general body of shareholders,
and in my opinion the proposed transaction was legal-
ly questionable, improper, and unfair to them.

"I immediately brought the subject before the executive committee of the company, some of the members of which were former Powell River directors
involved in the deal. I told them that their conduct
savoured of the highest degree of impropriety and
that they were no longer suitable persons to sit on the
board, representing the interests of all the shareholders. I told them that I would not recommend the
nomination of any of the directors who were involved in the deal at the annual meeting of the
company, which was to take place the following
month, and that I would give the shareholders the
reasons why I did not think they should be so nominated. This was done, and all the directors who had
been willing to sell their shares to St. Regis were
not nominated and shareholders were informed of the
reasons."

It was during this squabble that Clyne performed what
remains as one of the grand spontaneous gestures in Canadian business annals, which Establishmentarians across
the country still whisper about. During a party at the house
of Jack Shakespeare, a Vancouver lawyer, he got into an
argument with the former Powell River chairman. It
ended with Clyne dumping his glass of rye over Harold
Foley's elegant head.

IV

Money Power

CHAPTER EIGHT

The El Dorado Crowd

No matter how often the politicians may
proclaim that Canada's economic system
spreads abundance among the many, in reality,
it creates wealth for the few.

Their skin belongs to the afternoon sun. They hold common assumptions so deeply that they communicate through raised eyebrows and shared silences. They view Pierre Trudeau as a dangerous socialist, worship John Turner, and refer to Quebec separatism as "René Lévesque's show." They breed horses and mid-Atlantic accents, having mastered the trick of looking down their noses and talking through them at the same time.

They live in graceful ante-bellum mansions with white fluted pillars, twilit, book-lined studies, fastidious gardens, and drawing rooms awash with fragile antiques, Adam sideboards, Sheraton tables, the warming lustre of burnished bronze. They are surrounded by hangers-on—surrogate offspring with small lives, fusty bachelors and ladies-always-in-waiting, pretenders all, distinguished by their pettiness, an odd mixture of admiration, envy, and malice.

Most of their decisions evolve from the style in which they allow things to happen. Their lives are lived as a series of throw-away gestures, so that all the pleasures and all the splendour are made to seem effortless rather than planned, ordinary instead of ostentatious. They spend little time in self-evaluation and keep few records of their inward transactions.

They are the Canadian rich. The men and women who realize that no matter how often the politicians may proclaim that Canada's economic system spreads abundance among the many, in reality, it creates wealth for the few.

As a group, the Establishment rich are among the most envied of Canadians, with the climbers and the reachers constantly scouting their habits and their habitats, trying to define their essence, to grab a little of their magic for themselves. But like moths banging softly against a Coleman lamp in the moonlight, the upstarts are attracted to and kept away from the heart of the flame. Few newcomers make it into the magic circle. They don't know the rules and are too easily dismissed. ("Tell them we're busy, Peg. They're not our kind of people.")

The very rich enjoy a surprisingly stylized if highly sybaritic existence, one that touches only tangentially the mainstream of Canadian life. They are insulated from the economic jolts that can shake the merely prosperous, and their idea of hunger is being served a slightly rancid *filet de sole meunière* at a declining French restaurant. Most of their conversations spin around two topics: politicians and their perfidies, servants and their idiosyncrasies.* They feel entirely at home only in each other's company, where everyone has money—vast sums, otherwise they're considered vaguely quaint. Connections are paraded, but discreetly. Nearly everybody is somebody's cousin. They all know each other's children, now in their bursting thirties and taking over family firms. The eldest offspring is often described as "a decent chap," meaning that he may be none too bright but at least he hasn't turned out to be a rebel or anything unfortunate like that. "He's done his homework" is the ultimate accolade, "he's blotted his copybook" the ultimate insult.

They still drink Madeira after dinner. They live in very English houses—very low key with lots of old chintz, not much colour sense, nervous maids, walls decorated with endless variations on bloodless hunting scenes, and dinners consisting of oyster soup, raw roast beef, and frozen strawberries on meringue, preceded by hors d'oeuvre of Triscuits and canned pâté. They're intensely interested in all things British and have usually met various minor baronets at the Marquess of Blandford's or somebody else's country house. London, not New York, is their spiritual home.

---

*Prize catch is Thomas Cronin, a former butler to Princess Margaret, now employed by the McMahons at their mansion in Palm Beach.

"Where do you get your cigars now?"

"Well, Fortnum and Mason has a good tobacco selection."

"I'm certain they do. What about Dunhill's? Are they still in business?"

"Oh yes, but owned by Rothmans now."

"I used to go to a place on Jermyn Street. Haven't seen it lately. Hmm," puff, puff, *"yes. Excellent. Fortnum's. I'll remember."*

MONEY CAN BE A GREAT COMFORT. In large quantities, there is nothing transitory about it, as there is about power. Yet even wealth doesn't put a wall between the individual and his fear of hurt and death, doesn't provide any automatic inner confirmation of one's existence. Unlike their corporate cousins who deal in power plays and can look themselves up in the *Canadian Who's Who* to check on their current standing and past achievements, the merely rich have no ready tally of accomplishments. They have little sense of irony to deal with life's mysteries.

The rich have a strange image of themselves. Senator Norman McLeod Paterson, the Fort William grain merchant who owned 109 elevators and one of the largest fleets on the Great Lakes, once had his picture taken in front of the Senate with his foot on the running board of his tug-sized Rolls-Royce, bellowing at the camera: "What do you mean, we're rich old men?"

The fear of giving away the source or sum of their fortune, of committing themselves to offers of friendship, gradually fills their minds with smoky, ill-defined resentments. They begin to feel alienated and suspicious, spying on themselves, becoming everybody's mercenary and no one's intimate. And so, furtively and without really meaning to do so, they withdraw into themselves even further and begin to desire not just wealth but limitless riches. Instead of being appreciated for what it can buy, money becomes despised for all the problems it didn't resolve, the magical expectations it didn't fulfil.

At the point where money ceases to have real meaning —and the limits of personal consumption are reached astonishingly quickly—the compounding of further wealth becomes a game. The objective of the game is not more money but the playing of the game itself, which takes on something close to sexual connotations. Roy Thomson, the press lord, has become one of the game's most successful players: "I mean, hell, I eat three meals a day (and I should probably eat two), and I'm not very particular about my dress anyway. I can spend only a small fraction of what I make. So what the hell am I doing? I'm not doing it for the money. *It's a game and I enjoy myself.* I like to look at another paper and think, 'Jesus, if only that was mine. Let's see the balance sheet.' "

What really separates the very rich from everyone else is the time frame in which they live. They seldom need to defer desires. Their money gives them the authority to purchase the time and services of others—in bed, at the office, around the house. Because time is a more precious (and much more exhaustible) commodity than money, they place great emphasis on its expenditure. This leads the very rich to worship efficiency in all things, whether it's a new computer that will streamline their personal accounting systems or a gadget that will heat their swimming pools a little faster.

It's because they hate to see anything wasted that the very rich are so stingy. One of Eric Harvie's accountants recalls that the Calgary millionaire once objected to being charged $3.00 instead of the previous $2.50 for his weekly car wash* and that when an elderly couple who had spent twenty years as caretakers at his ranch left his employ, Harvie deducted five dollars from their final pay for some groceries they had taken with them. E.P. Taylor successfully sued the British government in the late sixties after the Board of Inland Revenue disallowed his claimed deduction for eight thousand pounds in transatlantic business trips. When John David Eaton's private plane was forced down near Winnipeg during a storm, he walked four miles through the snow with his pilot, Ralph Spadbrow, to send a telegram from the nearest railway station.

---

*The extra fifty cents turned out to be for cleaning the whitewall tires Harvie had recently had installed.

Spadbrow remembered that they had to retrace their steps for several hundred yards when the station agent shouted after them that he had overcharged Eaton by fifteen cents.

THESE STRANGE PALADINS OF WEALTH OBVIOUSLY DON'T ENJOY SIMPLE LIVES. One problem is that having exceptional fortunes no longer guarantees much personal distinction. That's why the rich are so zealously class conscious. No other class has the time or money to uphold such rigid common standards; at no other level are class distinctions so minutely observed. Established money is obsessed with the notion of keeping the parvenus at bay —those cigar chompers and haunch grabbers in their silk suits and pomaded haircuts, whose status lust hangs out like a dirty shirt tail.

The difference that counts is between being Old Rich and New Rich. Adherents of both groups give themselves away in all sorts of subtle ways—where they summer or winter, how they decorate their houses and offices, what they wear, drive, and eat, whom they marry and sleep with. What the New Rich can never quite grasp is that the surest way of being excluded is to compare possessions. By specifying the exact length of their Chris-Craft, boasting about their latest car, gadget, mistress, or French Impressionist painting, they betray a gauche insecurity the true Establishmentarian never feels.

It all depends on what makes the blood pump. New Money likes Cadillacs with elk-grained cabriolet tops and regency custom grilles; Old Money prefers Rolls-Royces.* Old Money follows the supermarket ads and knows when cans of B.C. salmon are on special. New Money tips lavishly. Old Money prefers subdued shades of brown; New Money loves primary colours, offices with red walls, and cigar lighters shaped like Model Ts. (You twist the spare tire and it belches forth a xylophone version of "The Impossible Dream.") Old Money goes with affected shabbiness, sailing trophies, lost duck-hunting hats, and grand-

---

*About seventy Rolls-Royces are sold in Canada every year, half of them in Toronto.

father's walking stick. New Money has stuffed fish mounted
on its recreation room walls.* The New Rich buy a house,
call in a professional, and order him to "decorate it."
They talk about drapes, chesterfields, and homes. The
Old Rich will employ decorators only to find specific pieces
and talk about curtains, sofas, and houses. Old Money
purchases the seagoing family pet a life preserver; New
Money outfits him in a yachting jacket.†

New Money buys his wife a necklace‡ made of rubies
and gold to wear over a brocade dress with sable cuffs.
Old Money cultivates lapel orchids in the colours of his
hunt. New Money builds an indoor snorkling tank and
keeps pogo sticks at poolside for additional exercise. Old
Money turns to public service if it gets really exercised
or really bored. Old Money in Europe seeks out neighbour-
hood left-bank hotels, enduring draughts and inferior
food as an annual adventure. New Money flies to the Paris
Hilton and orders two cheeseburgers-with-the-works. Old
Money knows not to wear diamonds before lunch, not
to carry unfinished cocktails to the dinner table, that
Thursday is maid's night out. Old Money's chauffeurs never slam doors or walk around the *front* of a car.

Old Money gets the children to help groom the horses,
wearing worn T-shirts, jeans, and very expensive riding
boots. New Money keeps careful profit-and-loss tallies on
each animal and sells off the yearlings that aren't likely to
make back their investments. Old Money plays tennis and
squash and skies hard; New Money hires a masseuse to
call at the house every morning. New Money gets the best
tickets to the Super Bowl, the Indianapolis 500, and the
Army-Navy Game. Old Money rents boxes at the Kentucky Derby and arranges foursomes at Burning Tree.
New Money uses caterers and invites a few business as-

---

*This is not always a dependable indicator. John Craig Eaton keeps a
stuffed blue marlin that he caught off Bimini in his office.

†Or goes even further and opens up a bank account for him. Herron's
Peppi, an eight-year-old poodle owned by retired Calgary oil millionaire
Bill Herron, not only has a bank account but is the registered owner of
a Cadillac with steer horns on the bonnet and seven hundred flashing
Canadian silver dollars imbedded in its coach-work. The best-dressed dog
in Canada is Sir Terence Wellington Whippet, owned by Mrs. David
Coulter, daughter of M.J. Boylen, the mining magnate. He has a morning
suit, a camel's-hair coat, and a tuxedo as well as a yachting jacket.

‡Probably at Secrett's in Toronto, Cavelti's in Vancouver, or Gabriel
Lucas's in Montreal.

sociates so that it can write off its cocktail parties. Old Money engages a combo and refers to them as "the music"; New Money boasts, "We've got the Short Circuits!" Old Money buys expensive winter topcoats that endow their wearers with a faintly conspiratorial air. New Money buys leather or suede jackets.

New Money buys paintings by their dominant colours and pretends to understand modern art; Old Money collects "pictures" and hangs them in dark rooms with little dinky lights over them. Old Money will produce the occasional jeroboam of Château Mouton-Rothschild 1929 without drawing attention to the fact that it costs $8,000 a bottle; New Money boasts about his T'ang Dynasty vase—the dealer wanted $30,000 for it, but he got it for $25,000.

Old Money treats waiters as slightly retarded errand boys; New Money tries to impress them by speaking broken French with the intimacy of a Resistance fighter explaining the location of an arms drop. Old Money makes elaborate (and unsuccessful) attempts to treat servants benignly, knows exactly what happened to poor Emma's first cousin, and sends her a Christmas food parcel from Eaton's. New Money haggles with the maid about overtime. Old Money marries the right girl (and ogles cocktail waitresses); New Money marries the wrong girl, starves her to perfection, and sends her to Holt, Renfrew with a charge account. Old Money refers to an errant partner's affair with his secretary as "Jimmy is having a little thing with Gloria." New Money trades in his wife.

THE RICH HAVE A DIFFICULT TIME SEPARATING THEIR MONEY FROM THEIR MANLINESS. In the proving ground of their souls the two are indivisible. Money is God; the man makes the money; therefore the man is in charge. (There's almost always trouble if the money comes by inheritance from the woman's side of the family.) Most wives are relegated to being baubles. In this kind of partnership even pretty women seem flesh without magic. Attempting to fulfil their decorative function, they do the rounds of slimming classes, Maine Chance, beauty studios, skin specialists, face-lift surgeons. (But age remains the final conqueror, and, having been cheated so long, is seldom kind in victory.)

Wives try hard to keep up with whatever conversation is going and give glad little cries of interest at nearly everything mentioned. ("Kuwait—oh, fascinating! How primitive those Arabs must be!") They complain about trying to keep servants happy, their daughter's Italian fiancé (they fear he isn't "stable"), the new rug being woven in Portugal that hasn't been delivered yet—all the time glancing around the room to see how they're doing. Gradually they become non-persons, no longer decorative, no longer needed as mothers, no longer anything much but burdens their husbands uneasily bear.

Much of their excitement comes from the rumours and facts of endogamy—the who-married-whom-and-merged-with-what game. The rich are constantly intermarrying, replanting the forests of family trees.* The list is endless.†

The "family" is a kind of sacred institution in these circles, not as the result of any unusual filial feelings but because it is the vessel that passes on the money. Most of the families that might have become great financial dynasties have petered out. They failed to establish systems of succession that would force the incapable to make way for those who could maintain and expand family investments. Family fortunes, no matter how great, were dispersed, the families left headless, without cohesion or thrust. When George Gooderham, a sixth-generation descendant of what was once a dominant Canadian family, was married, Lady

---

*The only Canadian family that keeps a complete, up-to-date record of changes is the Southams. A green-covered booklet is issued to all the descendants of William Southam and updated annually.

†Dean Acheson's mother was a Gooderham. Lord Beaverbrook's first wife was Bud Drury's aunt. Sir George Parkin's daughters married Vincent Massey, J.M. Macdonnell, and W.L. "Choppy" Grant. Eric Phillips's first wife, Eileen, one of Sam McLaughlin's daughters, ran away on Christmas Eve with the father of Frank McEachren (who is a Flavelle and who married John David Eaton's sister). Lord Atholstan's grandson is Hugh Hallward, whose wife is Gordon Fisher's sister, while Gordon Fisher's wife is W.A. Arbuckle's daughter. Colin Webster's wife is Charles Frosst's daughter. Eric Harvie's wife was a Southam and his daughter married a Maclaren. Col. Clifford Sifton's granddaughter married Ian William Molson Angus, whose mother is a Molson and whose father was master of the Lake of Two Mountains Hunt. Hal Jackman married Jimmy Duncan's daughter. Phyllis Laidlaw McCullagh Drew is the widow of both the newspaper publisher and the Opposition leader. Geoffrey Massey, Raymond's son, married Ruth Killam, of the Vancouver branch of the family. Bora Laskin's daughter married Beryl Plumptre's son.

Gooderham, his great-aunt, gave a shower for his bride. The more than a hundred women relatives who turned up had to be identified with name cards. Mrs. Jules Timmins has twenty-nine grandchildren.

An exception to this kind of scattering of resources is the Southam family. Before any member is given an executive job he must clearly establish his credentials. "We're fortunate that the family is so loyal to the company," says St. Clair Balfour, current head of the clan. "We wouldn't hesitate to ask a family member to leave if he wasn't working out, though we would remove him in as nice a way as possible."

"Inherited wealth," complained William K. Vanderbilt in 1905, "is a big handicap to happiness. It is as certain a death to ambition as cocaine is to morality." Many sons simply take over the desks of their fathers, uncles, or fathers-in-law.* Charles L. Gundy, chairman of Wood Gundy, the Toronto investment house, inherited most of the twenty directorships in the companies financed by his father, including Canada Cement Lafarge, Massey-Ferguson, and Dominion Steel and Coal Corporation. Their family position did not save other sons from dreary years spent learning the business. G. Blair Gordon, who became president of Dominion Textile, worked as a fitter's helper in one of his father's mills, in spite of his preference for playing polo. He still has a scar on his brow from an inkwell hurled at him by a striker at Montmorency Falls in 1938. John David Eaton spent twelve years selling men's underwear and being moved through other departments before he was named to head Canada's largest retailing chain in 1942.

Johnny F. Bassett, son of the former *Telegram* publisher, who has inherited his father's nerve and bluntness, spoke for the new generation of rich men's sons when he told a journalist: "It's not a handicap being John Bassett's boy. I've had an excellent relationship with dad. He's a hell of a sounding board and he's a bright, bright son of a

---

*Other families that pass on their corporate assets from father to son include the Eatons, the Molsons, the Batas, the Steinbergs, the Woodwards, the Davises (Alcan), the Birkses, the Bronfmans, the Rogerses (B.C. Sugar), the Burtons (Simpsons), the Westons, the Jefferys (London Life), the Iveys, the Macdonalds (Confederation Life), the Bentleys (Canadian Forest Products), and the McLeans (Canada Packers).

bitch. He's a great family guy; he'll back you. You can make a terrible mistake, and still he'll back you up. I don't remember ever feeling the pressure from being John Bassett's son. We're two different people. I mean there are two John Bassetts in Toronto now . . . . I suppose everybody in Toronto regards the Bassetts as Establishment. I don't. I regard the Establishment as being people who founded here in the 1880s, third and fourth generation. In 1952 my old man didn't have a pot to piss in when he bought a newspaper—thanks to Mr. Eaton—that was losing a million dollars a year."*

BEFORE CORPORATIONS REPLACED FAMILIES AS THE BASIC UNITS OF ECONOMIC POWER, money was much more visible, simpler to track toward its ultimate source. The first Canadian fortunes grew out of the fur trade and landholdings, the early shipping lines, the merchant ventures that supplied the young colony. Then there emerged, during the last half of the nineteenth century, the railway barons, who altered the main mode of financial operation from the partnership to the stock corporation. They were the first to master the intricacies of manipulating stock to gain control over enormous capital resources. Unlike their successors, the men who founded the industrial trusts,† they didn't divorce themselves from management but knew how to use other people's (and government) money for their own purposes. Some thirteen hundred railroads were eventually chartered in Canada, many of them wellheads of family empires. The flowering of these fortunes never equalled similar developments in the U.S. "Canada has always been undercapitalized, because most industrial development took place after taxation and the welfare

---

*Quoted from an article by John Gault in *Toronto Life*, November, 1973. When Johnny F. was eight, he invented a dice baseball game based on the National League teams and sold franchises to fellow classmates at Bishop's College School for ten cents each. His investment income is now derived from the Telegram Corporation, a trust set up by his father and John David Eaton in the name of the three Bassett sons and the four Eaton boys. The corporation, which owned the *Tely*, controls 51 per cent of Baton Broadcasting Inc. (which includes CFTO-TV) among its multiple holdings.
†Between 1909 and 1913 alone, fifty-six major industrial mergers involving 248 companies were negotiated.

state had started," the late Neil McKinnon of the Commerce once noted. "In the U.S., on the other hand, most of the growth took place during the nineteenth century, when large pools of private capital could still be collected. Here, most capital was provided by financial institutions, mainly the banks, rather than individuals."

The original tycoons didn't feel properly attired without a cane, cigar, and morning coat. Their "name" was their proudest asset, their wealth the source of their distinction. Conspicuous waste and conspicuous leisure—not to mention conspicuous consumption—were all necessary parts of their ritual. (Leisure in a world where everyone had to work was conspicuous enough. But the point was driven home by their clothes—hoop skirts, corsets, high silk hats—all palpably inconsistent with any form of toil.)

It was an age before the rich were transformed into frightened men, hunting for salvation in the fine print of the income-tax manuals. These old-style tycoons regarded themselves as contemporary inheritors of that mantle of esteem once borne by gladiators, nobles, and bishops—walking proof to an invidiously competitive society that ability and application could be spectacularly repaid. They owned private railway cars that carried pianos, bathtubs (with gold-plated taps), wine "cellars" (cushioned to protect the vintages from the thump of railbeds), fireplaces, and Tiffany lamps. They lived in capricious castles filled with the icy nuances of their class, monuments to their self-indulgence. They spent money without thought* and developed pernickety habits to certify their power. Sir Joseph Flavelle, for example, who grew up as a small flour miller in Peterborough, Ontario, and eventually headed the Grand Trunk, the National Trust, and the Bank of Commerce, wouldn't allow cigars to be served at his Toronto mansion unless the governor general was in attendance. But after an evening's entertainment, his footman would deliver one expensive Turkish cigarette to each departing guest.

---

*John McMartin, a millionaire gold miner, spent $70,000 decorating the dining-room ceiling of his summer house in Cornwall, Ontario, with a five-foot-wide frieze depicting a lakeside scene. It had real bulrushes gummed against the plaster and stuffed flying ducks impaled on invisible wires.

This life style flourished nowhere more conspicuously than in Montreal's "Square Mile."* From 1860 until the stock market collapse of 1929, there was created within these chilly boundaries a non-Canadian enclave that was forever England. Rich Montrealers looked to the late Victorian and Edwardian era for inspiration to divine their own universe—a convoluted, self-contained world populated by its own itinerant muffin-man. A host was judged by how he disposed of his cherry pits.

The most prestigious receptions were held at Ravens-crag, the baronial cloister built by Sir Hugh Allan (ship-ping) on the slope of Mount Royal in 1861,† and the home of Sir Mortimer Davis (tobacco) just along Pine. The streets were filled with the residences of barons: Mount Stephen (CPR), Strathcona (CPR), Shaughnessy (CPR), and Atholstan (*Montreal Star*); baronets and knights: Abbott (prime minister), Allan (shipping), Mere-dith (law and banking), Tait (law), Gordon (textiles), Drummond (sugar and banking), Beatty (CPR), Holt (everything), Hingston (medicine and banking), Macdon-ald (tobacco), Van Horne (CPR), and Forget (stockbrok-ing); and mere millionaires: Angus (CPR), Caverhill (hardware), Linton (shoes), McIntyre (CPR), Green-shields (wholesale drygoods, law, and stockbroking), Ross (CPR and streetcars), Beardmore (leather), Workman (hardware and railways), Workman (steel and coal), Reford (shipping), Drummond (steel), Timmins (mining), MacDougall (stockbroking), Mackay (wholesale dry-goods), Learmont (hardware), Pillow (CPR connection), Hosmer (CPR connection), Molson (brewing), Dawes (brewing), Paton (cartage), Mackenzie (stockbroking), Killam (finance), Ogilvie (flour), Birks (jewellery), and Morgan (department stores).

---

*A term used by Hugh MacLennan to denote the area bounded by University Street on the east, Pine Avenue and Cedar Avenue on the north, Côte des Neiges Road and Guy Street on the west, and Dorchester Street on the south. Its mainstream was a mile-long section of Sherbrooke Street. (The fashionable streets extended a bit beyond these boundaries, in fact, and encompassed the blocks of Dorchester west of Guy that included the mansions of Lord Strathcona and Lord Shaughnessy.) Mrs. MacLennan recalls the complaint of one Square Miler: "I never thought I'd live to see my daughter having to live in Westmount."

†When the ruling family of Luxembourg was offered refuge in Montreal during World War II, they turned down the offer of Ravenscrag because they didn't wish to live in "such a palace." It now houses the Allan Memorial Institute, attached to McGill.

Children who inhabited the Square Mile had a Spartan upbringing, confined to nurseries and their own dining rooms. They went to school at the Study, Miss Edgar's and Miss Cramp's, or Selwyn House and Lower Canada, and afterwards to McGill, where they clubbed together for ski outings to St. Sauveur, either with the Penguins (founded by the Dawes family) or the Redbirds (established by the Molsons). As teen-agers, they came out at one of three balls—the St. Andrew's, the Hunt Club, or the Charity. Families summered together at Magog, Tadoussac, Montebello, St. Andrews, or Murray Bay. Their social ties ran straight south to the eastern American seaboard, seldom to Toronto.

Perhaps the most pretentious Montrealer was Donald Alexander Smith, who rose from junior fur trader in the Hudson's Bay Company to become its governor, president of the Bank of Montreal, and chief financial agent of and chief profiteer from the CPR's construction. Along the way, he also settled the initial Riel rebellion, toppled Sir John A. Macdonald's first administration, established the force preceding the RCMP, was tossed out of Parliament for bribing voters to re-elect him, and came close to being jailed on at least one occasion. Invitations to the largest of his four houses—a baronial red stone castle at 1157 Dorchester Street—were sought by every social climber in Montreal. Smith slavishly followed the official order of precedence and kept a private guest tally that classified his visitors according to rank.* The dining room of the house opened into a garden for summer teas, often attended by more than two thousand guests. When the future king and queen of England stayed with Smith, he built a special balcony off the second floor so that the royal couple might have a better view of the fireworks display exploded from the top of Mount Royal in their honour. The furniture was custom made of bird's-eye maple; bisecting the

---

*The impressive roll call included George V and Queen Mary who came to Canada in 1901 as the Duke and Duchess of Cornwall and York, a prince and princess, eight dukes, seven marquesses, twenty-one earls, six viscounts, six governors general, twenty-six lieutenant-governors, seven prime ministers, twenty-seven provincial premiers, four archbishops, seventeen bishops, fourteen chief justices, twenty-nine supreme court judges, thirty-one mayors, and fifty-eight generals. Smith's list even separated this last group into forty-seven generals of the Imperial Army and eleven colonial troop commanders.

house was a dramatic three-story staircase, all its mahogany components faultlessly dovetailed. Below stairs and out of hearing, a row of eight rooms was partitioned off for the dozen or more maids and flunkeys.

Smith ruled his household with humourless arrogance. Once while eating breakfast with Dr. Wilfred Grenfell, he watched the lamp under the hot-water kettle falter and die. When the missionary wanted to relight it, Smith stopped him and angrily summoned his butler. "Remember, James," he said, "you have only certain duties to perform. This is one. Never, under any circumstances, let such an omission occur again."

One of the richest Canadians of his day (the CPR shares he acquired for $25 reached $280 in his lifetime), Smith spent the last eighteen years of his long life in London as Canadian High Commissioner to the United Kingdom, where Queen Victoria created him Baron Strathcona and Mount Royal. In 1900, he donated a fully equipped mounted regiment of six hundred North West Mounted Police veterans to help the British fight the Boer War. He became the ultimate Anglophile; his snobbery extended even beyond the grave. His will directed that money be set aside for the establishment of a leper colony. But it had a strict entrance requirement: only leprous English gentlemen of good standing could be admitted.

The most powerful of the Montreal set was, without any doubt, Sir Herbert Holt, who controlled some three hundred companies on three continents, worth nearly three billion dollars. Originally the engineer in charge of punching the CPR through the sliding-earth passes of the Rockies and the Selkirks, in 1914 he designed the railway transportation network that supplied the ammunition to halt the Kaiser's initial thrust across France. During the sombre beginnings of World War II, he quietly gave Britain a full squadron of Spitfires.

His mills turned out 10 per cent of the world's newsprint. Just before the 1929 crash, he was on the verge of putting together a utilities combine that would have become the world's richest corporation. His Montreal Light, Heat and Power was the largest privately owned utility then in existence; he established Famous Players Corporation, Consolidated Paper, and Dominion Textile, spent

twenty-six years as head of the Royal Bank (multiplying
its assets fifteenfold), and became such a dominant influence that the mention of his name could affect a whole
stock market. When shareholders of Brazilian Traction,
Light and Power panicked during the revolution of 1925
in São Paulo, rumours were leaked to the floor of the
Montreal Stock Exchange that Holt was becoming a company director. The sell-off stopped although the revolution
continued and Holt never did join Brazilian's board.

An unpleasant man whose face resembled a carefully
washed Irish potato punctured by pinched, garter-blue
eyes, he was so hated that during the 1931 strike of the
Canadian Union of Linesmen and Helpers against his
power companies he marched to work through downtown
Montreal enclosed in a square formed by four guards
with cocked rifles. A year earlier he had ducked under his
mahogany desk barely in time to avoid the bullets of a furious stockbroker.

A Renaissance man among the Square Milers was Sir
William Van Horne, hero of the CPR's construction who
turned the debt-ridden pioneer line into one of the world's
great transportation systems, then flung railroads across
Cuba and Guatemala. He also invented a grasshopper
killer, an avalanche deflector, and a submarine detector;
he became an outstanding amateur botanist, palaeontolo-
gist, and landscape painter.

Van Horne loved to deflate the stuffier members of his
set with elaborately planned practical jokes. During an
inspection tour of the Rockies, he had the train stopped
when he suggested to Sir William Peterson, a CPR director
and principal of McGill University, that he might find
some Indian statues at a nearby gorge interesting. While
the professor was poking around the "statues"—which
turned out to be piles of rocks left over from construction
—Van Horne ordered the train to start. Peterson was nearly injured jumping onto the accelerating last coach as Van
Horne cheered him on, smacking his large thighs in glee.

Another favourite was his cigar prank. A firm of cut-
rate tobacconists had capitalized on his fame by calling a
five cent brand the "Van Horne." He ordered hundreds of
the leafy horrors, removed their bands, mixed them in his
humidor with expensive perfectos, and then palmed them

off on his guests. His visitors, wishing to acknowledge his reputation as a connoisseur, would inhale the tarry fumes and exclaim: "Ah, Sir William, what a delightful aroma!" They could only smile icily at Van Horne's crude guffaw, which followed his explanation. He once hired a man simply because he had butted one of the dud cigars and said: "How much does the stable boy charge you for these things?"

Van Horne's study was hung with models of fifteenth-century ships; his fifty-two-room mansion housed one of the largest collections of Japanese porcelain in North America and two hundred paintings, valued at $30 million. Velvet wall hangings provided the mellow backdrop for his works by Rubens, Titian, Murillo, Velasquez, El Greco, Renoir, Reynolds, Goya, Hogarth, Turner, and Courbet. He had four Rembrandts, two Goyas, a Leonardo da Vinci study of a woman's head, and four paintings by Franz Hals.

During his last sickness in 1915, doctors limited Van Horne strictly to three cigars a day. He meekly agreed. But by next morning he had a box of specially rolled two-foot perfectos brought to his hospital bed, and puffed contentedly the prescribed three cigars a day, for four hours each, waiting to die.

The prime example of the idle rich who populated wealthy Montreal in its heyday was Elwood Hosmer, who spent much of his life drinking gin and smoking $1.25 Coronas in one of the lobby lounge chairs at the Ritz-Carlton Hotel, often answering nature's calls in the pot of a nearby palm tree. His days were climaxed at six o'clock in the evening, when Hosmer—his chair surrounded by the accumulated droppings of his day's sojourn—would pass out, half-covered by the funny papers which were his favourite reading. Bellboys would then carry him outside, where a chauffeur would transfer him to his limousine for the two-block drive to his home, which housed four of the finest Canalettos in any private collection.*

---

*This routine was seriously disrupted only once. In 1927, Elwood suddenly decided he wanted to fly the Atlantic. The attempt ended when his aircraft, the *Flying Whale*, crashed after takeoff from the Azores. He and three companions spent twelve hours drifting in the ocean until they were picked up by the liner *Minnewaska*. Elwood soon returned to the more stable Ritz-Carlton armchair.

The Ritz had been originally financed in 1912 by a group that included Elwood's father (Charles Hosmer, who founded CP Telegraphs and became president of Ogilvie Flour Mills), and soon became the gathering place for the Montreal elite. They lunched in the Oak Room, took tea in the Palm Court, dined in the Oval Room, held debut parties in the Grand Ballroom, and moved in if they had a row at home, to dine on caviar Astrakhan and Grande Fine Champagne de Napoleon 1800.

The most extravagant of the Montrealers was J.K.L. Ross, son of James Ross who amassed a large fortune as leader of the "Big Four" contracting team that pushed the CPR through the mountains.* Between 1913, when his father died, and 1928, when he was declared bankrupt, Ross exhausted a fortune estimated at $16 million. His extravagances included travel, wherever possible, by private train (not just a private car) and wagers of $5,000 or $10,000 (he once bet $50,000 on a single horse race —and won). He had up to eight Rolls-Royces at any one time; his forty-room house on Peel Street was staffed by thirty servants; the *Gloria*, one of his seven yachts, was in the same class as the *Britannia* of King George V, and he raced her out of Cowes as a member of the exclusive Royal Yacht Squadron. He maintained two big racing stables and one of his horses, Sir Barton, became the first Triple Crown champion when he won the Kentucky Derby, the Belmont Stakes, and the Preakness in 1919. Although he was officially declared bankrupt on November 1, 1928, and was left with only three hundred dollars in cash, a codicil to his father's will set him up with a relatively modest income that allowed Ross to spend the last two decades of his life (he died in 1951) in Montego Bay, Jamaica, on an estate that was eventually sold to Lord Beaverbrook.

Another extravagant though much more private spender was Izaak Walton Killam, president of Royal Securities, who used to carry a fresh egg down to the Mount Royal Hotel barbershop for special shampoo treatments. His wife, Dorothy, once instructed a senior vice-president of Royal Securities to engage a suite on a train to bring her

---

*The others were Sir Herbert Holt, Sir William Mackenzie, and Sir Donald Mann.

dog down to New York, carefully specifying that the animal was to sleep only on a lower berth. She owned jewellery worth more than $4 million and died in 1965 at a villa on the French Riviera she had bought for three million dollars from Count Giovanni Agnelli, head of the Fiat motor works. An avid baseball fan, in 1956 she unsuccessfully bid six million dollars to keep the Dodgers from moving out of New York.

The Square Milers continued to intermarry, ride to hounds, give balls, have tea at the Ritz, and blackball each other at the Mount Royal Club. But their dominance declined rapidly after World War I. Nearly every one of the great houses lost at least one son in the "right" regiments, recruited so that the Square Milers could go into battle surrounded by their own. By 1926, when Frank McKenna opened a florist's shop in the old Paton house, the mansions began to be converted and the Square Mile was never the same again.*

ASKING A MAN HOW MUCH MONEY HE'S WORTH is a little like demanding which sex position he prefers. No candid reckoning is possible.

Estimates are made very much more difficult by the fact that the fortunes of many of the great financial dynasties have been reduced to large quietly administered estates. The money that once talked now only whispers. The financial presence of the Cawthras, Gooderhams, Mulocks, and Oslers in Toronto, the Carlings and Labatts in London, the Seagrams in Waterloo, the Booths in Ottawa, the Cassilses, Redpaths, Galts, Gaults, McCalls, and Davises in Montreal, the McRaes and Buckerfields in Vancouver, and the Dunsmuirs, Rithets, Priors, Pembertons, and Pendrays in Victoria survives mainly in trust company ledgers.† Some families have ensured absolute secrecy for

---

*Despite the decline of the old families and the obvious shift of power to Toronto, there's still a lot of money in Montreal. During a $25-million fund-raising drive by McGill University in 1974, some seven million was subscribed on the first day: $4 million by the McConnell estate, $2 million from the Bronfman family, $500,000 from the Websters, and $250,000 each by the Royal and the Bank of Montreal.

†The Mortimer Davis and Elwood Hosmer estates still warrant their own listings in the Montreal telephone directory.

their transactions by operating their own trust companies.*
Other holdings are handled by professional investment
managers.†

Big wealth doesn't consume. It builds. The really rich
don't capitalize their gains. They keep reinvesting. Some
of the Old Money lives on the income from reinvested
interest; the basic fortunes remain intact. Others flee to
the lush havens of Grand Cayman, the Bahamas, and Bermuda, where their wealth never emerges to be counted,
taxed, or recorded. Family fortunes show up in strange
places. When the late Joseph Kennedy distributed one
million dollars to each of his children on their twenty-first
birthday, the gift received world-wide publicity. But Jules
Brillant, a little-known Quebec industrialist who spent his
whole life in Rimouski, gave his five kids *ten* million dollars each when they reached majority.‡

Most of the surviving great fortunes belong to families
that have retained ownership of the large companies they
operate. Their money doesn't lie in trust company safes;
it's out in the marketplace multiplying itself. Their incomes, as audited by Ottawa tax inspectors, are meaningless, only indicating how much they decided to take out
during any particular year. A labyrinth of family foundations, "street" names, investment trusts, Swiss bank
accounts, and income deferment schemes efficiently camou-
flages any reckoning of their exact holdings.

Yet by a mysterious process of osmosis the rich can
pinpoint the extent of one another's fortunes quite accurately. The estimates that follow are based, for the most
part, on how the rich rank each other, checked by bank
officials and other sources. They can be divided into three
main categories:

---

*The McConnell estate owns Commercial Trust; the Webster family
has Imperial Trust; Steve Roman controls Standard Trust; Nova Scotia's
Stanfield clan runs Acadia Trust in Truro; the Morgan family of Montreal
has Morgan Trust.

†The most active of these is Bolton, Tremblay & Co. of Toronto, run
by Arthur Labatt, managing about $700 million for two hundred clients.
Other firms include Jarislowsky, Fraser & Co. Ltd. in Montreal; Elliott &
Page Ltd., Toronto; Scudder, Stevens & Clark of Canada Ltd., Toronto;
and Phillips, Hager & North Ltd., Vancouver.

‡Brillant made most of his money selling the Lower St. Lawrence Power
Co. to Hydro-Québec and Québec-Téléphone to the U.S.-controlled Anglo-
Canadian Telephone Co. Aubert Brillant, his eldest son, was declared
bankrupt in 1969 at the age of forty-four. The $15,000 diamond ring
Aubert wore to court represented a third of his remaining assets.

1. The centi-millionaires: men and families owning assets worth more than $100 millions;*
2. The $50-million group;
3. The $20-million group.

The Centi-Millionaires

Steve Roman. You can visualize him as a rich peasant in one of Tolstoy's later novels, with dimpled stocky body, chubby capable hands, and a glittery, glittery eye, in a country tavern in the evening of a market day, drinking beer and wiping chicken grease off his chin. His elegant suits don't camouflage much of anything and he conveys the impression that this gives him no pain.

His house has this same feel. Set in a twelve-hundred-acre estate at Unionville, twenty-five minutes by limousine from downtown Toronto, it reflects accurately a Slovak version of grandeur. Roman hasn't attempted to floss it up by turning it into an English country seat or a French château, or with any of the kind of nonsense that the decorators foist on the New Rich. There's a big Slovak painting in the hall, marble in the foyer, crystal chandeliers, red velvet chairs, a fireplace worthy of a feudal castle, lots of liquor of the best kind (which he himself rarely drinks), rich food, huge floral arrangements. It's spending on an unabashed scale, but Roman isn't vulgar about it—doesn't point out his acquisitions except with pleasure in them or in acceptance of a guest's admiration.

The family ties (four sons and three daughters) are strong. The kids yell at him and he yells back. If he makes a joke about his wife's age, she makes a joke about his: gives as good as she gets. He talks with a mild accent and drops his *the's*, as in "Let's go around table and talk about election." One of the few non-Wasps or non-Jews to be allowed a toehold in the Establishment, Roman has a couple of honorary degrees and is on the boards of the Royal Ontario Museum and the Royal Agricultural Winter Fair, but his only Toronto club affiliation is the Empire,

---

*To place these fortunes in a world context, they can be compared with the $500-million estimate of Aristotle Onassis's estate and the $62.5 million in assets declared by Nelson Rockefeller during the 1974 confirmation hearings that led to his assuming the U.S. vice-presidency.

which is no club at all but a Royal York Hotel luncheon group that sells tickets at the door.

He has proved to be terrific at cattle raising, a certified Establishment hobby that he's turned to profit. (One of his three-year-old Holsteins, Romandale Reflection Cristy, made the *Guinness Book of World Records* when it sold for $65,000.) In fact, everything he's touched for the past couple of decades has turned to profit, which may be as big a part of his personal catechism as his belief in the Holy Trinity.

He loves to tell the story about a cattle auction in the late sixties at the Royal Winter Fair, when he was trying to thin his herd. To add a little excitement to the bidding, he conceived the idea of putting up for sale two animals at a time: one great, one merely good, with the highest bidder taking his choice. The first time he tried it, he lost only one breeder he wanted to keep. But he did it again more recently, and this time the buyers had caught on and cleaned him out of his best stock. He accepts the loss with belly-pumping laughter: *"That'll teach me something: don't use a trick more than once."*

Stephen Roman came to Canada from his native Slovakia in 1937, worked for a while as a tomato picker near Oshawa, drifted into a munitions plant during World War II, played the stock market, and eventually built up a ten-thousand-dollar nest egg. He struck oil in North Dakota, sold out, and in 1953 bought 900,000 shares (at 8½ cents each) of North Denison Mines, a speculative mining operation. He changed its name and in February, 1954, purchased (for $30,000 and 500,000 shares of his stock) the claims in the Algoma uranium strike staked by A.W. Stollery, near Quirke Lake, which turned out to be the largest uranium ore body ever discovered. It was Roman's peculiar skill that he was able to put together the $59 million to bring Denison into production without losing control of his property. Within four years, he owned the richest uranium mine in the world and by the mid-seventies had amassed forward orders worth more than five billion dollars.

Since the uranium properties seem almost to run themselves, Roman has expanded into ownership of other enterprises: Lake Ontario Cement, Pacific Tin Consolidated, coal properties in B.C. and Alberta, an oil field off Spain, the Strathcona Paper Company in Napanee, Ontario, and Main Iron Works of Houma, Louisiana, builders of ocean-going tugs. Directly and through his holding and exploration company, Roman Corporation, he retains a third of Denison's stock, worth about $100 million. (Every time Denison moves up a point on the stock exchanges, Roman is $1.5 million richer.) He is a director of the Royal Bank, Crown Life, and Guaranty Trust but is chiefly concerned with expanding his own enterprises. His crowning venture will be the $1-billion oil refinery he is planning to build jointly with Arab money men in the Bahamas.

Unlike many of his confreres, Roman isn't afraid to defend capitalism publicly. "If we want to remain free," he says, "we must work towards the ultimate in human initiative, help to present clear and more definite ways in which free enterprise can function." He pursues what he calls "logic," preaching that "the trouble with most people is that they follow emotion, but emotion doesn't lead them to the truth."

During the first thirteen years of its existence and after producing net profits of more than $100 million, Denison proposed to pay not a cent in federal taxes.* Roman despises politicians and their flossy ideas. He was particularly incensed when Lester Pearson cancelled a $90-million uranium contract he'd negotiated with France and when Pierre Trudeau disallowed Denison's sale to an American mining and oil conglomerate.† Roman has tried to counter Ottawa's influence by retaining an occasional politician on his board. At first it was Senator Harry Willis, then the chief Tory bagman; he was succeeded by the Honourable George Drew, following his retirement as Canadian high commissioner to the United Kingdom; then came Senator Keith Davey; and currently, it's the Honourable Alvin Hamilton.‡

---

*Ottawa challenged Roman's accounting methods and won the drawn-out court battle that ensued. The thirteen-year period included the three tax-exempt years that a mining company is allowed after entering production.

†Roman promptly sued Trudeau for $104 million in damages but lost both the original case and an appeal.

‡None of these appointments worked too well. Willis didn't have much real power; Drew kept falling asleep at board meetings (even though Roman had assigned one of his flunkeys to sit beside him and whisper,

He has twice run unsuccessfully as a federal Tory in York North, trying to collect on the pledge of a cabinet post from Robert Stanfield. But the only politician who ever enlisted Steve Roman's complete sympathy was Richard Nixon. Roman was one of the largest non-American financial contributors to Nixon's election campaigns, and when Trudeau turned down his scheme to sell off Denison, the American president telephoned to say that two officials of the U.S. consulate in Toronto had been delegated to whisk him off to the States if he needed a political refuge. "It took me exactly one second to say 'No,' " Roman recalls. "I want to stay in Canada."

Relaxing around his villa at Lyford Cay in the Bahamas or at his Unionville mansion, Roman enjoys entertaining the Wasps who flock to his parties, partly out of admiration and mostly out of curiosity. But he listens to their conversation with ill-concealed foot-tapping boredom. He hates theory, obfuscation, refinement. He loves plain talk, big money, making deals. His eyes sparkle, his hands work at the scar on his forehead, and he seems to be thinking: *"You're some smart, Steve."*

Howard Webster must be the most unusual millionaire in the country. He looks like a retired streetcar conductor —a big, heavy man in a plain navy-blue raincoat, a durable and not very expensive suit, and a fedora, all three of which could easily have been bought in 1952. He once flew out to settle a strike at the *Vancouver Sun* wearing tennis shoes and carrying his clothes in a Loblaws shopping bag. His hands are freckled, his eyes blue, his hair thinning and white; and he has a smile that's as ingenuous as a child's. He may be the shyest tycoon in Canada—taciturn, a model Scot who gets physical relish from the making of money. He is a lonely man who finds himself continually being misunderstood, not quite connecting with those around him, partly because his mind is continually outracing his manner.

He seldom allows himself to do things just because they might be fun and instead has made it fun to do

---

"Wake up, George," at the appropriate moments); and Keith Davey resigned soon after he was appointed on an issue of principle, when he disagreed with Roman's cavalier treatment of Ottawa's tax assessments.

what's profitable. The golf course he bought on Lake
Champlain and the cattle ranch he owns on P.E.I. are
both moneymakers. He remembers the details of every
proxy fight, where each meeting took place, who said
what to whom, the dollar value at the bottom of every
balance sheet. These deals are his passion, his recreation,
his children, his everything. The men who jostle to be
near him keep watching to see if he'll reveal some trick,
some special moneymaking secret. But he never does.

The Webster holdings, probably worth in excess of
$400 millions, are controlled through the privately held
Imperial Trust in Montreal. The family fortune was built
up by Howard's father, Senator Lorne Webster, who
started business life as a clerk in his Scottish family's
small Quebec City coalyard. He eventually put together a
string of 250 companies (under an umbrella corporation
called Canadian Import) that gained so tight a monopoly
on the sale of British coal in Canada that he was found
guilty of restrictive trade practices during a government
investigation in 1933.* The Senator built up an industrial
empire in steel, sugar, furs, and insurance. In 1924 he
bought the Montreal Water and Power Company for nine
million dollars and sold it, unchanged, to the city two
years later for six million more. When he died in 1941,
the elder Webster's meticulously drafted will created a
dynasty. He divided his fortune among his five sons and
one daughter,† though they didn't come into their full
estates until they were forty, and any Webster who
brought disgrace to his name was automatically excluded.
Twenty per cent of each inheritance was to be pooled in
Imperial Trust so that the family would survive as a
financial unit. The Senator was very precise about how
the Webster patrimony should be preserved. "I com-
mend my soul to Almighty God and urge all my children
to be active followers of Jesus Christ," he stated in his last
testament. "It is also my earnest desire and request that
my children shall continue actively interested in church,
religious and charitable works and make generous contributions to such works. . . . I further request them to

---

*The Websters' lawyer during the hearings was Louis St. Laurent.
†Mrs. John H. Taylor of Toronto, whose husband ran Liquefuels Ltd.,
Weaver Coal Co., and Seaway Terminals and is a corporate director.

remain united in their transactions and live in harmony together."

Canadian Import was sold to Shell for $80 million in 1967, and four of the five brothers—Colin, Eric, Stuart, and Richard—have since faded from business prominence. Howard was always the special one. He studied economics at McGill under Stephen Leacock and attended the Babson Institute of Business Administration near Boston. ("I was set to go to the Harvard Business School, but it was a two-year course and Babson's was only nine months, so I went there.") He took a six-month tour around the world on the *Empress of Britain* in 1933. ("There were all these widows wanting to meet George Bernard Shaw, who was aboard. I said, 'Sure, I'll introduce you to my friend Bernard.' So I took this lady, who had been married three times, and said, 'Mr. Shaw, this is the widow of R.W. Lock.' All he replied was, 'And whose widow are you now?' ")

The Senator assigned his son to see if he could cure the financial troubles of Holt, Renfrew, one of his companies. Instead, young Howard discovered Annis Furs of Detroit, then one of the largest U.S. fur houses but not a particularly well-managed business, and persuaded his father to buy it for him. Howard turned it into a profit-maker and at one point managed to corner the world market in monkey furs. ("They said, 'Do you want the monkeys?' I said, 'How many monkeys?' They said, 'A hundred and fifty thousand!' I said, 'Jesus, dead or alive?' They told me the furs were a bargain at twenty cents each because monkey fur was then selling at a buck each as trimming for coats. I made the deal, but I forgot all about them. A long time later, in 1947, I got a call from the German government asking whether I had some monkeys stored in Paris. Meanwhile, the monkey market had gone sour, so that one didn't turn out too well.")

Webster moved to the U.S., bought sheep ranches in Uruguay, the patent rights for Claude Neon lights, a big chunk of Central Coal and Coke (which owned twenty-three oil wells in Louisiana), and Southwest Lumber Company in Arizona. He managed to get control of Schick's, the razor people, and wrested control of Eversharp from its founder, Martin Strauss II. He bought huge subdivisions near Los Angeles and Detroit and a ranch just north of San Diego, where he grew alfalfa and alligator pears. In 1952, he purchased the forty-seven-storey Penobscot Building, Detroit's largest skyscraper (for $17.5 million with a twenty-one-year mortgage at 4 per cent), which he still owns.

Howard Webster's main interests now are control of Burns Foods in Calgary (which he bought for $3.4 million), Quebecair (bought from the Brillant family), parts of Maclaren Power and Paper in Quebec, Detroit Marine Terminals, two hotels (the Windsor in Montreal and the Lord Simcoe in Toronto),* his large ranch in P.E.I. (which at its first auction sale of European-breed cattle in 1973 grossed $857,950), several large shopping centres in Eastern Canada, and a block of the FP newspaper chain. Webster entered Canadian publishing abruptly in 1955 (when he bid $10.9 million for the *Globe and Mail* —"I figured it would keep me on my toes a little more than just watching my stocks go up and down"). He folded the *Globe* into the FP chain in 1965 because "after Oakley Dalgleish died it was hard to get tough publishers, and I needed the kind of protection against strikes you can get from a larger unit."

Webster never interferes editorially in any of his papers, but he enjoys the prestige of being the *Globe*'s chairman and president. ("I fell for the *Globe*," he says, as though it was a love affair, and in a way it is.) He runs his business empire through the offices of Imperial Trust and at sixty-five continues his unorthodox wheeling and dealing, enjoying life, making things turn.

The most likely heir to the Webster mantle is Colin's energetically brilliant son Lorne, the 45-year-old head of the Prenor Group, which manages assets of $800 million. The second-largest shareholder in the Montreal Expos, he recently bought Northern Life in London, Ontario, from the Ivey family and runs large insurance, real estate, and investment interests. A few years ago, Lorne offered his Uncle Howard ten thousand dollars for ten min-

---

*At one annual meeting of Lord Simcoe shareholders, Webster arrived in a light blue suit and dark brown shoes but had no annual report. When a shareholder inquired why, Webster replied: "I've got one, but I left it in my room because the figures are so lousy."

utes of his time to discuss the secrets and strategy of business acquisition. The bid was gently refused.

"We always knew that Eaton's Santa was the real one," recalls Toronto-born Rick Rabin, now living in Gander. *"You can't fool kids about anything as important as that."**

The Eatons Canadians have always felt a special relationship with the Eaton family, the closest we've come to having an aristocracy of our own. They are the country's fifth-largest employers (after the government, the railways, and Bell Canada); their catalogues have an annual circulation of eighteen million; their sixty-two stores sell $25 millions' worth of goods a week.

The private company was founded in 1869 by Timothy, brought to its initial flowering by Sir John Craig, extended to cross-country dimensions by Robert Young Eaton, and modernized by John David. Probably the best-known Eaton of them all was Florence McCrea (better known as Flora), youngest daughter of a carpenter from Omemee, Ontario, who married Sir John in 1901. As a token of her special status, Lady Eaton always retained the fifty-cent cheque issued to her when she served an hour behind the ribbon counter during the opening ceremonies of the family's Winnipeg store. She built a Norman castle with seventy rooms at King, just north of Toronto, leased a villa in Florence (originally built for Queen Elizabeth of Romania),† and travelled about the country in her private railway car.

"The Eaton name, as a general rule of thumb, appeared in the press only when an Eaton wanted it to," wrote Ron Haggart in the *Toronto Daily Star.* "When a holdup man murdered a finance company manager on Yonge St., fleeing through Eaton's store and then Simpson's in an attempt to get lost in the crowds, the dramatic chase was

---

*Quoted from *The Store That Timothy Built,* by William Stephenson (Toronto: McClelland and Stewart, 1969).

†In a 1927 interview with the *Toronto Daily Star,* after her return from a summer in Italy, Lady Eaton praised Mussolini's reforms ("No more do the beggars around the cathedrals annoy anyone") and lamented that the dictator "is not really in good health, and the only relief is in distracting his thoughts by playing the violin."

delicately described in the press as being 'through a down-town department store and south across Queen St. into another downtown department store.' "

John David Eaton* was raised in a Toronto mansion called Ardwold, a house with fifty rooms, fourteen bath-rooms, and its own hospital that stood a little to the northeast of Casa Loma. In 1933 he married Signy Hildur Stephenson, whom he courted while he ran the family's Winnipeg store. He served as the president of Eaton's from 1942 until 1969, and maintained a large house in Toronto's Forest Hill Village, a country seat in the Caledon Hills, a villa in Antigua, and an island in Georgian Bay, commuting to work in a helicopter he'd learned to fly. The *Hildur*, a diesel yacht with accommodation for six passengers (and six crew), was considered his prize possession.

Three of John David's sons, Fred, John, and George, have taken an active interest in the store.† "They are rich men's sons of the most attractive sort," wrote Alexander Ross in *Maclean's*. "Handsome, soft-spoken, unobtrusively well-mannered, utterly assured, and quietly confident of the fact that being born an Eaton is nothing to be ashamed of. They would not be out of place as constitutional monarchs of some clean little country like Denmark or Holland."

Fred, who is president of Eaton's of Canada, lives in Forest Hill and has a summer Rolls (a 1950 model with a space specially provided by the maker for a picnic hamper) and a 1962 Rolls for winter driving. Young John, who is the firm's chairman, lives in a Rathnelly town-house, drives a maroon Rolls, and works hard at his calling. "There *is* something special about being an Eaton," he says. "It's a feeling I've had all my life. Canada

*John David was chosen to head the firm over Sir John's eldest son, Timothy Craig, who lives in England pursuing his hobby of operating model trains. Timothy's prize possession is a replica, one-eighth of the actual size, of the locomotive that pulled Sir Winston Churchill's funeral train. A life-size portrait of his father hangs in his house at Tunbridge Wells, beside a portrait of himself in hunting pinks. "My father's portrait is exactly six inches higher than my own," he says.
†The family also founded its own Toronto church, Timothy Eaton Memorial on St. Clair Avenue, now worth about $7.2 million in real estate alone. Its current minister (who receives a salary of $21,000 and free use of a $150,000 house) is George Morrison, a former comptroller of IBM World Trade Corp. who left the corporation at the age of forty-one to join the United Church and became secretary of its general council.

has given a lot to us and we should give a lot back. That doesn't mean just money, but time spent in community efforts." George recently became a vice-president.

Eaton's has never gone to the market for investment capital; being a provincially chartered corporation, it is not required to make public disclosures of its operations or board membership. Eaton's of Canada, the chief holding apparatus, which owns T. Eaton Company (the operating arm), has twelve directors: the four Eaton boys; their mother, Signy; Thor Stephenson (Signy Eaton's brother, who is president of Pratt and Whitney Aircraft of Canada in Montreal); Budd H. Rieger, a vice-president of Canadian Corporate Management; Dick Thomson, president of the TD Bank; David Kinnear, a director of the Bank of Montreal and former chairman of T Eaton Company; Allan Beattie, a partner in the Osler, Hoskin and Harcourt law firm; R.J. Butler, chairman of T. Eaton Company; and Brigadier Gordon Dorward de Salaberry ("Swotty") Wotherspoon, a lawyer and Eaton confidant. On top of this hierarchy is the family trust, which has the authority to choose (by the autumn of 1975) which of the four sons will succeed to John David's mantle.* The estate's trustees are his widow, her brother Thor, Beattie, Thomson, and Wotherspoon.

One of the great mysteries about the Eaton empire is how the family manages to pass it on from generation to generation without paying the succession duties that cripple enterprises many times smaller.† The secret is a process called "estate freezing," which involves hiving off assets to a holding company (Eaton's of Canada), which controls all the common stock, placed in the hands of each succeeding generation after payment of a relatively modest gift tax.

Despite its size, Eaton's has not been keeping pace with the expansion of Canada's retail trade.‡ The company lost heavily on its pocket computer investment (Rapid Data), and several gifted executives, including Don

---

*Eaton's will calls for the succession to occur when the youngest son reaches the age of thirty.
†Lady Eaton died at ninety-one in July, 1970, John David Eaton died at ninety-three in August, 1973.
‡Simpsons-Sears Ltd. had a 1974 income of $1.3 billion and its average sales per square foot were $134, compared with $100 at Eaton's.

McGiverin and Alan Marchment, left in frustration. Earl Orser, a Clarkson, Gordon grad, was appointed the new president of Eaton's operating company in the spring of 1975.

Perhaps it's a sign of the family's declining grandeur that John David Eaton's most prized (and most secret) possession, the 506-ton *Chimon,* a luxurious diesel yacht he quietly kept in the Mediterranean, is now lying in Southampton, for sale to the highest bidder. Built in 1938 for another owner by Camper and Nicholsons (and refitted in 1973–74 at a cost of $625,000), the 173-foot vessel was so roomy that she carried eight tenders of various sizes and had accommodation for twelve guests and a crew of sixteen.

E.P. Taylor. He sits there, all smiles and forgiveness, his cherry-cheerful face grooved by lines of mellowing pugnacity, and it's not easy to think of E.P. Taylor as a symbol of anything except the pleasures of aging gracefully. But for twenty years he stood out in the struggle between Canada's haves and have-nots as the ultimate personification of riches gained and power wielded. Through his founding and control of Argus Corporation, he became an acknowledged master of the capitalist theology, using the free-enterprise system as a successful arrangement of human affairs that allocates maximum benefits to the most adroit. "Eddie can read a balance sheet like a poem and tell you where it doesn't scan," they used to say along Bay Street.

But in 1969, on his sixty-eighth birthday, Taylor severed most of his board-room connections and began his planned withdrawal to Nassau, where he had been developing his Lyford Cay millionaires' subdivision. Except for his appearances in the sports pages, where he always seemed to be wearing that half-moon smile of his, he virtually disappeared from Canadian mention.

Six years later, Taylor still moves like the most expensive tropical fish in the tank, so that when he walks into a room its occupants become a trifle more self-conscious. His resources have only multiplied, so much so that during the 1974 market break he suffered a paper loss of between thirty and forty million dollars and treated the

event as a bad joke. The brew of laughter is never far
below the surface of his banter. ("I was offering forty-
four horses in Saratoga last night; sold thirty. Put my
reserves a little too high, but sold a million dollars' worth
anyway. . . . Bought two horses worth over a million
dollars each in the past two weeks.* One of them won the
United Nations Derby in Atlantic City. There was a lot of
booing after the race. Didn't know who they were booing,
me or the horse. Turned out to be the Governor of New
Jersey. Crowd didn't like him for some reason. Miss
America was with him. When I presented her in the
winners' circle, I whispered: 'Would you give me a kiss,
dear?' So I was kissed in front of twenty-five thousand
people by Miss America!")

He now operates out of his breeding farm in Maryland
(just south of the Delaware border), his beach villa at
Lyford Cay, or the remodelled gatehouse he maintains
off Bayview Avenue in North York. Taylor has become a
bit disillusioned with the Bahamas' black government.
("I've got a meeting with the Prime Minister a week today
to see whether I can get some action on things that would
help the country. I've a little advantage there in that the
Royal is the government's banker and I'm in charge of
that area for the bank.")

His main interest has shifted to a deal that dates from
a meeting with Daniel Ludwig, the great mystery man of
American finance, described by Taylor as "probably the
richest white man in the world." Ludwig's wealth, estimated to be about three billion dollars, easily exceeds the
combined fortunes of the original Vanderbilts, Morgans,
and du Ponts. His two hundred interlocked corporations
operate in fifty countries and include ownership of the
world's largest tanker fleet, salt mines, orange groves, oil
refineries in Panama, a monster river dredge at the
mouth of the Orinoco, a 15,000-head cattle ranch in
Venezuela so vast it has never been surveyed, coal mines
in West Virginia, Canadian oil wells, a marine insurance
company and hotels in Bermuda, potash mines in Ethio-

*Between 1960 and 1969, Taylor was the leading North American
breeder (in races won); in 1970 he became the world's leading horse
breeder (in money won); and in 1973 he was voted Racing's Man of the
Year.

pia, shipping operations in India, a $20-million cargo transfer complex in Japan, the former Japanese naval shipyard at Kure, where the world's greatest battleship, the *Yamato*,* was built; the Princess Hotel in Bermuda; condominiums in Australia; the $40-million Acapulco Princess Hotel; and much of Brazil's great rain forest.

He runs his enterprises with obsessive cost-cutting discipline, registering his ships in Panama (which imposes no taxes and few safety regulations) or other flag-of-convenience countries like Liberia and crewing them with Cayman Islanders. When his designers reported that they couldn't comply with his request that they find a way of storing oil in tankers' masts, Ludwig ordered them to eliminate the masts. Navigation lights are mounted on steel pipes instead.†

Ludwig's only luxury is his 257-foot *Danginn* (registered in Monrovia), and it was aboard this yacht that he entertained E.P. Taylor in 1960. "I wasn't impressed, particularly," Taylor remembers, "because Ludwig is a vegetarian and there wasn't much food. But a few years later he asked me to the opening of his hotel in Acapulco. It's magnificent, built just like an Aztec pyramid. Ludwig invited four hundred people from around the world for four days. I was busy, so I couldn't stay long. On the first morning he said, 'Eddie, I want to show you something. Get into the wagon.' So I got into a blue station wagon, and he took me around about a mile away and showed me three houses and workmen building other houses on a production-line basis.

"I said, 'I'm very interested in this.' They were built production line. They'd start a house on Monday and it would be finished Saturday. The equipment would move once a day: pour the foundation the first day, the walls the second day, roof it in the third day; the fourth day, the plumbing; the fifth day, the painters; the sixth day, the landscapers; the seventh day, the house would be

---

*The *Yamato* (72,809 tons displacement) sank with a loss of 2,498 of her crew of 2,778 on April 7, 1945, on her way to Okinawa after taking five bomb hits and ten torpedoes; she carried nine 18.1-inch guns.

†At the same time, Ludwig asked the designers to substitute exhaust pipes for ship's funnels because they cost less. He once bought a tanker called the *Anahuac*. Nobody could pronounce her name, but Ludwig decided to keep it anyway. "It would have cost $50 to paint it out," he explained.

demonstrated and put up for sale. I decided to try it in the Bahamas. I built a hundred of them and cut costs by 40 per cent."

Following drawn-out negotiations with one of Ludwig's partners, Taylor acquired use of the patent in 1973 and set up his own International Housing in the Cayman Islands through a Panamanian trust in which he had $35 million. During 1974, its first full year of operation, the company built five thousand houses worth $20 million in Mexico, Costa Rica, Brazil, Nigeria, Venezuela, and the Caymans. By the summer of 1975 he was negotiating deals with the Shah of Iran, the King of Saudi Arabia, the President of Indonesia, and the dictator of Nicaragua that will make Eddie Taylor, at seventy-five, the world's largest house-builder.

Charles Rathgeb. The half-dozen bracelets of gold and leather jangle like a belly-dancer's baubles when he moves his left arm. It's the BIG SIX! Each bangle (awarded by the Explorers' Club in London) denotes that Rathgeb has shot, single-handed, one of the great animals: a lion, a leopard, an elephant, a buffalo, a tiger, and a rhino.*

Rathgeb's office at the Toronto headquarters of Comstock International is the size of two tennis courts. Decorated in various shades of brown, it has floor-to-ceiling blowups of himself hunting, parachuting, tuna fishing, bobsledding, car rallying, ballooning, mountain climbing, racing motorboats, aeroplanes, horses, and several other speedy conveyances. As president and sole shareholder of Canada's largest contracting company (with annual revenues well in excess of $300 million), Rathgeb likes to live a little.

Here is the Canadian Establishment's champion jock. "That was our boat in the London-to-Monte Carlo power race," he says, glancing around his office. "That was the bobsled we used in the 1964 Olympics. In 1967, I was the first Canadian to fly over the Alps by balloon, from Zurich to Milan. Haven't done much lately, because we had a crash and I broke my leg rather badly. I've got a

---

*He bagged the tiger in the Himalayan hills, the others in either Kenya or Tanzania.

steel pin through my ankle, and if I were to land hard, the pin might shatter it."

Rathgeb's sporting bent goes back to his days at Upper Canada College, when he represented this country on the Commonwealth Cricket Team, which played matches against English public schools in the summer of 1935. He then spent two years as an RCMP constable in the High Arctic and during World War II served in the RNC, with thirty-six Atlantic crossings to his credit. An experienced climber, he abandoned his 1975 assault on Mount Everest only because Ottawa wouldn't lend him enough aircraft. In 1973, at the age of fifty-two, he became the first Canadian to drive in the Targa Florio road race in Sicily; his car finished tenth out of eighty entries. A year later he took part in the arduous Trans-Sahara World Cup Rally. He has flown jets solo across the Atlantic, operates racing stables, and captained the first Canadian entry in the International Tuna Championships.

Since he inherited Comstock from his father in 1965, Rathgeb has significantly expanded its overseas activities so that it has become one of Canada's important multinationals,* employing a peak work force of twelve thousand. He is also a director of the Royal Bank, Canadair, and the Olympic Trust, and his wife is the former Rosemary Clarke (steamships). One of the few businessmen in his league who doesn't believe in tax havens or offshore subsidiaries, he runs a computer-oriented highly centralized operation. "I own Comstock," he says, "because I believe that a construction firm is best run as a benevolent dictatorship."

Tom Bata. He should have been born a cardinal in fourteenth-century Florence, privy councillor to the Pope, travelling the world as special envoy from the palace of

---

*Comstock's Canadian contracts have included work on the National Arts Centre in Ottawa, the Banff Springs Hotel, Maple Leaf Gardens, the Southgate Shopping Centre in Edmonton, Toronto International Airport, the Trans Mountain pipeline from Edmonton to Vancouver, and many of the DEW Line installations. U.S. jobs include the New York headquarters of the Chase Manhattan Bank, many of the Cape Kennedy space installations, and the U.S. Steel headquarters in Pittsburgh. Overseas assignments have included renovations to the Panama Canal; construction of the Intercontinental Hotel in Bangkok; the Volta River power dam in Ghana; and an increasing number of large projects in Kuwait, Dubai, Bahrain, and several other Arab countries.

the Doge in Venice, spreading the word, distributing the tithes, negotiating the quotas, punishing the heretics.

The Bata empire—ninety plants in eighty countries—has about it a kind of divine fervour, a ritualistic devotion both to the product and to the man that marks few Canadian enterprises. Towns take on the brand name (Batawa in Canada, Batapur in India, Bataville in France); the organization maintains its own college courses, roving inspectors, codes, and communications networks.*

Tom Bata manufactures more footwear than anyone else in the world. He employs 85,000 workers, manages 5,000 retail outlets, and makes 350 million pairs of shoes worth roughly a billion dollars a year.

"Tomas Bata felt he was sent out by God Almighty to shoe mankind," Karel Capek, the Czech philosopher, wrote about Bata's father, who founded the family firm in Zlin, Czechoslovakia.† Young Tom escaped the Nazis in 1939 and brought out enough craftsmen and equipment to start a small factory in the Bay of Quinte area of Southern Ontario. After the war, he took over his father's embryonic world network of factories and began to expand it. The whole organization is now run by Bata and his energetic wife, Sonja (an architect, she also does much of the designing for both shoes and stores), out of a modernistic Parkin-designed building in Toronto's Don Mills suburb. Subsidiaries and associated companies submit monthly balance sheets, which are fed into computers to spot weak areas and suggest remedies. Profits of Bata Limited, the basic holding company (which is wholly owned by the Bata family), are distributed among a private foundation in Switzerland (which acts as a banking house for the whole organization) and two Bermuda-based trusts (which are the repositories of the Bata family fortune).

Bata commutes about 150,000 miles a year between his various factories, is a director of CP Air, IBM Canada,

---

*The Bata world is split up into seven regional offices coded with such abbreviations as LATAM (Latin America), CARO (Central Africa), MERO (Middle East), ANZAR (Canada).
†The elder Bata had one of his offices built inside a huge elevator so that he wouldn't waste any time between inspections. Work Is a Moral Necessity was the slogan he placed on factory gates.

and IBM World Trade Americas/Far East Corporation, and deliberately stays out of much involvement with the Canadian Establishment. The family's Toronto home, a Georgian house on Park Lane Circle off Bayview Avenue, has an impressive assortment of art objects, including Signac watercolours, an Utrillo, Tanka Temple hangings from Tibet, bronze horsemen from the T'ang Dynasty, and a Pietro Annigoni portrait of the hostess.

Garfield Weston. His annual reports read like telephone directories. Associated British Foods, the worldwide food merchandising operation Garfield Weston and his son Garry run out of London, lists 127 bakeries, 76 flour mills, 1,901 shops and supermarkets, 63 warehouses, 189 food manufacturing and processing plants in England, Ireland, New Zealand, and Australia—all Weston subsidiaries. The 1974 sales of George Weston Limited amounted to $4.7 billion, making it the largest corporation ever put together by a Canadian.* Altogether, the Weston enterprises employ about 160,000.

There is something untidy and incomplete about the Weston operations, reflecting the impulsive nature of their founder. Garfield Weston once bought an Irish castle because he saw two donkeys at the gate. When he inquired about their names, he was told that they were called Fortnum and Mason, after the great London provisioners. Weston, who happens to own the store, was so delighted that he bought the property on the spot.

"My father," says Galen Weston, who now heads the Canadian operation, "is deeply concerned with Commonwealth affairs. He believes that English-speaking peoples should look after each other, see to their own well-being. The main reason he started acquiring the bakery business in England was to provide an overseas market for Canadian wheat. He became the world's greatest baker, and one of his motivating forces was to sell Canadian wheat. He's a tremendous salesman, has great flair, is religious to

---

*George Weston Ltd. is controlled by the W. Garfield Weston Charitable Foundation through Wittington Investments Ltd. Nearly all the Weston companies have only inside directors. In 1974, the ten George Weston Ltd. directors held sixty-three seats on the boards of their various affiliated companies.

'a point. Methodist. Very good personal living habits and unbelievable stamina, enthusiasm; he's great at conceptualizing new situations. He was one of the first conglomerate operators, back thirty years ago. Ruthless in cleaning up after his own mistakes and others'. Yet very proud of his origins as a baker's son here in Toronto. Very proud of his own ability to make biscuits personally."

Weston's father began as a bread-wagon driver. In 1884 he established a small bakery, which was netting $25,000 a year by the time his son inherited it in 1924. Young Garfield had gone off to war and spent his leaves inspecting the under-financed biscuit factories of England. After his Canadian bakery began to flourish,* he bought out the well-known Scottish biscuit-making firm of Mitchell and Muil, and Chibnall's of London. He moved to England in 1934 and started on a rampage of food firm acquisitions. When Matthew Halton, the Canadian journalist, toured one of his plants, Weston pointed out a small air jet he had installed at the end of the production line. "I see, that's blowing the extra chocolate off," Halton observed. "Oh, no," Weston replied. "It's blowing the profit on!"

In 1939, Weston became Conservative M.P. for Macclesfield in an uncontested by-election. He never ran again and during his time at Westminster made only one speech, defending the policies of Lord Beaverbrook. He lives on a large estate beside the Thames, opposite Eton, and loves to race up the river in a speedboat. His receiving room is covered by a 250-year-old carpet once owned by the Shah of Persia.

In 1947, Weston purchased the Loblaw grocery operations in Canada and later those in the U.S. During the mid-fifties he acquired the National Tea Company of Chicago, then the fourth-largest U.S. supermarket chain.

Weston has always run his companies with a conspiratorial air, using code names to designate subsidiaries†

---

*One of Weston's purchases was the Eddy Paper Co. mill in Hull, overlooking the Parliament Buildings. The final instructions from R.B. Bennett, the mill's previous owner, who had been beaten by the Liberals in 1935 and had withdrawn to Britain and a peerage, were to "keep blowing the smoke into Mackenzie King's eyes."

†B.C. Packers, for instance, was referred to as "Phish" and Power Super Markets as "No. 1" in internal communications.

and sending most of his instructions to their operating heads' homes rather than offices. Intercompany relations were so Byzantine that even the men who ran the firms often weren't sure how they related to the holding group. Before Galen Weston's current reorganization, for example, Atlantic Wholesalers was 96 per cent owned by Harbour Investments, a subsidiary of Food Markets Holdings. Food Markets was owned by Loblaw Groceterias Company, which was controlled by Loblaw Companies, a subsidiary of Perrin Investments, which in turn was owned by George Weston Limited, which was controlled —through still another holding company and a charitable foundation—by W. Garfield Weston.

He barred his executives from taking any part in community affairs, exempting only George Metcalf, who headed his Canadian operations, by allowing him to teach a weekly men's Bible class.

As well as his castle in Ireland, his country seat on the Thames, and a town house in London, Weston maintains an apartment at the ManuLife Centre in midtown Toronto. He remains as elusive and mysterious as ever. When architects were completing the blueprints for his company's new head office on St. Clair Avenue, about a mile to the north of his apartment, he had them instal a private elevator strictly for his own use, so that he could come and go without being seen.

Roy Thomson. The only self-made billionaire on the list, Roy Thomson cultivates the image of himself as a living embodiment of the profit motive. Seated next to Princess Margaret at a London fashion show, he spots a lamé gown on one of the models and exclaims: "My favourite colour—gold!" During a 1963 audience with Nikita Khrushchev, the Russian dictator teasingly asks what use Thomson's money is to him.

"You can't take it with you," says Khrushchev.

"Then I'm not going," Thomson replies.

Thomson had to renounce his Canadian citizenship when he was created a baron in 1964, but his son will inherit both his title and his fortune. "My father has a good chance of becoming a billionaire," says the younger Thomson, "but as of the moment that figure includes a certain amount of poetic licence." (The family will probably go over the magic mark in 1976 when the full dimensions of their oil strike in the North Sea—drilled in partnership with J. Paul Getty—are confirmed.)

Thomson owns 192 newspapers (from *The Times* of London to the *Council Bluffs* [Iowa] *Nonpareil*); 148 magazines (from the *Illustrated London News* to the *Brewers' Guardian*); seven book-publishing houses; hotels, airlines, insurance firms, trucking fleets, cable television companies, and a host of other enterprises, employing about thirty-five thousand around the world. Ken Thomson, his 53-year-old son and heir, owns 70 per cent of the Canadian operation through a tier of holding companies, while the family has 81 per cent of the British operation. He lives in the finest example of Georgian house architecture in Toronto, collects paintings (he has the best Joshua Reynolds outside a museum), married a beautiful model (whose picture he first saw in an Eaton's catalogue), buys his shoes at Wildsmith's on Duke Street in London, and efficiently runs his father's empire.

Wildly unassuming compared with his father, "young Ken," as he continues to be called, has mounted an astonishing bronze statue behind the desk of his office. It depicts a young tiger battling an old elephant. "When you live in the shadow of a legend, you don't go flashing mirrors," Sidney F. Chapman, the company's financial consultant, once commented. "Kenny is no mere figurehead. When it comes to making a deal, he has a cool mind of his own."

Poldi Bentley. The third Czech clan among Canada's centi-millionaires, the Bentley family's holdings constitute the second-largest private company in Canada—second only to Eaton's, though their profit ratios are very much higher. Leopold Lionel Garrick Bloch-Bauer owned cotton mills in prewar Czechoslovakia, immigrated to Vancouver in 1938, changed his name, and started, along with his brother-in-law, John Prentice (originally called Pick), a small veneer and plywood mill called Canadian Forest Products, which employed twenty-eight men. Their big push came in 1940, when they got a contract to build wing assemblies for Mosquito bombers. Instead of paying out dividends, they re-invested profits and never went to the public for capital, preferring short-term loans from the Bank of Montreal.

Canadian Forest Products (including Cornat Industries,* which was taken over in 1974) has consolidated annual sales of $400 million, employs eleven thousand, paying out about $120 million in wages. The second generation is now taking over—Peter Bentley, Poldi's son, is president, J. Ron Longstaffe, Prentice's son-in-law, is executive vice-president. There is only one outside director, Sir Don Ryder, chairman of Reed International, the *Daily Mirror* group, with which Canadian Forest Products has a joint interest in a large Prince George pulp mill. (A partner of Canfor's in another pulp mill at Prince George is Feld-mühle AG, part of the empire of the late Friedrich Flick, who made Mercedes-Benzes.) "We like the atmosphere in which we can make fast decisions with nobody looking over our shoulder," says Longstaffe.

Poldi Bentley is special. Highly cultured without being intellectual, he goes around done up as a sport in what looks like a 1937 polo coat, hand-sewn by the best tailor in Vienna. He has a hunting estate in Salzburg (where he feeds the game all winter) and advocates establishment of hunting preserves in B.C. where gentlemen could bag their elk. He is as avid for Mozart as he is for the Vancouver Canucks, is fanatically anti-Barrett, proud of having been a charter member at the Capilano Golf and Country Club, snobbish in the most unaffected and unabashed way of any tycoon in the country.

David Stewart. The office is crowded. It contains, among other things, a globe of the world; an honorary colonel's commission from the Queen's York Rangers; a statue of Napoleon; a Scottish broadsword; a porcelain pig; the model of a Rolls-Royce; a toy elephant; a cigar-store Indian; a map of Canada East and Canada West; the wood-carving of a 1725 grenadier of the Third Foot

---

*Cornat, which was acquired by a $17-million share offer in the fall of 1974, is a holding and management company that builds, repairs, and docks ships, warehouses steel, freezes vegetables, manufactures aluminum products, lends out mortgage money, runs truck lines, and until recently sold pizza pies. Revenues in 1974 were $107 million. The company has made a bid to take over Canadair Ltd. and de Havilland Aircraft of Canada Ltd.

Regiment; a 1621 British Admiralty flag; the tape made at a national sales conference of Macdonald Tobacco, the company that until recently was owned and run by the office's occupant, David Stewart. He shuffles around the room, overlooking Montreal's Victoria Square, wearing his favourite uniform—a pale blue sweater with a cigarette hole burned in it.

Probably the most unusual object in this unusual office is the twin-passenger seat from an old Fairchild flying boat. Stewart has never forgotten the great sleep he had flying across the Atlantic in the late forties aboard one of these planes. So he bought a Fairchild, salvaged a seat, and now, when he feels like it, can strap himself in, lower the backrest, put on an eye-mask, and snooze away.

The most retiring millionaire in the country, David Macdonald Stewart may be the gentlest man ever to control more than $100 million. There is a sad cast to his drooping grey moustache as he reminisces about his father and how he had to establish his own sense of independence through studying military history. Stewart has one of the world's finest collections of toy soldiers, and he personally finances the Montreal Military and Marine Museum as well as two ceremonial regiments.*

David Stewart doesn't precisely fit the stereotype of your average centi-millionaire. But he's a lot less eccentric than either of his predecessors. The company was established in 1858 by Sir William Macdonald, a loony skinflint from P.E.I. who amassed a considerable fortune from his tobacco factories but couldn't abide anyone smoking "the vile stuff" in his presence. Although he gave away about $15 million during his lifetime, he continued to wear the same shabby black coat long after it had turned green with age and furnished his office with a six-dollar deal table and a kitchen chair. He wouldn't allow installation of a telephone ("The public could have me by the ear any time they wished") and was so adamant in his moral stances that he insisted extra money be spent to put in marble partitions between the toilet stalls at Macdonald College, one of his gifts to McGill. ("More young men

---

*They are Fraser's Highlanders (the 78th Regiment, which fought under Wolfe against Montcalm) and La Compagnie Franche de la Marine, probably Canada's first permanent military force.

have been corrupted by what they have seen written on lavatory walls than many of us imagine. Writing on marble is easily effaced.") He was so disliked, even by his family, that no relatives turned up for his funeral in 1917.

Since Macdonald had no children, the company was left to Walter Stewart, who had been his bookkeeper and whose father had been his secretary for fifty years. Walter Stewart, David's father, headed the firm for the next fifty years, ruling it in the same spirit as Sir William. He rode to work on the back of one of his trucks, continued to use Macdonald's desk, and except for promoting Lassie, the Highland girl in the myrtle-green bonnet who was imprinted on the company's Export brands, refused to advertise. For tax reasons he folded ownership of the firm into a foundation. In 1974, six years after he took over from his father, David Stewart sold Macdonald's (which by then had annual sales of $250 millions) to R.J. Reynolds Industries of Winston-Salem, North Carolina, adding the funds to the family foundation. Stewart has stayed on as vice-chairman, but he is much more concerned with his philanthropic activities. That and cats. He is devoted to Himalayan females with green eyes, and when one was lost recently he searched as far as Bancroft, Ontario, to find a suitable replacement. David Stewart's family crest, which sits on the desk in his office (the same desk Sir William used), is a Himalayan cat rampant, grasping a tobacco leaf in its forepaw.

Eric Harvie. A lean figure with close-cropped hair, he carried a handkerchief up his left sleeve, favoured one of those miniature cowboy lassoes instead of a tie around his neck, and walked with the aid of a vicious-looking cane, which he tapped lightly against the ground as if keeping time to some private drummer. He amassed a greater personal fortune from petroleum than any other Canadian, yet was not an oilman, stayed in the industry only eleven years, and exhibited none of the free-wheeling traits that characterize the breed.

Harvie seemed totally indifferent to power, casually abandoning the opportunity of becoming the only Canadian to put together a fully integrated major oil company, and even though he went on amassing a fortune of well over $100 millions, he used little of the money for himself. Instead of going about Calgary in one of those burnished-arc Cadillacs oilmen seem to prefer, he drove an old Studebaker, so banged up that its undercarriage was a sheet of solid bronze.

Born in Orillia, Ontario, on April 1, 1892, Harvie studied at Osgoode Hall and the University of Alberta, graduating with a law degree in 1914. After enlisting in the 15th Light Horse, he sailed for Europe and was severely wounded on the Somme. Invalided home, he re-enlisted in the Royal Flying Corps and was finally demobilized as a captain in 1919. He joined a Calgary law firm and married Dorothy Jean Southam.

Back in 1906 the CPR sold off half a million of the acres it had originally been granted as part of its construction charter to the London-based Western Canada Land Company.* Unlike most of the railway's transfers, this purchase included mineral rights, and in 1931, the British firm set up Anglo-Western Oils to explore its properties. After drilling a few dry holes, it was wound up. When the Alberta government introduced its Mineral Taxation Act in 1942, the British land company was hit with a $25,000 annual tax bill and ordered its Canadian agent, Harry M.E. Evans (a former mayor of Edmonton), to seek a buyer for its franchise. On January 17, 1944, Harvie became the new owner (for a rumoured $110,-000) of the mineral rights and established Western Minerals to hold them as well as Western Leaseholds, which became his exploration vehicle. In November of 1946 Harvie leased 480 acres southwest of Edmonton to Imperial Oil and three months later this turned out to be the site of the great Leduc strike. The Vermilion and Redwater fields that followed were also largely on Harvie's mineral rights. By 1951, Harvie's companies owned a part-interest in 82 producing oil wells and had expanded their land holdings to two million acres. Four years later, Harvie abruptly sold Western Leaseholds to Canadian

*The company changed its name to British Dominions Land Corporation in 1925.

Petrofina for about $50 million, and in 1973 Western Minerals was purchased by Brascan for $30 million.

Harvie may be the only rich Canadian who leaves behind a popular legacy. His magpie instinct for collecting anything and everything he happened to see has endowed his foundations with the finest collection of western artifacts and general trivia anywhere. A random walk through the storage area of the Glenbow-Alberta Institute will reveal, among other objects, a set of Queen Victoria's royal bloomers; the last Model T Ford built; a 1900 steam-operated locomotive; the drum that boomed at Sitting Bull's command before the Battle of the Little Big Horn; a roomful of the possessions of Colonel Garnet Wolseley, who crushed the first Riel Rebellion in 1870 and later led a whaleboat expedition piloted by Canadian *voyageurs* up the Nile to Khartoum; Sir Robert Peel's penny-farthing bicycle; sets of matched duelling pistols; a barroom from Keremeos, B.C., complete with a brass foot-rail and dented brass spittoons; bullets found after Custer's last stand; ten thousand butterflies from the Duke of Bedford's collection; the bar of the courtroom where R.B. Bennett used to argue cases in Calgary; the brand of Max Bell's cattle; rodeo bronzes by Bob Scriver from the Montana Cowboy Hall of Fame; paintings by A.J. Casson, A.Y. Jackson, and J.F. Kernan (who did *Saturday Evening Post* covers); a Maya sun god made out of jade; the panelling from a French château; Earl Grey's decorations; CPR conductors' badges; and the Gatling gun used in the Riel Rebellion, which fired fifteen hundred rounds a minute and was commanded by a U.S. National Guard officer.*

Eric Harvie died on January 11, 1975. He seldom gave interviews. But a few months before his death, when he was already very ill, he talked to this book's author and reminisced about the early days. Out of the fulness of his life he was willing to impart only one sage bit of advice: "Never throw away old socks, old underwear, or old cars."

---

*Most of these and other items will be housed in the Glenbow Centre, due to be opened in Calgary during 1976.

Max Meighen. The Colonel is angry. "I don't trust the media," he is saying. "I've no use for them. I don't trust them. I find them completely dishonest and without character. . . . The politicians? Much the same. But at least the percentage of honest ones is greater than in the media."

This is an unusual stance for Max Meighen: he rarely finds a group for whom his contempt is greater than for politicians. (Meighen is one of the few men to list himself as a "Conservative" in the *Canadian Who's Who,* pinpointing his conviction that *Progressive* Conservatives have subverted his philosophy.)

By now, Meighen—metallurgist, son of the former prime minister, director of a dozen corporations with assets of close to two billion dollars—is in full spate. "Of course, the best government is the least government. Ottawa should be responsible for defence; for the courts; for tariffs. I don't think government should ever be in business. Their history proves this. Not just Liberal government in Ottawa but the Conservative government that was in Nova Scotia and the Conservative government that is in New Brunswick, the Conservative government that was in Manitoba."

An upright, military man (he served with distinction as a full colonel in World War II), Meighen speaks in clipped, nasal tones, checking his facts on a slide rule, trying to fit an increasingly confusing world into manageable patterns. "The trouble is," he confesses, "I have no faith in democracy. I wrote my father in 1944 that in my normal life expectancy all western nations would be under dictatorship and the form in the United States would be military. My nephew accused me of advocating dictatorship. I said, 'I don't advocate it at all. I say it's just bound to occur. There are more have-nots than there are haves, and you're going to end up in a German post-first-war type of inflation.' "

Max Meighen, in brief, is not overwhelmingly happy with the state of public affairs in this (or any other) country.* He may well be the most careful investor in the

*He spends three and a half weeks in winter and twelve days in summer at "Favouring Winds," his villa in Jamaica.

nation. "I haven't owned a bond, any life insurance, or anything like that since the war," he says. "That still doesn't protect me against the market going down. But at least I've done better than the market."

When his father left the Commons after his defeat in 1926, he helped establish a series of closed-end investment trusts, of which Canadian General Investments and Third Canadian General Investment Trust (the two companies with net assets of about $150 million that Max Meighen now heads) are the survivors. Meighen's companies hold 15 per cent of Huron and Erie Mortgage Corporation* and its subsidiary Canada Trust Company, which has large and growing operations across the country. A major shareholder in Argus Corporation through its holding trust, Ravelston, he is very much a part of the McDougald group, serving as chairman of Domtar, chairman of the executive committee of Argus, and member of the executive committees of Massey-Ferguson, Dominion Stores, and Standard Broadcasting.

The Colonel practises what he preaches. He literally refuses to sanction the federal government with his official recognition. Since the end of the war, he has visited Ottawa only once. In 1952 he flew in, issued an ultimatum to the National Revenue Department on a tax ruling he wanted changed, and flew out again.

The Molsons. There is no higher-grade Old Money in the country than that of Senator Hartland de Montarville Molson, whose father, it was said, "spoke French with a Bank of Montreal accent." He belongs to the fifth generation in Canada of the Lincolnshire family that settled in Montreal in 1782. They built Canada's first steamboat, first railway, largest brewery and distillery; they worshipped at their own church, founded their own bank, and even printed their own currency.

"To me, power and wealth are perfectly synonymous," Senator Molson once declared. "I think the words can be used interchangeably. It used to be quite fashionable to mention wealth some years ago. Nowadays it's not men-

_____
*Along with two other large shareholders (London Life and Mutual Life); this gives the group control of Huron & Erie and Canada Trust.

tioned very frequently; the word 'power' is used. If a man
is in a position of sufficient power, he either accumulates a
great deal of wealth with it or he doesn't need the wealth
in that position."*

A graduate of the Royal Military College, Hartland
Molson flew a Hurricane in the Battle of Britain. "Once I
was chasing two Jerries," he recalled later. "I got a burst
into one and he went down in flames. But I didn't happen
to look back, and another one crept up behind me and
sat on my tail. He hit me, and I bailed out"—twenty-three
thousand feet over London, with three bullets in his right
leg. Molson dropped twelve thousand feet before his
parachute opened. Invalided home, he was promoted to
group captain and made an honorary ADC to the governor
general.

After the war, he headed the family brewery and in
1955, at the age of forty-eight, was appointed to the
Senate. The family wealth is now concentrated in the Molson Companies, a Toronto-based conglomerate that had
sales of $741 million in 1974. But Molson money can still
speak for itself. When John Nichol was collecting funds
for the Lester Pearson College of the Pacific, Senator Hartland Molson gave him a cheque for $250,000.

Charles Bronfman. "Dad wanted things very badly,"
Charles Bronfman is saying. "After all, he was a kid who
came from nowhere, and did a lot of things. He wanted to
be recognized for what he had done. But I didn't want
anything, and to me it's come very easily. The things that
have happened I don't really give a damn about—whether
I'm a director of the Bank of Montreal is not very important in my life. Whether I'm a member of the Mount
Royal Club is not very important. But to him it was very
important, and I feel sort of sad that life happens this way:
that when you don't want it, you get it, and when you do
want it so very badly, you have to have great wars and
battles."

At forty-four, Charles Rosner is *the* Canadian Bronfman, president and chairman of the executive committee

*From a transcript of the CBC broadcast, "Men at the Top," aired as
part of the "Explorations" series on October 2, 1958.

of the Seagram Company, the world's largest distillers, chief owner of the Montreal Expos, heir to Samuel Bronfman's billion-dollar fortune. Introspective, unspoiled, a lively and engaging character, he doesn't treat his position lightly. "You always wonder," he says, "if people are friendly because they like you or because they want something. But you get over it after a while. A great friend of mine used to say that one of my protections was that I happened to have a fairly healthy level of paranoia. I never really sought power. I used to do things, and people would say to me, 'Do you realize what you just said?'

"I'd say, 'Oh, I just said something.'

"And they'd say, 'Yes, but *you* said it. Don't you realize who you are?'

"And I used to say, 'Well, no, I'm just another guy.'

"And they'd say, 'No. You're not just another guy.' And then I had to start learning about how to keep myself in control, to measure my words. And I found that quite difficult for a while. Even today, in certain areas I sometimes don't realize the so-called power that's at my command. Sometimes it can be a little bit frightening. Sometimes it can be damn pleasurable."

Bronfman went through the standard Canadian upper-class upbringing: Selwyn House (1937–45), Trinity College School at Port Hope (1945–48), and McGill (1948–51), but it didn't really take. "It was a disaster. I should never have gone to TCS. Not that the school was bad, but it was just terrible for me. I was much too immature. My parents sent me and I didn't have the gumption to resist. So then I went to university, but I wasn't ready for McGill, either. It was interesting. I could do certain things, other things I couldn't do. I could write papers. Anything that had a certain degree of bullshit, I was all right with. When it came to exams, I'd get panic attacks. So I left after two and a half years, before I was going to fail, and went to work on March 12, 1951."

It was at twenty-three, as head of the newly acquired Thomas Adams Distillers, that he first began to assert himself. The psychic breakthrough came in 1955, when he recommended a new bottle design for his subsidiary's premier stock. "Dad was against what he called 'fancy packaging,' but I told him, 'I want this bottle,'" Bronfman remembers. "He looked at me for a long time and then he said, 'So you want to go into fancy packages.' I said Yes, and stuck to my guns. Within half an hour the whole thing was settled. It was the first time in my life I'd ever convinced my father of anything. In two years that brand moved from 19,000 to 100,000 cases. In those days, I was frightened of my father. It was my problem, not his, and winning my point with the Adams bottle helped solve it."

But it was his purchase of the Expos in 1968 that permanently liberated the young Bronfman: "Eventually, eventually what you've got to try and do is become a person in your own right, for whatever purpose. It was the Expos that did that for me, as a human being. That was something of my own. I acquired them by a fluke, an accident. We were down in Puerto Rico, my wife and I, at a Young Presidents convention. The vice-chairman of the executive committee for the city of Montreal called me up, and said the Mayor wanted ten people to put a million dollars each into major-league baseball. Well, I figured it would happen anyway, so I said, 'Okay, we'll be in, if that's what the Mayor really wants,' as one of the ten. And next thing I knew about it was when I heard that the franchise had been awarded to Montreal. So then I found out that there weren't ten, there were six. And of the six, there were only three with real money—the Websters, Louis Lévesque, and ourselves. When Lévesque, who was going to be the chairman, backed out, I had to make a decision.

"I remember I shut myself in my office for two hours, and told my secretary, 'Just leave me alone. Even if my father wants in, anybody wants in, tell them I'm sick, I'm dead, or anything you want.' I sat there and I thought and thought and thought, and said to myself: 'This just has to be. It's very good for the city,' and so on. I never even thought about whether it might be good for me, particularly. That didn't seem to enter my mind. But I guess it was somewhere in the background, because I don't believe that people have these great, altruistic ideas. Something always says, 'There's something in it for me'—as a person, or the monetary reward, or whatever. So I said, 'It's got to be done.' And we did it."

Samuel Bronfman died on July 10, 1971, at eighty. Born in Brandon, third son of a prosperous grist-mill owner from Bessarabia (a territory shuffled between Russia and Romania in the nineteenth and twentieth centuries), he bought a small Winnipeg hotel, got into the interprovincial liquor mail-order business, and in 1924 established a small distillery in a Montreal suburb. Three years later he acquired the financially troubled Joseph E. Seagram and Sons. In 1928 he merged them into Distillers Corporation-Seagrams. During Prohibition in the U.S., the Canadian government unofficially sanctioned cross-border exports by refunding the seven-dollar-a-gallon excise tax paid on whisky intended for Canadian consumption. Bronfman never denied that Prohibition made him rich. "We loaded carloads of goods, got our cash, and shipped it," he once told the *New York Times*. "Of course, we knew where it went, but we had no legal proof. And I never went to the other side of the border to count the empty Seagram's bottles."

Following repeal, Bronfman flooded the U.S. market and won such immediate acceptance that his Seven Crown and Seagrams V.O. eventually became the largest- and second-largest-selling brands of whiskies in the world. By 1974, Seagrams had consolidated net sales of $1.8 billion and was branching out (through Texas Pacific and Seafort Petroleum) into world-wide oil exploration.

The company is now controlled by Seco-Cemp, which holds 32.6 per cent of the stock and is in turn owned by Sam's heirs: Charles, Edgar (who runs the U.S. operation),* Phyllis Lambert (who persuaded her father to retain Ludwig Mies van der Rohe as architect of the Seagram Building in New York and later took up architecture herself), and Minda, the wife of Baron Alain de Gunzburg, a partner in the Dreyfus Bank of Paris. Set up as a trust for the Bronfman children by Lazarus Phillips, Cemp is ably managed by Leo Kolber, who is also

---

*Edgar Bronfman's first wife was Ann Margaret Loeb, daughter of John L. Loeb, senior partner in the Wall Street investment house of Loeb, Rhoades & Co. Divorced in 1972, they came together in August of 1975 when their eldest child, Sam, was kidnapped. The $4.5-million ransom demand ($2.3 million was paid, and all of it was recovered) drew public attention to both the Bronfman family and the nature of the crime. Kidnap insurance became a fashionable buy among the rich.

vice-chairman of Cadillac Fairview, Canada's largest developer, 38 per cent owned by Cemp. Besides its real estate interests, Cemp has radio and TV stations (through its computer service company, Multiple Access), Warrington Products (including Greb Shoes, which makes Hush Puppies and Bauer Skates, and Eddy Match, which it bought recently for Eddy's office-furniture division and then resold the match operations to their former British owners), a significant chunk of Metro-Goldwyn-Mayer and Panarctic Oils, and 12 per cent of the world-wide Club Méditerranée.

Sam never did quite make it into the Canadian Establishment. But at the company's 1974 annual meeting in Montreal, the Bronfmans were finally embraced as insiders. The signals were unmistakable. The motion to change the company's name from Distillers Corporation-Seagrams to the Seagram Company was put forward by none other than Senator Hartland de Montarville Molson. The appointment of Price Waterhouse and Company as auditors was moved by J. Michael Scott, resident Wood Gundy director in Montreal, and seconded by Brian Drummond, the head of Greenshields. The motion to adjourn came from Peter Dixon, a partner in A.E. Ames, whose father was the Anglican Bishop of Montreal. Amen.

The McConnell Estate. Unlike the fortunes of most wealthy men, the McConnell estate has survived its founder's death to remain an active corporate and philanthropic entity. Although John Wilson McConnell gave away at least $100 million during his lifetime, some estimates suggest there's still up to $600 million left in his foundation and various investments associated with Commercial, the family trust company.* The estate is operated under the direction of Peter Laing, whose wife, Kit, is the last surviving child of J.W. McConnell. A first-class lawyer who lost both his legs at El Alamein, he turned down a judgeship out of a sense of duty to his father-in-law. He is a

---

*As well as a partnership in the FP chain, McConnell investments are thought to include control of Sucronel Ltd. (one of whose divisions is St. Lawrence Sugar), the National Casket Co., and large blocks of stock in Crush International, Canada Cement Lafarge, Belding-Corticelli, Algoma Steel, Canadian Pacific, Consolidated-Bathurst, and the Bank of Montreal.

nephew of the late Ross McMaster, who from 1926 to 1957 was president or chairman of Stelco. Operating head of the *Montreal Star* is Derek Price, who married Jill, one of McConnell's grandchildren.

John A. McDougald, the chairman and president of Argus Corporation, whose personal fortune (described in Chapter 1) runs in the vicinity of $300 millions.

Nelson Davis, who heads a conglomerate of medium-sized companies, almost all of which he privately owns. His fortune and life style are the subject of Chapter 9.

George Richardson, current godfather of the Winnipeg family whose activities are detailed in Chapter 7.

K.C. Irving, the king of New Brunswick, now a resident of Bermuda, whose strange empire is outlined in Chapter 7.

The $50-Million Group

Dr. Charles Allard, Edmonton (physician, developer, and chemical industries investor); Sam Belzberg, Vancouver (financing); Prentice Bloedel, Bainbridge Island, Washington (MacMillan Bloedel); Crosbie family, St. John's (Newfoundland's most important conglomerate); Nathanael Davis, Montreal (owns largest single block in Alcan Aluminium); Paul Desmarais (Power Corporation); Hunter family, Toronto (chief shareholders, through Hunco Limited, of Maclean-Hunter); Ivey family, London, Ontario (fortune originated with the establishment in 1906 of Empire Manufacturing, later Empire Brass, and still later Emco; family branched out into life insurance and packaging; Allpak Products is its main holding company); Henry Newton Rowell "Hal" Jackman, Toronto (chairman, Empire Life Insurance; also controls Dominion of Canada General Insurance, E-L Financial Corporation, Victoria and Grey Trust; recently named youngest director of Argus Corporation); Captain Joseph Jeffery, London, Ontario (former naval officer, now controls and runs London Life, founded by his grandfather); John Jodrey, Hantsport, Nova

Scotia (inherited and has expanded his father's investment portfolio); Karl Landegger, Eleuthera (owns large pulp mills in Saskatchewan and New Brunswick; has been known to dispatch his private jet to Fort Lauderdale to pick up his favourite swimming-pool cleaner; was married to a Chinese princess of the Manchu dynasty); Jack Leitch, Toronto (controls Upper Lakes Shipping and has large shareholdings in Dofasco and other companies); Loeb family, Ottawa (M Loeb; wholesale grocers and supermarkets); Fred Mannix, Calgary (construction, mining, and pipeline complex); McCain family, Florenceville, N.B. (French-fried potatoes); W.F. McLean, Toronto (controls Canada Packers through family foundation); Frank McMahon, Palm Beach and Bahamas (from the mining town of Moyie, B.C., he made it in oil, gas and pipelines, became a Broadway angel and a racehorse owner); Miron family, Montreal (sold their construction business to Genstar but have since put up $50 million cash for a new cement mill); Deane Nesbitt, Montreal (head of Nesbitt, Thomson; owns large shareholdings in Royal Bank, TransCanada PipeLines, and Power Corporation); Alexis Nihon, Montreal (Belgian-born industrialist and developer; yachtsman; heavyweight wrestler with the Bahamas team in the 1968 Olympics in Mexico City; too heavy for the 1972 Games); Reichmann brothers, Toronto (own Olympia and York Developments, downtown Toronto's largest builders); Simard family, Sorel and Montreal (industrial duchy at Sorel based on shipbuilding); Southam family, Toronto (publishing and printing); Steinberg family, Montreal (controls supermarket chain); Tanenbaum brothers, Toronto (York Steel Construction, Pinetree Development, and other investments); Timmins family, Montreal (their wealth mostly offshore now; operates Chromasco Limited through Timmins Investments); Ray Wolfe, Toronto (controls the Oshawa Group; is a director of Canadian Pacific and Bank of Nova Scotia); Woodward family, Vancouver (department stores and cattle ranch).

The $20-Million Group

John Aird, Toronto (lawyer, ex-senator; investments);
Beauchemin family, Montreal (Sullivan Mining Group);
Bentall family, Vancouver (real estate and construction); Joseph Berman, Toronto (real estate development);
Billes family, Toronto (Canadian Tire Corporation);
Drummond Birks, Montreal (his private company clears
$4 million a year selling old-fashioned sterling silver in pale
blue boxes); George Black, Toronto (partner in Ravelston,
the Argus holding company); Walter Blackburn, London,
Ontario (owns the city's major newspaper, radio and TV
stations); Leonard Blatt, Toronto (developer); Block
brothers, Vancouver (real estate); Brillant family, Rimouski (investments); Bernard Brynelsen, Vancouver (brought
Brenda Mines and others into production); Burton family,
Toronto (has joint control of Simpsons Limited with Wood
Gundy); Robert Campeau, Ottawa (real estate); Carmichael family, Toronto (Argus links; equipment leasing);
Lou Chesler, Toronto and Bahamas (one-time stock salesman who promoted mines, Florida real estate, movies,
and Grand Bahama gambling); Clarke family, Montreal
(shipping); R.L. Cliff, Vancouver (investments); Edwin
Cogan, Toronto (Greater York Group; developer); Cohen
family, Winnipeg (Canadian distributors of Sony products); George Cohon, Toronto (McDonald's hamburger
franchise); Fred Connell, Toronto (one of Canada's original mining entrepreneurs, controls Conwest Exploration);
Roy Crabtree, Montreal (runs Wabasso Limited); Crothers family, Toronto (equipment dealers, hotels); Cummings family, Montreal (sold out its real estate holdings
to Trizec Corporation); John Daniels, Toronto (real estate development); Mortimer Davis estate, Montreal
(founded by former head of Imperial Tobacco); Dawes
family, Montreal (former brewers; sold out to Canadian
Breweries in the early 1950s; also in construction; active
in Olympics and other sports ventures); Graham Dawson,
Vancouver (real estate and construction); Del Zotto family, Toronto (real estate and construction); Reuben Dennis, Toronto (real estate); Senator Paul Desruisseaux,
Montreal and Sherbrooke (Melchers Distilleries and in-

vestments); Eph Diamond, Toronto (real estate development); Gordon Farrell, Vancouver (telephone and cement); John Fraser, Toronto (administers the Samuel McLaughlin Foundation; he won't give any more grants to doctors—the last batch he sent to Austria forgot to send him postcards); Gardiner family, Oakville and Toronto (investments); George Gardiner, Toronto (oil and other investments, including the Colonel Sanders franchise for most of Ontario and Quebec); Gerstein family, Toronto (jewellery stores); Ben Ginter, Vancouver and Prince George (brewing, construction); Goldlist family, Toronto (developers); Duncan and Walter Gordon, Toronto (Clarkson, Gordon); F. Ronald Graham, Montreal (investments; also involved with George Gardiner in fried chicken); Green family, Toronto (Greenwin Construction; developers); Alex Grossman, Toronto (Belmont Construction; developer); Charles Gundy, Toronto (chairman of Wood Gundy; has large private stock holdings); Hugh Hallward, Montreal (Lord Atholstan's grandson; heads Argo Construction); Sam Hashman, Calgary (real estate and construction;) Bill Hatch, Toronto (investments); Clifford Hatch, Windsor (president, Hiram Walker–Gooderham and Worts); W. Bernard Herman, Toronto (parking lots); Sydney Hermant, Toronto (controls Imperial Optical Company); Ivanier family, Montreal (Ivaco Industries; nuts and bolts, metal fabricators); Keevil family, Vancouver (formerly Toronto; mining and oil through Teck Corporation); Michael Koerner, Toronto (manages his family trusts and controls medium-sized steel companies); Murray Koffler, Toronto (Shoppers Drug Mart and is rapidly expanding into new ventures); Kruger family, Montreal (own large newsprint and other paper operations in Quebec and South America as well as an aluminum extrusion plant in Holland); LaBine family, Toronto (Eldorado discoverer; sold out to Bovis Corporation); Laidlaw family, Toronto (fortune based on lumber business); Latner family, Toronto (Greenwin Construction; developers); Lawson family, Oakville and London, Ontario (printing and packaging); Irwin David Leopold, Montreal (Mondev Corporation; developers of Westmount Square and other major projects), J. Louis Lévesque, Montreal (investments and horses); Levy brothers, Toronto (widespread holdings built on auto parts); Lundrigan family, Corner Brook (construction); Charles E. MacCulloch, Halifax (real estate development); Maclaren family, Ottawa (lumber, pulp and paper; largest shareholders in the Bank of Nova Scotia); H.R. MacMillan holdings, Vancouver (original lumber fortune now distributed to heirs); George Mara, Toronto (investments); Mashaal family, Montreal (builders); McCall family, Montreal (steel suppliers); McCutcheon holdings, Toronto (residue of former Argus partner's fortune); S. Bruce McLaughlin, Mississauga (his company owns big chunks of Mississauga, on Toronto's western border, and the Caledon Hills to the north; associated in ventures with the Edper Bronfmans); McMartin brothers, Bermuda (Hollinger heirs); Merkur brothers, Toronto (Meridian development group); Gerhard Moog, Toronto (developer); Bartlett Morgan, Montreal (sold his department store to Hudson's Bay Company; now operates Morgan Trust and owns the mountain on which the James Bond picture *On His Majesty's Secret Service* was filmed); Graham Morrow, Toronto (financial and insurance companies; one holding, Imperial Life, was sold to Paul Desmarais); Odette family, Toronto and Windsor (builders); Phrixos Basil Papachristidis, Montreal (has a fleet large enough so that in 1974 when the Greek government suggested all of the country's shipowners donate one dollar per ton toward the war effort against Turkey over Cyprus, it cost him one million dollars); Senator Norman Paterson, Thunder Bay (shipping and grain handling); Jim Pattison, Vancouver (glittery conglomerate); Pigott family, Hamilton (builders); Pitfield family, Montreal and Toronto (investments); Poole family, Edmonton (builders); John Prusac, Toronto (important funnel for foreign funds into Canadian real estate through his Deltan Corporation); Irving Rocke Ransen, Montreal (Mondev Corporation); Reitman family, Montreal (women's clothing stores); Dr. K.A. Roberts, Toronto (real estate and finance); Guy Rogers, Toronto (family sold Elias Rogers Company to Texaco; operates St. Marys Cement and Canada Building Materials); Rogers family, Vancouver (sugar refining and packaging); Ted Rogers, Toronto (broadcasting); Philip Roth, Toronto (Meridian; developer); Rudberg family, Montreal (builders); Russel

family, Montreal and Toronto (steel suppliers); Schwartz
family, Halifax (spices); Seaman family, Calgary (oil drilling); Searle family, Winnipeg (folded their grain company
into Federal Industries, a conglomerate); Seitz family,
Toronto (introduced the typewriter to Canada; Ernest
wrote "The World is Waiting for the Sunrise"; his brother
Joseph switched to Royal after Olivetti bought Under-
wood); Jerry Shefsky, Toronto (Greater York Group;
developer); Sifton family, Toronto (newspapers and television); Sobey family, Stellarton, N.S. (supermarkets and
theatres); Southern family, Calgary (Atco Industries);
Tabachnick family, Windsor and Toronto (sold holdings
in Cambridge Leaseholds to Oxford Development Group);
Peter Thomson, Montreal (controls Warnock Hersey conglomerate); Torno family, Toronto (wine and arts); A.
Murray Vaughan, Montreal (chairman of British American Bank Note; administers Hosmer and Pillow estates);
Weldon family, London, Ontario (investments); Arthur
White, Toronto (Dickenson Mines, Kam-Kotia Mines);
Bud Willmot, Toronto (Molson Companies; investments);
Charles Wills, Vancouver (lawyer; heir to Reifel fortune);
Walter Zwig and Jacob Hendeles, Toronto (co-developers
of office buildings).

CHAPTER NINE

The Immaculate Passions
of Nelson Morgan Davis

He has sought all his life not
so much the fact of becoming
personally wealthy as the *sensation*
of enrichment. He has tried to
achieve this rare ecstasy
through the expenditure of a
fortune in the endless careful
pursuit of perfection
in its many forms.

Any journey of exploration deep into the country of the Canadian rich eventually leads the traveller to the unusual driveway of a Federal-style mansion overlooking the Rosedale Golf Club. Running off at right angles from one of those fashionable cul-de-sacs that lattice Toronto's northern reaches, the driveway is carefully designed, with sharp twists that slow a car down precisely to the speed at which it will glide to a noiseless stop before the front door of the million-dollar house.

What really sets off this driveway—and gives a clue to both the riches and the character of its owner—is that the crunch beneath the tires of the visitor's car is strangely muted. Even on the driest day, the slightly yellowed "gravel" yields not a speck of dust. And for good reason.

When Nelson Davis, who is probably this country's most interesting and certainly its least-visible multimillionaire, was building this house (an enterprise that took seven years to complete), he decided to take no chances on having visitors trail dirt into his living room. He covered the driveway with the only rock that produces no dust: meteorite. It is chemically inert, so hard that it's occasionally used to polish stainless steel. After a long search, Davis discovered some available meteorite that had plummeted to earth thirty miles southeast of Cleveland, Ohio.

343

He paid $10,000 to have it crushed and brought to Toronto. Now he has no dust in his living room.

Nelson Morgan Davis ("Nels" to his friends) looks and sometimes acts like a character straight out of a late John O'Hara novel. Yet he stands out among the super-rich Canadians of his generation as a man with unique ideas about money and its uses. Most of the Canadian wealthy are obsessed with the sheer "moneyness" of money—their fascination is in watching their investments reproduce themselves through an endless series of more and sometimes less immaculate financial transactions. They are much more interested in *making* money than in spending it.

Not Nelson Davis. He has sought all his life not so much the fact of becoming personally wealthy as the *sensation* of enrichment. He has tried to achieve this rare ecstasy through the expenditure of a fortune in the endless careful pursuit of perfection in its many forms. "Every time I make a dollar," he explains, "I spend a quarter of it on myself. There's nothing wrong with that." (Nelson Davis's gross personal income probably approaches $12 million a year.)

Striving for perfection in all things is an obsession with Davis: the perfect house (he has four); the perfect car (he drives six); the perfect servant (he employs eighteen); the perfect boat (he owns twenty); and the perfect golf course. A long-time member of the Rosedale Golf Club, Davis had second thoughts about belonging in the early fifties when a duffer's ball nicked his nose. "I'll build my own," he said (Nelson Davis is a man of few words). He promptly bought a 350-acre tract near Markham, north of Toronto, dammed up streams, moved trees, threw up hills, and built himself Box Grove, one of the best eighteen-hole golf courses in the country. Although Davis was the club's only member, he employed his own pro (Jimmy Johnstone), and Arnold Palmer flew up frequently to play at Box Grove.*

Davis still owns a 1933 Alfa Romeo in mint condition and not long ago sold one of his antique cars for $100,-

---

*Box Grove was sold for $3 million to IBM Canada in 1966 for use as the company's private country club. Davis now plays most of his golf at the Laurel Valley Golf Club on the Mellon estate in Pennsylvania.

000. But his most valuable vehicle was a 1904 Royce, made before Charles Rolls joined the firm. Because it was one of only two such cars in existence, a few years ago Rolls-Royce attempted to obtain it for the company museum. Never having heard of Nelson Davis and presuming him to be a not very well-informed colonial, the company wrote him a mildly condescending letter, suggesting he trade his ancient car in on a more contemporary model at their expense. Davis, who had three new Rolls-Royces at the time, replied with a one-line riposte that may be a classic of its kind: "What would I do with a new Rolls-Royce?"*

If Nelson Davis has one passion besides his never-ending search for perfection, it is his yearning for anonymity. Men of great wealth are always shielded by unlisted telephones, family retainers, phalanxes of lawyers and counsellors. But Davis carries his insistence on privacy to breathtaking lengths. His Toronto house has *five* unlisted telephone numbers. His entry in the *Canadian Who's Who* gives no personal information whatever. Even inside the higher echelons of the business Establishment he is a figure of speculation and mystery. "Nelson is an enigma," says Charlie Burns, Toronto's Establishment stockbroker. "I've known him a little all my life, but I really don't know very much about him." American journalists who occasionally stumbled across his name and glimpsed the extent of his fortune offered to place him on the covers of *Fortune, Time,* and the old *Saturday Evening Post* if he would only speak to them. But he refuses to be interviewed.†

Davis is possessed of a strong inner sense of identity. He does not require any public presence to remind himself of who he is and how far he has come. There are those rich men who need publicity so that they can read about themselves and be comforted that they are indeed alive and doing well. Nelson Davis is a keeper of distances. He views the world with the undistracted gaze of a sentinel scan-

---

*Nelson Davis eventually donated the Royce to an American automotive museum.

†The only time that his name appeared prominently in Canadian newspapers was in 1969, when he provided the $200,000 in cash demanded by the kidnappers of his niece, Mary Nelles. "I have always believed in keeping myself anonymous," he told the *Globe and Mail* at the time, "and I don't want to change that policy now."

ning distant fields through the battlement of a castle wall.

He has a slightly ruddy complexion and colourless eyes, the kind of looks and bearing that make it difficult to pick him out of a crowd. Exquisitely mannered, precise to a fault, his formality is that of an Anglican deacon on Palm Sunday. He is a warm, honest, and kind man who places great stock in friendships ("You're judged by the friends you have," he says). But at large parties, where men bear-hug each other and women kiss people they barely know, his politeness can be cool. He won't have alcohol consumed in any of his houses. When the late Eric Phillips, who loved a drink, was spending a weekend at Davis's large island home in Muskoka, the host insisted that the Argus Corporation partner climb aboard one of the many motor-boats before "imbibing." Davis has never been known to swear. His strongest oath is "The h—— with it." His sense of perfection even intrudes on his eating habits. One evening when he was taking a group of guests to the Sunday night buffet at the Paradise Valley Country Club in Scottsdale, Arizona, he insisted on tackling the food precisely at the opening hour of six o'clock so they could all have the pick of the fare before anyone else had messed with it.

Davis belongs to a dozen of the most prestigious private clubs in North America and is proud of the fact that he was the first Canadian invited to join the Rolling Rock Country Club built on the great Mellon family preserve at Ligonier in Westmoreland County, Pennsylvania. He doesn't use his other club memberships very often, preferring to entertain a few close friends in one of his homes. He divides his year approximately into thirds, spending about four months each at his houses in Arizona, Muskoka, and Toronto.

Davis's first abode in Arizona was the rambling, six-bedroom Phoenix villa of pink stucco and tile roofing he acquired from Clare Boothe Luce. (She had bought it for $250,000 from Tommy Manville, the asbestos-fortune heir whose only distinction was that he married eleven times.) A few years ago, Nelson Davis built himself another Arizona property, which he calls the Eagle's Nest, at Sedona, 105 miles north of Phoenix. "This time I'm going first-class all the way," Davis told a friend when he began work on his mountain hideaway.

Bud McDougald, who has been a guest in both houses, maintains that just about all the furnishings of Davis's retreat "seem to have belonged to Napoleon." He also experienced at first hand the Davis security system. McDougald was retiring for the night in the Phoenix house when he opened a window for some fresh air. "The whole place went off like a rocket," he recalls. Security guards appeared as if by magic and the Great Danes belonging to Adele Astaire (now Mrs. Kingman Douglass and formerly Lady Charles Cavendish), who lived next door, began howling in the night.*

Davis's showpiece is his Toronto house on Riverview Drive, a gallery of craftsmanship, furnished with the sort of rarefied objects museums display behind stretched red velvet cords. Called Eagle House, and built exactly to Federal specifications (this was the American interpretation of Georgian architecture), it has eagles perched everywhere—on walls and the back verandah, over the garage, on car doors. It took seven years to finish—three years being researched, one year being planned, and three years being built.† (The house was decorated by John Gerald of New York, the garden and driveway planned by Stuart Ortloff, who executed most of the landscaping for the mansions lining the fashionable coast of Long Island.)

Everything about the dwelling is the product of one man's perfectionism. There are hand-made mouldings from New York, complete fireplaces purchased in England, gold door fittings taken out of Fifth Avenue mansions that were pulled down. Glass cases line the halls to display priceless collections of Georgian silver and Meissen china, which Davis takes out and allows guests to heft. The downstairs furniture is entirely English—some satinwood, some mahogany, all of museum quality—a huge Sheraton table in the dining room and Adam chairs. There are silk hangings framing the windows, all in pale colours, with everything immaculate, somehow untouched and untouch-

---

*Nelson Davis doesn't leave anything to chance. In the winter of 1974, when the energy crisis caused a gasoline shortage in Arizona, he bought two service stations.

†Before moving into Eagle House, Davis lived at Graydon Hall, a Toronto residence second in opulence only to Casa Loma. The centrepiece of a 96-acre property, the house had 14 bedrooms, a 10-car garage, and a 9-hole golf course. It was originally built in 1933 for a million dollars by H. Rupert Bain on the proceeds of gold stock promotions.

able. Upstairs is a collection of American glass and American furniture; the only Canadian objects in the house are two bedside tables in a guest room. Mrs. Davis's bedroom is all done in pink; his suite resembles the quarters of a battleship captain, with a ship's light, dark wood, and small, flush drawers. One cupboard holds thirty pairs of shoes, made mainly out of various reptile skins.*

It takes a staff of eighteen maids, gardeners, chauffeurs, and cooks to operate Nelson Davis's various establishments. He has an easy-going relationship with his servants, despite the occasional strains. When his two children were growing up, their governess, a Miss Parker, who drove them to school and did the family shopping, felt she had to have a new car. Davis bought her a Buick station wagon. He then was asked for an audience by Warren, his chauffeur, who came in long-faced and said, "I may not have pleased you, sir, but what did I do so terrible that you would want to hurt me like this?" It evolved that he was insulted, couldn't hold his head up with the other staff, because he had to drive an Oldsmobile 88 while the governess had the new Buick. Davis's wife, Eloise, said this was nonsense, that the chauffeur should be fired. But Davis decided that Warren was just too knowledgeable about the cars, the pipes, and the wiring in all the various households. Some time later they were entertaining dinner guests when the cook sent word via the butler that the stove fuse was blown so that she couldn't do the vegetables. Warren was sent for; he arrived in white tie and tails (there was some kind of function at his lodge, and he was dressed for it) to make the repair. Eloise was angry all over again, but Nelson was adamant. Warren would stay.

NELSON MORGAN DAVIS GREW UP IN SHAKER HEIGHTS, OHIO, THE SON OF A MANUFACTURER who served as deacon of a Congregationalist assembly. Everything his family had was of the best. He recalls, for example, that

---

*In another storeroom Nelson Davis keeps the forty-eight reminders of a practical joke Bud McDougald played on him in 1949. Davis had been to Herbert Johnson, the famous London hatter, and liked a new style of headgear. He ordered twenty-four hats, one in every second shade the store had on display. McDougald heard about the purchase and on his next visit ordered the other twenty-four, suggesting that the hatter send his friend Nels the bill.

the only recordings allowed into the house were luxury sets on the Victor Red Seal label. Young Nelson's main interest was mathematics. "When I went to high school in Cleveland," he remembers, "the assistant principal, who was a lady and an excellent mathematician, invited six of us to take a special course in higher mathematics which involved trigonometry, spherical geometry, analytics, and calculus. We were a fortunate group. In fact, I can remember my first year at Cornell University, when I took the three-hour final examination in trigonometry and handed in my paper to the professor in twenty minutes and left the room to good-natured boos and catcalls from my fellow students. Fortunately, I never missed a problem during the whole year. I also learned a trick way of addition so that I could add three columns of figures at one time."

At Cornell, instead of attending the required sixteen hours of lectures a week he went to thirty and in his graduating year could have taken a degree in mechanical engineering, general arts, civil engineering, or honours science, depending on which set of exams he chose to write. He also earned considerable pocket money, some of it by selling off the catering contract for the senior prom to the highest bidder.

All through his teens he worked on expanding his remarkable memory for figures. "It was a skill I originally developed by studying the old Railway Guide—a book two inches thick which had the timetables for every passenger train in the U.S. and the main ones in Canada," he remembers. "I used to go through the guide and memorize some of the tables for the main railroads in the country such as the New York Central, Pennsylvania, Illinois Central, Santa Fe, Union Pacific, Southern Pacific, Rock Island, etc. One of my favourite trains was the Twentieth Century Limited, an extra-fare train running from Chicago to New York. This train invariably ran in several sections, one every couple of minutes apart, running at times as close as a block behind one another. Other trains that I used to like were the Broadway Limited between Chicago and New York on the Pennsylvania, the Panama Limited running between Chicago and New Orleans, the City of San Francisco, the City of Los Angeles, and the

City of Portland on the Union Pacific running between Chicago and the aforementioned cities, and the Super Chief on the Santa Fe between Chicago and Los Angeles, the Lark on the Southern Pacific between Los Angeles and San Francisco, and the Golden State between Phoenix and Chicago which was the Rock Island's crack train for many years.

"All of these trains were made up of Pullman cars. No coach passengers were carried. They would vary in length from eight to fourteen cars of various types, from two-drawing room, four-compartment, eight-section cars to all roomettes, all compartments, and various other combinations. I used to know the numbers designated for this equipment on all of the trains I've mentioned, such as Cars 201 through to 212 or 214. Passenger trains fascinated me when I was a youth. I can remember standing at the 105th Street Station in Cleveland during the Christmas holidays and watching the Century and the Southwestern Limited come in, from four to seven sections, one right after the other, and head east, chugging away."

After young Nelson left college, family legend has it that his father decided he should head for Canada, sending him on his way with fifty dollars, a railway ticket, and his blessing. Nelson did arrive in Toronto just after the 1929 crash with few assets, but he came on a specific mission. His father-in-law owned Chainway Stores, a group of cut-rate variety outlets in southern Ontario that had been badly hit by the depression. Davis restored their financial health and liked the country so much that he decided to stay. He began buying up middle-sized companies, financing his deals through loans from the old Imperial Bank. When he went to borrow his first $250,000, the bank manager had allotted Davis only a fifteen-minute appointment to state his case. He stayed three hours, outlining five different ways in which he could repay the money ("the sixth was up my sleeve"), and ended up borrowing an eventual $13 million, all of which was paid back within seven years. He spent all profits from his expanding operations buying up blue-chip stocks at their depression lows. These investments provided one source of his large fortune. The other was his adroit application of Section

92A of the Income Tax Act, which allowed him to take over surpluses held by the corporate treasuries of family-held companies whose owners couldn't extract their cash without raising themselves into impossible tax brackets. By selling their firms to Davis for fair market value (based on assets rather than the frozen surpluses), the former owners were able to raise enough cash to pay off their expected succession duties, and Davis (because he was a third party) got unimpeded access to all of their retained earnings. Though there was nothing illegal about this (until the tax act was changed in 1963), Davis was, in effect, buying up the companies with their own money.

What really made these transactions so unusually profitable was the skill with which Davis picked the companies he went after. "What I look for in buying companies," he explains, "are certain ratios in addition to certain facts. When I'm presented with statements for the first time covering a company we might possibly be interested in acquiring, I first consider the various factors of the industry in which the proposed acquisition operates, then try to get an idea of how powerful the company is in its particular industry, how it rates with its competitors and what the possibilities are for its rate of growth. If the working capital position looks interesting and the company, on a cursory examination, looks to be in a healthy condition, I then proceed to pull the various balance sheets apart and compare various assets and liabilities with the comparable figures over a five- or ten-year period. You do the same with the earnings statements so that you have a pretty good idea of whether the business looks interesting, and you try to compare the figures with other businesses with which you have to compete. You always try to make sure that the earnings are not too cyclical.

"I've found from years of experience that you are wise to contact a dozen or so of the company's main customers and sources of supply. Many times we changed our views regarding an acquisition when the news from these particular sources didn't stand up. Most firms put their best foot forward for their shareholders at the end of the year when they convert lots of their receivables and inventories into cash, paying off their liabilities and bank loans if possible. This is called 'window dressing.'

"If everything looks pretty good at this stage, I then like to get hold of several years' operating statements and see how high the peaks and how low the valleys are for the main items in the operating statement. From there on it becomes a question of negotiating price, having in mind how long it's going to take to get your money back, how much new capital you might need in excess of that being generated through operations in order to get the maximum profit from the company in question.

"It's a question of judgement as to whether or not you're going to make a good deal or a bad deal, and no matter how definite certain assets and liabilities may be, there are many variables that must still be contended with during the years in which the business is operated. When it comes to making the final decision, I play no hunches. I list all the favourable factors on one side of a sheet and all the unfavourable ones on the other side. Unless it is at least two to one in favour of the favourables, I discard the proposition."

He hasn't always been right, but his winning average has been excellent. "I have never had a business which was losing money at some time or other which we could not work around to a profitable operation, providing our executives put enough effort behind it," he says. "Sometimes it wasn't worth it. On several occasions we sold or closed businesses because we felt that with the same effort and management in a new company, or by using the funds from the sale or liquidation to further develop an already existing company, we would prove to be more profitable in the long run."

Nelson Davis's current empire consists of about fifty companies engaged, among other things, in paving highways, transporting new cars, lending money, and manufacturing paint, varnish, and nylon stockings.* The com-

---

*The N.M. Davis Corp. subsidiaries and affiliates include: Admiral Acceptance, Arrow Leasing, Atlantic Distributing, Automobile Transport, Blue Ridge Holdings, Box Grove Realty, Brennan Paving, C & H Transport, Canvar Industries, Cartran Manufacturing, Carwil Transport, Cataract Transport, Central Chevrolet (Toronto), Chain Store Equities, Coloron Corp. (Canada), Dayco (Canada), Don Mills Golf Centre, Don Valley Ski Centre, Eastern Properties, Fast Freight Service, Fleet Express Lines, Glenelda Properties, Glenwood Carriers, Glenwood Park Holdings, Grant Cartage & Forwarding, Great Lakes Supply, Hi-Mar Holdings, Industrial Tankers, Inter-City Truck Lines, Intercontinental Securities, Markham Sand and Gravel, Miller Gravel (Northern), Miller Paving, Monarch Engineer-

plex is held together by N.M. Davis Corporation, which produces an annual sales volume of more than $200 million. At average profit levels, this would probably yield an estimated gross income of about $12 million a year —and Nelson Davis is the only shareholder of substance. "We could be a lot bigger if we went public," he says. "But if you do, you live in a goldfish bowl, and I don't want anybody chasing me."

Davis administers his unique conglomerate from yet another mansion (called Penryn House) at the bottom of a dead-end street in Toronto's Bayview district.* He works in the Tudor mansion's former living room near a fireplace with a hand-carved mantel, surrounded by precious furniture (there is the inevitable large Sheraton table in the dining room) and walls hung with canvases by English masters. There's not much evidence on the main floor that this is an office instead of a residence. Monthly and annual operating statements from each of the fifty companies he owns are kept behind a yellow curtain in a mahogany cabinet. The telephone seldom rings. "I get paid for what I know, not for what I do," he says. "You get more leading than you do driving." The half-dozen accountants and lawyers who make up his holding company staff work on the second floor. "Never do anything if someone can do it for you," Davis believes. He hires the best legal and auditing talent available in the country to act as his consultants.

Although he seldom sees the operating heads of his various companies except at their annual meetings, Davis is extremely careful about the kind of men he chooses. "One of the secrets of my business success," he says, "is that I never had a contract with any of my executives. If a man wants to quit, he can leave on five minutes' notice. If he is not doing a good job, I can dispense with his services at my discretion." The Davis companies have a

---

ing, Morgan Industries, North-South Investment, Parkwood Central, Parkwood-Yonge Holdings, Penryn House, Promotion Products, Roadway Transport, Stanley Allied Products, Stanley Manufacturing, Talon Construction, Trans-Canada Highway Express, West Markham Industrial Estates, Windsor Auto Forwarders, Wyandotte Enterprises, and Yonge-Blythwood Realty. Nelson Davis's brother, Marshall, is in charge of trucking operations. His son, Glen, is vice-president of administration and a director of N.M. Davis Corp.

*The eagle motif crops up even here. The wallpaper in the executive washroom at Penryn House is ablaze with eagles.

generous profit-sharing plan to provide their chief operating officers with additional incentive.

WHEN F. SCOTT FITZGERALD COINED HIS FAMOUS APHORISM, "the rich are different from us," he could have had Nelson Davis in mind. For nearly forty years (he turned sixty-nine in 1975), Nelson Davis has hunted perfection, placing few limits or conditions on its achievement. Only he knows how close he has come. His face is not the visage of a man much given to ecstasies. But neither does it bear the ravaged cast of misanthropy that distorts the look of so many men of his persuasion and wealth. He is neither lonely nor unhappy, but a man whose universe is unfolding as he thinks it should.

Yet somehow it seems symbolic that with all their possessions, their houses, and their money, the Davises' favourite roosting place is their upstairs study at Eagle House in Toronto. It's a modest, exquisitely bourgeois den—a television room, really, that wouldn't look out of place in any suburban bungalow. Nelson and Eloise retire there after supper most evenings, watch a little TV, fetch each other some milk or pop, and go to bed early. Maybe Fitzgerald was wrong after all.

V

Network Power

CHAPTER TEN

Present at the Creation:
CD's Boys

It was the network of connections and
interconnections between business and
government, fathered by Clarence Decatur
Howe, that became the Canadian
Establishment—its great dynasties
spreading into every form of commercial
enterprise across the country.

The autumn of 1945 was a fine, feisty time for Canadians.
We had gone to war six years before as emotional colonials
still, the dutiful inhabitants of a dull, depression-worn,
agricultural hinterland, morbidly attached to the mother
country and her imperial pretensions. We had emerged
from World War II in a remarkably different mood—
confident, spirited, clearly admirable in our own eyes because of the impressive contribution we'd made to the
Allied victory. We felt like true citizens of the world at
last, living in a modern industrialized state, looking forward to our share of peacetime's rewards. The country
was like some young giant stirred by the feeling of power
that comes to the late adolescent not yet daunted by the
failures and misgivings of maturity.

All that summer and fall, porches were festooned
with Union Jacks and homemade banners that bore such
messages as "Welcome Home, Sam" or "Your Mom and
Dad are proud of you, Son!" By September, thousands of
returning veterans were scrambling for places in the universities, living in trailers, grabbing at degrees in engineering, law, physics, geology, or commerce so that they could
tool up and operate the new industrial machine. The
women's magazines warned about the pitfalls facing veterans having to readjust, and a new issue of Dominion of
Canada bonds was advertised everywhere as a sure way to
prevent future wars.

Shortages were still acute; a can of B.C. sockeye salmon

was a prize second in value only to a pair of nylon stockings with dark brown seams. Women not only had bosoms but also wore bras. They continued to wear the skimpy skirts and grotesque padded-shoulder jackets of wartime, with page-boy hair, blood-red nails, and little dabs of Evening in Paris behind their ears. No one but actresses and prostitutes used eye shadow, and the Pill ("that rules the waves") was a seasickness remedy. Only cellists had long hair. Milk-wagon horses still plodded city streets. Kids put nickels in their loafers, danced cheek to cheek, the big bands were swinging high.

A few earnest Canadians hesitantly began to advance the idea of fostering a distinct culture. But what most people really wanted was a suburban bungalow, a new car, four kids, an electric refrigerator, a bedroom radio in a cream-coloured case, and the right to their unassailable dreams.

In Ottawa, Mackenzie King hinted that he wouldn't be contesting another election and Igor Gouzenko defected from the Russian embassy with documents whose secrets would eventually heat up the Cold War. But in the rest of the country, no one talked very much about what had been going on in the capital.

Certainly nobody realized—not even the participants themselves—that there had formed in that city during the war years an Establishment whose members and ideas were to dominate the nation's business and public affairs for most of the next quarter century and, in many ways and some places, dominate them still.

THIS ESTABLISHMENT WAS MADE UP OF FEWER THAN A THOUSAND MEN, nearly all of them Wasps, most of them well educated when a university degree was still a privilege. A little older than their confreres who were rushing to enlist as officers in the navy, army, and air force, by 1939–40 they had already found places in the country's cautious, penny-pinching business firms or in the middle reaches of Ottawa's tiny public service. More than most men their age, they were full of ginger and ambition, set on getting ahead, not burdened with the inner conflicts people who grew up earlier and later endured. Their prewar professional lives had been muted by the pervasive Canadian colonialist mentality of the period, the feeling that this country was smalltime, a place where nothing important ever had happened or was ever likely to happen. They had been taught—and they had learned their lesson well—that history was made across the sea, that business acumen and manufacturing know-how existed below the border, and that the best we could manage here was bound to be an imitation.

As they first began arriving in wartime Ottawa, these men found themselves catapulted into a hothouse atmosphere that was confusing, frustrating, occasionally absurdist, but unmistakably alive. The excitement of those times and friendships was to feed the nostalgia of its participants for the rest of their lives.

When he was into his seventies, E.P. Taylor could vividly recall, on the afternoon of his first day in Ottawa, walking into the cramped office of Henry Borden, the Toronto lawyer turned dollar-a-year man. Borden was on the telephone. He gestured for Taylor to sit down and continued his conversation with what turned out to be the sales manager of North American Aviation Incorporated in California.

"Yes! Yes!" Borden was shouting into the mouthpiece of the old-fashioned upright instrument. "Yes, we damn well need those trainers or we can't get our air force going. We'll buy them from you. Cash on the barrel head. We've got the money. . . . Of course I know about your Neutrality Act. But I've got this scheme. You deliver the planes to North Dakota, right by the Saskatchewan boundary line. Have your men taxi them right up to the border. We'll have our fellows on the Canadian side throw ropes across. . . . Yes, *ropes*. You just attach them to the undercarriages and we'll pull them into Canada. Got it? Thanks. It's a pleasure doing business with you. . . ."

FOR MANY OF THE DOLLAR-A-YEAR MEN, WORLD WAR II WAS TO BE the most creative season of their professional lives. Their innovative talents flourished as they learned to extend the boundaries of their self-reliance, to manage the world at large without having to copy or feel inferior to the British or the Americans.

The man who set the style for the members of this select group, who became their deity—both as a model for its members to follow and as a depositary for the ideas they could believe in—was C.D. Howe, the shrewd Yankee from Port Arthur, Ontario.

He taught them an important insight: that knowledge is power. In first reviving, then operating, a diverse economy flung across an unlikely hunk of geography, Howe's protégés deliberately set out to learn where all the important pieces were; who counted and who didn't; how to deal with each other, with cabinet ministers, and with the political system. (At the same time, there was forming a significant community of interest between the dollar-a-year men and the upper echelons of the public service, where the group of mandarins who would run Canada's permanent sub-government well into the 1970s began to emerge.)

It was the network of connections and interconnections between business and government, fathered by Clarence Decatur Howe, that became the Canadian Establishment—its great dynasties spreading into every form of commercial enterprise across the country. It turned out to be an astonishingly resilient structure, with large remnants of the original group or their heirs still exercising the power that counts. When the dollar-a-year men fanned out at the close of World War II to run the nation they had helped to create, the attitudes, the working methods, and the business ethic they took with them determined the country's economic and political course for the next three decades.*

They had come to Ottawa as individuals; they left as an elite.

A measure of this remarkable group's accomplishment was the dramatic speed with which they managed to convert the rustic, dormant Canadian economy of 1939 into

---

*For a selected list of dollar-a-year men who worked under C.D. Howe and their later appointments in the corporate hierarchies of postwar Canada, see Appendix E.

the free world's fourth most powerful industrial state. At the start of the war, Canada counted barely eleven million people. A decade had elapsed since the onset of the Great Depression, but 600,000 people were still out of work; only 658,000 Canadians had jobs in manufacturing. Ottawa resembled a sleepy colonial outpost, with diplomatic representation abroad limited to missions in Washington, Paris, Tokyo, and London. "The mainspring of Mackenzie King's conception of the national effort," wrote C.P. Stacey, the historian, "was his fear of conscription for overseas service, its adverse effects on the country's unity and, doubtless, his party's chances of continuing in power. . . . He saw the Canadian contribution to the war as centring in the development of war industry."*

Under C.D. Howe's direction, the country's defence output grew so fast that by 1943 war-related industries were employing 1,100,000 Canadians, compared with a peak enrolment of 1,086,000 men and women in the armed forces. The gross national product leapt from $5 billion in 1939 to $12 billion by 1945. "Even the construction of the CPR didn't approach the daring of Canada's undertaking in the summer of 1940," wrote Bruce Hutchison.† "It was less an act of mobilization than an act of faith by a handful of people prepared for it by their lonely conquest of half a continent. And it was one of the chief ingredients of the Allies' victory."

Many start-up problems during the war's early days were complicated by the "mother knows best" attitude of the beleaguered British. On October 15, 1939, when the first official United Kingdom delegation arrived in Ottawa to set up the Commonwealth Air Training Plan, Arnold Heeney, then secretary to the Cabinet, and Clifford Clark, the deputy minister of finance, went to welcome them in their suite at the Chateau Laurier Hotel. Just before the talks got under way, Sir Arthur Balfour, a Sheffield industrialist who was the chief British negotiator, drew the

---

*C.P. Stacey, *Arms, Men and Governments: The War Policies of Canada, 1939–1945* (Ottawa: Queen's Printer, 1970).

†Bruce Hutchison, *The Incredible Canadian; A Candid Portrait of Mackenzie King, His Works, His Times, and His Nation* (Toronto: Longmans, 1952).

two Canadians aside and solemnly presented each of them with a tissue-wrapped penknife.*

A MORE INTRIGUING GAME WAS BEING PLAYED AT THE OF-FICES of the hastily set up Foreign Exchange Control Board, which was charged with controlling export and import currency transactions.† A group of high-ranking Bank of England officials had moved into the board's offices without informing Graham Towers, its chairman, of exactly what they were doing. They took the Canadians for granted and icily ignored all inquiries about their purpose.

Walter Gordon, who had been called to the FECB from his father's Toronto accountancy firm, was walking up Fifth Avenue during a brief business visit to New York when he happened to meet the British banker second in command of the mysterious contingent. "I was determined to find out what they were doing in Ottawa," Gordon later recalled, "so I invited him to the Algonquin Hotel for a drink. I took the waiter aside and told him, 'This guy really likes his martinis. Keep bringing them, but make his twice as strong as mine.'

"After a few rounds I asked the Englishman why he was looking so woebegone. He finally broke down and said that his mistress was in Belgium, which had recently been overrun by the Germans, and he couldn't find out whether she was all right. He said he knew of only one man in England influential enough to be able to help. 'But,' he confided, 'I'm in no position to approach him, even though he's a director of the Bank of England.' So I

---

*During the war's early phases, British industrialists deliberately withheld blueprints, designs, and secret processes from the Canadians, in case they might lose some profitable defence orders. The initial response of the Canadian business community was equally chauvinistic. Writing in *Quarterly Review of Commerce*, John C. Kirkwood, a Toronto business consultant, advised readers that "it is not always wrong to turn other persons' misfortunes to one's personal advantage. And by the same token, it is not wrong for Canadian enterprises to turn to profitable account their advantageous position and opportunity in respect of the current war. Our enterprises would be blameworthy if they failed to use their present opportunity to sell, to the maximum of possibility, all that they can and to sell at prices established by the law of supply and demand."

†The Foreign Exchange Control Board functioned efficiently through and beyond the war period, but its most lasting contribution may well have been to bring together eighteen of the mandarins who ran postwar Ottawa. ̶ey included Lester Pearson, James Coyne, John Deutsch, Arnold Heeney, ⸳nne Plumptre, Louis Rasminsky, and Max Mackenzie. For a complete ̶ing, see Appendix F.

asked him who it was. He told me it was Sir Edward Peacock.

" 'Well,' I said, 'I know Sir Edward well. He's a great friend of my father's. I'll write to him and see if he can find out.'

"We talked about this for a while, and then, just before the guy passed out, I pressed him on what he and his colleagues were doing in Ottawa, taking over all our good offices and so on. 'Oh,' he said, 'we don't talk about it because we feel mildly embarrassed, but we're there to set things up in case the Germans invade and the bank has to get out of England.' "

Gordon's methods were as unorthodox then as they were twenty years later when he returned to the capital as minister of finance. "As soon as I got back to Ottawa from New York," he remembers, "I saw people lined up outside the FEC Board's offices and nobody was doing much for them, so I started to deal with their problems on an *ad hoc* basis. I'd been the auditor at Falconbridge Nickel, and I recognized the company's executive treasurer in the line-up. I asked him what his problem was, and he said he had a ship full of nickel ore bound for the company's refinery in Norway being held up by red tape in Montreal. So I sent a wire to the director of customs ordering him to release the vessel, and signed it FOREIGN EXCHANGE CONTROL BOARD. A few days later we started to get urgent internal communications from the minister and deputy minister of customs trying to find out who'd sent the wire that had released the ship. I just put all the memos in a wastebasket and never told Towers what I'd done until the day I left. He said: 'Why didn't you let me know?'

"I told him, 'You would have had to fire me, and then who the hell would have organized this thing for you?' "

AT MIDNIGHT, ON APRIL 8, 1940, AS WORD WAS FLASHED TO OTTAWA that Adolf Hitler had hurled his *Wehrmacht* into Norway, the Department of Munitions and Supply Act was put into effect and C.D. Howe was sworn in as the department's minister. His mandate was to mobilize and expand the country's minuscule manufacturing sector to produce not only the materials and supplies required by

Canada's armed services but also the goods to fulfil the contracts beginning to pour in from allied nations.

The minister's primary assignment was to recruit efficiency-minded men who could carry out his orders. The casual nature of E.P. Taylor's enlistment was fairly typical of the process. Howe was lunching at the Rideau Club on the day after his appointment with Henry Borden and Gordon Scott, a Montreal accountant, and complaining about how hard it was to find a bright young executive to become one of his senior advisers. Borden looked around the lounge and spotted Taylor sitting with his father.

"There's Eddie Taylor over there," he said. "You know him, CD?"

Howe had heard of the brewing combine the young Taylor had been putting together but hadn't met him. When Scott vouched for his business acumen, Howe asked Borden to bring him over. Taylor listened to Howe's proposition and agreed on the spot to report for his new assignment the following Monday morning. Some time later, Howe asked his latest recruit whether he knew anybody who could look after the procurement of naval guns. "Sure," said Taylor. "I'll get Eric Phillips. He's very capable and he knows all about boats. He's got a big yacht in Georgian Bay and another one in the Bahamas." That tenuous recommendation was enough to place Phillips, who up to then had been running an Oshawa glass factory, in charge of obtaining the Royal Canadian Navy's large-bore armaments.*

E.P. Taylor's war turned out to be an intense, exhilarating time. In December of 1940 he was accompanying Howe on a war supply mission to England when their ship, the *Western Prince,* was torpedoed, and they had to spend a night and most of a day in a lifeboat.† When

---

*Phillips was soon promoted to take charge of Research Enterprises Ltd., a Crown corporation that co-ordinated wartime industrial development. A fringe benefit of Taylor's recommendation was that during their time in Ottawa, the two men got to know each other more intimately, and at war's end Phillips became one of the senior partners in Taylor's new holding company, Argus Corporation. Other dollar-a-year men Taylor recruited within the Argus orbit included M.W. McCutcheon, H.J. Carmichael, Wilfrid Gagnon, George Black and, less directly, James Duncan of Massey-Harris.

†Fortunately for him, Taylor was equipped with a special waterproof duckhunting outfit that his wife had bought him at Abercrombie & Fitch before he embarked on his transatlantic crossing.

they returned to Canada, Howe assigned Taylor to help resolve the shortage of U.S. dollars that was hampering Canada's defence requirements. President Franklin Delano Roosevelt had agreed to meet Mackenzie King at his country house in Hyde Park, N.Y., on Sunday, April 21, 1941, to negotiate an agreement which would, in effect, barter Canadian resources and surplus war goods for American manufactured products—despite nominal adherence by the U.S. to its Neutrality Act.

Along with Clifford Clark, the deputy finance minister, and J.B. Carswell, a former building contractor then acting as Canada's director-general of purchasing in the U.S., Taylor was delegated to brief the Canadian prime minister on the morning before the historic conference. Mackenzie King, who had been vacationing in Virginia, picked a symbolic spot for the rendezvous: the billiard room on the top floor of the Harvard Club, off New York's West 44th Street. It was an unusually hot day and the trio worked in shirt-sleeves, expounding from their *aide-mémoire* how King might parry some of FDR's more probing queries. The P.M. left for Hyde Park on a special train at noon and, as it turned out, the President asked no questions at all. Monday's *New York Times* described the entente, all too prophetically, as "a virtual merging of the economies of the United States and Canada."

Howe telephoned Taylor the next day with a typical message: "Eddie, we've just formed a Crown corporation called War Supplies Limited. You're the chairman. Go to Washington, live at the Willard Hotel, and sell our stuff. I've given your old job here to Harry Carmichael."

"So I told CD," Taylor later recalled, "that was fine and that Harry could have my carpet. Having a carpet in the temporary office buildings where we worked was a great sign, and Carmichael didn't have one. When I got to Washington, I realized right away that the Hyde Park agreement was completely illegal. It had no authority at all. It merely called for the Americans to supply us with 'numerous defence articles' and for Canada to make available to the Americans about $300 millions' worth of 'munitions, strategic materials, aluminum, and ships.' But it hadn't been passed either by our Parliament or the U.S. Congress. I overcame that one pretty fast.

"My first day in Washington, I went to see Frank Knox, U.S. Secretary of the Navy, General Brehon Somervell, head of the U.S. Army Services of Supply, and the heads of all the other big procurement agencies. 'Sure, we want those things you've got,' they told me, 'but what authority can we use?' So I'd bring out my copy of the *New York Times,* and they'd read the story describing Roosevelt's pledge, and they'd say, 'Well, looks as if you have something there. Come back tomorrow.' I told them to call Harry Hopkins in the White House if they had any doubts."

Eventually, War Supplies sold $1.3 billions' worth of Canadian goods; in the meantime, Taylor, at the personal request of Winston Churchill, had moved on to head the British Supply Council, co-ordinating all of Britain's American purchases.

THE DOLLAR-A-YEAR MEN WHO SPENT THE WAR IN OTTAWA considered themselves grossly overworked, but what came out of their mutual experience was a great sense of comradeship: a terrific knotting together of people making common cause and, above all, the fact that they really got to *know* each other. Eating lunch and often dinner with the same group for five years produced in the participants, for the first time in the experience of most of them, a consensus about the kind of country they wanted after the war, the sort of business practices they believed in, early glimmerings that Toronto and Montreal were not the only commercial centres in Canada that mattered. They began to exchange confidences, to sponsor one another for club memberships, to share perceptions and ambitions. It was an enduring trust, and even though the business Establishment has many strains within it, no badge of honour carries more prestige than the phrase: "I put in time under CD."

The men and one woman* who ran Ottawa's civilian

---

*The most senior and highest paid ($4,500 a year) woman in wartime Ottawa was Mrs. Phyllis Turner, who was chief of the Oil and Fats Administration branch in the Wartime Prices and Trade Board. Frank Ross, her husband-to-be, was director-general of naval armaments production in the Department of Munitions and Supply. She lived in the Sandy Hill area of town and when her teen-aged son, John, walked the family dog, he would often meet and converse with Mackenzie King.

war machine could be categorized by the places where they went to have meals. Most of the cabinet ministers went to the Rideau Club, along with the senior dollar-a-year men, though James Ilsley, the dour Maritimer who spent the war years as minister of finance, came to work by streetcar and gulped most of his lunches at the hash counter of Bowles Restaurant on Sparks Street. The mandarins held a daily roundtable free-for-all in the cafeteria of the Chateau Laurier Hotel, while the Honey Dew at the corner of Bank and Sparks streets became a favourite hangout for the Wartime Prices and Trade Board administrators. Everyone waited for invitations to Government House, where the chef had somehow managed to maintain a steady supply of French Brie, just ripe enough to eat. The favourite dinner spot was Madame Burger's restaurant in Hull. Those who could afford it lived either at the Chateau or in the Roxborough Apartments, at Laurier Avenue and Elgin Street.

It was a happy time, but they frequently found their efforts hampered by the bureaucratic framework in which they had to operate, despite the urgency of the *ad hoc* decisions they were daily forced to make.* H.R. Mac-Millan, who came to Ottawa on June 24, 1940, to become timber controller for the WPTB, found that he had to wait four months before the government would reimburse him for the salary he was paying his secretary. One rule that particularly angered the newcomers was that, according to civil service regulations then in effect, only ministers were allowed cradle telephones. Everyone else had to use the old-fashioned stand-up kind.

Probably the most delicate problem handled by the Wartime Prices and Trade Board, which was run with high good humour by Donald Gordon, the former deputy governor of the Bank of Canada, concerned a Hamilton housewife's application for a thousand dollars in U.S. funds so that she could spend a week in New York to have herself artificially inseminated. Because of Canada's short-

*When Philip Chester, later managing director of the Hudson's Bay Company, left Ottawa because he found the regulations insufferable, his wife gave a glittering dinner party to celebrate his return to Winnipeg. As the guests sat down, they found that all the food on the table was tied with red tape. There was also a set of forms at each setting that they had to fill out in triplicate before they could begin eating.

age of U.S. currency, regulations limited American visits to business trips, with very few pleasure jaunts allowed. For weeks the lady's application circulated around WPTB offices, with some raunchy comments pencilled in the margin. Gordon finally settled the matter by scribbling across her papers: "OBVIOUSLY NOT FOR PLEASURE PURPOSES —APPROVED."*

At another level, the Ottawa war machine was not quite so altruistic as it was portrayed at the time. At the height of the war, Munitions and Supply was placing six hundred contracts a day for millions of dollars' worth of supplies and equipment. There was little time for tenders.† The Liberals used the award of defence orders to help fill party coffers. "Howe was the greatest bagman the Grits ever had," Senator Grattan O'Leary complained afterwards. "There were some fifteen hundred war contracts out in 1944, and everybody the Tories went to for election expenses would say they'd already given to the Liberals. We found out that whenever the Liberal bagman arrived, he'd casually remark that CD had told him: 'Be sure to tell Charlie [or Ed or Bill] I was asking for him.' The clear implication—whether Howe was aware of it or not —was that CD would be told the size of the man's donation." (Wallace R. Campbell, a former president of the Ford Motor Company of Canada who served as chairman of the War Supply Board, resigned because political pressure was brought on him to put through a contract at $100,000 in excess of its value.)

Another touchy area was the opportunity for conflict of interest, because the basic recruiting procedure both Howe and Donald Gordon followed was first to get the

---

*The Wartime Prices and Trade Board was one of the government's most successful operations. Canada's cost of living rose only 20 per cent, compared with 55 per cent during World War I. For a selected list of dollar-a-year men who served with the WPTB and the positions they achieved in the postwar economy, see Appendix G.

†Doug Ambridge, the bombastic engineer who served for a time as director of shipbuilding under Howe and became president of Abitibi Paper, later recalled that when he arrived, Desmond Clarke, his predecessor, was operating on a tendering system. "If you wanted a ship, even a goddamn little minesweeper, you had to put out a tender on it," Ambridge complained. "Well, for Christ's sake, what difference did that make? It took three times as long. So I went to see CD over Desmond's head, and I said, 'Look, I'm not going to have any more of these damn tenders. We can't have tenders and get the boats at the same time. I'm going to give the contracts to anybody I think will do them.' Howe told me that was okay as long as I got the damn ships. A few weeks later, Desmond was named some kind of special assistant to Howe and I never saw him again."

best expert in his field, then to place him in charge of the price and procurement management for his whole industry. In his memoirs, James Duncan, the former Massey-Harris chairman, remarked: "One day C.D. Howe invited me to Ottawa and asked me to draw up recommendations covering the allocation of raw materials to the Canadian farm-implement industry. It was unusual that I should be asked to submit a plan restricting our own and our competitors' operations, but CD knew that I would not take advantage of the situation. In the course of time my recommendations were adopted, including the proviso that no restriction should be imposed on Britain's requirements for farm machinery as these were essential to the success of that country's intensive food-producing program. As a result of these restrictive measures, the 1942 and 1943 manufacturing programs for farm machinery were seriously hampered. Our war production, however, was correspondingly increased, and our company in 1942 went through a period of great expansion."*

Although Canadian companies were subject throughout the war to fairly severe excess-profits taxes, Howe allowed manufacturers to write off their capital investments pretty well as they saw fit.† Between September, 1939, and August, 1945, some $3.5 billion was invested in new manufacturing facilities, at least half of the sum financed through special Ottawa tax credits and allowances. A grand total of $28 billion was spent on the war effort, and the Canadian economy was forever altered in the process.‡

---

*James Duncan, *Not a One-Way Street* (Toronto: Clarke, Irwin, 1971).
†The system of accelerated depreciation provisions was first suggested to Howe by his friend R.E. "Rip" Powell, president of Aluminum Company of Canada, whose firm also became one of the scheme's chief beneficiaries. Alcan was able to write off its entire $193-million ingot and hydro development at Shipshaw, Quebec, in three years. As soon as he retired from politics, Howe was named a director of Aluminium Ltd., parent company of Aluminum Company of Canada.
‡This rapid expansion also helped to perpetuate the concentration of industry in central Canada. Speculating about the alienation of the Western Provinces in the 1970s, E.B. Osler, a former Liberal M.P. from Winnipeg, wrote in *Maclean's*: "Perhaps what has happened to us (or what has *not* happened) can best be understood by looking at the lasting effects produced in Canada by the Empire Air Training Scheme of World War II. Between 1940 and 1945, Air Force stations sprang up all over the West, quickening the economic and social pulse of many a prairie town. Simultaneously, in central Canada, factories employing many people were built to turn out uniforms, engines and airframes, radios, flight instruments and the like. Then, in 1946, after fulfilling its purpose, everything was cranked down. The result? Prairie towns went back to handling grain and sustain-

C.D. HOWE WAS NOT ONLY THE PIVOTAL FIGURE IN THIS TRANSFORMATION: he became the founder of modern, industrialized, Americanized Canada. During the time of his flowering, he represented an exciting new force in Canadian affairs. He was very different from the old Wasp elites that ruled Toronto and Montreal, whose members were British in their orientation, turning towards Government House, the Crown, and the Empire for guidance. Howe was middle class, self-made, a tough, American get-up-and-go engineering type. The dollar-a-year men who came to aid in the war effort had grown up with Hollywood movies, the first generation to do so. They were in love with the American style of easy-going brashness, the "get things done without a lot of stuffy nonsense" attitude that Howe so perfectly epitomized.

Howe put in place the infrastructure of the Canadian economy that still exists today, allocating the resources, granting the tax write-offs, directing the wartime buildup, fostering the postwar prosperity.

His most enduring political legacy probably was to lend some measure of credibility to the myth of the Liberal party as an expression of the national will. During his time in Ottawa, the Liberal party became, in Jack Pickersgill's immortal phrase, "the *government* party," and everybody else was left on the sidelines. "The unreflecting acceptance of this belief," wrote Denis Smith, "smoothed the way for the integration of senior civil servants and businessmen into the Liberal national system: for they could play their cooperative roles without making any overt political commitment to the party."*

It is not easy now to realize what a great influence Howe was able to exercise over national initiatives during his twenty-two years in public service. Most of his policies —at least until the mid-fifties—were looked on as something close to God's own truth. Only Mackenzie King was

ing an ever-diminishing population of farmers, while the factories in central Canada, converted to civilian production, embarked on an expanding cycle of prosperity which is still being maintained. In other words, central Canada emerged from the war with an augmented industrial base—just as it had emerged originally from the 'opening' of the West—while western Canada (especially midwestern Canada) came out of it with nothing more lasting than the memory of some charming visitors and a temporarily increased cash flow."

*Denis Smith, *Gentle Patriot: A Political Biography of Walter Gordon* (Edmonton: Hurtig, 1973).

able to stop him from taking Canada into a free-trade arrangement with the U.S., a step that would have muted any chance for this country's long-term independence.

A curious combination of simplicity and directness, on the one hand, and susceptibility to riches and prestige on the other, Howe gloried in the company of the powerful and felt himself to be their equal. He liked nothing better than to visit London and dine with Lord Beaverbrook. But he himself lived simply and didn't bother with ostentatious trappings. When he was congratulated on getting an honorary doctorate from the Massachusetts Institute of Technology, he shrugged and said: "It's not that I give a damn for the degree, it's the impression it'll make on my wife's Boston relatives that I care about."

His New England heritage as a doer with a hard rock belief in himself and his capacities remained the dominant strain in Howe's character. Born at Waltham, Mass., in 1886, Howe graduated from MIT in 1907 and stayed on as an engineering instructor for a few months until his professor recommended both him and a fellow graduate for a full-fledged lectureship at Dalhousie University. They tossed a coin to see who would apply, and Howe won.* After five years in Halifax, he moved to the Lakehead as chief engineer with the Board of Grain Commissioners and three years later established his own engineering firm. During the next decade and a half, Howe built grain storage facilities worth $125 million at harbours from Canada to Argentina, including the Port Arthur Saskatchewan Pool Seven, the largest grain elevator in the world.

The depression cut into his business, and although Howe's previous political activity had been limited to a brief (1922–25) term on the Port Arthur Board of Education, he now began to move into the highest circles of the Liberal party, which had been temporarily put out of office by R.B. Bennett in 1930. One of his friends was Norman Lambert, a former secretary of the Canadian Council of Agriculture, who had recently been named the party's national organizer. During the winter of 1933,

*Howe once confided to Stanley Knowles, the NDP M.P. from Winnipeg, that he had never been sure who had actually won that toss. "Maybe I lost it," he said. "The other fellow went on to be the head of a large American corporation."

Lambert invited Howe to dine at the Chateau Laurier with Vincent Massey, then president of the National Liberal Federation. Convinced by the two men that he should stand for the Port Arthur seat in the next election, Howe set one condition: that if elected, he would immediately be taken into the Cabinet. Mackenzie King promptly invited him to Laurier House and enthusiastically endorsed both his candidacy and the pledge of a portfolio. The seat went Liberal by a comfortable margin in the 1935 campaign, and Howe was named Minister of Railways and Canals. Some of his prewar initiatives, such as establishing the CBC and Trans-Canada Air Lines, gave an early indication of his practical approach.

Graham Spry, head of the Radio League of Canada which had been lobbying for a government broadcasting system, recalls that "in everything Howe did he was motivated by the capitalist ethic; free enterprise was a magic phrase for him, and when he was first approached about the CBC he was quite hostile. But we kept pressing him very hard. Eventually he came round, asked Brooke Claxton, who was acting as the league's lawyer, to write the act, and public broadcasting triumphed. Howe was responsive to the right kind of approach. He may have been the epitome of the big businessman, but when he saw that it was more practical, more efficient, to do something like the CBC or TCA, he would deal with it in those terms."*

Those hybrid creatures, the Crown corporations, represented perfectly the way Howe liked to conduct the government's business. Crown corporations provided both the kind of legal entity to which businessmen were accustomed and a degree of bureaucratic decentralization no government department could attain, yet their directors were chosen by the minister in charge, their accounts

---

*Spry later moved to London and eventually became personal assistant to Sir Stafford Cripps, who was in charge of aircraft production in Winston Churchill's wartime coalition. Spry introduced Howe to his minister and they hit it off immediately. Cripps told Spry afterwards that Howe was "one of the most sensible people of his acquaintance." Howe thought the whole encounter was hilarious. "Here I am," he told Spry, "a supposed capitalist, and Cripps is a socialist, yet I'd sooner deal with him than anybody else in Churchill's government." Spry concluded that this was the secret of Howe's success: "CD was a fully integrated man. The fact that Cripps was a teetotaller, a vegetarian, and a left-winger, while he was a man's man who liked bourbon, steaks, and fishing, didn't blind him to Cripps's abilities."

were vetted by the Auditor-General, and the issued capital shares were held by the government. When Howe decided in 1937 that Canada should have its own national airline, he invited CPR, CNR, and Canadian Airways (then the largest private air operation, owned by the Richardson family of Winnipeg) to form a joint venture, with the government supplying airport and communications facilities. When Canadian Airways and CPR turned down the offer, Howe launched TCA as a purely government enterprise.*

During the war, the number of Crown corporations multiplied so rapidly (twenty-eight were eventually established) that Howe ran out of appropriate names and finally told his dollar-a-year men to pick titles from the exchanges in the Montreal telephone directory. This was how such operations as the Plateau Company (set up to buy raw silk for parachutes), Citadel Merchandising (created to buy machine tools), and the Fairmont Company (established to handle crude and synthetic rubber and hides) got their names.

Howe's critics, both in government and in business, kept trying to find a suitable ideological label for him, to pin him down, to determine some pattern in the welter of policies he sponsored. John Deutsch, who was probably the most remarkable and certainly the most practical of the great Ottawa mandarins, watched Howe operate at close hand for more than two decades. "The fact is," says Deutsch, "that CD didn't know a policy when he saw one. He knew how to run a railroad, how to make the thing go—but *why* you had a railroad, that is a question he did not ask. He never had any decisive input in general policy matters. Someone responsible told him, 'This is what we need,' and he went and did it. He was an operating executive—one of the greatest this country has ever had."

Despite his lack of any definable ideology, Howe was

*TCA (now Air Canada) was Howe's favourite child. He held onto it as he moved through his various portfolios, personally recruited its executives, and loved to fly on its planes. In the summer of 1957, a few days after he was defeated and responsibility for the airline was switched to the Department of Transport, he was sitting by himself on the steps of the East Block, waiting for a taxi. John Baldwin, Deputy Minister of Transport, walked by, and Howe yelled after him: "Take care of TCA for me!"

very certain of what he thought. And one of the things he genuinely believed was that the willingness of the Americans to invest so much of their capital in Canada was the best possible indicator of progress.* Neither Howe nor his disciples, who had taken so much pride in throwing off the British yoke, seemed even vaguely aware that by their actions they were exchanging one kind of dependence for another. Part of Howe's continentalism was based on his action-oriented approach to business. He was irritable and impatient with the cautious ways of Canadians. He felt that they hung back, had little zest, demanded assurance of a big return on their money before they'd start anything. The boys with the risk money—American enterprise—*theirs* was the language he understood.

Howe hated inaction. He couldn't stand being in the company of External Affairs types who, he figured, thought up a problem and then entertained themselves by discussing its paradoxes. His method of running men and departments was wholly unbureaucratic. He was given to issuing terse oral instructions—the first important Canadian politician who preferred the telephone to writing letters. For him, a fifteen-page memo, no matter how beautifully worded or reasoned, was simply an indication that you didn't know what you wanted (given a bulky report, he'd usually grin at its bearer and ask, "What's it say?").† He was exasperated with underlings who protested that what he wanted to do was administratively impossible. "Nothing is administratively impossible," he would say, and when they explained that the department's legal adviser said it couldn't be done, Howe would shoot back: "Then get me a lawyer who says it *can* be done."

Howe's rapport with businessmen was based on something more than decisiveness. He implanted in them the

---

*In 1948, when a series of secret negotiations about a reciprocal free-trade arrangement between the U.S. and Canada was initiated by Washington officials, Howe was the most enthusiastic booster of the plan in the Cabinet. In his diary, Mackenzie King (who vetoed the scheme) wrote: "Howe has the absurd idea that what complete freedom of trade would mean is that Canada would be piling her manufactured goods into the United States."

†Howe had no patience with written documents of any kind. At the Rideau Club where he lunched, members are expected to write out their orders on a pad brought by the waitress. One of his luncheon companions remembers glancing at Howe's fast, phonetic scribble and reading: "Plane omelet & rasin pie."

gift of self-confidence. He taught them that a $50-million decision is not necessarily more difficult to make than one involving $50,000. To make nine important decisions a day, even if only five of them turn out right, was far better than making no decisions at all. He had the ability to assess people, to persuade them to like him and work for him at full tilt.

When a fledgling dollar-a-year man once breathlessly asked Howe (almost saluting as he said it): "What are your instructions, CD?" Howe calmly replied: "I never give instructions, I just give responsibilities." That wasn't strictly true, but he did delegate tremendous leeway to his subordinates and respected their recommendations. In the fall of 1942, when Dr. C.J. Mackenzie, then head of the National Research Council, wanted to establish the first Canadian nuclear research unit jointly with British scientists, he had to see Howe for permission, because the minister reported to Parliament for the organization. "I went to CD's office and discussed the idea," he later recalled. "Howe sat there and listened; then he turned to me and said: 'What do you think?' I told him I thought it was sound. He nodded a couple of times and said: 'Okay, let's go.'"

His weakness as an administrator was that he could rarely bring himself to fire anybody. Howe's deputy minister in the Department of Munitions and Supply was G.K. Sheils, a former bookkeeper from New Brunswick, whose abilities and temperament were totally incompatible with those of his minister. Howe never let Sheils go, but he promoted all his important dollar-a-year men to be directors-general of their various divisions, which allowed them to report directly to him over Sheils's head; he put his deputy in charge of "support staff." (Sheils, who knew exactly what was happening but didn't want to give up his pension, spent the war filling in requisitions and allocating pencils.)

Annette Saint-Denis, a slender, aristocratic woman now in her sixties who served as Howe's secretary for twenty-one years, used to feel that everybody who was anybody came to see her boss. They would sit there in her office, talking to her on the way through, so that it seemed like the centre of the universe. Ottawa ran on a smaller scale then; the world seemed manageable, with government departments all within walking distance of Parliament Hill. When Howe was moved into the temporary buildings hastily put up for the wartime expansion, she was dismayed by the inadequacy of her minister's quarters. But he didn't give a damn. After he'd occupied the office for three years and a crew from Public Works came in to lay a new carpet, he told them just to mend the worn spots in the old one.

She was constantly after him to replace his worn-out clothes, to get new shoes or a new hat. Her worst moment came at Mackenzie King's funeral when she noticed Howe among the cortège of cabinet ministers in a morning coat that was literally green with age. Afterwards, she chided him about it, but Howe seemed unimpressed. Next morning he came in and apologized. "Listen, young lady," he said, "you were right. That's the coat I wore to my wedding forty years ago."

Going home and reading, listening to the radio, or playing bridge were Howe's main relaxations. He enjoyed fishing at Colonel R.S. McLaughlin's lodge near Cap Chat, Quebec, and maintained a summer home at St. Andrews in New Brunswick. But he was strangely impersonal with most people. He never lost his dignity, didn't slap backs, was not given to garrulous boasting or partying—a purposeful man, firmly in command of his worth.

PARADOXICALLY, IT WAS C.D. HOWE WHO IN THE SPRING OF 1945 sponsored the White Paper on Employment and Incomes in which was enshrined the idea that government should be *the* prime factor in the creation and disposition of a major share of the national wealth. The document, now almost forgotten, was to set the climate in which both government and business would operate for the next thirty years.

By the autumn of 1944, when victory seemed assured, Mackenzie King and his ministers came to fear, in about equal proportions, two possibilities: the postwar prospect of massive unemployment as war production was wound down and the emergence of socialism as a burgeoning political force that would benefit from the dissatisfactions of the returning veterans. To the Liberal pragmatists who populated Mackenzie King's cabinet, the solution seemed obvious. The government's legislative priorities would have to be diverted temporarily toward helping the common man. An Unemployment Insurance Act and the Family Allowance Act that established the controversial "baby bonus" system had been put in place during the war.

As early as 1941, Ian Mackenzie, then minister of pensions and national health, had organized the Committee on Reconstruction, headed by F. Cyril James, principal of McGill University. Its research director was Leonard Marsh, who had studied at the London School of Economics under Sir William Beveridge, author of a report on social insurance that had recommended universal pensions for Great Britain. Marsh's report, presented to the House of Commons Committee on Reconstruction and Rehabilitation on March 15, 1942, called for "a total security programme designed for the modern industrial state" that would cost between $100 million and $500 million a year. At first nothing much happened, but in December of that year a Gallup Poll revealed that the Liberals, who had won more than half the votes cast in the 1940 election, had slipped to 36 per cent. The CCF's share of public support had leapt from 8½ per cent to 23 per cent. Then, on August 3, 1943, Ontario's Liberal government was overwhelmed at the polls and the CCF (which had only four fewer M.L.A.s elected than the Conservatives) became the official opposition.* National public opinion polls later that year reported a CCF surge to 29 per cent, with the Liberals and Conservatives down to 28 per cent each. The Liberals decided to act. "The Tories could have the right, the CCF the left," Professor Jack Granatstein wrote in an analysis of the period. "Mackenzie King and the Liberal Party would hold to the centre and prevent the polarization of Canadian politics along class lines."†

The man who provided the Liberals with the theoretical base for this doctrine was John Maynard Keynes, the wide-ranging Cambridge don whose *The General Theory of Employment, Interest, and Money*, published in 1936,

*Saskatchewan elected its first socialist government on June 15, 1944.
†J. L. Granatstein, *Canada's War: The Politics of the Mackenzie King Government, 1939–1945* (Toronto: Oxford University Press, 1975).

revolutionized applied economics. Keynes amassed $2 million by staying in bed an extra half hour each morning and speculating in the world's gyrating currency and commodity markets by telephone; he collected modern art, ran a theatre, and married Lydia Lopokova, the leading ballerina of Diaghilev's Russian ballet company; he was a director of the Bank of England and chairman of a large insurance company; he dabbled in half a dozen disciplines and was at the centre of the avant-garde Bloomsbury set of writers and painters. Half dilettante, half Renaissance man, he was a prolific genius who wrote so many books and papers that one unannotated listing of them takes up twenty-two pages. Something of an eccentric, he never stopped amassing knowledge, however esoteric. (When Keynes met H.G. Wells for the first time, the two men immediately began to compare notes on why chimpanzees use their knuckles for walking.)

The General Theory was attacked at the time of its publication as a subversive, radical document, but Keynes was in fact a high-caste Establishment figure who condemned Marxists for being "illogical and oh, so dull." He saw himself as an economic saviour, providing a way of pulling the world out of the Great Depression without fatally damaging the free enterprise system.

Despite his commitment to massive state intervention, Keynes was vigorously opposed to the nationalization of industry. He was the first economist to demonstrate convincingly that governments have not only the ability but the *responsibility* to use their power for increasing the general levels of production, income, and employment. This was the great Keynesian heresy: that man could control his economic fate—the very opposite of the doctrine preached by Adam Smith, that the economy was naturally regulated by the "invisible hand" of the marketplace.* Keynes founded macro-economics, which deals with aggregate rates of saving and consumption instead of individual entrepreneurial decisions. He evolved the concept of anticyclical budgeting: the idea that in times of recession

---

*Keynes made a profound impression on his generation. In his biography, *Stanfield* (Toronto: McClelland and Stewart, 1973), Geoffrey Stevens paints an evocative portrait of the future Conservative leader on a bicycling holiday in Europe, carrying *The General Theory* in his knapsack.

governments should increase expenditures and reduce taxes, incurring budgetary deficits that will stimulate the economy.

Through a combination of personalities and circumstances, Canada became, according to John Kenneth Galbraith, "the first country to commit itself to a firmly Keynesian economic policy." The man who brought the message home was Bob Bryce. A gaunt figure with sagging eyes under outrigger glasses with lenses as thick as bottle bottoms, he eventually became the quintessential mandarin, a pervasive Ottawa behind-the-scenes influence as clerk of the privy council, as deputy minister of finance, and later as chairman of the Royal Commission on Corporate Concentration. But in 1932, he had just graduated in mining engineering from the University of Toronto. Because no one was hiring engineers, he switched to economics and decided to attend Cambridge. "I had done four years of economics in Toronto and thought I was pretty good," recalls Lorie Tarshis,* who went to Cambridge with Bryce, "but Bob took the summer to study the subject, and by the fall he was up to any of us. At Cambridge, we were fortunate enough to be invited into the Political Economy Club from our very first year, and it was there that we came directly under Keynes's influence."†

The Political Economy Club, which convened five times a term in Keynes's rooms at King's College, consisted of his favourite faculty members and ten promising undergraduates. The meetings began at about eight o'clock with guests drawing numbers from a hat. Those holding slips numbered 1 to 6 spoke extemporaneously on that evening's topic. "I remember one rainy night Bob and I were the only two who appeared, and the paper had something to do with the history of the East India Company in the 1690s," Tarshis recalls. "Keynes would always serve tea and cookies by 10.30, make a few complimentary remarks about the presentation and discussion, and then till

---

*Tarshis is now chairman of the social sciences division of Scarborough College of the University of Toronto.

†The two young Canadians found themselves chosen for the honour not by chance but because Wynne Plumptre (later an assistant deputy minister of finance) had preceded them to Cambridge. It was he who recommended Bryce and Tarshis for membership. Keynes had been Plumptre's personal tutor for two years.

the time until 11.50 (when we had to leave to get back to our digs) with great insights and pronouncements." Bryce's memory of those evenings and their consequences is very specific:

"After a year or two, I was convinced that Keynes was on the track of something really important. In the winter of 1935, I went to the London School of Economics two days a week as a missionary to convert the heathen. I wrote a longish paper on what I understood Keynes's basic concepts to be. It circulated in mimeographed form (before Xerox) very widely. I sent it to Keynes who endorsed it as a correct version of his ideas and was surprised that I was able to set them forth so briefly. I took this with me when I went to Harvard (on a Commonwealth Scholarship) in September, 1935. By that time, I suppose, I was more of a disciple than most of his students. This was only about five months before *The General Theory* appeared. I didn't take the advice Richard Kahn [Keynes's assistant and executor] gave me, to forget the professors and stay in the library at Harvard, and spent most of my two years there in controversy—attending various seminars, clubs, and other groups, trying to get some of the faculty and graduate students, including a bright young junior fellow by the name of Paul Samuelson, to understand what it was all about.* Years later I had to explain that, to get some of the Marxists (like Paul Sweezey and Shigeto Tsuru) to attend my study group on Keynes, I had to attend their group on Marxist thought. It was wonderfully interesting stuff, because so many of us thought that Keynes's theory was going to make economics meaningful in dealing with the depression.

"I left Harvard in mid-1937. Clifford Clark had heard about me through Jim Macdonnell,† who was

---

*As chairman of the economics department at MIT, Paul Samuelson won a Nobel Prize in 1970.

†J.M. Macdonnell was president of National Trust and later a Diefenbaker cabinet minister.

a friend of my father's.* He offered me a summer
job, which was the normal way of sizing a fellow up
in those days. But I didn't want something temporary, so I went with the investment department of
Sun Life in Montreal. They beat him by about an
hour. Clifford caught up with me in 1938 and said:
'It isn't as much fun as you expected, is it? We'll
open up a position in the Department of Finance
for you and have a competition for it, if you'll put
in.' And so I got into Finance after facing a very
formidable board of examiners that included Clark
and Graham Towers.

"Clark was not a Keynesian by then but was open-
minded and wanted exposure to those ideas. I suppose he had some familiarity through reading Keynes
and a few contacts like Wynne, who then was secretary of the Macmillan Commission, which Clark set
up to recommend the establishment of the Bank of
Canada. I found Clark willing to learn and use
Keynes's analysis, though sceptical of some of his
generalizations about the way the world worked.

"One of the first clearly Keynesian measures in
Canada was the tax credit for investment expenditures proposed in the budget of the spring of 1939,
in which Eaton† and I worked with Clark. The initial extended application of Keynes's method of analysis was in the first wartime budget speech of September, 1939, most of which I wrote as everyone
else then around was busy on other things. The fact
that we got into Keynesian analysis under wartime
conditions, when justifying more public expenditures
and government deficits didn't look like reckless
spending for economic policy purposes, made it
much easier to get acceptance. It really hit Ottawa,
hit the country, hit the politicians, the business community and Canadian economists at a time when it
seemed like a fairly responsible attitude.

---

*R.A. Bryce, a mining engineer, was president of Macassa Mines and
a director of several major Canadian corporations, including the Toronto-
Dominion Bank and National Trust.
†Ken Eaton, a Canadian Ph.D. from Harvard, joined the finance department in 1934 and eventually became an assistant deputy minister.

"Keynes visited Ottawa several times during 1944 as a representative of the U.K. treasury to discuss financing of the post-European phase of the war and the prospective financial position of the U.K. after the war. I was secretary at most of the meetings. His brilliance in thought and word led Canadian ministers to be on their guard against this spellbinder. One night, on the anniversary of the founding of the Bank of England, Keynes put on a wonderful dinner at the Chateau Laurier, despite wartime austerity, and spoke for nearly two hours about the history of the bank. I had such a good dinner I can recall very little of what he said."

THE KEYNESIAN IDEAS FOUND THEIR FIRST COHESIVE PUBLIC EXPRESSION in the White Paper prepared under the instructions of C.D. Howe in the spring of 1945. CD, who had by this time switched his portfolio to Reconstruction and Supply,* was busy giving away the nation's war plants to private industry, sometimes at thirty-five cents or less on the dollar. The huge Canadair plant near Montreal, for example, which cost Ottawa $22 million to build, was sold to Electric Boat Company (later General Dynamics Corporation) of Groton, Connecticut, for fifty cents on the dollar. To give a further boost to the changeover to peacetime manufacturing, he continued the wartime accelerated depreciation allowances, which permitted companies to write off new assets against profits for a total of $1.4 billion between November 10, 1944, and March 31, 1947.

One Thursday late in March, 1945, when Bill Mackintosh, then director-general of research in Howe's new department, was walking back to the temporary buildings from Parliament Hill with his minister, he suggested they put together a clear, integrated statement of the govern-

---

*Howe accepted the new posting on the condition that Mackenzie King would transfer to his department two of his senior advisers, Bill Mackintosh and Jack Firestone. Mackintosh was a Queen's University economist with a Ph.D. from Harvard who had been an assistant to Clifford Clark. Firestone had been the senior research assistant on the Marsh report; later he became director of economic research for the Department of Reconstruction and Supply as well as the Department of Trade and Commerce.

ment's economic intentions. Howe told him to have a shot at it, and Mackintosh produced a draft by the following Monday. Howe approved it with only one significant modification.*

The document was considered so important that, before it went to full Cabinet, it was studied by a special committee of ministers consisting of Howe, Louis St. Laurent (then in Justice), and James Ilsley, from Finance. "These were the ablest and most influential ministers of the day," Mackintosh later recalled. "We spent the greater part of a day on it. I was forearmed with a text in which I had underlined in different colours the specific commitments, the general statements of policy, the implied commitments, and all statements in the name of the Government. I required specific approval of each or, alternatively, amended wording. By the end of the day, they were visibly wearied by my schoolmasterish drill, but they approved the text for formal acceptance by the Cabinet, having made no change of substance, though they asked here and there for a more familiar word and rounded a sentence or two. Over such changes I did not cavil for a second, for I knew I was accomplishing my prime object, that no important paper should ever have gone to Cabinet with a fuller understanding and realization on the part of the key ministers of what they were committing the Goverment to."

The White Paper on Employment and Incomes was tabled in the Commons on April 12, 1945. Because this was also the day Franklin Delano Roosevelt died, the document received little attention. Yet it represented the first outright acceptance by any government anywhere of Keynes's economic principles and set out a specific plan for a government-managed economy from which no Canadian government has since deviated.

---

*His main change was to alter the phrase that pledged the government to maintain "full employment" to "a high level of employment." Jack Firestone, who was closely involved with Howe at the time, said later: "CD was not a Keynesian in the sense that he would subscribe to making up deficiencies in demand through the kind of fiscal instruments which Keynes's policies led us to adopt. Rather, he was a pragmatist who was willing to accept an increasing role for government in economic affairs of whatever form was required. As it turned out, this was true not only in an anti-cyclical sense but, in many instances, a structural sense as well. The financing of the trans-Canada pipeline was one of the outstanding examples."

THE PLEDGE OF MASSIVE INTERVENTION IN THE ECON-
OMY MAY HAVE BEEN Keynes's idea, but it paralleled
exactly the notion of the country held in the minds and
souls of Ottawa's senior public servants. They saw the
Keynesian prescription as a way of purging capitalism of
its defects without having to turn toward socialism. They
were, most of them, intellectuals, mildly radicalized in the
style of the thirties, academics *manqué* who satisfied their
reform instincts by manipulating fiscal policies and drafting social welfare legislation. Lord Keynes was their high
priest, but pragmatism was their religion.*

The identifying quality that stood out in any composite
portrait of the Ottawa mandarins who began to emerge as
a cohesive establishment after the war was their consciousness of belonging to an elite. It was this knowledge that
imbued them with a sense of effortless superiority. They
seemed to view their mission as that of sentries on the
ramparts of Canadian democracy, guarding it from both
the selfishness of the citizens and the short cuts of the
politicians. They prided themselves on their non-partisan
approach in a highly political environment. But, given a
choice, they much preferred the Liberals, partly because

---

*Merril Menzies, the Winnipeg economist who provided the Diefenbaker
government with one of its few sources of intellectually sound advice,
believes that the Ottawa mandarins subverted Keynes's purposes. According to Menzies, "Keynes warned that the world is ruled by the thoughts
and precepts of dead economists. He was too wise not to know that his
General Theory would have to evolve as the world economy underwent
accelerated change. Most of his disciples did not possess this wisdom.
. . . They confirmed their understanding of his teachings by their skilful
management of the Canadian economy during the war and reconstruction
years. But after 1950 there was nothing but the marketplace to shape the
future of Canada. Instead of adapting Keynes's theory, developed within
the context and experience of the British economy of the 1930s, they simply adopted it in the apparent belief that, without any significant altera-
tion, it was equally applicable to Canada. But in almost every essential,
the two economies stood in marked contrast. Instead of the mature industrial economy Keynes built his theory on, ours was immature and
heavily resource based. Instead of a homogeneous economy, we had one
of the most regionalized economies in the world. Instead of an economy
understandably more concerned about stability than growth, we had to
plan for growth as well as stability, or growth would be determined by
the priorities of others. Instead of an economy with highly favourable
terms of trade and balance of payments (true of Britain before the war),
our terms of trade for primary resources were frequently seriously adverse compared to the industrial giants, and we were following policies
which could only ensure in perpetuity an adverse balance of payments, at
least on capital account. One can see why fiscal, and later monetary,
policy loomed large in Keynes's thinking about the management of the
U.K. economy. To assume that fiscal and monetary forces could alone
deal adequately with Canada's quite different problems seems as absurd
today as it did then. But this is exactly what was assumed by the Establishment of the 1950s, and only marginal modifications could be de-
tected in the 1960s."

so few Conservatives showed enough trust in their impartiality to heed their counsel.*

Cultivated, clever, and cordial, they lacked ideology; their passions were as dry as winter leaves. Life for most Ottawa mandarins held few surprises. They saw most problems as intellectual tumbling exercises and didn't particularly like to mingle with people outside their own magic circle. Away from Ottawa on flash forays to the busy hinterland beyond the capital, they resembled shy woodland animals caught rashly far from the undergrowth.

Probably the group's most striking characteristic was its uncanny ability to reach a consensus on daily problems without the aid of any formal meeting. Although they appeared to have few connecting links, they were quietly engaged in a process of continuous consultation. "If you picked the thirty or so men who matter in this town and put radioactive tracers in their pockets, then watched their daily movements on a giant fluoroscope, you'd be amazed how often their paths cross," a deputy minister of that era theorized. "And out of these comings and goings constantly flow memoranda with limited but important circulation."

Many of these exchanges took place over lunch, first in the basement cafeteria of the Chateau Laurier Hotel, then at the Rideau Club,† and more recently again at the Chateau in the alcove seats of the Grill.

A more private and much more important forum for the exchange of mandarin views remains the Five Lakes Fishing Club, located in the Gatineau hills about an hour's drive from the capital. The property was originally acquired by Bill Mackintosh, Donald Gordon, and Clifford

---

*The congenial relations between the bureaucrats and their Liberal masters burst into the open when some senior civil servants shattered the line of demarcation between themselves and the politicians by joining the Liberal cabinet. At the 1948 press conference where Mackenzie King (who had himself gone into politics after a stint as deputy minister of labour) announced that Lester Pearson would leave his job as undersecretary of state for external affairs to become the department's minister, King frankly acknowledged that "the civil service should be regarded as the stepping-stone to the ministry." Eight civil servants became Liberal ministers between 1940 and 1957. After the 1963 election, seven more former civil servants joined Cabinet.

†A German ambassador who left Canada in the early sixties confided to his successor: "Whenever you want to report on the reactions to any important policy, all you have to do is wander into the Rideau Club, take a seat at one of the large tables for members without guests, and chat with the senior civil servant inevitably eating next to you. This is the only capital in the world where you can gauge the government's attitude over one lunch."

Clark (who wanted to call it the Fiscal Piscal Club) in the early days of the war to provide senior civil servants with a private place to relax. Dues were set at $150; membership was limited to forty. The club consists of a primitive lodge (which can sleep up to twenty-five) beside a fished-out lake. But it continues to be a status-laden sanctuary where members can meet on summer evenings and weekends to swim and talk. Half a dozen places are still held by ex-civil servants who want to maintain live links with their former associates. They include Harvey Perry, until recently executive director of the Canadian Bankers' Association; David Mansur, a Toronto real estate consultant; and Fraser "Scotty" Bruce, formerly president of Alcan.*

Another factor that allowed the original mandarins to reach their lightning consensus on most issues was the similarity of their educational backgrounds.† Ten Oxford graduates, seven of them Rhodes Scholars, dominated the important civil service positions. High value was placed on scholarship, and nearly half of the group held academic doctorates. Norman Robertson, dean of the External Affairs undersecretaries, took the jackpot, because he was both a Rhodes Scholar and had taught at Harvard.‡

Only one Canadian institution, Queen's University at Kingston, became prominent in the undergraduate training of the Ottawa elite. Heads of the economics department at Queen's in turn assumed the major command posts of the federal bureaucracy, as if by royal succession. The line began in 1908 when Adam Shortt, the first chairman of economics at Queen's, was recruited by Sir Wilfrid Laurier to direct his newly established civil service commission. Shortt's successor in the Queen's economics chair, O.D. Skelton, was in turn enlisted by Mackenzie King in 1925 to follow Sir Joseph Pope as undersecretary of state. During the next sixteen years, Skelton founded and built up Canada's External Affairs

---

*For a recent list of members of the Five Lakes Fishing Club, see Appendix H.
†For a selected list of the Ottawa Mandarins, see Appendix I.
‡The only member of the tribe who had no university degree was Davidson Dunton, who headed the CBC. This condition was ameliorated somewhat by the fact that he went on to become president of Carleton University.

department and as Mackenzie King's closest adviser became the most important civil servant in Ottawa.

Skelton's university job had been taken over by Clifford Clark, a Queen's- and Harvard-trained economist who was appointed deputy minister of finance in 1932. No man left a more profound imprint on the Ottawa bureaucracy. During the two decades Clark spent in the finance post, he served under six ministers and dominated them all. Ken Eaton, one of his assistant deputies, said about him: "He was a king in his office and reluctant to attend other people's meetings. We were his ambassadors, fighting his battles with other departments and proud to do so."

Clark's successor at Queen's, Bill Mackintosh, author of the White Paper, was called in to help Clark during World War II and, not surprisingly, filled in as acting deputy minister of finance in 1945 when Clark, who had worked himself to exhaustion, took a leave of absence. John Deutsch, who succeeded Mackintosh at Queen's, carried on the tradition as chairman of the Economic Council of Canada. This unusual quintet of Queen's economists not only set the tone of Ottawa's mandarinate but recruited most of its members. They scoured the universities for suitable candidates and continually exchanged lists of bright young lecturers and students.*

THIS GROUP OF REMARKABLE BUREAUCRATS HELD SWAY between the mid-thirties and the mid-sixties. They fashioned the policies that kept the Liberals in power for thirty-four of those forty years, but there was little doubt that the most powerful Ottawa presence during most of that time (next to the Prime Minister himself) was Clarence Decatur Howe.

Howe had a curiously different relationship with each of the two P.M.s he served. He was Mackenzie King's appointee, and King was the boss of everybody in Cabinet, including Howe. "King could usually control his willful

---

*The name of a young University of Toronto history lecturer, L.B. Pearson, first appeared on such a list sent to Skelton by Mackintosh in 1928.

colleague," Bruce Hutchison wrote. "Once, returning to Ottawa and finding that Howe had dared to call the Cabinet together in his absence, King lectured him as if he were a schoolboy. Howe accepted the chastisement and sheepishly told his friends that he deserved it." King wouldn't allow smoking during Cabinet. On one occasion when he unexpectedly walked into the privy council chamber, Howe stuffed his lit pipe into a hip pocket and burned himself.

Howe's relations with Louis St. Laurent were very different. The two men ran the government as partners. Early in 1948, when King announced his resignation and the lawyer from Quebec City was being urged by his family not to remain in politics, one of the chief arguments that persuaded him to run for the Liberal succession was Howe's word that *he* would get out of public life unless St. Laurent stayed. St. Laurent felt that he couldn't cope without Howe. Although he was never called St. Laurent's "Lieutenant from English Canada," Howe had far more power than the Quebec lieutenant of any English-speaking prime minister. Under St. Laurent, Howe had become more assertive in Cabinet, grown testy with his colleagues, and tried to extend the Liberal business-government axis into a closed corporation with himself as chief executive officer. Mitchell Sharp, who always managed to find a comfortable berth in both worlds, remarked of this period that "Howe knew every important businessman in Canada. They seemed to make a practice of talking to CD whether they wanted anything from Ottawa or not."

"He had business interests of a very wide kind," Doug Fisher, the CCF history teacher who defeated Howe in 1957, said in a radio interview. "He had a very close relationship with men like Sir James Dunn of Algoma Steel [and] R.S. McLaughlin of General Motors, with the American steel interests through the Hanna company and George Humphrey, who was later Eisenhower's Secretary of the Treasury. He consorted with these people. Now that's kind of a twisty word, 'consort,' but he was very, very close to them and he found this kind of man much more attractive and interesting than his political colleagues. Where did the boundary line come between

NETWORK POWER   389

these private business interests of his and government
business? There isn't really any answer. All we know is
that he moved with, if you want to use a loaded word,
the tycoons of North America, and to a degree he was
responsible for setting up and creating tycoons. The former lieutenant-governor of British Columbia, Frank Ross,
whom he tried to squeeze into Steep Rock Iron Mines
and then helped launch on a major career out in B.C.,
was one example. . . . If I have any criticism, whether
Howe was good or bad, I would like to know the real
story behind these relationships."*

Howe did indeed move in the highest circles of the
North American business universe. He had no hesitation
in placing his favourites in charge of large private corporations. One of his closest friends was Rodgie McLagan,
a bantam autocrat who had served as a gunner in World
War I and spent most of his career working himself into
the presidency of Canadian Vickers in Montreal. "After
the war," McLagan remembered, "CD decided I'd better
get a new job. He told me to call Sir James Dunn. 'He's
looking for a new president for Canada Steamship Lines;
he needs somebody like you because you know a lot
about shipbuilding and he's got all these shipyards. Go
and see him.'

"I called Sir James and of course he wasn't there; he
was supposed to be in London. So I decided, by Jesus,
I'll send him a telegram. Well, he wasn't in London; he
was in Paris at the Ritz. And he telegraphed back and
said, 'Come ahead, would love to see you.'

"So I went to London, saw a play, and the next day

---

*Howe's private investments were held by Penryn Securities and Penryn
Holding Company. They were set up in 1944, with Bill Bennett as secretary from 1944 to 1957. He was associated with Howe for twenty-two
years, first as his chief executive assistant and later as president of Eldorado Mines and Atomic Energy of Canada. Bennett later became president
of the Iron Ore Company of Canada. In 1958, when Douglas Fisher
placed a question on the parliamentary order paper regarding the details
of Penryn's investments, M.J. Coldwell, then leader of the CCF, asked him
to have it withdrawn. He said that it was the worst kind of muckraking,
that he knew and admired Howe, that Howe had phoned him, much
disturbed that his personal affairs should be brought into Parliament.
"Coldwell," Fisher recalls, "was very angry at my refusal to withdraw
the question and I discovered that Howe had compassionately intervened
to keep Coldwell's son from overseas service during the war and had later
got him a job in TCA. I then went to see Gordon Churchill about my
question. He was now the Minister of Trade and Commerce and expressed
great interest, but soon became neutral and unresponsive." Details of
Penryn's holdings have never been disclosed.

flew to Paris. Sir James was holding court in his room at the Ritz, overlooking Place Vendôme. He said, 'Tonight we're going to go and have dinner at Maxim's. I want you to accompany Lady So-and-so and I'm taking Lady Dunn. Be ready at seven o'clock, downstairs.'

"There I was, I didn't have any suit, black tie—I didn't know what to do, so I went down to the concierge and I said, 'What the hell do I do now?'

"She said, 'Go out to such-and-such a place and they'll fit you in fifteen minutes.'

"That night, when we got to Maxim's, there was this waiter, a great big tall fellow with a long white beard, fawning over us. Finally Sir James turns around and asks me, 'Are you a connoisseur of champagne?' Before I could answer, he says, 'I understand from my friend CD that you are. Why don't you order?'

"I didn't know a damn thing about champagne, but I remembered that in the play I saw in London, a fellow had ordered something called Bollinger '27. So I studied the list and said, 'We'll have some Bollinger '27.'

"The man looked at me, went to Dunn, and said, 'Very good vintage, Sir James.' He comes back in fifteen minutes and says, 'I'm terribly sorry, we have no Bollinger '27.'

"Sir James turns around and says, 'Well, Rodgie, what would you suggest now?'

"I decided to play the sevens. I said, 'How about Bollinger '37?' So the guy comes back and serves the champagne.

"We drank more champagne all the next afternoon and I was hired as president of Canada Steamship. Every Christmas after that Dunn would send me a case of Bollinger. He never found out that I didn't know a damned thing about champagne."

HOWE MADE THE NATION'S BUSINESSMEN FEEL LIKE SHARERS IN THE EXPERIENCES OF THEIR TIMES. Twice a year, usually in June and December, a select group of Canadian executives was shown draft forecasts on the state of the Canadian economy *before* they were sent on to government agencies for appropriate policy formulation. These secret, all-day briefings, which included about sixty senior economic advisers from both the private and the public sectors, were held in a large Trade and Commerce conference hall, with time off for lunch in one of the Rideau Club's private dining rooms. Among the participants were Bob Fowler,* president of the Canadian Pulp and Paper Association; Bill Harris, the Toronto investment dealer; Morgan Reid, a vice-president of Simpsons-Sears; Harry Edmison, secretary of Argus Corporation; and Dave Mansur, the ex-mandarin who became a Toronto urban development consultant.†

The outbreak of the Korean War in 1950 gave Howe a chance to reactivate at least part of his wartime coalition by bringing a few of his favourite dollar-a-year men back to Ottawa and reviving his accelerated write-off provisions for industrial expansion. The economy kept booming, even if U.S. investment funds had been cascading into Canada at a net rate of $3 million a day since 1945, and control of the country's most profitable sectors was slipping south of the border.

While the Trade and Commerce minister (who had by now also taken on the Defence Production portfolio) seemed to be at the top of his form, in fact his political position was being undermined—by no one more effectively than himself. In the mid-fifties, Walter Gordon, then regarded as one of the business Establishment's chief spokesmen, became concerned over the rapid build-up of foreign ownership in the country. He wrote an article questioning the open-handed welcoming of U.S. investment by the St. Laurent government and suggested that a royal commission be set up to examine the policy's consequences. Gordon sent a copy of his paper to Ken Taylor, the deputy minister of finance, pointing out that he was sure he could get it published in the journal put out by the Canadian Institute of International Affairs (because he was one of the organization's directors) but that he wanted first to make certain its appearance wouldn't unduly upset anyone in Ottawa.

Taylor phoned right back to report that he'd shown

---

*R.M. Fowler later became president of the C.D. Howe Research Institute.

†For a list of the business representatives who regularly attended these sessions, see Appendix J. The meetings ended in May, 1960, when Firestone, who conducted most of the sessions, left the public service.

the article to Walter Harris (the finance minister) and Louis St. Laurent. They wanted to take over Gordon's idea of setting up a royal commission on Canada's economic prospects (with Gordon as chairman) for inclusion in the budget speech, then only two weeks away. Howe was in Australia at the time, which was probably the only reason the proposal passed Cabinet. (He felt that any investigation of the Canadian economy was equivalent to staging a royal commission into C.D. Howe, and he was damned if he'd have any of that.) Gordon was warned to avoid Howe at all costs. But being Walter Gordon, as soon as he moved to Ottawa he made an appointment to see CD. It was a bristling encounter. The Minister of Trade and Commerce limited his remarks to one sentence: "Don't expect any help from me."

"I only want one guy from your department," Gordon replied, "Jack Davis, your research director."*

"You can have him. He won't be missed."

After the commission hearings had started, Howe saw Gordon at a wedding reception held in Ottawa's Country Club and deliberately snubbed him.†

This turned out to be only a minor preliminary skirmish in the assault on Howe's authority. He had, by now, been exercising his enormous influence on Ottawa and the country for twenty years. A succession of emergencies —dragging Canada out of the depression, waging World War II, heading the drive for reconstruction, re-arming for the Korean War—had allowed him to operate without much, if any, regard for Parliament. He enjoyed politics, up to a point. It was like a sport in which he had a small passing interest—the way you imagine most athletes feel about playing polo. But it didn't have much to do with his real passions, and he paid amazingly little attention to what went on in the House of Commons or in Cabinet that didn't directly concern his department.‡

---

*Davis later became Minister of the Environment in the Trudeau administration.

†The bitterness didn't survive the Liberal defeat. In 1959, Howe noticed Gordon lunching at the Rideau Club, came over, shook his hand, and said: "There are so few of us left, we might as well be friends."

‡Howe's main protégé, Robert Winters, once made a remark unintentionally revealing about both himself and his mentor: "CD really missed a bet by not appreciating how Parliament works. I always found it salutary to take something and have it approved by the Commons—it's the same feeling as having your board and shareholders behind you."

"He'd come into the Rideau Club at noon," Grattan O'Leary recalls, "and he'd sit at the members' [open] table and talk with complete candour about what was going on in Cabinet. He had a sort of relish for crises. Like a strong man being asked to lift a weight, he'd flex the muscles of his personality and bull ahead."

By this time the Liberal government had grown arrogant in office, with not a single minister still in Cabinet who had been through the chastening experience of time put in on the Opposition benches. Hugh MacLennan, the dean of Canadian novelists, wrote in *Maclean's:* "They treat the national mind much as the officials of a trust company treat the mind of a rich widow whose funds they have been hired to manage. To keep the widow from asking too many questions is always wise. Treat her with courtesy, of course. Talk to her with an occasional sally of ponderous avuncular humor, ply her with accurate reports couched in a jargon she cannot possibly understand, but whatever you do, don't let her get too inquisitive about what goes on behind the doors of the company." Howe behaved in this period as if he were determined to provide suitable quotes for his enemies.*

The Conservatives, under George Drew's leadership, first managed to demonstrate the full measure of Howe's contempt for Parliament to the country at large during the Defence Production Act debates in the summer of 1955. The government had moved an innocent-sounding motion, entitled "An Act to Amend the Defence Production Act," which included the clause: "Section 41 of the said Act is repealed." Section 41 happened to be the provision that stated that the entire act, passed during the Korean War, was to expire on July 31, 1956. In other words, Howe was demanding that the extraordinary powers he had wielded during a national emergency

---

*On May 21, 1951, during a House debate on trade agreements, Howard Green, the Vancouver Conservative, expressed concern over government action, indicating that it was trying to escape previous commitments. "Who would stop us?" Howe replied. "Don't take yourself too seriously. If we wanted to get away wth it—who would stop us?" During a question on April 21, 1953, concerning an Order-in-Council banning all Canadian shipping to North Korea and Chinese ports, Howe answered Opposition criticism by saying: "If we have overstepped our powers, I make no apology for having done so." During one debate on defence production estimates, Howe brushed off an opposition M.P.'s complaint with the comment: "If the services say they need a gold-plated piano, it's our duty to buy it."

should become a permanent part of the law. Under the provisions of the act, the Minister of Defence Production had, among other things, the right to compel anyone owning facilities suitable to defence work to accept defence contracts "on terms and conditions which the Minister deems to be fair and reasonable." It also gave the minister the right to put a controller into a business to direct all its operations, if in his judgement it wasn't performing efficiently enough. The controversial bill was brought up for second reading on June 7, and the fifty-one Conservatives in the Commons talked it to a standstill until July 11. J.M. Macdonnell, who led the Toronto onslaught, declared that it represented "an affront to a free parliament."

Howe had turned down a suggestion that the extraordinary power he was demanding be limited to a three-year term, declaring that this "would mean coming back to Parliament in three years, and I've more to do than spend my time amusing Parliament." This was how Grattan O'Leary later recalled the succession of events that led to the final Defence Production Act compromise: "I was having lunch at the Rideau Club when George Drew told me that an astounding thing had happened. St. Laurent had called him and said, 'George, we have to settle this thing. I'll write a memo to you listing my concessions, and then I'm going home for the weekend to St. Patrice. I'll call you at Stornoway on Monday at noon, and we'll fix it up.' Drew said that he wanted me to be there when the P.M. called but that he wouldn't tell his caucus, because they wouldn't believe him. I remember that CD was away in Sept-Iles on a fishing trip. I sat beside Drew on the Monday, and when he asked for one more concession, St. Laurent accepted it without changing a comma. For me, that telephone call marked the end of the Liberals' hold on power."

The pipeline debate that followed has been documented elsewhere.* Although Walter Harris and Jack Pickersgill had planned the government's ruinous tactics, it was C.D. Howe who got most of the blame. Even in

---

*The most complete description is in *PipeLine*, by William Kilbourn (Toronto: Clarke, Irwin, 1970).

retrospect, it is difficult to explain the Liberals' behaviour. Howe obviously saw the pipeline only in terms of a long steel conduit to carry natural gas. His attitude was best summed up in an unusually emotional interjection during the pipeline debate. "This may be the last big project I will be called upon to undertake," he said. "I want to assure the members that it is not my purpose to close my years by undertaking a project that will stand to my discredit. . . . I believe this pipeline will make my children proud that their father had a hand in it."

Why the Liberal cabinet went meekly along with Howe in degrading Parliament is even less easy to explain. Howe threatened to resign if the bill were not pushed through the House in the required time and St. Laurent made it clear that if he couldn't keep his cabinet together, he also would leave. That would have left the party leaderless for the general election, due in 1957.

On election night, informed he'd just been turned out by Douglas Fisher, Howe delivered himself of the opinion that the country was being swept by some strange disease and that *he* was going to bed. CD was defeated, but he was not destroyed. Always the realist, he got angry only once, when an underling at Trade and Commerce came pussyfooting into his office to say how sorry he was that Mr. Howe had to retire from politics. "Retire! Hell!" Howe shouted. "I was beat!"

He moved to Montreal, became chairman of Ogilvie Flour Mills, took up a dozen directorships,* and on New Year's Eve of 1960, fifteen days short of his seventy-fifth birthday, he died.

The business Establishment had taken its formal farewell of Howe during a grand banquet staged a couple of years earlier at the Mount Royal Club in Montreal. Howe's friend Grattan O'Leary had been asked to propose a toast, and the two men sat there at the head table, looking out over the assembled company.

"There's a lot of money out there, CD," O'Leary remarked.

---

*Besides Ogilvie, Howe's directorships included Aluminium Ltd., Bank of Montreal, National Trust, Dominion Tar and Chemical, Price Brothers, Crown Life Insurance, Atlas Steels, Rio Tinto Mining, Hollinger Consolidated, Ocean Cement, and the Chemical Corn Exchange Bank in the U.S.

"Grattan, I bet you I can put a figure on just how much," Howe replied, surveying the room. "Close to two billion dollars, I'd guess, give or take a million." Then CD reflected for a moment and said: "They're all great guys and they're all rich. But nobody's giving *them* a dinner."

CHAPTER ELEVEN

The Ties That Bind

No influence is more cohesive, no
bond more lasting,
than the time spent at the private
schools and other institutions that instill
Establishment values. Those early impressions,
absorbed through willing pores, set
lifetime priorities, prejudices,
presumptions, and above all, personal
partnerships.

Common patterns of forbearance and indulgence, shared attitudes and manners, a cultivated shabbiness of dress and decor, the mid-Atlantic accent (a nasal honk that tends to lift vowels and slur final consonants)—these and other subtleties identify the core group of the Canadian Establishment to one another. Automatic accreditation is gained through elusive signals that bespeak shared experience: those musty portraits in the hall at grandfather's Westmount mansion; the nickname of that fusty Latin teacher at Upper Canada who caned boys for conjugating the verb "to be" improperly; a summer together once at St. Andrews-by-the-Sea; the way the garden at the country place glowed that season of Dierdre's coming-out party; a friend in common who retired in disgust to Bermuda after Edgar Benson came out with his White Paper.

Perhaps because it comes early, when personalities are still malleable, no influence is more cohesive, no bond more lasting, than the time spent at the private schools and other institutions that instill Establishment values. Those early impressions, absorbed through willing pores, set lifetime priorities, prejudices, presumptions, and above all, personal partnerships. At a subconscious level, they perpetuate the idea that privilege exists and that it should be exercised; that rebellion, however fleetingly attractive, is ultimately self-defeating. One meets the right people. The latticework of connections begins to form, stretching all the way to the Order of Canada (the Canadian equivalent of the Queen's Honours List), honorary degrees, and other rewards that may eventually follow.

Canada's eighty-odd private schools* have a total enrolment of approximately twenty thousand boys and girls, only a small portion of whom are the Establishment's children. But according to the surveys of both John Porter and Wallace Clement, Old Boys and Old Girls of the private schools form a disproportionate number of the various groupings within the Canadian Establishment.†

Especially for the boys who find their circumscribed version of adult existence fairly dull, school days are often the emotional high point of their lives, a time to which they never cease looking back with nostalgia. Intense friendships are formed; rugged individualism gains its expression on the playing fields. It is an ordered world of rustling rhododendron leaves, common rooms with leather armchairs, posture classes, gowned masters, bullying prefects, cold showers, and milk doctored with saltpetre—exclusive, parched, remote, restricted. Not a *Viva Zapata* moustache in sight. Manners are taught; deportment is never taken for granted.

The aim of the schools is something their headmasters define as "development of character," which by implication at least includes collective and individual dedication to society's existing values and the desirability of perpetuating them by transmitting the traditions of its upper classes. "The schools all have old boys' associations," says Tom Hockin, headmaster of St. Andrew's College. "They're always trying to remind the boys how lucky they are to be at whatever school they're at, that they're part of a great tradition, in the path of hundreds of eminent old boys in whose footsteps they can follow. The phrase 'unlike the public schools' is never used, but the idea is implanted that the School has a glorious history. They

---

*A listing of most of these institutions, with locations, names of principals, enrolments, and fee schedules, appears in Appendix K.

†After John Porter's *The Vertical Mosaic* detailed the inordinate number of Upper Canada College graduates who had become comfortably ensconced in the board rooms of the nation, the very next UCC fund-raising brochure quoted his words verbatim with both pride and emphasis as the best reason yet for graduates to give the college their financial support.

have people on committees busy keeping the name glorious, raising money, having meetings, putting on dinners—and that doesn't go on at York Mills Collegiate, or whatever."

Although Canada's private schools retain many customs of the British public school system on which they are modelled, they have successfully escaped its tendency for what one critic describes as "perpetuating a race of languid duchesses and intrepid deerstalkers."*

There was a time when no headmaster of a Canadian private school was acceptable unless he'd studied at Oxford or Cambridge. Anglophilia permeated the institutions, with new boys having to serve as "fags" to seniors (the equivalent of being a batman in the army), canings inflicted for the slightest offence, and boys expressing their creativity through pranks dear to the Tom Brown tradition. The main legacy of the British influence is the prefect system. A headmaster of Ridley College at St. Catharines, Ontario, once described the advantages of becoming a prefect as "promoting a dawning understanding of the need for order in the community, of the burdens of leadership, and the place of proud humility in a man's life."† At Upper Canada, the head prefects of each of the college's eight houses‡ form a board of stewards, which meets the headmaster once a

---

*By shifting some emphasis from tradition to academic achievement, Canada's private schools have in recent years substantially improved their scholastic standings. The Canadian Headmasters' Association claims that more than 90 per cent of their matriculants receive university entrance qualifications, compared with 50 to 75 per cent of candidates from provincial high schools.

†The eight boys who achieved prefect status at Ottawa's Ashbury College in 1931–32, for example, were Robert Stanfield, later national leader of the Conservative party; John David Southam, who became secretary to Vincent Massey and executive vice-president of Southam Press in Montreal; Roger Rowley, who served as a major-general in the Canadian Army; Robert Coristine, a lieutenant-colonel in the Royal Canadian Artillery who later became an executive of Imperial Tobacco; Fraser Heubach, later executive vice-president of a large U.S. hotel chain; Norman Gillies, an Inco executive and consulting geologist; David Fauquier, who rode for the Canadian equestrian team and was general manager of a perfume factory; and John Magor, who became publisher of two B.C. newspapers.

‡Like most other private schools, UCC divides its pupils into "houses," only two of which (Seaton's and Wedd's) are actual buildings, where the boarders live. Each house, consisting of about sixty boys, has a senior and a junior housemaster and six prefects. The house becomes a kind of substitute family. It provides a group of boys with whom each pupil co-operates in games and from whom he will draw many of his friends. A boy remains in the same house during his entire school career. The housemaster provides the permanent liaison officer parents can approach on minor problems and to whom the boy can turn for advice or direction.

week "to discuss the life, the activities, and the discipline of the school."

One of the great Canadian private school pranks took place in 1964 when Elizabeth Taylor and Richard Burton were performing (on and off stage) in an O'Keefe Centre version of *Hamlet*. Mark Phillips, the eighteen-year-old grandson of Eric Phillips, a senior partner in Argus Corp., dressed up in what his mother, Nancy, described as "something like a cross between the dress regalia of the Persian Light Horse Infantry and the kitchen fatigue overalls of the Bolivian Heavy Anti-Aircraft Artillery." Young Phillips drove his motorcycle up Avenue Road to the school grounds, where six of his Upper Canada College chums, dressed in tuxedos, had crowded into a rented Cadillac. Phillips then escorted the limousine to the entrance of the O'Keefe, where there was a large crowd waiting to catch a glimpse of Elizabeth Taylor. Some sixty Upper Canada boys had been recruited to surge forward as the Cadillac slid to a ceremonious stop and Mark Phillips opened the door for the most distinguished of its young occupants. "My name is Monk Marr!" announced the UCC senior. "I am the great New York satirist. Make way, I beg of you. . . ." The instant crowd of college boys thronged around him, notebooks poised, begging for his autograph. Puzzled reporters, photographers, and onlookers parted ranks obsequiously for the mysterious Monk Marr and finally broke into applause as he and his cohorts made their way toward the cheapest seats in the house. Mark Phillips, who had planned the whole silly caper, rode his motorcycle home looking, according to McKenzie Porter, a *Telegram* columnist, "like a despatch rider for the Ethiopian Sanitary Corps, but feeling satisfied with the part he had played in the fooling of a very foolish mob. He cared not a whit for the fact that he had missed the official opening of *Hamlet*. He had seen the preview the night before and he looked upon the show as bloody awful."

Discipline is an essential ingredient of private school tutelage, much of it taking the form of rigid timetables and narrow codes of conduct designed to test the will of students instead of following the simpler rules of common sense.* The schools vehemently oppose the freedoms they feel have been advocated for secondary education by such studies as Ontario's Hall-Dennis Report. "It is bad education," Patrick Johnson, a former principal of Upper Canada, maintained, "to let boys and girls think they are not going to have to face the consequences of wrongdoing. Surely it is no kindness to let loafers continue loafing, cheats continue cheating, thieves get away with theft, and vandals with vandalism. What an appalling legacy we leave for the future if we do not drive home the lessons of good citizenship before these young people find themselves in jail. Some modern educational theorists seem to have replaced the Ten Commandments with a single commandment, 'Thou shalt not say, "Thou shalt not."'"

During his decade (1965–74) as principal of UCC, Patrick Johnson, an Oxford graduate and former captain in the 9th Gurkha Rifles, emerged as the most articulate defender of the private school ideal in Canada. "Many educational theorists," he said, "believe that comprehensive education is a panacea because all students will then have equal opportunity. Unfortunately, the egalitarianism they seek is the equal opportunity to be mediocre. If equality is what we are after, then I would be happier with the proposition that equality means equal opportunity to develop unequally." He also dared to speak out on behalf of the private schools' much-cherished conviction that competition is good for young souls, because it encourages excellence. "There *is* an important place for healthy competition in our schools," Johnson insisted. "It recognizes the realities of life and certainly, in my experience, ambitious, normal, well-adjusted boys and girls respond to it, without forgetting that co-operation also must have a place in their lives. Admittedly some competition is negative or unhealthy—for example, the competition to see which boy can grow the longest hair or wear the dirtiest jeans; the competition to see which student can push the most drugs in the locker room, the competi-

---

*"I am prepared to give the boys more liberties," Michael McCrum, headmaster of Eton, once declared, "providing they do not take them."

tion to see which school can give its students the most popular and the least challenging program, the competition to win games at all costs without regard to sportsmanship—and so on. But I see nothing wrong, and much that is right, in competing to be excellent at the level of excellence at which an individual student can perform. I see nothing wrong, and much that is right, in awarding scholarships for academic merit, a trophy to the boy showing the best team spirit, and merit pay to the teachers who contribute the most."

The school over which Johnson presided was founded in 1829 by Sir John Colborne (later Lord Seaton) when he was lieutenant-governor of Upper Canada. The college's military traditions go back to the charge of the Light Brigade during the Crimean War* and the Fenian Raids of 1866, when a company of lightly armed boys from the school provided Toronto's only military garrison. During World War II, 74 per cent of the 1,580 UCC Old Boys who enlisted won commissions; twenty-six of them eventually achieved the rank of brigadier or higher.

Spread over a forty-acre site athwart Avenue Road in Toronto's fashionable Forest Hill district, Upper Canada College is this country's most influential private school —the Eton or Groton of Canada. "If the role of UCC during the past and present could be reduced to four descriptive words," Viscount Alexander told a college prize-day audience in 1947 when he was governor general, "those words would be 'a school for leaders.' "† The Duke of Edinburgh is UCC's "school visitor" or patron. Harold Roberts, an Old Boy whose permanent avocation has been placing some two thousand UCC graduates in various positions of corporate influence, asserts that "the *Financial Post Directory of Directors* reads like

---

*Lieutenant Alexander Robert Dunn, a UCC Old Boy, was one of its survivors and became the first Canadian to win the Victoria Cross, receiving the VC from Queen Victoria herself. His sword and medals now hang in the college's entrance hall. Another Old Boy, Major Churchill Cockburn, won a VC during the South African War.

†Stephen Leacock, who was both a student and a master at UCC, once observed that in later life he was invariably encountering someone he'd caned at the college. "I have licked," he wrote, "two generals of the Canadian army, three cabinet ministers, and more colonels and majors than I care to count."

a roll call of our Old Boys."* About a third of Canada's most influential company directors are private school graduates, half of them from Upper Canada College.

To teach its pupils the value of money, UCC does not allow any boy, no matter how affluent his family, to bring cars to school and advises the parents of boarders to keep them on a strict five-dollar-a-week allowance. Supervised contact with girls is limited to four chaperoned dances a year. The college's football, hockey, rugger, and cricket teams are encouraged in their efforts by the most bloodthirsty school yell in their league:

Nigger, nigger hoe potater,

Half past alligator,

Ram, ram bulligator,

Chippewana duck.

College! College! Rush 'er UP!

Following Upper Canada's clear lead, the Ontario private schools most favoured by the Canadian Establishment are Trinity College School at Port Hope, St. Andrew's College at Aurora,† Ridley College at St. Catharines,‡ Lakefield College School in Lakefield, and Hillfield in Hamilton. Selwyn House, Lower Canada College, and Bishop's College School in Lennoxville are the boys' schools preferred by Quebec's English-speaking Establishment. In B.C., it's St. George's in Vancouver and Shawnigan Lake on Vancouver Island,|| while the Manitoba Es-

---

*Even some of the boys who fail at Upper Canada College seem to do well. Page Wadsworth's marks at the college couldn't get him past the junior matriculation stage. He hid his report from his father and became a banker instead. In 1973, he succeeded Neil McKinnon as chairman and chief executive officer of the Canadian Imperial Bank of Commerce.

†St. Andrew's has some kind of special relationship with the political elite of Newfoundland, its graduates having included Premier Frank Moores, Ed Roberts, the leader of the Liberal opposition, and two of the Crosbie brothers.

‡Ridley raised $3,500,000 during six months in 1973 as a result of a low-key campaign to increase its capital resources, run by Bud Willmot.

||Although it belongs to the world rather than to British Columbia, the Lester B. Pearson College of the Pacific near Victoria has gathered, under the direction of John Nichol, the former senator who is chairman of its board of governors, the most impressive committee of Establishment sponsors of any Canadian educational institution. They include Bruce

tablishment prefers St. John's Ravenscourt. Probably the most prestigious girls' school in the country is Bishop Strachan in Toronto. "I send my daughters to BSS," one Old Girl told a reporter from the *Canadian Magazine*, "because I don't want them to marry a plumber. Not because he *plumbs,* you understand, but because his background, upbringing, ideals for the present and future would be too different from theirs. He would simply have nothing in common with my girls." Situated on seven valuable acres near UCC, it is the oldest private school for girls in the country, producing the kind of ladies who can turn a curtsy into an effortless bob of good breeding.*

Several private schools have begun to recognize the advantages of co-educational classes, but the finishing schools that many Establishment boys and girls want to attend are in Switzerland. The best is Neuchâtel Junior College on Lac de Neuchâtel, which was founded in 1956 by Leonard Wilde, an Englishman who had been a master at Shawnigan Lake School. It has had an enviable academic rating and offers classes at the Ontario Grade 13 level. Another is the Canadian Junior College at Lausanne, on the north shore of Lake Geneva. The college teaches the equivalent of the final two grades in Ontario high schools (at an annual fee of $4,500). Classes

---

Hutchison, the editorial director of the *Vancouver Sun;* James W. Burns, president, Great-West Life Assurance Co., Winnipeg; Paul Desmarais, chairman, Power Corporation of Canada, Montreal; from Toronto, James Coutts, president, Canada Consulting Group, Rt. Hon. Roland Michener, Mrs. George Ignatieff, Trinity College, Doris Anderson, editor, *Chatelaine,* George Elliott, vice-president, MacLaren Advertising, John W. Holmes, research director, Canadian Institute of International Affairs, William P. Wilder, chairman, Canadian Arctic Gas Pipeline, William Harris, financier, John Robarts, former premier of Ontario, John Aird, lawyer and corporate director, and Kenneth Rotenberg, president, Y & R Properties; from Ottawa, Charles Ritchie, Muriel Fergusson, former Speaker of the Senate, Dr. Sylvia Ostry, deputy minister of Consumer and Corporate Affairs, Gordon Fairweather, M.P., Tony Abbott, M.P., Louis Rasminsky, retired governor, Bank of Canada, and Escott Reid, former Canadian high commissioner to India. Outside Canada there are Saul Rae, Canadian ambassador to the UN, Maurice F. Strong, executive director, UN Environment Program, Geneva, Richard O'Hagan, minister-counsellor, Canadian Embassy, Washington, and Richard G. Reid, executive vice-president, Esso Europe Inc., London. Non-Canadian governors are economist Barbara Ward (Lady Jackson), London, and James Reston, vice-president of the *New York Times.* One of the contributors is the Winspear Foundation, headed by the Edmonton industrialist and accountant Francis Winspear.

*In the summer, Establishment kids go to camp. The most popular are Taylor Statten's Camp Ahmek for boys and Camp Wapomeo for girls in Algonquin Park. Pierre Elliott Trudeau spent the summers of 1937 and 1938 at Ahmek perfecting his English and canoe-paddling.

are conducted like university seminars with enrolment limited to a maximum of fourteen; students spend their weekends travelling in Europe.*

Most of Canada's private schools had waiting lists throughout 1975, despite the recession. Graduates (operating genuine Old Boys' networks) seem to have little trouble raising money for college capital drives. In 1958, when the main buildings at Upper Canada College were condemned as structurally unsafe, the board of governors easily collected $2,930,000 to replace them.†

WHILE PRIVATE SCHOOLS PROVIDE BOTH A UNIFYING INFLUENCE AND A TRAINING GROUND for Canada's Establishment, at least two institutions of higher learning can bestow on their graduates the imprimatur they need to move into contention for Establishment consideration. The more traditional route is through a Rhodes Scholarship at Oxford University. The dozen university graduates chosen for the honour every year receive an education that fits many of them to be professional amateurs: men who have a judicial cast of mind that they can apply to all problems without getting too weighed down by technical details. "The importance of Oxford," Arnold Heeney, the Rhodes Scholar who became chairman of the International Joint Commission, once said, "is that it puts public service in the forefront as a possible career. You're imbued with the tradition that the service of the state is a desirable profession, particularly in Treasury or External."‡

Most Rhodes Scholars have, in fact, entered govern-

---

*The Canadian Junior College recently opened a branch on the island of Carriacou, in the Grenadines. Enrolment is limited to forty; fees are $3,650 a year.

†The Upper Canada College Foundation has a market portfolio worth about $1.5 million. Stocks held include Alcan, Domtar, Du Pont of Canada, Great Lakes Paper, Imperial Oil, Massey-Ferguson, Noranda, Southam Press, and Thomson Newspapers.

‡Told of the presence, at the signing of the Columbia River Treaty in Washington in 1961, of Arnold Heeney, then Canadian ambassador, and two of the Canadian negotiators, Davie Fulton, minister of justice, and A.E. Ritchie, assistant undersecretary for external affairs, General A.G.L. McNaughton snorted: "Three Rhodes Scholars—three blind mice." McNaughton was then chairman of the IJC; he was replaced the following year by Heeney.

ment service, returned to teach at universities, or gone into law. Only a few are active in business.* A more modern and increasingly significant path to attention within the Canadian business community is through the Harvard University Graduate School of Business Administration.†

THE HARVARD BUSINESS SCHOOL IS THE WEST POINT OF AMERICAN CAPITALISM. Just as squires were once coached toward knighthood, Harvard's eight hundred carefully selected yearly recruits (aout 7 per cent of them Canadians) are groomed for a career of bossing other people. Unlike Oxford, where professors wander around the mouldy elegance of historic buildings in gowned authority, HBS has classrooms with the impersonal air of ships' engine rooms, and the standard teaching uniform is a white shirt with rolled-up sleeves. Rhodes Scholars study possibilities and problems; the guys at Harvard are interested only in applying solutions. "Around the Business School," wrote a recent graduate, "it's not how you play, it's whether you win the goddamn game."

It is more than symbolic that the business school is separated from the main Harvard campus by the Charles River. On the main campus, you see what you always thought of as Harvard types—gentle boys with long scarves and thoughtful, committed expressions; serious-looking girls with manes of jittery hair, all looking, despite their deliberately casual clothes, very aristocratic, very much in command of themselves. Even the names of HBS's neo-Georgian buildings—Mellon Hall, Baker Library, Morgan Hall, Kresge Hall, Dillon Hall, Burden Hall, Chase Hall—reflect a different ethic. Few students

---

*They are L.C. Bonnycastle, vice-chairman of Canadian Corporate Management Co.; Henry Borden, a director of Brascan Ltd.; Michael Brown, president of Brown, Farris & Jefferson Ltd., Vancouver, and his father, W. Thomas Brown, president of Odlum Brown & T.B. Read Ltd.; E.R.E. Carter, president, Hambro Canada Ltd.; N.E. Currie, vice-president and economic adviser to the Bank of Montreal; and James Sinclair, chairman, Lafarge Canada Ltd.

†The distinction of becoming the first Canadian to turn down a Rhodes Scholarship in favour of attending the Harvard Business School belongs to Gary Bowell, who rose to become president of Rayonier Canada Ltd. and later head of Weldwood of Canada Ltd., a subsidiary of Champion International Corp. and this country's largest producer of plywood.

'wear beards; everyone seems to be carrying a briefcase 'and a pocket calculator; there's the odd Mercedes in the parking lot.* In the Baker Library, which forms the core 'of the business school, students lounge around reading the *Wall Street Journal,* the *Economic Times of Bombay,* the *Australian Financial Review, Business Week,* and the *Financial Post.* The library itself includes such titles as *Aesop's Fables in the Executive Suite,* by John S. Morgan ("Shows how the lessons taught in *Aesop's Fables* can be put into practice in your daily, professional life").

At least four thousand university graduates from every part of the world contend for the eight hundred places in each class. The HBS admissions board evaluates their "demonstrated leadership qualities, managerial competence, academic background, personal career goals" and scores on a special test. But the key document is a seventeen-page self-evaluation form designed to give the 'school's administrators clues to the motives and ideology of each applicant. "You wouldn't even think of going to the Harvard Business School, you wouldn't even want to apply, unless you were a tough, fairly intelligent, action-oriented person," says Professor Donald Thain, an HBS graduate and professor of business administration at the University of Western Ontario.† "It's intelligence and track record that really count. If a guy's fairly bright, has been on a university football team and can make the leather crack, knows what competition's all about, and isn't interested in mental masturbation, then he'll probably get in."

HBS's two-year courses go under such nebulous titles as Control, Human Behavior in Organizations, and En-

---

*Even the resident graffiti artists have a certain uninspired technocratic flavour to their humour. In one washroom stall on the third floor of the Baker Library, way down in the left-hand corner, someone has lettered in neat handwriting: "You are now shitting at an angle of 45 degrees."

†Western models itself on Harvard more than any other graduate business school in Canada. Its most important program has been to develop a comprehensive library of Canadian case histories (based on the Harvard model), including a study of business problems ranging from Albert's Barber Shop in London, Ontario (which didn't have enough daytime customers and was advised to institute reduced prices for slack-hours trade), to the details of the negotiations that led to the nationalization of an Alcan subsidiary by the government of Guyana in 1971. One of the few Harvard cases that mentions Canada is called the Beleaguered Brewery. It deals with a Canadian subsidiary's response to Walter Gordon's 1963 budgetary measures, entirely from the U.S. corporation's point of view.

vironmental Analysis for Management. But the core of each class is not so much its subject matter as the teaching method. There are no lectures and few textbooks, only the case system, a process pioneered at Harvard in 1911. The typical "case" is a fifty-page mimeographed bundle of lumpy prose that traces the evolution of a company's affairs up to a crucial decision point. Students must attempt to devise valid courses of action for top management, even if they haven't been given enough facts or working time. "We were all deliberately given more work than we could do, because in a real-life situation you're always running out of time to study a question," says Laurent Picard, the former head of the CBC and new president of Marine Industries Limited, who has a doctorate from the Harvard Business School. "You're forced to make a choice in your priorities all the time. The worst thing you can do is act uncertain and say you need more information." The ultimate testing ground for each student is when he's called upon to discuss a case in class. "The way you get good grades," says Professor Thain, "is by being very rough. You get your hand up and you say, 'Now, the second last guy who spoke, he made a couple of interesting points, but he really doesn't understand what the case was all about. He tried, but he really didn't get it. The previous speaker, over there,' then you wait till all the chairs have swivelled, everybody's looking the guy right in the eye, and you go on, 'his problem is that of the four major factors, he only saw one. Now, let me lay this out for you. . . .' You have to score points fast because you know the next guy who speaks is going to dump on you, or else one of the two guys you've just maligned is going to say, 'Wait a minute, you son of a bitch, your problem is you never listen. If you'd only unblock your bloody ears you'd understand what my point was. . . .' "

The high-pressure seventy-four weeks, the ruthless competition for grades* are part of a deliberately fostered atmosphere to test the strong and reject the introspec-

---

*Harvard's intricate marking system provides minute incentives for students. In their middle range, for example, marks are High Pass Plus; High Pass; High Pass Minus; Pass Plus; Pass; Pass Minus; Low Pass Plus; Low Pass; and Low Pass Minus.

tive.* "You realize they haven't got faith in anything except pressure, fear and terror," Peter Cohen, a Harvard MBA, wrote in a recent memoir.† "Students, professors, even the secretaries—it was as if everybody were fighting to get out of some corner, and they were not worried too much about habits of thinking or questioning anything, but content to accept that the maximization of long-range profit is why God hath created the earth. . . . So you learn not to give a shit if the people you climb over are weak or sick or small or blind. You understand that everybody is your enemy, and you learn to fear and hate people, to live in crowded isolation for the rest of your days."

Most learn to cope with this Darwinian environment; some quietly depart, others crack up. The school employs two full-time psychiatrists; suicide attempts average 3 per cent a year. "The problem," says Laurent Picard, "is that nearly everybody who arrives was first in his class somewhere and now somebody's got to be last and somebody's got to be in the middle. This creates tremendous pressures. When I was there, about 20 per cent of the students sought psychiatric help, even though some of them later led their class."

"What the Harvard Business School did for me," recalls Bill Wilder, later the head of Wood Gundy and chairman of Canadian Arctic Gas Pipeline, "was to point up that if you're going to be a success in business you've got to be able to reach decisions even when you don't have all the facts. I find that Canadian executives are frightened by the very thought of making decisions. Harvard was also a great eye-opener for me in terms of the fact that I was exposed to people who worked much harder than I thought possible. McGill was like a cocktail circuit compared to Harvard. We really rolled up our sleeves and went to work. I found that a very humbling experience and I came out of there with a sense of humility, a sense of self-confidence, and a sense of discipline."

The greatest single influence on Wilder and most of the

---

*Everything at the Harvard school is organized, even the marijuana trade, with rigid inspections of merchandise, low overhead, and dealer's choice.
†Peter Cohen, *The Gospel According to the Harvard Business School* (New York: Doubleday, 1973).

HBS alumni who went through the school during the late forties and the fifties was Professor Georges Doriot, who taught industrial management. Doriot, a brigadier-general in the U.S. Army from 1941 to 1947, arrived in the United States from France in 1921 and joined the school in 1926. He used to pace up and down his classroom, challenging conventional wisdom in all its forms ("Why do boxcars have to be box-shaped?") and dispensing some unusual advice ("When you go to bed at night, look in the mirror and say to yourself: 'What have I done today; am I really any better than I was this morning—how can I spend the day more productively?' "). He also suggested that Americans don't work hard enough and that students should read *New York Times* obituaries to see who had died so they could tell where to apply for executive openings.

HARVARD BUSINESS SCHOOL GRADS ARE UNCTUOUSLY COURTED BY NORTH AMERICAN INDUSTRY. In 1973, for instance, 322 companies sent their personnel managers to woo the 777 graduates; they held 6,994 interviews. One particularly hot group, the class of '49, now has a quarter of its graduates ensconced in the presidential suites of large corporations; 16 per cent are millionaires.*

Approximately a thousand Harvard Business School graduates, half of them MBAS, function in various executive and managerial capacities in Canada.† The pattern

---

*The most interesting Canadian in the group was C. Peter McColough, from Halifax. He went to HBS after graduating from the Dalhousie Law School. After he had a brief stint as vice-president, sales, with the Lehigh Coal & Navigation Co. in Philadelphia, a fellow Harvard Business School grad put him in touch with Joseph Wilson, head of the Haloid Company in Rochester. On his first visit, McColough found a rundown plant whose sales manager came to work carrying a black lunch box. But when Wilson showed him a new dry-copying process that Haloid had developed, McColough took a five-thousand-dollar pay cut and joined the company as assistant to the vice-president in charge of sales. By 1966, he had become president of the company, which in the interval had changed its name to the Xerox Corporation.

†Analysis of the Canadian section of the *Harvard Business School Directory of Former Students, 1973,* shows about five hundred MBAS on the job in Canada, about 215 holders of its Advanced Management Program Certificate, and about seventy holders of its Program for Management Development Certificate; most of the twenty-five-odd Doctors of Business Administration are shown in academic positions, notably at the University of Western Ontario's School of Business Administration and York University's Faculty of Administrative Studies. For a selected list of Harvard MBAS, DBAS, and holders of the AMP Certificate, with their current positions in Canadian business, see Appendix L.

followed is that the Harvard grad who becomes head of his company then goes after others. Alcan Aluminium provides a classic example of the Harvard network in operation, starting in 1939 when Nathanael Davis, now Alcan's chairman and chief executive officer, joined the company. Davis graduated from Harvard in 1938, the year that Dana Bartholomew (Harvard Business School, 1928–29) joined the organization; Bartholomew served as its chief financial officer from 1949 to 1970, when he was succeeded by John H. Hale (Harvard Business School, 1948–49). In the 1972 reorganization of Alcan's top management, it was Paul Leman (Harvard Business School, 1937–38) who became president when Davis moved up to the new position of chairman and chief executive officer. In 1975 Leman was succeeded in the presidency of the principal operating subsidiary by David Culver (Harvard MBA, 1949). Apart from all this, Alcan has about a dozen Harvard Business School MBAS and certificate holders in executive positions.

The HBS network is in place in several other major Canadian organizations. Consolidated-Bathurst, whose president, Bill Turner, came out of the school (with High Distinction) in 1953, has three MBAS and three Advanced Management Program Certificate holders in important jobs. At Wood Gundy there are eight MBAS and an AMP Certificate holder. Bill Wilder, who got his Harvard MBA in 1950, became president of Wood Gundy in 1967 but left in 1972 to be chairman of Canadian Arctic Gas Pipeline. (Also at Canadian Arctic Gas Pipeline, as vice-president, finance, is John Yarnell, a graduate of Consolidated-Bathurst's Harvard MBA roster.) The Steel Company of Canada, whose president, Peter Gordon, attended an HBS Advanced Management Program in 1966, has ten other AMPs and two MBAS in executive and managerial positions. Imperial Oil lists five MBAS and four AMPS among its executives. MacMillan Bloedel in Vancouver has four MBAS, a couple of AMPS, and a group vice-president, Bruce Howe, who got a Program for Management Development Certificate in 1970. Prentice Bloedel, a former vice-chairman who retired from the board in 1972, attended HBS in 1924–25. Two of Canada's Big Five chartered banks have Harvard MBAS as presidents, William Mulholland at the Bank of Montreal and Dick Thomson at the Toronto-Dominion. With Thomson at the TD are six AMPs and another MBA.

There are still many more Rhodes Scholars than Harvard MBAs in the public service, but this is being offset, in part at least, by cabinet wives and consultants.* At the provincial level, HBS's most distinguished alumnus is Peter Lougheed, the Premier of Alberta. His next-door neighbour, Allan Blakeney of Saskatchewan, is a Rhodes Scholar.

The Harvard Business School's chief booster in Canada is Harry Jackman (MBA, 1926), president of Dominion and Anglo Investment Corporation, who took part in establishing the Mackenzie King Chair of Canadian Studies at Harvard University and in 1954 organized the Harvard University Associates in Canada Inc.† At their monthly meetings of Harvard Business School clubs in Toronto, Montreal, and Vancouver, graduates keep close tabs on each other's careers.

"The Harvard Business School does have an Old Boys' network and it's very strong," says Bill Dimma, a former executive vice-president at Union Carbide Canada who went back to the school for a doctorate and is now dean of administrative studies at York University. "Most of the people who go to the Harvard Business School have accepted the system, they want to be part of it, want to be an important part of it, want to be near the top of it. But the school is changing as society evolves. I had two stints there fifteen years apart. The assumptions underlying the program used to be fairly simple: that the business sector is the critical sector of the system, that efficiency and profit are everything. But it's become more subtle lately; there are all sorts of undercurrents and at the moment I think the school is hesitating about what its real role in life should be."

---

*In August, 1975, Jim Coutts left his Toronto-based Canada Consulting Group, which had four Harvard MBAs, to become principal secretary to Pierre Trudeau. John Turner's wife, Geills, holds a certificate from the Harvard Business School, as does Ruth Macdonald, who was a bond trader for Greenshields Inc. in Montreal before her marriage to Donald Macdonald, now energy minister.

†The legal work to set up this fund-gathering organization was done free of charge by Roland Michener, a Rhodes Scholar and later Governor General of Canada.

Most Harvard grads aren't as sensitive to social change as Dimma is. For them, the school remains what it has always been: a solid first step in the climb up the long ladder to meaningful corporate power. Like private schools, HBS provides a shortcut, a buzzword that spells WATCH ME within the business Establishment world.

ONE OF THE CANADIAN ESTABLISHMENT'S UNRESOLVED FRUSTRATIONS IS THAT THIS COUNTRY persists in maintaining vestiges of egalitarianism in its honours systems. The brokerage devices between money and status are creaky at best. There is always, of course, membership on the boards of the main regional and national theatres, symphonies, ballet companies, and other cultural institutions. But with governments having to finance an increasing share of these institutions' deficits, the awkward process of democratization has begun to take hold. The chief Establishment honours remaining are the Order of Canada, honorary degrees, and entry in the *Canadian Who's Who*.

Canadian recommendations for titles from the United Kingdom were abolished in 1919, except for a brief revival in 1934 and 1935 under R.B. Bennett's sponsorship.* In 1943, on Mackenzie King's recommendation, George VI approved the issuing of a Canada Medal, but it was never awarded. The most detailed recommendation for an honours system is the still-secret appendix to the 1951–53 Royal Commission on the Arts, Letters and Sciences, headed by Vincent Massey. It urged awarding of an Order of St. Lawrence consisting of six grades.

The Order of Canada was established on April 17, 1967, as a direct result of Lester Pearson's experiences as a diplomat when he felt the frustration that existed among Canada's representatives abroad because we were the only nation of major or minor status that had no distinctive way of honouring its citizens for meritorious ser-

*When Roy Thomson accepted his barony in 1964, he had to give up his Canadian citizenship. "I didn't give it up, they took it away from me," he complained. "They gave me the same reward that you give a traitor. If I had betrayed my country, that's the reward I would get—taking away my citizenship. Canada should allow titles. If you get a title from the Pope, there's no trouble accepting that."

vice. It was Pearson who fought the idea through his doubtful cabinet, which finally approved it on December 5, 1966, with many ministers still voicing their objections.

Pearson had sought Vincent Massey's advice on the project and received from him a long private letter on February 3, 1966, which stated in part: "An honours system is a normal piece of national equipment as an examination of the practice in other countries shows. The institution of such a system in Canada would make, I think, a definite contribution to Canadian unity." Another important influence on the P.M.'s thinking was a detailed communication from Major-General Bruce Matthews (a former president of the National Liberal Federation and a partner in Argus Corporation), who had become conscious of the absence of Canadian orders while acting as honorary pallbearer during the funeral of General H.D.G. Crerar in 1965. "Canada has rarely paid appropriate tribute during the lifetime of its outstanding citizens to the persons involved," Matthews wrote, and went on to suggest an appropriate national order.

After Pearson had made up his mind to establish the honours system, John Matheson, the Liberal M.P. for Leeds, set out to make heraldic inquiries in England. The ribbon for the new decoration was based on the Canadian General Service Medal, granted to Canadian militia veterans during the Fenian Raids of 1866–71. The motto for the new order, "Desirous of a Better Country," came out of a sermon Matheson heard preached by Rev. Herbert O'Driscoll, rector of the Anglican Church of St. John the Evangelist in Ottawa, to a meeting of the Canadian Council of Churches on February 8, 1966.

The semi-annual Order of Canada award lists are divided among Companions, Officers, and Members with no discernible pattern.* In December, 1973, for example, Bill Twaits, then chairman of Imperial Oil, was made a Companion while Vacy Ash, the former chairman of Shell Canada, became merely an Officer. An unpublished

---

*Candidates for the Order of Canada are sifted and weighed by an advisory council consisting of the Chief Justice of Canada, the Clerk of the Privy Council, the Undersecretary of State, the chairman of the Canada Council, and the presidents of the Royal Society of Canada and the Association of Universities and Colleges of Canada.

study by Wilfred W. McCutcheon of Ottawa of the men and women named to the Order between July 1967 and June 1970 shows that their median age was 66.3 and that sixty-eight of the recipients—a disproportionate share of the total—were businessmen associated with 329 firms.*

The McCutcheon survey demonstrates a high correlation between awards, with 583 of his Order of Canada candidates having also been granted honorary university doctorates. At the same time, some 87 per cent of the Order bearers had been listed in the *Canadian Who's Who* before their appointments. The arbiter for the past forty-four years of just who gets into the *Canadian Who's Who*† is Arthur L. Tunnell, a sprightly and devastatingly dedicated eighty-year-old former journalist who bought Canadian rights to the reference volume from Lord Northcliffe in 1931. Tunnell's book lists two thousand business executives; he drops between three and four hundred names per edition, because in his view they are no longer reference-worthy. "If a man goes to jail, for instance, he's got to come out of the next volume," Tunnell says. "There's a notable instance that I can think of just after the war, when a broker, a vice-president in a big brokerage house, one of the biggest, defaulted in the sum of about 80,000 smackers and went to prison. That man was a grandson of a Father of Confederation. There isn't anything more pitiful. But he had to come out. We can't accept Kingston Penitentiary as an official address."

*Of these, thirty were connected with at least one of Canada's hundred largest corporations. Twenty two winners had connections with one of the twenty-five largest financial institutions, including nine associated with the chartered banks and seven with the largest life insurance firms.
†The *Canadian Who's Who* is published every three years. It costs fifty-five dollars and weighs three pounds; it has twelve hundred pages and a print run of about three thousand copies. No one can buy his way into the Tunnell book.

CHAPTER TWELVE

Clubland on the Rocks

By joining the exclusive clubs
that still count, members of the Canadian
Establishment can pretend to themselves that
they are part of a select assemblage of men
who *are*, instead of men who merely *do*.

It is not the food that distinguishes the sombre clubs
where the Canadian Establishment dines and deals most
working days. The passably fresh oysters with their scat-
ter of limp sea biscuits and the ceremonial Tabasco bottle;
the hot or jellied *consommé madrilène au sherry;* the
bloody roast beef accompanied by cold potatoes and the
inevitable squash; the "fresh" strawberries with rhubarb;
the wrinkled baked apples—the snobbish non-fanciness
of the menu can be matched and easily surpassed at any
good downtown restaurant. Nor is it the service, which
once drove club members to the very limits of their con-
descension but nowadays leaves them merely waiting im-
patiently for the weary shuffle of retainers grown old and
feeble in their employ. It isn't the beamed ceilings of
natural oak or the endless halls lined with fading litho-
graphs of English country life that bespeak proud
colonialism; it isn't the fat Uppmann cigars passed round
in mahogany humidors, or the reading rooms featuring
the *very* latest *Illustrated London News;* it isn't even the
cigar holders affixed (at the exactly appropriate level) on
the marble partitions that divide the stalls of the basement lavatories.

It is none of these things that makes club life unique.
It is the peculiar quality of the hush that sets these
places apart—the heavy hush of privilege that intim-
idates even the most self-confident regulars. They try to
deal with it by greeting each other in over-hearty voices,
with a clubman's gestures—the possessive pat on the
shoulder, the tight grip on the forearm, the whole panto-

417

mime of being one of the chosen. But the sound of their assertion lies in the air. It does not fade or echo. It just lies there; and so they modify their tones three sentences into any conversation, and the holy hush endures undisturbed.

It is a hush and a mood that contain an element of imposture, since Canadian clubmen have even less reason than their British archetypes for feeling that their membership denotes anything more worthy than the fact that they have the right connections and the price of admission. Yet that very special feeling is there, just the same, and it produces a strange alchemy in those who share it. By joining the exclusive clubs that still count, members of the Canadian Establishment can pretend to themselves that they are part of a select assemblage of men who *are,* instead of men who merely *do.* George Grant, a former principal of Queen's University, expressed this thought perfectly at the turn of the century when he told a meeting of Toronto's National Club: "A club like this affords a platform for calm discussion by men who stand in the daylight. Each of us speaks for himself, and will have due weight given, not only to what he says, but what he *is.*"

The basic purpose of these institutions is little changed since their beginnings in seventeenth-century England, where they sprang up as congenial meeting places for men of mutual interests. This tradition had its start in Canada with the original Beaver Club, which operated intermittently in Montreal between 1785 and 1827 and was comprised of adventurers who had made fortunes in the country's early fur trade. An unalterable condition of membership was proof of having spent at least one winter in "the primitive struggle for wealth in the wilderness." Meetings would open with the handing round of an Indian peace pipe as one of the retired adventurers recalled his hardships, after which the members would start drinking. At some point in the evening they would be moved to seize fire tongs, pokers, and walking sticks, sit on the floor, and, with appropriate sound effects, re-enact the drama of a canoe being swept down turbulent rapids.

NOT SO VERY LONG AGO, AT LUNCHTIME ON ANY GIVEN
WEEKDAY, the nation's Establishment conducted most of
its charitable, commercial, and political liaisons inside
club dining rooms. This is no longer true. The new-breed
wheelers are dealing downtown in the smart places
where they can sniff out the fast money, looking past
their luncheon companions' shoulders to see who's breaking bread with their competitors. The time is long past
when the maître d' of the Albany Club in downtown
Toronto could complain to City Hall that the King streetcars should be obliged to reduce speed when passing his
premises, because they jostled the cellar stocks of port.

But even if conviviality and the fast money have
moved on, prestige and the really big money still reside
in the clubs. They act, according to Wallace Clement's
study of the economic elite of Canada, as badges of
" 'social certification' . . . a place where friendships are
established and old relationships nourished. A person's
'contacts' are important in the corporate world because
they affect the ability to have access to capital, to establish joint ventures and to enter into buyer and seller relationships with the men who control the nation's largest
corporations. . . . Canadian clubs are one of the key institutions which form an interacting and active national
upper class."*

Once he is a member, the typical clubman becomes so
integrated with his environment that he takes it completely for granted, except perhaps to wonder occasionally
why everyone else he knows doesn't belong also. "What
I like about these places," a Toronto Club regular once
confided to a friend, "is their essentially egalitarian spirit.
There's no distinction whatever made between a man
with half a million dollars and another with $50 mil-
lion." In his survey of the American upper crust, Cleveland Amory summed up the club ethic in terms of its
freedoms. "It is here and only here," he wrote, "the
member can find his four freedoms: freedom of speech
against democracy; freedom of worship of aristocracy;

---

*Wallace Clement, *The Canadian Corporate Elite: An Analysis of Eco-
nomic Power*, Carleton Library Original, No. 89 (Toronto: McClelland
and Stewart, 1975).

freedom from want of tipping; and, above all, freedom from fear of women."*

A little-known advantage of club adherence is that it plugs members into an impressive international network of similar institutions.† These affiliations provide a measure of instant accreditation in contacting the elites of other cities and other countries, though club membership alone guarantees very little. Both the Vancouver and the Rideau clubs have an interesting exchange arrangement with the Travellers' in London, founded in 1819. One of the Travellers' traditions is that members do not speak to each other, even at luncheon or dinner, when they wander into the dining room reading books and magazines.‡ Other cross-affiliations allow Canadian clubmen into the Rand at Johannesburg, the Salisbury in Rhodesia, Le Nouveau Cercle in Paris, Circolo della Caccia in Rome, the Kildare Street Club in Dublin, and the highly prized Grande Société in Bern.||

Over and above these automatic exchanges, more than a hundred members of the Canadian Establishment pay

---

*Cleveland Amory, *Who Killed Society?* (New York: Harper and Bros., 1960). A fifth freedom worth mentioning might be freedom from embarrassments caused by subscribing to the double standard. It is a sacred tradition that extra ladies in a gentleman's life write to or telephone his club rather than his home or office. Tactful hall porters deliver such messages on silver trays, address-side down, just in case the affair might involve a fellow member's wife or mistress.

†Members of the Vancouver Club, for instance, enjoy reciprocal visiting privileges at the Halifax Club; the Union Club in Saint John; the Garrison Club, Quebec; the St. James's Club, Montreal; Club St. Denis, Montreal; the Rideau Club, Ottawa; the National Club, Toronto; the Hamilton Club; the Manitoba Club, Winnipeg; the Edmonton Club; the Ranchmen's Club, Calgary; the Travellers' Club, London; the Caledonian Club, London; the Junior Carlton Club, London; the Rag, London; the Australian Club, Sydney; the Australian Club, Melbourne; the Christchurch Club, New Zealand; the Auckland Club, New Zealand; the Outrigger Canoe Club, Hawaii; and the Hong Kong Club.

‡Most Travellers get to know each other only during August, when the club closes for staff holidays and its members are admitted to the Garrick, where they can talk. The best-known break in the Travellers' custom of silence occurred during the Battle of Britain when Air Marshal Sir Charles Portal, Chief of the Air Staff, was joined by Lord Cecil Manners on a sofa in the club's morning room. Sir Charles jumped up in shocked surprise when Lord Cecil remarked: "Extraordinarily well the Flying Corps is doing these days, wouldn't you say?" There was, of course, no reply.

||The ultimate international club was the Tres Vidas en la Playa, built near Acapulco in 1969 for $30 million. Founded by Prince Bernhard of the Netherlands, Prince Franz Joseph of Liechtenstein,and Prince Rainier of Monaco, it owned three private miles of Pacific beach, four fresh-water lakes, and two golf courses. Members included Count Giovanni Agnelli, chairman of Fiat; Antenor Patino, the world tin magnate; Count Ferdinand von Bismarck; Robert Anderson, a former secretary of the U.S. Treasury; and the Duke of Cadaval, Portugal's second-largest landowner. The only Canadian ever asked to join was the late Robert Winters, then president of Brazilian Light and Power.

dues to clubs of their choice outside the country. New York's Metropolitan has the largest contingent, including Bud McDougald of Argus Corporation, Arnold Hart of the Bank of Montreal, George Sinclair, chairman of MacLaren Advertising, and John J. Mooney, president of the Ontario Jockey Club. E.P. Taylor is the only Canadian member of The 29 Club, an exclusive New York lunching society. Probably the most prestigious social club in the U.S. is Rolling Rock, at Ligonier, fifty miles east of Pittsburgh. Located on fifty thousand acres of the huge Mellon estate,* with a serried complex of swimming pools alone worth $3 million, a luxurious stone clubhouse, fishing streams, and a magnificent steeplechase course, it has a dozen or so Canadian members, including Nelson Davis, Bud McDougald, William Mulholland (president, Bank of Montreal), Beverley Matthews (senior partner of the McCarthy and McCarthy law firm), Allen McMartin (chairman, Hollinger Mines), Nathanael Davis (chairman, Alcan Aluminium), Major-General Bruce Matthews (executive vice-president, Argus), Bob Scrivener (chairman, Bell Canada), F.C. Wallace (retired chairman, Canadian Pittsburgh Industries), Harold Crang (the Toronto stockbroker), John McKee (chairman of Stone and Webster Canada), and Charlie Burns (chairman of Burns Brothers and Denton).

LUNCHEON CLUBS IN CANADA FUNCTION AS SANCTUARIES, PROTECTING THEIR INCUMBENTS, however briefly and artificially, from the distasteful realities of contemporary society. Members use their lunch hours to keep continually expanding their circles of like-minded acquaintances. Most clubs keep "open" tables, where diners without guests can meet, explore each other's psyches, talk shop, and further mutual ambitions. One club habitué expresses their philosophy succinctly: "Belonging to clubs takes the guesswork out of friendships."

Among Canada's most important lunching clubs are

---

*The Mellons hold one of America's great family fortunes, estimated at $3 billion. Their assets include control of Gulf Oil, Aluminum Co. of America, Mellon Bank, General Reinsurance, Carborundum Co., Koppers Co., and the First Boston Corp.

the Halifax Club, the Union Club in Saint John, the Garrison Club in Quebec City, the St. Denis and the Mount Stephen in Montreal, the Hamilton Club, the London Club, the Manitoba Club in Winnipeg, the Assiniboia in Regina, the Edmonton Club, the Ranchmen's and the Petroleum in Calgary,* the Terminal City Club in Vancouver, and the Union Club in Victoria.† But the clubs that really count, the only *national* institutions, are the York, Toronto, and National in Toronto, the Mount Royal and the St. James's in Montreal, the Rideau in Ottawa, and the Vancouver Club.

THE TORONTO CLUB

Founded by the Family Compact of Upper Canada in 1835, this is still the most difficult private lunching club in the country to join. Initially, it barred anyone engaged in trade. Even after he had become a titled millionaire, Sir Joseph Flavelle got in only following a long wait because he had once been a vice-president of the Robert Simpson Company. The club is housed in a Victorian brick pile at Wellington and York streets, and its specialty is undiluted, precisely measured (four to one) martinis served in carafes set in ice for pouring into chilled glasses.

A combination of the Great Depression and bad management brought the Toronto Club close to bankruptcy in 1941, when its executives met in emergency session upon discovering that they didn't have enough cash to meet the weekly payroll. Bud McDougald, who had been an active club member since 1933, was asked whether

---

*The Ranchmen's, which was founded in 1891, maintains in its archives a boiled tuxedo shirt autographed by the future King Edward VIII and all the club members who attended a wild party to mark his visit as Prince of Wales. To the Ranchmen's also belongs the distinction of having had the member longest in residence. Dudley Ward, whose wife took up with the Prince of Wales, left England in order not to embarrass the royal family and spent much of the last twenty-five years of his life living on the club premises.

†Canada's greatest clubman may have been the late James Ross, a Scottish engineer who achieved his first success in the railway construction of the seventies and eighties and later made two more fortunes by establishing streetcar systems and building up the country's steel and coal industries. His memberships included the Mount Royal, the St. James's, the Royal St. Lawrence Yacht, the Forest and Stream, the Montreal Curling, the Montreal Hunt, the Montreal Jockey, the Montreal Racket, and the Royal Montreal Golf, the Rideau, the Manitoba, the Toronto, the Royal Canadian Yacht, the York, the Union of Saint John, the Halifax, the Royal Cape Breton Yacht of Nova Scotia, the Manhattan of New York, and the Constitutional Club of Manchester.

he would head a committee to reorganize its finances. "The only kind of committee I join is a committee of one," McDougald declared and was promptly handed the job. He issued a series of interest-free first-mortgage perpetual debentures to members which have since turned the Toronto into the country's wealthiest private club (total revenue in 1974 was $430,575). Even though many more members might easily be accommodated, McDougald insists on keeping the Toronto's roster below four hundred. "This has been a policy of mine since I took on the club," he says. "What good is a club if you've got to line up to go to lunch? The Toronto Club is run at about 60 per cent of capacity on purpose. We could take in twice as much revenue by having twice as many members, but this isn't my idea of a club. My idea is to be able to take your friends to lunch at any time you like and know you can have a table. The people who usually want to join are the same kind of people who are willing to pay for that under-capacity so they can go to lunch when they want to."

Whenever an important international business celebrity arrives in Toronto, his itinerary almost always includes a private dinner at the Toronto Club. One such occasion was the reception given on March 18, 1973, by Jack Brent, chairman of IBM Canada, and Jim Kerr, chairman of TransCanada PipeLines, for John Connally, who was briefly secretary of the treasury under Richard Nixon. Guests included Bill Twaits, then chairman of Imperial Oil, Neil McKinnon, then chairman of the Commerce, Allen Lambert, chairman of the Toronto-Dominion Bank, Bob Scrivener of Bell Canada, and John Bassett, president of Baton Broadcasting. Only two toasts were proposed that evening, one to the Queen, the other to the President of the United States.*

Access to the Toronto Club is guarded by Bud McDougald. Although he is listed on the club's executive only as chairman of the finance committee, no one gets in without his approval. He has been known to bear grudges beyond one generation. When John T. DesBrisay, Q.C., a

---

*At similar dinners when Nixon was sinking into the morass of the Watergate scandals, the second toast was amended to salute only "the office of the President of the United States."

well-placed partner in the Toronto law firm of Cassels, Brock, wanted to join, his application languished for two years. He finally discussed the matter with the friend who had put up his name and was told that Bud probably had something against him, though no one seemed to know exactly what it might be. After months of discreet inquiries, it turned out that thirty years before, when McDougald used to be sent on underwriting trips to New York with Bud Wisener, a fellow broker, Wisener preferred taking Ginger Rogers to dinner, leaving McDougald to do most of the work. Wisener's daughter had married John DesBrisay, and *that* seemed to be why—three decades later—the gates of the Toronto Club remained closed.

THE YORK CLUB

Club lore has it that when one of the Gooderhams of the Canadian distilling dynasty moved into the mansion that now houses the York Club at the corner of St. George and Bloor streets, his wife expressed a distinct aversion to the chilly morning walk to her bathtub. To solve this ticklish dilemma, a manservant would fill the tub with steaming water in the bathroom and discreetly withdraw. With a flourish, the obliging husband would then push a bedside button, and the tub, mounted on narrow-gauge rails, would pull itself up to the bedside, so that his lady could descend directly into its comforting warmth.

Always house-proud, the host was once taking a group of friends on a pre-dinner tour. To show them how the "world's smallest railway" worked, he pushed the button, and out lumbered the tub, full of steaming water and his screaming wife.

The York's membership in 1974 was only 265. Regular lunching members include the Eaton boys, two of the Oslers and one Gooderham, the philanthropist-publisher Floyd Chalmers, Gordon Fisher, the dynamic head of Southams, and Walter Gordon, the former minister of finance. The York is the only club that deliberately attempts to mix its membership by admitting "supernumeraries" to represent the various arts. Among them are the literary critic Northrop Frye, the author-architect Eric

Arthur, the economist Vincent Bladen, and the conductor-composer Boyd Neel. It has a relatively small roster of non-resident (out-of-town) members, including Montrealers Paul Desmarais and Viscount Hardinge of Lahore, and such world travellers as Lord Thomson of Fleet and Garfield Weston. York members don't drink very hard; the 1973 bar bill totalled $82,000. The club can exercise quiet clout if the occasion arises. When the Toronto Transit Commission was building the St. George subway station next door, the York quietly arranged to have the diesel air compressors used only after midnight, so that members would not be disturbed.

THE NATIONAL CLUB

With 1,015 members, the National is what Barbara Moon once described in the *Globe and Mail* as "a bullpen for the Toronto Club." The only institution of its kind established for political reasons (to house the Canada First party under the leadership of Goldwin Smith in the 1870s), the National has since been declining both in prestige and in cuisine. It does maintain the distinction of having its own songs for special occasions.*

Other Toronto clubs don't carry much Establishment weight.† The Albany is a hangout for superannuated Tories and hasn't shown much life since a memorable evening in the early fifties, when a group of relatively young members decided that the bust of Sir John A. Macdonald, the Albany's patron saint, needed cleaning. They placed it in an upstairs bathtub. The statue turned out to be not bronze but plaster of Paris, and immediately began to crumble. In their hazy, alcohol-inspired wisdom, the group thought up a delicious solution. They

---

*This sample verse of a National Club Christmas carol is to be sung, accompanied by jingling glasses, to the tune of *Jingle Bells:*

Ginger ale, ginger ale, ginger ale today,
Oh! how hard it is to sing on ginger all the way,
It's very fine to quench your thirst, so join me in this lay,
Mix it with a little Scotch and shout hip, hip, hur-ray!

†The listing in the *Canadian Who's Who* of a man's club affiliations places him at the appropriate Establishment level of acceptance as irrevocably as his street address. Eric Phillips, for example, belonged to the National, University, and Toronto clubs while still running a glass factory in Oshawa during the mid-thirties. When he moved to Toronto after the war to assume a senior partnership in Argus Corporation, he dropped the National and substituted the York.

would raid Queen's Park, pinch a similar-looking bust of Sir Wilfrid Laurier, and put it in Sir John A.'s place. No one noticed the substitution for four months.

The more sedate University Club has a first-class kitchen and is the most used of all the clubs. It also *looks* most like a London club, its design having been based on Boodle's in St. James's Street. The membership is younger and less stuffy than it is in any of its Toronto counterparts. Moving up the fastest in both popularity and prestige is the Badminton and Racquet, on St. Clair Avenue. It already has an Eaton, a Webster, and a Seagram on its roster and boasts the longest waiting list in town.

THE MOUNT ROYAL CLUB

Housed in a club building designed by the U.S. architect Stanford White (who also designed the Metropolitan Club in New York), Montreal's Mount Royal is the most snobbish club in the country. It was originally established by some prominent members of the St. James's who found their surroundings too crowded and no longer in keeping with their ideal of club life. The legend persists that the main reason Max Aitken, the future Lord Beaverbrook, left Montreal for England in 1910 was that he couldn't get into the Mount Royal. Izaak Walton Killam, Aitken's old business associate, didn't even try; he just sat in his mansion across Sherbrooke Street and glared out—though he did make it into the St. James's and the Toronto clubs.

The Mount Royal's ashtrays still come equipped with silver toothpicks. Its greatest crisis occurred during a bridge tournament in 1931, when the stern-visaged financier Sir Herbert Holt socked a dull partner on the jaw. The game continued without explanation or apology.*

---

*Hugh Paton, Sir Herbert Holt's brother-in-law, was such a stuffy character that according to Montreal socialites he could strut while sitting down. At a formal dinner party given by Alfred Baumgarten, the German-born capitalist who then controlled St. Lawrence Sugar Refining, a group of Mount Royal members decided they would play a practical joke on the lumpish Hugh. The Baumgarten home (now the McGill Faculty Club) had a swimming pool. Half a dozen guests lined up at the pool's edge, pledging that at a given signal they would all take three steps forward—though they had previously agreed in secret not to make a move. When the signal was given, Paton was the only one who plunged into the pool. Quickly realizing what had happened, he pretended to be drowning, and five dinner-jacketed men jumped in to save him.

The Mount Royal had a membership in 1974 of 530. In addition to listing just about every member of Montreal's Wasp Establishment, it also has a small representation from the city's French community, including Senator Louis Beaubien and Senator Louis Gélinas, both investment dealers; Philippe de Gaspé Beaubien, president of Télémedia; lawyers Jacques Courtois and Louis-Philippe de Grandpré; Paul Desmarais; André Bisson, general manager of the Bank of Nova Scotia, Quebec region; André Charron, an investment dealer; Paul Paré, president of Imasco; and Marcel Vincent, retired chairman of Bell Canada. The 178 non-resident members are a representative cross-section of the Toronto, Vancouver, Maritime, and British establishments. Among them are Allan Burton, chairman of Simpsons; Bud Willmot, chairman of Molson Companies; Edmund de Rothschild of the English banking family; Sir Val Duncan of the Rio Tinto group; Allen Lambert; Bud McDougald; Victor Oland of the Halifax brewing family; Charles Gundy, chairman of Wood Gundy; Bruce Matthews; Frank McMahon, the oil and gas entrepreneur; Maurice Strong, Undersecretary-General of the United Nations; Alf Powis, president of Noranda Mines; and Frank Sobey of Sobeys Stores. The club's 1974 bar bill totalled $71,559.

THE ST. JAMES'S CLUB

"The St. James's Club," wrote Charles Vining, a Canadian commentator, in 1935, "is a somewhat airless institution having two classes of members: those who wish they belonged to the Mount Royal and those who are glad they don't belong to the Mount Stephen." The club was founded in 1857 by a group of Montreal businessmen fed up with having waiters eavesdrop on their noonday chatter, and its charter provided that servants were to show "attention to their general appearance and dress and avoid loud talking and other disagreeable noises." Early minutes indicate some unexplained problems with a barmaid, dealt with only when a resolution was passed "that it be fully explained that her continuance in the service of the club be ruled by her good behaviour and that she retire nightly at ten o'clock." The great clubhouse at

Dorchester and University, completed in 1864, was torn down to make way for William Zeckendorf's Place Ville Marie. Conscious of the sensibilities he was ruffling, the New York real estate tycoon raised the top floor of his skyscraper's main tower an extra two feet and extended the St. James's an invitation to occupy his premises. But its members voted to move into the Union Street building, owned by the Mashaal brothers, across the road instead. Ever since, the St. James's, like Toronto's National Club, has gained in members and lost in prestige.

The best French-Canadian club is the St. Denis (which has the noblest kitchen and a bowling alley). The Mount Stephen, once the home of the CPR's first president, has a five-inch-thick front door adorned with a knob and hinges plated in 22-carat gold, but not much else. The Montreal Racket Club, its enrolment limited to a hundred members, quietly carries the most prestige. It has one large luncheon table where no discussion of business matters is allowed.

THE RIDEAU CLUB

The Rideau Club was founded in 1865 by Sir John A. Macdonald, and its location—right across Wellington Street from the Parliament Buildings—has always symbolized its purpose: to provide a discreet meeting place where men representing business power and political authority can exchange favours. Every Canadian prime minister (except John Diefenbaker and Pierre Trudeau) has belonged and made extensive use of the club's facilities. The processional staircase, with its Corinthian pillars and ruby-red carpet, sweeping upwards to its drawing rooms and dining lounges lends the Rideau a distinctive air missing from some of its lesser cousin institutions.

Up until the end of the St. Laurent regime, there was a regular "Cabinet" table in the left-hand corner of the dining room.* But ministers are too busy now, preferring

*R.B. Bennett particularly enjoyed continuing his discussions begun in Cabinet at this table. But in 1934, when Harry Stevens resigned his Trade and Commerce portfolio, broke with the Bennett government, and started up his own Reconstruction party, he located himself every noon hour in the club lounge right at the top of the staircase, so that Bennett couldn't enter the dining room without passing him. Rather than acknowledge his former minister's presence, Bennett stopped using the club, taking lunch instead at his suite in the Chateau Laurier Hotel.

to eat in their offices or the Parliamentary Dining Room. For an annual fee of $335, diplomats (ambassadors and heads of missions) are allowed to become privileged members, as are royal commissioners and heads of government boards whose appointments do not exceed ten years. For the fiscal year ended February 20, 1974, the Rideau Club bar bill amounted to $99,073, with cost of sales being $39,127 and the gross profit $59,946.

One Rideau tradition concerns the formation of the Last Post Club (on Armistice Day, 1958) by a group of regulars who sat around the pillar closest to the reading room. Their rules were simple: no strangers, no shoptalk, and a round of drinks. At their annual meeting, held at noon every December 24, the Last Poster who performed the most worthwhile deed during the preceding twelve months was presented with a replica of the pillar mounted on an oak base.*

Club lore seems limited to a nameless Exchequer Court judge who brought a frozen turkey into the club after a round of Christmas parties. For reasons that remain obscure, he decided to express his Yuletide spirit by swinging the bird around his head a few times. Its neck snapped and the flying body smashed a bust of the Marquis of Lorne, which was supposed to be made of marble but turned out, under the turkey's impact, to be tinted plaster. The judge lost both his turkey and his Rideau Club membership.

THE VANCOUVER CLUB

In the fall of 1955, a shipping broker and Vancouver Club regular, the late Bill Hurford, said to nobody in particular: "The Arabs are a Semitic race." The remark caused great consternation among those present; two lawyers debated it in increasingly heated language. The argument became so nasty that eventually Hurford himself got fed up and, to drown out the disputatious law-

---

*A much more prestigious, now defunct, organization was the dining-out club that functioned in Ottawa through the forties and fifties and into the early sixties. Over the years its members included Senator Grattan O'Leary, Sir Lyman Duff, Norman Robertson, Arnold Heeney, Frank Underhill, M.J. Coldwell, Ivan Rand, John Stevenson, Donald Gordon, Duncan Campbell Scott, and Norman Lambert. They met one Tuesday a month at the Ottawa Country Club to dine and talk.

yers, began to sing "Cock Robin," with other members joining in. That didn't resolve the situation, so the songsters took up "Green Grow the Rushes," all twelve verses of it, which finally drowned out the embattled lawyers. Club life has its own peculiarities, and for reasons best known to themselves the participants in this silly incident decided to commemorate it by founding the Witenagemot (Anglo-Saxon for assembly of wise men) Society, with the idea of holding an annual gourmet dinner, between the courses of which the assembled company would sing the two ballads, in their entirety, in unison and without fluffs. The Vancouver Club has always been a bit different.* Drinks, for example, are not ordered from a central bar but are poured out of members' own bottles, which they keep in their lockers. At the end of 1974, the Vancouver had 1,163 members, the highest entrance fee ($1,500) of any dining club, and a waiting list of thirty-five. Its roster of out-of-towners included John Aird, the Toronto lawyer; Arthur Child, president of Burns Foods; Charles Gundy; Fred Mannix, the construction executive from Calgary; Yves Pratte, chairman of Air Canada; Jake Moore, president of Brascan; and Bill Wilder, chairman of Canadian Arctic Gas. The Terminal City Club has tried without much success to challenge the Vancouver, but it is at the Lawn Tennis and Badminton Club that the second-generation Vancouver Establishment prefers to spend its time.†

The Lawn Tennis was started in 1897 by Vancouver's leading families of the time—the Springers, the Boultbees, the Crickmays, the Heathcotes, the Gardner

---

*Club minutes recall a squabble over the feeding of dogs which continued for some years. A typical complaint from a member, dated July 9, 1904, reads: "I beg to draw the attention of the Committee to the fact that one of the members persistently feeds his dog on the front steps of the Club, which is to say the least anything but cleanly, besides it has the tendency of making the dog in question snap at members coming in or going out of the Club. If every member exercised the same right, the front of the Club would soon have the appearance of kennels. The BACK YARD is the proper place for all dogs to be fed." Another distinction of the Vancouver Club is that not a single one of its members was killed in World War II.

†This follows the pattern of what's been happening in other cities. Clubs on this circuit include the Montreal Badminton and Squash Club, the Winnipeg Squash Racquet Club, the Quebec Winter Club, the Glencoe Club, Calgary, the Racquet Club of Victoria, the Badminton and Racquet Club of Toronto, the Montreal Amateur Athletic Association, the Royal Glenora Club in Edmonton, the Multnomah Athletic Club, Portland, and the Olympic Club, San Francisco.

Johnsons, the Cambies, the Tatlows, the Townsends, the Cave-Browne-Caves, the Senklers, the Maranis, the Marpoles, the Malkins, the Bell-Irvings, the Beechers, and the Jukeses. Its original lawn-bowling turf came from the gardens of Col. Victor Spencer, who with his brother Chris sold the family department stores to Eaton's in 1948 and whose house is now the B.C. area officers' mess.

Club life in Vancouver trails in significance behind that of other Canadian cities. Local clubmen plug themselves into the national scene in the first-class cabins of the Vancouver-Toronto CP Air and Air Canada flights.

BEYOND THE DOWNTOWN LUNCHING CLUBS THERE EXISTS IN CANADA a covey of sportsmen's hideaways that lure the international business celebrities. The most renowned and most inaccessible of these are the Ristigouche Salmon Club, in northern New Brunswick, and the Long Point Company, on the north shore of Lake Erie.

Membership in both these clubs is dominated by the select group of Americans that winters on Hobe Sound, an island resort twenty-five miles north of Palm Beach. With its 150 houses and rigid admission requirements, Hobe is one of the most reticent resorts in the world. It has no hotels, no "native" population, a yacht club but no dock, a hunt club but no horses, a skeet club but no pigeons, a golf club but no bar. Cottages cannot be sold until the buyer has been accepted by a vote of all the other residents, who number various branches of the Pryors from Greenwich, the Whitneys from Long Island, the Fords from Detroit, the Armours from Chicago, the Strawbridges from Philadelphia, the Ayerses from Cleveland, the Bullocks from Cincinnati, and the Scrantons from Scranton, Pa., among others. Former U.S. cabinet officers who favoured Hobe Sound are Robert Lovett and Averell Harriman (who used to call up Harry Truman between croquet shots). Thursdays are party nights, and according to one old Hobe Sound hand, "you dress for dinner, but you don't put on your diamond tiara."

Few Canadians winter at Hobe Sound, though the families of William C. Harris, the Toronto financier, and David Chandler, chairman of Galt Malleable Iron, have year-round residences there. Graham Towers, the former governor of the Bank of Canada, was a frequent guest on the island, and it was to the Harris compound that Lester Pearson flew in the fall of 1972, when he knew he was dying. The main connection of most Hobe Sounders with Canada is through their fishing and hunting jaunts to Ristigouche and Long Point.

The Ristigouche Fishing Club, which insists on using the old spelling of the river's name, owns exclusive fishing rights up to the so-called Million Dollar Pool at the mouth of the Matapedia River. It costs $25,000 to join plus $6,000 in annual dues.* Most vacancies occur at the death of a member. A recent recruit was J.K. Jamieson, the Canadian-born chairman of Exxon Corporation. In addition to its main clubhouse at Matapedia, on the Quebec side of the river, it maintains four lodges. Only seven of the twenty members are Canadians: Doug Peacher, president of Simpsons-Sears; Allan Burton; Brian Magee, chairman of A.E. LePage; Charles Gundy; Mike Scott, a vice-president and director of Wood Gundy and son of the late William Pearson "Pete" Scott, former honorary chairman of Wood Gundy; Dave Weldon, chairman of Midland Doherty; and Beverley Matthews, the Toronto lawyer, who is also a vice-president and director of the Toronto-Dominion Bank and a director of a dozen other major companies.

Most of the American Ristigouche crowd also belong to the Long Point Company.† Its membership is similarly limited to twenty, though the Canadians who belong are a different group that now includes R.A. Laidlaw, whose family made a fortune in lumber; John Hale, executive vice-president, finance, of Alcan Aluminium; Jim McConnell, a former Toronto advertising man; and Bill Harris, the son of the former chairman of Harris and Partners. Most memberships are inherited. The Ameri-

---

*The club's leases, currently held under the name of Spencer Olin of East Alton, Illinois, were acquired at an auction in 1883. Payments made to the New Brunswick government amount to only $34,215 in angling fees and property taxes a year.

†Originally settled by United Empire Loyalists in 1794, the Long Point peninsula which juts out into Lake Erie was sold at public auction by the government of Canada West in 1866 to a group of duck shooters for $19,000. They received perpetual rights to turn it into a private hunting preserve.

can roster counts the Cabots of Boston and the Morgans, Whitneys, and Winthrops of New York, as well as half a dozen other Hobe Sounders. Every member has his own lodge, built on stilts jack-hammered into the marshland that provides an ideal halfway resting station for the continent's migrating ducks. One English member, J.T. Lord, boasted of having shot 3,300 in one season, but club rules have since been amended in accordance with Canadian game laws.

Less exclusive but offering equally good hunting is the Griffith Island Club, situated off the Bruce Peninsula in Georgian Bay, between Wiarton and Owen Sound. Purchased in 1952 by General Motors of Detroit as a sporting lodge for its top executives, the island was abruptly sold when Ralph Nader began his attacks on the company's extravagances. Now it is run by a private company headed by John Robarts, the former premier of Ontario, and is stocked annually with deer, partridge, and some ten thousand pheasants. The Griffith Island Club allows its fifty members to bring along wives and girl friends during the last week of every month.

The Tadenac, another private club on Georgian Bay, about halfway between Honey Harbour and Parry Sound, occupies twenty square miles originally owned by Sir William Mulock, Sir Henry Pellatt, and Sir Edmund Osler. It has only twenty members, including Bill Wilder, Dr. John Evans, president of the University of Toronto, and Alastair Gillespie, minister of Trade, Industry and Commerce in the Trudeau government.

Similar clubs exist in other provinces. One of the most attractive is the Pennask Lake Club, between Merritt and Kelowna and 272 road miles northeast of Vancouver. It was established by the late James D. Dole, the Honolulu "pineapple king," who searched the world for the best trout fishing and built a lodge at the lake (altitude 4,660 feet) in 1929. At the other end of the country, in St. John's, the most exclusive place is the Newfoundland Game Fish Protection Society at Murray's Pond, a few miles from the provincial capital. The entry fee is $200 and annual dues are $125, and the waiting list is very long because most memberships are obtained through inheritance.

Other important hunting and fishing clubs include three just north of Toronto, the Caledon Mountain Trout Club, the Goodwood (near Stouffville), and the East Hill Gun Club (on Harold Crang's estate, near Aurora), and a number in Quebec, including the Maganassippi Fish and Game Club (in Témiscamingue County), the Moisie Club (near Sept-Iles), the Bras Coupé (near Maniwaki in the Gatineau valley), and the Saguenay Club (fifty miles east of Chicoutimi), which has guards equipped with German shepherds and Mace spray guns to keep out poachers.*

A few corporations still maintain fishing and hunting clubs mainly to entertain their customers and contacts. Fraser Companies of Edmundston, New Brunswick, for example, owns a lodge on the Kedgwick River and is host to eight guests for three days at a time throughout the angling season. It is the largest fishing club in the province, with seventeen full-time employees.

PROBABLY THE MOST PECULIAR ASPECT OF CLUB LIFE IS THAT BELONGING is at least as important as attending any club functions. It's as though the point of joining a club is not so much to get in as to see whether you *can* get in. Membership is seldom restricted by written rules, but each institution's admission committee acts as a fine-mesh screen against those who aren't wanted.† A sign on the portals of an exclusive Paris club on the Rue Rabelais expresses this sentiment with the words, It Is Useless to Knock. According to one member of the Mount Royal, admission committees should guarantee "that when you walk in, you need ask no questions about anyone you may meet. He is someone you will be glad to know, merely because you find him there."

The "blackball" system, which keeps out the undesirables, works in subtle ways. Most club applications are carefully worded to allow even the sponsors of candidates

---

*On July 1, 1971, François Couture was shot to death by a guard at the Grand River Fishing Club, near Chandler, Que., for alleged poaching.
†In the early nineteenth century, the Duke of Portland, an eccentric British landowner, decided that the clubs he belonged to were being populated by the wrong sort. He staffed his own club and, setting himself up as its membership committee, began to screen his friends and acquaintances. No one measured up to all of his qualifications and for twenty years until his death, he remained the club's only member.

to downgrade their choices. A typical club application will carry this warning:

> Members are reminded that in all matters pertaining to the nomination of new members the first responsibility of the sponsors is to their Club and not to the nominee.

> If you are prepared to support this application is your interest based on:

> ——business considerations
> ——desire to oblige a friend
> ——the candidate's public prestige
> ——the candidate's congeniality with the membership
> ——close personal friendship
> ——other

> Having regard to the number of persons seeking admission to membership, would you inform the Club whether in your opinion the candidate is:

> ——deserving of priority
> ——congenial and acceptable but no special claim to priority
> ——my support was sought for this applicant, and while I agreed to the use of my name, I did so with some hesitation
> ——not a particularly suitable applicant

The actual blackball is applied during the vote taken on each new membership. The quota for rejection differs. At the Toronto Club, for instance, one negative ballot in every ten is enough to guarantee ostracism. Sometimes a quiet rebuff by one of the club's eminent members is enough to quash an application. Few candidates actually suffer the humiliation of being blackballed, because before anyone's name is formally proposed enough club members have been sounded out to ensure his election. The Rideau Club, for example, has rejected only forty prospective members since 1882.

The element of club life most seriously under attack is its antediluvian attitude toward women, which hasn't changed much since the Chicago Club opened its doors in 1869 with the unofficial motto, No Dogs, Democrats, Women, or Reporters Allowed. Members' wives and lady friends are still treated as backstairs creatures, being admitted only under the cover of darkness through separate doors into segregated quarters with washrooms done up with marble sinks, tortoise-shell combs, silver powder boxes, flecked wallpaper, and Pears soap. There has been some softening (the Ranchmen's Club of Calgary allows women in on New Year's Day), but it took the Rideau Club exactly forty-five years to act on a 1918 resolution calling for the opening of a ladies' dining room. At a 1964 reception tendered by the Department of External Affairs to U Thant, Secretary-General of the United Nations, two women M.P.s, Pauline Jewett and Margaret Konantz, were not allowed to enter the club's main premises and were hustled out of sight through a pantry. Possibly the most ridiculous example of such extravagant male chauvinism occurred in the Vancouver Club at a dinner given for George Vanier on June 10, 1965. The club had a long-standing tradition of entertaining every new governor general of Canada on his first journey to the West Coast. Club executives were thrown into a tizzy when the G.G. quietly informed them that he didn't go anywhere without Mme Vanier at his side. The club was about to cancel the festivities when the president of the day, T.E. Ladner, resolved the problem by also inviting Mrs. George Pearkes, the wife of the Lieutenant-Governor of British Columbia, and the members' wives.

The Canadian Establishment's younger generation finds such antics mildly amusing. A more serious issue is the anti-Semitism inbred in the older club members, although no written rule gives the slightest hint of discrimination. The invisible barriers have come down slightly at the Mount Royal Club, but only when the quality of the potential Jewish members has been beyond refusal. In 1966, Lazarus Phillips, who probably has the best legal mind in Canada and was the first Jew to become a vice-president of the Royal Bank, became a member after being proposed by Senator Hartland de Montarville Molson, Senator Louis Beaubien, and Earle McLaughlin, the Royal Bank's chairman. Sam Bronfman, the distiller, tried re-

peatedly to gain admittance without success, but his son
Charles made it in 1970, under the sponsorship of
Arnold Hart of the Bank of Montreal and Bill Bennett, presi-
dent of the Iron Ore Company of Canada, who was also the
Mount Royal Club's chairman that year. Phillips's son Neil
got in two years later, but no Jews have been put up since.

One successful assault on club anti-Semitism took place
at the Rideau Club in the summer of 1964. The story
has it that two very prominent Ottawa residents had been
denied entry or blackballed because they were Jewish. Some
of the more enlightened members quietly passed the word
that if their forthcoming slate was rejected, they would
resign and make a public issue of the club's attitude.
Their first step was to alter the club's admission rules.
Previously, each new candidate had needed at least
twenty-one votes in his favour, while either one negative
ballot in ten or a total of fifteen blackballs was sufficient
to exclude him. Under the new system, a membership
subcommittee was formed to review all nominations,
which were then posted. This was the notice that went
up on July 21, 1964:

Louis Rasminsky Governor, Bank of Canada, Ottawa, Canada	Proposer, Blair Fraser; Seconder, A. Davidson Dunton
Simon Reisman Deputy Minister, Department of Industry, Ottawa, Canada	Proposer, H.B. McKinnon; Seconder, C.M. Drury, C.B.E., D.S.O., E.D., M.P.
Lawrence Freiman Executive, A. J. Freiman Limited, Ottawa, Canada	Proposer, Commander F.J.D. Pemberton, C.D., R.C.N.; Seconder, J. Ross Tolmie, Q.C.
Bernard Alexandor* Lawyer, Ottawa, Canada	Proposer, C.J. Mackenzie, C.M.G., M.C.; Seconder, Mr. Justice D.C. Abbott

---

*A wing commander in the RCAF reserve, Alexandor served as Assistant
Judge Advocate General and member of the Court Martial Appeal Board.
He is Lawrence Freiman's brother-in-law.

David A. Golden*   Proposer,
Air Industries Association   A. Davidson Dunton;
  of Canada,   Seconder,
Ottawa, Canada   Dr. O.M. Solandt, o.b.e.

Under the combined weight of such sponsorship, the Rideau Club relented.

The saddest case of discrimination was probably that of Walter Koerner, the Czech millionaire; Koerner and other members of his family were among British Columbia's most generous philanthropists. Not only could he never gain admission to the Vancouver Club, but eventually he became embarrassed to go there even as the guest of Jack Clyne, then the West Coast's most powerful industrialist. They would lunch instead at the Shaughnessy Golf Club, telling each other that it was probably more convenient anyway.

The most obdurate holdouts have been the Manitoba and the St. Charles Golf clubs in Winnipeg. This is particularly ironic because in no Canadian community is the cultural life more vitally dominated by Jews than in Winnipeg. In 1968, Sol Kanee, a leading Winnipeg miller, a long-time director of the Bank of Canada, past chairman of the Royal Winnipeg Ballet, and one of the city's most civic-minded citizens, was taken to lunch at the Manitoba Club by George McIvor, then chairman of the Canadian Wheat Board. "Four days later," Kanee remembers, "McIvor called me back and said he wanted to have lunch with me again. He told me he'd been reprimanded for taking me to the club and wanted to take me again so he could thumb his nose at his fellow members. But I wouldn't go." That same year, Kanee had been approached by James Richardson (then head of the Richardson financial complex) and Stewart Searle, a grain merchant who became president of Federal Industries. They proposed that Kanee, along with Albert Cohen (president of General Distributors, which represents the Sony interests in Canada) and Samuel Freedman, make an attempt to break the Manitoba Club's anti-Jewish barrier. Searle and Richardson pledged that

---

*Golden is a former deputy minister of Industry and was a Hong Kong prisoner of war; he later became president of Telesat Canada Ltd.

they would resign if the trio was turned down. "I told Jim," Kanee said later, "for me, no problem. For Albert there's no problem. But that Mr. Justice Samuel Freedman, chancellor of the University of Manitoba [he became Chief Justice of Manitoba in 1971], should be exposed to having his application turned down—thank you very much, but the answer is No."

Richardson dropped the idea, but resigned from the St. Charles for the same reasons. The president of the golf club at the time was Alan Sweatman, a talented Winnipeg lawyer and a director of both the Toronto-Dominion Bank and Hudson Bay Mining and Smelting. He tried to get Allan Waisman, a local architect, into the club. When he was rejected, Waisman left town to take up practice in Vancouver. Sweatman then attempted to alter the St. Charles by-laws according to the Rideau Club model and was able to get the changes approved (on division) by the club's directors. They then had to be ratified at the annual midwinter meeting, held at the Manitoba Club.

The proposal was turned down, and Sweatman remembers: "I had a couple of people lined up to make the appropriate motion from the floor that evening, but when we got to the meeting, instead of the usual turnout of fifty, there were three times that many. It was damned obvious what was going to happen. So both my mover and my seconder came to me and backed out. I couldn't really blame them. The upshot of it was that the only person in the room who was fully in favour of the idea was me."

The Manitoba Club did finally admit its first Jew in 1972 (Gerry Libling, another architect) and in 1974 passed a non-discriminative by-law. But Sweatman resigned his membership in the Manitoba anyway. "Some committee members phoned and asked me why I quit," he recalls. "I said, 'Look, I like playing golf with the Jews, but if you think I'm going to sit and have lunch with them, you're crazy.' I don't think they even got the joke."

THE DOWNTOWN LUNCHING CLUBS ARE A DECLINING INFLUENCE. The action is moving elsewhere. For one thing, the whole tenor of that kind of club life depended on a long-vanished master-servant relationship. The Union Club in Victoria still has in its house rules a clause that reads: "No member shall give any gratuity whatsoever to any servant. The receipt of any gratuity shall render the servant liable to immediate dismissal without notice and with forfeiture of any wages then due."*

Canada's quintessential club servant was Joseph Arthur "Archie" Lacelle, who served as the Rideau Club's hall porter for fifty-seven years. One of his daily assignments was to walk over to the Chateau Laurier and collect specially baked breakfast rolls. The only mistake he seems to have made was in 1908, when he readdressed a letter that had arrived for a member to his home, letting his wife in on the husband's secret love affair. "It is to Archie's everlasting credit," notes the Rideau Club's official history, "that he accepted the rebuke in the proper spirit and thereafter would never admit to a female enquirer that a member was even in the club until he had checked and found out the desired reply." There are few Archies left, and yet the clubs require disproportionately large operating staffs. The Vancouver Club, for instance, has sixty-six full-time employees.†

With mounting costs and an altered income tax act that doesn't allow members to write off their dues as a business expense, the clubs are facing financial difficulties.‡ The Vancouver Club's 1973 surplus of $892 turned into a $34,242 deficit in 1974, over and above a $63,000 bank loan. The Rideau Club recently decided to hold back members' chits to eliminate a second monthly mailing, thus saving sixty dollars in postage. The mighty Mount Royal

---

*During the fifties there was a retired railway steward called Richards who served senior members of the Toronto Club. He complained about the abusive treatment meted out to him by Sir James Dunn, but he found an appropriate solution. Whenever he served him soup, he spat into it first.

†Twenty-three former staff members share in total annual pension payments of $35,543, which works out to $1,545.35 each.

‡The 1971 budget based on Edgar Benson's White Paper effected this change. Previously, an estimated 90 per cent of members' fees had been paid by their corporations. In 1952, the national revenue department had challenged Royal Trust's deductions for seventy-eight memberships for its executives, but the Exchequer Court ruled that club fees were deductible because they were held for reasons of business promotion rather than pleasure.

suffered a $22,466 deficit in 1973 and barely went into the black ($7,043) in 1974.

EVEN IF IT HAS BECOME OUTDATED AND SLIGHTLY RIDICULOUS, the club game continues, played according to the rules of its intricate caste system and the arcane codes of exclusion under which the outsider never quite finds out exactly why he wasn't good enough to get in.

And so they sit around their dreary sanctums of privilege, and in their muted seclusion the clubmen reflect on the various stages of their lives, looking back to judge how far they have come. They feel at home here, but every once in a while a few among them will recall their true origins and feel a chill: primeval flashes from their predatory past when they treated each other as prey instead of comrades—a time when their dreams of conquest were still dreams and they regarded the hush of club life as merely a clearing in their path to power.

They have become tribal elders now, gathering about the great unlit fireplaces to rage against the upstarts and the politicians gnawing at their authority, usurping their rightful influence. Some possess the instincts of hunters still, but should they truly listen to themselves, the sound they would hear might be the gurgle of dinosaurs. The dominance of the Canadian Establishment's great business dynasties draws inexorably to a close.

The pale sunlight filters through the club windows, with the dust motes dancing in it, dyeing the gloom under the ox-blood leather chairs, glancing off the much-waxed oak of the staircases leading to the dining areas. The clubmen sip their Scotch, claim their reserved tables, order steak (medium rare), wash it down with an amusing little St. Emilion, and light up their cigars.

CHAPTER THIRTEEN

The Canadian Establishment: A Tentative Sounding

> Power tends to connect; absolute
> power connects absolutely.

Viewed through a working journalist's hourglass, the exercise of power is essentially a spectacle of personalities in conflict. Authority cannot exist without someone to wield it. Power in the abstract is merely a potential; it becomes a social process only when some individual uses his authority to challenge or change the course of events. Once this happens, power flows subtly, like mercury, to where it can be used.

Power fascinates us all because it sets in train the most compelling of human emotions, whether the witness to its exercise abhors it, hungers after it, shrinks from its toils, suffers its cruelties, or enjoys its pleasures. The Indians have a word for this sensation: *darshan*—that glow of warmth and light one gets from the propinquity of the powerful. That old curmudgeon Malcolm Muggeridge made up an epigram about it: power is to the collective what sex is to the individual. And every cab driver in every Canadian city has a theory about it, some of them cock-eyed in their individualism, some uncannily correct in their perceptiveness, but all of them displaying the same fascination with "THEM"—the powerful, the men who run our lives—a response as old as human society itself.

"The men who really wield, retain and covet power in New York," Nicholas Pileggi wrote in *New York* magazine, "are the kind of men who answer bedside telephones while making love." Other peculiarities define business power on this side of the 49th parallel. It is reptile quiet, characterized by self-effacement, self-denial, a kind of "Who, me?" quality that has to do with propitiating the Protestant deity that has presided over English Canada's brief history. This attitude goes back to the individualism of the frontier, the raw land's harsh geography and staple economy. Senior members of the current Establishment grew up in a small-time business nation, the prewar Canada that, during the fifties, was revealed as an undeveloped depository of fabulous resources. As descendants of the original settlers in this treasure house, they came to think it was their natural right to grow rich.

The country changed around them, but until recently the main effects of the change were merely to entrench them in their positions. The powerful here have always lived with a colonial mentality which deems that *real* power (and real excellence, for that matter) lies somewhere else—over the water, below the border, among the imperial interest groups who must be viewed with awe, emulated with care, but on no account challenged lest they withdraw their dollars and their moxie. Northrop Frye sees our colonial status as frostbite on the roots of the Canadian imagination. "Colonialism," he has written, "produces a disease for which I think the best name is prudery. By this I do not mean reticence in sexual matters. I mean the instinct to seek a conventional or commonplace expression of an idea." What he might have been describing is the prudery of spirit, the snobbish modesty, the unwillingness to take risks that characterize all branches of the Canadian Establishment as it has existed through most of the twentieth century.

The Establishmentarians' own public abnegation of power and the absence of any popular understanding of how they do, in fact, exercise an inordinate influence in running this country is rooted in the fact that Canadian society has been too new, too busy becoming, too unstable in its immigration-emigration patterns, too engrossed in survival to develop the self-consciousness necessary for the evolution of its own myths and theories about power or anything else. It was not until 1965 that the power structure of this country was examined in detail. That was the year when John Porter, the Carleton University sociologist, published his monumental *Vertical Mosaic* and banished forever from the Canadian psyche the comfortable notion that this is a classless (or at any rate an entirely middle-class) country. Porter's original thesis was ex-

panded and brought up to date a decade later by Wallace
Clement in his *Canadian Corporate Elite*. He concluded
that "Canada has been and remains a society controlled
by elites. With increasing economic concentration over
the past twenty years, the structure has become increasingly closed thus making it more difficult for those outside the inner circles of power to break through."

While it is obvious that economic forces left to themselves help mainly the powerful, authority and morality do
not necessarily reside on opposite sides of the economic
teeter-totter. The men who belong to the Canadian Establishment have little need to conspire. They think the
same way *naturally*. Most of their ideas mesh perfectly.
They recognize so few conflicts of interest because their
broad interests seldom conflict. That what is good for
them, their careers, and their bank accounts might not
also be good for some of Canada's less exalted citizens is
not a proposition they are prepared to entertain.

The mere idea of such a cabal—the notion of the existence of an undemocratic class structure—comes as a
profound shock to many Canadians. It negates the popu-
list belief in the wide open spaces, the notion of Canada
as a land of freely accessible opportunities. Because the
Establishment we have is not reinforced by an aristocracy (as it is in Britain) or based on several generations
of wealth (as it is in the U.S.), most Canadians tend to
view the designations upper, middle, and lower class as
referring mainly to life styles and levels of sophistication.
But even if the Canadian Establishment that exists is considered to be highly ephemeral (comparable in the loose-
ness of its structure to the floating crap-game crowd
described by Damon Runyon), Canada does have classes
that are much more than temporary way-stations. "In all
societies, two classes of people appear," wrote the Italian
sociologist Gaetano Mosca when he was a student at the
University of Palermo, "a class that rules and a class that
is ruled."

Paradoxically, this does not mean that all members of
the Canadian Establishment necessarily belong to or come
out of the upper strata. Many if not most of them are
part of what George Orwell once described as "the lower

upper middle class"—a class that could give its offspring the advantages of education and the right entree but not necessarily inherited wealth.

HOW AN ESTABLISHMENT ORGANIZES ITSELF DETERMINES HOW A NATION WILL PURSUE ITS OBJECTIVES. Canada's Establishment consists of a surprisingly compact self-perpetuating group of perhaps a thousand men who act as a kind of informal *junta,* linked much more closely to each other than to their country.

Although their power is waning, they still possess the ability to compel obedience, to shape events and trends— political and cultural as well as economic—in their favour. Their exercise of authority is subtle, not always successful, but constantly aimed at fulfilling Bertrand Russell's definition of power as "the production of intended effects." Operating outside the constitutional forms, the Establishment's adherents exercise a self-imposed mandate unburdened by public accountability.

Without being a social compact, the confederacy of Canadian Establishments—loosely knit yet interlocking— forms a psychological entity. Its members share habits of thought and action, common sets of values, beliefs, and enemies. They consider themselves an untitled aristocracy whose virtue has been certified by their elevation to one of the dominant elites.

They are, therefore they rule.

Although the Canadian Establishment is coming increasingly under American control (a phenomenon that will be explored in a later volume of this series), it remains dominated by Old Canada Wasps,* holding proud and together through the right career histories and, most emphatically, the right connections. Power tends to connect; absolute power connects absolutely.

There exists no single monolithic Establishment in this country, but rings of establishments, and the most important of them all—because it is so concentrated, so powerful, and influences so many others—is that formed by the

---

*More precisely, as Don McGillivray of the *Financial Times* has pointed out, the Canadian equivalent of this short form for "White Anglo-Saxon Protestants" should probably be "White Anglo-Celt Protestants" or Wacps.

businessmen who control the Canadian economy's private sector.

Canada's Establishment is dominated by the corporate elite, partly because its members move freely from function to function, sliding in and out of Liberal cabinets, filling the seats on the boards of the main cultural institutions, making themselves felt within the governing bodies of the universities, running most of the institutions that count. "Corporate power is not tangential to Canadian society," James Eayrs, the University of Toronto political scientist, has concluded. "Corporate power *is* Canadian society."

Like the members of any other elite, the Canadian business Establishment's adherents disavow the possession of power, even if they value its exercise. They are too busy to hold political office but like to think they determine who does. They are accustomed to running things—promoting those men (and groups of men) they regard as reliable, blocking the interlopers and all too frequently the innovative, deciding what is good and desirable for the society in which they operate. Much of their influence operates in the form of negative sanctions: invisible barriers unaccountably raised against people and policies they don't accept.

Despite their remarkably similar habits, theirs is a paradoxical kinship, for they belong to an elite that maintains its dynamism through incessant jousting for position within its own careful confines. Even when the occasional bitter feud erupts into public view (such as the Argus-Power row), these games of power are played to a particular set of rules that are not laid down, even if they are well understood.

Members of this business Establishment touch and greet each other on a wide spectrum of intimacy depending on the commonalty of their objectives at any given moment. But no matter how much their goals may temporarily conflict, *they always take one another into account.* They accept, understand, and protect each other. ("Make certain you see him before noon," runs the gentle admonition about one of the Establishment's most distinguished power-holders who has a drinking problem.)

Yet it is an Establishment in a state of unprecedented transition. The great business dynasties—except for some

Molsons and Eatons—which so recently dominated Canada's economy have all but vanished from contention. Power shifts according to the ways money is made. Leaving behind the railway and banking barons, the mining and oil fortunes, wealth is now flowing out of very different fashions and life styles. There are many more millionaires ("people one hardly knows"); the influence of money grows much more diffuse. Education, breeding, and manners have become deflated currencies among the business elite.

At the same time, Canada's economic centre of gravity is shifting from Montreal to Toronto and pushing westward. Power still accrues to the centre, and the central economic authority clearly remains anchored in Toronto, where most of the business Establishment lives, deals, and maintains and spreads its roots. But Calgary and Vancouver are moving up fast. The impatient Western power barons are refusing to integrate themselves into the Eastern elites as their independent influence expands to challenge the incumbents.

Part of this phenomenon—whose implications for the Canadian social structure have yet to be realized—is that the wealth and authority once organized around families (as they still are in some regional pockets, mainly in the Maritimes) have been replaced by the national power grips of the huge corporations. The most influential men in most Canadian cities and towns no longer belong to local power clusters. Instead, they are the smooth ambassadors of large multinational or transnational corporations. Careers are made in companies, not communities. The equations of power are changing.

THINGS HAVE A WAY OF COMING MOST SHARPLY INTO FOCUS NEAR THE END OF THEIR HISTORIC CYCLES. Canada was run well into the sixties by a tightly knit single elite—the business/government axis forged during World War II by C.D. Howe. Gradually these twin components grew apart, at first forming an uneasy alliance and more recently beginning to struggle for supremacy. The corporations, if they are big and powerful enough, have learned that no government will allow them either to go bankrupt or to shut plants and increase unemployment. So they raise their prices and profits with equanimity, and governments protect them with subsidies and by increasing the money supply. In return, they are charged higher taxes and their freedom of action is being drastically reduced. Confrontations are resolved through uneasy reconciliations of private and public power in the interests of saving the system.

But the smell of rapidly achievable authority is attracting the young into government (not corporate) service, and they do not want to save the system; they want to change it. They view the Royal Commission on Corporate Concentration as an exercise in identifying their targets. The great, system-bending confrontation that was to come between management and labour is taking place between business and government.

Faced with these and other unexpected onslaughts on its tranquil possession of power, Canada's business Establishment is suffering a crisis of nerve and faith, a partial loss of the easy self-confidence that has always marked its passage.

The members of Canada's various Establishments are caught between two diverse and contrary incarnations: one as the traditionally calm overlords of the Canadian manor and the other as the besieged barons of castles that are being overrun by noisy rebellious strangers from the other side of the wall. Besides the invading hordes of politicians and bureaucrats, there are beginning to be heard other dissenters, other voices: the newly educated middle class, the newly confident Western Canadians, the new nationalists, the Jews, the Establishment's own sons and daughters, disenchanted with its scale of values. (But the Waterloo—or Vietnam—of the Canadian Establishment may well be its failure to comprehend what has been happening in Quebec, where popular rage has been mistaken for a "quiet revolution.")

Classes in possession of what they believe to be unchallengeable doctrine do not change. They become extinct.

The Canadian Establishment has not yet lost its enduring sense of safety and survival. But there is a warning of fever in their Wasp souls as its members brood in their drawing rooms, dispatching sullen butlers to draw noiseless curtains against the gathering night.

Appendices

APPENDIX A
The Sturgeon Lake Pack

This is the guest list of the 1973 Sturgeon Point business and government conference held by Toronto stockbroker Robert Wisener.

Name	Affiliation	Title	Location
Peter N. Breyfogle	Massey-Ferguson Ltd.	Vice-President, Corporate Operations	Toronto
Doug Caldwell	Smith & Caldwell Ltd.	President	Toronto
Jim Cole	Guardian Capital Group	Vice-President	Toronto
E. Kendall Cork	Noranda Mines Ltd.	Vice-President and Treasurer	Toronto
Lewis B. Cullman	Lewis B. Cullman Inc.	President	New York
Glenn H. Curtis	Glenn H. Curtis & Associates Ltd.	President	Toronto
John T. DesBrisay, Q.C.	Cassels, Brock	Lawyer	Toronto
Senator Douglas D. Everett	Royal Canadian Securities Co. Ltd.	President	Winnipeg
Douglas H. Fullerton	Special Study on the National Capital	Director	Ottawa
Pierre Genest, Q.C.	Cassels, Brock	Lawyer	Toronto
Edwin A. Goodman, Q.C.	Goodman & Goodman	Lawyer	Toronto
James F. Grandy	Department of Industry, Trade and Commerce	Deputy Minister	Ottawa
Barry P. Hayes	Toronto Carpet Manufacturing Co. Ltd.	Vice-President	Toronto
Stewart Jamieson	British Metal Corp. (Canada) Ltd.	President	Toronto
Richard Jeffrey	Cyrus J. Lawrence Inc.	Vice-President	New York
Douglas N. Kendall	Kenting Ltd.	Chairman	Toronto
Robert M. MacIntosh	Bank of Nova Scotia	Executive Vice-President	Toronto
Jack P.S. Mackenzie	Canada Permanent Trust Co.	Vice-President, Investments Division	Toronto
George S. Mann	United Trust Co.	Financial Consultant	Toronto
Alan R. Marchment	Guaranty Trust	President	Toronto
James W. McCutcheon	Shibley, Righton & McCutcheon	Lawyer	Toronto
Jock S. McLeod	T. Eaton Co. Ltd.	Investment Manager	Toronto
Richard C. Meech	Borden & Elliot	Lawyer	Toronto
Milan Nastich	Ontario Hydro	Assistant General Manager, Finance	Toronto
John F. Nelson	Kleinwort, Benson Inc.	Vice-President, Corporate Finance Department	New York
Alfred Powis	Noranda Mines Ltd.	President and Chief Executive Officer	Toronto
Simon S. Reisman	Department of Finance	Deputy Minister	Ottawa

Name	Affiliation	Title	Location
Charles F. Robbins, Jr.	Marine Midland Bank	Vice-President	New York
L. John Rothwell	Southam Press Ltd.	Vice-President, Engineering and Production	Toronto
Philip S. Schiliro	Wisener & Associates Co. Ltd.	President	New York
Lionel H. Schipper, Q.C.	Goodman & Goodman	Lawyer	Toronto
T.G. Sheard	Martin, Lucas & Co. Ltd.	Vice-President	Toronto
Selby Sinclair	Toromont Industries Ltd.	Chairman	Toronto
Richard H. Wilson	Colonial Management Associates Inc.	President	Boston
Wilfred J. Wilson	Teachers Insurance and Annuity Assoc. of America	Vice-President	New York
John R. Yarnell	Canadian Arctic Gas Pipeline Ltd.	Vice-President, Finance	Toronto

APPENDIX B
The Jet Set

This is a list of the private jets owned by Canadian business firms. It was compiled for this book by Les Edwards, Director of Industry and Government Relations, the Air Transport Association of Canada, Ottawa, and Hugh Whittington, editor of Canadian Aviation. Speeds are in knots and ranges are in nautical miles.

Type of Aircraft	Owner	Operates from
Grumman Gulfstream II:	Denison Mines Ltd.	Toronto
Seats 12 (normal) to 19	Falconbridge Nickel Mines Ltd.	Toronto
Cruising speed 512 kts.	Imperial Oil Ltd.	Toronto
Range 3,000 miles	International Nickel Co.	
Price about $5 million	of Canada Ltd.	Toronto
equipped	Noranda Mines Ltd.	Toronto
	Northern Electric Co. Ltd.	Montreal
Lockheed Dash 8 JetStar:	Power Corp. of Canada Ltd.	Montreal
Seats 9 (plus 2 crew)	Royal Bank of Canada	Montreal
Cruising speed 468 kts.	Texasgulf Inc.	Toronto
Range 2,800 miles	TransCanada PipeLines Ltd.	Toronto
Price $3.75 million plus		
equipment		
Dassault/Breguet Falcon	Argus Corp. Ltd.	Toronto
(various models):	Canadian Superior Oil Ltd.	Calgary
Seats 7 to 12	Glenway Home Builders Ltd.	Toronto
Cruising speed to 500 kts.	Seagram Co. Ltd.*	Montreal
Range 1,650-2,450 miles	Tele-Direct Ltd.	Montreal
Price $1.14 million to		
$2.25 million		
Rockwell Sabreliner:	R. Angus Alberta Ltd.	Edmonton
Seats 8 (normal)	Northern & Central Gas	
Cruising speed 445 kts.	Corp. Ltd.	Toronto
Range 1,950 miles		
Price $2.084 million		
HS-125:	Alberta Gas Trunk Line	
Seats 8 (normal)	Co. Ltd.	Calgary
Cruising speed 450 kts.	Alcan Aluminium Ltd.	Montreal
Range 1,500 miles	Bank of Montreal	Montreal
Price $1.6 million	Bank of Nova Scotia	Toronto
	Peter Bawden	Calgary
	Canada Packers Ltd.	Toronto
	Canadian Imperial Bank	
	of Commerce	Toronto
	Churchill Falls (Labrador)	
	Corp. Ltd.	Montreal
	Domtar Ltd.	Montreal
	T. Eaton Co. Ltd.	Toronto
	Fiberglas Canada Ltd.	Toronto
	Ford Motor Co. of Canada Ltd.	Toronto
	Gulf Oil Canada Ltd.	Toronto
	Interprovincial Pipe Line Ltd.	Edmonton
	K. C. Irving	Saint John
	Kaiser Resources Ltd.	Vancouver
	Labrador Mining & Exploration	
	Co. Ltd.	Toronto
	Molson Companies Ltd.	Toronto
	Ontario Paper Co. Ltd.	Toronto
	Pacific Petroleums Ltd.	Calgary
	Price Co. Ltd.	Montreal

*Formerly Distillers Corporation-Seagrams Ltd.

Type of Aircraft	Owner	Operates from
	Shell Canada Ltd.	Toronto
	Simpsons-Sears Ltd.	Toronto
	E. P. Taylor	Nassau
	Toronto-Dominion Bank	Toronto
	Woodward Stores Ltd.	Vancouver
Gates Learjet:	B.C. Forest Products Ltd.	Vancouver
Seats 8	Dominion Road Machinery	
Cruising speed 464 kts.	Co. Ltd.	Goderich
Range 2,500 miles	High Line Electric	Prince Albert
Price $1.079 million	John Labatt Ltd.	Toronto
	Mannix Co. Ltd.	Calgary
	Oshawa Group Ltd.	Toronto
	Powell Equipment Ltd.	Winnipeg
	Ranger Oil (Canada) Ltd.	Calgary
	George Weston Ltd.	Toronto
Jet Commander/	Belzberg family	Vancouver
Westwind 1123:	Burns Foods Ltd.	Calgary
Seats 8-10	Central & Nova Scotia Trust Co.	Moncton
Cruising speed 450 kts.	Comstock International Ltd.	Toronto
Range 2,000 miles	Du Pont of Canada Ltd.	Montreal
Price $1 million	Hudson Bay Mining &	
	Smelting Co. Ltd.	Toronto
	International Nickel Co.	
	of Canada Ltd.	Toronto
	Jean-Louis Lévesque	Montreal
Cessna Citation:	BACM Industries Ltd.	Winnipeg
Seats 7	B.C. Telephone Co.	Vancouver
Cruising speed 350 kts.	Canadian Forest Products Ltd.	Vancouver
Range 1,150 miles	Canadian International	
Price $850,000	Paper Co.	Montreal
	Pratt & Whitney Aircraft of	
	Canada Ltd.*	Montreal

APPENDIX C
The Top 100 Club

This list, compiled by the Financial Post, ranks Canada's largest manufacturing, resource, and utility companies on the basis of their 1974 sales. A few of the larger firms, such as Canadian International Paper, have been omitted because they are provincially chartered and do not file financial statements with the Department of Consumer and Corporate Affairs. (Crown corporations like Polysar, CNR, and Air Canada have been excluded.) Sixty-six of the hundred corporations are controlled or substantially controlled by foreign interests. Separate tabulations list the twenty-five largest financial institutions, the ten top merchandisers, and subsidiaries that consolidate their accounts with parent companies. Combined earnings for the top hundred totalled $4.394 billion, with American Motors (Canada) Limited coming in with the largest return (38.7 per cent) on invested capital. Combined assets were valued at $62.022 billion. The top profit-maker in 1974 was Inco, with $303 million.

Company	Sales or operating revenues in thousands of dollars	Assets in thousands of dollars	Net income in thousands of dollars	%	Foreign Ownership Owner
Ford Motor Co. of Canada Ltd.	4,259,400[a]	1,462,300	154,300	87.8	Ford Motor Co., Dearborn
Imperial Oil Ltd.	3,645,000	2,701,000	290,000	69.4	Exxon Corp, New York
General Motors of Canada Ltd.	3,613,544[a]	1,093,053	106,097	100.0	General Motors Corp, Detroit
Canadian Pacific Ltd.	3,112,846	5,434,527	181,276	35.7	U.S. 17.7%, British 9.5%, other 8.5%

457

Company	Sales or operating revenues in thousands of dollars	Assets in thousands of dollars	Net[1] income in thousands of dollars	%	Foreign Ownership Owner
Bell Canada	2,665,606	5,820,597	224,436		
Alcan Aluminium Ltd.[3]	2,391,883	2,932,802	140,601	54.6	U.S. 44.1%, other 10.5%
Chrysler Canada Ltd.	1,929,170[2]	522,028	18,601	100.0	Chrysler Corp., Detroit
Massey-Ferguson Ltd.[3]	1,757,142	1,589,096	67,359	13.4	U.S. 12.2%, other 1.2%
International Nickel Co. of Canada Ltd.[3]	1,670,457	2,773,142	303,432	50.0	U.S. 35%, other 15%
Shell Canada Ltd.	1,601,523[4]	1,475,950	142,039	71.0	Royal Dutch/Shell Group
Gulf Oil Canada Ltd.	1,476,800[4]	1,631,200	161,000	68.3	Gulf Oil Corp., Pittsburgh
Canada Packers Ltd.	1,453,749	273,117	16,242[5]		
Noranda Mines Ltd.	1,147,041	1,707,296	154,870		
MacMillan Bloedel Ltd.	1,396,330	1,200,063	72,299		
Steel Co. of Canada Ltd.	1,133,163	1,340,336	110,861		
Moore Corp. Ltd.[3]	1,023,522	734,987	72,114		
Domtar Ltd.	897,652	683,363	82,479		
Seagram Corp. Ltd.[3]	866,902[4]	1,728,618	79,845		
Brascan Ltd.[3]	792,701	1,903,289	118,222		
Texaco Canada Ltd.	754,018[4]	711,693	55,049	68.2	Texaco Inc., New York
Canadian General Electric Co. Ltd.	709,913	563,754	26,043	91.9	General Electric Co., Schenectady
Consolidated-Bathurst Ltd.	689,009	636,632	47,712	12.9	Associated Newspapers Group Ltd., London

Company				%	Foreign parent
Dominion Foundries & Steel Ltd.	681,636	791,181	70,402		
IBM Canada Ltd.	668,013	423,536	66,840	100.0	International Business Machines Corp., Armonk, N.Y.
Genstar Ltd.	645,868	606,723	35,074		
Molson Companies Ltd.	613,632⁴	407,052	19,620	60.0	Europe 50%, U.S. 10%⁵
Burns Foods Ltd.	568,752	108,962	4,521⁷		
TransCanada PipeLines Ltd.	567,942	1,500,794	45,582		
Imasco Ltd.	558,891⁴	332,271	30,805	53.0	Britain⁸
Abitibi Paper Co. Ltd.	551,893	846,903	45,880		
International Harvester Co. of Canada Ltd.	550,022	430,937	23,640	100.0	International Harvester Co., Chicago
Canadian Industries Ltd.	517,586	361,204	34,842	75.4	Imperial Chemical Industries Ltd., London
Hiram Walker-Gooderham & Worts Ltd.³	501,377⁴	852,758	65,422		
John Labatt Ltd.	479,600⁴	376,685	22,564		
Falconbridge Nickel Mines Ltd.	457,827	773,936	21,976	14.5	Superior Oil Co., Houston⁹
Swift Canadian Co. Ltd.	452,032	111,506	9,037	100.0	Esmark Inc., Chicago
BP Canada Ltd.	445,551⁴	559,151	39,511	65.6	British Petroleum Co. Ltd., London
Husky Oil Ltd.	435,306⁴	393,471	33,679	20.5	G.E. Nielson & Associates, U.S.
Mobil Oil Canada Ltd.	410,361	446,163	65,397	100.0	Mobil Oil Corp., New York
Westinghouse Canada Ltd.	402,878	209,419	10,789	75.2	Westinghouse Electric Corp., Pittsburgh
Rothmans of Pall Mall Canada Ltd.	398,383⁴	457,143	8,856	59.2	Rembrandt Controlling Investments Ltd., South Africa
Rio Algom Ltd.	390,571	472,311	43,824	51.3	Rio Tinto-Zinc Corp., London
Anglo-Canadian Telephone Co.	374,139	1,340,277	19,629	34.0	General Telephone & Electronics Corp., New York
Dominion Bridge Co. Ltd.	370,368	279,850	21,695		

Company	Sales or operating revenues in thousands of dollars	Assets in thousands of dollars	Net income in thousands of dollars	%	Foreign Ownership Owner
Du Pont of Canada Ltd.	368,425	321,533	20,497	74.9	E.I. du Pont de Nemours & Co., Wilmington
Petrofina Canada Ltd.	356,746[4]	454,673	31,047	71.8	Petrofina SA, Belgium
Northern & Central Gas Corp. Ltd.	344,040	737,617	23,953		
Crown Zellerbach Canada Ltd.	342,644	279,340	20,235	89.0	Crown Zellerbach Corp., San Francisco
Union Carbide Canada Ltd.	341,357	316,528	45,085	75.0	Union Carbide Corp, New York
Dominion Textile Ltd.	336,243	244,668	18,753		
Canada Cement Lafarge Ltd.	330,734	460,168	23,257	54.5	Lafarge SA, Paris
Maple Leaf Mills Ltd.	328,591	158,842	8,381	73.7	Norris Grain Co., Chicago
Canron Ltd.	325,718	207,591	11,212		
Hawker Siddeley Canada Ltd.	325,015	273,517	9,261	59.3	Hawker Siddeley Group Ltd., London
Ensite Ltd.	322,789	182,852	(4,278)	100.0	Ford Motor Co., Dearborn
Price Co. Ltd.	320,147	363,503	31,868[20]		
Dow Chemical of Canada Ltd.	307,000	350,000	n.a.	100.0	Dow Chemical Co, Midland, Mich.
Reed Paper Ltd.	303,201	296,705	34,045	86.3	Reed International Ltd., London
Consumers' Gas Co.	282,756	681,672	27,142		
Kraft Foods Ltd.	281,324	115,043	10,112	100.0	Kraftco Corp., Glenview, Ill.
Goodyear Canada Inc.	280,926	208,209	7,701	88.5	Goodyear Tire & Rubber Co., Akron
British Columbia Forest Products Ltd.	279,054	358,345	21,086	41.8	U.S., Mead Corp., Scott Paper Co.[11]

Company				
Sun Oil Co. Ltd.	268,838[4]	418,736	22,068	100.0	Sun Oil Co., Philadelphia
Amoco Canada Petroleum Co. Ltd.	268,766	577,763	28,600	100.0	Standard Oil Co. (Indiana), Chicago
Weldwood of Canada Ltd.	266,708	182,104	9,720	73.6	Champion International Corp., New York
Westcoast Transmission Co. Ltd.	266,600	664,277	26,731	14.8	Phillips Petroleum Co., Bartlesville, Okla.[13]
American Motors (Canada) Ltd.	265,184	42,222	7,368	100.0	American Motors Corp., Detroit
Hugh Russel Ltd.	262,800	115,471	15,665		
Ennock Corp. Ltd.	254,710	164,463	10,921		
Celanese Canada Ltd.	250,403	218,715	12,83-	56.6	Celanese Corp., New York
Comstock International Ltd.	250,000[13]	n.a.	n.a.		
General Foods Ltd.	248,304	137,188	10,801	100.0	General Foods Corp., White Plains, N.Y.
Continental Can Co. of Canada Ltd.	241,188	173,012	15,493	100.0	Continental Can Co., New York
Union Gas Ltd.	240,800	429,895	14,213[14]		
Canadian Hydrocarbons Ltd.	240,041	204,047	4,881	51.9	U.S. 17.7%, Europe 34.2%[15]
Neonex International Ltd.	235,200	104,100	3,500	9.3	U.S.
Lever Brothers Ltd.	233,162	105,677	8,105	100.0	Unilever Ltd., London
Canadian Corporate Management Co. Ltd.	231,738	111,444	9,331		
Pacific Petroleums Ltd.	229,950[4]	596,729	45,395	48.4	Phillips Petroleum Co., Bartlesville
Silverwood Industries Ltd.	229,080	70,889	1,355		
Standard Brands Ltd.	225,087	167,069	8,517	100.0	Standard Brands Inc., New York
Redpath Industries Ltd.	223,708	163,929	5,712	55.8	Tate & Lyle Investments Ltd., England
Canada Steamship Lines Ltd.	223,492	394,458	34,063		
White Motor Corp. of Canada Ltd.	222,000	85,605	6,661	100.0	White Motor Corp., Cleveland
Southam Press Ltd.	221,920	115,835	19,2-0		

Company	Sales or operating revenues in thousands of dollars	Assets in thousands of dollars	Net[1] income in thousands of dollars	%	Foreign Ownership Owner
Texaco Exploration Canada Ltd.	219,198	609,090	106,914	100.0	Texaco Inc, New York
Hudson Bay Mining & Smelting Co. Ltd.	217,301	403,973	38,579	36.7	Anglo American Group, South Africa
Total Petroleum (North America) Ltd.[3]	215,429	183,946	1,852	46.5	Cie Française des Petroles, France
Uniroyal Ltd.	202,883	128,736	1,689	100.0	Uniroyal Inc, New York
J.M. Schneider Ltd.	202,270	45,741	3,286		
Robin Hood Multifoods Ltd.	194,634	85,917	3,959	100.0	International Multifoods Corp., Minneapolis
Sherritt Gordon Mines Ltd.	192,958	189,843	23,046	39.7	Newmont Mining Corp, New York
Interprovincial Pipe Line Ltd.	192,944	617,222	35,585	22.9	Exxon Corp., New York[10]
Canadian Johns-Manville Co. Ltd.	191,981	245,507	20,179	100.0	Johns-Manville Corp, Denver
Canadian Cellulose Co. Ltd.	191,501	148,180	28,991		
Firestone Tire & Rubber Co. of Canada	191,210	193,948	(7,884)	100.0	Firestone Tire & Rubber Co., Akron
Rockwell International of Canada Ltd.	187,847	108,543	10,683	100.0	Rockwell International Corp., El Segundo, Calif.
Hudson's Bay Oil & Gas Co. Ltd.	183,200	487,349	58,352	53.1	Continental Oil Co., Stanford, Conn.
Atco Industries Ltd.	180,055	89,274	14,367		
Thomson Newspapers Ltd.	175,396	229,450	29,707		

¹On "deferred tax" basis, excluding extraordinary items.

²Figures for automobile companies include sales to parent and affiliated companies: General Motors $1,391 million, Ford $1,519.9 million, Chrysler and American Motors unstated. Also, Ford consolidates $1,038.7 million in sales of overseas subsidiaries.

³Accounts stated in U.S. funds have been converted at rate prevailing at fiscal year-end.

⁴Excise taxes deducted. For Molson Companies, as estimated by Financial Post Computer Services.

⁵Includes net investment income etc., totalling $598,000.

⁶Includes 10.6% owned by Associated International Cement Ltd., London, 5.8% owned directly by Société Générale de Belgique, Brussels, and its subsidiaries, and 15.7% by companies in which SGB and its subsidiaries have minority interests. Remainder widely distributed and based on the assumption that the majority of bearer-share warrants are owned in Europe. Stock is internationally listed.

⁷Includes capital loss $49,876.

⁸British-American Tobacco Co. Ltd., London, through a subsidiary, owns 45%. Tobacco Securities Trust Co. Ltd., London, 50% owned by British-American Tobacco, owns 9%.

⁹Indirect interest through McIntyre Mines Ltd., which owns 37% of Falconbridge. Superior directly and through 53.3%-owned Canadian Superior Oil Ltd. owns 39.4% of McIntyre.

¹⁰Includes investments, profits, etc., totalling $206,000.

¹¹53.3% owned directly by Mead Corp., Dayton, Ohio; 26.5% owned by Brunswick Pulp and Paper Co., Brunswick, Ga., which is owned 50% by Mead and 50% by Scott Paper Co., Philadelphia.

¹²Through 48.4% interest in Pacific Petroleums Ltd.

¹³Financial Post estimate.

¹⁴Company uses "deferred tax" method of accounting. Had the "flow through" method fused by the majority of public utility companies) been applied, net income would have been $22,537,000, and ranking would have been 53rd. The Canadian Institute of Chartered Accountants recommends the deferred tax method for most companies, but makes an exception for certain regulated companies such as public utilities.

¹⁵Iwill Development Ltd. owned 53.7%. Ownership of Elwill on full dilution: two U.S. residents, Raymond A. Rich and David R. Williams, Jr., 10% and 15%, respectively, a U.S. institution 8%, and Elican Development Co. Ltd. 67%. About 5% of Elican is owned in Canada, the remainder in Europe by Belgian, German, and French interests.

¹⁶Through 59.4% interest in Imperial Oil Ltd.

463

The 25 Largest Financial Institutions

Company*	Assets in thousands of dollars
Royal Bank of Canada	21,669,880
Canadian Imperial Bank of Commerce	18,946,881
Bank of Montreal	17,650,974
Bank of Nova Scotia	13,462,476
Toronto-Dominion Bank	11,857,017
Sun Life Assurance Co. of Canada	4,329,866
Banque Canadienne Nationale	4,125,868
Royal Trust Co.	3,121,967
Manufacturers Life Insurance Co.	2,755,872
Banque Provinciale du Canada	2,556,839
Huron & Erie Mortgage Corp.	2,223,552
Canada Permanent Mortgage Corp.	2,212,834
London Life Insurance Co.	2,187,981
IAC Ltd.	2,139,457
Great-West Life Assurance Co.	2,106,428
Canada Life Assurance Co.	1,705,931
Mutual Life Assurance Co. of Canada	1,596,585
Confederation Life Insurance Co.	1,267,176
Crown Life Insurance Co.	1,106,400
General Motors Acceptance Canada†	1,098,555
Victoria & Grey Trust Co.	1,072,799
Guaranty Trust Co. of Canada	1,034,722
National Trust Co. Ltd.	1,027,725
Traders Group Ltd.	983,879
North American Life Assurance Co.	939,037

*Figures for banks, National Trust, and Victoria & Grey are for year ended Oct. 31, 1974; all others, Dec. 31, 1974.
†Wholly owned by General Motors Corp., Detroit.

Major Subsidiaries

Company[1]	1974 sales in thousands of dollars	Parent company
Aluminum Co. of Canada Ltd.[2]	1,497,589	Alcan Aluminium Ltd.
Northern Electric Co. Ltd.	970,711	Bell Canada
Cominco Ltd.	781,898	Canadian Pacific Ltd.
Algoma Steel Corp. Ltd.	474,102[3]	Canadian Pacific Ltd.
British Columbia Telephone Co.	302,873	Anglo-Canadian Telephone Co.
Canadian Pacific Air Lines Ltd.	276,787	Canadian Pacific Ltd.
BACM Industries Ltd.	275,370	Genstar Ltd.

464

Carling O'Keefe Ltd. .... 274,713[4]   Rothmans of Pall Mall
                                                  Canada Ltd.
Ogilvie Flour Mills Co. Ltd..... 195,206   John Labatt Ltd.

[1]These firms had sales during 1974 that could have ranked them on the main list of the one hundred largest companies, but their financial results are consolidated with those of their parent organizations.
[2]Accounts, stated in U.S. funds, have been converted at rate prevailing at fiscal year end.
[3]Consolidated from July 8, 1974.
[4]Excise taxes deducted.

The 10 Top Merchandisers

Company[1]	1974 sales in thousands of dollars	Assets in thousands of dollars
George Weston Ltd.[2]	4,733,355	1,294,307
Dominion Stores Ltd.	1,649,502	240,856
Canada Safeway Ltd.[3]	1,547,398[4]	372,035
Simpsons-Sears Ltd.[5]	1,341,128	941,083
Steinberg's Ltd.	1,197,319	389,003
Hudson's Bay Co.[6]	1,013,562[7]	771,178
M. Loeb Ltd.	898,060	138,962
Oshawa Group Ltd.	866,518	236,122
F.W. Woolworth Co. Ltd.[8]	841,834	329,622
Woodward Stores Ltd.	504,491	205,086

[1]This list excludes T. Eaton Co. Ltd., which does not publish its figures. Its annual sales are estimated at $1.4 billion.
[2]Consolidates Loblaw Companies Ltd. and U.S. operations of Loblaw subsidiaries.
[3]Wholly owned by Safeway Stores Inc., Oakland, Calif.
[4]Excludes $984,633 in sales to parent.
[5]Voting shares owned 50% by Simpsons Ltd. and 50% by Sears, Roebuck & Co., Chicago.
[6]Share distribution: Canada 59.4%, Britain 37.2%, other foreign, 3.4%.
[7]Excludes fur consignments, $175,661,000.
[8]Wholly owned by F.W. Woolworth Co., New York.

The Canadian Business Establishment

This is a selected list of Canada's national business Establishment.

John B. Aird
Partner
Aird, Zimmerman & Berlis
Toronto

Donald S. Anderson
Corporate Director
Toronto

William A. Arbuckle
President
Investment Secretariat Ltd.
Montreal

John A. Armstrong
Chairman and CEO
Imperial Oil Ltd.
Toronto

Lewis H.M. Ayre
Chairman and President
Ayre & Sons Ltd.
St. John's

Robert A. Bandeen
President
Canadian National Railways
Montreal

Ian Barclay
President
B.C. Forest Products Ltd.
Vancouver

Alex E. Barron
President
Canadian General Investments Ltd.
Toronto

Thomas J. Bell
Chairman and CEO
Abitibi Paper Co. Ltd.
Toronto

Roy Bennett
President
Ford Motor Co. of Canada Ltd.
Oakville

William J. Bennett
President
Iron Ore Co. of Canada
Montreal

Robert Blair
President
Alberta Gas Trunk Line Co. Ltd.
Calgary

Edmund C. Bovey
Chairman and CEO
Northern & Central Gas Corp. Ltd.
Toronto

Charles R. Bronfman
President
House of Seagram Ltd.
Montreal

Charles F.W. Burns
Chairman
Burns Bros. and Denton Ltd.
Toronto

J.W. Burns
President
Great-West Life Assurance Co.
Winnipeg

G. Allan Burton
Chairman and CEO
Simpsons Ltd.
Toronto

Robert Burns Cameron
Chairman
Maritime Steel & Foundries
Ltd.
Halifax

Alistair M. Campbell
Chairman
Sun Life Assurance Co. of
Canada
Montreal

Donald G. Campbell
President
Maclean-Hunter Ltd.
Toronto

F.R.F. Carter
President
Hambro Canada Ltd.
Toronto

André Charron
President
Lévesque, Beaubien Inc.
Montreal

Arthur J.E. Child
President
Burns Foods Ltd.
Calgary

John V. Clyne
Director
MacMillan Bloedel Ltd.
Vancouver

Albert D. Cohen
President
General Distributors of
Canada Ltd.
Winnipeg

H. Reuben Cohen
Corporate Director
Moncton

John H. Coleman
President
JHC Associates Ltd.
Toronto

Jacques Courtois
Partner
Laing, Weldon, Courtois,
Clarkson, Parsons,
Gonthier & Tetrault
Montreal

Frank M. Covert
Partner
Stewart, MacKeen & Covert
Halifax

Kenneth Cox
President
New Brunswick Telephone
Co. Ltd.
Saint John

Andrew Crosbie
Corporate Director
St. John's

Peter D. Curry
President and Chief Operating
Officer
Power Corp. of Canada Ltd.
Montreal

Nelson M. Davis
Chairman and President
N. M. Davis Corp. Ltd.
Toronto

Graham Dawson
President
Dawson Construction Ltd.
Vancouver

Jean de Grandpré
President
Bell Canada
Montreal

Paul Desmarais
Chairman and CEO
Power Corp. of Canada Ltd.
Montreal

John Herbert Devlin
Chairman
Rothmans of Pall Mall
  Canada Ltd.
Toronto

A.E. Diamond
Chairman and CEO
Cadillac Fairview Corp. Ltd.
Toronto

John Craig Eaton
Chairman
Eaton's of Canada Ltd.
Toronto

R. Fraser Elliott
Partner
Stikeman, Elliott, Tamaki,
  Mercier & Robb
Montreal

Douglas D. Everett
President
Royal Canadian Securities
  Co. Ltd.
Winnipeg

Gilbert Finn
President
Assomption Mutual Life
  Insurance
Moncton

Gordon N. Fisher
President
Southam Press Ltd.
Toronto

August Franck
Chairman and CEO
Genstar Ltd.
Montreal

Douglas Gardiner
Deputy Chairman
Royal Bank of Canada
Toronto

J. Douglas Gibson
Corporate Director
Toronto

Kelly Gibson
Chairman and CEO
Pacific Petroleums Ltd.
Calgary

John M. Godfrey
Partner
Campbell, Godfrey & Lewtas
Toronto

Duncan Gordon
Partner
Clarkson Gordon & Co.
Toronto

J. Peter Gordon
President
Steel Co. of Canada Ltd.
Toronto

A.G.S. Griffin
Corporate Director
Toronto

L. Edward Grubb
Chairman and Chief Officer
International Nickel Co. of
  Canada
Toronto

Charles L. Gundy
Chairman
Wood Gundy Ltd.
Toronto

Conrad F. Harrington
Chairman
Royal Trust Co.
Montreal

W.B. Harris
Corporate Director
Toronto

Russell E. Harrison
President
Canadian Imperial Bank of
Commerce
Toronto

Claude Hébert
Chairman and CEO
Bombardier Ltd.
Montreal

George C. Hitchman
Deputy Chairman of the
Board
Bank of Nova Scotia
Toronto

G.H.D. Hobbs
President
Cominco Ltd.
Vancouver

Beland H. Honderich
President and Publisher
Toronto Star Ltd.
Toronto

Donald F. Hunter
Chairman
Maclean-Hunter Ltd.
Toronto

Arthur, Jack, and J. K. Irving
Irving Holdings
Saint John

Richard M. Ivey
Partner
Ivey & Dowler
London, Ontario

Neil Ivory
President
Pembroke Management Ltd.
Montreal

Henry N.R. Jackman
Chairman
Empire Life Insurance Co.
Toronto

Stephen Jarislowsky
President
Jarislowsky, Fraser & Co. Ltd.
Montreal

Capt. Joseph Jeffery
Chairman and CEO
London Life Insurance Co.
London, Ontario

John J. Jodrey
President
Minas Basin Pulp & Power
Co. Ltd.
Hantsport, N.S.

Robert Jones
President
Investors Group
Winnipeg

Edgar F. Kaiser, Jr.
President
Kaiser Resources Ltd.
Vancouver

Sol Kanee
Chairman
Soo Line Mills (1969) Ltd.
Winnipeg

James W. Kerr
Chairman and CEO
TransCanada PipeLines Ltd.
Toronto

Michael Koerner
President
Canada Overseas Investments
Ltd.
Toronto

Murray Koffler
Chairman and CEO
Koffler Stores Ltd.
Toronto

Leo Kolber
President
Cemp Investments Ltd.
Montreal

Thomas E. Ladner
Partner
Ladner, Downs
Vancouver

C.M. Laidley
Senior Vice-President (Loans
  and Investments)
Canadian Imperial Bank of
  Comm.
Toronto

Peter M. Laing
Partner
Laing, Weldon, Courtois,
  Clarkson, Parsons, Gonthier
  & Tetrault
Montreal

Allen Thomas Lambert
Chairman and CEO
Toronto-Dominion Bank
Toronto

Howard J. Lang
Chairman and CEO
Canron Ltd.
Montreal

John D. Leitch
President
Upper Lakes Shipping Ltd.
Toronto

Joseph Likely
President
Jos. A. Likely Ltd.
Saint John

A.J. Little
Corporate Director
Toronto

Charles E. MacCulloch
Chairman
MacCulloch & Co. Ltd.
Halifax

Peter Macdonnell
Partner
Milner & Steer
Edmonton

Alexander John MacIntosh
Partner
Blake, Cassels & Graydon
Toronto

Robert MacIntosh
Executive Vice-President
Bank of Nova Scotia
Toronto

J. Douglas Maitland
Chairman
Hastings West Investment Ltd.
Vancouver

Brig. Richard S. Malone
President
FP Publications Ltd.
Toronto

Ernest C. Manning
Corporate Director
Edmonton

Fred Mannix
President
Loram Holdings Ltd.
Calgary

David Mansur
Corporate Director
Toronto

George Mara
Corporate Director
Toronto

Alan Marchment
President
Guaranty Trust Co. of
  Canada
Toronto

Maj.-Gen. A. Bruce Matthews
Executive Vice-President and
Director
Argus Corp. Ltd.
Toronto

Beverley Matthews
Partner
McCarthy & McCarthy
Toronto

Jerry McAfee
President
Gulf Oil Canada Ltd.
Toronto

Andrew McCain
Vice-President
McCain Produce Co. Ltd.
Florenceville, N.B.

H. Harrison McCain
Chairman
McCain Foods Ltd.
Florenceville, N.B.

John Leighton McCarthy
Vice-President and Director
Canada Life Assurance Co.
Toronto

John A. McDougald
Chairman and President
Argus Corp. Ltd.
Toronto

F.G. McDowell
Executive Vice-President
(Credit)
Toronto-Dominion Bank
Toronto

Peter M. McEntyre
President
Commercial Trust Co. Ltd.
Montreal

Donald McInnes
Partner
McInnes, Cooper & Robertson
Halifax

Donald Alexander McIntosh
Partner
Fraser and Beatty
Toronto

W. Earle McLaughlin
Chairman and President
Royal Bank of Canada
Montreal

William F. McLean
President
Canada Packers Ltd.
Toronto

Frederick H. McNeil
Deputy Chairman and CEO
Bank of Montreal
Montreal

Charles Edward Medland
President
Wood Gundy Ltd.
Toronto

Col. Maxwell Meighen
Chairman
Canadian General Investments
Ltd.
Toronto

Hartland de M. Molson
Honorary Chairman
Molson Companies Ltd.
Montreal

John H. Moore
President
Brascan Ltd.
Toronto

William D. Mulholland
President
Bank of Montreal
Montreal

J. Dean Muncaster
President
Canadian Tire Corp. Ltd.
Toronto

Pierre Nadeau
President
Petrofina Canada Ltd.
Montreal

Deane Nesbitt
President
Nesbitt, Thomson & Co. Ltd.
Montreal

John Nichol
President
Springfield Investment Co.
   Ltd.
Vancouver

J. Angus Ogilvy
Partner
Ogilvy, Cope, Porteous,
   Hansard
Montreal

Philip Oland
President
Moosehead Breweries Ltd.
Saint John

Victor Oland
Corporate Director
Halifax

Jean P.W. Ostiguy
President
Crang & Ostiguy Inc.
Montreal

Paul Paré
President
Imasco Ltd.
Montreal

Douglas Peacher
President
Simpsons-Sears Ltd.
Toronto

Lazarus Phillips
Partner
Phillips & Vineberg
Montreal

Ward C. Pitfield
President
Pitfield, Mackay, Ross & Co.
   Ltd.
Toronto

Gérard Plourde
Chairman and CEO
UAP Inc.
Montreal

Alfred Powis
President
Noranda Mines Ltd.
Toronto

John Prentice
Chairman
Canadian Forest Products Ltd.
Vancouver

Louis Rasminsky
Corporate Director
Ottawa

Charles I. Rathgeb
Chairman and CEO
Comstock International Ltd.
Toronto

George T. Richardson
President
James Richardson & Sons Ltd.
Winnipeg

J. Ernest Richardson
Chairman and CEO
B.C. Telephone Co.
Vancouver

B.H. Rieger
Vice-President and Director
Canadian Corporate
   Management
Toronto

Conrad S. Riley
President
Dominion Tanners Ltd.
Winnipeg

T. Stewart Ripley
President
Metropolitan Trust Co.
Toronto

Cedric E. Ritchie
Chairman, President, and CEO
Bank of Nova Scotia
Toronto

John P. Robarts
Partner
Stikeman, Elliott, Robarts &
   Bowman
Toronto

R.G. Rogers
President
Crown Zellerbach Canada Ltd.
Vancouver

Lucien Rolland
President
Rolland Paper Co. Ltd.
Montreal

Robert Carlton Scrivener
Chairman and CEO
Bell Canada
Montreal

Joseph Sedgwick
Counsel
Seed, Long, Howard, Cook &
   Caswell
Toronto

Gordon R. Sharwood
Chairman and CEO
Guaranty Trust Co. of Canada
Toronto

Frank Howard Sherman
President
Dominion Foundries & Steel
   Ltd.
Hamilton

Ian David Sinclair
Chairman and CEO
Canadian Pacific Ltd.
Montreal

William Sobey
Chairman and CEO
Sobeys Stores Ltd.
Stellarton, N.S.

James A. Soden
Chairman and CEO
Trizec Corp. Ltd.
Montreal

George Charles Solomon
President
Western Tractor Ltd.
Regina

Ronald Southern
President
Atco Industries Ltd.
Calgary

Sam Steinberg
Chairman and CEO
Steinberg's Ltd.
Montreal

Alan Sweatman
Partner
Thompson, Dorfman,
   Sweatman
Winnipeg

J. Allyn Taylor
Chairman
Canada Trust Co.
London, Ontario

Kenneth Thomson
Chairman and President
Thomson Newspapers Ltd.
Toronto

Richard M. Thomson
President
Toronto-Dominion Bank
Toronto

D.W. Timmis
President
MacMillan Bloedel Ltd.
Vancouver

James M. Tory
Partner
Tory, Tory, DesLauriers &
    Binnington
Toronto

John A. Tory
President
Thomson Corp. Ltd.
Toronto

William Ian Mackenzie Turner
President
Consolidated-Bathurst Ltd.
Montreal

Jack Turvey
President
Interprovincial Steel & Pipe
    Corp.
Regina

William Osborn Twaits
Corporate Director
Toronto

Page Wadsworth
Chairman and CEO
Canadian Imperial Bank of
    Commerce
Toronto

Douglas H. Ward
Chairman
Dominion Securities Corp.
    Harris & Partners Ltd.
Toronto

Donald C. Webster
President
Helix Investments Ltd.
Toronto

Lorne Webster
President
Prenor Group Ltd.
Montreal

R. Howard Webster
President
Imperial Trust Co.
Montreal

David B. Weldon
President
Midland Doherty Ltd.
Toronto

W. Galen Weston
Chairman
George Weston Ltd.
Toronto

Kenneth A. White
President
Royal Trust Co.
Montreal

H. Richard Whittall
Deputy Managing Partner
Richardson Securities of
    Canada
Vancouver

James William Whittall
President
Reed Shaw Osler Ltd.
Toronto

William P. Wilder
Chairman and CEO
Canadian Arctic Gas Pipeline
    Ltd.
Toronto

Donald G. Willmot
Chairman
Molson Companies Ltd.
Toronto

Ray D. Wolfe
Chairman and CEO
Oshawa Group Ltd.
Toronto

Harold E. Wyatt
Senior Vice-President (Credit)
Royal Bank of Canada
Montreal

APPENDIX E
The Munitions and Supply Gang

This is a selected list of people, some of them dollar-a-year men, who worked in the Department of Munitions and Supply under C.D. Howe during World War II. It shows some of the later activities in which they were involved.

Name	Wartime Position	Later Activities
Ainsworth, A. Lee	Director, Cutting Tools and Gauges Ltd., 1941–45	Vice-President, John Inglis Co. Ltd.; President, Ainsworth Motors Ltd.
Aitken, Allan A.	Director, Federal Aircraft Ltd., 1940–47	Vice-President, Price Bros. & Co. Ltd.
Ambridge, Douglas W.	Director-General, Shipbuilding, 1941–44	President, Abitibi Paper; Director, Montreal Trust
Ament, Arthur R. G.	Treasurer, Research Enterprises Ltd., 1945–47	Treasurer, Brascan Ltd.
Anderson, Alfred Clare	Deputy Controller, Steel, 1941–45	Vice-President, Dominion Foundries and Steel Ltd.
Arscott, Allan E.	Director, Wartime Merchant Shipping Ltd., 1941–45	Chairman, Canadian Bank of Commerce
Banks, Charles A.	U.K. Representative, 1940–45	Managing Director, Placer Development Ltd.; Lieutenant-Governor of B.C., 1946–50
Barrett, Henry	Director, Melbourne Merchandising Ltd., 1940–47	President, Dominion Woollens and Worsteds Ltd.
Baxter, Lionel D. M.	Director, Wartime Oils Ltd., 1943–45	President, Calgary & Edmonton Corp.; Anglo-Canadian Oils Ltd.
Beaubien, De Gaspé	Director, Defence Communications Ltd., 1943–45	President, De Gaspé Beaubien & Co.

Name	Wartime Position	Later Activities
Bell, Ralph P.	Director-General, Aircraft Production, 1940–44	President, Halifax Insurance Co., National Sea Products Ltd.
Belnap, LaMonte J.	Vice-President, Citadel Merchandising Co. Ltd., 1940–46	Chairman, Consolidated Paper Corp., Dominion Glass Co.
Berkinshaw, Richard	President, Polymer Corp. Ltd., 1942–45	President, Goodyear Tire and Rubber Co. of Canada Ltd.
Bickell, J. P.	President, Victory Aircraft Ltd., 1942–44	Chairman, McIntyre Porcupine Mines Ltd.
Birchard, Eslie Russell	Deputy Controller, Motor Vehicle Control, 1941–45; Controller, 1945; Vice-President, War Assets Corp., 1945–47	Vice-President, National Research Council
Birks, Ray T.	Director, Eldorado Mining and Refining Ltd.	President, Sterling Trusts
Bishop, Arthur L.	Director, Polymer Corp. Ltd., 1942–43	President, Coniagas Mines Ltd., Consumers' Gas Co.
Borden, Henry	Chairman, Wartime Industries Control Board, 1942–43	Lawyer; President, Brascan Ltd.
Brillant, Jules	Director, Defence Communications Ltd., 1943–45	Chairman, Provincial Bank; President, Lower St. Lawrence Power Co.
Brunning, Ernest John	Member, Production Board, 1941–45	President, Consumers Glass Co. Ltd.
Campbell, Douglas	Director, Signals Production Board, 1944–45	President, St. Lawrence Flour Mills
Carmichael, Harry	Co-ordinator of Production Board, 1942–45	Director, Massey-Ferguson and Argus Corp. Ltd.
Cockshutt, C. Gordon	Director, Plateau Co. Ltd.	President, Cockshutt Farm Equipment Ltd.

Name	Wartime Position	Later Activities
Common, Frank	General Counsel, Allied War Supplies Corp., 1940–46	Lawyer; Director, Ciba Ltd.
Connell, Frederick	Controller, Metals, 1944–45	Chairman, Conwest Exploration Co. Ltd.; President, Central Patricia Gold Mines Ltd.
Cope, F. Campbell	Secretary, Defence Communications Ltd., 1943	Lawyer; Director, Corby Distilleries, Hiram Walker
Cottrelle, George R.	Controller, Oil, 1940–45	Director, Canadian Bank of Commerce
Covert, Frank Manning	Solicitor, Legal Branch, 1940–42	Lawyer; President, Great Eastern Corp. Ltd., Maritime Paper Products Ltd.; Director, Royal Bank of Canada, Petrofina Canada Ltd.
Cowie, Alfred Henry	General Manager, Wartime Merchant Shipping Ltd., 1941–42	Vice-President, Dominion Bridge Co.; Director, Eastern Canada Steel and Iron Works
Crabtree, Harold	President, Allied War Supplies Corp., 1940–46	Chairman, Howard Smith Paper Mills Ltd., Fraser Companies Ltd.
Crandall, L. M.	Technical Adviser, Timber Control, 1941–43	Chairman, Eddy Match Co.
Crispin, Clifford	Control Officer, Timber Control, 1942–44; Assistant Controller, Timber, 1945	Vice-President, MacMillan & Bloedel Ltd.
Davey, John	Director, Wartime Merchant Shipping Ltd., 1941–45	President, International Paints (Canada) Ltd.; Director, Canada Steamship Lines
Dawes, A. Sidney	Vice-President, Federal Aircraft Ltd., 1940–47	Chairman, Atlas Construction Co. Ltd.

Name	Wartime Position	Later Activities
Donald, Robert	Solicitor, Legal Branch, 1942–45	Secretary, Brascan Ltd.
Eaton, John David	Member, Production Board, 1944–45	President, T. Eaton Co.
Eden, William Andrew	President, Fairmont Co. Ltd., 1940–41	President, Woods Mfg. Co.; Vice-President, Dominion Textile Ltd.
Elder, Aubrey	Director, Fairmont Co. Ltd., 1940–41	Lawyer; Director, Prudential Insurance Co. of America
Farish, David	Director-General, Organization and Personnel Branch, 1941	Vice-President, Northern Electric; President, Dominion Sound Equipments Ltd.
Filberg, Robert	President, Aero Timber Products Ltd., 1942–45	Chairman, Canadian Western Lumber Co.
Flemming, Hugh John	Director, Veneer Log Supply Ltd., 1942–45	Premier of N.B., 1952–60
Fogo, J. Gordon	Wartime Industries Control Board, 1942–44	Lawyer; President, National Liberal Federation; Senator
Fox, Edward	Vice-President, Victory Aircraft Ltd., 1942–43	President, Canadian Cottons Ltd.; Vice-President and Director, Brascan Ltd.
Fraser, Douglas M.	Assistant Secretary, Wartime Industries Control Board, 1944–45	Vice-Chairman, National Energy Board
Frith, John Rowland	Director of Supply, Coal Control, 1944–46	President, Lake Coal Division, M.A. Hanna Co.; President, Mullen Coal Co.
Gagnon, Wilfrid	President, Quebec Shipyards Ltd., 1943–45	Chairman, Dow Brewery, Canadian Aviation Electronics

479

Name	Wartime Position	Later Activities
Gaine, Arnold	Secretary-Treasurer and Vice-President, Research Enterprises Ltd., 1940–45; Treasurer, Turbo Research Ltd., 1944–45	Vice-President, Brascan Ltd.
Gavsie, Charles	Associate General Counsel, 1942–45	Lawyer; Deputy Minister of National Revenue; President, St. Lawrence Seaway Authority
Godsoe, J. Gerald	Associate Co-ordinator, then Chairman, Wartime Industries Control Board, 1942–45	Lawyer; Director, International Trust, Crown Life, RCA Ltd.
Gold, Eric Rae	Secretary, Wartime Housing Ltd., 1942–46	Lawyer; Secretary CMHC
Goldenberg, H. Carl	Director-General, Economics and Statistics Branch, 1940–45	Lawyer; Senator
Gordon, Crawford, Jr.	Director, Organization, 1942–45	President, A. V. Roe (Canada) Ltd.
Gordon, G. Blair	Director, Federal Aircraft Ltd., 1940–47	President, Dominion Textile Ltd.
Gourley, Robert	Director, Wartime Housing Ltd., 1941–42	President, Beaver Lumber Co.
Hackett, William T. G.	Secretary, Wartime Industries Control Board, 1941–43	Economic Adviser, Bank of Montreal
Hahn, James E.	Vice-President, Victory Aircraft Ltd., 1944–46	President, John Inglis Co. Ltd.
Harris, Kenneth	Director of Research, 1942–45	Assistant Professor, Harvard Business School
Heasman, George Robert	Assistant to Director, Canadian Mutual Aid Board, 1941–45	Director, Trade Commission Services, 1946–53; Ambassador to Indonesia, 1953–57

Name	Wartime Position	Later Activities
Hewett, F. V. C.	Executive Assistant, Metals Control 1941–45	President, McIntyre Porcupine Mines; Chairman, Ventures Ltd.
Horsey, J. William	Director, War Assets Corp., 1945–46	Chairman, Dominion Stores Ltd.; Director, Argus Corp. Ltd.
Hyde, G. Miller	Director, Federal Aircraft Ltd., 1940–47	Judge, Court of Queen's Bench, Quebec
Jennison, G. L.	Director, Priorities Board, 1941–45	President, Wills, Bickle and Co. Ltd.; Director, Canada Permanent Trust
Johnson, John David	Director, Citadel Merchandising Ltd., 1940–46	Chairman, Canada Cement Co.; Vice-President, Royal Bank of Canada
Jolley, Malcolm	President and Director, Small Arms Ltd., 1941–46	President, Russell Industries
Kelley, W. A. G.	Director, Atlas Plant Extension Ltd., 1940–43	Lawyer; Director, Brascan Ltd.
LaBine, Gilbert	Director, Eldorado Mining and Refining Ltd., 1942–46	President, Gunnar Gold Mines
Lamprey, John	Deputy Controller, Timber Control, 1942–45	President, Yorkshire Corp.
Lang, Louis L.	Director, Fairmont Co. Ltd., 1940–41	President, Mutual Life; Vice-President, Bank of Montreal; Director, Steel Co. of Canada
Leitch, Gordon	Managing Director, Toronto Shipbuilding Co. Ltd., 1941–42	President, Upper Lakes Shipping Ltd.; Director, Bank of Montreal
Leman, Beaudry	Director, Allied War Supplies Corp., 1940–46	Chairman, Banque Canadienne Nationale; Vice-President, General Trust of Canada

Name	Wartime Position	Later Activities
Little, Elliott	Director, Quebec Shipyards Ltd., 1943–45	President, Anglo-Canadian Pulp & Paper Mills
Logan, S. H.	Director, Victory Aircraft Ltd., 1942–44	Chairman, Canadian Bank of Commerce
MacAulay, John	Director, Eldorado Mining and Refining Ltd.	Lawyer; Director, Canada Safeway, Bank of Montreal
MacLaren, Ian	Associate Controller, Coal, 1943–46	Chairman, Rochester & Pittsburgh Coal Co. (Canada) Ltd.
MacMillan, H. R.	Controller, Timber, 1940; President, Wartime Merchant Shipping Ltd., 1941–43	Chairman, MacMillan & Bloedel; Vice-President, Canadian Bank of Commerce; Director, Canada Trust Co.
MacTavish, Duncan	Secretary, Canadian Mutual Aid Board, 1943–45	Lawyer; President, National Liberal Federation; Director, Canadian Bank of Commerce; Senator
Mansur, David	Assistant Chairman, National War Finance Committee, 1942–45	President, Kinross Mortgage Corporation; Director, Guaranty Trust
McCrimmon, Murray	Assistant to Director, Canadian Mutual Aid Board, 1943–45	Vice-President, Canadian Foreign Investment Corp.
McCurdy, Fleming	Director, Wartime Merchant Shipping Ltd., 1941–45	President, *Halifax Chronicle*, Eastern Trust Co.
McCurdy, J. A. D.	Aircraft Production Board, 1940–44	Lieutenant-Governor of N.S.; President, Montreal Aircraft Industries Ltd.
McKeen, Stanley	Director, Park Steamship Co. Ltd., 1946–47	Senator; Chairman, Straits Towing Ltd., Union Steamships
McMaster, Ross	Director, Allied War Supplies Corp., 1940–46	Chairman, Steel Co. of Canada; Director, CPR

Name	Wartime Position	Later Activities
Mockridge, Harold	Director, Fairmont Co. Ltd., 1941–44	Lawyer; Director, International Nickel Co. of Canada; President, Anglo-Canadian Mining & Refining
Morrison, D. M.	Director, Chemicals and Chemical Warfare, 1942–44	President, Trans Mountain Oil Pipe Line Co.
Morrow, Frederick	Director, Citadel Merchandising Co. Ltd., 1940–46	Vice-President and Director, Bank of Toronto; Director, Consumers Glass Co. Ltd.
Munro, Hector	Assistant to Controller, Timber Control, 1942–45	President, B.C. Forest Products Ltd.
Murdoch, J. Y.	Director, Allied War Supplies Corp., 1940–45	Lawyer; Chairman, Noranda Mines; Vice-President, Bank of Nova Scotia
Nicholson, A. S.	Controller, Timber, 1941–42	Chairman, Halton & Peel Trust & Savings Co.; President, Nicola Valley Sawmills Ltd.
Nicholson, John	Polymer Corp. Ltd., 1942–45	Lawyer; Director, Brascan Ltd.; Lieutenant-Governor of B.C.
Norris, John S.	Director, Allied War Supplies Corp., 1940–46	Director, Imperial Life Assurance Co.
O'Leary, A. T.	Director, Defence Communications Ltd., 1943–45	President, Inter-Provincial Steamship Co.
Paradis, Alfred	Director, Wartime Merchant Shipping Ltd., 1941–45	President, Harricana and Gatineau Telephone Co. Ltd.
Phillips, W. Eric	President, Research Enterprises Ltd., 1940–47	President, Duplate Canada Ltd.; Director, Argus Corp. Ltd.; Chairman, Massey-Ferguson

Name	Wartime Position	Later Activities
Pigott, Joseph	President, Wartime Housing Ltd., 1941–45	Chairman, Pigott Construction Co. Ltd.
Rainville, Gustave	Director, Research Enterprises Ltd., 1940–47	President, Consolidated Quebec Gold Mining & Metals Corp.
Rea, W. Harold	Liaison Officer, Oil Control, 1942–45	President, Canadian Oil Companies Ltd.; Chairman, Great Canadian Oil Sands Ltd.
Read, John	President, Atlas Plant Extension Ltd., 1942–45	Chairman, Canadian Westinghouse
Redfern, Charles	Vice-President, Wartime Merchant Shipping Ltd., 1943	President, Redfern Construction, Canadian Dredge & Dock
Reid, Fraser	Director, Eldorado Mining and Refining Ltd.	Director, Gunnar Gold Mines
Ross, Frank	Director-General, Naval Armaments and Equipment, 1940–46	Co-Chairman, Canada Cement Lafarge Ltd.; Lieutenant-Governor of B.C.
Ross, James Gordon	Director, Wartime Metals Corp., 1942–46	Director, Asbestos Corp.
Ross, Phyllis Gregory Turner (Mrs. Frank Ross)	Controller, Fats and Oils, 1941–45	Chancellor of UBC; mother of finance minister John Turner
Scully, Hugh	Controller, Steel, 1940–41	Director, IBM Canada Ltd.; Canadian Consul-General, New York
Scully, Vincent	Treasurer (later President), War Supplies Ltd., 1941–44; President, Victory Aircraft Ltd., 1944–46	President, Steel Co. of Canada

Name	Wartime Position	Later Activities
Shaw, Ralph	Assistant to Controller, Timber Control, 1942–44	President, MacMillan & Bloedel
Sheppard, G. Harry	Director-General, Organization and Personnel Branch, 1943	President, IBM Canada Ltd.; Director, Imperial Life Assurance Co.
Simard, Joseph	Director, Quebec Shipyards Ltd., 1943–45	Chairman, Marine Industries Ltd.
Simpson, J. I.	Director, Small Arms Ltd., 1940–46	Chairman, Dunlop Canada Ltd.
Spratt, J. Grant	Vice-President, Wartime Oils Ltd., 1943–45	President, Trans Mountain Oil Pipe Line Co.
Stavert, R. Ewart	Director, Wartime Metals Corp., 1942–46	President, Consolidated Mining and Smelting Co.
Stewart, James McGregor	Coal Control, 1939–43	Lawyer; Chairman, Mersey Paper Co.; Vice-President, Nova Scotia Light and Power Co.; Director, Royal Bank of Canada
Symington, H. J.	President, Trans-Canada Air Lines, 1941–47	Lawyer; Chairman, Price Bros. and Co. Ltd.; Director, CNR
Taylor, Austin	Vice-President, Wartime Merchant Shipping Ltd., 1941–45; Vice-President, Wartime Shipbuilding Ltd., 1941–45	President, Bralorne Mines; Director, B.C. Forest Products Ltd.
Taylor, E. P.	President, War Supplies Ltd., 1941; President, British Supply Council in North America, 1941; Canadian Chairman, U.S.-Canada Joint War Aid Committee, 1943	President, Argus Corp. Ltd.

Name	Wartime Position	Later Activities
Taylor, John Howard	Associate Director, Bituminous Coal Supply, 1945–46	President, Canadian Fuel Marketers Ltd.; Chairman, Bramalea Consolidated Developments
Timmins, Jules	President, Wartime Metals Corp., 1942–46	Chairman, Hollinger Consolidated; Director, Noranda Mines
Turnbull, David	Director, Allied War Supplies Corp., 1940–45	General Manager, Acadia-Atlantic Sugar Refineries; Vice-President, Eastern Canada Savings & Loan; Director, Dominion Steel & Coal Corp.
Turnbull, Hugh	Solicitor, 1940–41	Lawyer; President, Montreal Life Assurance
Uren, Wilbur Edward	Director-General, Priorities Branch, 1940–45	Chairman, Dominion Coal Board
Walker, William	Managing Director, Melbourne Merchandising Ltd., 1940–44	President, Canadian Chemical and Cellulose Co. Ltd.
Wallace, F. C.	Vice-President, Production, Research Enterprises Ltd., 1944–47	President, Canadian Pittsburgh Industries Ltd.
Weldon, J. A.	Controller, Allied War Supplies Corp., 1942–45	Vice-President, W. C. Pitfield & Co. Ltd. and Rolland Paper Co. Ltd.
Williamson, Alan	Vice-Chairman, Wartime Industries Control Board, 1942–45; Controller, Rubber, 1942–45; Controller, Timber, 1942–45	Joint Chairman, Wood Gundy & Co.
Wilson, Ernest Albert	Director, Allied War Supplies Corp., 1940–45	President, Ingersoll Machine & Tool Co.

Name	Wartime Position	Later Activities
Wilson, Hedley	Director, Wartime Housing Ltd., 1941–46	Vice-President, Maritime Trust Co.
Wood, Frank Edgar	Chief Cost Accountant, Audit Division, 1940–47	Secretary-Treasurer, Marathon Corp. of Canada
Young, Maj.-Gen. Hugh	President, Wartime Housing Ltd., 1946	Deputy Minister, Dept. of Public Works
Zimmerman, Adam	Director, Small Arms Production, 1940–43	Chairman, Defence Research Board

APPENDIX F
The Exchange Control Board Alumni

This is a list of the members of the senior staff of the Control Board during World War II, also showing some of their later activities.

Name	Wartime Position*	Later Activities
Beattie, John Robert	Adviser, Statistics and Research	Senior Deputy Governor, Bank of Canada
Bull, W. Frederick	Member	Deputy Minister of Trade and Commerce
Clark, W. Clifford	Member	Deputy Minister of Finance
Coyne, James Elliott	Adviser, Securities	Governor, Bank of Canada, 1954–61
Deutsch, John J.	Alternate Member	Chairman, Economic Council of Canada; Principal of Queen's University, 1968–74
Gordon, Donald	Chairman, WPTB	Chairman and President, CNR; President, Brinco Ltd.
Heeney, Arnold	Member	Chairman, International Joint Commission
Mackenzie, Maxwell	Member	Deputy Minister of Trade and Commerce, 1945–51; President, Canadian Chemical and Cellulose Co. Ltd.
Pearson, Lester B.	Member	Prime Minister of Canada
Plumptre, A.F. Wynne	Alternate Member	Assistant Deputy Minister of Finance

*The most interesting career of anyone associated with the FECB was that of Eric George Adams, head of the Statistics and Research Section. Adams graduated in Engineering from McGill in 1929 and took an MBA from Harvard in 1931. In 1940 he became technical adviser to the Wartime Requirements Board. He joined the FECB on March 24, 1941. Following Igor Gouzenko's disclo-

Name	Wartime Position	Later Activities
Rasminsky, Louis	Alternate Member	Governor, Bank of Canada, 1961–73
Saint-Amour, L.P.	Assistant to Chairman	Deputy Governor, Bank of Canada
Scott, W.E.	Statistics and Research Adviser	Inspector-General of Banks
Scully, Hugh	Member	Canadian Consul-General, New York
Sim, David	Member	Deputy Minister, Customs and Excise
Taylor, R.F.B.	Toronto Office	Treasurer, Trans Mountain Oil Pipe Line Co.
Towers, Graham	Chairman	Governor, Bank of Canada, 1934–54
Wilgress, L. Dana	Member	Canadian Ambassador to USSR

sures about Russia's wartime espionage in Canada, Adams was charged with being a member of the espionage organization of Col. Nicolai Zabotin, the military attaché of the USSR Embassy in Ottawa. The Royal Commission on Espionage says that the commissioners were satisfied that Adams was an important unit in the Zabotin organization, although he was acquitted in October, 1946.

489

APPENDIX G
The Wartime Prices and Trade Grads

This is a selected list of people, some of them dollar-a-year men, who worked on the Wartime Prices and Trade Board under Donald Gordon during World War II. It shows some of the later activities in which they were involved.

Name	Wartime Activity	Later Activities
Armer, James Cameron	Metals Administration, 1941–44	Vice-President, Dominion Forge Ltd.
Arnup, John D.	Prices and Supply, 1942–44	Judge, Supreme Court of Ontario; Treasurer, Law Society of Upper Canada
Ashbaugh, F.K.	Metals Co-ordinator, 1944–46	President, Lake Erie Tobacco Co. Ltd.
Austin, William	Information Branch, 1945–46	Assistant to the President, General Motors of Canada
Baker, George	Luggage and Small Leather Goods, 1941–46	President, Canadian Leather Products
Barbour, George	Prices and Supply, 1942–43	Minister of Public Works, P.E.I., 1943–49; Senator, 1949–62
Beaudoin, René	Information Branch, 1943–44	Speaker of the House of Commons, 1953–57
Bentley, D.F.	Prices and Supply, 1942–44	Vice-President, Texaco Canada Ltd.
Bloom, Herbert	Metals Administration, 1941–45	Vice-President, Massey-Harris Co. Ltd.
Boivin, P. Horace	Cotton Administration, 1941–45	President, Granby Elastic and Textiles
Brenan, Ralph	Foods Administration, 1942–46	President, G. E. Barbour Co. Ltd.; Vice-President, Fraser Companies Ltd.
Brimble-combe, W.H.	Footwear Administration, 1943–45	President, Blachford Shoe Manufacturing Co.

Name	Wartime Activity	Later Activities
Brown, Arthur	Electrical Equipment and Supplies, 1941–43	President, Dominion Sound Equipments
Brunning, Ernest John	Coal Administration, 1943–47	President, Consumers Glass Co. Ltd.
Bryant, J.S.	Prices and Supply, 1942–46	Vice-President, Simpsons Ltd.
Burroughes, Frank	Prices and Supply, 1943–45	President, Union Acceptance Corp.
Burton, Edgar	Retail Trade, 1941–44	Chairman, Simpsons Ltd.
Carter, Kenneth	Hides and Leather, 1944–47	Chairman, Royal Commission on Taxation
Chisholm, Robert	Wholesale Trade, 1941–44	Vice-President, Dominion Stores Ltd.; Chairman, William Mara Co. Ltd.
Clarke, Kenneth	Non-Ferrous Metals, 1944–45	Vice-President, International Nickel Co. of Canada
Connell, Frederick	Non-Ferrous Metals, 1944–45	Chairman, Conwest Exploration Co. Ltd.; President, Central Patricia Gold Mines Ltd.
Cottrelle, George R.	Oil Controller, 1941–45	Director, Canadian Bank of Commerce
Coyne, James Elliott	Deputy Chairman, 1942	Governor, Bank of Canada, 1954–61
Croft, James Randolph	Services Administration, 1943–46	Vice-President, Traders Finance Corp.
Crowlie, Hugh	Plant Machinery, 1941–44	President, Dominion Engineering Works; Director, Dominion Textile Ltd.
Cruikshank, Donald	Metals Administration, 1941–44	President, Steel Equipment Co. Ltd.

Name	Wartime Activity	Later Activities
Day, Robert	Jewellery Administration, 1941–46	Vice-Chairman, Bulova Watch Co. Ltd.
Deschatelets, Jean-Paul	Enforcement Counsel, 1942–51	Minister of Public Works, 1963–65; Speaker of the Senate
Duffett, Walter	Research Statistician, 1942–44	Dominion Statistician
Dugal, Armand-Joseph	Retail Trade, 1941–45	Director, Dupuis Frères Ltée
Ferrabee, Francis Gilbert	Plant Machinery, 1942–44	President, Canadian Ingersoll-Rand Co.
Flahiff, Terrence	Timber Administration, 1946–47	Chairman, Manicouagan Power Co. Ltd.; Vice-President, Ontario Paper Co. Ltd.
Fowler, Robert	Industrial Division, 1942–45	President, Canadian Pulp and Paper Assoc.; Chairman, BP Canada Ltd.
Frith, John Rowland	Director, Supply, Coal Control, 1944–46	President, Lake Coal Division, M.A. Hanna Co.; President, Mullen Coal Co.
Gibson, J. Douglas	Research Statistician, 1942–47	Deputy Chairman, Bank of Nova Scotia; Chairman, Eddy Match Co., Consumers' Gas Co.
Gordon, Donald	Chairman, WPTB, 1941–47	President, CNR
Griffin, Anthony	Emergency Shelter, 1946–47	Chairman, Home Oil Co. Ltd.; President, Triarch Corp. Ltd.
Guthrie, Albert	Furniture and Bedding Control, 1941–47	President, Simmons Ltd.
Henderson, Maxwell	Comptroller, 1942–46	Auditor-General of Canada
Horton, Edward	Textiles and Clothing, 1941–45	Deputy Minister of Municipal Affairs, Ontario

Name	Wartime Activity	Later Activities
Howard, Wilbert Harvard	Co-ordinator, Pulp and Paper, 1941–48	Lawyer; Chairman, Montreal Trust, Anglo-Newfoundland Development Co., Canadian Petrofina
Johnston, I.K.	Foods Administration, 1941–42	President, Imperial Bank of Canada
Langford, Henry	Counsel, 1944–45	Lawyer; Managing Director, Chartered Trust Co.
LeBel, Arthur	Senior Advisory Counsel, 1943–44	Judge, Supreme Court of Ontario
Levy, Herman	Administrator, 1941–45	President, Levy Bros.
Leybourne, Harold	Deputy Administrator, Wool, 1941–45	President, Artex Woollens Ltd., Majestic Woollens Ltd.
Macdonald, Ian	Publishing Administration, 1942–46	Deputy Chairman, Thomson Newspapers Ltd.
Mackenzie, Maxwell W.	Deputy Chairman 1942–44	Deputy Minister, Trade and Commerce; President, Canadian Chemical and Cellulose Co. Ltd.
Mc-Cutcheon, M. Wallace	Services Administrator, 1941–45	Vice-President and Managing Director, Argus Corp. Ltd.; Senator
McGregor, Fred	Member, 1939–47	Chief, Combines Investigation Branch
McLean, Alexander Neil	Fishery Products, 1940–45	President, Connors Bros. Ltd.; Senator, 1945–67
Mohan, Richard Thomas	Tea, Coffee, and Spices Administrator, 1941–45	Chairman, General Foods Ltd.
Morris, Michael	Fur Skins and Fur Garments, 1941	President, Hollanderizing Corp. (Canada) Ltd.
Morrow, C.J.	Fishery Products, 1942–44	President, National Sea Products Ltd.

Name	Wartime Activity	Later Activities
Nicholson, John	Supplies Administration, 1941–42	Vice-President, Polymer Corp. Ltd.; Director, Brascan Ltd.; Lieutenant-Governor of B.C.
Palm, William H.	Pulp and Paper Administration, 1941–44	President, Hinde & Dauch Ltd.
Plumptre, A.F. Wynne	Secretary, 1945–47	Assistant Deputy Minister of Finance
Rapmund, J.L.	Business Machines, 1942	General Manager, Burroughs Adding Machine Co. of Canada
Reid, Morgan	Wool Requirements, 1942–45	Vice-President, Simpsons-Sears Ltd.
Ross, Howard	Administrator, Rationing, 1943–45	Chartered Accountant; Chancellor, McGill University
Sim, David	Tobacco Administrator, 1940–45	Deputy Minister of Customs and Excise
Sinclair, Adelaide	Economist, 1942	Executive Assistant, Deputy Minister of Welfare
Spence, Ernest J.H.	Prices, 1942–47	President, Canadian Food Products Ltd.
Stanfield, Robert	Rent Control, Halifax, 1942–45	Premier of N.S., 1956–67; National Leader of Progressive Conservative Party
Stewart, James	Administrator, Services, 1941–43	Chairman, Canadian Bank of Commerce
Symington, H.J.	Controller, Power, 1941–46	Chairman, Price Brothers & Co. Ltd.; Director, CNR
Taggart, James Gordon	Controller, Food, 1941–43	Deputy Minister of Agriculture
Taylor, Kenneth	Co-ordinator, Foods Administration, 1943–46	Deputy Minister of Finance

Name	Wartime Activity	Later Activities
Uren, Wilbur Edward	Steel and Timber Control, 1943–45	Chairman, Dominion Coal Board
Walton, William Ralph	Rubber Control, 1941–45	President, International Silver Co. of Canada
Wells, Dalton	Enforcement Counsel, 1941–44	Chief Justice, Supreme Court of Ontario
Wemp, Grant	Licensing, 1942–43	President, Industrial Acceptance Corp.
Williamson, Alan	Controller, Timber and Rubber, 1942–45	Joint Chairman, Wood Gundy & Co.
Wilton, Richard	Pulp and Paper, 1943–44	President, Bathurst Power and Paper Co. Ltd.

APPENDIX H
The Five Lakes Fishing Club Crowd

This is a membership list (as of February 15, 1973) for the Five Lakes Fishing Club, located in the Gatineau hills near Ottawa.

Name	Date of Membership	Position
J.R. Beattie	1941	Former Deputy Governor, Bank of Canada
J.R. Brown	1969	Senior Tax Adviser to Department of Finance
F.W. Bruce	1941	Ex-Chief Executive Officer, Aluminum Co. of Canada Ltd.
R.B. Bryce	1941	Former Clerk of Privy Council and Deputy Minister of Finance
W. Frederick Bull	1953	Former Deputy Minister of Trade and Commerce
L.F. Burrows	1953	Secretary-Manager, Canadian Horticultural Council
H.M. Carscallen	1972	Former Chief of Air Operations, Air Force Headquarters, Ottawa
Louis Couillard	1965	Former Deputy Minister of Manpower and Immigration; Chairman of Tariff Board
James E. Coyne	1953	Former Governor, Bank of Canada
John Deutsch	1961	Former Chairman, Economic Council of Canada; Principal of Queen's University
C.M. Drury	1951	Former Deputy Minister of Defence; President of Treasury Board; Minister of Science and Works
A. Davidson Dunton	1962	Former Chairman of CBC
Mrs. A.K. Eaton		Widow of Assistant Deputy Minister of Finance

Name	Date of Membership	Position
John Eaton	1972	Ken Eaton's son
C.F. Elderkin	1946	Former Inspector-General of Banks
Jean Fournier	1972	Head of Quebec House; former official, External Affairs
Douglas M. Fraser	1971	Vice-Chairman, National Energy Board of Canada
Ed Gallant	1965	Chairman, National Capital Commission
W.F. Ganong	1953	Chief Meteorological Adviser to federal government
Dr. J.H.S. Geggie	1972	Local doctor at Wakefield, P.Q.
Allan Gibbons	1943	Former Administrator of Foreign Exchange Control Board and Reeve of Rockcliffe
John Gnaedinger	1953	Former Senior Engineer, Alcan
James F. Grandy	1971	Deputy Minister of Trade and Commerce
George R. Heasman	1943	Former Director, Trade Commission Service
Mrs. A.D.P. Heeney		Widow of Clerk of Privy Council
Claude Isbister	1962	Former Assistant Deputy Minister of Finance
Robert Johnstone	1971	Adviser to the Governor, Bank of Canada
L.S. Killaly	1943	Former Mortgage Manager, Sun Life Assurance
D.H.W. Kirkwood	1964	Former Assistant Secretary to Cabinet
David Mansur	1941	Former Chairman, Central Mortgage and Housing Corp.
W.R. Martin	1955	Former Assistant Secretary to Cabinet
D.W.R. McKinley	1943	Vice-President, National Research Council

Name	Date of Membership	Position
Frank Milligan	1971	Former Assistant Secretary to Cabinet
J. Harvey Perry	1969	Executive Director, Canadian Bankers' Assoc.
J.W. Pickersgill	1941	Former Clerk of Privy Council; Liberal cabinet minister
S.D. Pierce	1946	Former Assistant Deputy Minister of Trade and Commerce
A.F.W. Plumptre	1951	Former Assistant Deputy Minister of Finance
Louis Rasminsky	1941	Former Governor, Bank of Canada
Simon Reisman	1964	Deputy Minister of Finance.
Mrs. Alfred Rive		Widow of former Canadian Ambassador to Ireland
Guy Roberge	1964	Deputy Chairman, Canadian Transport Commission
J.A. Roberts	1962	Former Deputy Minister of Trade and Commerce
Gordon Robertson	1953	Former Clerk of Privy Council
Mrs. Norman Robertson		Widow of former Undersecretary of State for External Affairs
Blair Seaborn	1971	Acting Deputy Minister of Consumer and Corporate Affairs
David Sim	1941	Former Deputy Minister of Revenue
Mrs. Finlay Sim		Widow of Finlay Sim, former Comptroller-Secretary, Department of Trade and Commerce, and brother of David
Mrs. Margaret Sproule		Widow of Clifford Clark, former Deputy Minister of Finance
Ernest Steele	1961	Former Deputy Minister of Consumer and Corporate Affairs

Name	Date of Membership	Position
Kenneth Taylor	1941	Former Deputy Minister of Finance
Ross Tolmie	1941	Ottawa lawyer
P.M. Towe	1965	Ambassador and Permanent Representative to OECD
D.R. Yeomans	1971	Assistant Deputy Minister of Supply and Services

The Ottawa Mandarins

This is a selected list of some of the men who made up the Ottawa bureaucratic Establishment between the late thirties and late sixties.

Name	Graduate studies at Oxford	Graduate studies at Cambridge	Graduate studies at Harvard	Studied or taught at London School of Economics	Rhodes Scholar	Has a Ph.D or has been a professor	Member or ex-member of Five Lakes Fishing Club	Member of Rideau Club	Is or has been with Department of Finance	Is or has been with Department of External Affairs	Most prominent Public Service appointment
John Baldwin						●	●			●	Deputy Minister of Transport
J.R. Beattie			●	●		●		●			Deputy Governor, Bank of Canada
Bob Bryce	●	●				●	●	●			Deputy Minister of Finance
Clifford Clark		●		●		●	●	●	●		Deputy Minister of Finance
George Davidson		●				●		●			Deputy Minister of Health and Welfare
John Deutsch			●			●	●	●	●	●	Chairman, Economic Council
Bud Drury						●	●			●	Deputy Minister of National Defense
Davidson Dunton						●	●	●			President, CBC
Ken Eaton		●				●	●	●	●		Assistant Deputy Minister of Finance

Name	Graduate studies at Oxford	Graduate studies at Cambridge	Graduate studies at Harvard	Studied or taught at London School of Economics	Rhodes Scholar	Has a Ph.D or has been a professor	Member or ex-member of Five Lakes Fishing Club	Member of Rideau Club	Is or has been with Department of Finance	Is or has been with Department of External Affairs	Most prominent Public Service appointment
A.D.P. Heeney					●	●	●			●	Chairman, International Joint Commission
Claude Isbister		●				●	●	●	●		Deputy Minister of Immigration
Al Johnson		●				●		●			President, CBC
C.J. Mackenzie		●	●			●		●			President, National Research Council
W.A. Mackintosh		●	●			●	●	●	●		Acting Deputy Minister of Finance
Hector McKinnon								●	●		Chairman, Tariff Board
Lester Pearson	●					●	●	●		●	Undersecretary of State for External Affairs
Jack Pickersgill	●					●	●	●		●	Clerk of the Privy Council
Wynne Plumptre		●				●	●		●		Assistant Deputy Minister of Finance
Louis Rasminsky			●			●	●	●			Governor, Bank of Canada
Simon Reisman			●			●	●	●			Deputy Minister of Finance
Ed Ritchie					●			●		●	Undersecretary of State for External Affairs
Gordon Robertson					●	●	●	●		●	Clerk of the Privy Council

Name	Graduate studies at Oxford	Graduate studies at Cambridge	Graduate studies at Harvard	Studied or taught at London School of Economics	Rhodes Scholar	Has a Ph.D	Member or ex-member of Queen's University	Is or has been a professor	Member of Rideau Club	Member of Five Lakes Fishing Club	Is or has been with Department of Finance	Is or has been with Department of External Affairs	Most prominent Public Service appointment
Norman Robertson		●			●	●	●	●				●	Undersecretary of State for External Affairs
Mitchell Sharp			●					●	●		●		Deputy Minister, Trade and Commerce
David Sim							●	●					Deputy Minister, Customs and Excise
O.D. Skelton				●		●		●				●	Undersecretary of State for External Affairs
Ernie Steele			●				●	●	●				Undersecretary of State
Ross Tolmie	●				●		●	●			●		Solicitor, Department of Finance
Graham Towers			●				●	●	●				Governor, Bank of Canada
Jake Warren			●						●	●			Deputy Minister, Trade and Commerce
Dana Wilgress							●	●		●		●	Deputy Minister, Trade and Commerce

APPENDIX J
C.D. Howe's Secret Insiders

This is a list of the regular participants in the confidential briefing sessions conducted between 1947 and 1957 by Dr. O.J. Firestone and other Trade and Commerce officials under the auspices of C.D. Howe.

R.M. Fowler, President, Canadian Pulp and Paper Association, Montreal.

John Pemberton, Assistant Treasurer, Sun Life Assurance Co., Montreal.
(Jack Popkin, Economist, Sun Life Assurance Co., Montreal— alternate.)

J. Douglas Gibson, Economist, Bank of Nova Scotia, Toronto.
(R.M. MacIntosh, Economist, Bank of Nova Scotia, Toronto— alternate.)

William T.G. Hackett, Economist, Bank of Montreal, Montreal.
(Ted Walton, Economist, Bank of Montreal, Montreal—alternate.)

Jack Brydon, Treasurer, North American Life Assurance Co., Toronto.

W.C. Harris, President, W.C. Harris & Partners, Toronto.

S.H. "Jack" Sutherland, Economist, Ford Motor Co. of Canada, Toronto.

Eugene Forsey, Director of Research, Canadian Congress of Labour, Ottawa.

Harry Purdy, Treasurer and Economist, B.C. Electric Co., Vancouver.

A.B. Brown, Economist, Great-West Life Assurance Co., Winnipeg.

Stuart Armour, Economist, Steel Co. of Canada, Hamilton.

R.B. McPherson, Economist, Du Pont of Canada Ltd., Montreal.

Donald Marsh, Economist, Royal Bank of Canada, Montreal.

Morgan Reid, Economist, Simpsons-Sears.

Courtland Elliott, Investment Adviser, Toronto-Dominion Bank, Toronto.

Tim Martin, Investment Adviser, Toronto.

Douglas Wahn, Economist, CNR, Montreal.

Fred Brebner, Treasurer and Economist, Ontario Hydro, Toronto.

W. Harold Poole, Economist, Young and Rubicam Ltd., Toronto.

Arthur Smith, Economist, Canada-U.S. Committee, Montreal.

Harry Edmison, Secretary and Economist, Argus Corp., Toronto.

William Lougheed, Economist, Canadian Bank of Commerce, Toronto.

Bruce Shaw, Investment Adviser, A.E. Ames and Co., Winnipeg.

D.B. Mansur, Consolidated Toronto Development Corp., Toronto.

W.C. Hopper, Economist, Canadian Federation of Agriculture, Ottawa.

The Private School Fraternity

This is a list of private schools in Canada (not including Quebec's classical colleges) with their locations, principals, enrolments, and fee structures.

Boys' Schools

Name	Date Founded	Co-ed	Location	Head of School	Boarders	Day Students	Ages	Staff	Boarders' Fees	Day Students' Fees
Albert College	1857	X	Belleville, Ont.	Lorne L. Shewfelt, M.A.	85	10	11-18	16	$3,900-4,200	$1,900
Appleby College	1911		Oakville, Ont.	Edward R. Larsen, B.A., M.A.	195	165	9-18	35	$3,700-3,900	$2,050
Ashbury College	1891		Rockcliffe Park (Ottawa)	W.A. Joyce, D.S.O., E.D., B.Sc.	130	225	10-18	32	$3,600-3,650	$1,925-1,975
Bishop's College School	1836	X	Lennoxville, Que.	John D. Cowans, M.A.	165	16	11-18	26	$4,000	$1,800
Brentwood College School	1923	X	Mill Bay, B.C.	D.D. Mackenzie, M.A., F.R.S.A.	220	10	13-18	24	$3,850	$1,500
Crescent School	1913		Willowdale, Ont.	Christopher B. Gordon, B.A.	None	285	10-19	22		$1,550-1,650
De La Salle College "Oaklands"	1870		Toronto	Brother Edgar	None	900	11-18	40		$475-680
Halifax Grammar School	1958	X	Halifax	Douglas Williams, M.A.	None	160	5-19	20		$815-1,060
Hilfield-Strathallan Colleges	1901	X	Hamilton	M.B. Wansbrough, B.A.	None	400	3-19	55		$735-1,700
King's College School	1788		Windsor, N.S.	T.T.Menzies, M.A.	130	30	12-18	13	$3,300	$750

School			Location	Headmaster			Ages			
Lakefield College School	1879		Lakefield, Ont.	J.T.M. Guest, B.A.	205	28	10-18	21	$3,700-3,850	$1,650
Lower Canada College	1909		Montreal	G.H. Merrill, M.A.	None	585	8-18	45		$1,375-1,825
Pickering College	1842		Newmarket, Ont.	Harry M. Beer, B.A.	150	None	11-18	6	$3,700	
Ridley College	1889		St. Catharines	Richard A. Bradley, M.A.	380	100	10-18	42	$3,800-4,000	$2,050-2,250
Rothesay Collegiate School	1877		Rothesay, N.B.	Rev. Terence Davies, B.A., L.Th.	90	40	12-18	15	$2,600	$900
St. Andrew's College	1899		Aurora, Ont.	T.A. Hockin, B.A., M.P.A., Ph.D.	275	85	11-18	29	$4,075	$2,175
St. David's School for Boys	1971		Squamish, B.C.	Christopher Goodwin	75	None	13-18	15	$3,900-4,100	
St. George's College	1961		Toronto	John L. Wright, E.D., B.A.	None	346	9-18	22		$1,300-1,550
St. George's School	1931		Vancouver	Alan C.M. Brown	100	500	7-17	40	$3,195-3,645	$860-1,495
St. George's School of Montreal	1930	X	Montreal	Vincent P. Skinner	None	255	3-17	45		$930-1,650
St. John's-Cathedral Boys' School	1961		Selkirk, Man.	Frank Wiens, B.A., B.Ed.	100	None	13-17	10	$2,000	
St. John's School of Alberta	1967		Stony Plain, Alta.	David Neelands, B.Sc.	100	None	13-17	10	$2,000	
St. John's Ravenscourt School	1820	X	Winnipeg	H.J.P. Schaffter, M.A.	90	310	6-17	34	$3,435	$980-1,770
St. Michael's College School	1852		Toronto	Father Norman Fitzpatrick, M.A., S.T.B.	None	900	13-18	47		$400*
St. Michael's University School	1910		Victoria	P.A. Caleb, LL.B.	145	300	8-17	34	$2,725-2,875	$800-980
Selwyn House School	1908		Montreal	Alexis S. Troubetzkoy, B.A.	None	430	6-18	36		$950-1,350

*Fees are paid only by students in Grades 11 to 13.

Name	Date Founded	Co-ed	Location	Head of School	Boarders	Day Students	Ages	Staff	Boarders' Fees	Day Students' Fees
Shawnigan Lake School	1916		Shawnigan Lake, B.C.	H.C. Wilkinson, B.Com., M.B.A., M.Sc., P.Eng.	200	20	13-18	20	$3,900	$2,065
Stanstead College	1817		Stanstead, Que.	N. Thomas Russell	187	24	12-20	23	$3,100	
Strathcona-Tweedsmuir School	1934	X	Okotoks, Alta.	W.A. Heard	None	200	6-17	25		$1,000-1,350
Trinity College School	1865		Port Hope, Ont.	Angus C. Scott, M.A.	340	10	11-18	34	$3,775-3,975	
Upper Canada College	1829		Toronto	Richard Sadleir, M.A.	173	715	8-19	69	$4,610	$2,380
Weston School	1917	X	Montreal West	Mrs. Elizabeth A. Goddard, B.Sc.(Hons.)	None	50	5-17	20		$690-1,380

Girls' Schools

Name	Location	Head of School	Number of Students	Boarders' Fees	Day Students' Fees
Albert College	Belleville, Ont.	Lorne L. Shewfelt, M.A.	75	$3,900-4,200	$1,900
Alma College	St. Thomas, Ont.	Miss M.E. Bone, B.A.	140	$2,600	
Balmoral Hall School	Winnipeg	R. Martin Kenney, C.D., B.A., M.Ed.	240	$1,900	$995-1,810
Bishop's College School	Lennoxville, Que.	John D. Cowans, B.A., M.A.	85	$4,000	$1,800
Bishop Strachan School	Toronto	E.S. Jarvis, B.A., B. Paed.	670	$4,200	$1,600-1,950
Branksome Hall	Toronto	Miss Allison Roach, B.A.	670	$3,200	$500-1,600
Brentwood College School	Mill Bay, B.C.	D.D. Mackenzie, M.A., F.R.S.A.	50	$3,800	$1,500

School	Location	Head	Enrolment	Boarding fee	Day fee
Convent of the Sacred Heart	Montreal	Sister Margaret Johnson, R.S.C.J., B.A.	340	$1,425	$355
Crofton House School	Vancouver	Miss Rosalind W. Addison, B.Sc. (Hons.), Dip.Ed.	380	$3,135-3,575	$875-,475
Miss Edgar's and Miss Cramp's School	Montreal	Miss Jean C. Murray, M.A., Dip.Ed., Cert. Soc. Sc.	260		$1,150-,250 / $350 (senior students)
Edgehill School	Windsor, N.S.	Miss Gail Ann Emmerson, M.A.	80	$2,400	$550
Elmwood School	Rockcliffe Park (Ottawa)	Mrs. J.C. Whitwill, M.A. (Hons.)	160		$1,400
Halifax Grammar School	Halifax	Douglas Williams, M.A.	70		$815-1,060
Halifax Ladies' College	Halifax	Miss Carol F. Salton, M.A.	160		$465-755
Havergal College	Toronto	Mrs. Audrey G. Southam, B.A.	620	$4,200	$874-2,050
Hillfield-Strathallan Colleges	Hamilton	M.B. Warsbrough, B.A.	250		$735-1,700
Loretto Abbey	Toronto	Sister Evanne Hunter	500		$475*
Loretto College School	Toronto	Sister Ann Manuel	380		$300*
Netherwood (Rothesay School for Girls)	Rothesay, N.B.	Miss Lynda A. Heffernan, B.Sc., B.Ed.	75	$3,000	$1,000
Norfolk House	Victoria	Miss A. Winifred Scott, B.Sc.	240		$700-1,050
Ontario Ladies' College	Whitby, Ont.	Dr. Reginald C. Davis, M.A., M.Mus., M.Ed., Ph.D.	115	$2,730-2,850	$1,144
Queen of Angels Academy	Dorval, Que.	Sister Rose Dorothy Beauvais, S.S.A., B.A., B.Ed., M.A.	160	$1,365-1,465	$365
Queen Margaret's School	Duncan, B.C.	Peter Josselyn, B.A., Dip.Ed.	185	$3,400	$1,250*
St. Clement's School	Toronto	Miss Hazel W. Perkin, M.A.	330		$675-1,250
St. George's School of Montreal	Montreal	Vincent P. Skinner	170		$930-1,650
St. John's Ravenscourt School	Winnipeg	H.J.P. Schaffter, M.A.	40		$980-1,770

*Fees are paid only by students in Grades 11 to 13.

Name	Location	Head of School	Number of Students	Boarders' Fees	Day Students' Fees
St. Joseph's College School	Toronto	Sister Mary Kenneth	730		$425*
St. Joseph's Convent High School	Toronto	Sister Anne Schenck	720		$300*
St. Margaret's School	Victoria	Mrs. Lorna T. French, B.A. (Hons.)	240	$2,695-3,124	$700-1,070
St. Mildred's-Lightbourn School	Oakville, Ont.	Sister Mary Michael, C.S.C., B.A., B.Ed.	345		$400-1,100
Strathcona Lodge School	Shawnigan Lake, B.C.	Miss Angela J.V. Brown, B.A. (Hons.); Dip.Ed.	120	$3,100-3,350	
Strathcona-Tweedsmuir School	Okotoks, Alta.	W.A. Heard	150		$1,000-1,350
The Study	Montreal	Mrs. Jean C. Scott, B.A., M.A.T.	240		$900-1,350 $350 (senior students)
Trafalgar School for Girls	Montreal	Miss Jean E. Harvie, M.A.	240		$700 $350 (senior students)
Weston School	Montreal West	Mrs. Elizabeth A. Goddard, B.Sc. (Hons.)	50		$690-1,380
York House School	Vancouver	Bryan Peet, A.D.Ed., M.Ed.	330		$450-1,700

*Fees are paid only by students in Grades 11 to 13.

508

APPENDIX L
The Harvard Business
School Clan

This list is a selection of Canadian executives who hold degrees from the Harvard Business School or who have completed courses at the school; it includes Doctors and Masters of Business Administration and holders of the Advanced Management Program Certificate.

Aitken, David E.
: General Manager, Converting Operations, Canadian International Paper Co.

Albino, George R.
: President and Chief Operating Officer, Rio Algom Ltd.

Alexander, Edward R.
: Vice-President, Corporate Planning, Timmins Investments Ltd.; son of E. Ryckman Alexander, former vice-president and treasurer of Sun Life Assurance Co. of Canada (also a Harvard graduate)

Allan, John D.
: Executive Vice-President and Director, Steel Co. of Canada Ltd.

Alsop, David
: Director, Administration and Corporate Development, Burrard/Yarrows Group, Cornat Industries Ltd.

Bales, Ronald C.
: Former vice-president, Aluminum Co. of Canada Ltd.; now with Alcan subsidiary in Argentina

Ballon, Edward M.
: Vice-President, Retail Operations, and Director, Henry Birks & Sons Ltd.

Barford, Ralph M.
: President and Chief Executive Officer, Valleydene Corp. Ltd.; Chairman, GSW Ltd.

Bata, Thomas G.
: General Manager, Bata Schuh AG, Switzerland; son of Thomas J. Bata, Chief Executive Officer of the Bata shoe organization

Beadon, R. Perry
: Vice-President and Director, Procter & Gamble Co. of Canada Ltd.

Beale, Roy E.
: Vice-President and Director, Operations, Wood Gundy Ltd.

509

Beaubien,
  Philippe de
  Gaspé   President, Télémédia (Québec) Ltée

Becket, R.   Vice-President and General Counsel,
  Wilson   Canadian International Paper Co.

Bees, Robert M.   Vice-President and General Manager,
                   Link-Belt Division, FMC of Canada Ltd.

Berghuis,   Vice-President and Director,
  William W.   Jones Heward & Co. Ltd.

Berry,   Vice-President, Office and Education
  George C.   Products, Molson Companies Ltd.

Bertrand,   Manager, Public Relations,
  Gaston   Provincial Bank of Canada

Beutel,   Partner, Beutel,
  Austin C.   Goodman & Co.

Bilodeau,   Chairman,
  Rodrigue J.   Honeywell Ltd.

Birkett,   President, Osler, Geoffrion, Norris &
  E. Roy   Gélinas Inc.

Birks,   Managing Director, Vancouver Operations,
  Thomas M.   Henry Birks & Sons Ltd.

Bisson, André   General Manager (Quebec), Bank of
                   Nova Scotia

Blaine,   Vice-President, Finance,
  Lawrence W.   Northern & Central Gas Corp. Ltd.

Blasdale,   Vice-President, Finance, and Treasurer,
  Brian C.   American Can of Canada Ltd.

Blaser,   Senior Vice-President, Gulf Oil
  Lorenz P.   Canada Ltd.

Blatchley,   Assistant Secretary, Treasurer and
  Raymond W.   Comptroller, Rayonier Canada Ltd.

Blazek,   Regional Co-ordinator, Bata Ltd.,
  Slavomir J.   Paris

Block, Arthur J.   Chairman, Block Bros. Industries Ltd.

Blumenauer,   Chairman and President,
  George H.   Otis Elevator Co. Ltd.

Bongard,
   Gordon R.P.
Chairman and President,
Bongard Leslie & Co. Ltd.

Bonnycastle,
   Michael K.
Principal, Woods,
Gordon & Co.

Bourquin,
   R. Mark
Chairman,
Bulova Watch Co. Ltd.

Bowell,
   G.S.J. Gary
President,
Weldwood of Canada Ltd.

Bradstock,
   John H.
Superintendent of National Accounts,
Toronto-Dominion Bank

Bream,
   Kenneth G.
Executive Vice-President,
Cadillac Fairview Corp. Ltd.

Breyfogle,
   Peter N.
Executive Vice-President, Europe,
Massey-Ferguson Ltd.

Brown,
   David H.
Director, Corporate Underwriting,
Burns Bros. and Denton Ltd.

Brown,
   Donald C.
Salary Administration,
Canadian Pacific Ltd.

Brown,
   Norman J.
Vice-President,
Finance, Steel Co. of Canada Ltd.

Buckley,
   Douglas G.
General Manager, Western Region,
Hudson's Bay Co.

Burns, James
   William
President,
Great-West Life Assurance Co.

Cadham,
   Thomas
Vice-President, Management Information
Services, John Labatt Ltd.

Cartwright,
   Alton S.
President, Canadian General Electric Co.
Ltd.

Chalmers,
   David B.
President,
Windward Petroleum Ltd.

Chapman,
   C. Norman
President,
Emco Ltd.

Chater,
   Leslie H.
General Engineering Manager, Hilton
Works, Steel Co. of Canada Ltd.

Cheeseman,
   Edgar W.
Vice-President, Underground Mining
Operations, Rio Algom Ltd.

Chick,
Wilfred C.
Vice-President, Treasurer, Steel Co. of
Canada Ltd.

Child,
Arthur J.E.
President,
Burns Foods Ltd.

Chin, Thomas
Secretary and Controller, Raytheon Canada
Ltd.

Christ,
Alexander
President, Industrial Growth Management
Ltd.

Christner,
William C.
Vice-President, Operations, and Director,
Thos. J. Lipton Ltd.

Cloutier,
Sylvain
Deputy Minister of
Transport

Coker,
James L., IV
President,
Sonoco Ltd.

Cooke,
Dewar B.
Manager, Market Research, MacMillan
Bloedel Ltd.

Cooper,
Peter H.
General Manager of Operations,
Toronto-Dominion Bank

Côté, Marcel
Manager, Credit Department,
Banque Canadienne Nationale

Coutts,
James A.
Pierre Elliott Trudeau's campaign manager,
1974 general election; named principal
secretary to P.M. in August, 1975; formerly
partner, Canada Consulting Group

Cronyn,
John B.
Vice-Chairman,
John Labatt Ltd.

Culver,
David M.
President, Aluminum Company of Canada
Ltd., and Director, Alcan Aluminium Ltd.

Currie,
George B.
Chairman,
MacMillan Bloedel Ltd.

Currie,
Richard J.
Executive Vice-President,
George Weston Limited.

Currie,
William M.
Former vice-chairman and president,
Canadian Imperial Bank of Commerce;
retired 1974

Curry, Steele
President, Revelstoke Companies Ltd.; son
of Peter D. Curry, President of Power Corp.

Curtis,
Glenn H.

President,
Glenn H. Curtis & Associates Ltd.

Daniher,
E. Clayton

Chairman, Baker, Lovick Ltd.; President,
Comcore Communications Ltd.

Davidson,
Melville W.

President,
Canadian Sugar Institute

Dickinson,
John G.

General Manager, Ventures Group,
MacMillan Bloedel Ltd.

Diggory, T.J.

Partner, Peat, Marwick & Partners

Dimma,
William A.

Dean of Faculty of Administrative Studies,
York University; company director; Ontario
government adviser

Doering,
Lyle H.

Vice-President, Marketing Administration,
Steel Co. of Canada Ltd.

Drummond,
Kevin

Minister of Agriculture,
Quebec

Drury,
Chipman H.

Chairman, Avis Transport of Canada Ltd.;
brother of C.M. Drury, Minister of Public
Works and Minister responsible for Science

Dunn, Hubert

Assistant General Manager,
Banque Canadienne Nationale

Eaton, Alan Y.

Director, Burns Bros. and Denton Ltd.;
former vice-president, T. Eaton Co. Ltd.

Eberts,
Lindsay F.

Assistant Vice-President, Marketing and
Planning, Guaranty Trust Co. of Canada

Erlindson,
Melvin E.

Corporate Treasurer,
Polysar Ltd.

Fair,
W.J. Harold

Vice-President,
Consolidated-Bathurst Ltd.

Fisher, Alex D.

Vice-President, Facilities Planning,
Engineering and Research Division, Steel
Co. of Canada Ltd.

Fisher,
James C.

Partner,
Canada Consulting Group

Fortin, Georges

Assistant General Manager,
Provincial Bank of Canada

Gallagher,
John P.

Chairman,
Dome Petroleum Ltd.

Galloway, David A.	Partner, Canada Consulting Group
Gardiner, George R.	President, Gardiner, Watson Ltd.
Gentles, Roy A.	Group Vice-President, Alcan Aluminum Corp. (U.S. subsidiary of Alcan Aluminium Ltd.)
Gibson, Gordon F.	Liberal MLA in B.C.; former assistant to Pierre Elliott Trudeau; son of Vancouver millionaire J. Gordon Gibson
Godkin, D. Jack	Manager, Personnel Development and Administration (Sales Division), Ford Motor Co. of Canada Ltd.
Godsoe, Peter C.	General Manager, International, Bank of Nova Scotia
Gordon, John Peter	President, Chief Executive Officer, Steel Co. of Canada Ltd.
Gould, Keith P.	Former vice-president, general district manager, and director, Otis Elevator Co. Ltd.; now Vice-President, Domestic Sales, Otis Elevator Co., New York
Graham, David R.	President, Cablecasting Ltd.
Green, K. Gordon	Vice-President, Corporate Finance Department, Morgan Stanley Canada Ltd.
Griffith, Harold M.	Chairman of the Board, Steel Co. of Canada Ltd.
Griffiths, Anthony F.	President, Canadian Cablesystems Ltd.
Gross, Ronald M.	President, Canadian Cellulose Co. Ltd.
Gunther, Mark H.	President and Chief Executive Officer, Prince George Pulp and Paper Ltd. and Intercontinental Pulp Co. Ltd.
Harris, Allen J.	Vice-President, Manufacturing, Primary Operations, Steel Co. of Canada Ltd.
Harvie, Donald S.	Senior Vice-President, Petrofina Canada Ltd., son of the late Eric Harvie, Alberta oil millionaire

Hatch, H. Clifford	Manager, Market Control, Hiram Walker-Gooderham & Worts Ltd.
Heisey, W. Lawrence	President, Harlequin Enterprises Ltd.
Hemmans, George E.W.	President and General Manager, TDRI Ltd. (Toronto-Dominion Realty Investments)
Henderson, Ian A.	Supervisor, Financial Planning and Analysis, Royal Bank of Canada
Hernndorf, Peter A.	Head, Current Affairs, CBC
Hilliker, John A.C.	Senior Vice-President and Regional General Manager, British Columbia, Canadian Imperial Bank of Commerce
Hurd, Edwin Cecil	Chairman, Trans Mountain Pipe Line Co. Ltd.
Hurst, F. Warren	Executive Vice-President and General Manager, Commercial Operations, and Director, Consumers' Gas Co.
Ivey, Peter J.	Director and former chairman, Emco Ltd.
Jackman, Henry R.	President, Dominion & Anglo Investment Corp. Ltd.
Jarislowsky, Stephen A.	President, Jarislowsky, Fraser & Co.
Jones, D. Carlton	President, Hudson's Bay Oil & Gas Co. Ltd.
Kearney, Francis G.	Vice-President, Peat Marwick Ltd.
Kelley, W. Allen	Vice-President, Distribution, T. Eaton Co. Ltd.
Kennedy, Ernest F.	Assistant Comptroller, Canadian International Paper Co.
King, John Erlin	Vice-President, Texaco Canada Ltd.
Koerner, Michael M.	President, Canada Overseas Investments Ltd.
Korthals, Robert W.	Vice-President, Administration, Toronto-Dominion Bank

Kratzer, William S.	Vice-President, Beverage-General Packaging, American Can of Canada Ltd.
Lakie, David	Senior Vice-President, Corporate Relations, Molson Companies Ltd.
Lang, Ted E.	President, Carnation Co. Ltd.
Lavoie, Léo	President, Provincial Bank of Canada
Leclerc, René	Former Vice-Chairman of the Board, Banque Canadienne Nationale; retired 1975
LeMesurier, J. Ross	Vice-President and Director, Wood Gundy Ltd.
Lennard, Gordon H.	Vice-President and Regional General Manager, Quebec Region, Canadian Imperial Bank of Commerce
Leroux, Jean-Jacques	Executive Vice-President, Operations, Northern & Central Gas Corp. Ltd.
Levine, William H.	Executive Vice-President, Chief Financial Officer and Secretary, Daon Development Corp.
Loewen, Charles B.	President, Loewen, Ondaatje, McCutcheon & Co. Ltd.
Lougheed, E. Peter	Premier of Alberta
Lounsbury, Thornton B.	Vice-President, Marketing, Westinghouse Canada Ltd.
Ludwick, Arnold M.	Treasurer, Cemp Investments Ltd.
Lyman, Peter F.E.	Consultant, Peat, Marwick & Partners
Macdonald, Ian	Partner, Haskins & Sells Associates
Mackenzie, Michael A.	Partner, Clarkson Gordon & Co.
MacLaren, Roy	Chairman and Chief Executive Officer, Ogilvy & Mather (Canada) Ltd.
MacLean, Ralph S.	Vice-President and Director, Emco Ltd.

Maxwell,
John S.
Executive Vice-President, Finance, and
Director, Canadian International Paper Co.

McArthur,
Duncan R.B.
President,
Inland Cement Industries Ltd.

McCarthy, W.J.
Senior Vice-President, Finance,
Sun Life Assurance Co. of Canada

McCaskill,
Donald B.
President,
Algonquin Management Ltd.

McCulloch,
Murray D.
Assistant Mill Superintendent,
Steel Co. of Canada Ltd.

McDonald,
W. Scott
Executive Vice-President,
Bank of Nova Scotia

McDougall,
J.H.
President,
International Capital Corp. Ltd.

McGrail, K.W.
Vice-President and Assistant General
Manager, and Director, Nova Scotia Power
Corp.

McIntyre,
John G.W.
Vice-President,
Hudson's Bay Co.

McKendy,
John S.
Vice-President,
National Trust Co. Ltd.

McLellan,
Graham R.
Vice-President and Comptroller,
Imperial Oil Ltd.

McLeod,
Ian H.
Principal,
McKinsey & Co. Inc.

McMurrich,
Arthur R.
Vice-President, Marketing Division,
Steel Co. of Canada Ltd.

Meekison,
Dougal M.
Finance Manager,
B.C. Telephone Co.

Meekison,
James D.
Chief Financial Officer and Director,
Cablecasting Ltd.

Mercure, Gilles
Vice-President, International,
Provincial Bank of Canada

Miller,
John O.
Director, Administrative Services,
MacMillan Bloedel Ltd.

Mitchell, Bruce
Senior Consultant, Woods, Gordon & Co.

Mohr,
Lionel C., Jr.
Vice-President,
Toronto Star Ltd.

Moreton,
A. George
Vice-President, Imperial Oil Ltd., and
President, Esso Chemical Canada

Mulholland,
William
President,
Bank of Montreal

Murray,
Alan M.
Vice-President, Finance,
Cominco Ltd.

Murray,
J. Richard
Former managing director, Hudson's Bay
Co.; appointed Commissioner, Foreign
Investment Review Agency, 1974; President,
Federal Business Development Bank, 1975

Nelson,
Richard C.
Executive Vice-President and Director,
Crown Zellerbach Canada Ltd.

Nelson,
Richard I.
President,
British Columbia Packers Ltd.

Newell,
James
Vice-President,
Westinghouse Canada Ltd.

Nickerson,
Terry M.
Controller,
IBM Canada Ltd.

Norsworthy,
Hugh H.
Senior Public Relations Officer,
Aluminum Co. of Canada Ltd.

Nose,
Roy H.
Director, Osler, Geoffrion, Norris &
Gélinas Inc.

Oland,
Sidney M.
General Manager, Labatt's Saskatchewan
Brewery; son of Victor Oland, former
president of Oland's Brewery Ltd., Halifax

Oliver,
Alfred R.
Vice-President, Procurement,
Steel Co. of Canada Ltd.

Oliver,
Joseph J.
Vice-President, Merrill Lynch,
Royal Securities Ltd.

Orloff,
Roger B.
Manager, Planning and Economic Analysis,
Reed Paper, Ltd.

Ostrander,
Harry S.
Group Vice-President, Products, Sun Oil Co.
Ltd.

Panabaker,
D. Deane
Vice-President, Production, and Director,
Otis Elevator Co. Ltd.

Pangman, Peter M.	Vice-President and Director, McLean, Budden Ltd.
Pearson, George L.	Vice-President, Pulp and Paper Group, Crown Zellerbach Canada Ltd.
Pecho, Verne D.	Vice-President, Finance, and Secretary-Treasurer, Okanagan Helicopters Ltd.
Picard, Laurent	President, Marine Industries Ltd.; formerly President, CBC
Pitts, John W.	Chairman and President, Okanagan Helicopters Ltd.
Pollock, John A.	President, Electrohome Ltd.
Poole, William C.	General Manager, National Accounts, Toronto-Dominion Bank
Porter, R. Keith	President, Thos. J. Lipton Ltd.
Poyen, John S.	President, Canadian Petroleum Association
Radford, J.E.	Assistant General Manager, Bank of Nova Scotia
Reimer, Borge	President, Hayes-Dana Ltd.
Richardson, John E.	Partner, Clarkson Gordon & Co.
Ronald, T. Iain	Treasurer, Hudson's Bay Co.
Ronson, John C.	Organization Development Manager, Steel Co. of Canada Ltd.
Ross, Alastair H.	President, Western Decalta Petroleum Ltd.
Rubess, Bruno R.	President, Volkswagen Canada Ltd.
Salter, J.H.	Executive Vice-President, Operations, Cominco Ltd.
Saumier, André R.	Assistant Secretary, Ministry of Urban Affairs
Scholes, J.M.	Group Vice-President, Investments, Royal Trust Co.
Shelton, Howard B.	Retired in 1975 as President and Director, Canadian Occidental Petroleum Ltd.

Shoults,
Arthur M.

Advertising executive, communications entrepreneur; Chairman, Comcore Communications Ltd.; former chairman, Baker, Lovick, BBDO Ltd.

Smithson,
George A.

Vice-President and General Manager of Ontario Southwest, Toronto-Dominion Bank

Snell, Paul F.

Vice-President and General Manager, International Division, Toronto-Dominion Bank

Speakman,
Glenn C.

Director,
Midland Doherty Ltd.

Spencer,
Elden E.

Assistant Vice-President,
Canada Permanent Trust Co.

Steinberg,
H. Arnold

Executive Vice-President, Administration and Finance, and Treasurer, Steinberg's Ltd.

Stevens,
Robert A.

Vice-President, Valleydene Corp. Ltd.;
President, GSW Ltd.

Stewart,
Peter B.

Executive Vice-President, Operations,
Molson Companies Ltd.

Stoneham,
Herbert E.C.

Vice-President, Human Resources, Molson Companies Ltd.

Sundstrom,
Roland L.

Former vice-president, Timber, and director, Crown Zellerbach Canada Ltd.; now Chairman, Board of Management, Van Gelder Papier (a Crown Zellerbach affiliate in Holland)

Sweeney,
John B.

Vice-President,
Consolidated-Bathurst Ltd.

Theriault,
George H.

Vice-President and Director,
Atlantic Richfield Canada Ltd.

Thomson,
Richard M.

President,
Toronto-Dominion Bank

Townsend,
Harold V.

Group Vice-President, Packaging Division, MacMillan Bloedel Ltd.

Turner, William
I.M., Jr.

President,
Consolidated-Bathurst Ltd.

Urquhart,
Howard B.

President,
Rayonier Canada Ltd.

Vyoral, Josef

President, Bata Industries Ltd.

Wagg,   Director, Planning,
    Timothy J.   Consolidated-Bathurst Ltd.

Walker,   President, Canadian Gas and Energy Fund
    Edward   Ltd.; President, Canadian Security Growth
    Arthur   Fund Ltd.; Vice-President, Investment
                    Research, Canadian Security Management
                    Ltd.

Weaver,   President,
    Arthur G.   Eaton Financial Services Ltd.

Widdrington,   President,
    Peter N.T.   John Labatt Ltd.

Wilder,   Chairman, Canadian Arctic Gas Pipeline
    William P.   Ltd.; former president, Wood Gundy Ltd.

Winser,   Vice-President,
    Frank C.   Aluminum Co. of Canada Ltd.

Wood,   President,
    Neil R.   Cadillac Fairview Corp. Ltd.

Wosk,   Vice-President,
    Larry   Planning and Development, Wosk's Ltd.

Yarnell,   Vice-President, Finance, Canadian Arctic
    John R.   Gas Pipeline Ltd.; former vice-president,
                    Administration, Consolidated-Bathurst Ltd.

Young,   Senior Vice-President, and Director,
    Alan B.   Hamilton Group Ltd.

Young,   Senior Vice-President, and Director,
    David M.   Hamilton Group Ltd.

Index

Index

Abbott, D.C., 437
Abbott, Sir John, 296
Abell, John, 34–35
Aberfoyle Mines, 220
Abergavenny, Marquess of, 9, 28
Abitibi Paper Co. Ltd., 82–85, 93, 112, 267n
Acadian Lines Ltd., 203n
Acadia Trust Co., 303n
Acadia University, 258
Acapulco, Mexico, 316, 420n
Acheson, Dean, 292n
Acklands Ltd., 201n
Acres Ltd., 141n
Adams, Thomas, Distillers Ltd., 332
Aetna Factors Corp., 141n
Agnelli, Count Giovanni, 139, 302
Agra Industries Ltd., 231n
Aikins, MacAulay & Thorvaldson, 182
Air Canada, 214, 430
Aird, Sir John, 241
Aird, John B., 59, 117, 149, 165, 241–42, 244, 338
Aitken, Max, see Beaverbrook, Lord
Ajax Petroleums Ltd., 75
Alaska Highway, 167n, 168n
Alaska Pine & Cellulose Ltd., 267n
Alaska Pine Co. Ltd., 267n
Albany Club, 419, 425
Alberta, 208, 231, 247, 248, 250–53, 327–28
Alberta Energy Co. Ltd., 95, 250
Alberta Gas Ethylene Co. Ltd., 250
Alberta Gas Trunk Line Co. Ltd., 94, 95, 250, 455
Alberta Liberal Association, 141
Alberta Power Ltd., 253
Alberta Ranches Ltd., 251
Alcan Aluminium Ltd., 94, 111, 219, 336
Alexander, Bernard, 437, 437n
Algoma Central Railway, 95, 228, 242
Algoma Steel Corp. Ltd., 80, 93, 112, 220, 222, 464
Allan, Sir Hugh, 211–12, 296
Allan family, 211–12
Allan Memorial Institute, 296n
Allarco Developments Ltd., 253

Allard, Dr. Charles, 200n, 253, 336
Allen, John C.L., Ltd., 245
Allen, Peter, 245
Allen, Ralph, quoted, 259–60
Allendale Mutual Insurance Co., 252
Allied Wheat Commission, 234
Aluminium Ltd., 395n; see also Alcan Aluminium Ltd.
Aluminum Co. of America (Alcoa), 205n
Amax Inc., 242
Ambridge, Douglas W., 369n
American Airlines Inc., 144
Ames, A.E., and Co., 115n
Amory, Cleveland, Who Killed Society?, 419–20
Amyot, René, 214
Anderson, Donald S., 113, 123, 205, 466
Anderson, Robert, 420n
Anderson, Ronald, quoted, 207–8
Anglin, James P., 29
Anglo-Canadian Telephone Co., 237n, 303n, 459, 464
Anglo-Western Oils Ltd., 327
Angus, Ian William Molson, 292n
Angus family (Montreal), 296
Anne (Princess), 9
Annigoni, Pietro, 14, 320
Annis Furs Inc., 309
Anslaux, Baron Hubert, 139
Anthes Imperial Ltd., 188, 227
Anti-combines Legislation, 166–70
Anticosti Island, 55–56
Antigua, 312
Arbor Corp., 22
Arbour, Pierre, 214
Arbuckle, William A., 77, 111, 205, 219, 292n, 466
Arbuckle Govett & Co., 111
Archibald, A. Gordon, 227
Ardwold, 312
Argo Construction Ltd., 93
Argus Corp. Ltd., 7–37 passim, 81n, 83–84, 93, 111, 114, 125, 156, 192, 201n, 206n, 314, 455
Armstrong, John A., 183n, 243, 466
Art, collections of, 13, 60–61, 182, 300, 320, 323
Arthur, Eric, 424–25
Asbestos Corp. Ltd., 93, 112

Ascot, 9, 14
Ash, W.M. Vacy, 10, 112, 207, 414
Ashbury College, 268, 504
Asselin, Hon. Édouard, 28
Assiniboia Club, 422
Associated British Foods Ltd., 320
Associated Newspapers Group Ltd., 84, 85, 458
Assomption Mutual Life Insurance Co., 254, 468
Astaire, Adele, 347
Atchison, Clarence, 231
Atco Industries Ltd., 249n, 250, 462
Athabasca Columbia Resources Ltd., 273
Atholstan, Lord (Hugh Graham), 292n, 296
Atlantic Acceptance Corp. Ltd., 76, 162
Atlantic City, 315
Atlantic Wholesalers Ltd., 322
Atlas Corp., 20
Atlas Steels, 395n
Atomic Energy of Canada, 389n
Augsbury, Frank, 43n
Australian International Finance Corp., 99n
Avco Corp., 8, 38, 40n
Avis Rent-a-Car, 49
Avon River, 227
Ayers family, 431
Ayre, Fred, 237
Ayre, Lewis H.M., 28, 237
Ayre family, 236–38
Ayre & Sons Ltd., 95, 237–38
Ayre's Ltd., 238

BACM Industries, 233, 455
BAC One-Eleven [airplane], 183
B.A. Oil Co., 70, 71
B.C. Electric Co., 74, 503
B.C. Forest Products Ltd., 26, 93, 116n, 206, 265, 268
B.C. Jockey Club, 269
B.C. Lions, 269
B.C. Packers Ltd., 267, 321n
B.C. Petroleum Corporation, 276
B.C. Pulp & Paper Co. Ltd., 267n
B.C. Sugar Refinery Ltd., 94, 116n, 268, 272, 273
B.C. Telephone Co., 94, 112, 116n, 265, 266
Babich, L.P., 163n
Babson Institute of Business Administration, 309
Bache Co. Canada Ltd., 180, 252
Badminton and Racquet Club, 426
Bahamas, 76, 217, 260, 266, 303, 305
Baillie, A.W., 114
Bain, H. Rupert, 347n
Baker, Charles "Bud," 246
Baird, David G., 28
Balfour, R. James, 231n
Balfour, St. Clair, 293
Ball, George, 242
Ball, Gordon, 124
Ballard, Harold, 154n, 200n
Ballem, John, 250, 253
Baltzan, Dr. David, 231n
Bandeen, Robert A., 219
Banff Springs Hotel, 318n
Bank Act, 118, 120, 129n, 131n;
  1967 revision, 51n, 131, 207;
  1977 revision, 124n
Bank of America, 58, 80, 98n, 109n
Bank of British Columbia, 98, 116
Bank of British North America, 105
Bank of Canada, 26, 102, 127, 129–
  131, 146–47, 162, 231, 254
Bank of Commerce, 212, 241, 295;
  see also Canadian Imperial Bank of Commerce
Bank of England, 362–63
Bank of France, 132
Bank of Montreal, 92, 94–95, 98, 99, 103, 106, 109–12, 117–22, 160, 179, 197, 208, 211, 213, 219, 243, 302n, 324
Bank of Nova Scotia, 92, 95–96, 97n, 98, 99, 99n, 109, 116n, 117–120, 125–28, 228
Bankes, Jack, 69, 123
Banque Canadienne Nationale, 66–68, 98, 117n, 215
Banque Nationale de Belgique, 139
Banque Provinciale du Canada, 98, 254
Barbaro, Ron, 245n
Barbeau, Jacques, 276
Barclay, Ian, 116n, 268, 466
Baring, Maurice, 10
Barran, Sir David, 139
Barrett, Premier David, 263, 265n, 268
Barron, Alex E., 27n, 28, 29
Barrow, J.C., 113, 165n
Bartholomew, Dana T., 411
Basford, Ronald, 164, 206n
Bassett, Doug, 245
Bassett, John, 138, 172n, 245, 293–294
Bassett, John F. (Jr.), 245, 293–94
Bassett family, 199n
Bata, Sonja, 319
Bata, Thomas J. (Tom), 319–20
Bata, Tomas, 319
Bata family, 293n, 319–20
Bata Ltd., 319
Bath and Tennis Club (Palm Beach), 11
Bathurst Paper Ltd., 75; see also Consolidated-Bathurst Paper Co. Ltd.
Baton Broadcasting Inc., 172, 244, 294n
Baum, Daniel, 97
Baumgarten, Alfred, 426n
Bauslaugh, W.P., 71
Bawden, H.N. (Harry), 18, 19
Bawden, Peter, 252, 253n
Bawlf family, 230
Bay, Charles Ulrick (Rick), 10
Bay Street (Toronto), 19, 91, 172–173, 229, 253
Beardmore family, 296
Beattie, Allan, 245n, 313
Beattie, R. Leslie (Les), 66–67
Beatty family, 296
Beaubien, Senator Louis, 214, 427
Beaubien, Philippe de Gaspé, 214, 427
Beauchemin family, 338
Beaudoin, Laurent, 214
Beauharnois scandal, 16
Beaulieu, Roger, 214

Beaupré, T.N., 112
Beauregard, Senator Elie, 216n
Beaverbrook, Lord (Max Aitken), 292n, 301, 321, 426; *Men and Power*, 4
Beaver Club (Montreal), 418
Beck, Frederick A., 29
Beecher family (Vancouver), 431
Bélanger, Marcel, 205
Bélanger, Michel, 214
Belding-Corticelli Ltd., 335n
Belkin, Morris, 268
Belkin Packaging Ltd., 268
Bell, Max, 80, 200n, 251–52
Bell, Ralph P., 225, 477
Bell, Russell Davenport, 204–5
Bell, Thomas J., 82, 112, 165n, 243, 465
Bell family, 237n
Bell Canada, 93, 94, 96, 110, 144, 187, 206n, 214, 219, 226–27, 254n, 458
Belliveau, J.E. (Ned), *quoted*, 260
Bell-Irving family, 267
Belmont Stakes, 301
Belzberg, Sam, 200n, 336
Benidickson, Senator William, 234n
Benidickson, Mrs. William (Agnes Richardson), 234n
Ben's Bakery, 116
Ben's Holdings Ltd., 225
Bennett, R.B., 164n, 168, 321n
Bennett, Roy, 165n, 191n, 192n, 202n, 244, 466
Bennett, Stewart G., 28
Bennett, W.A.C., 166n
Bennett, William J. (Bill), 161, 219
Benson, Edgar, 164, 397, 440n
Bentall, Charles, 266, 274
Bentall, H. Clark, 116n, 268
Bentall family, 338
Bentley, L.L.G. (Poldi), 200n, 268, 323–24
Bentley, Peter, 200n, 268, 324
Bentley family, 293n
Berger, Sam, 200n
Berle, Adolf A., Jr., *quoted*, 203
Berlin, Richard, 57
Berman, Joseph, 246–47, 338
Bermuda, 177, 261, 303
Bernhard, Prince, 192n
Berthierville, Que., 168
Berton, Pierre, 212; *National Dream*, 212n
Bethlehem Copper Corp., 271, 276
Beurling, George (Buzz), 275
Beveridge, Sir William, 377
Bherer, Wilbrod, 57
Big Five [banks,] 93n, 97–98, 99–109, 111–130, 231
Bilderberg Group, 192n
Billes, Fred, Jr., 246
Billes family, 338
Birks, Drummond, 338
Birks family, 293n, 296
Bishop's College School, 140, 294n
Bishop Strachan School, 404
Bismarck, Count Ferdinand von, 420n
Bisson, André, 128, 214, 427
Bisson family, 70
Black, Conrad, 245

Black, George Montegu, 21n, 30, 114, 177, 195, 231, 338
Black Angel Mine, 220
Blackburn, Walter, 338
Black's Harbour, 235
Bladen, Vincent, 425
Blair, S. Robert, 250–51, 465
Blake, Cassels & Graydon, 112, 242, 470
Blakeney, Allan, 412
Blakeny Concrete Products Ltd., 93
Blatt, Leonard, 338
Bleckwell, E.H., 113
Block family, 338
Bloedel, Prentice H., 280, 336
Blue Peter Steamships Ltd., 238
Blumenauer, George H., 111, 510
Board of Inland Revenue, 288
Boel family, 139
Boer War, 298
Bolton, Thomas G., 28, 165n
Bolton, Tremblay & Co., 303n
Bombardier Ltd., 214, 217
Bongard, Gordon R.P., 245
Bonner, Robert, 165n
Bonnycastle, L.C., 406n
Bonsecours Market, 210
Boodle's (Club), 426
Booth family, 302
Borden, Henry, 28, 161n, 359, 364
Borden, Sir Robert, 161n
Bouey, Gerald, 231
Boultbee family, 430
Bourassa, Robert, 52, 216–17
Bovey, Edmund C., 244
Bovis Corp. Ltd, 162n, 340
Bowaters Mersey Paper, 225n
Bowell, Gordon S.J. (Gary), 406n
Bowes Co. Ltd, 93, 114
Bowfort Services Ltd., 113
Bowring family, 236
Bowring Brothers Ltd., 237
Bow Valley Industries Ltd., 253
Box Grove (golf course), 344
Boyce, H.M., 266
Boyd, Robert, 214
Boylen, M.J., 290
Brading Breweries Ltd., 20
Bradfield, John, 182–83
Brascan Ltd., 51n, 94, 110, 120, 143, 185–86, 200, 201n, 206n, 328, 458
Bras Coupé Club, 434
Bratty, Rudy, 245n
Brazilian Light & Power Co., 161n, 185; *see also* Brascan Ltd.
Brazilian Traction, Light & Power Co. Ltd., 299; *see also* Brascan Ltd.
Breakers Hotel (Palm Beach), 11
Bremner, Bill, 245n
Brenda Mines Ltd., 265, 238
Brewers' Guardian, 323
Brewing Corp. of Canada, 20
Briarmeade Farm, 234
Brillant, Aubert, 303n
Brillant, Jules, 303, 477
Brillant family, 310, 338
Brinco Ltd , 51n, 94, 166n
British Columbia, 180n, 262–67
British Dominions Land Corp., *see* Western Canada Land Co.

British Steel Corp. (Canada) Ltd., 96
Brittain, A. Code, 68
Brocklesby, John N., Transport Ltd., 82
Bronfman, Allan, 79
Bronfman, Charles Rosner, 114n, 165n, 177, 181, 197, 219, 331–35
Bronfman, Edgar, 43n, 334
Bronfman, Edward, 79
Bronfman, Minda (Mrs. Alain de Gunzburg), 334
Bronfman, Peter, 79
Bronfman, Phyllis, (Lambert), 334
Bronfman, Samuel, 217, 332, 436–437
Bronfman, Samuel II, 334n
Bronfman family, 79, 119n, 293n, 302n
Brook, Thomas, 253n
Broughton, Philip, 178
Brown, Albert, 104
Brown, Colin, 192n, 200n
Brown, Douglas McK., 268
Brown, Fred, 266, 269
Brown, Michael, 276n
Brown, R.A. (Bobby), 251
Brown, W. Thomas, 266n, 268, 276n
Brown, Farris & Jefferson Ltd., 276
Bruce, F.W., (Scotty), 386
Bruce, Harry, quoted, 238, 257
Bruce, Hugh, 140
Bruce, Maxwell, 29
Bryce, R.B. (Bob), 124, 241, 379, 380
Brynelsen, Bernard, 338
Buckfield family, 302
Buckerfield's Ltd., 235
Buckley, Mrs. William F. (Patricia Taylor), 274
Buck's [club], 9
Buckwold, Sidney L., 231n
Buckwold's Ltd., 94, 231
Budd Automotive Co. of Canada Ltd., 94
Bulk-Lift Systems, 245n
Bulloch, John F., 165n
Bullock family, 431
Burchill, John, 254
Burden, William A.M., 242
Burke, Carl, 236n
Burke, F.E., 116n, 165n
Burns, Charles F.W. "Charlie," 56n, 199n, 222, 228–29, 243, 246, 345
Burns, James William, 165n, 232
Burns, Latham, 245
Burns, Pat, 273
Burns Bros. and Denton Ltd., 243, 245n
Burns Foods Ltd., 179, 184, 185, 252, 310, 459
Burnside, 106n, 107n
Burnside, Mrs. T.D.M. (Josephine Eaton), 106n, 107n
Burrage, Patrick, 233n
Burton, G. Allan, 113, 143, 244
Burton, Richard, 400
Burton, Ted, 245
Burton family, 243n, 293n, 338
Bury, Sir George, 180

Bushnell Communications Ltd., 7, 33
Butler, Robert J., 165n, 313

CBC, 215, 372
CCF, 160, 168, 247, 377
CFRB, 7n, 34
CIL, see Canadian Industries Ltd.
CJAD, 21n
CKAC, 73, 74
CNR, 212, 279
CP Air, 220, 265, 270, 319, 431
CPR, 17, 47, 78, 143, 144, 199, 206n, 211, 212, 220, 221, 251, 296–99, 327; see also Canadian Pacific Ltd.
CP Telegraphs, 301
CRTC, 33, 226
Cadaval, Duke of, 420n
Cadillac Fairview Corp. Ltd., 244, 246, 335, 468
Caisse de Dépôt, 85, 214, 215
Caisses Populaires, 215
Caledon Hills, 246, 312
Caledon Mountain Trout Club, 434
Calgary Albertan, 251
Calgary Power Ltd., 253
Calvan Consolidated Oil & Gas Co. Ltd., 251
Cambie family, 431
Cameron, J.W., 165n
Cameron, Robert Burns, 226, 467
Camp Ahmek, 404n
Campana [yacht], 252
Campbell, Alistair M., 165n, 219, 467
Campbell, D. Chester, 254
Campbell, Des, 84n
Campbell, Donald G., 244
Campbell, Pete, 19
Campbell, Robert, 252
Campbell, Robert, K.C. Irving—The Art of the Industrialist, 258–259
Campbell, Robert W., 29
Campbell, Wallace R., 368
Campeau, Robert, 76, 338
Camper & Nicholsons Ltd., 314
Campo, Alfredo F.M., 53
Camp Wapomeo, 404n
Canada Bud Breweries, 20n
Canada Cement, see Canada Cement Lafarge Ltd.
Canada Cement Lafarge Ltd., 94, 110, 116n, 144, 170n, 201n, 275, 293
Canada Consulting Group, 412n
Canada Development Corp. (CDC), 53, 116n, 162n, 201n, 226, 269
Canadair Ltd., 318, 324n
Canada Life Assurance Co., 94, 95, 109, 113, 144, 270, 471
Canada Medal, 413
Canada Packers Ltd., 94, 113, 144, 155, 177, 185, 195, 205
Canada Permanent Trust Co., 83, 109, 255, 453
Canada Safeway Ltd., 232, 275, 465
Canada Steamship Lines Ltd. (CSL), 50, 53, 59, 60, 61, 75, 80, 81, 113, 153n, 215

Canada Trust Co., 268, 330
Canada Veneers Ltd., 259
Canadian Airways, 373
Canadian Arctic Gas Pipeline Ltd., 411
Canadian Aviation Electronics Ltd., 219
Canadian Bank of Commerce, 105; see also Canadian Imperial Bank of Commerce.
Canadian Bankers' Association, 124, 131
Canadian Breweries Ltd., 20, 21n, 26, 177, 195; see also Carling O'Keefe Ltd.
Canadian Cablesystems Ltd., 186n
Canadian Corporate Management Co. Ltd., 95, 173, 244, 313
Canadian Dredge & Dock Co., 162n
Canadian Economic Policy Committee, 192n
Canadian Forest Products Ltd., 95, 116n, 271, 324
Canadian Fuel Marketers Ltd., 93
Canadian General Electric Co. Ltd., 111, 144,
Canadian General Investments Ltd., 27n, 330
Canadian General Securities Ltd., 141n
Canadian General Service Medal, 413–14
Canadian Headmasters' Assoc., 399n
Canadian Imperial Bank of Commerce, 7, 36, 47, 78, 79, 92–94, 106n, 107, 109, 110–14, 116, 118–122, 125, 136, 140–48, 161n, 186, 207, 235
Canadian Import Co. Ltd., 110, 308, 309
Canadian Indemnity Co., 231
Canadian Industrial Gas and Oil Ltd., 75, 252
Canadian Industries Ltd. (CIL), 95, 140, 459
Canadian Institute of International Affairs, 391
Canadian Insurance Shares Ltd., 141n
Canadian Junior College, 404
Canadian Keyes Fibre Co. Ltd., 225n
Canadian Liquid Air Ltd., 93
Canadian Manufacturers' Assoc., 162n
Canadian Maritime Commission, 278
Canadian National Railways, 18, 219, 222; see also CNR.
Canadian Northern Railway, 212
Canadian Oil Companies Ltd. (White Rose), 74, 75
Canadian Pacific Investments Ltd., 78, 80, 201n, 220
Canadian Pacific Ltd., 93, 95, 102n, 110, 177, 192, 193, 220, 231n, 265, 465, 468
Canadian Pacific Pension Fund, 85
Canadian Petrofina Ltd., 327–28; see also Petrofina Canada Ltd.

Canadian Petroleum Association, 253
Canadian Premier Life Insurance Co., 232
Canadian Propellers, 21n
Canadian Pulp and Paper Association, 391
Canadian Radio League, 372
Canadian Salt Co., Ltd., 227
Canadian Shell Ltd., 113; see also Shell Canada Ltd.
Canadian Stock Exchange, 192–93
Canadian Tire Corp. Ltd., 246, 338, 471
Canadian Transport Commission, 199, 498
Canadian Union of Linemen and Helpers, 299
Canadian Utilities Ltd., 253
Canadian Vickers Ltd., 57, 389
Canadian Westinghouse Co. Ltd., 188; see also Westinghouse Canada Ltd.
Canadian Wheat Board, 114, 230, 233
Canadian Who's Who, 287, 329, 415
Canaus Investments Inc., 82
CanDel Oil Ltd., 253
Canning Investment Corp., 225n
Canron Ltd., 94, 111, 144, 219, 251, 460
Canso area, 224
Capek, Karel, 319
Cape Kennedy, 318n
Capilano Golf and Country Club, 324
Capital Radio, 33
Capozzi, Herb, 200n
Cara Inn, 203
Cariboo Cattlemen's Assoc., 266
Carleton University, 199, 386n
Carling family, 302
Carling O'Keefe Ltd., 201n
Carlson, Don, 170–71
Carlyle Hotel (London), 17
Carlyle Hotel (N.Y.C.), 139
Carmel Valley Tennis Club (Calif.), 142n
Carmichael, H.J., 28, 364n, 365
Carmichael, John, 245
Carmichael family, 338
Caron, Marcel, 214
Carriacou (Grenadines), 404n
Carte Blanche, 38
Carter, E.R.E., 406n
Carter, James B., Ltd., 233
Cartwright, Sir Richard, 160
Casa Loma, 247, 347n
Cassiar Asbestos Corp. Ltd., 208
Cassils family, 302
Catelli Food Products Ltd., 120n
Cave-Browne-Cave family, 431
Cavelti, Toni, Ltd., 290n
Caverhill family, 296
Cawthra family, 240, 302
Cayman Islands, 242, 318
Cay West SA, 30n
Cazavan, Marcel, 214
Cedar Avenue (Montreal), 296n
Cemp Bronfman group, 200

Cemp Investments Ltd., 47, 85, 96, 114n, 156, 193, 201n, 219, 334–335, 469

Centennial Properties Ltd., 227

Central & Nova Scotia Trust Co., 227, 254, 255

Central Coal & Coke Corp., 309

Central Leduc Oils Ltd., 251

Central Mortgage and Housing Corp. (CMHC), 53, 497

Century Insurance Co. of Canada, 270

Century Sales & Service Ltd., 95, 253

Chalmers, Floyd, 103, 205, 244, 424

Champlain, Lake, 308

Chandler, David, 431

Chant, Dixon S., 29

Chapman, H.V., and Associates, 179–80

Chapman, Sidney F., 323

Charbonneau, Guy, 214

Charity Ball (Montreal), 297

Charlottetown Hotel, 213n

Charron, André, 314, 427

Chase, George, 225

Chase Manhattan Bank, 99n, 121, 201n, 318n

Chateau Laurier Hotel, 23, 367, 385

Cheesman, W.J., 165

Chemcell Ltd., 111

Chercover, Murray, 245

Cherniavsky, Peter, 273

Cherry, Zena, 246

Chesler, Lou, 338

Chester, Philip, 165n, 367n

Chibnall's Bakeries Ltd., 321

Chicago Club, 436

Chieftain Development Co. Ltd., 253

Child, Arthur J.E., 165n, 179, 184–185, 252, 467, 512

Chisholm, Ronald, 245n

Chrétien, Jean, 53, 55

Christopher, Arthur B., 113, 116n, 268–69

Christopher Enterprises Ltd., 93, 116n

Chromasco Ltd., 337

Churchill, Gordon, 389n

Churchill, Winston, 366

Circolo della Caccia, 420

Citadel Merchandising Co. Ltd., 373

Claridge's Hotel (London), 9, 24

Clark, Donald M., 266n

Clark, W. Clifford, 278n

Clarke, Brock, 219

Clarke, Desmond, 368n

Clarke, Rosemary (Mrs. Charles Rathgeb), 318

Clarke family, 338

Clarkson, Thomas, 200

Clarkson, Gordon & Co., 143, 185, 200–1, 214

Claude Neon, 309

Clauremiand Ltd., 217

Clausen, Alden Winship (Tom), 58

Claxton, Brooke, 161, 372

Clement, Wallace, The Canadian Corporate Elite, 204, 419n, 445

Clerihue, William, 165n

Cliff, Ronald L., 269, 338

Cloverlawn Investments Ltd., 245n

Club aux Brigands, 43n

Club Mediterranée, 335

Club St. Denis (Montreal), 57, 422, 428

Cluett, W.G. "Bill," 31

Cluett, Peabody & Co. Inc., 31

Clyne, John Valentine (Jack), 111, 165n, 166n, 172, 199, 264, 276–81, 438

Coallier, Rev. J.H., 64

Cobalt, Ontario, 136, 212

Cockburn, Major Churchill, 402n

Cocoa Terminal Market Association, 235

Cogan, Edwin A., 338

Cohen, Albert D., 232, 236, 438–39, 467

Cohen, H. Reuben, 254, 467

Cohen, Harry, 252

Cohen, Hersh, 218

Cohen, Lazarus, 218

Cohen, Peter, Gospel According to the Harvard Business School, 409

Cohen family, 339

Cohon, George, 245, 338

Colborne, Sir John (Lord Seaton), 402

Coldwell, M.J., 168, 389n

Cole, Jim, 453

Coleman, Jim, 252

Coleman, John H., 101, 110, 115, 244, 467

Coleman, Alta, 208

Coleman Collieries Ltd., 209

Collier, David C., 157–58, 165n

Collingwood family, 237n

Collins, A.F. "Chip", 249

Coloron Corp. (Canada) Ltd., 352n

Columbia Life Assurance Co., 79n

Columbia Match Co., 168

Columbia River Treaty, 405n

Comac Communications Ltd., 245

Combines Investigation Acts, 167–168

Combines Investigation Branch, 168–70

Cominco Ltd., 95, 96, 116n, 220, 265, 270, 465

Commerce Capital Corp. Ltd., 186n

Commerce Court (Toronto), 122, 138

Commercial Bank of Scotland, 187n

Commercial Developments Ltd., 226

Commercial Trust Co. Ltd., 80, 303n, 335

Committee on Finance, Trade and Economic Affairs, 98

Commodity Exchange (Winnipeg), 232n

Commonwealth Air Training Plan, 361

Commonwealth Cricket Team, 318

Commonwealth Match Co., 169

Compagnie de Charlevoix Ltée, 217

Compagnie Franche de la Marine, 325n

Comstock International Ltd., 93, 112, 115, 197, 317, 318
Concourse Building (Toronto), 208n
Confederation Life Insurance Co., 109, 144, 270, 464
Conference Board, 175n, 205
Connally, John, 57
Connell, Frederick, 338
Connolly, Senator Harold, 224
Connor family, 226
Connors Bros. Ltd., 255
Connor-Smith-Morrow holdings, 226
Conservative party, of Alberta, 166n, 249; of Canada, 53–54, 36Y, 393–94; of Newfoundland, 166n, 236–37
Consolidated-Bathurst Ltd., 50, 53, 56, 77–78, 84–86, 101, 219, 241, 474
Consolidated Exporters Ltd., 267
Consolidated Paper Corp. Ltd., 75, 299; see also Consolidated-Bathurst Ltd.
Constellation Hotel (Toronto), 203
Consumers' Gas Co., 96
Continental Can International Corp., 96
Conventures Ltd., 253
Conwest Exploration Co., Ltd., 338
Cooper, Marsh A., 112, 183n, 244
Cooper, Ralph W., 111
Cooper, Sydney, 200n
Cooper Construction Co. Ltd., 94, 111
Copper Cliff, Ont., 63, 67
Coral Harbour Yacht Club, 76
Corbet, J.M. Richard, 56n
Cornat Industries Ltd., 268, 271, 273, 323
Cornell University, 219n, 349
Cosulich family, 271
Côté, Julien, 97
Côte des Neiges Road, 296n
Coulter, Mrs. David, 290n
Courtois, Jacques, 214, 427, 467
Couture, François, 434n
Coutts, James A. (Jim), 56, 165, 245, 404n, 412n
Covert, Frank Manning, 110, 116, 224–25, 242, 467, 477
Cowdray family, 139
Cowes, England, 301
Cox, Kenneth, 254, 467
Coyne, James Elliott, 126, 130, 230, 362n
Crabtree, H. Roy, 111, 338
Cran, W.C. Thornton, 25
Crandall, L.M., 478
Crang, Harold, 246, 421, 434
Crang, Jim, 200n
Crang & Ostiguy Inc., 94
Crathorne, Lord, 9, 28
Crédit Foncier Franco-Canadien, 215
Crevier, Etienne, 214
Crickmay family, 430
Crimean War, 218, 223, 402
Cripps, Sir Stafford, 372n
Crittenden, Harold A., 231n
Crompton, George, 165n

Cronin, Thomas, 286n
Crosbie, Andrew, 238, 467
Crosbie, Mrs. Andrew, 239
Crosbie, Chesley, 239
Crosbie, Sir John Chalker, 239
Crosbie, John, 239
Crosbie family, 236, 238, 239, 336
Crosbie & Co. Ltd., 238
Crosbie Services Ltd., 95
Cross, James, 43
Cross, James [rancher], 252
Crothers family, 338
Crown Life Insurance Co., 109, 228, 306
Crown Trust Company, 7, 77n, 20, 37n, 58, 206, 254
Crown Zellerbach Canada Ltd., 94, 111, 116n, 206, 265, 273, 460
Crows Nest Industries Ltd., 272
Crump, N.R. (Buck), 78, 110, 220, 222, 252
Crush International Ltd., 337
Culver, David M., 219, 513
Cummings family, 338
Cunard, Samuel, 223n
Currie, George B., 165n
Currie, N.B., 406
Currie, William M., 140
Curry, Peter D., 61, 84n, 116, 211, 231, 467

Dafoe, John W., 230
Daigle, Pierre, 29
Daily Gleaner (Fredericton), 259
Daily Mail (London), 84
Daily Mirror (London), 324
Dalgleish, Oakley, 310
Dalhousie University, 225, 258, 272
Dali, Salvador, 14n
Daniels, John, 338
Daon Development Corp., 267n, 272
Dartmouth, N.S., 226
Davey, Senator Keith, 165n, 306
Davidson, I.D., 113
Davie Shipbuilding Ltd., 50
Davis, Arthur Vining, 205n
Davis, Glen, 253n
Davis, Jack, 392
Davis, Marshall, 353
Davis, Sir Mortimer, 296, 302n, 338
Davis, Nathanael V., 111, 219, 336, 411
Davis, Nelson Morgan (Nels), 110, 147, 198, 244, 336, 421
Davis, Mrs. Nelson (Eloise), 348, 354
Davis family (Alcan), 293n
Davis, N.M., Corp. Ltd., 94, 114, 147, 353, 467
Dawes family, 296, 297, 338
Dawson, Graham, 116, 267n, 269, 272, 338, 467
Dawson Construction Ltd., 95, 116n, 269, 467
Dawson Developments Ltd., 272; see also Daon Development Corp.
Day & Ross Ltd., 256n
Dayco (Canada) Ltd., 352n
Dean, Arthur, 242

Defence Production, Ministry of, 363–76
de Grandpré, Jean, 214, 467
de Grandpré, Louis-Philippe, 427
de Gunzburg, Baron Alain, 334
de Havilland Aircraft of Canada Ltd., 142, 324n
Delbridge, Clayton Boston (Slim), 200n, 269
Delray Beach, Fla., 56
Del Rio Producers Ltd., 251
Deltan Corp., 340
Del Zotto family, 338
Demers, Charles, 214
Demers, Robert, 214
Denison Mines Ltd., 182, 183n, 305–7, 455
Dennis, Reuben, 338
de Pencier, Michael, 245
de Puyjalon, Henry, 165n
Dernière Heure, 73
DesBrisay, John T., 423–24
Deseronto, Ont., 7n
Desmarais, Jean Noel, 49, 50
Desmarais, Louis, 44n, 53, 60, 67, 214–15
Desmarais, Paul, 31–34, 36–37, 101, 165, 195, 197, 211, 212, 213, 219, 242, 336, 404n, 425, 427
Desmarais, Pierre, 49
Desrochers, Louis A., 253
Desruisseaux, Senator Paul, 112, 338
Detroit Marine Terminals Inc., 310
Deutsch, John J., 112, 373, 387
DEW line, 281n
Dewees, Willis P., 267n
Dhavernas, Marc, 215
Diamond, A.E., 244, 468
Diamond, Eph, 335
Diamond, Jack, 200n, 269
Dickie, William, 252
Dickson, George, 177
Diefenbaker, John, 162, 231, 248, 270
Dimanche-Matin, 73
Dimma, William A., 412, 513
Dinkel, Robert S., 250
Distillers Corporation-Seagrams Ltd., 79, 334–35, 455, 458; see also Seagram Co. Ltd.
Dixon, Peter, 335
Dlouhy, Dominik, 219
Dofasco, 251; see also Dominion Foundries & Steel Ltd.
Doig, Ian, 252
Dome Exploration, 75; see also Dome Petroleum Ltd.
Dome Petroleum Ltd., 252
Dominion & Anglo Investment Corp. Ltd., 173
Dominion Bank, 115
Dominion Construction Co. Ltd., 96, 116n, 266, 269
Dominion Fertilizers Co. Ltd., 170
Dominion Foundries & Steel Ltd. (Dofasco), 95, 144, 337
Dominion Glass Co. Ltd., 75, 78
Dominion Life Assurance Co., 109
Dominion Safety Fund Assoc., 79n
Dominion Securities Corporation Ltd., 15, 18, 19, 115n

Dominion Securities Corp. Harris & Partners Ltd., 243, 474
Dominion Steel & Coal Corp. Ltd., 226, 228, 293
Dominion Stores Ltd., 7, 7n, 21n, 22, 26, 28, 35, 144, 237, 330
Dominion Tanners Ltd., 94, 113, 116, 232
Dominion Textile Co. Ltd., 298; see also Dominion Textile Ltd.
Dominion Textile Ltd., 201n, 227, 293, 460
Domtar Ltd., 7, 7n, 21n, 27, 83, 85, 86n, 94, 112, 183n, 330, 455
Dorchester, Frank, 274n
Dorchester Street (Montreal), 296n
Doriot, Georges, 410
Douglas Lake Ranch, 275
Doyle, John C., 237
Drapeau, Jean, 99n
Drayton Group of Investment Trusts, 94
Drew, Hon. George, 168, 306, 394
Drew, Mrs. George, 135, 292n
Dreyfus Bank, 334
Drummond, Brian, 335
Drummond family [sugar], 296
Drummond family [steel], 296
Drury C.M. (Bud), 71, 292n, 437
Dublin, 420
DuMoulin, P. Anthony, 29
Duncan, James, 23, 292n; Not a One-Way Street, 369n
Duncan, Sir Val, 427
Dundas Farms Ltd., 236n
Dunlap, David M., 29
Dunn, Lieut. Alexander Robert, 402n
Dunn, Sir James, 153n, 175, 389–90
Dunsmuir family, 302
Dunton, A. Davidson, 205, 386, 438
Du Pont of Canada Ltd., 96, 110, 113, 455, 460
du Pont, Felix, 33
du Pont family, 10
Duquet, John E.L., 29, 111
Duquet, MacKay & Weldon, 111

E-L Financial Corp. Ltd., 336
Eagle House, 347
Eagle's Nest, 346
East, John, Iron Works Ltd., 114
East, M.A., 114
East Coast Smelting & Chemical Co. Ltd., 261
Eastern Air Lines Inc., 93
Eastern & Chartered Trust Co., 109
Eastern & Western Land Corp., 16
Eastern Canada Savings & Loan Co., 225, 254
Eastern Provincial Airways Ltd., 238
Eastern Telephone & Telegraph Co., 225n
East Hill Gun Club, 434
East Kootenay Power Co. Ltd., 74
Eaton, A.K. (Ken), 381n, 387
Eaton, Lady (Flora McCrea), 311, 311n, 313n,
Eaton, Fredrik S., 245, 312
Eaton, George, 245n, 312, 313
Eaton, Sir John Craig, 311

Eaton, John Craig, 195, 245, 290n, 312, 468
Eaton, John David, 288, 293, 312, 313, 314, 479
Eaton, Mrs. John David (Signy Stephenson), 311
Eaton, Robert Young, 311
Eaton, Timothy, 106–7n, 311
Eaton, Timothy Craig, 312n
Eaton family, 199, 292n, 293n, 294n, 311–14
Eaton, T., Co. Ltd., 95, 96, 114n, 125n, 201n, 232, 313, 455
Eaton's of Canada Ltd., 195, 245n, 312, 313, 468
Eayrs, James, quoted, 447
Eby, Peter, 245n
Economic Council of Canada, 251, 268, 387
Eddy, E.B., Co. Ltd., 168
Eddy Match Co. Ltd., 168–69, 335
Eddy Paper Co. Ltd., 321n
Edinburgh, Duke of, 402
Edmonton Club, 422
Edper group (Edward and Peter Bronfman), 182n
Edper Investments Ltd., 79
Edwards, Les, 455
Edwards, Lou, 56
Effinger, C.N., 244
El Dorado Club, 32
Electric Boat Company, 382
Electric Reduction Co. of Canada Ltd., 170
Electrohome Ltd., 113
Ellen, Leonard, 254
Elliott, R. Fraser, 58, 114, 219, 468
Elliott & Page Ltd., 186n, 303n
Ellis, A. John, 116n, 269
Emco Ltd., 336
Empire Brass Manufacturing Co. Ltd., 336
Empire Club, 305–6
Empire Co. Ltd., 227
Empire Development Co. Ltd., 250n
Empire Life Insurance Co., 37n, 243
Empire Manufacturing Co. Ltd., 336
Employers' Council of B.C., 270
Engineering Consultants Ltd., 260n
English, Fred, 17
Epley, Marion, 12n
Epsom, 9, 251
Erickson, Arthur, 263
Evangeline Savings and Mortgage Co., 226
Evans, Harry M.E., 327
Evans, Dr. John, 433
Evening News (London), 84
Everett, Senator Douglas D., 232n, 453, 468
Everglades Club, 11, 31–32, 39
Everglades Protective Syndicate, 11
Eversharp Inc., 309
Excelsior Life Insurance Co., 96
Exploram Minerals Ltd., 250n
Explorers' Club, 317

FLQ, see Front de Liberation du Québec

FP newspapers, 74, 310
FP Publications Ltd., 80, 245, 251, 470
Fairley, Albert L., Jr., 28, 110
Fairmont Co. Ltd., 367
Falconbridge Nickel Mines Ltd., 94, 108, 162, 363, 455
Family Allowance Act, 377
Famous Players Corp., 241–42, 298
Faribault, Marcel, 45
Farrell, Gordon, 266, 271, 339
Farris, J. Haig deB., 276n
Fauquier, David, 399n
Federal Grain Ltd., 111, 231; see also Federal Industries Ltd.
Federal Industries Ltd., 95, 232
Feldman, Zane, 200n
Feldmühle AG, 324
Fenian raids, 402
Ferguson, Harry, 23, 24
Ferneley, John, 14
Fidelity Life Insurance Co., 270
Filion, Gérard, 162n
Financial Executives' Institute, 171
Financial Post, 18, 23, 103
Financial Post's Directory of Directors, 204, 402
Financial Times of Canada, 170
Finlay, John, 245n
Finlay, Percy, 8
Finlayson, Jock, 99n, 219
Finn, Gilbert, 254, 468
Finning, Earl B., 275
Finning Tractor & Equipment Co. Ltd., 96, 116n, 275
Firestone, O.J. (Jack), 382n
First National City Bank (New York), 98n, 129n
First National Bank (Palm Beach, Fla.), 7–8, 12
First Toronto Corp. Ltd., 186n
Fisher, Douglas, 388
Fisher, Gordon N., 199n, 245, 292n, 468
Five Lakes Fishing Club, 385–86, 496–99
Flavelle, Sir Joseph, 296, 422
Flavelle family, 292
Flick, Friedrich, 324
Flood, Allan, 245n
Florence, Italy, 311
Florenceville, N.B., 229n, 257
Florida, see Delray Beach, Hobe Sound, Palm Beach
Foley, Harold, 280, 281
Food Markets Holdings, 322
Ford, President Gerald, 32
Fording Coal Ltd., 220, 265
Ford Motor Co., 202n, 457
Ford Motor Co. of Canada Ltd., 94, 113, 191n, 202n
Foreign Exchange Control Board (FECB), 362, 363, 490–95
Foreign Investment Review Act, 156
Forest and Stream Club, 422
Forest Hill Village, 312, 402
Forget family, 296
Fortnum and Mason, 287, 320
Foster, Sir George, 160
Fotheringham, Allan, 264, 269, 272

Fowler, Robert M., 290, 391, 391n, 492

Franck, August, 219, 468

Francoeur, Jacques, 73, 74, 215

Franklin, Mitchell, 255

Franz Joseph, Prince, 420n

Fraser, Blair, 437

Fraser, John, 339

Fraser Companies Ltd., 228, 434

Fraser's Highlanders (78th Regiment), 325n

Frazee, Rowland (Rowlie), 99n, 128, 178, 219

Freedman, Samuel, 439

Freeman-Attwood, E.C., 201n

Free Press (Winnipeg), 79, 230, 231, 251

Freiman, Lawrence, 437

Frenette, Claude, 53, 74, 215

Front de Liberation du Québec (FLQ), 43, 44, 214

Frosst, Charles, 292n

Frye, Northrop, 424; *quoted*, 444

Fuller, D.L., 231n

Fuller, John A. (Jack), 70

Fullerton, Douglas H., 196, 206, 453

Fulton, Davie, 405n

Gagnon, Wilfrid, 364n, 479

Gairdner family, 339

Galbraith, John Kenneth, 379; *New Industrial State*, 203n

Gallagher, John P. (Jack), 252, 513

Galt, Thomas, 219

Galt family, 302

Galt Malleable Iron Ltd., 431

Galvin, Edward A., 242, 252

Gambles Canada Ltd., 233

Ganong, R. Whidden, 254

Gardiner, George R., 200n, 246, 339

Gardiner, Percy, 246

Gardiner, W. Douglas H., 99n, 243, 468

Garrison Club, 420n, 422

Garson, Stuart, 168, 279

Garwood, Joseph, 245n

Gatineau Bus Co., 68–70

Gatineau Power Co., 68, 72

Gault, John, 294n

Gault family, 302

Gelco Entreprises Ltd., 49, 72, 73, 76, 81n

Gélinas, Senator Louis P., 32, 215, 427

Geneen, Harold, 176

General Bakeries Ltd., 22, 112

General Bearings Ltd., 274n

General Distributors of Canada Ltd., 232n, 252, 438, 467

General Dynamics Corp., 282

General Investment Corp., (Quebec), 217

General Motors Acceptance Corp., 129n

General Motors Corp., 102n

General Motors of Canada Ltd., 70, 157, 457

General Telephone & Electronics Corp., 265n, 459

General Theory of Employment, Interest, and Money, 377–79

Genest, Pierre, 43–45, 56, 63, 68, 453

Geneva, Switzerland, 139, 235

Genstar Ltd., 47, 102n, 219, 237, 459, 468

George V (King), 297, 301

George VI (King), 122n, 413

Georgian Bay, 312, 433

Gerald, John, 347

Gerstein, Irving, 245n

Gerstein family, 339

Gesca Ltée, 73–74, 76

Getty, Donald, 249

Getty, J. Paul, 323

Gibbings, C.W., 114

Gibson, J. Douglas, 165, 205, 244, 468, 492, 503

Gibson, Kelly, 252, 468

Gignac, Jean-Paul, 53, 215

Gill, E.C., 113

Gillespie, Alastair, 433

Gillespie family, 230

Gillies, Norman, 399n

Ginter, Ben, 339

Giroux, Roland, 215

Glad Tidings Temple, 272

Glassco, J. Grant, 161n, 201n

Glenbow-Alberta Institute, 328

Glenbow Centre, 328n

Glencoe Club, 430n

Globe and Mail (Toronto), 37, 141, 207, 228, 246, 251, 310, 425

Globe and Mail Ltd., 246

Globe Magazine, 200n

Godbout, Adélard, 216

Godfrey, John M., 165, 244

Godwin, Ernest T., 29

Golden, David A., 438

Good Samaritan Hospital (Palm Beach), 11

Gooderham, Bill, 199n

Gooderham, George, 199n, 292–93

Gooderham, Ted, 19–20

Gooderham, Lady, 292–93

Gooderham family, 230, 292n, 302, 424

Goodwood Club, 434

Goodyear Tire & Rubber Co. of Canada Ltd., 96

Gordon, Donald, 279, 367, 368

Gordon, Duncan, 201, 339

Gordon, G. Blair, 293, 480

Gordon, Col. H.D.L., 201

Gordon, J. Peter, 165, 171, 198, 244, 411

Gordon, Walter L., 132, 172–73, 200, 339, 262–63, 391, 392, 425

Gordon family (Montreal), 296

Gormley Investments Ltd., 21n

Gouin, Sir Lomer, 99n

Gouzenko, Igor, 358, 488–89n

Government House, 367

Graham, F. Ronald, 251, 339

Graham, Peter, 200n

Graham family, 267

Granatstein, J.L., *Canada's War*, 377

Grand Cayman, 235, 303

Grand Falls, N.B., 256n

Grand River Fishing Club, 434n

Grand Trunk Pacific Railway, 212, 296

Grand Trunk Railway, 212
Grande Société, 420
Grant, George, 418
Grant, Robert, 199n
Grant, William Lawson (Choppy), 16, 250, 292n
Gratsos, Panos, 271
Gray, Gordon, 245n
Graydon Hall, 347n
Graymont Ltd., 267
Great Canadian Oil Sands Ltd., 95
Great Eastern Corp. Ltd., 225n
Great Glen cattle ranch, 267n
Great Lakes Paper Co. Ltd., 220
Great Lakes Supply Co., Ltd., 352n
Great Plains Development Co. of Canada Ltd., 250
Great-West Life Assurance Co., 50, 58, 78–80, 109, 154, 231, 232, 464, 466
Great West Saddlery Co., 79
Greb Shoes, 335
Green family, 339
Greene, Dick, 237n
Greenshields family, 296
Greenshields Inc., 34, 35, 71, 192
Greenshields & Co. Inc., 204; see also Greenshields Inc.
Green Valley Fertilizer & Chemical Co. Ltd., 235
Greenwood, L.G., 114, 140
Grenfell, Dr. Wilfred, 298
Grew Ltd., 21n
Greyhound (bus line), 72
Griffin, Anthony G.S. (Tony), 118, 165n, 205, 244, 468
Griffin, Melvin W. (Mel), 177n
Griffith Island Club, 433
Griffiths, Frank, 269–70
Griffiths, W.F., 232
Grossman, Alex, 339
Grubb, L. Edward, 165n, 183, 191n, 192n, 244, 468
Grumman Gulfstream II [aircraft], 183, 455
Grundy, Norm, 84n
Guaranty Trust Co. of Canada, 141n, 198, 201, 243, 306, 453, 470, 473
Guest, Gowan, 274n, 276
Guinness, A.E., 216
Guinness Book of World Records, 305
Gulf Oil Canada Ltd., 95, 96, 125, 455, 458
Gundy, Charles L., 28, 181, 243, 293, 339
Gundy, J.H., 23
Gunn, Sir James, 14, 40n
Gutta Percha & Rubber Ltd., 200
Guy Street (Montreal), 296n

Hager, Roger T., 29
Haggart, Ron, quoted, 311–12
Haldenby and White, 19
Hale, John H., 411, 432
Halifax Club, 422
Hall, Coleman E. (Coley), 200n
Hall Corporation Shipping Ltd., 43n
Hall-Dennis Report, 401
Hallward, Hugh, 292n, 339

Haloid Company, 410n
Halton, Matthew, 321
Hamber, Eric, 267n
Hambro Canada Ltd., 95
Hamilton, Alex D., 29, 165n
Hamilton, Hon. Alvin, 306
Hamilton, Eric, 165n
Hamilton, Hon. William, 165n, 270
Hamilton Club, 422
Hamilton Harbour affair, 176, 217
Hampson, H. Anthony, 53, 269
Hanbury family, 267
Hanson, Horace, 255
Hantsport, N.S., 228
Harbour Investments, 322
Hardin, Herschel, quoted, 160
Harding Carpets Ltd., 96
Hardinge of Lahore, Lord, 36, 219, 425
Hardinge, Field Marshal Sir Henry, 36
Hargraft family, 230
Harlequin Enterprises Ltd., 245
Harmsworth, Vere, 84
Harney, John, 39n
Harquail, F.J., 209
Harradence, A. Milton, 248
Harriman, Averell, 431
Harrington, Conrad F., 219, 468
Harris, Joseph, 231
Harris, William B. (Bill), 240, 432
Harris, William C. (Bill), 165n, 391, 431, 432
Harris, Hon. Walter Edward, 392, 394
Harrison, Russell E., 141, 146, 243, 469
Hart, G. Arnold, 99n, 110, 123, 127, 208, 219, 242, 421, 437
Harvard Business School, 52, 60, 75, 101n, 140, 184–85, 249, 272, 309, 406–13, 509–21
Harvard University, 217, 219, 266, 268, 406–7
Harvard University Associates in Canada Inc., 412
Harvey family, 237
Harvie, Donald S., 252, 514
Harvie, Eric, 252, 288, 292n, 327–328
Hashman, Sam, 183, 339
Hastings West Investment Ltd., 270, 470
Hatch, H. Clifford, 339, 514
Hatch, W. Douglas, 199n
Hatch, William M. (Bill), 339
Hatch family, 200n
Hatfield, Richard, 261
Hatskin, Ben, 200n
Hawaii, 45
Hawke, J. Howard, 180
Hearn, Dr. Richard, 188
Hearst Corporation, 57
Heathcote family, 430
Hebdos Métropolitains, 73
Hébert, Jean-Claude, 166n, 214, 469
Hébert, Louis, 68–69, 215
Heeney, A.D.P., 230, 361, 405n
Heffelfinger, George, 232
Heffelfinger family, 230
Heidrick & Struggles Inc., 179
Heimbecker family, 230

Helix Investments Ltd., 196, **474**
Hendeles, Jacob, 341
Hendrie, George, 199*n*
Hennigar, David, 227
Herman, W. Bernard, 199*n*, 339
Hermant, Sydney M., 113, 120, 339
Hermes of Paris, 183, 211
Hernando Island, 263, 271
Herring, J.F., 14
Herron, W.S., 290*n*
Herschorn, Peter, 255
Heubach, Fraser, 399*n*
Hickman, E.L., 114
Hickman, A.E., Co. Ltd., 94, **114**
Hickman family, 237*n*
Hicks, A.R., 113
Highcroft Enterprises Ltd., 232
Hill, Dr. F. Marguerite, 118*n*
Hillcrest Collieries Ltd., 209
Hillcrest Mohawk Collieries Ltd., 209
Hillfield-Strathallan College, 403
Hilton of Canada, 51*n*, 203, 273
Hi-Mar Holdings Ltd., 352*n*
Hingston family, 296
Hitchman, George C., 210, 243, 469
Hobbes, Thomas, 4
Hobbs, Gerald H.D., 116*n*, 270, 469
Hobbs, J.W. (Joe), 267*n*
Hobe Sound, Fla., 431
Hockey Canada, 269
Hockin, T.A. (Tom), 398
Hodgson, W.R. (Bill), 200*n*
Holbrook, D.S., 112
Holiday Inns, 158*n*
Hollinger Mines Ltd., 7, 8, 22, 26, 37*n*, 94, 110, 238
Holmes, Thomas B., 209
Holmes, Dr. Thomas H., 209
Holt, Sir Herbert, 59, 135, 175, 296, 298, 299, 426
Holt, Renfrew & Co. Ltd., 309
Home Bank, 101*n*
Home Care Properties, 225*n*
Home Oil Co., Ltd., 118, 250, 251, 253, 253*n*
Honderich, Beland H., 245, 469
Honeywell Ltd., 12*n*
Hong Kong Stock Exchange, 235
Horner, Dr. Hugh, 249
Hosmer, Charles, 301
Hosmer, Elwood, 300, 302*n*
Hosmer family, 296
House of Seagram Ltd., 95, 114*n*, 163*n*, 197, 208, 219
Housser family, 241
Howard, Ken, 83*n*, 85
Howard Johnson's Motor Lodges, 203
Howe, Bruce I., 276, 411
Howe, Clarence Decatur, 38, 141, 157, 168, 225, 278, 279, 363–76, 382–96, 448
Howe, C.D., Research Institute, 192*n*, 391*n*
Hudson's Bay Company, 75, 143, 160, 185, 186, 231, 233, 235–36, 251, 465
Hudson's Bay Oil & Gas Co. Ltd., 228–29, 237, 462
Hughes, Gordon, 226

Hughes, Howard, 272
Hughes, Samuel, 165*n*
Humphrey, Gilbert, 28
Hunco Ltd., 336
Hunt, Russell, *K.C. Irving,* 258
Hunt Club Ball (Montreal), 297
Hunter, Dick, 232*n*
Hunter, G.R., 114
Hunter family, 336
Huntsman's, 6
Hurford, William, 429
Huron & Erie Mortgage Corp., 330
Husky Oil Ltd., 221, 469
Hutchison, Bruce, *Incredible Canadian,* 361*n*
Hyde Park, N.Y., 365
Hydro-Québec, 215, 303*n*
Hyland, J. Norman, 206, 266*n*
Hyndman, Louis, 249
Hyndman, Walter, 236*n*

IAC Ltd., 211, 225; *see also* Industrial Acceptance Corp.
IBM Canada Ltd., 96, 319
IBM World Trade Corp., 202
IBM World Trade Americas/Far East Corp., 320
ITT, 52, 176, 265*n*
IU International Corp., 186*n*; *see also* International Utilities Corp.
Ibn Saud, King, 10*n*
Ile aux Ruaux, 43, 43*n*, 44 44*n*
Ile d'Orléans, 43, 217
Illustrated London News, 323
Ilsley, James, 225, 367, 383
Imasco Ltd., 93, 113, 314
Imperial Bank of Canada, 101*n*, 350; *see also* Canadian Imperial Bank of Commerce
Imperial Life Assurance Co. of Canada, 50, 73, 78, 109
Imperial Oil Ltd., 93, 112, 114, 179, 202*n*, 250, 258, 455, 457, 466
Imperial Optical Co. Ltd., 94, 113, 339
Imperial Tobacco Co. of Canada Ltd., 338; *see also* Imasco
Imperial Trust Co., 303 *n*, 308, 310, 474
Inco, *see* International Nickel Co. of Canada Ltd.
Income Tax Act, 350–51
Independent Broadcasting Authority, 33
Industrial Acceptance Corporation, 67, 70–71, 465; *see also* IAC Ltd.
Industrial Development Bank, 254
Industrial Estates Ltd., 226
Inland Cement Industries Ltd, 253
Inland Natural Gas Co. Ltd., 269
Institute for Research on Public Policy, 241
Institute of Canadian Bankers, 106*n*, 127
Intercolonial Trading Corp. Ltd., 234*n*
Intercontinental Hotel (Bangkok), 318*n*
International Business Machines Corp., *see* IBM
International Housing Ltd., 317

International Joint Commission, 405n, 488
International Multifoods Corp., 94, 462
International Nickel Co. of Canada Ltd. (Inco), 63, 66–67, 95, 96, 110, 179, 191n, 206n, 235
International Paper Co., 93
International Telephone & Telegraph Corp., see ITT
International Tuna Championships, 318
International Utilities Corp., 186, 253; see also IU International Corp.
Inter-Ocean Grain Co. Ltd., 95, 232
Interprovincial Steel & Pipe Corp. Ltd., 231n, 270–71, 474
Interprovincial Trading Corp. Ltd., 234n
Inverlochy Castle, 267n
Investors Diversified Services Inc., 78
Investors Group, 50, 58, 78, 80, 84, 185, 232, 469
Investors Syndicate of Canada Ltd., 231
Irish Derby, 251
Iron Ore Co. of Canada, 7n, 219, 389n, 466
Irving, Arthur, 261, 469
Irving, J.K., 261, 469
Irving, Jack, 261, 469
Irving, Kenneth Colin (K.C.), 224, 256, 258–61, 336, 455
Irving family, 258–61, 469
Irving, J.D., Ltd., 260n
Irving, K.C., Ltd., 238
Irving newspapers, 170, 259, 261
Irving Oil Co. Ltd., 258n
Irving Ours Polaire [tanker], 260
Irwin, Spike, 84n
Isbister, Claude, 230, 497, 501
Island Telephone Co. Ltd., 227
Ivaco Industries Ltd., 339
Ivanier family, 339
Ivey family, 293n, 310, 336
Ivory, Neil, 219, 469

JAMM, 213
Jack, Mel, 161
Jackman, Henry N.R. (Hal), 37n, 243, 292n, 336
Jackman, Henry R. (Harry), 173
James, F. Cyril, 377
James Bay Energy Corp., 214
Jamieson, J.K., 432
Jannock Corp. Ltd., 180, 201n, 461
Jarislowsky, Stephen A., 117, 157, 194–95, 219, 469, 515
Jarislowsky, Fraser & Co. Ltd., 303n, 469
Jefferson, Jack R., 276n
Jeffery, Capt. Joseph, 336, 469
Jeffery family, 293n
Jennings, R.F., 252
Jet Commander/Westwind, 183, 455
JetStar, 32, 56
Jodrey, John J., 227, 336
Jodrey, Roy, 116, 225, 227–29
Jodrey family, 227–28
Johnson, Gardner, family, 430–31

Johnson, Premier Daniel, 45, 52
Johnson, Daniel, Jr., 52n
Johnson, Oscar, 25
Johnson, Patrick, 401
Johnson, Wallace, 158n
Johnstone, Jimmy, 344
Jolivet, L.C. (Jolly), 274n
Jones, Robert, 232, 469
Jonlab Investments Ltd., 185, 186
Jukes family, 431
Juneau, Pierre, 33–34
Junior Associates of the Montreal Museum of Fine Arts, see JAMM
Jupiter River, 55, 56

Kaiser Resources Ltd., 51n, 265, 269, 455, 469
Kalles, Sam, 17
Kalmus, Herbert, 234
Kamarin Investments Ltd., 234n
Kane, Joseph, 245n
Kanee, Sol, 231, 236, 438–39
Keate, J.S. (Stu), 165, 270
Keevil family, 339
Kelly, Grace, 216
Kelly, Douglas & Co. Ltd., 265, 270
Kelowna, B.C., 433
Kennedy, John F., 10, 57, 266
Kennedy, J. Taylor, 165n
Kennedy, Joseph P., 303
Kennedy, Robert (Bobby), 39–40
Kent family, 257
Kent Line Ltd., 260n
Kentucky Derby, 252, 301
Kenwal Enterprises Ltd., 232
Kerr, James W. (Jim), 110, 188, 243, 469
Kerrigan, Harold F., 28
Keynes, John Maynard (Lord Keynes), 163n, 171, 377–82
Khrushchev, Nikita, 322
Kilbourn, William, 394n
Kilburn, Peter, 219
Kildare Street Club, 420
Kilgour, David, 58, 79, 154, 231
Killam, Dorothy (Mrs. Izaak W.), 301–2
Killam, Izaak Walton, 86n, 301, 426
Killam, Larry, 276
Killam, Lol, 199n
Killam, Ruth, 292n
Killam family, 267n, 297
Kimber, J.R., 83
King, Egerton W., 253
King, W.L. Mackenzie, 164, 167, 358, 361, 365, 370–72, 376, 377, 382n, 386–88, 413
King Street (Toronto), 91, 92, 419
King, Ont., 246, 311
King's College (Cambridge), 379
Kingsway Transports Ltd., 50
Kinnear, David, 114n, 313
Kirkpatrick, John G., 30
Kirkwood, John C., 362n
Kitcat & Aitken, 36
Kleinwort, Benson Inc., 453
Knob Hill Farms, 245n
Knowles, Frank, 61, 84n
Knowles, Stanley, 371n
Knowlton, Gerald, 252
Knowlton, W. Leo, 29

Knudsen, Semon E. (Bunkie), 12n, 34
Koerner, Iby, 271
Koerner, Leon, 267n
Koerner, Michael, 240, 245, 267, 339, 469, 515
Koerner, Walter, 267, 438
Koerner family, 267
Koffler, Murray, 339, 469
Kolber, E. Leo, 114n, 156–57, 193, 219, 334–35, 469
Korean War, 391
Korthals, Robert W., 245
Kosygin, Alexei, 139n
Kramer, Bob, 200n
Kramer, Donald, 231n
Kramer Tractor Ltd., 231n
Kreuger, Ivar, 168
Kroft, Charles, 232
Kruger family, 339

Labatt, Arthur, 303n
Labatt, John, Ltd., 120, 125, 143, 185–86, 226, 456, 459
Labatt family, 302
LaBine family, 339
Labrador [icebreaker], 216
Labrador Mining & Exploration Co. Ltd., 7n, 455
Lacelle, Joseph Arthur (Archie), 440
Lacroix, Camille, 29
Ladner, Leon, 270
Ladner, Thomas E., 270, 436
Lafarge Canada Ltd., 406; see also Canada Cement Lafarge Ltd.
Lafferty, Richard G.D., 77, 98
Laidlaw, R.A., 432
Laidlaw family, 339
Laidley, C.M., 210, 243, 470
Laing, Peter M., 219, 335
Laing, Mrs. Peter (Kathleen McConnell), 335
Laing, Weldon, Courtois, Clarkson, Parsons, Gonthier & Tetrault, 470
Laiterie Laval Ltée, 95
Lake family, 237n
Lakefield College School, 403, 505
Lake of the Woods Milling Co. Ltd., 168n
Lake Ontario Cement Ltd., 305
Lake Rosseau, 149
Lalonde, Marc, 44, 55
La Malbaie, Que., see Murray Bay
Lamarre, Bernard, 215
Lambert, Allen Thomas, 111, 117, 122, 165, 182n, 243, 423, 427
Lambert, Norman, 371–72
Lambert, Phyllis, see Bronfman, Phyllis
Landegger, Karl, 337
Landry, Alfred, 255
Lang, F.A., 232
Lang, Howard J., 111, 144, 219, 470
Langelier, Joe, 66
Langford, Henry, 79, 493
Lank, Herb H., 110, 219
Lapalme, Georges-Emile, 216
La Patrie, 73
Laporte, Pierre, 44
La Presse, 45, 47, 73, 74, 76, 217
Laskin, Chief Justice Bora, 292n
Last Post Club, 429

Latner family, 339
La Tribune, 73, 74
Laura Secord Candy Shops Ltd., 120
Laurel Valley Golf Club, 344n
Laurentian Mutual Assurance, 215
Laurentide Financial Corp. Ltd., 50, 75, 76, 265
Laurier government, 218
Lausanne, Switzerland, 404
Lavoie, Léo, 215, 516
Lavoie, Raymond, 215
La Voix de L'Est, 73, 74
Lawn Tennis and Badminton Club (Vancouver), 430–31
Lawson family, 339
Lazard Frères, 139
Leach, A. Searle, 111, 232, 241
Leach family, 230
Leacock, Stephen, 309, 402n
Learmont family, 295
Lecky, Mrs. John, 266
Le Devoir, 127
Leduc field, 327
Lee, Robert H. (Bob), 275–76
Lehman Brothers, 91
Leitch, John D. (Jack), 111, 144, 244, 246, 337, 470
Leitch, Mervin, 249
Leman, Paul, 165n, 219, 411
Le Nouvelliste, 73–74
Leopold, Irwin D., 339
LePage, A.E., Ltd., 245n
Le Petit Journal, 73
Lesage, Jean, 215, 216
Les Journaux Trans-Canada Ltée, 73
Le Soleil, 52
Lester B. Pearson College of the Pacific, 331, 403–4n
Létourneau, Roger, 29, 113, 215
Létourneau, Stein, Marseille, 111, 113
Letson family, 267
Lévesque, Jean-Louis, 71, 73, 200n, 215, 333, 339, 456
Lévesque, René, 285
Lévesque, Beaubien Inc., 214
Levy brothers, 339, 492
Lewis, Derek, 237n
Lewis, W. James D., 29
Lewtas, James L., 29
Liberal Federation, National, 30, 271, 414
Liberal Federation, Quebec, 53n
Liberal party, Canada, 241, 244; Manitoba, 231; Newfoundland, 237n; Quebec, 214, 216, 219n; P.E.I., 236n
Libling, Gerald, 439
Ligonier, Pa., 346, 421
Likely, Joseph, 255
Likely, Jos. A., Ltd., 95, 470
Lindwood Holdings Ltd., 225n
Linton family, 296
Liquefuels Ltd., 308n
Little, A.J. (Pete), 200, 205, 244, 470
Little Pond Ltd., 236n
Liverpool Plains Pastoral Co. Proprietary Ltd., 82
Lobb, John, 183n
Loblaw Companies Ltd., 322, 464n

Loblaw Groceterias Co. Ltd., 322
Lockhart, Leonard, 255
Lockharts Ltd., 255
Loeb, Ann Margaret (Mrs. Edgar Bronfman), 334n
Loeb, David, 199n
Loeb family, 337
Loeb, Rhoades & Co., 334n
Lombard Place (Winnipeg), 233, 234
London Club, 422
London Life Insurance Co., 96, 109, 330n, 336
Longchamps [racetrack, Paris], 124
Longden, Vance, 251
Long Point Company [club], 432
Longstaffe, J. Ron, 268, 324
Lopokova, Lydia, 378
Loram Construction Inc., 250n
Loram International Ltd., 250n
Lord, J.T., 433
Lord Nelson Hotel (Halifax), 255
Lord Simcoe Hotel (Toronto), 310
Lornex Mining Corp. Ltd., 265
Loubier, Gabriel, 74n
Lougheed, D.D., 250
Lougheed, E. Peter, 249, 412, 517
Love, G. Donald, 253
Love, Richey B., 249n
Lovett, Robert, 431
Lower Canada College, 297, 403, 505
Lower St. Lawrence Power Co., 303n
Lowson, Sir Denys, 242
Lucas, Gabriel, Ltée, 290n
Luce, Clare Boothe, 346
Ludwig, Daniel K., 315–17
Lumbers, Leonard G., 56n, 112
Lundberg, Ferdinand, The Rich and the Super-Rich,184
Lundell, Oscar, 206
Lundrigan, Arthur Raymond, 237, 238
Lundrigan, William James, 237
Lundrigan family, 237, 340
Lundrigans Ltd., 237
Lycoming Division of Avco, 40n
Lyford Cay, Bahamas, 307, 314

M & M Systems Research Ltd., 94, 111
Macadam, Robert, 13
Macassa Mines Ltd., 381n
MacAulay, John, 182, 231
MacRan Sales Agency Ltd., 256n
MacCulloch, Charles E., 226, 340, 470
MacCulloch family, 225
MacCulloch & Co. Ltd., 95
Macdonald, Angus L., 225
Macdonald, Sir John A., 223, 233n, 297, 425, 428
Macdonald, Ruth (Mrs. Donald S. Macdonald), 412n
Macdonald, Sir William, 325–26
Macdonald College (McGill), 325
Macdonald family (Confederation Life), 293n
Macdonald family (tobacco), 296
Macdonald Tobacco, 325
Macdonnell, J.M. (Jim), 249, 292n, 380–81, 394

Macdonnell, Peter L.P., 113, 249–250, 470
MacDougall, Hartland, 243
MacDougall family, 295
MacIntosh, Alexander John, 112, 244, 470
MacIntosh, Robert M., 125–26, 128, 243, 253, 470
Mackasey, Bryce, 53
Mackay, David, 236n
Mackay, Hugh Hazen, 255
Mackay family, 296
MacKeen, John C., 113, 226
Mackenzie, Dr. C.J., 375, 437, 501
Mackenzie, Ian, 377
Mackenzie, Maxwell W., 111, 362n, 488, 493
Mackenzie, Sir William, 301n
Mackenzie King Chair of Canadian Studies, 412
Mackenzie family, 296
Mackenzie Valley, 220, 250, 275
MacKimmie, Matthews, 253
Mackintosh, William A. (Bill), 382–83, 385, 387
Maclachlan, Peter, 199n
Maclaren family, 292n, 340
MacLaren Advertising, 421
Maclaren Power & Paper Co., 95, 310
MacLauchlan, Harry, 236n
Maclean-Hunter Ltd., 96, 103, 336, 467
Maclean's, 104n, 236n, 257, 276n, 312, 369n–70n, 393
MacLennan, Hugh, 296n; quoted, 393
MacLennan, Mrs. Hugh, 296n
MacMillan, H.R., 265–66, 279, 280, 340, 367, 482
MacMillan, K.B., 232
MacMillan, Norman, 222
MacMillan Bloedel Ltd., 94, 111, 116n, 166n, 180, 206, 206n, 221, 265, 266, 269, 474, 276, 411
MacMurray, James, 255
Macpherson family, 236
Mac's Milk, 245n
Maganassippi Club, 434
Magee, Brian, 432
Magor, John, 399n
Main Iron Works, 306
Maine Chance, 291
Maisonrouge, Jacques, 202
Malkin family (Vancouver), 267, 431
Malkin, W.H., Ltd., 270
Malone, Cliff, 219
Malone, Richard C., 232n
Malone, Brig. R.S. (Dick), 165n, 231, 245, 470
Manalta Coal Ltd., 250n
Manalta Holdings Ltd., 250n
Manark Industrial Sales Ltd., 250n
Mandel, Jerri, 245
Manitoba, 229–36
Manitoba Club, 231, 420n, 422, 438
Manitoba Pool Elevators, 233
Mann, Maj.-Gen. Churchill, 246
Mann, Sir Donald, 301n
Mannesmann AG, 222
Manning, Ernest C., 111
Manning, Fred, 225

Mannix, Fred C., 32, 43n, 113, 250, 337, 430, 470
Mannix Co. Ltd., 93, 456
Mansur, David B., 386, 391
Manufacturers Life Insurance Co., 109, 464
ManuLife Centre, 322
Manville, Tommy, 346
Maple Leaf Gardens, 154n, 245n, 318n
Maple Leaf Mills Ltd., 272
Mara, George, 56n, 200n, 205, 244, 339, 470
Marani family, 431
Marathon Realty Co. Ltd., 220, 265
Marchment, Alan R., 243, 314, 453, 470
Margaret (Princess), 286n, 322
Marine Industries Ltd., 162n, 215–217, 408
Marine Pipeline Construction of Canada Ltd., 235
Maritime Accessories Ltd., 225n
Maritime Central Airways, 236n
Maritime Life Assurance Co., 226, 254
Maritime Paper Products Ltd., 225
Maritime Steel & Foundries Ltd., 93, 225n, 226, 467
Maritime Telegraph & Telephone Co. Ltd., 96, 227, 272
Markborough Properties Ltd., 236
Marlfair Holdings Ltd., 274
Marpole family (Vancouver), 431
Marsh, Leonard, 377
Marshall, Ben, 14
Martin, Danae (Mrs. Hugh), 271
Martin, Hugh, 162n, 270
Martin, Lorry, 69
Martin, Paul Jr., 53, 56, 61
Martineau, Jean, 219
Marwell Dredging Ltd., 162n
Maryland, 246, 315
Mashaal brothers, 340, 428
Mason, Col. James Cooper, 101n
Massachusetts Institute of Technology, 275, 371, 380n
Massé, M.A., 99n
Massey, Geoffrey, 292n
Massey, Raymond, 292n
Massey, Vincent, 250, 292n, 372, 414
Massey-Ferguson Ltd., 94, 113, 144, 293, 330, 453, 458
Massey-Harris Co. Ltd., 23–24
Massey-Harris-Ferguson Ltd., 24
Masters' Golf Tournament, 192n
Matheson, John, 414
Matthews, Maj.-Gen. A. Bruce, 26–28, 30, 201n, 244, 414, 421
Matthews, Beverley, 110, 244, 421, 471
Matthews, Richard, 253
Mauro, Arthur, 232
May, Mrs. Marjorie Post, 10, 10n
Mayberry, T.M., 111
Mayer, Louis B., 6
Mayne, A.F. (Art), 43n, 110
Mayne, A.F., and Associates, 110
McAfee, Jerry, 244, 471
McAlpine, Robert, 95
McArthur, Duncan R.B., 253, 517
McArthur, Jack, quoted, 248

McCabe family, 230
McCaig, J.R., 250
McCain, Andrew, Sr., 256n
McCain, Andrew, 255, 471
McCain, H. Harrison, 165n, 201, 256–57, 258n, 471
McCain, Mrs. Harrison (Billie McNair), 258n
McCain, Robert, 256n
McCain, Wallace, 256n, 258n
McCain, Mrs. Wallace (Margaret Norrie), 258n
McCain family, 256–58, 337
McCain Foods Ltd., 95, 256n, 471
McCain Produce Co. Ltd., 256n, 471
McCall family, 302, 340
McCarthy, Don, 245
McCarthy, John Leighton, 244, 471
McCarthy & McCarthy, 110, 471
McClelland, T.H., 116n
McCloy, John J., 121
McColough, C. Peter, 410n
McConnell, John Wilson, 335
McConnell estate, 219, 303n, 335
McCormack, Thomas G., 27n, 28
McCrum, Michael, 401n
McCuaig Desrochers, 253
McCullagh, George, 228
McCurdy, Hollis T., 29
McCutcheon, M. Wallace (Wally), 21n, 23, 37n, 340, 493
McCutcheon, Wilfred W., 415
McDaniel, Rod, 250
McDonald's Restaurants of Canada Ltd., 245n, 338
McDougald, D.J., 6n, 15–16
McDougald, John Angus (Bud), 3–34, 36–41, 81n, 83, 111, 147, 156, 192, 198, 204, 206–7, 244, 336, 421, 422–24, 427
McDougald, Mrs. John A. (Jimmy), 14, 19, 25, 33
McDougald, Senator, W.L., 16
McDougald, D.J., and Company, 15
McDowell, F.G., 243, 471
McDowell, Ted, 210
McEachren, Frank, 292n
McElman, Charles. 260
McEntyre, Peter M., 219
McFadzean, Lord, 139
McGavin, Allan, 116n, 271
McGavin ToastMaster Ltd., 95, 116n
McGill University, 140, 272, 296n, 297, 299, 302n, 309, 332, 409
McGillivray, Don, 446n
McGiverin, Donald, 231, 314
McGowen, Kenneth, 245n
McGovern, Senator George, 39n
McGregor, Fred, 167–68
McGregor, William S., 253
McInnes, Donald, 226, 471
McIntosh, Donald Alexander, 28, 205, 244
McIntyre family, 296
McIntyre Mines Ltd., 75
McIvor, George, 438
McKee, John, 421
McKeen, Senator Stanley, 271, 482
McKenna, Frank. 302
McKibben, J.H., 249n
McKinnon, Hector B., 437

McKinnon, Neil John, 79, 106, 111, 120, 122, 126, 161n, 186, 295, 403n
McLagan, T.R. (Rodgie), 113, 389
McLaughlin, Eileen (Mrs. Eric Phillips), 292n
McLaughlin, Col. R.S. (Sam), 21n, 115, 292n; Foundation, 339
McLaughlin, S. Bruce, 245, 340
McLaughlin, W. Earle, 33, 99n, 101–2, 110, 117, 120, 122, 124, 165n, 177, 181–82, 192n, 219, 436, 471
McLean, C.M., 236n
McLean, Donald, 255
McLean, William F. (Bill), 113, 144, 147, 155, 165n, 177, 195, 205, 244, 337, 471
McLean family (Canada Packers), 293n
McLean family (Charlotte, N.B.), 257
McLelland, Hugh, 245n
McMahon, Frank M., 49n, 113, 180n, 200n, 251, 266, 337, 427
McMartin, Allen, 27n, 28, 38n
McMartin, Duncan, 38n
McMartin, Jack, 37n
McMartin, John (Sr.), 37n, 295n
McMartin, Melba, 38n
McMartin family, 340
McMaster, Ross, 336, 482
McNair, John B., 258n, 261
McNamara, Harold, 162n
McNamara family, 200n
McNamara Corp. Ltd., 162n, 217
McNaughton, Gen. A.G.L., 405n
McNeil, Frederick H., 128, 165n, 219, 471
McPherson, A.R., 29
McQueen, Neil, 251
McRae family, 302
Mead Corp., 268, 460
Means, Gardiner C., *Modern Corporation and Private Property*, 203n
Medjuck, Ralph, 227
Medland, Charles Edward, 243, 471
Meighen, Arthur, 164n, 329
Meighen, Col. Maxwell, 27–29, 329–30, 471
Melady family, 230
Melchers Distilleries Ltd., 93, 112, 338
Mellon estate, 344n, 421
Menier, Henri, 55
Menzies, Merril, 384n
Mercantile Bank of Canada, 98, 128n, 129n
Merchants' Bank of Canada, 213
Mercier, François, 219
Meredith family, 296
Meridian development group, 340
Merkur brothers, 340
Metcalf, George C., 322
Metro Centre Developments Ltd., 93, 113
Metro-Goldwyn-Mayer Inc., 5, 335
Metropolitan Club (N.Y.), 11n, 421
Metropolitan Life Insurance Co., 102n, 109, 161, 181n
Metropolitan Stores, 232n

Metropolitan Trust Co., 116n, 243, 473
Meyer, André, 139
Michener, Rt. Hon. Roland, 412n
Micmac Mall, 226
Midland Bank (England), 139
Midland and International Banks Ltd., 99n
Midland Doherty Ltd., 243, 474
Mies van der Rohe, Ludwig, 334
Miller family, 257
Milner, Stanley A., 253
Milner & Steer, 113, 250
Minas Basin Pulp and Power Co. Ltd., 96, 225n, 226, 228, 409
Minchin, Gordon, 79n
Mineral Taxation Act, 1942 (Alberta), 327
Mining Corporation of Canada Ltd., 228
Minnekhada Stock Farms, 267n
Minto Coal Co., 256
Miron family, 337
Miron Co. Ltd., 96
Miss Edgar's and Miss Cramp's School, 297, 507
Mitchell, A. Hoadley, 253
Mitchell, David, 250
Mitchell, J.E., 28
Mitchell & Associates Ltd., 253
Mitchell & Muil Ltd., 321
Mizner, Addison, 11
Mobil Oil Canada Ltd., 96, 112, 253, 459
Mockridge, Harold C.F., 113, 483
Mohawk Navigation Co. Ltd., 235
Moir's Chocolates, 116
Moisie Club, 434
Molson, Senator Hartland de Montarville, 112, 165n, 219, 330–31, 335, 436, 471
Molson family, 199n, 211, 292n, 293n, 296, 297, 448
Molson Companies Ltd., 95, 96, 112, 155, 194, 201n, 225, 231n, 241, 270, 331, 459, 474
Molson Industries Ltd., 177, 188
Monarch Life Assurance Co., 109, 231, 233
Monast, André, 28, 110, 144, 215
Monroe family, 237n
Montreal Alouettes, 200n
Montreal Canadiens, 199n
Montreal Council of Orthodox Rabbis, 218
Montreal Curb Market, 213
Montreal Expos, 181, 199n, 310, 332, 333
Montreal Light, Heat & Power Consolidated, 298
Montréal-Matin, 74
Montreal Military and Marine Museum, 325
Montreal Racket Club, 422n, 428
Montreal Star, 202n, 251, 296, 336
Montreal Stock Exchange, 109, 213, 214, 299
Montreal Trust Co., 50, 51n, 54, 58, 61, 78, 109
Montreal Water & Power Co., 308
Moog, Gerhard, 199n, 340
Moon, Barbara, *quoted*, 200, 425
Mooney, John J., 200n, 421

Moore, John Henderson (Jake), 110, 120, 143, 165, 185–86, 201*n*, 244, 430, 471
Moore, T.F., 114
Moore Corp. Ltd., 96
Moores, Premier Frank, 239, 403*n*
Moosehead Breweries Ltd., 94, 255
Morgan, Bartlett, 340
Morgan family (Montreal), 296, 303*n*
Morgan, Ostiguy & Hudon Inc., 111; *see also* Crang & Ostiguy
Morgan Trust Co., 95, 303*n*, 341
Morgan's [department store], 212
Moriyama, Raymond, 247
Morrison, George, 312*n*
Morrow, Graham, 340
Morrow family, 226
Morrow, R.E. (Bob), 84–86
Morton, Paul, 231*n*
Mosca, Gaetano, *quoted*, 445
Moscow, USSR, 251
Mother's Own Bakery Ltd., 254
Mounfield, W.K., 165*n*
Mount Royal Club, 57, 104, 161, 302, 331, 442, 426–27
Mount Stephen, Lord, 296
Mount Stephen Club, 422, 427
Muggeridge, Malcolm, *quoted*, 443
Muir, James, 99*n*, 105, 121–24 126, 187
Mulholland, William D., 211, 219, 412, 421, 471, 518
Mulock, Sir William, 433
Mulock, Tom, 246
Mulock family, 302
Multiple Access Ltd., 335
Muncaster, J. Dean, 244
Munitions and Supply, Dept. of, 225, 363–64, 375, 476–87
Munnings, Sir Alfred, 14, 25
Murchison group, 123
Murdoch, J.Y., 183, 483
Murray, William Allan, 16, 30*n*
Murray family, 236
Murray Bay, 44, 57, 297
Murray's Pond, Nfld., 433
Mutual Home Security Assoc., 79*n*
Mutual Life Assurance Co. of Canada, 109, 115, 330*n*

NDP, 130, 166*n*
Nadeau, Pierre, 53, 214, 472
Nader, Ralph, 433
Nassau, Bahamas, 314
National Arts Centre, 318*n*
National Capital Commission, 196, 206
National Casket Co., 335*n*
National Club (Toronto), 160, 425–426
National Life Assurance Co. of Canada, 94, 109
National Sea Products Ltd., 225*n*, 226
National Tea Co., 321
National Trust Co. Ltd., 109, 249*n*, 249, 296
National Westminster Bank, 99*n*
Naylor, R.T., 159
Neel, Boyd, 425
Nelles, H.V. (Viv), *quoted*, 159
Nelles, Mary, 345*n*

Nelsons Laundries Ltd., 113, 268–269
Neonex International Ltd., 201*n*, 272, 461
Nesbitt, Deane, 35, 35*n*, 219, 242, 337, 472
Nesbitt, Thomson and Co. Ltd., 35–36, 75, 192, 337
Neuchâtel Junior College, 404
Neufeld, E.P., *quoted*, 117
New Brunswick, 71, 72, 102, 170, 201, 223, 254–59, 261, 434
New Brunswick Railway Co., 259
New Brunswick Telephone Co. Ltd., 96, 254, 255
Newfoundland, 197, 236–39
Newfoundland Telephone Co. Ltd., 238
Newfoundland Game Fish Protection Society, 433
New Providence Development Co. Ltd., 93, 112
New York, N.Y., 184, 235, 362, 421
New York (magazine), 443
New York Times, 259, 334, 365, 410
New York Yacht Club, 11*n*
Nichol, David, 165*n*
Nichol, John 165*n*, 205, 242, 271, 331, 403*n*, 472
Nicholls, Sir Harmar, 8
Nickle, Carl O., 253
Nicks, William, 100*n*
Nielsen, Arne, 112, 253
Nihon, Alexis, 337
Nixon, Richard M., 307, 423*n*
Noranda Mines Ltd., 7*n*, 93, 94, 96, 111, 143, 157, 183, 198, 201*n*, 228, 268, 453, 455, 458, 472
Nordair Ltd., 236
Nordex Ltd., 49
Noronic [ship], 153*n*
Norrie, Senator Margaret, 258*n*
North American Life Assurance Co., 109, 250, 254, 464, 503
North Denison Mines Ltd., 305, 306; *see also* Denison Mines Ltd.
Northern & Central Gas Corp. Ltd., 76, 78, 94, 182, 221, 455, 460, 466
Northern Electric Co. Ltd., 275, 455, 464
Northern Industries Ltd., 114
Northern Life Assurance Co. of Canada, 310
Northern Quebec Power Co., 74–75
Northern Paint Co., 272
North Sea, 84, 322
North West Mounted Police, 79, 298
North York, 13, 315
Nouveau Cercle, 420
Nova Scotia, 323–28
Nova Scotia Light & Power Co. Ltd., 113, 227
Numac Oil & Gas Ltd., 96, 253

OSF Industries Ltd., 245*n*
O'Brien, George, 199*n*, 272
O'Brien, John, 205
O'Brien, William L.S., 29, 43*n*, 44*n*
Ocean Cement & Supplies Ltd., 266
O'Connell family, 56

Odette family, 340
Odlum, Floyd, 20
Odlum Brown & T.B. Read Ltd., 266n, 268
O'Driscoll, Rev. Herbert, 414
Ogilvie Flour Mills Co. Ltd., 120n, 301, 395, 465
Ogilvie family, 296
Ogilvy, J. Angus, 113, 219
Ogilvy, Cope, Porteous et al., 84, 113, 472
O'Hagan, Richard, 404n
Oilman's Golf Tournament, 123–124
Okanagan Helicopters Ltd., 268, 272
Oland, Philip, 255, 473
Oland, Victor, 227, 427, 472
Oland family, 199n
O'Leary, Senator Grattan, 161n, 218, 368, 393, 395–96
Olympia & York Developments Ltd., 337
Olympic Lottery, 97
Olympic Trust, 318
Onassis, Aristotle Socrates, 216, 304n
Onassis, Jacqueline, 139
O'Neill, E.R., 232
Ontario, 46, 72, 97, 248
Ontario Agricultural College, 266, 271
Ontario Hydro, 166, 188
Ontario Jockey Club, 125, 246
Ontario Securities Commission, 79, 81n, 83, 107n
Oppenheimer, Harry F., 139
Order of Canada, 398, 413–15
Orion banking group, 99n
Orser, Earl H., 201n, 314
Ortloff, Stuart, 347
Orwell, George, 445–46
Osgoode Hall, 63, 64, 97, 327
Oshawa Group Ltd., 96, 337, 456, 465, 475
Osler, E.B., 369–70n
Osler, Sir Edmund, 433
Osler, Gordon, 231
Osler family, 302, 424
Osler, Hammond & Nanton Ltd., 231
Osler, Hoskin & Harcourt, 113, 313
Ostiguy, Jean P.W., 111, 214, 472
Otis Elevator Co. Ltd., 93, 111
Ottawa Journal, 251
Ottawa Rough Riders, 200n
Outerbridge family, 236
Overbeck, Egon, 222
Overwaitea Ltd., 272
Oxford Development Group Ltd., 253, 339
Oxford University, 141, 199, 217, 406

Pacific Logging Co Ltd., 220, 265
Pacific Petroleums Ltd., 93, 251, 266, 455, 461, 468
Pacific Press Ltd., 206, 269
Pacific Tin Consolidated Corp., 305
Pacific Western Airlines, 166n, 249
Packard Motor Car Co., 6, 40n
Paderewski, Ignace, 40–41
Paine, Paul, 60

Palm Beach, Fla., 8, 10–13, 31–34, 266, 286n
Palm Desert, Calif., 32, 263
Palmer, Arnold, 344
Panama Canal, 318n
Panarctic Oils Ltd., 335
PanCanadian Petroleum Ltd., 220, 252
Papachristidis, Phrixos Basil, 340
Paradise Valley Country Club, 346
Paragon Business Forms Ltd., 217
Paré, Paul, 113, 214, 427
Paris, Jean-Michel, 215
Parisien, Jean, 61, 67, 84n, 215
Parizeau, Gérard, 215
Parkin, Sir George, 249–50, 292n
Parkin, John C., 197, 246, 319
Parrish family, 230
Parrish & Heimbecker Ltd., 230
Paterson, Senator Norman McLeod, 267n, 287, 340
Paterson family, 230
Paterson, N.M., & Sons Ltd., 96
Patino, Antenor, 420n
Patino, Simon, 259
Patio Group, 249
Paton, G.W., 169
Paton, Hugh, 426n
Paton, W.J.R., 180
Paton family, 297, 302
Patricia Contractors Ltd., 235
Pattillo, Arthur, 83
Pattison, James A., 200n, 271–72, 341
Peacher, Douglas, 244, 432
Peacock, Frederick, 249n
Pearson, H.J. Sanders, 253
Pearson, Lester B., 30, 165n, 218, 222, 306, 413–14, 431, 488, 501
Pearson government, 53, 199
Pei, Ieoh Ming, 121
Peladeau, Pierre, 215
Pellatt, Sir Henry, 247
Pemberton, Commander F.J.D., 437
Pemberton family, 267, 302
Pemberton Securities Ltd., 275
Pembina Pipe Line Ltd., 250n
Pendray family, 302
Penhale, Maj.-Gen. A.I., 109, 112
Pennask Lake Club, 433
Penobscot Building, 310
Penryn Holding Company, 389n
Penryn House, 309
Penryn Securities, 389n
Peoples Jewellers Ltd., 245n
Pepin, Jean-Luc, 53
Perlin family, 236
Permanent Joint Defence Board, 241
Perrault, Charles, 165n
Perrault, Germain, 98n, 215
Perrin Investments Ltd., 322
Perry, J. Harvey, 124, 386
Peruvian International Airways, 21
Peterborough, Ont., 295
Peters, Joseph, 245n
Peters Wiles Co., 245n
Peterson, Sir William, 299
Petrofina Canada Ltd., 53, 93, 95, 215, 225n, 251, 252
Petroleum Club (Calgary), 123
Phelan, Paul, 199

Philip, Duke of Edinburgh, 7, 9, 44n, 402
Phillips, Mrs. Eric (Doris Eustace Smith), 9n, 14n
Phillips, Lazarus, 218–19, 334, 436, 472
Phillips, Capt. Mark, 9
Phillips, Mark (grandson of Eric), 400
Phillips, Nancy, 400
Phillips, Neil, 437
Phillips, Ross, 253
Phillips, Lt.-Col. W. Eric, 21n, 22, 30, 207, 346, 425n
Phillips & Vineberg, 217
Phillips, Hager & North Ltd., 303n
Phoenix Assurance Co. of Canada, 225n
Photo Journal, 73
Picard, Laurent, 215, 408, 409, 519
Piché, Marcel, 215
Pickard, Walter, 236
Pickersgill, J.W. (Jack), 191, 230, 498, 501
Pierce J.M. (Jack), 253n
Pierce, Robert, 242
Pigott family, 340
Piggott family, 199n
Pileggi, Nicholas, quoted, 442
Pillow family, 296
Pinder, Herbert C., 114, 231n
Pine Point Mines Ltd., 220
Pioneer Grain Co. Ltd., 230, 231, 234, 236
Pirie family, 257
Pitblado, James, 219
Pitblado & Co., 114
Pitcairn, Nathan, 29
Pitfield, Ward C., 243
Pitfield family, 340
Pitfield, Mackay, Ross & Co. Ltd., 244, 255, 256
Pitts, John W., 272, 519
Place d'Armes, 123
Place Ville Marie, 120–22, 182, 213, 428
Placer Development Ltd., 94, 113, 116n, 265
Plourde, Gérard, 215, 472
Plateau Co. Ltd., 373
Plumptre, A.F. Wynne, 240, 379n, 381
Plumptre, Beryl, 292n
Poitras, Jean-Marie, 215
Political Economy Club, 379–80
Pollock, C.A., 113
Poole, George E., 253
Poole, John E., 253
Poole, John W., 272
Poole family, 341
Poole Construction Ltd., 96, 253
Port Arthur, Ont., 360
Port Hope, Ont., 402
Portelance, Léo, 64
Porteous, John G. (Jack), 57, 70, 219
Porter, John, 192, 398, 444
Porter, Julian, 245
Porter, J.P., Co. Ltd., 176, 217
Porter, McKenzie, 246, 400
Portland, Duke of, 434n
Powell, K.A., (Canada) Ltd., 231
Powell, Kenneth A., 231, 232

Powell, R.E. (Rip), 369n
Powell River Co. Ltd., 280–81
Power Corp. of Canada, 43, 44, 49, 50, 52–54, 59–62, 74–86, 101
Power Super Markets, 321n
Powis, Alfred, 111, 157, 165n, 172, 183n, 191–92n, 198, 244, 427
Poyen, John, 252, 519
Pratt, Calvert, 238
Pratt, Ewart, 238
Pratt family, 236, 238
Pratt & Whitney Aircraft of Canada Ltd., 313, 456
Pratte, Claude, 111, 215
Pratt, Yves, 214, 430
Preakness, 301
Premier Cablevision Ltd., 267n
Premier Trust Co., 209
Prenor Group Ltd., 95, 310
Prentice, John G., 116n, 268, 323, 472
Price, Derek, 219, 336
Price, Mrs. Derek (Jill McConnell), 336
Price Co. Ltd., 82–86
Price Waterhouse & Co., 336
Prince Edward Island, 236n, 308, 310
Princess Hotel (Acapulco), 316
Princess Hotel (Bermuda), 316
Prior, Frank, 12n
Prior family, 302
Procter & Gamble Co. of Canada Ltd., 96
Producers Pipelines Ltd., 231n
Progressive (party), 247
Provigo Inc., 215
Provincial Transport Co., 62, 71–73, 80
Provincial-Voyageur, 50
Prudential Insurance Co. of America, 109
Prusac, Rifet John, 340
Pryor family, 431
Purchase, Gregory, 232
Purity Flour Mills, 22
Purves, R.P., 232
Purves family, 230

Quaker Oats Co. of Canada, 167n
Quebec, province of, 43–48, 72, 74, 214, 215, 248, 434, 449
Quebecair, 102, 310
Québec Autobus, 62, 70, 71
Quebec Deposit and Investment Fund, see Caisse de Dépôt
Quebec Securities Commission, 214
Québec-Téléphone, 303n
Queen's University, 112, 250, 382n, 386–87
Quinine cartel, 166

RCAF, 38n, 225
RCMP, 176
RVYC [Royal Vancouver Yacht Club], 263
Raborn, Smiley, 253
Rae, John, 53, 56, 61, 84, 85
Rae, Saul, 53, 404n
Rainier, Prince, 216, 420n
Ranchmen's Club, 422n
Rand Club (Johannesburg), 420n
Ransen, Irving Rocke, 340

Rapid Data Systems & Equipment Ltd., 313
Rasminsky, Louis, 124, 127, 132, 205, 362n, 404n, 437
Rathgeb, Charles I. (Chuck), 112, 115, 165n, 197–98, 200n, 244, 317–318, 472
Rathgeb, Mrs. Charles (Rosemary Clarke), 318
Rattenbury, Nelson, 114
Ravelston, Scotland, 30n
Ravelston Corp. Ltd., 30, 37, 330
Ravenscrag, 296
Rawlinson, E.A., 231n
Rayonier Canada Ltd., 265n, 267n
Rayonier Inc., 265n
Reconstruction and Rehabilitation, Committee on, 377
Reconstruction and Supply Department of, 382
Reconstruction party, 428n
Redpath family, 302
Redwater oilfield, 251, 327
Reed International Ltd., 324, 460
Reed Shaw Osler Ltd., 243, 275, 474
Reford family, 296
Regan, Gerald, 226
Reichmann family, 180n, 337
Reid, Escott, 404n
Reid, Richard G., 166n, 404
Reifel, George C., 267
Reifel, George H., 267
Reifel family, 267, 341
Reisman, Simon S., 55, 172, 437, 453, 497, 501
Reitman family, 340
Reliance Grain Co. Ltd., 231
Research Enterprises Ltd., 364n
Restigouche River, 260
Reynolds, Patrick M., 276
Reynolds, R.J., Industries Inc., 326
Rhodes Scholarships, 199, 250, 386, 405
Rhodes, James, 276
Richardson, George, 233–34
Richardson, George Taylor, 111, 232–36, 242, 336
Richardson, Senator Henry W., 234
Richardson, J. Ernest, 111, 116n, 272, 472
Richardson, James, 234
Richardson, James [Trudeau cabinet minister], 234
Richardson, James (founder of family), 233–34
Richardson, Mrs. James (Muriel Sprague), 234
Richardson, Kathleen, 234n
Richardson, Robert J., 165n
Richardson family, 230, 231, 233–235
Richardson, James, & Sons, 75, 232, 234n
Richardson, James, & Sons Ltd., 94, 111, 234n, 473
Richardson Securities of Canada, 95, 116n, 234n, 235, 274, 474
Rideau Club, 107, 279, 364, 367, 374n, 385n, 428–29
Ridley College, 185, 399–400, 505
Rieger, Budd H., 344, 313
Riel, Maurice, 215

Riel Rebellion, 297
Riley, Conrad S., 113, 116, 232, 236, 472
Riley, Culver, 231
Rimouski, Que., 303
Rindress, Horace, 176
Rio Algom Ltd., 141, 221, 459
Rio Tinto-Zinc Corp. Inc., 96, 459
Ripley, T. Stewart, 243, 473
Ripley, Wilder, 200n, 251
Ristigouche Salmon Club, 260, 431, 432
Ritchie, A.E. (Ed), 405n
Ritchie, Cedric E., 99n, 243
Ritchie, Charles, 404n
Rithet family, 302
Ritz-Carlton Hotel (Montreal), 300, 301
RivTow Marine Ltd., 271
RivTow Straits Ltd., 271
Rix, W.A., 236n
Robarts, John P., 53, 56n, 199, 205, 244, 433, 473
Roberts, Ed, 403n
Roberts, Harold, 402–3
Roberts, Dr. K.A., 340
Roberts, Norman, 199, 386, 502
Roblin, Duff, 231
Rocca, Patrick, 256
Roche, David, 177
Rockefeller, Nelson, 304n
Rockefeller brothers, 139
Rockefeller family, 168
Roger, W. Erle, 231n
Rogers, D.T., 273
Rogers, Donald S., 233
Rogers, Elias, Co., 340
Rogers E.S. (Ted), 245, 340
Rogers, Forrest, 116n, 273
Rogers, Ginger, 424
Rogers, Guy, 340
Rogers, Robert G., 111, 116n, 273, 473
Rogers family, 293, 240
Rohmer, Richard, 194
Rolland, Lucien G., 110, 214, 242, 473
Rolland Paper Co. Ltd., 95, 110, 473
Rolling Rock Country Club, 346, 421
Rolls-Royce Ltd., 40n, 345
Roman, Stephen, 182, 183n, 303n, 304–7
Roman Corp. Ltd., 306
Roosevelt, Franklin Delano, 163n, 365, 383
Rosedale Golf Club, 240, 344
Ross, Alexander, quoted, 276–77, 312
Ross, Arthur, 29
Ross, Frank, 366n, 389, 484
Ross, Mrs. Frank (Phyllis Gregory Turner), 366n, 484
Ross, J.K.L., 301
Ross, James, 301, 422n
Ross, Dr. Murray, 205
Ross family, 296
Roth, Philip, 340
Rothermere, Viscount, 84
Rothmans of Pall Mall Canada Ltd., 26, 95
Rothschild, Edmund de, 237, 427

Rotstein, Abraham, *quoted*, 162–63
Rouleau, Alfred, 215
Rowley, Roger, 399n
Royal Agricultural Winter Fair, 9, 40n, 202n, 304, 305
Royal Bank of Canada, 33, 36, 43n, 47, 65, 69, 71, 73, 78, 80, 81, 84, 85, 92, 93, 98, 99, 101, 102, 109–128, 143, 178, 187–88, 192, 207, 211, 218, 219, 225, 226, 250, 299, 302n, 306, 315, 318, 455, 464, 471, 475
Royal Bank Trophy, 123–24
Royal Canadian Naval College, 171
Royal Canadian Securities Co. Ltd., 232n, 453
Royal Commission on the Arts, Letters and Sciences, 413
Royal Commission on Banking and Finance, 120n, 268
Royal Commission on Corporate Concentration, 53, 379, 449
Royal Flying Corps, 327
Royal General Insurance Co. of Canada, 273
Royal Military College, 185, 200, 331
Royal Ontario Museum, 304
Royal Securities Corp. Ltd., 301
Royal Trust Co., 85, 109, 130, 206n, 211, 219, 464
Royal Yacht Squadron, 301
Royal York Hotel, 305
Royce, E.A., 107
Royce [automobile], 345
Roythree [nominee company], 75n
Rubiales Mine, 220
Rudberg family, 340
Rudolph, John, 248
Runciman, A.M., 28, 233
Russel, Hugh, 256
Russel family, 340
Russell, Bertrand, 446
Russell & DuMoulin, 268
Rust, Thomas, 116n
Ryan, Claude, 127–28
Ryder, Sir Don, 324

Safeway Stores Inc., 275
Saguenay Club, 434
Sahara Desert Canoe Club, 245n
St. Andrews N.B., 297, 376
St. Andrew's Ball (Montreal), 297
St. Andrew's College, 17, 403, 505
St. Andrews Club (Delray Beach, Fla.), 56n
St. Charles Golf and Country Club (Winnipeg), 438
Saint-Denis, Annette, 375, 376
St. Denis Club, *see* Club Saint Denis
Ste Adèle, Que., 56
St. James Street (Montreal), 213
St. James's Club (Montreal), 57, 427–28
Saint John Shipbuilding & Dry Dock Co. Ltd., 259
St. John's Ravenscourt School, 404, 505
St. Laurence Corporation, 22, 86
St. Laurent, Louis, 39, 144, 161, 278, 383, 388, 392, 394
St. Laurent government, 273

St. Laurent, Monast & Waters, 110
St. Lawrence River, 43, 55, 210, 217
St. Lawrence Sugar Refining Co., 335n
St. Louis, Mo., 40
St. Michael's Hospital (Toronto), 40n
St. Pierre, Maurice, 44n
St. Regis Paper Co., 280
Salisbury Club (Rhodesia), 420
Saltsman, Max, 130
Salzburg, Austria, 324
Sampson, Anthony, *Anatomy of Britain*, 9
Samuelson, Paul, 380
Sandwell, Percy Ritchie, 116n, 273
Sandwell & Co. Ltd., 93, 116n
Sanford, Mrs. Stephen (Laddie), 10n
Sangamo Co. Ltd., 38
Sangster, John B., 231n
São Paulo, Brazil, 299
Saratoga, N.Y., 315
Sartre, Jean-Paul, 164n
Saskatchewan, 231, 231n
Saskatchewan Pool Seven [elevator], 371
Saskatchewan Roughriders, 200n
Saskatoon Trading Co. Ltd., 93, 114
Saunders, Peter Paul, 273
Sauvé, Maurice, 53
Savary Island, B.C., 263, 269
Scales, Austin, 236
Schick razors, 309
Schlitz, Jos., Brewing Co., 185
Scholes, J.M., 219, 519
Schurman, Michael, 165n
Schurman Construction Ltd., 236n
Schurman family, 236n
Schwartz family, 341
Scotia Bond Co. Ltd., 226
Scotia Square, 226
Scott, J. Michael, 219, 335, 432
Scott, William Pearson, 432
Scrivener, Robert Carlton (Bob), 111, 144, 192n, 219, 423
Scudder, Stevens & Clark of Canada Ltd., 303n
Scully, Vincent W.T., 111, 201n, 484
Seaboard Lumber Sales Co. Ltd., 266
Seaboard Shipping Co. Ltd., 266
Seafort Petroleum Ltd., 334
Seagram, J.E. Frowde, 200n
Seagram, Joseph E., & Sons, 334
Seagram Co. Ltd., 332, 334, 335, 455; *see also* Distillers Corp.-Seagrams Ltd.
Seagram family, 302
Seaman, Daryl, 29, 253
Seaman family, 341
Searle, Stewart, 438
Searle family, 230, 341
Seaway Terminals, 308
Seco-Cemp Ltd., 334, 335
Secrett, C.V., 290n
Securities and Exchange Commission (U.S.), 32
Sedgwick, Joseph, 244, 473
Seitz, Burke, 199n

Seitz, Ernest, 341
Seitz, Joseph, 341
Selkirk Holdings Ltd., 253
Sellers, Henry E. (Harry), 231
Sellers family, 230
Selwyn House School, 140, 297, 332, 505
Senga Ltd., 234n
Senkler family, 431
Servan-Schreiber, Jean-Jacques, 57
Service, Robert, 105
Servotronics Inc., 245n
Shaheen, John M., 237
Shaker Heights, Ohio, 348
Shakespeare, Jack, 281
Sharp, Mitchell, 124, 230, 388, 502
Sharwood, Gordon R., 106, 140–42, 198–99, 201, 240, 243
Shaughnessy, Lord, 296
Shaw, George Bernard, 309
Shawinigan Water and Power, 70, 74
Shawnigan Lake School, 403, 506
Sheen, Bishop Fulton J., 5–6
Shefsky, Gerald (Jerry), 341
Sheils, G.K., 375
Shell Canada Ltd., 10, 75, 207, 309, 456, 458
Sherbrooke Street (Montreal), 219, 296n, 426
Sherman, Frank Howard, 165n
Shields, Michael, 84
Shier, Harry, 245n
Shoppers Drug Mart, 339
Shortt, Adam, 386
Shrum, Gordon, 264
Sidbec-Dosco Ltd., 215
Sidney Sussex College, Cambridge University, 17
Siebens, William W., 253n
Siebens Oil & Gas Ltd., 235
Sifton, Clifford, 292n
Sifton, Victor, 251
Sifton family, 341
Simard, Andrée (Mrs. Robert Bourassa), 217
Simard, Claude, 217
Simard, Edouard, 216
Simard, Jean, 162n, 217
Simard, Joseph, 215–16, 485
Simard, Ludger, 216
Simard, Michelle, 217
Simard, René, 217
Simard family, 215–17, 278, 337
Simkin, Saul, 233
Simmonds, J.A., 236n
Simon Fraser University, 263, 269
Simpson, Robert, Co. Ltd., see Simpsons Ltd.
Simpsons Ltd., 93, 143, 243n, 465, 466
Simpsons-Sears Ltd., 94, 113, 313n, 456, 472
Sinclair, George, 421
Sinclair, Ian David, 78, 110, 155, 177, 182, 188, 192, 199, 201n, 211, 219–22, 265n, 473
Sinclair, Hon. James (Jimmy), 110, 116n, 161, 170n, 273, 275
Sir Barton [horse], 301
Skelton, O.D., 386–87, 502
Sloan, Peter, 267n

Smallwood, J.R. (Joey), 237
Smallwood government, 238, 239
Smathers, Senator George, 57
Smith, Arthur, 253
Smith, C. Gordon, 231
Smith, Donald Alexander, see Strathcona, Lord
Smith, Denis, Gentle Patriot, 370n
Smith, Herb, 142–43
Smith, J.H., 111
Smith family, 226
Smith family (grain merchants), 230
Smythe, Conn, 200n, 246
Sneath, Harold, 233
Sobey, David, 227
Sobey, Donald, 227
Sobey, Frank Hoyse, 227, 427
Sobey, William, 227, 473
Sobey family, 225, 227, 341
Sobeys Stores Ltd., 95, 473
Social Credit party, 247, 274
Soden, James A., 219, 473
Solandt, Dr. O.M., 438
Solomon, George Charles, 231n, 473
Somerville, J.L. (the Duke), 16n–17n
Sony Corp., 232n, 438
Soo Line Mills (1969) Ltd., 231, 469
Sorel, Que., 215, 216
South African War, 402n
Southam, Dorothy Jean (Mrs. Eric Harvie), 327
Southam, Mrs. Gordon, 266
Southam, John David, 399n
Southam, William, 292n
Southam family, 293, 337
Southern, Ronald, 249n, 250, 473
Southern family, 341
Southgate Shopping Centre, 318n
Southwest Lumber Co. Inc., 309
Sovereign Life Assurance Co. of Canada, 231
Spadrow, Ralph, 288–89
Spellman, Francis Cardinal, 5
Spencer, Barbara, 266–67
Spencer, Col. Victor, 431
Spencer family, 266
Spragins, Frank, 253
Sprague, Daniel, 233
Springer family, 430
Springfield Investment Co. Ltd., 271. 472
Spry, Graham, 372
Square Mile (Montreal), 214, 296–297
Stacey, Col. C.P., Arms, Men and Governments, 361
Stafford, Jack, 199n–200n
Staiger, J.G., 28
Standard Brands Ltd., 51n, 201n, 225n, 461
Standard Broadcasting Corp. Ltd., 7, 21n, 26, 33, 330
Standard-General Construction Ltd., 252n
Standard Life Assurance Co., 85, 95, 109
Standard Oil Co. of California, 259
Standard Stock and Mining Exchange, 213

Standard Trust Co., 303n
Stanfield, Robert, 54, 161n, 307, 399n, 494
Stanfield family, 303n
Stavro, Steve, 245n
Steel Co. of Canada Ltd., 95, 111, 171, 201n, 206n
Steep Rock Iron Mines Ltd., 389
Steer family, 236
Steers Ltd., 238
Steinberg, Sam, 219, 473
Steinberg family, 293n, 337
Steinberg's Ltd., 219
Steiner American Corp., 269
Stelco, 198, 201n, 336; see also Steel Co. of Canada Ltd.
Stephenson, Signy Hildur (Mrs. John David Eaton), 312
Stephenson, Thor, 313
Stephenson, William, *Store That Timothy Built*, 275n
Stevens, Geoffrey, *Stanfield*, 378n
Stevens, H. H. (Harry), 428n
Stewart, David Macdonald, 325–26
Stewart, Walter, 326
Stewart, Walter, *Hard to Swallow*, 256n
Stewart, MacKeen & Covert, 110, 467
Stikeman, Elliott, Tamaki, Mercier & Robb, 114, 468
Stollery, A.W., 305
Stott, Jack, 245n
Straits Towing Ltd., 271; see also RivTow Straits Ltd.
Strathcona, Lord (Donald A. Smith), 160, 296, 297–98
Strathcona Paper Co. Ltd., 306
Strauss, Martin, II, 296
Streeter, Joseph, 256
Strong, Maurice F., 53, 75, 427
Study, the (Montreal), 296
Sturgeon Lake Conferences, 171–172, 453–54
Sudbury, Ont., 47, 62–64, 70, 71, 162, 214
Sudbury-Copper Cliff Suburban Electric Railway Co., 63
Sugra Ltd., 12
Sully, Bruce, 199n
Sun Life Assurance Co. of Canada, 95, 109, 113, 142–44, 206n, 219, 225n, 464
Sweatman, Alan, 233, 236, 439, 473
Sweeney, W.R. "One-Share", 208n
Sweezey, Paul, 380
Swinden, James N., 28, 29
Sydney Engineering & Dry Dock Co. Ltd., 225n
Sydney Steel Corp., 226
Syncrude Canada Ltd., 253
Systems Equipment Ltd., 235

Tabachnick family, 341
Tadenac Club, 433
Tait family, 296
Tait family (Shediac, N.B.), 257
Tanenbaum family, 337
Targa Florio race (Sicily), 318
Tarr, A.E., 231
Tarshis, Lorie, 379, 379n
Tatlow family, 431
Taylor, Austin C., 273–74, 485

Taylor, Austin G.E., 273, 274
Taylor, Charles, 199n
Taylor, E.P., 3–4, 9n, 14, 20–23, 25–26, 30n, 36–37, 112, 125, 176–177, 179, 182, 199n, 202, 246, 288, 314–17, 359, 364–66, 421, 456
Taylor, Elizabeth, 400
Taylor, Mrs. John H., 308n
Taylor, McDougald Ltd., 22
Taylor, Pearson & Carson Ltd., 253
Taymac Investments Ltd., 22
Tatam, John, 29
Techman Ltd., 250n
Technicolor, 234
Telegram (Toronto), 138
Telegram Corp., 294n
Telegraph-Journal (Saint John), 261
Télémédia (Québec) Ltée, 214
Terminal City Club, 422, 430
Teron, William (Bill), 49
Texaco Canada Ltd., 144, 211, 227, 458
Texas Pacific Oil Co., 334
Thain, Donald, 408
Thames River, 321, 322
Thant, U, 436
Thatcher, Ross, 161
Thaw, Harry K., 11n
Third Canadian General Investment Trust Ltd., 330
Thomas Equipment, 256n
Thompson, Harold, 233
Thompson, Dorfman, Sweatman, 233, 473
Thomson, Kenneth, 182, 245, 322–323, 473
Thomson, Peter N., 75, 111, 341
Thomson, Richard M. (Dick), 99n, 101n, 128, 193–94, 243, 313, 412, 473, 520
Thomson of Fleet, Lord (Roy Thomson), 57, 158, 164, 288, 322, 323, 413n
Thomson Newspapers Ltd., 74, 93, 96, 245, 462, 472
Thornbrough, A.A., 28, 29
Thorncliffe (racetrack), 17
Thorne's Hardware Ltd., 258n
Thornton, Sir Henry, 213
Threadneedle Street, 91
Time Canada Ltd., 270
Times, The (London), 323
Timmins, J. Thomas, 29
Timmins, Mrs. Jules, 293
Timmins family, 296, 337
Timmins Investments Ltd., 337
Timmis, Denis W., 116n, 274, 474
Timothy Eaton Memorial Church, 312n
Tittemore, C.R., 83–85
Todgham, Ron W., 29
Topnotch Feeds Ltd., 235
Torchinsky, Benjamin, 231n
Torno family, 341
Toronto Argonauts, 200n, 241
Toronto Club, 8, 141, 198, 240, 422–24
Toronto Daily Star, 311; see also *Toronto Star*
Toronto-Dominion Bank, 92–126 *passim*, 193, 313, 456, 471

Toronto-Dominion Centre, 122, 124, 125, 181, 182n, 240
Toronto Globals, 245n
Toronto Maple Leafs, 135, 222
Toronto Life, 294n
Toronto Star, 248
Toronto Star Ltd., 245, 469
Toronto Stock Exchange, 25, 83, 109, 171, 212–13
Toronto *Sun*, 245n, 246
Torrey, David, 219
Tory, James M., 244, 474
Tory, John A., 83, 112, 244
Tory, Tory, DesLauriers & Binnington, 112, 474
Touche, Rodney, 253
Towers, Graham, 103, 362, 432
Traders Group Ltd., 141n
Transair Ltd., 232
Trans-Canada Air Lines, 372, 373; *see also* Air Canada
Trans-Canada Corporation Fund, 73–74, 75
TransCanada PipeLines Ltd., 94, 110, 164n, 188, 206n, 221, 455, 469
Trans-Sahara World Cup Rally, 318
Travellers' Club, 420
Trbovich, Nick, 245n
Tres Vidas en la Playa (club), 420n
Triarch Corp. Ltd., 72, 185
Trimac Ltd., 250
Trinity College School, 403, 506
Trizec Corp. Ltd., 219, 225
Trouw of Canada Ltd., 235
Trudeau, Pierre Elliott, 6, 32, 44, 53n, 54–56, 142, 164, 164n, 165, 166, 218, 219, 248, 273, 285, 306, 428
Trudeau government, 54, 81, 170, 234
Truman, President Harry, 431
Trumbull, J. Lyman, 266n
Trusts and Guarantee Co., 37n
Tryton Investment Co. Ltd., 232
Tsuru, Shigeto, 380
Tunnell, Arthur L., 415
Tupper, Sir Charles Hibbert, 270
Turf (club), 9–10
Turmel, Antoine, 215
Turner, E.K., 165n
Turner, Geills, 412n
Turner, John, 58, 165n, 263–64, 273, 285, 366n
Turner, William Ian Mackenzie, Jr. (Bill), 60, 75, 78, 84, 85, 219, 520
Turner Valley, Alta., 251
Turvey, Jack, 231n, 474
Twaits, William Osborn (Bill), 112, 165n, 202n, 244
Twenty-Nine Club, 421
Tyerman, David M., 231n

UAP Inc., 96, 215
Union Carbide Canada Ltd., 96, 221, 460
Union Club (Saint John), 422
Union Club (Victoria), 422
Union Club (N.Y.), 11n
Union Nationale, 45
Unionville, Ont., 304, 307

Unité-Québec, *see* Union Nationale
United Aircraft of Canada Ltd., *see* Pratt and Whitney Aircraft of Canada Ltd.
United Farmers of Alberta, 247
United Grain Growers Ltd., 233
United Nations, 53
United Nations Derby, 315
United States, 72, 195–96, 201, 202, 295
U.S. Steel Corp., 12n, 318n
United Terminal Sugar Market Association, 235
Unity Bank of Canada, 98, (table)
Universal Sales Ltd., 260n
University Club (Toronto), 426
University of Alberta, 327
University of British Columbia, 199
University of Toronto, 101n, 163
University of Western Ontario, 407
University of Winnipeg, 276n
University Street (Montreal), 296n
Upper Canada College, 16, 17, 30, 135, 200, 241, 250, 271, 318, 399–403
Upper Lakes Shipping Ltd., 94, 111, 144, 470
Urquhart, George, 256
Urquhart, Howard B., 265n, 520

Vaccari, Victorio, 57
Valdmanis, Alfred, 237
Valley Investments Ltd., 234n
Vancouver Canucks, 270, 324
Vancouver Club, 263, 272
Vancouver Foundation, 266
Vancouver *News-Herald*, 269
Vancouver *Sun*, 165, 251, 270, 307
Vancouver Symphony Association, 269
Vanderbilt, William K., 293
Van Dusen, W.J., 266
Van Horne, Sir William, 299–300
Van Horne family, 296
Vanier, George, 30
Van Nest, Gary, 245
van Roggen, George, 275
Vencedor [yacht], 267n
Vermilion, Alta., 327
Vickers & Benson Ltd., 245n
Victoria, Queen, 298, 402
Victoria Cross, 402n
Vincent, Marcel, 110, 165n
Vogel, Garson, 233
Vrai (magazine), 166

Wabasso Ltd., 95, 111
Wadsworth, J. Page R., 107n, 113, 140, 144, 145, 243, 403n, 474
Wagg, Timothy J., 84n, 321
Waisman, Allan, 439
Walkem family, 267
Walker, Jim, 70
Walker, Hiram,–Gooderham & Worts Ltd., 96, 339, 459
Wall Street (N.Y.), 91
Wallace, Sister Catherine, 118n
Wallace, Clarence, 267n
Wallace, Stuart, 267n
Wallace family, 267
Wall & Redekop Corp., 275
Wall Street Journal, 18
Walton, Alexander, 274

Walton, Sir William, 274
Ward, Douglas H., 243, 474
Ward, Dudley, 422
Ward, Walter G., 166n
Wardell, Brig. Michael, 259
Warnock Hersey International Ltd., 54, 76
Warren, Eric, 200
Warrington Products Ltd., 335
War Supplies Ltd., 366
Wartime Prices and Trade Board, 168, 367–68
Wasik, Mitchell L., 28
Water Street (St. John's), 237
Weaver Coal Co., 308n
Webb & Knapp (Canada) Ltd., 78
Webster, Colin W., 28, 110, 292n, 309
Webster, Donald C. (Ben), 196–97, 474
Webster, Eric, 309
Webster, Jack, 264
Webster, Senator Lorne, 308–9
Webster, Lorne, 199n, 310, 474
Webster, R. Howard, 184, 185, 199n, 236n, 307–10, 474
Webster, Richard, 309
Webster, Stuart, 309
Webster family, 102, 302n, 303n, 333n
Weldon, David B., 243, 474
Weldon family, 341
Wellington, Duke of, 10
Wesley College (Winnipeg), 199
Westcoast Transmission Co Ltd., 93, 113, 180n, 266, 461
Westdeutsche Landesbank, 99n
Western Approaches Ltd., 271
Western Breweries Ltd., 21n, 231
Western Broadcasting Co. Ltd., 269–70
Western Canada Land Co., 327
Western Co-operative Fertilizers Ltd., 250
Western Empire Life Assurance Co., 79n
Western Leaseholds Ltd., 327
Western Minerals Ltd., 327, 328
Western Tractor Ltd., 95, 231n, 473
Westfair Foods Ltd., 232
Westinghouse Canada Ltd., 96, 459
Westmead Ltd., 234n
Westmount Life Insurance Co., 112
Weston, Garry, 320
Weston, George, 321
Weston, W. Galen, 244, 320, 322, 474
Weston, W. Garfield, 320–21, 425
Weston family, 293n
Weston, George, Ltd., 270, 320, 322, 456, 474
Weston, W. Garfield, Charitable Foundation, 320n
Weyburn Livestock Exchange Ltd., 94, 231
Weyburn Security Bank, 101n
Weyerhaeuser Canada Ltd., 96, 116n
Whistler Mountain, 263
White, Arthur, 18, 341
White, Kenneth A., 130–31, 219, 474

White, Stanford, 11n
White Motor Corp., 34
White Paper on Employment and Incomes, 376, 383
White Paper on Tax Reform (1970), 164, 173, 397, 440n
White Rose, see Canadian Oil Companies Ltd.
White's [club], 9
Whitmore, Norman, 231n
Whittall, Diana (Mrs. George van Roggen), 275
Whittall, H. Richard, 116n, 242, 274–75, 474
Whittall, James William (Judd), 243, 275, 474
Whittington, Hugh, 431
Wilder, William P. (Bill), 165, 243n, 244, 409, 411, 430, 474, 521
Wilde, Leonard, 404
Williams, Marshall M. (Marsh), 253
Williams, Ron, 232n
Williams-Taylor, Sir Frederick, 57n, 103–4
Willis, Senator H.B., 236n, 306, 306n
Willmot, Donald G. (Bud), 56n, 155–56, 165n, 177–78, 180, 188, 194, 244, 246, 341, 427, 474
Wills, Charles (Chuck), 267, 341
Willys-Overland Export Corp., 75
Wilson, J.O., 266n
Wilson, Joseph, 410n
Wilson, W.A., quoted, 202
Win-Bar Insurance Agencies, 245n
Windfall Oils & Mines Ltd., 208
Windfields Farm Ltd., 30n
Windsor Hotel (Montreal), 310
Windsor Star, 172n
Windsor Station (Montreal), 123
Wingate, H.S., 110
Winkler, Ed, 245n
Winkler Lighting, 245n
Winnipeg Agreement, 127
Winnipeg Grain Exchange, 230, 232n
Winnipeg Tribune, 231n
Winspear, Francis, 205, 404n
Winters, Robert, 140–42, 161, 186, 201n, 392n
Winters family, 236
Wisener, Philip A. (Bud), 424
Wisener, Robert, 171–72, 195–96
Witenagemot Society, 430
Wittington Investments Ltd., 320n
Wolfe, Ray D., 244, 337
Wood, David, 250
Wood, E.R., 18
Wood Gundy Ltd., 34, 36n, 83, 115n, 181, 293
Woodruff, A.G., 169
Woods, Elmer, 230n
Woodward, Charles Namby Wynn (Chunky), 112, 116n, 275
Woodward family, 293n, 337
Woodward Stores Ltd., 93, 112, 116n, 456, 465
Workman family (hardware and railways), 296
Workman family (steel and coal), 296

World War I, 21n, 212, 266n, 298, 302, 321, 327
World War II, 14, 21n, 30, 38n, 160, 161, 215, 222, 259, 267, 298, 305, 318, 329, 331, 358–69, 373, 402, 430
Wotherspoon, Brig. Gordon D. de S. (Swotty), 313
Wyatt, Harold E., 210, 475
Wyman, Robert, 275

Xerox Corp., 410n

Yarnell, John R., 411
Yorath, D.K., 253
York Club, 131, 422, 424–25
York Street (Toronto), 91
Yorkshire Trust Co., 266n
York University, 103, 410, 412
Young, W. Maurice (Maury), 116n, 275

Zeckendorf, William, 105, 121, 428
Zlin, Czechoslovakia, 319
Zwig, Walter, 199n., 341

ABOUT THE AUTHOR

PETER C. NEWMAN, having been editor-in-chief of both Canada's largest newspaper (*The Toronto Daily Star*) and Canada's largest magazine (*Maclean's*) as well as the Ottawa commentator whose syndicated column reached an unprecedented two million readers, has been a backstage witness to the exercise of power in all its many manifestations. He came to Canada from Vienna in 1940 and was educated at Upper Canada College and the University of Toronto, where he received his B.A. and M.B.A. degrees. He spent five years with *The Financial Post,* learning how Canadian business works. His four previous books, including the immensely successful *Home Country,* of 1973, have all been bestsellers. *Renegade in Power* and *The Distemper of Our Times* set new standards in Canadian journalism by illuminating some of the darker, private corners of the Canadian political process. One of Canada's most honoured journalists, Peter Newman has been a visiting professor of political science at McMaster University and a director of Maclean-Hunter Publishing Company and Macmillan's of Canada Ltd. Currently in the process of turning *Maclean's* from a monthly into Canada's first indigenous newsmagazine, he is busy researching the second volume of his series on *The Canadian Establishment* and writing a new history of Canada.

WATCH FOR THIS EXCITING NEW SEAL BOOK

Canada's most celebrated novelist.
Author of The Diviners-
Margaret Laurence

A Jest of God

Her moving novel of a sensitive woman yearning for love.

SEAL BOOKS

Bringing to readers throughout Canada
the finest and bestselling works
of Canadian writers.